Flexible Benefits Answer Book

Fourth Edition

This is a new edition of *Flexible Benefits Answer Book*. It replaces the Third Edition of *Flexible Benefits Answer Book*. Please discard all previous editions and supplements.

Flexible Benefits Answer Book

Fourth Edition

Robyn C. Morris

A Panel Publication

ASPEN PUBLISHERS

1185 Avenue of the Americas, New York, NY 10036
www.aspenpublishers.com

Permissions
Aspen Publishers
1185 Avenue of the Americas
New York, NY 10036

ISBN 0-7355-3198-6

Printed in the United States of America

1 2 3 4 5 6 7 8 9 0

About Aspen Publishers

Aspen Publishers, headquartered in New York City, is a leading information provider for attorneys, business professionals, and law students. Written by preeminent authorities, our products consist of analytical and practical information covering both U.S. and international topics. We publish in the full range of formats, including updated manuals, books, periodicals, CDs, and online products.

Our proprietary content is complemented by 2,500 legal databases, containing over 11 million documents, available through our Loislaw division. Aspen Publishers also offers a wide range of topical legal and business databases linked to Loislaw's primary material. Our mission is to provide accurate, timely, and authoritative content in easily accessible formats, supported by unmatched customer care.

To order any Aspen Publishers title, go to *www.aspenpublishers.com* or call 1-800-638-8437.

To reinstate your manual update service, please call 1-800-638-8437.

For more information on Loislaw products, go to *www.loislaw.com* or call 1-800-364-2512.

For Customer Care issues, email CustomerCare@aspenpublishers.com; call 1-800-234-1660, or fax 1-800-901-9075.

Aspen Publishers
A Wolters Kluwer Company

SUBSCRIPTION NOTICE

This Aspen Publishers product is updated on a periodic basis with supplements to reflect important changes in the subject matter. If you purchased this product directly from Aspen Publishers, we have already recorded your subscription for this update service.

If, however, you purchased this product from a bookstore and wish to receive future updates and revised or related volumes billed separately with a 30-day examination review, please contact our Customer Service Department at 1-800-234-1660, or send your name, company name (if applicable), address, and the title of the product to:

ASPEN PUBLISHERS
7201 McKinney Circle
Frederick, MD 21704

To my mother

Preface

The *Fourth Edition* of *Flexible Benefits Answer Book* streamlines and updates the *Third Edition* with new text, discussion of recent developments, and new appendixes providing relevant excerpts from regulations and other guidance. The *Fourth Edition* gives the reader a ready reference for flexible benefit plan design, implementation, communications, and compliance. In addition to flexible benefit plan design, the book also offers alternative employee benefit strategies and concepts.

Until fairly recently, the IRS and Congress had not made significant changes to the original Internal Revenue Code Section 125 text and older regulations that, for many years, defined the guidance used by employers for flexible benefit plans. The two oldest sets of regulations, Treasury Regulations Sections 1.125-1 and 1.125-2, were both published in the 1980s and remain in proposed form. Treasury Regulations Sections 1.125-3 and 1.125-4 were finalized in 2001 after being proposed in the late 1990s. In addition, other regulations having an impact on employee benefits (such as certain fringe benefits and COBRA rules) have been finalized since the last edition of the *Flexible Benefits Answer Book*.

The *Fourth Edition* includes updates and new material in the following areas:

- Application of final Treasury Regulations Section 1.125-4 to changes in election in a Section 125 Plan
- Application of final Treasury Regulations Section 1.125-3 to Family and Medical Leave Act situations within a Section 125 Plan
- Application of COBRA rules to employee benefits plans, and in particular to medical reimbursement accounts and health reimbursement arrangements
- All new text on Health Reimbursement Arrangements as outlined in June 2002 releases of Revenue Ruling 2002-41 and IRS Notice 2002-45
- Discussion of parking and mass transit programs, with application of final Treasury Regulations Section 1.132-9.

Although the *Flexible Benefits Answer Book, Fourth Edition* concentrates on flexible benefit plans operated under Code Section 125, it also contains several sets of questions on areas not typically offered within a Section 125 Plan, such as parking and mass transit benefits and the new Health Reimbursement Arrangements. There is also discussion of other tax preferred programs such as Archer MSAs and tuition savings programs.

The concise, specific answers—along with the helpful appendixes—provide plan sponsors, benefits consultants, attorneys, accountants, and insurance professionals with the guidance necessary to design, implement, and maintain flexible benefits plans.

Robyn C. Morris
November 2002

About the Author

Robyn C. Morris is president and owner of R. C. Morris Incorporated, Chagrin Falls, Ohio, an employee benefits consulting firm with a 15 year history. R. C. Morris Incorporated is known throughout the region for its expertise in flexible benefits plan design, implementation, and communication. The firm also provides other employee benefits and compliance consulting, including COBRA compliance and third party administration of specialized medical reimbursement arrangements.

Prior to starting her own firm, Ms. Morris was a consultant for a major employee benefits consulting firm. She has also been employed in the compensation and benefits departments of two major steel companies.

Ms. Morris is the past president and one of the founding board members of the American Society of Pension Actuaries (ASPA) Benefits Council of Cleveland. She continues to serve on the Board of Trustees of that organization. In addition, Ms. Morris is a member of the ASPA Benefits Council subcommittee of the ASPA National Board of Trustees. She holds the designation CFC, Certified in Flexible Compensation, from the Employers Council on Flexible Benefits.

Ms. Morris has authored and coauthored articles on flexible benefits issues and is a contributor to various publications. She conducts educational sessions on flexible benefits and other topics pertaining to employee benefits.

She received an MBA with a concentration in finance from the University of Pittsburgh in 1986 and a Bachelor of Arts degree from Oakland University in Rochester Hills, Michigan in 1976.

Acknowledgments

I wish to acknowledge the support and encouragement of my family, friends, and co-workers as I set aside other activities in order to work on this book. I especially wish to acknowledge the editorial staff at Aspen Publishers who are always helpful and patient.

Robyn C. Morris
September 2002

How to Use This Book

The *Flexible Benefits Answer Book, Fourth Edition* is designed for professional advisors and business executives who need quick and authoritative answers to help them decide whether to institute or continue a flexible benefits plan, how to choose and design the type of plan that best suits their needs, and how to comply with the growing number of federal requirements and tax rules that apply to these plans.

This book uses simple, straightforward language and avoids technical jargon wherever possible. The question-and-answer format, with its breadth of coverage and plain-language explanations, effectively conveys the complex and essential subject matter of flexible benefits plans. In addition, the book provides numerous examples that illustrate specific applications and situations as well as practice pointers that highlight recent interpretations of IRS regulations, and provides cautions concerning common pitfalls.

Citations of authority are provided as research aids to those who need to pursue particular items in greater detail. To provide additional assistance in locating related topics, the book makes use of an extensive system of cross referencing.

List of Questions. A detailed List of Questions is designed to help the reader locate specific items of immediate interest.

Examples and Practice Pointers. Throughout the text, numerous examples illustrate specific applications and real-life situations, and practice pointers highlight practical steps to take in administering flexible benefits plans.

Appendixes. For the subscriber's convenience, a series of supplementary reference materials is contained within the Appendixes that appear at the end of the book.

New to the *Fourth Edition* are Appendix K, which provides the text of Final Treasury Regulations Section 1.125-3, Effect of FMLA on the Operation of Cafeteria plans, and Appendix N, which provides the text of IRS Notice 2002-45 and Revenue Ruling 2002-41 dealing with HRAs.

Index. An index is provided as a further aid to locating specific information. All references in the index are to question numbers.

Abbreviations. Numerous statutes, regulations, and regulatory agencies govern and administer flexible benefits arrangements, and a number of these rules and statutes are abbreviated or referred to by acronym throughout this book. These abbreviations and acronyms are identified on their first use in each chapter.

Contents

List of Questions

Chapter 1 Overview

Eligible Employees

Plan Design Considerations

Anticipating Change

Effect of Poor Planning

Dependent Care Assistance

Deferred Compensation Plans

Vacation days

Adoption Assistance

Benefits Not Permitted Under Section 125

Restrictions on Qualified Benefits

Chapter 4 Choice-Only Plans

Plan Design

Implications for Employees

Implications for Employers

Elections

Chapter 6 Flexible Spending Accounts

Overview

Use-It-or-Lose-It Rule

Tax Implications

Form 5500

Chapter 7 Fully Flexible Benefits Plans and Total Compensation

Overview

Plan Design

Operational Issues

Credit Methodology

Pricing Methodology and Models

Chapter 8 Welfare Benefit Plan Options: Health/Life/Disability

Medical Plans

Dental Plans

Vision Plans

Medical Flexible Spending Accounts

Life Insurance

Disability Coverage

Change in Status

Form 5500

Adoption Assistance Programs

Employee Participation

State Laws

Chapter 10 Cash and 401(k) Deferrals

Cash as a Plan Benefit

401(k) Plan Deferrals

Administrative Considerations

Chapter 11 Rules For Cafeteria Plan Operation

ERISA

Form 5500

Cafeteria Plans

401(k) Plans

Dependent Care FSAs

Adoption Assistance FSAs

Compliance

Changes to Elections

Chapter 13 Enrollment and Related Administrative Issues

Enrollment

New Technologies

Key Employee Concentration Test

Timing of Testing

Other Nondiscrimination Rules

Chapter 15 Other Laws Affecting Flexible Benefits Plans

Consolidated Omnibus Budget Reconciliation Act of 1985 (COBRA)

Family and Medical Leave Act of 1993 (FMLA)

Parking and Mass Transit Benefits

Archer Medical Savings Accounts (MSAs)

Chapter 1

Overview

Not very many years ago, flexible benefits plans were exciting new benefits arrangements, experimented with by only the largest of plan sponsors. In recent years, however, such arrangements have become common among plan sponsors of all sizes and types. The popularity of flexible benefits plans can be attributed to the ability of a plan sponsor to share benefit costs with participants on a tax-preferred basis and to the element of choice offered to plan participants.

Another reason that flexible benefits plans have become more popular is that more people know about them. More than ever, benefits consultants, accountants, attorneys, and insurance brokers are advising their clients to implement such arrangements; in some cases, the impetus for installation comes directly from employees. This chapter presents an overview of flexible benefits plans and defines the terms and concepts that figure in the development and implementation of such plans.

History

Q 1:1 What is a flexible benefits plan?

In broadest terms, a *flexible benefits plan* is one in which an employer offers its employees a choice between a variety of benefit options. Thus, a flexible benefits plan allows each participant to create a benefits program that meets his or her personal needs within the limits of available funds.

The options offered might include tax-preferred and non-tax-preferred benefits. They might instead include a choice between two or more benefits—but without a cash option. A plan that offers a choice between two or more qualified benefits but no cash or taxable options need not comply with the provisions of Section 125 of the Internal Revenue Code (Code). Such a plan may still deliver specific benefits on a nontaxable basis, however, and be referred to as a flexible benefits plan.

Most often, the term *flexible benefits plan* is used synonymously with a plan intended to qualify as a *cafeteria plan* as defined by Code Section 125(see Q 1:4).

> **Practice Pointer.** Flexible benefits plan terminology can be confusing. Those designing the plan should clarify early in the process whether a plan provides a choice of benefits options, the possibility of a cash option, and whether or not the plan is tax advantaged.

Q 1:2 How did flexible benefits plans (as we know them today) come into being?

The Revenue Act of 1978 created two kinds of flexible compensation under Code Sections 401(k) and 125. Code Section 125 allows for the establishment of cafeteria plans and permits plan participants to choose between (1) taxable benefits, such as cash; and (2) nontaxable, qualified benefits, such as medical coverage. If it were not for Code Section 125, such a choice would violate constructive receipt rules and result in taxable income to plan participants (see Q 1:13). Code Section 125 also allows for very simple types of flexible benefits plans, for example, premium conversion (sometimes called premium-only) plans (see Q 2:31). In a plan intended to operate under the protection of Code Section 125, employees can pay for certain benefits using pretax contributions, without recognizing the value of that benefit as taxable income. Taxes avoided by the participant on pretax contributions to the plan include federal income tax, FICA (Social Security and Medicare) tax, state income tax for most states, and often, local income tax. At the same time, the employer is also able to reduce tax liability for the matching FICA tax, Federal Unemployment Tax (FUTA), and other payroll taxes at the State Level. (See Appendix A.)

The Miscellaneous Revenue Act of 1980 expanded the scope of flexible benefits and Code Section 125 by permitting employees to deposit income into a 401(k) plan as part of their flexible compensation program.

Guidance

Q 1:3 What rules and regulations govern cafeteria plans?

Flexible benefits plans that are true cafeteria plans are described in Code Section 125 as offering participants a choice between taxable benefits (generally cash) and permitted nontaxable (qualified) benefits. In addition to Code Section

125, five sets of Treasury regulations directly affect the operation and administration of a cafeteria plan:

1. Proposed Treasury Regulations Section 1.125-1;
2. Proposed Treasury Regulations Section 1.125-2;
3. Final Treasury Regulations Section 1.125-3;
4. Final Treasury Regulations Section 1.125-4; and
5. Temporary Treasury Regulations Section 1.125-2T (limited application).

The first two proposed Treasury regulations sections focus on general issues related to plan design, such as eligibility, allowable options under a cafeteria plan, reporting and disclosure requirements, coverage periods, employee election rules, and the tax treatment of benefits. Although they are not final, the proposed regulations sections should be followed by plan designers to avoid problems with plan compliance.

Proposed Regulations Section 1.125-1 was published in 1984. It has been amended three times, most recently in 2001, but has not been finalized. Proposed Regulations Section 1.125-1 offers guidance in the general operation of Section 125 cafeteria plans, and in particular, answers several questions on the issue of nondiscriminatory and discriminatory plans. These Proposed Regulations state certain operating rules that are an important and required part of any Section 125 cafeteria plan.

Proposed Regulations Section 1.125-2 was published in 1989. It also has been amended a few times, but not finalized. It clarifies some points made in Proposed Regulations 1.125-1, and offers further guidance in areas such as Flexible Spending Accounts.

Both sets of proposed regulations provide guidance and interpretation of Code Section 125 in operation. The fact that they are still in proposed state does not render them irrelevant when seeking to comply with the requirements of the Code.

The third set of regulations covers the effects of the Family and Medical Leave Act (FMLA) on the operation of a cafeteria plan. Regulation Section 1.125-3 was finalized in 2001.

Treasury Regulations Section 1.125-4 describes permitted changes to elections made under a cafeteria plan. These regulations replace portions of the language formerly in Sections 1.125-1 and 1.125-2, and were finalized in 2001.

Temporary Treasury Regulations Section 1.125-2T clarifies which benefits are permissible under a cafeteria plan and which benefits must be excluded. (Proposed Treasury Regulations Section 1.125-2 also covers those topics.)

Other guidance, such as revenue notices and revenue rulings issued by the Internal Revenue Service (IRS), also affects the design and operation of cafeteria plans.

A Section 125 cafeteria plan is nothing more than a tax savings structure for delivery of benefits to participants. One way to view a cafeteria plan is as an umbrella. Various qualified benefits are offered under the plan's structure. Each qualified benefit option has specific rules and regulations that apply to it.

For example, dependent care assistance options must qualify under Code Section 129, which defines eligibility, dependent status, reimbursable care or assistance, applicable nondiscrimination rules, and permissible maximum benefits. Although those rules do not affect the cafeteria plan directly, they do affect the shape and scope of the choices that are offered. For instance, the design of a dependent care assistance plan must take into consideration that the maximum permissible benefit is $5,000 (for a married couple filing separately, the amount drops to $2,500). Another consideration is that not all care providers are qualified under Code Section 129; employees who use dependent care services that do not qualify under Code Section 129 cannot receive benefits under the dependent care assistance option of the cafeteria plan.

Caution. If a benefit option offered under a cafeteria plan is supposed to meet qualification requirements under a separate Code section but fails to do so, noncompliance may disqualify not only the benefit but also the entire plan.

Q 1:4 What other legislation impacts the operation of a Section 125 plan?

Other legislation has also had an impact on the operation of Section 125 plans. The Family and Medical Leave Act of 1993 describes how a participant may remain in a medical plan (including a Medical Flexible Spending Account) while on FMLA Leave. The Consolidated Omnibus Budget Reconciliation Act of 1985 (COBRA) has also had a direct impact on medical coverage and medical spending accounts within a Section 125 plan. And the Health Insurance Portability and Accountability Act of 1996 (HIPAA) [PL 104-191] provided for a number of changes that directly or indirectly impact flexible benefits plans. HIPAA introduced the Medical Savings Account (MSA) (not to be confused with a medical flexible spending account), and it clarifies treatment of long-term care insurance within a Section 125 plan.

Much has lately been written about the idea of "defined contribution" health and welfare benefits plans, under which employees are offered a fixed dollar amount within the employer's benefits arrangement to spend on company-sponsored benefits. This concept is not new to cafeteria plan design, but has gained greater exposure recently because of employer concerns about continued financing of benefits plans and about employer liability for the benefits plans chosen for employees and retirees.

Q 1:5 Is a cafeteria plan subject to ERISA?

No. A Section 125 plan (i.e., a cafeteria plan) is not subject to ERISA. A cafeteria plan is similar to an umbrella benefits plan that encompasses the underlying life insurance, health, disability, dependent care, and 401(k) plans. ERISA may, however, govern the individual benefits options that are "covered" by the flexible benefits umbrella.

The "benefit" provided by a Section 125 plan is the ability to pay toward the cost of options within the plan on a pretax basis. The ability to make a pretax payment—in and of itself—is not described as an ERISA plan.

> **Practice Pointer.** A Section 125 plan need not meet the communications requirements of an ERISA plan (i.e., a summary plan description), but it is highly advisable to fully describe the plan in writing to participants and eligible employees. It is important to remember, however, that underlying benefits very likely have an ERISA requirement to summarize the benefit in writing for plan participants.
>
> Also, a Section 125 plan is not required to file a Form 5500 or Schedule F. (Relief from this requirement was granted by IRS in April, 2002. See Appendix J.) However, underlying benefits, including a medical flexible spending account, may have a Form 5500 reporting obligation as a welfare benefit plan.

A medical FSA is a self-funded health arrangement described in Code Section 105. It *is* an ERISA plan and therefore must also comply with the summary plan description requirements, the claims review provisions, and other requirements of ERISA.

Q 1:6 Is a flexible benefits plan subject to coverage continuation protection under COBRA?

Although a Section 125 plan itself (as a tax structure that may include many benefit options) is not subject to the Consolidated Omnibus Budget Reconciliation Act of 1985 (COBRA), the underlying health benefits offered in a Section 125 plan are subject to COBRA under the same rules that apply to healthcare coverage outside of a Section 125 plan. Therefore, a group health benefits option offered in a Section 125 plan as an underlying health plan, is subject to COBRA. Even if the only group health benefits option offered under the cafeteria plan is a medical FSA, the medical FSA is subject to COBRA, and employees electing health benefits made available under the cafeteria plan may have a right to COBRA protection to the same extent as beneficiaries of other group health plans. It is important to note that medical FSAs operate under COBRA continuation regulations that differ from those applicable to other health plans (see chapter 15).

If the participant's spouse or dependent elects COBRA continuation of group health plan coverage, or if the coverage is elected on such an individual's behalf, that individual must be given the same rights as the participant.

Q 1:7 What federal laws other than ERISA and COBRA regulate or interact with flexible benefits plans?

The Code and Treasury regulations contain the rules that govern cafeteria plans (see chapter 11). In addition, certain laws that mandate benefits or otherwise have an impact on the administration of a flexible benefits plan must be considered. Statutes such as the Family and Medical Leave Act (FMLA) affect how flexible benefits plans can be designed and administered.

Cafeteria plans under Code Section 125 have also been affected by the Tax Reform Act of 1986 (TRA '86) and the Health Insurance Portability and Accountability Act (HIPAA). HIPAA made only one minor change that applied directly to Section 125 plans; however, it made several changes regarding long-term care insurance and MSAs that indirectly affected flexible benefits plans. (See chapter 15 for a discussion of how other laws affect flexible benefits plans.)

HIPAA also added claims procedures and privacy rules for third-party administrators and plan sponsors of certain plans, including medical reimbursement accounts. Some of these requirements are still being developed.

Q 1:8 Which federal agencies have jurisdiction over employees in flexible benefits plans?

The Department of the Treasury, the IRS, and the Department of Labor all have some jurisdictional claims over certain legal and operational aspects of cafeteria plans.

Q 1:9 Are there state laws that regulate Section 125 cafeteria plans?

No. State laws do not regulate cafeteria plans. Most states, however, have laws that govern the garnishment of wages, which, in turn, may have a direct or indirect effect on the enrollment of employees in a cafeteria plan. Of greater concern is the fact that every state that levies income taxes has made a determination as to whether it will follow the federal government in granting special tax treatment to salary reduction amounts under a cafeteria plan. Most state income tax laws are patterned after federal law. This means that salary reduction amounts are generally not considered taxable income for most state income tax purposes; however, there are exceptions to that generalization and a state may change its position at any time. Appendix A outlines each state's definition of taxable income for state income tax purposes.

In addition, some municipal tax laws do not allow an exemption for a salary reduction. Generally, most municipalities do not consider salary reduction amounts to be taxable income. In some cases, however, municipalities are permitted to define taxable income independently of the state's definition. This means that, although the state might exclude Section 125 plan wage reductions from taxable income, the locality might not. States that are known to permit localities to define taxable income independently of the state's definition are indicated in Appendix A; however, it is best to reconfirm this information at the time of plan implementation, and periodically thereafter.

Practice Pointer. With regard to state and municipal taxation, the plan sponsor need not be concerned with the location of the workplace (i.e., the state in which plan participants work) but, rather, with the state in which the plan participants reside. A legal advisor should be consulted regarding the tax treatment of salary reductions in a particular location. Alternatively, the appropriate state or local authority should be contacted.

Definitions

Q 1:10 What is a cafeteria plan?

An employee benefits plan that offers an employee certain options or choices and is structured in accordance with Code Section 125 is technically referred to as a *cafeteria plan*, per Code Section 125.

Paraphrased, Code Section 125 states that if an arrangement is nondiscriminatory (with respect to key and highly compensated employees; see chapter 14), no amount will be included in the gross income of a participant solely because the participant can choose among the benefits of the plan. Code Section 125(d)(1)(B) states that in a qualified cafeteria plan, the participants can choose among two or more benefits consisting of cash and qualified benefits.

A flexible benefits plan must meet the basic legal requirements of a cafeteria plan to deliver the tax advantages allowed by Code Section 125. Generally, the legal requirements of a cafeteria plan are as follows:

1. The plan must be in writing;
2. All participants must be employees;
3. The plan must provide employees with a choice between two or more benefits. At least one of the choices must include cash or a cash equivalent and the other choice or choices must be nontaxable, qualified benefits as defined by the Code (see chapter 3);
4. The plan must meet nondiscrimination standards and not discriminate in favor of the highly compensated participants; and
5. When the plan includes a component governed by the Employee Retirement Income Security Act of 1974 (ERISA), the plan must meet the requirements of ERISA, such as making specific communications to employees and including certain language in the plan documents. A medical reimbursement account is an ERISA plan, because it is a Welfare Benefit Plan.

Q 1:11 What terms are commonly used for a cafeteria or flexible benefit plan?

Code Section 125 uses the term *cafeteria plan*. Other names in common use for a flexible benefits program are *flexible benefits plan, flexible compensation plan, choice plan, flex plan*, and *Section 125 plan*. Plans that have only a pretax premium component are often called *premium conversion plans* or *premium-only plans* (POPs).

Proposed Treasury Regulations Section 1.125-2 employs the term *flexible spending arrangement* to describe an account that is funded by the employee or employer (or both) and is used to reimburse an employee for qualified expenses on a tax-preferred basis. Other terms used for a flexible spending arrangement are *flexible spending account* (FSA), and *flexible reimbursement account*. The underlying account names referred to in the proposed and final regulations are *health FSA*, *dependent care assistance*, and *adoption assistance*. Terms in common use for a health FSA include *medical spending account* (MSA), *health care spending account*, and *medical reimbursement account*. Commonly used terms for a dependent care assistance account are *dependent care assistance plan* (DCAP), *dependent care spending account*, and *dependent care reimbursement account*.

A plan that includes premium conversion, spending accounts, and an option to direct employer-provided cash or benefits credits toward benefits purchase might be referred to as a *full-flex plan*. Such a plan typically permits plan participants to pay for benefits on a pretax basis.

> **Note.** When the term *cafeteria plan* is used in communications materials, it is most likely describing a plan with many options. However, a cafeteria plan might be a plan as basic as a pretax health insurance premium contribution plan.

Q 1:12 Do the terms *flexible benefits plan, cafeteria plan*, and *Section 125 plan* all mean the same thing?

For many practitioners, the terms *flexible benefits plan, cafeteria plan*, and *Section 125 plan* are interchangeable. In this book, the term *flexible benefits plan* is generally defined to mean a qualified cafeteria plan under Code Section 125. It is possible, however, to design a "flexible benefits plan" that is not intended to be qualified under Code Section 125—with benefits not permitted under that section. For example, a benefits plan may offer employees a choice of benefits for which they pay with after-tax dollars, such as financial planning, automotive and mortgage insurance, and whole life insurance. Other types of benefits that cannot be included in a qualified cafeteria plan might be permitted to be paid with pretax dollars; they include premiums for long-term care coverage (but see Note) and expenses for parking and mass transit. Although such benefits are not permitted in a cafeteria plan under Code Section 125, they might be constructed to be part of an overall flexible benefits approach (see chapters 7 and 16).

Note. Congress has been reviewing long-term care insurance and its possible inclusion under a Section 125 plan. As this book goes to press, such coverage is not a permitted benefit under a Section 125 plan. Although long-term care insurance premiums may be considered a business expense for an employer, an employee cannot pay toward such premiums on a pretax basis. Plan designers and plan sponsors are urged, however, to revisit the matter upon implementation of either a Section 125 plan or a long-term care plan.

Q 1:13 What is constructive receipt, and how does it relate to cafeteria plans?

All taxpayers must report as taxable income any compensation or earnings realized during the year. In most instances, the term *taxable income* refers to amounts actually paid to and received by an individual. In some cases, however, amounts can be constructively received. This means that money need not be actually received by or paid to the individual to be considered taxable income.

A person is deemed to be in constructive receipt of income or property if he or she has a nonforfeitable right to such income or property and can take possession of it at any time. In such situations the IRS takes the position that whether or not an employee exercises his or her right to take possession of the income or property, the mere fact that the employee can take possession means that he or she must pay taxes on such income or property.

An important advantage of a Section 125 plan is that it provides a statutory exemption to the doctrine of constructive receipt. In other words, a participant in a Section 125 plan who can choose either cash (or some other taxable benefit) or a nontaxable, qualified benefit will not be in constructive receipt when he or she chooses the nontaxable benefit. Of course, if the participant chooses cash or another taxable benefit, he or she must pay taxes on its economic value.

Note. Unless an employer has a Section 125 plan in place, it cannot offer an employee the choice between cash and benefits without the employee's being in constructive receipt of the full value of the benefit. For example, if an employer that does not have a Section 125 plan offers a new hire the choice between "full" compensation of $30,000 without health insurance coverage or reduced compensation of $26,000 with health insurance coverage, the employee who selects health insurance coverage will be in constructive receipt of the value of the health insurance coverage. That is, if the employer does not offer the choice in the context of a Section 125 plan, the employee should be taxed on $30,000 even though his or her wages amount to only $26,000. This situation is easily remedied by the implementation of a qualified Section 125 plan before an employer offers such a choice to employees.

Q 1:14 What is total compensation?

In a total compensation framework, the issue of *how* employees are rewarded becomes relatively unimportant. Instead, the issue of *how much* employees are rewarded, when one combines all the various compensation elements, becomes essential.

Total compensation refers to the package of wage and benefits offered to an employee. Some employers also include their statutory obligations such as workers compensation or unemployment tax when considering the total compensation of an employee. However, most employees who are thinking in terms of total compensation will measure their wage combined with benefits of value to them, such as employer-provided health insurance, life insurance, disability coverage, retirement plan funding, etc.

The employer-employee relationship has been changing in recent years. Employees are seeking more than cash compensation as reward for performance. Many employees now see themselves as entrepreneurs who are selling their skills, talents, and services to their employers. They are looking less for a defined job and more for opportunities to grow and further enhance their marketability and skills (a career opportunity). The compensation paid to such "employee-entrepreneurs" must be flexible and meaningfully exchangeable for alternative types of compensation. Consequently, an employer's emphasis should always be on the total compensation package—not just on the direct cash compensation paid as wages or salaries, or the deferred cash compensation paid into savings or retirement programs, or the group benefits plans that protect or replace income. The total compensation objectives delineated by the organization represent a very important part of any flexible benefits program.

With or without a flexible benefits plan, an employer will want to measure the total compensation paid to employees in all of its various forms, not merely the cash wages. When a flexible benefits plan is offered, the employee-entrepreneur will decide for himself or herself the best way to allocate the total compensation received among cash, deferred compensation, and fringe benefits.

Q 1:15 What is cost sharing and cost shifting?

Cost sharing occurs when an employee shares the burden of the cost of benefits with his or her employer. *Cost shifting* occurs when an employer shifts some of its cost for employee benefits to employees.

Cost shifting often takes place at the same time premium conversion is introduced. When an employer implements a premium conversion plan, it may also raise the amount that employees are required to contribute. Ideally, the amount of employee tax savings approximates the amount of additional cost, and many employees will take home the same amount of pay.

Cost shifting may also take place from year to year as an employer determines its benefits budget and benefit credits (see chapter 7) allowed in a flexible benefits plan.

Example. In 2003 Ferrous Unlimited offers full-time employees annual benefits credits amounting to $3,000. At the end of the year, Ferrous knows that benefits costs will increase by an average of $300 per person. It decides to increase the annual allowance by $50. The shortfall ($250) will be cost shifted to employees.

Q 1:16 What is adverse selection?

Adverse selection occurs when participants select against a flexible benefits plan by choosing only those benefits that they are most likely to use or by exchanging those benefits that they are least likely to use for cash or other benefits. That undermines the strategy of having many low-risk participants help cover the costs of relatively few high-risk or high usage participants.

Examples of adverse selection are as follows:

- An employee anticipating major surgery may select the highest level of medical coverage, even if the premiums cost more.
- An employee who makes only occasional visits to a doctor chooses the lowest-cost option available.
- Only those individuals who have impaired vision select vision coverage.
- Only those individuals who need (or have dependents who need) braces select orthodontia coverage.

Tax Treatment

Q 1:17 What are the federal and state tax advantages of a cafeteria plan?

Under a qualified cafeteria plan, employees reduce their gross income by the amount of their salary reduction. That reduction in turn reduces their federal income and FICA tax liability (and usually their state and local income tax liability) because the taxes are calculated on a smaller amount (gross income less salary reduction). (See Appendix A for how states and municipalities treat pretax salary reductions under Code Section 125.) A cafeteria plan that complies with all the rules and regulations that govern a Section 125 plan, including the nondiscrimination rules, protects plan participants against constructive receipt (see Q 1:13) so that when employees have the opportunity to choose between cash and qualified benefits under the plan, they will not be required to include the value of the benefit they selected in gross income. In addition, when an employee reduces his or her income to pay for a qualified employee benefit, it can be done on a pretax basis.

Cafeteria plans provide a tax savings for the employer as well as the employee. The employer reduces its FICA contribution (provided the employee's earnings were below the Social Security taxable wage base) because the employee's salary reduction lowers the basis of the FICA tax. The FICA tax savings for an employer can be substantial. Further, the employer does not have to pay federal unemployment taxes required under the Federal Unemployment Tax Act (FUTA) on the amount of the salary reduction. Because the FUTA wage base is quite low, actual employer FUTA tax savings are minimal. In some cases, the employer also saves on various payroll taxes at the state level, such as state unemployment tax and workers compensation premiums, or other state sponsored insurance programs based on employee wage.

Example. Amy, an employee of Mixed Media, Inc., earns $33,000 per year and contributes $5,000 per year toward the cost of family medical coverage. That expenditure can be paid by Amy in two ways:

1. *After-tax.* Under this method, Amy pays taxes on the $33,000 of income. If Amy pays 33 percent of her income to cover all federal, state, and local taxes, her annual tax bill is $11,000. That leaves Amy with $22,000 of income after taxes, of which $5,000 goes to pay for medical coverage. Amy is left with $17,000 of income after health care costs and taxes.
2. *Pretax.* Under this method, Mixed Media allows Amy to pay the $5,000 contribution toward her family's medical coverage with pretax dollars, so Amy's medical plan contribution reduces her annual salary to $28,000. Since Amy pays taxes on only $28,000, her tax bill is $9,332. Amy therefore has $18,668 of income after health care costs and taxes. Since Mixed Media pays FICA tax on $28,000 instead of $33,000, it saves about $383 in taxes for Amy alone.

This example simplifies actual application of taxes to income, but accurately illustrates how a cafeteria plan can be used to reduce an employee's tax bill and thereby increase spendable income. The difference in spendable income between the two methods is directly attributable to not paying taxes on the health insurance premium contribution. The pretax method leaves Amy with an additional $1,650 of spendable income over the year. The $1,650 increase in spendable income can be estimated in advance by multiplying the total tax rate (33 percent) by the premium contribution amount ($5,000).

Considerations for the Employer

Q 1:18 Why might an employer provide a flexible benefits plan?

Most employers are motivated to take any action because of their desire to 1) make money, 2) limit expenses, and/or 3) spend wisely. Implementing a flexible benefits plan might result in a positive cash flow for the employer, but "making money" cannot be the primary reason for implementing such a plan. On the other hand, a flexible benefits plan will almost certainly allow an employer to limit expenses and to spend wisely when costs are incurred.

Through a flexible benefits plan, an employer can determine a benefits budget as a function of any number of factors—for example, as a percentage of revenue or earnings, as a fixed amount per employee, or even as a percentage of some performance goal. When the actual cost of providing benefits exceeds the employer's budget, the remaining expense is passed on to employees in the form of a choice: Does the employee want to elect the benefit and pay for the cost not covered by the employer, or does the employee prefer to forgo the benefit or choose a less expensive option?

Offering a flexible benefits plan is spending wisely if the employer determines that such a plan is important to employees and thus will help the employer attract and retain desirable employees. A survey titled "Two Careers, One Marriage, Making It Work in the Workplace," which was conducted in 1998 by Catalyst, a not-for-profit research firm in New York, asked respondents what programs they would look for if they were switching jobs. Cafeteria-style benefits was the second most common response. (The first was flexible work schedule.) Clearly, flexibility in the workplace is becoming more and more desirable, and even necessary to attract and retain quality talent.

Recently, a lot has been written about a "defined contribution" approach to health and welfare benefits. Many believe that taking this approach to health and welfare plans will change the entire health care delivery system. According to a survey published by Defined Care in 2000, 100 percent of employers and 50 percent of consumers answering the survey believe that "the entire health care system will change as defined contributions become more widespread." (This survey was one in which the reader was self-nominated to respond, and may not have statistical validity, but it shows the thinking of those who responded.)

A defined contribution approach to health care benefits is an underlying plan design in many flexible benefits plans. Even a premium conversion (or premium-only) plan introduces this idea when the employer states that it will pay a fixed dollar amount toward the cost of premiums, and plan participants pay the excess to make up the full cost.

Q 1:19 What is the economic value of a flexible benefits or cafeteria plan to an employer?

To an employer, the economic value of a flexible plan is that it can be used to control or contain the cost of the employee benefits program. It does so in a number of ways, but underlying each approach is the same basic premise: An employer can define the level of contribution it is willing or able to make available and is no longer in the business of providing a defined benefit regardless of its cost. It therefore becomes possible for an employer to do the following:

1. Fix benefits cost as a flat dollar amount or as a percentage of payroll;

2. Relate expenditures of benefits costs to organizational productivity or profits;
3. Introduce new benefits at no additional cost to the employer by capping the amount of contribution toward all benefits paid by the employer;
4. Determine which benefits options to make available; and
5. Manage employees' selection of benefits by controlling the price tag of each benefit being offered.

In addition to managing benefits expense, an employer might also expect to see some payroll tax savings because of employee salary reductions that result from participation in a flexible benefits plan. Although the payroll tax savings to an employer may not be the primary motivation for the employer to implement a flexible benefits plan, those savings will help offset the cost of plan implementation and administration. They may even, in some cases, create additional savings for the employer.

Q 1:20 How can an employer help ensure that a flexible benefits plan will save it money?

A flexible benefits plan can save money for an employer if planning goes into the design and implementation of the program. At no time should a benefits department seek to add benefits without analyzing and reviewing the strategic value of the addition for both the employer and the employee. Very often, an organization that introduces a flexible benefits plan has unrealistically high expectations of what the program is going to achieve, particularly in cost savings.

It is important to remember that the first year of implementation requires a commitment of energy and resources to both setting up the program and educating the employees. Because employee behavior is unlikely to change dramatically during the first year the plan is in place, short-term savings are not likely to occur without significant benefits cutbacks or cost shifting to employees. In fact, in a large organization, the complexity of a flexible benefits program often requires the cooperation of several departments and generates significant administrative and communication start-up costs. Such start-up expenses can usually be offset by savings realized by the flexible benefits plan in its first three years of operation.

Many employers that have installed flexible benefits plans have found good communications (see chapter 12) to be essential for saving money. Because such a plan has a cost associated with it, greater savings will be realized when more employees participate in the pretax elements of the plan, which save the employer costs on payroll taxes. When a program includes employee choices, the employer has an obligation to provide information about options available to the employees. Only when both the employer and the employees adequately understand how the plan affects employee decision making can an employer be assured of realizing any long-term savings from the program.

Today, increasing numbers of employers are looking at cost-containment measures as part of their flexible benefits planning. Some of the more commonly used cost-containment techniques include competitive bidding among insurance companies, the use of third-party administrators to lower administrative costs, and wellness programs and employee-assistance plans that reduce future medical claims and minimize absenteeism.

Q 1:21 What value does a flexible benefits or cafeteria plan have to an employer apart from its economic value?

From an employer's vantage point, presenting employee benefits through a flexible benefits plan offers four distinct advantages in addition to those related to cost control:

1. Such plans provide options to employees that they would not otherwise have.
2. Such plans remove the employer from the paternalistic position of declaring the best selection of benefits for all employees.
3. Such plans are considered by many to be enlightened benefits delivery vehicles that will help to attract and retain better employees.
4. Such plans allow employers, through careful planning, to construct the enrollment form as a sort of "benefits statement," displaying the various benefits offered through the employer. This communications piece may help employees to better understand and appreciate their benefits as part of their total compensation.

Q 1:22 How does a flexible benefits plan help control medical premium cost increases?

To understand how a flexible benefits plan can help control medical plan costs at the employer level, it is first necessary to consider a traditional indemnity health insurance arrangement with premiums (or self-funding) fully paid by the employer. The structure of a traditional benefits program promotes cost increases each year for two reasons. First, the underlying costs of many medical and dental plans are based on reasonable and customary charges, which are self-inflating. Second, medical costs are increasing faster than the consumer price index. Without a flexible benefits plan, a plan sponsor's commitment is to provide the full cost of a plan of benefits, rather than a defined dollar allowance. Therefore, the employer is, in effect, buying into automatic cost-of-living adjustments in health care. Without a flexible benefits plan, it is the employer's obligation to select the health insurance options that are most cost effective.

The introduction of a flexible benefits plan helps to shift some of the obligation to select cost-effective benefits to plan participants. Flexible benefits plans define the contribution of the plan sponsor, not the benefit (see Q 1:19). In the short term, that means an employer can use a flexible benefits plan to shift costs to employees. In the long term, however, using such a plan merely to shift costs will not be successful. The ultimate cost-controlling mechanism of a flexible benefits plan is its introduction of a strategic set of options and its use of appropriate pricing of those options to support and encourage use of the cost-efficient programs by plan participants.

An article in the August 13, 2001, issue of *Business Insurance* states that a "consumer-driven" system may be the most promising option. A consumer-driven model would, in theory, lower the demand for health care. If consumers develop an attitude toward health care spending that matches their attitude toward purchase of other items such as computers and cellular phones, the overall cost of health care might decrease. However, not all experts agree that a consumer-driven model is the answer to lower cost health care.

Each health insurance option under a flexible benefits plan should represent a different set of trade-offs that employees must weigh. That is, employees must decide if they would rather have more or less managed care, must choose between higher or lower levels of coverage, and must determine how much they would be willing to pay for the right to select their health care providers. Ultimately, those choices boil down to one key issue: cost. Under a flexible benefits plan, the message to employees is, "Choose the plan you want, but know that if you select the most expensive plan with little or no constraints, you will end up paying a lot more out of your own pocket."

Practice Pointer. The long-term strategy of a flexible benefits plan is to encourage appropriate consumer behavior by offering cost-effective choices and by giving the consumer an economic interest in the selection process.

Considerations for the Employee

Q 1:23 What role does the concept of employee choice play in a flexible benefits plan?

At its most basic level, the choice for an employee participating in a flexible benefits plan is whether to be covered by benefits or to take cash as compensation. Even a premium conversion plan (see chapter 5), which may not appear to have a "cash" component, offers that basic level of choice. Under a premium conversion plan, employees can opt either to be covered by the employer's plan with a pretax contribution toward benefits or to pay for benefits on an after-tax basis—or to waive coverage under the benefits program completely. If an employee chooses not to pay for benefits on a pretax basis, that employee chooses cash, even if he or she chooses to pay for benefits on an after-tax basis. As far as a flexible benefits plan under Code Section 125 is concerned, the employee's choice is to pay for benefits on a pretax basis or take cash for an after-tax use.

Offering the right array of options in a fully flexible benefits plan is essential to a successful long-term strategy. The trade-offs offered must enable the majority of employees to choose options that meet their needs. Less efficient options should cost more than more efficient options. The cost of high-option plans must be higher than the cost of medium- or low-option plans. Thus, although choice is initially used to introduce employees to new options, choice is ultimately used to help employees understand, appreciate, and value their benefits. To communicate the value of those benefits, the employer needs to create and implement a sensible pricing strategy, and if appropriate, to subsidize the preferred plan or to overcharge for inefficient plans, or both.

Because employees generally try to get the most benefits for their money, a flexible benefits plan uses economic choice to control costs. Employees should be encouraged to view the purchase of benefits as they view the purchase of other goods or services. If they do so, most can be expected to behave rationally and select the most cost-effective plans for their personal situations.

Q 1:24 Can a flexible benefits plan save employees money?

Absolutely. When employees use pretax dollars instead of after-tax dollars to purchase benefits, they will avoid federal income tax, FICA tax, and state income tax (in most states) on those dollars. For the majority of employees, that tax savings ranges from 25 percent to 40 percent for every pretax dollar spent on benefits (see Q 1:17).

A flexible benefits program can also save employees money by reducing the duplication of benefits under different plans. Employees are encouraged to enroll in only those benefits that they truly need; as a consequence, neither the employer nor the employee wastes money providing unnecessary or duplicate benefits. (See the discussion regarding adverse selection in chapter 2.) Cost savings realized by the employer in pricing can be returned to the employee in the form of a greater range of benefits offerings or might be used to increase wages.

Q 1:25 What value does a flexible benefits or cafeteria plan have to employees apart from its economic value?

From an employee's vantage point, choice is a valuable benefit in and of itself. Traditional benefits plans developed a few decades ago are simply not appropriate for today's family. Recent data indicate that less than 15 percent of families conform to the 1950s model of a father who works outside the home as the sole income provider and a mother who stays at home with two or more children. Two-income and single-parent families, as well as employees with no dependents, have a variety of needs that render single-program designs inappropriate. Employees look for benefits that help to alleviate work and family pressures and that therefore offer greater value for working family members than pure economics would indicate.

When offering employee benefits plans, employers must take into account a number of considerations that may lead to a very complex employee benefits structure. A single, rigidly structured traditional benefits formula cannot respond meaningfully to such a wide range of parameters as benefits costs, demographics, family composition, tax status, new legal requirements, employee satisfaction, the competition's benefits package, and new designs in employee benefits. All those factors can be taken into account under a flexible benefits plan.

Many employers believe that their employees do not recognize or appreciate the substantial financial contribution made by employers to provide health insurance and other benefits plans. Typically, as costs increase, the level of employees' appreciation may remain neutral or even decline. In addition, as benefits offerings increase in both number and complexity, employers providing and paying for health insurance options may feel less confident that they are in the best position to decide for employees which benefits and how much of each benefit to offer. Employees may prefer to make such decisions for themselves.

Although employers are concerned that their benefits packages may no longer be meeting competitive pressure from outside plans, there is a limit on how much financial support they can provide. By having employees decide which benefits are most important to them, based on family and personal needs, an employer not only remains competitive with other employers but also allows each employee to reap the greatest return on every dollar of benefits money that is spent. The relationship between employer and employee becomes a dynamic one in which both share in the responsibility of reaching solutions that are satisfactory—and affordable.

Another reason an employer should contemplate the use of flexible benefits plans is demographics. A company's demographics may indicate, for example, that more elder care and less child care would be both responsive and competitive. Employee benefits need to meet not only age-related demographic diversity but also the expectations of employees. With higher educational levels come higher economic expectations for long-term growth and personal development within a company. It is not uncommon to find employees who want to have more control over how their benefits funds are spent.

Practice Pointer. In many organizations, the growth of flexible benefits plans has a direct relationship to the professional growth of individual employees. A flexible benefits plan not only helps an employer meet its employees' personal needs but also recognizes employees' psychological development and need for increased control.

Q 1:26 What are the economic incentives for an employee to participate in a flexible benefits plan?

Employees enjoy the economic incentive of being able to pay for employee benefits with tax-free dollars. Paying with pretax dollars rather than after-tax dollars will always result in more spendable income for the plan participant. (In certain circumstances, however, factors such as age and expected Social Security benefits will outweigh this economic incentive.)

Section 125 cafeteria plans can also be designed so that employees have the option of converting employer-provided benefits dollars into personal savings (or vice versa). If an employer links a method for funding the 401(k) savings plan option to its Section 125 plan, for example, the value of the plan to employees will increase. An employer that allows employees to choose among vacation time and other benefits is allowing employees to design a benefits program that meets their family needs on an individual basis. Thus, an employee can funnel dollars or credits toward benefits that are important to that employee and away from benefits that are less important.

Chapter 2

Plan Design and Implementation

To make the best use of its time, money, and other resources, it is crucial that an employer consider the variety of plan design options before implementing a flexible benefits plan. Further, the employer must give careful consideration to enrollment and maintenance issues such as communications and payroll deduction coding. Although planning considerations will vary significantly among employers of various sizes and greater or lesser resources, there are common factors all employers should take into account when considering a flexible benefits plan. This chapter reviews those factors and offers advice targeted at employers of specific sizes. This chapter also reviews the steps to plan implementation.

Employer Objectives

Q 2:1 What are some of the most frequently stated goals of employers seeking to implement a flexible benefits plan?

Most plan sponsors (i.e., employers) that have installed a flexible benefits plan or that are considering such a program are trying to achieve one or more of the following goals:

- Controlling or containing benefits costs

- Mitigating increases in medical plan costs
- Introducing new benefits at no cost to the employer
- Introducing tax-effective pretax benefits
- Attracting and retaining key personnel
- Meeting diverse employee population needs
- Demonstrating to employees the value of the organization's benefits plan
- Moving from paternalism in benefits to a partnership with employees

Q 2:2 What basic planning questions should be asked when designing a flexible benefits plan?

Although every employer is different, there are a number of basic planning questions that need to be considered when establishing the overall design of a flexible benefits plan:

1. What does the employer want to achieve with a flexible benefits plan?
2. What are the employer's financial goals?
3. Does the employer want a benefit plan that is less than, equal to, or greater than the plans of its competitors?
4. What is the minimum level of coverage an employee should have?
5. How much should an employee pay for benefits?
6. Are benefits intended strictly for the financial protection of employees, or does the employer take the approach that benefits are part of total compensation? (While the same benefits might be offered under either approach, the employer motivation is different between the two.)
7. Should individual business operating units have their own benefits programs?
8. Does the employer face any communications challenges such as multiple languages or small numbers of employees in several locations (e.g., in a retail environment)?

Q 2:3 What objectives should an employer establish before implementing a flexible benefits plan?

An employer should establish specific objectives in certain areas before implementing a flexible benefits program. Those objectives include the following:

1. Financial objectives—
   - Total employer contributions to the plan, and
   - Total employee contributions to the plan.
2. Budget guidelines, and growth of employee benefits expenditures (see note below).
3. Employee relations objectives—

- Employee acceptance,
- Employee understanding, and
- Employee appreciation of the benefits package.

4. Administrative objectives—
   - Ease of administration,
   - Cost of administration, and
   - Administrative accuracy.

Note. The growth of employee benefit expenditures can be measured in terms of percentage growth or in terms of real dollar growth. For example, an employer may specify that the employer's expenditure for benefits should not grow by more than a specified percentage or should not increase by more than a certain dollar cap per year. Such specific objective measurements can be established before the implementation of a flexible benefits program.

Q 2:4 Why is it crucial to plan a flexible benefits plan carefully?

A flexible benefits program that is carefully planned allows an employer to strategically manage its entire benefits program. Strategic management includes the ability to estimate and project costs associated with changes to the benefits plan options and changes in premiums. Strategic management also encourages increased employee involvement in and awareness of the employer's long-range goals regarding total compensation expenditures.

From the viewpoint of the employer, one obvious advantage of a flexible benefits program is its ability to control and contain employee benefits costs. Rising medical costs have led to higher and higher premiums every year. In the past several years, rising premium costs have created a dilemma for most employers; that is, the value of medical insurance coverage has become a greater and greater part of total compensation—possibly more than employers find desirable. Flexible benefits plans have been quite successful in helping employers initially shift more of the premium costs to employees, present more appropriate design trade-offs in health benefits, and develop pricing strategies that encourage employees to select cost-efficient health plans that tend to reduce utilization patterns.

In addition, a successful flexible benefits plan helps an employer meet diverse employee needs, maximize the tax savings that can be realized by the employee benefits program, meet competitive pressures in the marketplace, reduce its paternalism, and create a sound basis for partnership with employees in a zone of mutual interest—employee benefits.

Appropriate Plan Sponsors

Q 2:5 What size of employer is likely to sponsor a Section 125 (cafeteria) plan?

When flexible benefit plans operating under Code Section 125 first became popular, they were implemented by primarily the largest of employers. This was due, in part, to the level of expertise and resources available to larger employers, but not typically to smaller groups.

Today, knowledge of Code Section 125 and its application within employee benefit plans has become widespread. Advisors to large and small employers understand how these plans work, and the benefits offered to both employers and employees. In addition, many employees have already participated in a Section 125 plan, either through a former employers, or through a spouse's benefit plan.

It is standard practice for medium-sized employers (400–5,000 employees) to offer flexible benefits plans. In fact, many smaller employers with employee populations ranging from 25 to 400 have implemented flexible benefits plans. Even employers with fewer than 25 employees should consider a premium conversion plan when employees contribute toward the cost of employer-sponsored insurance. It should be noted, however, that one of the biggest challenges for a very small employer is satisfaction of nondiscrimination rules. Indeed, the smaller the employer, the more difficult it can be to satisfy the requirements of the Code.

Although the plan design for a small organization often includes only premium conversion and Flexible Spending Accounts, many companies with fewer than one hundred employees are also offering employer benefits credits, a choice of medical plans (e.g., HMO, PPO, or traditional) through a single carrier, and the buying and selling of vacation days.

Q 2:6 How does a Section 125 plan impact different types of employers?

Any business entity organized for-profit may find a Section 125 plan to be a moderately low-cost benefit to implement. This is because the employer will save on the matching FICA tax, along with employees.

Not-for-profit organizations and churches may also benefit from both the employee satisfaction, and the employer tax savings offered by an employer-sponsored Section 125 plan.

Employers and employees who do not participate in the Social Security portion of FICA will see less financial motivation to implement a cafeteria plan, but their employees will still save on federal and, in most cases, state income tax. Therefore, these types of employers are increasingly offering some level of Section 125 to their employees.

Note. Employers and employees who do not participate in Social Security include those who are in the Public Employee Retirement System (PERS) and those in a State Teachers Retirement System (STRS). Contributions to these plans are calculated based on *unreduced*wages, even if an employee participates in a Section 125 plan, and reduces pay on a pretax basis.

Q 2:7 Can a flexible benefits plan be inappropriate for an employer that has union employees?

Yes. Although flexible benefits plans are subject to collective bargaining, there is nothing inherent in organized labor that renders a cafeteria style of benefits ineffective or less valuable. Inasmuch as flexible benefits plans traditionally have been used to control, contain, and shift employee benefits costs, unions have generally viewed them with great skepticism. Nonetheless, there are a number of situations in which employees who collectively bargain have negotiated for and enjoy flexible benefits plans. There are instances where the staff of a union has a flexible benefits plan, and there are also multiemployer trust funds that offer plan participants benefits through a flexible benefits plan.

To the organization considering a flexible benefits plan, having union employees generally means that a decision needs to be made early regarding whether to directly involve the union in the design of the plan or to install the flexible benefits plan for nonunion workers only. If the latter approach is taken, only nonunion workers are given the flexible benefits plan. If the collectively bargained employees subsequently decide they want the plan, they will have to negotiate for flexible benefits.

Q 2:8 May a flexible benefits plan be installed in a Taft-Hartley multiemployer trust fund?

Yes. A flexible benefits plan, including a Section 125 plan, may be installed in a Taft-Hartley multiemployer trust fund. (A Taft-Hartley trust is a trust fund jointly administered by employers and unions, and established pursuant to Section 302(c)(5) of the Labor Management Relations Act.) The primary design concern is how to perform salary reductions in situations in which a union member reports to a job site and may work for a different employer each day. In trade unions (e.g., carpenters, laborers, or roofers), a design dilemma arises because of the administrative complexities of correctly reducing a worker's salary and maintaining the records of such a program. For industrial unions in which a union employee works for one employer at a time throughout his or her career, that dilemma is obviously not an issue. In those multiemployer plans under which salary reduction is administratively problematic, however, salary reduction typically does not become part of the flexible benefits plan design.

The single most essential technical concern in a multiemployer trust fund is whether or not a participant may exchange cash for benefits. For example, if the fund wishes to allow a member to opt out of medical coverage for $650, can the opt-out benefit be paid out of an employee benefit trust? If so, how does the employer handle the tax and withholding requirements? Under the law, cash in an employee benefit trust may be used to pay for only specific health and welfare benefits and "other" benefits. Although the IRS has not ruled on whether cash constitutes an "other" benefit, many benefits practitioners take the position that it does and that it is therefore permissible to pay a multiemployer plan participant cash in lieu of benefits.

Note. Those trust funds that pay out cash generally withhold the appropriate federal and state tax amounts and forward such funds to the correct governmental authority. At year-end the fund must issue a Form W-2 to the participant.

Eligible Employees

Q 2:9 Who is eligible to participate in a cafeteria plan?

One of the basic requirements of a Section 125 (cafeteria plan) is that only employees can participate. Thus, in a sole proprietorship, partnership, or a limited liability company organized as a partnership that comprises both employees and partners, only the employees are eligible to participate in a cafeteria plan. Partners and sole proprietors are not considered by the IRS to be "employees" for plan eligibility purposes. A self-employed person, as defined in Code Section 401(c), and an owner of 2 percent or more of an S corporation are not considered to be employees under a cafeteria plan (see Q 2:12). Certain full-time nonemployee sales personnel, however, are considered to be employees. [IRC § 7702(a)]

The fact that all employees are eligible to be plan participants does not mean that an employer must include or will include all employees in a plan. An employer may elect to exclude any group from the plan if the plan design and operation are nondiscriminatory. For example, an employer might exclude from a plan all employees who work for a particular division of the employer, all employees who participate in collective bargaining, all employees who are newly hired, or all employees who work at a particular plant or geographic location.

When an employer begins to exclude eligible employees from participating in a cafeteria plan, the immediate concern is whether the plan will meet the nondiscrimination tests. A cafeteria plan may be exclusive, but if proportionately too many non-highly compensated employees are excluded, the plan will not be able to qualify under the nondiscrimination rules. The Code does allow a cafeteria plan to exclude certain individuals and yet pass nondiscrimination testing. For instance, union employees and employees who have less than three years of service may be excluded from the plan and disregarded for purposes of eligibility testing if certain conditions are met. A nonexcludable employee group, however, is not necessarily required to be eligible for the plan—as long as the plan can pass the required nondiscrimination tests. For example, it may be possible to exclude all employees from division Z from the plan, even though they must be considered in the tests to determine the nondiscriminatory status of the plan. (See chapter 14 for information on nondiscrimination testing.)

Q 2:10 May a cafeteria plan cover the dependents of an employee?

Yes. Proposed Treasury Regulations Section 1.125-1, Q&A 4, indicates that even though dependents of an employee may not be treated as employee participants in a cafeteria plan (unless, of course, the spouse or dependents are themselves employees of the employer), they may nonetheless have an interest in the benefit selections made by the employee. A spouse, dependent, or beneficiary will not, however, be treated under a cafeteria plan as an active participant with the same rights as the employee, even though such an individual has rights upon the death of a participant in a life insurance or 401(k) plan, benefits economically under a medical plan by being a member of the family when family coverage is selected by the employee, or is covered under a dependent care assistance plan (including participation for a limited time in a medical reimbursement account).

> **Note.** In some cases, a COBRA beneficiary of a participant (see chapter 15) might have independent rights to participate in the benefits provided under a cafeteria plan, including rights to participate for a limited time in a medical reimbursement account.

Q 2:11 May a cafeteria plan cover former employees?

Yes. For purposes of a Section 125 plan, Treasury Regulations Section 1.125-1, Q&A 4, defines *employee* to include former employees; thus, they may enjoy coverage under such a plan. Nevertheless, a cafeteria plan may not be created for the exclusive benefit of former employees, and former employees may not reduce their pension income as if it were wages or salary. Any contributions by former employees must be made with after-tax dollars.

Furthermore, the design of a cafeteria plan that includes former employees must not inadvertently allow those former employees to violate the prohibition under cafeteria plan rules against deferring compensation to a future plan year. [Prop Treas Reg § 1.125-2, Q&A 5(a)]. Under a cafeteria plan, active employees are not permitted to defer the employer's cafeteria plan contributions beyond the end of the year in which they terminate in order to have more flexible dollars available after they terminate, and former employees may not elect benefits that defer compensation (e.g., they may not allocate retiree flexible dollars to the defined benefit pension plan).

Although this was probably not anticipated when the Code was written, COBRA continuants in a Section 125 plan may be former employees. And in some cases, COBRA continuants are individuals who were never employees, but have a COBRA right to participation in the plan. (See chapter 15.)

Q 2:12 May a cafeteria plan cover a partner, a sole proprietor, or a shareholder of a Subchapter S corporation?

No. Self-employed individuals as described in Code Section 401(c), partners who draw earned income as described in Code Section 1402(a), and shareholder employees of a Subchapter S corporation who directly or indirectly own more than 2 percent of the company's outstanding stock on any day during the taxable year of the S corporation [IRC § 1372(a)] are not considered common-law employees for purposes of participating in employee fringe benefit plans. They are therefore ineligible to participate in a Section 125 plan. By rules of attribution (Code Section 318) the spouse, child, grandchild, and parent of a shareholder will also be ineligible to participate in a Section 125 Plan. A partnership, a sole proprietor, or a Subchapter S corporation may, however, offer a cafeteria plan to its eligible employees.

> **Note.** Because participation in a cafeteria plan by sole proprietors is strictly forbidden, a 100 percent tax-preferred method of payment for health insurance premiums is seemingly unavailable in 2002. (In 1999 through 2001, the permitted deduction was equal to 60 percent of health insurance expenses for self-employed individuals. The allowable deduction rises to 70 percent for 2002, and 100 percent for 2003 and thereafter.)

Yet ownership in a sole proprietorship is not attributed to a spouse under Code Section 318 (unlike spouses of partners or greater than 2 percent shareholders in a Subchapter S corporation). Therefore, if a spouse of a sole proprietor is also a bona fide employee of the sole proprietorship, the nonowner spouse can elect family health insurance coverage and the sole proprietorship can expense 100 percent of the cost (or the nonowner spouse can pay premiums on a pretax basis under a nondiscriminatory cafeteria plan). Therefore, it is possible for a sole proprietor to receive 100 percent tax-preferred health insurance coverage through a spouse working for the sole proprietorship. It will be important to make sure that the plan meets nondiscrimination testing requirements, in this case.

Plan Design Considerations

Q 2:13 What underlying principles are considered cornerstones in the design and implementation of a flexible benefits plan?

There are four basic principles that must figure in the design and implementation of a flexible benefits plan:

1. A flexible benefits plan is an ongoing benefit that requires continued maintenance. Because each year employees must select their options anew, the employer cannot install a flexible benefits plan and then ignore the responsibility of maintaining and renewing it (especially in light of the fact that the employer may wish to revise the pricing communicated to employees from year to year).

2. Simplicity is vital for a flexible benefits plan. The plan should include those options that are important to the employer and the employees, but it should not add on extra options simply for the sake of display.
3. Communicating all aspects and features of the flexible benefits plan to employees is essential to its success. The importance of a strong communications program cannot be underestimated.
4. The employer must know how the flexible benefits plan is to be administered if it is to be operated and maintained successfully. The employer's payroll or benefits department, which will certainly have some administrative tasks related to the plan, will need proper training. Claims administration will have to be provided if reimbursement accounts are offered. (Claims can be handled in-house or sent to a third party administrator.)

Q 2:14 What essential planning factors must an employer consider when developing a flexible benefits plan?

Key internal factors that an employer must consider when developing a flexible benefits plan include the following:

1. Employer's financial ability to provide benefits;
2. Employer's philosophy regarding employee participation and individual decision making;
3. Employee demographics;
4. Long-range benefits goals (e.g., benefits in relation to total compensation);
5. Top management support;
6. Adequate human resources and benefits expertise within the organization to manage the plans and employee information needs;
7. Appropriate employee meeting times and effective methods of communicating with employees;
8. Computer and payroll ability to support employee choices and recordkeeping requirements; and
9. Other employer programs that can be tied to the flexible benefits plan (e.g., an employee assistance plan or a wellness program).

Key external factors include the following:

1. The extent to which other employers in the same industry are using flexible benefits plans;
2. Whether the employer's competitors (whether or not in the same industry) use flexible benefits programs to recruit highly qualified employees;
3. Applicant and employee inquiries about flexible benefits programs;
4. Changes in the tax laws; and

5. The extent to which the business environment of the employer is subject to change (e.g., new regulatory, audit, or SEC requirements).

Q 2:15 How important are employee demographics to a flexible benefits plan?

Employee demographics play a major role in the design of a flexible benefits program. Reevaluating an organization's demographic makeup will help an employer to begin both the evaluation of the current benefits structure and the development of a workable design for the flexible benefits plan. For example, the design and cost considerations of a flexible benefits plan for an employer that predominately employs women (as in the typical hospital) will be very different from the design and cost considerations of a flexible benefits plan for an employer that predominately employs men (as in the typical construction company).

Practice Pointer. If an employee population tends to be homogeneous, the employer (and its benefits advisors) should question whether a flexible benefits program is needed to address issues that usually arise as the result of employee diversity. Even in a homogeneous population, however, employees may request a flexible benefits plan to address other issues important to them.

To help focus on how the demographics of an employer will affect a flexible benefits plan, the plan designers should categorize employees based on the following factors:

- Age
- Gender
- Eligibility for full-benefit program
- Full-time and part-time status
- Level of compensation
- Having working spouses employed full-time
- Having very young children
- Having dependents ages 6 through 21
- Having elderly parents to support

In addition, the following demographic statistics must be considered:

- Annual turnover rates
- Current retirements and prospective retirements over the next five years

Strategic planning for a flexible benefits plan may require a benefits or human resources manager to conduct a current demographic analysis and use it to project how the demographics of the employee population will change and what the needs of that population will be over the next five years. Such a long-range projection provides the employer with a road map of benefit planning assumptions based on a changing workplace.

Even if an employer does not undertake a long-term strategic projection, demographics are important to the design of a flexible benefits program because they provide a starting point for planning. Based on the information provided by the organization's demographics, an employer may decide not to offer child care or adoption assistance options but may instead feel compelled to provide elder care options, long-term disability insurance, and a 401(k) retirement savings program.

Q 2:16 What are the major steps in developing and implementing a flexible benefits plan?

In broad terms, the steps to developing and implementing a flexible benefits plan are as follows:

1. *Determine whether or not a flexible benefit plan meets the needs of the employer and employees.* In determining needs, be sure to address eligibility limitations and cost of implementation. For example, if the shareholders of a company may not participate, will that limitation dampen the idea of implementing a plan? If the cost of implementation is not recovered for many years, does the company have other reasons (i.e., employee satisfaction) to go forward anyway?
2. *Assemble a team of advisors and an internal assistance team.* The internal team might consist of the finance and human resource department staff, with input from top levels of management. The external advisors might include an ERISA attorney, tax accountant, employee benefits consultant, and insurance broker.
3. *Determine plan design.* With the help of advisors, develop a plan design that best meets the overall needs of the employer.
4. *Develop a calendar.* Communications development and delivery is often the one element that takes the most time. Be sure to leave plenty of time for communications development and editing, as well as production and employee benefits meetings. Then, enrollment must take place with enough lead time for participants to enroll, and for the payroll department to enter elections. If plan options such as insurance vehicles are not already established, include adequate time for review and acceptance of the insurance programs that will be offered by the plan.
5. *Assemble documentation.* A Section 125 cafeteria plan will need to be described in a Plan Document. Underlying plans often also have documentation requirements. In addition, the plan must provide written materials describing the plan to eligible employees. In the short-run, the communications materials may suffice, but a Summary Plan Description is required of many underlying plans, and should be distributed to plan participants.
6. *Conduct employee benefit meetings and enrollment.* Ensure that all eligible employees have had ample opportunity to learn about the provi-

sions of the plan, and have time to consider options before returning the enrollment form.

7. *Enter, audit, and confirm data.* Make entry to the payroll system or other flexible benefit tracking system. After audit for accuracy, send confirmation statements to plan participants, with enough time remaining for corrections, if necessary, before first payroll is run.

Q 2:17 What are the specific steps in developing and implementing a flexible benefits plan?

The development and implementation of a flexible benefits program involve every level of the employer organization. It is essential that top management endorse the conversion from traditional benefits delivery to a flexible benefits environment. (Some larger employers consult their boards of directors and request preliminary approval of the flexible benefits concept before proceeding.) Middle managers need to understand the plan design so they can discuss it in an effective and supportive way with their subordinates. Human resources and benefits specialists need to integrate their work with that of the information systems department, finance department, and other administrative departments to create the cost projections for plan options. Employees should be part of the initial needs assessment, as well as the communication, design, selection, and enrollment processes.

Small employers without several levels of management and departmentalization must still follow several steps to implement a flexible benefits plan. The steps in the design process for a flexible benefits plan outlined below, however, are directed at a large employer. (Remarks about their application to a small employer are included.)

1. *Establish a design team.* The design team should consist of human resources and benefits specialists and representatives from the information systems and finance departments, along with representatives from employee and supervisory groups who can help bring issues to the committee and assist in building a consensus around a specific design. For a small employer, the design team might consist of the company owner or chief financial officer, along with such advisors as an employee benefits consultant, an attorney or accountant (or both), and an insurance agent or broker.
2. *Determine whether outside assistance is needed to develop the design, legal documentation, and government reporting.* Some employers have sufficient in-house expertise to develop and submit the required documentation and government filings. If that expertise is not available, the design team should seek appropriate outside assistance with the project. Many small employers do not retain in-house staff to perform legal and compliance work, communications, or claims administration. Such duties will likely be assigned to outside providers.

3. *Assess employees' needs.* Many employers begin with an employee benefits survey to determine the perception and value of current benefits as well as employees' expectations and needs. The survey should be carefully worded and presented to employees as a measurement tool: employees who mistake a survey for a wish list can develop expectations so high that the ultimate success of the plan is jeopardized. An employee benefits survey is a valuable tool for an employer of any size.

4. *Develop flexible benefits goals and objectives.* The design team should determine the employer's compensation-related strategic goals, and then determine how those goals can be translated into the flexible benefits plan. At that point, the design team can submit its recommendations to top management for consensus.

5. *Analyze data.* The data to be analyzed include (a) demographic information, (b) statistics regarding the current benefits plan participation, (c) responses from the employee benefits survey, and (d) benchmark data from other corporations. Once collected, the data should be developed into a matrix that highlights which components will be part of the new plan design and how they will be part of it. Advisors such as employee benefits consultants and accountants can assist small employers with such an analysis, if necessary.

6. *Create the preliminary plan design and characterize the flexible benefits plan.* To develop the specific underlying design, it must be decided which benefits will be brought under the flexible umbrella, what number of options will be offered, and what the character of each option will be; then the characterization model (see chapter 7), the credit allocations, and the purchase price tag for each option must be determined. Next, using current benefits costs, current participation levels, and applicable underwriting constraints, a comprehensive cost projection of the entire benefits plan should be developed. For a small employer, the most likely underwriting constraint will be the percentage of employees covered. Some health and dental plans will require coverage of, for example, 75 percent, or even 100 percent of all employees who do not have coverage elsewhere. (A requirement that *all eligible* employees be covered will affect the inclusion of a benefit in the plan; see Q 5:2.)

7. *Make a final cost projection.* After a final plan design has been agreed upon, a closing cost analysis should be undertaken. A closing cost analysis incorporates all the projected underlying plan design costs and the expense of the plan itself. In addition, it should evaluate several employee migration models and the effect that participation levels within a specific benefit will have on the plan's cost projections.

    Planning Pointer. It is possible that, because of budgetary constraints, the final cost projections will not be acceptable. If that happens, the design team must be reconvened to make alterations in the plan design. It is not uncommon for steps 5, 6, and 7 to be repeated several times until a plan design and a cost projection that meet the employer's goals emerge.

8. *Develop an implementation plan.* The specific steps that various departments must undertake to successfully introduce flexible benefits to the employer (including the information systems, finance and accounting, legal, and employee or industrial relations departments) must be determined. Each department must establish a plan of action that can be coordinated with other departments to ensure completion by the scheduled employee enrollment date. For a small employer, it is likely that the payroll and finance staff (and probably the company's office manager) will be involved, as well as outside advisors such as an insurance agent, an accountant, a benefits consultant, and an attorney.

9. *Present the plan to management for final approval.* Depending on the formality of the employer's decision-making process, the design team should present its final plan design, cost projection, and implementation plan to senior management for a decision to continue with the implementation of the plan. Up to this point in the process, employer investment consists of the time and energy of the design team plus any consultant costs. It is important that management review the long-term cost projections, the timetable for implementation, budgets and communication costs, and any tax and legal issues before proceeding.

   Planning Pointer. If senior management is receiving information on the design, cost, and implementation steps at this point in the process for only the first or second time, a final decision is not likely to be made at one meeting. Therefore, there should be some mechanism for keeping senior management informed (e.g., monthly meetings) throughout steps 4 through 8 so as not to produce an information overload when final approval is sought.

   Note. For a small employer, step 9 is likely to be bypassed. Typically, senior management would be involved in the decision making and analysis throughout the entire process.

10. *Test the new plan.* Employee testing includes an assessment of employees' reactions to the plan design, to the types of choices available to the employees, and to the proposed communication program. Testing is usually accomplished through a focus group. It is important to listen to employees' opinions and to determine whether employees display unanticipated reactions (positive or negative) to the plan. Such reactions may require the employer to reevaluate the information being communicated, how it is being communicated, or, if a serious problem emerges, whether last-minute modifications to the plan design should be considered. Although employee testing is extremely valuable and is part of a well-conceived implementation program, most small employers bypass this step. Communications materials are often reviewed and edited by the few individuals responsible for employee relations and then finalized for distribution to all employees.

11. *Solicit proposals from carriers or vendors.* If no further modification to the plan is necessary, the next step is to bid out all the necessary services. The process may involve obtaining insurance coverages, selecting a third-party administrator, purchasing or leasing flexible benefits claims or payroll tracking software, and so on. The most current information (design, demographics) should be used when this stage is initiated to ensure that bids are both as accurate and as cost effective as possible. In addition, any unanticipated administrative or underwriting problems with the plan should be identified at this juncture.

    Note. This step may be one of the areas of greatest divergence between small and large employers. The large employer might design the plan first and then request proposals from vendors, whereas the small employer is likely to arrange relationships with vendors and advisors first and then design and implement the plan with their help.

12. *Develop all administrative systems.* Procedures, recordkeeping systems, and legal documentation all should be completed before employee enrollment. Depending on the exact nature of the plan design, it may be necessary to modify seemingly unrelated plan documents (e.g., the 401(k) plan or the pension plan) to clarify their relationship to the new plan. That is true for employers of all sizes.

    Planning Pointer. Many benefits plans are pay-related plans (i.e., the benefits they provide are predicated on the amount of an employee's compensation). Depending on the definition of salary or compensation used by the other benefits plans, employees who reduce their salaries under a cafeteria plan (as defined by Section 125 of the Internal Revenue Code (Code)) may also be reducing their retirement plan benefits, life insurance coverage, or disability protection. Some employers intend that result because it produces some savings that offset the expense of installing a flexible benefits plan. Other companies aim to amend the definition of pay so that it includes any amounts reduced from salary under the cafeteria plan.

13. *Conduct employee enrollment.* At enrollment, employees are now given the opportunity to make choices based on their individual needs. Enrollment can be accomplished either with paper forms or electronically via the Internet or a voice response system. Regardless of how the enrollment process is performed, a detailed workbook should be created to help the enrollee understand his or her choices. Another highly recommended procedure is to set up a telephone hot line or Internet Q&A site with e-mail response to specific questions so that enrollees may have any questions answered promptly.

14. *Assess the flexible benefits plan and the entire implementation process.* It is important that the design team review its methodology and assess the need to make changes arising from the experiences of the first open enrollment period. It may also be necessary to reevaluate all the employee options to determine if they are still appropriately priced and

meet employee needs. In addition, a first-year attitude survey should be conducted to evaluate which features of the flexible benefits plan employees like and dislike.

Q 2:18 What budgetary constraints apply to the implementation of a flexible benefits plan?

A flexible benefits plan can be costly to implement—especially during the first year, when all the design and implementation costs are incurred. Once the plan is finalized, employees have been educated about making their annual selection of benefits, and legal documentation is complete, however, a flexible benefits plan need not be significantly more costly to administer than any traditional benefits plan.

Nonetheless, in the first year, the employer needs to consider additional costs in computer programming, legal fees, communications materials, and outside advisors. Administrative and staffing requirements may also increase in the short term. For example, additional data entry clerks, benefits analysts, and employee relations or communications personnel may be required to get a new cafeteria plan up and running.

Even for a small employer, implementation of a flexible benefits plan may require additional time and effort of the payroll, finance, human resources, and administrative staff. Although the implementation cost for a small employer is quite a bit less than it is for a large employer, the relative cost may still be quite high when considered as a percentage of the benefits budget or on a per-employee basis.

Q 2:19 What is a realistic timetable for implementing a flexible benefits plan?

Naturally, the length of time required to implement a flexible benefits plan increases as the complexity of the plan increases. It should be noted however, that the reaction time of a small employer and a large employer are drastically different.

A realistic estimate for implementation of a premium conversion plan for a very large employer is three to four months; a plan with flexible spending accounts (FSAs) might take five to nine months to implement. Implementing a fully flexible benefits plan can take 12 to 18 months for a large employer. The longer time periods allow for the development and implementation of computer software that will monitor employees' choices.

Effective employee communications are essential to the success of the process. For a large organization, two to five months should be allocated to the development of communications materials, and four to eight weeks should be allowed for employee selection and enrollment. (See Appendix C for a sample nine-month timetable.)

For a small employer, implementation of a premium conversion plan might take six weeks (most of that time being communications development, enrollment, and response); a plan with FSAs might take two to three months. Implementing a fully flexible benefits plan might take six months for a small employer. The bulk of the time will be spent in making decisions about plan design, communications development and delivery, and in altering administrative systems (e.g., payroll) as necessary.

Q 2:20 How should recordkeeping and claims processing be dealt with when designing a flexible benefits plan?

The decision whether to outsource recordkeeping and claims processing for a flexible benefits plan or to conduct those administrative tasks in-house is fundamental to the planning process. Obviously, different cost and timing issues must be considered and resolved. Because an employer's training, personnel, and equipment needs will be affected by the decision, the sooner in the planning process it can be made, the better.

To evaluate the trade-offs between administering a flexible benefits plan in-house or outsourcing it, an employer should take four analytical steps:

1. *Develop criteria for decision making.* What is the business vision of the employer and how does the decision fit into that framework? The goal is to ensure that all decisions support the employer's competitive advantage.
2. *Formulate a cost-benefit analysis.* What is the cost (in time and money) for keeping plan administration in-house versus outsourcing those tasks?
3. *Evaluate customer reaction.* If an employer considers its employees as the customers of its human resources department, then the question of where they will be better served is crucial to the decision.
4. *Assess the philosophy of the various recordkeepers.* Will an outsourcing company share the attitudes about employees that in-house administrators have? What will happen if it does not?

A final strategic analysis should take into account all the criteria introduced in steps one through four above. Often, it should be noted, the final decision depends on who sets organizational priorities: those priorities will dictate whether outsourcing or in-house administration will appear more or less favorable.

Q 2:21 Can an employer design a flexible benefits plan that addresses the concerns of its different divisions, locations, or strategic business units?

Yes. Many large employers use a flexible benefits plan to address the stratification of employee groups within their organizations. In fact, the more environments an employer has, the greater the appeal of such a plan. (A tax-preferred plan under Code Section 125 must meet the nondiscrimination requirements set forth in the Code and related Treasury regulations, including coverage tests. (See chapter 14 for discussion of differing coverage for multiple groups of the plan sponsor.))

A flexible benefits plan offers two distinct advantages:

1. An employer can easily maintain separate programs within its flexible benefits plan at each location. It can differentiate on the basis of coverage levels (i.e., a different set of options) or coverage cost (i.e., different employer-paid portions), or both, for a particular benefit, depending on division, location, or strategic business unit.

2. A flexible benefits plan centralizes the administration of different plans within an employer (or controlled group of employers). This can result in substantial administrative cost savings.

   Caution. An employer that uses a flexible benefits plan to address the concerns of different locations, divisions, or strategic business units within its organization must recognize that creating many pricing differentials between groups may be counterproductive, especially if employees from different units share the same work area, the units do not compete in different industries (or marketplaces), or there are a number of regular transfers between the units.

Anticipating Change

Q 2:22 Should an employer anticipate changes in its flexible benefits plan?

Yes. In order to remain responsive to employee needs while continuing to meet employer objectives, a flexible benefits plan should be reviewed annually. Indeed, such a plan may need some design changes from year to year. A flexible benefits plan's initial design is by necessity based on the prior year's costs and the prior year's employee selection patterns. Even with the most accurate migration projections, some of the underlying benefits options will acquire more or less enrollment than was anticipated by the design team. As well, unless premium costs are guaranteed for a multiyear period, insurance carriers will eventually insist on higher renewal costs. Also, an employer can experience changes in its demographics or its workforce, or it may decide to offer new benefit plan options.

For all the foregoing reasons, a regular assessment of the cost of each benefit option—both the costs of employee participation and those of acceptance of the program—should be part of the annual update and renewal of a flexible benefits plan. Of course, an employer may decide not to make changes in a given year, especially if the desired changes are merely fine-tuning the plan.

Q 2:23 What annual planning process should be in place regarding the renewal of a flexible benefits plan?

An annual planning process that requires a review of the costs of each option under a flexible benefits plan against experience and employee participation should be in place. A number of conditions can necessitate changing benefits, including low participation in a specific option, requests for new benefits from employees, introduction of new programs by competitors that are attracting highly qualified employees, or the high cost of a particular benefit. An employer should not hesitate to make changes in the initial plan design, if warranted.

An employer should begin reviewing its flexible benefits plan at least four to six months before the next open enrollment period. That amount of time is necessary to gather data from insurance carriers and, if necessary, to return to the marketplace to rebid any insurance that seems too high. Furthermore, if, as part of the annual renewal process, the human resources department intends to conduct focus groups or an employee survey, the six months' time frame is a necessity.

Effect of Poor Planning

Q 2:24 Can poor planning cause a flexible benefits plan to lose its tax-favored status?

Yes, but only in the most extraordinary circumstances. If a flexible benefits plan is designed to comply with the provisions of Code Section 125, poor planning will probably not cause a loss of tax-favored status. Still, poor planning can cause a flexible benefits plan to fail nondiscrimination tests, and this will make the plan less attractive to highly compensated or key employees. Poor planning can also result in general employee dissatisfaction with the plan; in such a case the plan can be considered unsuccessful. Poor planning may even result in the Internal Revenue Service (IRS) or the Department of Labor (DOL) assessing monetary penalties against the employer for failure to meet certain compliance requirements (e.g., filing a Form 5500 series annual report). Unless a flexible benefits plan is in blatant violation of the law, however, it is unlikely that it would ever be disqualified (and thereby lose its tax-favored status). Examples of blatant legal violations are ignoring the use-it-or-lose-it rules (see Q 7:18) and offering benefits not permitted in the plan (e.g., parking expense reimbursement or tuition reimbursement (see chapter 16)).

Focus on Employees

Q 2:25 How does an employer determine which benefits to offer employees under a flexible benefits plan?

An employer's decision regarding which benefits to make available to employees under a flexible benefits plan depends on a number of factors. The design team should consider the following questions:

1. What were the findings of the employee survey?
2. What benefits arenas (e.g., group health and welfare, retirement, paid time off, cash compensation) should be open to employee choice?
3. What benefits does the employer feel compelled to offer because of the prior benefits offerings of the company?
4. How many ranges and options does the employer want to make available, and is the employer limited in number of options by, for example, the insurance carrier?
5. Are there demographic or geographic issues that may generate underwriting or adverse selection concerns?
6. By how much should variations of a single benefit option differ from one another?
7. Should the employer introduce flexible spending accounts?
8. Should the plan design include managed care?
9. Does the employer want to offer a choice that only a few employees will participate in?

Q 2:26 How does a flexible benefits plan allow an employer to shift cost while minimizing employee dissatisfaction?

In the short term, an employee who participates in a flexible benefits plan may pay more by contributing a greater percentage of premium cost or by choosing benefits within the plan that are cost-effective for the employee. It should be noted that cost-effective does not necessarily mean "least costly." An employee might opt for a benefit that requires a greater contribution from his or her pay (or a greater number of benefits credits) because that option provides the employee with better a value for the cost.

Also, a flexible benefits plan might allow an employee to shift employer dollars away from unneeded or less essential benefits to benefits that are more useful to the employee's family situation. For example, an employee may shift dollars away from group benefits such as life insurance or vacation pay to purchase the most expensive medical plan. A flexible benefits plan also allows an employee to reduce cash compensation or retirement benefits to purchase more of other benefits he or she wants.

If "total compensation" is a pie that represents the amount of money an employer may spend on remunerating each of its employees, a flexible benefits plan enables each employee to divide the pie as he or she pleases. For example, if an employee receives $25,000 in cash (salary), $2,500 in retirement benefits, and $4,000 in group health and welfare benefits, the employee's total compensation is $31,500. Under a flexible benefits plan the employee can choose to receive that $31,500 of total compensation in any combination he or she requires; for example, $6,000 in group health and welfare benefits; $1,000 in retirement benefits; and $24,500 in cash compensation.

When it comes to shifting costs through benefit plan cutbacks (almost always through the medical plan), a flexible benefits plan allows the employer to introduce such medical options as comprehensive and managed care preferred provider organizations (PPOs) or health maintenance organizations (HMOs). The communication to employees then becomes:

> There are only so many dollars the company can spend on medical insurance. If you want the plan that allows you to select the doctor or hospital you want, that has little or no case management, and that has high levels of insurance protection, you can have it, but you will have to pay for these privileges.

In other words, the employer gives employees a series of trade-offs, and each employee decides how best to allocate limited resources. For example, an HMO option provides employees with maximum coverage for a reasonable cost, but employees lose the right to choose any provider they wish and care is highly managed.

Practice Pointer. In the long term, if a flexible benefits plan is to help control or contain benefits costs, it should not be used merely to shift costs. Rather, a long-term strategy should be developed, under which pricing options (i.e., purchase price tags) encourage employees to seek the most cost-effective benefits plans. That is particularly true of health care where the only hope of controlling medical costs is through reduced utilization.

Adverse Selection

Q 2:27 What is the effect of adverse selection on a flexible benefits plan?

The problem with adverse selection is that, if left unchecked, it may increase the cost of any employee benefits program. There are a number of ways to negate the effects of adverse selection. Flexible benefits experts agree that adverse selection need not be a problem, although measures should be taken to combat it. That is, adverse selection need not have any long-term cost impact on a flexible benefits plan.

Cost increases are less likely to occur if a flexible benefits plan contains an economic (pricing) or design barrier that requires employees to make thoughtful, rather than easy, choices. Regardless of how an employer protects itself against adverse selection, the design and pricing of flexible benefits must take into account how employees are likely to choose their benefits and whether that selection may create cost swings or cost differentials not accounted for in the original purchase price tags (see chapter 7). Adverse selection may have the effect of limiting some types of plan designs and/or causing the employer to revise the purchase price tag cost of certain benefits.

Q 2:28 How can an employer minimize adverse selection?

An employer can never entirely avoid adverse selection. Still, adverse selection can be minimized by two primary methods.

Proper Plan Design. The controls instituted by proper plan design mitigate the effects of adverse selection by creating balances and mixtures of plan options. Specific elements of good plan design are as follows:

1. Elements of the benefits choices should not be easily segregated. For example, if an employer offers two dental plan options and the only difference between the two is orthodontic coverage, the employer has created an adverse selection problem because only those people who need braces will select the dental plan with orthodontic coverage. It is possible to compensate for the adverse selection, however, by pricing the plan with orthodontic coverage high enough to cover orthodontic benefits.
2. The employer may wish to link or tie two benefit options together. To avoid adverse selection in a prescription drug plan, an employer can tie it to a low-option medical plan or to the managed care medical option. By so doing, the employer makes the lower-option medical plan coverage or a managed care medical plan more appealing to individuals who routinely consume more pharmaceutical products. Those employees (who may be more regular users of health care) will be more likely to be grouped with healthier employees who might also choose the lower-option medical plan. The enrollment of healthier and less healthy employees together in a lower-option medical plan can save the flexible benefits plan more than enough money to offset any adverse selection costs.
3. An employer can require a core benefits selection of some kind; that is, the employer refuses to allow employees to opt out of coverage altogether. For example, all plan participants, whether they want it or not, must enroll in the core medical, life, and disability options. This method requires healthy employees, who might otherwise not elect coverage, to help subsidize coverage for less healthy employees. (*Note*: Required participation may not be used as an option in a Section 125 plan; see Q 6:2.)
4. If adverse selection is a major concern, an employer can always characterize the flexible benefits plan as a modular plan. Adverse selection or "anti-selection" costs can be handled easily by means of a modular

design, since modular designs are based on the three preceding design rules (provide difficult choices, link options, require participation). See Qs 8:13, 8:14 for a discussion on modular benefits design.

Pricing Mechanisms. The implementation of pricing control mechanisms protects a flexible benefits plan by focusing on the pure costs likely to be incurred by the plan and allowing for additional costliness owing to the effects of adverse selection.

By using a pricing strategy, the employer acknowledges the costs associated with adverse selection and introduces an adverse selection "load." In insurance jargon, a load for adverse selection is an incremental cost factor added to the pure premium or working rate that covers the cost of adverse selection. For example, if an employer determined that the adverse selection cost of offering both a high- and low-option long-term disability benefit (as opposed to offering only one or the other) is 3 percent, the employer can add a 3 percent load to each of the long-term disability rates to cover that cost. Alternatively, the employer could place more responsibility for covering the adverse selection cost on one plan or the other. Deciding which long-term disability plan shoulders the greater share of the cost may depend upon the pricing and long-term design strategies of the employer. One solution might be to introduce a 1 percent load to the high-option plan rates and a 5.5 percent load to the low-option plan rates. The intent of such a pricing solution is to lessen the savings of low-option plan participants and to use some of that money to protect the underwriting integrity of the plan.

Levels of Plan Design

Q 2:29 What levels of flexible benefits might be offered under a cafeteria plan?

Cafeteria plans offer varying degrees of flexibility and choice and include the following:

1. Premium conversion plans (tax advantaged for employers and employees; see chapter 5);
2. FSAs (tax advantaged for employers and employees; see chapter 6); and
3. Fully flexible plans that may require a credit methodology (most benefits are tax advantaged for employers and employees; see chapter 7).

As noted in Q 1:3, a cafeteria plan must meet a number of legal requirements to provide the favorable tax consequences that both the plan sponsor and the plan participant desire.

Q 2:30 What are the various approaches to designing flexible benefits plans?

It may be easiest to think of flexible benefits plans in "levels" that can build on one another. The most basic level of flexible benefits plan is a choice-only plan (not within the framework of Code Section 125). Within Section 125 plans, the simplest type of plan is a premium conversion plan (see chapter 5). A somewhat more complex level of plan includes FSAs (see chapter 6). A fully flexible benefits plan (see chapter 7) is often the most complex plan design of all.

Although plan design is often thought of in these levels of complexity, it is not necessary to build up a plan in the order of the levels identified here. For example, it is possible to have a plan that offers FSAs, but under which the employer pays for all of the health insurance (and thus the plan has no premium conversion component). It is also possible to have a fully flexible benefits plan with a complex credit methodology and yet not offer FSAs in the plan.

Following is an outline of Section 125 plan approaches, from simplest to most complex:

1. Premium conversion plans—
   - Premium contribution paid by employees on a pretax basis
2. FSAs—
   - Medical reimbursement account
   - Dependent care reimbursement account
   - Adoption assistance
3. Fully flexible benefits plans—
   - Choice among a menu of options
   - May include benefits credits to be spent within the plan or taken as taxable income
   - May require a credit methodology for pricing benefits and offering credits to spend within the plan

Q 2:31 What is a premium conversion plan?

A *premium conversion plan*, which is considered to be the simplest and most straightforward flexible benefits plan available, is a plan that permits employees to reduce compensation by an amount equal to their contribution toward the cost of the plan's premium. Employees make contributions toward the cost of the employer-sponsored health plan's premium, as well as contributions toward other kinds of employer-sponsored benefits, including dental coverage, prescription drugs, vision care, long-term disability, short-term disability, and group term life insurance. Under a premium conversion plan, employee contributions to a benefits program can be made with pretax, rather than after-tax, dollars. Pretax salary reduction refers to an employee's paying for benefits with "whole" earnings before taxes are withheld (see Q 1:17).

Note. Although premiums for most types of qualified employee benefits can be paid by employees on a pretax basis, some programs are specifically excluded from a Section 125 plan (see chapter 16).

Q 2:32 What is a flexible spending account?

A *flexible spending account* (FSA)—also known as a *flexible reimbursement account*—is a separate, individual account funded generally by employee salary reduction. An employer can also make contributions to such an account. Amounts placed in an FSA are used exclusively to reimburse the employee for qualified expenses incurred during the plan year (see chapter 6). Often, funding of each FSA is merely a recordkeeping function. All funds can be held together in a single claims paying account, or merely held in the general assets of the employer.

Q 2:33 What is a fully flexible benefits plan?

A fully flexible benefits plan, or a multiple option plan, offers participants a choice between several options and cash. Such a plan might include a complex formula for benefit credits or might offer only a combination of premium conversion for a variety of options combined with flexible spending accounts (see chapter 7).

A more intricate fully flexible benefit plan will require a series of exchange rates so that when, for example, an employee drops life or disability insurance for more medical coverage (or for cash), the methodology will be in place for calculating how many credits the employee will receive in place of the life or disability benefit and how many credits the employee needs in order to buy additional medical coverage. In simplest terms, the credit methodology is the price tag for a given benefit.

Another reason for having a credit methodology in place becomes apparent when an employee wishes to cash out a benefit: the methodology is applied to determine how much cash a credit is worth. Generally, benefit credits are used to spend within the plan on benefits; any amount converted to taxable income is considered to be "cash." It is possible to construct a plan so that benefit credits convert dollar for dollar or for a percentage; for example, 50 cents cash for every full benefit credit.

Q 2:34 What are some concerns with Total Flexible Compensation?

After a fully flexible plan, another "layer" of benefits could be added when an employer offers taxable benefits that may be offered outside of a Section 125 plan. However, the employer must be careful not to inadvertently provide reduction of income for a benefit not qualified for such a trade.

Example. Highlight Tours, Inc., wishes to enhance its employee benefits program. The company already offers premium conversion for medical and dental insurance, medical and dependent care FSAs, and the opportunity to buy and sell vacation days. The company offers Flexible Benefit Credits amounting to $4,000 per year for purchase of benefits within the plan.

Highlight Tours would like to add the option to receive financial planning. In addition, the company would like to offer employees the opportunity to take courses at the local college, in order to enhance their careers with the company. The company will make an additional allowance of $1,000 per year available for these options. Employees who do not spend the allowance will be able to receive the allowance as taxable income.

The value of financial planning is considered a taxable item, includible in wages. An employee who opts for financial planning will recognize that value in his or her income.

Educational Assistance Programs under Code Section 127 are not permitted to offer an employee a choice between the benefit and other taxable remuneration. Therefore, a plan that includes educational assistance in lieu of additional pay is not permitted. [Code Sec.127(b)(4)]

Therefore, before Highlight Tours implements their program, they must eliminate the Educational Assistance component of the program. They would want to re-think the allowance accordingly. The employer may offer Educational Assistance under Code Section 127, but they may NOT permit an employee to choose between the benefit and other taxable income.

It is important to ensure that, as a Total Compensation program is designed, it does not inadvertently run afoul of the requirements of Internal Revenue Code and Regulations.

Chapter 3

Benefits Permitted Under Section 125

Although a flexible benefits program may encompass a variety of taxable and tax-preferred benefits, a cafeteria plan as defined by Section 125 of the Internal Revenue Code may include only certain benefits. It is important to design a Section 125 plan to include only qualified benefits while meeting the needs of the employer and its employees.

This chapter outlines the benefits qualified to be included in a Section 125 plan. It also outlines the benefits that *cannot* be included in a Section 125 plan. These benefit options and exclusions are discussed in greater detail in other chapters of the book.

Overview

Q 3:1 Must a Section 125 plan offer participants a choice between qualified benefits and taxable benefits?

Yes. For a plan to qualify under Code Section 125(d), a participant in a cafeteria plan must be able to choose among two or more benefits consisting of cash and qualified benefits. Although the Code specifically refers to cash, a taxable benefit that results in taxable income is generally viewed as the equivalent of cash (see Q 3:4).

If a flexible benefits plan offers participants only choices between qualified benefits, then the plan is not a Section 125 cafeteria plan. If, for example, an employer offers employees a choice between an employer-paid health maintenance organization (HMO) plan or an employer-paid traditional plan, employees have a choice. However, the choice is between two benefits, with no cash option, including no pretax reduction in pay to purchase the benefit. Thus, in this case, Section 125 plan exists, even though the plan offers the flexibility of a choice between two benefits.

Q 3:2 Which qualified benefits are permitted under a Section 125 plan?

The Code prescribes those benefits that are "qualified" to be offered under a Section 125 plan. Only the benefit options specifically listed in Code Section 125 and the related Treasury regulations may be included as a qualified benefit under a cafeteria plan.

Generally, a qualified benefit is one that has special tax-favored status under the Code. Not all tax-preferred benefits may be included in a cafeteria plan, however. Furthermore, not all qualified benefits under a cafeteria plan are necessarily tax preferred.

Cafeteria plan benefits that are qualified for tax-favored treatment include the following:

1. Group term life insurance on an employee for death benefits up to the $50,000 gross income exclusion. (Group term life insurance that provides coverage in excess of $50,000 and results in additional imputed income is considered to be a taxable benefit.), [IRC § 79 Prop Treas Reg §§ 1.125-1, Q&A 5, 1.125-2, Q&A 4(a)(2)(ii)]
2. Accident and health insurance coverage, including all types of medical, vision, prescription, and dental plans, long-term disability, short-term disability, and accidental death and dismemberment, as well as medical reimbursement accounts, or flexible spending accounts (FSAs). [IRC §§ 105, 106]
3. Dependent care assistance plans that provide tax-favorable treatment for moneys spent on the care of certain dependents, provided such care is necessary and allows the employee to maintain his or her job. [IRC § 129]
4. Deferrals to a specified deferred compensation or 401(k) Plan. [IRC § 401(k)]
5. Purchase or sale of elective paid vacation days. [Prop Treas Reg § 1.125-2, Q&A 5(c)]
6. Adoption assistance for amounts paid or reimbursements made to an employee for the cost of such employee's adoption expense. [IRC § 137]
7. Cash is either an implied or explicit benefit in a Section 125 cafeteria plan. Of course, cash is always taxable income. Cash is the alternative when a plan participant chooses not to pay toward health insurance premiums on a pretax basis. This is not to say that the participant may not choose health insurance coverage, if not on a pretax basis. It is

possible to pay toward the cost of premium on an after-tax basis. In this case, under a Section 125 cafeteria plan, the election was for "cash." The cash was then spent (on an after-tax basis) to purchase benefits.

Q 3:3 What are taxable benefits under a Section 125 plan?

A *taxable benefit* under a Section 125 plan (i.e., a cafeteria plan) is one that results in taxable income for the employee when it is received and a tax deduction for the employer when it is given. The most common taxable benefit is cash; however, a taxable benefit need not be cash (see Q 3:4). Vacation pay in lieu of time off and group term life insurance coverage in excess of $50,000 are two examples of taxable benefits that are specifically permitted to be included in a cafeteria plan.

Q 3:4 Under what circumstances may an employer offer the cash equivalent of a taxable benefit as an option in a Section 125 plan?

An employer may offer a cash equivalent benefit under a Section 125 cafeteria plan if a participant must buy the benefit with after-tax dollars or have taxable income equal to the full value of the benefit. [Treas Reg § 1.125-2, Q&A 4(b)] Further, cash, property, or other benefits that create a current taxable event for the participant should be treated as cash and may be offered under a cafeteria plan. [Prop Treas Reg § 1.125-1, Q&A 5]

Q 3:5 What special consideration must a Section 125 plan take into account when offering group term life insurance?

An employer may offer group term life insurance as described in Code Section 79 on the life of the employee under a Section 125 plan (i.e., a cafeteria plan). It must be aware, however, that only the first $50,000 of such coverage is tax free. That includes tax deductible premium payments related to that $50,000 of coverage from all sources, including other employer-paid group term life insurance. Thus, for example, if an employer is providing a flat $15,000 in group term life insurance for all employees, the cafeteria plan will need to limit pretax payments to the premium amount relating to only the remaining $35,000 in a pretax benefit.

Practice Pointer. Because group term life insurance protection that is in excess of the $50,000 limit results in imputed income for the insured employee, many cafeteria plans provide an employer-paid life insurance benefit of one-times-salary up to $50,000 and then offer supplemental life insurance options to the employee. Often, a cafeteria plan allows supplemental life insurance to be purchased by an employee only with after-tax dollars.

Notice 89-110 indicates how the Internal Revenue Service (IRS) expects the amount includible in gross income for premiums in excess of a $50,000 benefit to be calculated: "The amount includible in the gross income of an employee who receives such insurance under a cafeteria plan is the greater of the employee's contributions toward the purchase of the insurance or the cost (determined under section 1.179(d)(2) of the regulations) of the insurance." [Notice 89-110, 1989-2 CB 447] Therefore, amounts of group term life insurance in excess of $50,000 paid by pretax dollars in a cafeteria plan will cause taxable income to the employee of the worst case scenario—the greater of the actual cost or the Table I rate. Such instruction is surprising because group term life insurance outside of a cafeteria plan includes an amount in the employee's gross income to the extent that the cost of insurance was greater than the Table I rate (i.e., the lesser of the employee's contributions or the cost determined by Table I). [Treas Reg § 1.79-3(d)(2)]

Accident and Health Plans

Q 3:6 What special consideration must a Section 125 plan take into account when offering disability insurance?

A Section 125 cafeteria plan may offer disability insurance such as accidental death and dismemberment and short- and long-term disability, provided it meets the requirements of Code Sections 105 and 106. (See Qs 8:69, 8:70)

A special tax consideration applies to disability insurance. If an employee receives disability insurance from his or her employer or pays for disability coverage with pretax dollars, any benefit received as disability income is taxable. If, however, the disability insurance is paid for with after-tax dollars, any disability income received will be tax free. Some benefits professionals believe that a cafeteria plan should allow disability options to be paid only with after-tax dollars. Others contend that for the vast majority of employees who will not receive any disability income, it is best to allow only for pretax employee contributions. A third alternative is to explain the matter to employees and let each plan participant choose whether to pay for disability benefits with pretax or after-tax dollars.

Q 3:7 What criteria must a Section 125 plan meet in order to offer a health insurance program?

An employer-sponsored health insurance program, as described in Code Sections 105 and 106, can be part of a Section 125 cafeteria plan provided that the following criteria are met:

1. The cafeteria plan must be a bona fide insurance program; that is, the premium payments and the medical reimbursements must reflect a shifting of risk between the covered individual and the entity that underwrites the plan (either an insurance carrier or the plan sponsor).
2. Medical expenses that are reimbursed must be incurred during the specified contract period (neither a health plan that reimburses 2002

incurred claims from the 2003 contract nor a health plan that reimburses a claim incurred after the close of the contract year are permissible).

3. Plan participants must buy coverage for a bona fide period of time, typically one year (a medical plan that allows an individual to purchase coverage on an expense-by-expense or on a month-by-month basis violates this requirement) or, in the case of a newly eligible employee, the remainder of the plan year.
4. If the health plan provides self-insured medical reimbursements under Code Section 105(h), the plan must meet the special nondiscrimination rules described in Code Section 105(h). [Treas Reg § 1.125-1, Q&A 17]

A medical FSA operates as a self-funded health insurance program under these rules.

Dependent Care Assistance

Q 3:8 What special consideration must a Section 125 plan take into account when offering a dependent care assistance plan?

A dependent care assistance plan that meets the qualification requirements under Code Section 129 may be part of a Section 125 plan (i.e., a cafeteria plan). Very often such a plan is presented as a dependent care Flexible Spending Account (see chapter 6).

A dependent care assistance plan is unusual in that it competes with the dependent care tax credit. For some taxpayers, the tax credit is worth more than the tax deduction they would receive under a cafeteria plan. Because an employee cannot use both the tax credit and the tax deduction, the employee must make an informed decision between the two. [IRC §§ 21, 129]

The Economic Growth and Tax Relief Reconciliation Act of 2001 (EGTRRA) increases the maximum amount of the tax credit for eligible dependent care tax credit for individual taxpayers beginning January 1, 2003. The dependent care tax credit will increase from $2,400 to $3,000 for one qualifying dependent and from $4,800 to $6,000 for two or more qualifying dependents. The percentage of qualifying expenses that can be claimed will increase from 30 to 35 percent. In addition, the income level at which the credit begins to "phase down" will rise from $10,000 to $15,000, so more taxpayers will receive the full benefit of the credit. As of this writing, the $5,000 maximum for a dependent care FSA has not been increased.

It is difficult to develop a rule for determining which federal income tax savings device—the credit or the deduction—is more advantageous for a particular individual. Generally, however, if an employee's family income is small and his or her federal income tax bracket is low, the tax credit is likely to save the taxpayer more than the tax deduction. An employee whose family income is below $20,000 will almost certainly want to take the tax credit; an employee whose family income is in excess of $30,000 will probably want to use the tax deduction; and an employee whose family income is between $20,000 and $30,000 will have to choose carefully between the two (see Appendix B). Added to this complexity is the fact that, since a Dependent Care FSA can offer a $5,000 benefit, even for one child, the Dependent Care FSA might be better than the Tax Credit, regardless of income, when only one child is in full-time day care.

State income tax savings will also have an impact on the choice between a credit and a deduction. A participant will receive a state income tax benefit in most states for contributions to a dependent care FSA, but may not see any state income tax savings on a personal income tax return through a specific credit. (NOTE: As of this writing, Pennsylvania and New Jersey do not offer state tax reduction for contributions to a Dependent Care Assistance Account.)

Deferred Compensation Plans

Q 3:9 What deferred compensation benefits may a Section 125 plan offer?

Code Section 125(d)(2)(A) clearly states that a Section 125 plan may not include any plan that offers deferred compensation. There are, however, two exceptions to that injunction:

1. Deferred compensation arrangements under Code Section 401(k).
2. Postretirement group life insurance plans maintained by certain types of educational institutions, provided that all contributions are made before retirement and the insurance does not have a cash surrender value at any time.

Note. Not all forms of deferred compensation are easy to identify (see Q 3:15).

Vacation days

Q 3:10 What special considerations must a Section 125 plan take into account when offering vacation days?

A participant in a Section 125 plan (i.e., a cafeteria plan) may be offered the option to buy or sell vacation days. It is important, however, that because the Code and Treasury regulations do not discuss any other paid time-off policies (e.g., holidays, sick time, or earned time), only vacation days should be offered as a paid time-off option. A cafeteria plan that allows participants to buy additional vacation days or sell unwanted vacation days must be able to distinguish between elective and nonelective vacation days.

Nonelective vacation days, as the name suggests, are not subject to election by the employee. For instance, if a plan sponsor gives employees three weeks of vacation and under the cafeteria plan employees may sell back one week, the two weeks that they cannot sell back constitute the nonelective vacation days. If a plan sponsor gives employees two core weeks of vacation and employees may purchase one additional week, the additional week that the employee may purchase constitutes elective time and the two core weeks constitute nonelective time.

As noted earlier (see Q 3:9), the prohibition against offering any type of deferred compensation in a cafeteria plan includes carrying over elective vacation days into another plan year. If unused elective vacation days are carried forward into the next plan year, then, by definition, the plan is not a cafeteria plan. There is, however, an interesting exception to the general operating principle of "use it or lose it." According to a proposed regulation:

> A plan does not permit the deferral of compensation merely because the plan permits a participant who has not used all elective, paid vacation days for a plan year to receive cash in the value of such unused days in exchange for such days if the participant receives the cash on or before the earlier of the last day of the plan year of the cafeteria plan or the last day of the employee's taxable year to which the elective contributions used to purchase the unused days relate. [Prop Treas Reg 1.125:2, Q&A 5(c)(3)]

Therefore, it is possible to cash out unused vacation days—before the end of the plan year (or employee's taxable year, if applicable.)

Practice Pointer. If a cafeteria plan includes the purchase of vacation days and the plan sponsor wishes to permit employees to receive the cash value of unused elective vacation days, the plan document should state that all unused elective vacation days will automatically be exchanged for cash as of a specified date near the end of the plan year. Without such a provision, an employee will forfeit all unused, elective vacation days as of the end of the plan year.

Under Treasury regulations, an employee may use his or her elective vacation days only after all nonelective vacation days have been exhausted. [Treas Reg § 1.125-2, Q&A 5(c)(2)]

Example. Rose, an employee of Pretty Petals, has two weeks of nonelective vacation and one week elective vacation (15 days total vacation time). If Rose uses 13 days of vacation during the 2002 plan year, the two unused days cannot be carried forward to 2003. By regulation, participants must use all nonelective vacation days before any elective days. In this example, the last five days are the elective days. If Rose does not use them during the plan year, she might forfeit the unused benefit. However, a different outcome is possible. Instead of compelling Rose to forfeit two days, Pretty Petal's cafeteria plan may provide that, before the end of the plan year, unused vacation days will automatically be exchanged for cash.

Q 3:11 May vacation day benefits be used as a cash equivalent?

For most practitioners, using (or viewing) vacation days as a taxable benefit and relying upon vacation time as a cash equivalent option is a risky position to take.

Although vacation pay is taxable, offering vacation days is not a taxable benefit. Letter Ruling 9635002 may give some understanding of how the IRS views vacation benefits. In that ruling, the IRS clearly envisioned vacation day benefits to be a qualified nontaxable benefit. The issue revolved around the taxability of an employee's choice between vacation day benefits and a contribution to the 401(k) plan. The IRS concluded that a choice between (1) vacation days, (2) a contribution to a 401(k) plan, or (3) forfeiture of unused vacation days did not create an employee election between cash or deferred income. In effect, the IRS said there was no cash option, even though it is understood that when an employee takes a vacation day and receives pay for that day, a taxable event takes place.

Adoption Assistance

Q 3:12 What adoption assistance may be offered under a Section 125 plan?

A Section 125 plan may offer an adoption assistance reimbursement account as an option. Under such an account, an employee may receive an exclusion from gross income for employer payments (including salary reduction payments) for qualifying adoption expenses. For plan years beginning on or before December 31, 2001, there was a dollar limit of $5,000 per child ($6,000 for a child with special needs, provided that the adoption was not a foreign adoption). [IRC § 137] EGTRRA extended and expanded the adoption assistance exclusion. Previously, the tax exclusion was scheduled to expire on December 31, 2001. Under EGTRRA, for plan years beginning on or after January 1, 2002, the dollar limit per adoption is $10,000. The income limit related to this benefit has also been increased (see chapter 6).

Benefits Not Permitted Under Section 125

Q 3:13 Which tax-favored benefits are not qualified benefits under a Section 125 plan?

An employee benefit may be tax preferred but not be a qualified benefit under a cafeteria plan as defined by Code Section 125. Code Section 125(f) describes several tax-favored employee benefit programs that are specifically excluded from cafeteria plans, including the following:

- Scholarships and fellowships. [IRC § 117]

- Educational assistance programs. [IRC § 127]
- Certain fringe benefit plans such as qualified employee discounts; working condition fringe benefits such as subsidized cafeteria-style employee restaurants; and *de minimis* fringe benefits that are too small to calculate on an employee-by-employee basis. [IRC § 132]
- Employer-provided group term life insurance on dependents of the employee. [Notice 89-110, 1989-2 CB 447]
- Medical savings account (MSA) contributions made at the election of the employee. [IRC §§ 106(b)(2), 125(f)]
- Long-term care insurance, even on an after-tax basis (even though premium payments for long-term care insurance are permitted as a pretax choice for employees in plans other than cafeteria plans). [IRC §§ 213(d), 125(f)]
- Parking and mass transit reimbursement (even though permitted as a pretax contribution by employees and a tax-free reimbursement in plans other than cafeteria plans).
- Contributions to a Section 529 College Savings Account.
- Contributions to a Health Reimbursement Arrangement with a rollover provision.

In short, the only benefits that may be included in a cafeteria plan are those specifically listed as includable in the Code and the related Treasury regulations (see chapter 2).

Restrictions on Qualified Benefits

Q 3:14 What are the limits on offering life insurance under a Section 125 plan?

Only group term life insurance may be offered under a Section 125 cafeteria plan. Other life insurance products such as whole life and universal life include the possibility of payment of a benefit beyond the period of coverage, thus deferring compensation in a prohibited manner.

It should further be noted that although individual term life insurance does not defer compensation to a future plan year, the Code and Treasury regulations specify only *group* term life insurance as a permitted benefit within a cafeteria plan. It would therefore be risky to design a cafeteria plan to include individual term life insurance

Q 3:15 May a Section 125 plan offer deferred compensation benefits?

A Section 125 cafeteria plan may include only two types of deferred compensation—401(k) arrangements and certain insurance plans maintained by educational institutions (see Q 3:9).

Not all forms of deferred compensation are easy to identify. Examples of prohibited deferred compensation itemized in Treasury regulations regarding cafeteria plans are as follows:

- Carryover of unused benefits, including elective vacation days [Treas Reg § 1.125-1, Q&A 7]
- Carryover of unused benefit credits [Treas Reg § 1.125-1, Q&A 7]
- Conversion of unused contributions or benefits for benefits that are different in the future [Treas Reg § 1.125-2, Q 5(a)]

Note. Treasury Regulations 1.125-2, Q&A 4(c) permits a "qualified cash or deferred arrangement (Section 401(k)" plan to be included in a Section 125 plan. The regulation does not use broad language and, in fact, specifically references only 401(k) plans. For this reason it is risky to interpret the regulations as also permitting other types of tax qualified plans, such as 403(b) or 457 plans, to be combined with a Section 125 plan.

Q 3:16 May a Section 125 plan offer group legal services?

No. The tax treatment for group legal services as an employee benefit changed in 1992. Although group legal services plans are reviewed by members of Congress for possible reinstatement to tax-preferred status from time to time, tax-qualified status does not currently extend to such plans. They may not be included in a Section 125 plan.

Q 3:17 May an employer substitute nonqualified benefits for cash in a Section 125 plan?

A taxable benefit that is not cash and also is not a qualified benefit (e.g., a health club membership or a financial planning option) should not be offered under a Section 125 cafeteria plan because it is not clear whether or not such a benefit can be deemed a cash equivalent.

For example, it may be dangerous for an employer to offer employees a choice between a high-option medical plan and a low-option medical plan with a financial planning option. The reason such a menu could pose difficulties is that the financial planning option may not be viewed, technically, as a cash equivalent taxable benefit—in which case the flexible benefits plan would not qualify. To maintain its qualified status, the cafeteria plan could frame the second option as being a low-option medical plan with cash and then outside the cafeteria plan let employees convert the cash to a financial planning benefit.

Q 3:18 May a Section 125 plan offer nonqualified benefits as options without risking its tax-qualified status?

No. If an employer is considering restricting the benefits offered to only nonqualified, after-tax benefits (e.g., group automobile insurance, financial planning services, mortgage assistance, and group homeowners' insurance), then it is not feasible to offer such benefits under a cafeteria plan. The only possible justification for including such benefits in a cafeteria plan is that they could be used as cash equivalent options. It must be noted, however, that there is no clear regulatory guidance to support using a nonqualified, after-tax benefit as a cash equivalent.

If, on the other hand, an employer desires to merely include after-tax benefits in a cafeteria plan design (i.e., not use them as a cash equivalent), then a non-tax-preferred flexible benefit arrangement may be readily designed that presents those options to participants without technically making them part of the cafeteria plan. By doing so, the integrity and tax-qualified status of the cafeteria plan is not jeopardized.

For instance, an employer can design a flexible benefit arrangement so that, as presented on the enrollment form, employees appear to be spending unused flexible credits or salary reduction dollars to purchase after-tax benefits while, in reality, the plan is structured so that unused flexible credits are first converted into cash and then the cash (after taxes are withheld) is used to purchase after-tax benefits. In such a manner, after-tax payroll deduction dollars (rather than salary reduction dollars) are used to purchase after-tax benefits. The plan looks totally integrated, but none of the after-tax benefit options are in fact part of the cafeteria plan.

Chapter 4

Choice-Only Plans

A choice-only plan allows employees to select from various types and levels of coverage, yet it does not constitute a cafeteria plan as defined in Section 125 of the Internal Revenue Code. This chapter explains which benefits can be offered through a choice-only plan and discusses the essential points of implementing such a plan.

Plan Design

Q 4:1 What are choice-only plans?

Choice-only plans allow employees to elect the types and levels of coverage they wish to receive. Employees select the benefits that best meet their needs, based on certain options offered by the employer. This type of plan is based on the employer's realization that employees have varying benefits needs, due to different demographic situations and lifestyles.

Sometimes, choice-only plans are structured so that both the employer and the employee contribute to defray the cost of benefits selected by the employee. When a choice-only plan is not intended to qualify under Code Section 125, any employee contribution for the benefit coverage must be made on an after-tax basis

In some cases, however, the choice-only plan is structured to give employees an opportunity to choose between equally priced benefits options, in which case a contribution by the employee may not be necessary. For example, if the employer provides fully employer-paid choices between a high-option medical plan and a low-option medical plan combined with dental coverage, this constitutes a choice-only plan. Such a choice-only plan need not satisfy the requirements of Code Section 125, because employees do not contribute toward the cost of the plan on a pretax basis.

The changing structure of the American family has contributed to the appeal of choice-only plans. In the last 20 years, the number of two-parent, single-worker families has decreased, while the number of families with two working parents and single-parent families has increased. Many employers have responded to these changes in the U.S. labor force by offering plans that provide employees with meaningful choices.

Q 4:2 What distinguishes a choice-only plan from a cafeteria plan?

A choice-only plan allows participants to choose from among various qualified group health and welfare benefits, such as medical, dental, vision, and disability and life insurance benefits. In some cases, a choice-only plan offers participants a choice of various after-tax, nonqualified benefits, such as legal services, financial planning, group universal life, and group automobile insurance. A choice-only plan can never allow a plan participant to trade pretax, qualified benefits for after-tax, nonqualified benefits (or vice versa).

In contrast, a cafeteria plan under Code Section 125 must offer participants a choice between two or more benefits consisting of cash and qualified benefits—at least one taxable benefit and one nontaxable benefit. (See chapters 2 and 4 for a detailed discussion of qualified benefits.)

Because a choice-only plan does not include the exchange of pretax, qualified benefits for a taxable benefit (usually cash), it does not qualify as a cafeteria plan.

Q 4:3 How does the employer determine which benefits to offer under a choice-only plan?

In determining which benefits should be offered under a choice-only plan, the employer should consider the following key factors:

- Which benefits will involve employee choice?
- How many choices will be available to employees?
- Will some current benefits be eliminated?
- Will certain coverages be required?
- What new benefits will be offered?
- How will plans of the same type (e.g., medical plans) differ from one another?
- How much should employees contribute for each benefits option?
- Will minimum levels of coverage be required (e.g., such as a low level of long-term disability coverage)?

Employer Considerations

Q 4:4 When a choice-only plan is introduced, is the amount the employer contributes usually less than the amount contributed under the current plan?

This depends on the employer's reason for introducing a choice-only plan. If the employer's goal is to achieve cost savings, and new choices are being introduced to mitigate the effect of this change, then the amount the employer spends on the new program will be less than the current cost. In this case, even though the employee may have to spend more dollars for the desired benefits, choice-only plans can increase the perceived value of selected benefits. On the other hand, the employer may be able to spend more on the program, so that additional choices are accompanied by the employer's willingness to fund new and/or existing benefits to a greater degree. In this instance, the plan provides increased economic value along with greater choice, which is a significant noneconomic value.

Given the cost of providing benefits to employees, it is important to recognize that many employers do introduce choice programs with the intent to control or contain the cost of the employee benefits program.

Q 4:5 Why might an employer want to offer a choice-only plan?

An employer might want to offer a choice-only plan to its employees for a variety of reasons, including the following:

- To respond to employees' diverse benefits needs
- To obtain greater control over benefits cost expenditures
- To make new benefits available to employees without increasing the employer's contributions
- To target shifts in plan enrollments
- To recruit and retain valued employees
- To increase employees' appreciation of benefits
- To develop the concept of benefits as a key component of total compensation
- To keep plan administration as simple as possible

Furthermore, a choice-only plan is not subject to the various administrative requirements that apply to a Section 125 plan, such as drafting a cafeteria plan document, performing nondiscrimination testing, and administering the rules governing the revocability of elections. Some employers are unwilling to take on those administrative requirements.

Administrative Rules

Q 4:6 Do special administrative rules apply to choice-only plans?

No. Unlike cafeteria plans, no special administrative rules (such as nondiscrimination testing or plan documentation requirements) apply to choice-only plans. However, the underlying benefits available through the plan may be subject to their own administrative rules, including ERISA's reporting and disclosure requirements, and the Code's nondiscrimination testing standards.

Q 4:7 Is a choice-only plan difficult to administer?

The administration of a choice-only plan depends on the complexity of its design. A plan that offers only a few choices requires little administration, while a plan that offers numerous choices in types and levels of coverage requires a complex recordkeeping system. Complicated designs also may require the services of an internal staff and a computer software program to administer the plan; alternatively, should the employer not have the staff to accomplish internal administration, the employer may use the services of an outside recordkeeper.

Q 4:8 What benefits may be included in a choice-only plan?

In its simplest form, a choice-only plan provides a choice among several benefits options, such as between an indemnity plan and a health maintenance organization (HMO). More complex arrangements allow participants to design their own benefits packages by choosing from a variety of benefits plans and options. Examples of benefits that may be included in a choice-only plan are dental, medical, life insurance, disability, and hearing and vision benefits, as well as more unusual benefits, such as long-term care and financial planning. However, choice-only plans do not permit participants to exchange pretax, qualified benefits for after-tax benefits (see Qs 4:2, 4:9).

Q 4:9 May an employee pay for benefits with pretax dollars in a choice-only plan?

No. If a plan is to remain outside of jurisdiction of Code Section 125, an employee must pay for benefits with after-tax dollars. Once an employee pays for benefits with pretax dollars, a premium conversion plan under Code Section 125 is created, and all the requirements that pertain to cafeteria plans (such as nondiscrimination testing and plan documentation requirements) would apply. (See chapter 5 for a discussion of premium conversion plans.)

Q 4:10 Can adverse selection affect a choice-only plan?

Yes. Adverse selection is the tendency on the part of employees to select against a program by choosing only the benefits they are most likely to use. Examples of adverse selection are as follows:

- Employees with severe health conditions will elect rich medical plans
- Employees with health conditions requiring drug treatment are likely to elect a plan with a strong prescription drug benefit
- Employees whose children need braces will elect orthodontia coverage

If left unchecked, adverse selection will increase the cost of a choice-only plan. (See Q 2:27 for a discussion of ways to mitigate the effect of adverse selection.)

Q 4:11 How does a choice-only plan differ from a cafeteria plan?

Table 4-1 offers a comparison of choice-only plans and cafeteria plans.

Table 4-1. Comparison of Choice-Only Plans and Cafeteria Plans

	Choice-Only	*Cafeteria*
Employee contributions	After-tax	Pretax or after-tax
Options available	Any and all	Only those cited in Code Section 125
Administrative rules	Generally, ERISA	Special Section 125 rules and ERISA rules for underlying plans
Section 125 nondiscrimination testing	Does not apply	Does apply
Benefits trades available	Among pretax benefits only or among after-tax benefits only[a]	Between pretax benefits and cash or cash equivalents[b]

[a] There is never an exchange between pretax and after-tax benefits.

[b] A cash equivalent benefit permitted by Code Section 125 can be included in a cafeteria plan, provided the participant buys the benefit with after-tax dollars or has taxable income equal to the full value of the benefit. (See chapter 3 for a discusssion of the benefits that constitute "taxable benefits" under a Section 125 flexible benefits plan.)

Q 4:12 Are taxable (non-qualified) benefits appropriate options under a choice-only plan?

Yes; they can be. Certain options that are not permitted under a pretax program represent the type of options one should consider for a choice-only plan. For example, it may be possible for an employer to offer a taxable allowance to all employees for selection among various benefits. In most cases, however, the employee's use of the allowance *may not* reduce his or her taxable income. The allowance is offered as an additional benefit, not an offset to pay. The basic concepts supporting choice-only plans are:

1 Employee demographics are changed forever;

2. The business environment requires employees to do more with less;
3. New delivery vehicles are being created all the time; and
4. The changing needs of employees put new demands on employers.

These basic concepts have all come together to promote freedom of choice, individualization, total compensation, and personal responsibility. In turn, a choice-only plan supports the use of nontraditional benefits to further these basic concepts.

Q 4:13 Is offering an after-tax allowance for purchase of taxable benefits appropriate for a choice-only plan?

Yes. A taxable benefits allowance is an excellent method for delivering the diverse array of options an employee can be offered in a choice-only plan. In most instances the taxable allowance is created specifically to provide nonqualified, after-tax or nontraditional benefits (or both).

Chapter 5

Premium Conversion Plans

In an effort to control their medical insurance costs, most employers now require employees to pay some portion of medical insurance premiums. Employees may also have to share the cost of other types of insurance, including dental, vision, group term life, and disability insurance.

A premium conversion plan allows employees to pay some portion of such insurance premiums with pretax dollars, thus creating a tax savings for both employer and employees. This chapter explains how a premium conversion plan works and how the operation of such a plan is regulated by Section 125 of the Internal Revenue Code

Plan Design

Q 5:1 What is meant by the term *premium conversion?*

Premium conversion is payment of a participant's portion of a benefits premium with pretax dollars rather than with after-tax dollars. For an employer to be able to permit employees to pay some portion of an insurance premium on a pretax basis, the employer must implement a benefits plan as described in Code Section 125. When a Section 125 plan includes only a pretax premium payment component, it is sometimes referred to as a *premium only plan* (POP).

When a plan participant uses pretax dollars for benefit payments, that participant avoids federal income tax, taxes imposed by the Federal Insurance Contributions Act (FICA) (if applicable), and, in most cases, state and local income tax on those dollars. Other tax savings, such as school district income tax, may also be available to the participant. Paying for benefits on a pretax basis rather than on an after-tax basis increases a participant's take-home pay.

At the same time, the employer avoids the matching FICA tax and Federal Unemployment Tax Act (FUTA) tax. In some states, the employer also saves on such taxes as the state unemployment tax or the state workers' compensation premium.

Q 5:2 How are premium conversion plans structured?

Some premium conversion plans are structured so that employees' premium payments for an elected benefit (e.g., medical coverage) must be made on a salary reduction (pretax) basis; other plans are structured so that employees may choose between making premium payments for elected benefits on a pretax or after-tax basis.

It is important to note that when payment for benefit coverage is only permitted on a pretax basis, employees must have the choice of opting out of coverage. For example, if an employer's dental insurance carrier required the employer to cover 100 percent of its employees under the dental policy, the employer could not require employees to pay a pretax contribution toward the plan. This is because the plan design does not contain a choice between cash and benefits, as required by Internal Revenue Code. Instead, the employer might opt to provide coverage at the individual level for all employees, but permit employees to add dependent coverage at an additional cost, which may be paid on a pretax basis. This arrangement offers employees the required choice between cash and benefits.

Q 5:3 In what context are premium conversion plans usually introduced?

Premium conversion plans are often introduced when an employer has decided to require employees to contribute toward the cost of benefits for the first time or when the employer is increasing the after-tax amount of premium contribution paid by employees. Implementing a premium conversion plan at the time an employer expects to increase the employee contribution has a double benefit for the employer. First, employees will be paying more toward the cost of coverage. Second, the employer will reap the payroll tax savings (FICA and possibly others) on the premium contribution paid on a pretax basis.

Premium conversion should be explored any time employees are paying part of the cost of a premium on an after-tax basis. Thus, even when employee contribution toward the cost of benefits is not new and a change in the employee contribution is not anticipated, an employer that requires employees to contribute toward the cost of coverage on an after-tax basis might wish to introduce premium conversion to help both the employees and the employer save on certain payroll taxes by converting premium payment to a pretax basis.

Q 5:4 What types of premiums may be paid on a pretax basis in a premium conversion plan?

Premium conversion plans typically permit payment of premium contributions on a pretax basis for health benefits qualified under Code Sections 105 and 106, although payment of premiums for other qualified benefits may also be permitted. (See chapter 3 for a definition of qualified benefits.) Health benefits for which premiums may be paid on a pretax basis include medical coverage, which encompasses preferred provider organizations (PPO) and health maintenance organizations (HMO), dental, prescription drug, vision care, and hearing plans. Although long term care insurance is a medical plan under Code Section 105, it is specifically excluded as a qualified benefit under a Section 125 plan.

Premium conversion may also be used by participants to purchase group term life insurance coverage, disability insurance (see chapter 8), and accidental death and dismemberment benefits.

To be considered a qualified benefit of the plan, the premium must relate to a plan provided by the plan sponsor. For example, premium conversion plans generally cannot be used to pay for COBRA premiums owed to another (i.e., former) employer, or to pay for a spouse's premium contribution. Depending on the plan design and the plans offered by the plan sponsor, it may be possible to be reimbursed on a pretax basis for premium expenses related to health and/or disability policies obtained independently by the participant. [Rev Rul. 61-148; Appendix L] The plan sponsor would need to consider these independent plans part of the coverage of the employer and permit any eligible employee to participate in premium reimbursement (see Q 5:16).

Q 5:5 What rules under Code Section 125 apply to premium conversion plans?

A premium conversion plan operates under Code Section 125 by offering a "choice between cash and benefits." That phrase is often a point of some confusion, however. The "cash" in the arrangement flows from the choice *not* to pay for benefits on a pretax basis, and thereby take taxable income. It is entirely possible for an employee to pay for benefit premiums on an after-tax basis. In such a case, the employee would have been deemed to have chosen cash, even though he or she paid for the premium with after-tax dollars. The "benefit" is the ability to pay for premium contribution on a pretax basis.

As a Section 125 plan, a premium conversion plan must follow all of the requirements of the Code and its supporting regulations, including description of the plan in a plan document, a salary reduction agreement, and nondiscrimination testing.

Q 5:6 What must a premium conversion plan document contain?

A premium conversion plan must be in writing [Prop Treas Reg § 1.125-1, Q&A 3], and the written document must include the following information:

1. A specific description of each of the benefits available under the plan, including the periods during which the benefits are provided (the periods of coverage);
2. The plan's eligibility rules governing participation;
3. The procedures governing participants' elections under the plan, including the period during which elections can be made, the extent to which elections are irrevocable, and the periods during which elections are effective;
4. The manner in which employer contributions can be made under the plan (e.g., a salary reduction agreement between the participant and the employer or nonelective employer contributions to the plan);
5. The maximum amount of employer contributions available to any participant under the plan; and
6. The plan year in which the cafeteria plan operates.

In describing the benefits available under the plan, the premium conversion plan document need not be self-contained. That is, the plan document can include by reference benefits established under other, separate written plans, such as coverage under a dependent care assistance plan, without describing in full the benefits established under such a plan. If, however, the other plan offers different maximum levels of coverage, the descriptions in the premium conversion plan document must specify the available maximums.

Q 5:7 Does the premium conversion plan document have to be filed with any government agencies?

No. Under current law, the premium conversion plan document does not have to be filed with any government agencies or submitted to the Internal Revenue Service (IRS) for a determination letter. However, the IRS and the Department of Labor (DOL) are free to audit the operations of Section 125 plans, and, during such a review, sponsors of such plans may be required to submit plan documents that meet the requirements of Code Section 125 (see Q 5:6).

Q 5:8 Must premium conversion plans satisfy any nondiscrimination rules?

Yes. Premium conversion plans are subject to two sets of nondiscrimination rules. First, nontaxable benefits offered under such a plan, such as accident or health benefits, may be subject to their own nondiscrimination standards. Second, the aggregate benefits of a premium conversion plan are subject to the Section 125 eligibility, contribution and benefits, and key employee concentration tests. (See chapter 14 for a detailed discussion of the nondiscrimination rules and requirements.)

Q 5:9 Are premium conversion plan contributions subject to the trust and audit requirements of ERISA?

No; not under current law. Section 125 cafeteria plans generally are exempt from the trust and audit requirements of the Employee Retirement Income Security Act of 1974 (ERISA) until final regulations addressing trust and reporting requirements for contributory welfare plans are issued.

On May 17, 1988, the DOL announced that participants' contributions to a cafeteria plan are plan assets within the meaning of ERISA Section 403(a). The DOL regulation required that salary reduction contributions be segregated from the employer's assets and placed in trust as soon as administratively feasible, but in no event later than 90 days after the payroll deduction or the date the participants would have received the amounts as cash. On August 12, 1988, however, the DOL announced that it would not enforce the trust requirement for cafeteria plans, although it did not exempt cafeteria plans from rules that plan assets held in trust be audited by an independent certified public accountant if a plan covers 100 or more employees.

In 1992, the DOL restated its previous (1988) policy that the trust requirement would not be enforced against cafeteria plans until after December 31, 1993, or, if earlier, not until after the adoption of final regulations providing relief from ERISA's trust and reporting requirements. The DOL further stated that the requirement that plans be audited by an independent certified public accountant would not be enforced against cafeteria plans that satisfy certain requirements. To be specific, the audit requirement will not be enforced against cafeteria plans with self-insured benefits arrangements without a trust, nor against cafeteria plans with insured benefits arrangements, provided that employee contributions are forwarded to the insurer or HMO within three months of receipt.

In August 1993, the DOL extended the relief from the trust and audit requirements of ERISA that had been afforded to cafeteria plans, until final regulations addressing trust and reporting requirements for contributory welfare plans are issued; however, the DOL required plans that do hold assets in trust to meet the ERISA audit requirement.

It is impossible to predict whether cafeteria plans will be exempted permanently from the trust and audit requirements because the issuance of final regulations regarding the matter does not appear to be a priority of the DOL. For the near term, it appears that the temporary relief will remain intact. [ERISA Technical Release 92-01, June 2, 1992, which superseded ERISA Technical Release 88-1, August 12, 1988]

Q 5:10 Is the relief from the trust and audit requirements provided by ERISA for cafeteria plans affected by the DOL's requirement for qualified plans to segregate plan assets as soon as administratively feasible?

Apparently not. In informal discussions, the DOL has stated that the trust and audit relief provided by ERISA Technical Release 92-01 remains in effect. Therefore, the accelerated schedule for depositing voluntary employee contributions made to an employee benefits plan effective as of 1997 will not apply to salary reduction contributions or employee after-tax contributions (including COBRA contributions) made to a Section 125 plan.

Implications for Employees

Q 5:11 What impact does a premium conversion plan have on employees' share of benefit costs?

If an employer has just implemented a premium cost-sharing program with employees, payment of that premium contribution on a pretax basis (i.e., through a premium conversion plan) can help employees lessen the cost through tax savings.

> **Example.** As of January 1, 2000, the Hope Manufacturing Company will require employees to contribute $50 per month toward the cost of medical and dental individual insurance premiums; employee contributions were never previously required. Because the $600 annual premium contribution ($50 x 12) will be paid through a premium conversion plan, a Hope Mfg. employee's take-home pay will in fact be reduced by *less than $600*. The premium payment amount is exempt from federal income taxes, FICA tax, and in this instance, state income taxes.
>
> Gretchen, an unmarried employee of Hope Mfg., earns $30,000 per year and pays federal income tax at the 15 percent rate, FICA tax at 7.65 percent, and state income tax at 5 percent. Tax savings for Gretchen as a result of the premium conversion plan will be $13.83 ($50 x 27.65%) per month. Thus, Gretchen's take-home pay will decrease only by approximately $36.17 per month—instead of $50.

Q 5:12 Is there any financial detriment for employees who participate in a premium conversion plan?

Possibly. With regard to benefits based on an employee's salary, such as life insurance, disability, and pension benefits, reduction of an employee's salary by the amount of contributions under a premium conversion plan may in turn reduce the value of future benefits payable to the employee under such programs. An employer should decide whether employees' salary reduction amounts will be included in or excluded from salary for purposes of calculating employees' life insurance, disability, and pension benefits.

Example. Bill, an employee of the Excellent Electricians Co., earns a gross salary of $30,000. Bill contributes $2,000 per year in pretax premium contributions. Excellent Electricians provides a life insurance benefit of one-times an employee's salary. Bill's benefit in the event of death is either $28,000 or $30,000, depending on whether Excellent Electricians includes the pretax premium contribution (in this case, $2,000) in its definition of salary.

Note. Most companies add back salary reduction amounts for calculation of benefit levels based on an employee's salary (but see Q 5:13).

It should also be noted that FICA taxes are paid on the reduced salary amount. For those employees close to retirement age, a lower reported salary might result in a slightly lower Social Security benefit.

Even if pretax premium payments result in a lower Social Security benefit or employer-provided life insurance, disability, or pension benefits, premium conversion is still valuable because of the increase in the employee's current take-home pay attributable to the plan's tax-savings feature. In most cases, the tax savings of today outweighs the possibly lowered future payout of certain benefit programs.

Q 5:13 May companies include salary reduction amounts in the calculation of retirement benefits that are based on an employee's salary?

Yes. As a result of the Small Business Job Protection Act of 1996 (SBJPA), for years beginning after December 31, 1997, Section 415(c) limits on contributions and benefits under defined contribution plans (currently the lesser of $40,000 or 100 percent of compensation) includes contributions to a Section 125 plan as part of compensation. [IRC § 415(c)(3)(D), added by SBJPA § 1434(a)] Section 415 compensation also now includes elective contributions to 401(k) plans, Section 403(b) tax-sheltered annuities, Section 457 nonqualified deferred compensation plans, and simplified employee pensions (SEPs).

In general, for years beginning before December 31, 1997, Section 125 salary reduction amounts are not treated as compensation for purposes of calculating an employee's maximum retirement plan contribution and benefits limits under Section 415.

Q 5:14 Is it possible to increase contributions paid by employees at the same time premium conversion is introduced without causing employees to pay more from their take-home pay?

Yes. If an employer knows the estimated tax rate of employees, it is possible to calculate the amount of increase to premium contributions that would approximately yield a neutral change in take-home pay. If the calculation is based on those employees in the lower tax bracket, those at a higher tax bracket might even see an increase in take-home pay with implementation of a premium conversion plan.

The method is as follows:

1. Determine the combined FICA, federal, and, if applicable, state and local tax savings rate for employees. The most conservative stance is to calculate the tax rate for lower-paid employees with lower tax rates.
2. To estimate the amount an employee in the lower tax bracket can pay and still take home the same pay, divide the current premium contribution amount by the inverse of the tax savings rate.

Example. Assume that a standard tax savings rate for employees is 27.65 percent. The current after-tax employee contribution for individual health coverage is $50 per month; for family coverage, $100 per month. Divide $50 by (1 minus 0.2765, or 0.7235), and divide $100 by (1 minus 0.2765, or 0.7235). The amount an employee could be asked to pay for single coverage and still take home approximately the same pay is $69.11. For family coverage, an employee could pay approximately $138.22 and still take home the same pay.

Q 5:15 What are the tax implications for an employee who participates in a premium conversion plan?

An employee who participates in a premium conversion plan sets aside an amount for premium payments that is not subject to federal income or, in most cases, state and local taxes. (See Appendix A for state and local treatment of pretax salary reductions under Code Section 125.) In addition, the amount of the salary reduction for employees who earn less than the Social Security wage base ($84,900 for 2002) is not subject to FICA taxes. Thus, when an employee makes pretax premium contributions instead of paying for premiums on an after-tax basis, the employee's taxable income is reduced and the employee's take-home pay is increased.

Q 5:16 May an employee pay the premium of an individual health plan policy through his or her premium conversion plan?

Yes, as long as certain conditions are met. Proposed Treasury Regulations Section 1.125-2, Q&A 7(b)(4), indicates that a medical flexible spending account (FSA) may not treat participants' premium payments for other health coverage as reimbursable expenses. More to the point, however, the regulation indicates that premiums for current health coverage can be paid on a salary reduction basis through the ordinary operation of a cafeteria (i.e., Section 125) plan.

In informal conversations, IRS officials have indicated that the arrangement allowing payment of premiums for an individual health plan policy must meet the following conditions:

1. The plan document for the premium conversion plan must indicate that it will provide for individual health insurance policies.

2. The policy in question must be an employee's individual health policy (e.g., not be a policy provided by the employer of the employee's spouse.)
3. There must be an accounting that provides significant proof that the outside premiums have been paid, as described in Revenue Ruling 61-146.

Note. It appears that COBRA premiums for a participant may not be paid through a premium conversion plan because they represent payments made for a group health policy of a different employer.

Revenue Ruling 61-146 (see Appendix L) sets forth the following standards for a proper accounting:

1. The employer reimburses each employee directly once or twice a year for the employer's share of the health premiums upon proof of prior payment of the premiums by the employee to the insurer;
2. The employer issues to the employee a check payable to the particular employee's insurance company, the employee being obligated to send the check to the insurance company; or
3. The employer issues a check as described in alternative (2), except the check is payable jointly to the insurance company and the employee.

Q 5:17 Must an employer file Form 5500 for a premium conversion plan?

No. IRS announced in April 2002 that the requirements of Code Section 6039D were no longer valid. (Previously, all Section 125 Plans were required to file Form 5500 and Schedule F.) This change is effective immediately and retroactively. A copy of the IRS News Release is included in Appendix J.

Implications for Employers

Q 5:18 What are the tax implications for an employer that sponsors a premium conversion plan?

Generally, an employer does not pay FICA taxes on the pretax amounts set aside by employees who earn less than the Social Security wage base. In addition, pretax salary reduction amounts are not subject to FUTA taxes. Other tax savings may also be available at the state taxation level. Those tax savings often result in significant cost savings for the employer, which may be used to help fund overall benefits costs.

Q 5:19 May an employer correct contributions to a Section 125 plan made in error?

Informal discussions with the IRS have indicated that it is theoretically possible to correct cafeteria plan elections made in error by a plan participant or by the plan administrator. IRS officials have cautioned, however, that strict standards would be applied, such as requiring strong proof of the legitimacy of the mistake. Internal Revenue Code and Regulations offer no guidance on fixing mistakes in the plan.

Example. A participant mistakenly believes that the Dependent Care FSA is an election for family medical coverage. The participant elects to contribute to the Dependent Care FSA, even though his children are all over the age of 13. The IRS would be likely to deem the election to be correctable if it could be proved that the participant had no dependents who would qualify for dependent care assistance benefits during the period of coverage.

Example. A participant erroneously elects to reduce his salary by $500 per month under a medical FSA; he says that he really intended to reduce his salary by $500 per year. A correction could be made if there was proof that his election was mistaken, such as a number of prior years' elections continually showing approximately the amount of the election the participant says he intended to make.

If contributions are mistakenly made to a Section 125 plan and there is clear and compelling evidence of the error, the IRS has informally indicated that the contributions that were mistakenly made may be refunded to the employee. If the employee receives a refund, the incorrectly contributed amount must be included in the employee's taxable wages. In such a set of circumstances, the employee may make a corrected election for the remainder of the plan year.

Q 5:20 What options for collecting pretax employee contributions are available to an employer whose workforce has seasonal layoffs?

Employee contributions to a Section 125 plan via salary reduction are possible only if the employee is receiving some taxable pay from the employer. In the course of a seasonal layoff during which employees are not paid, employee contributions can be made on an after-tax basis. There are, however, other options for collecting pretax employee contributions so that employees can continue to enjoy the tax advantages of a Section 125 plan. Treasury Regulations Section 1.125-4 allows employees to change their salary reduction elections upon taking an unpaid leave of absence. If a seasonal layoff is deemed analogous to a leave of absence, at least two courses of action appear to be acceptable from the standpoint of the requirements of Code Section 125 for making pretax contributions:

1. The employer can permit employees to make extra pretax contributions in the period immediately preceding a scheduled layoff; or
2. The employer can permit employees to make up any missed contributions on a pretax basis after they return from a scheduled layoff.

If the second approach is taken, the salary reduction contributions should be made in the same plan year as the employee's layoff. To do otherwise would enable employees to defer the receipt of compensation by carrying plan contributions forward, and that would violate Section 125 rules.

Caution. In the case of a self-insured health plan, any special arrangements for employees on seasonal layoffs must be offered on a nondiscriminatory basis.

Note. Teachers and other employees of a typical public school system routinely are not paid for the last week of June or the months of July and August (the annual summer vacation). It appears that such school personnel can make extra pretax contributions before the last week in June to cover the months in which no salary will be received. Alternatively, they can be allowed to make up missed contributions when they return in September, provided they do so before the Section 125 plan year ends. Of course, under the latter approach, the employer takes the risk that some employees will not return to work and it will not be able to recoup those employees' plan contributions.

Q 5:21 When would an employer not want to establish a premium conversion plan?

There are a few circumstances in which an employer would not want to establish a premium conversion plan:

1. The size of the workforce or the premium contribution amount is so small that the tax savings to the employer would not offset the cost of plan implementation, even after a reasonable cost recovery period.
2. The employer undertakes a preliminary analysis of the nondiscrimination testing requirements for a Section 125 plan and determines that if the plan were adopted, based on current data, it could not satisfy the nondiscrimination requirements. (The tests take into account the plan's eligibility rules as well as the contributions made to and the benefits received under the plan.) (See chapter 14.)
3. The employer may determine that premium payments for a particular benefit should be offered on an after-tax basis. For example, some employers permit long-term disability premiums to be paid on an after-tax basis, so that any benefit received is tax free (see Q 8:72).
4. The employer decides to continue to pay the full cost of premium payments. No premium conversion is required.

Elections

Q 5:22 What is the period of coverage for a premium conversion plan?

The period of coverage for a premium conversion plan must be 12 months, except under circumstances in which a short plan year is allowed. That is, coverage cannot be purchased on a month-by-month or expense-by-expense basis. A short plan year is permitted for a first plan year or when a plan year is being changed. [Prop Treas Reg §§ 1.125-1, Q&A 17 and 18, 1.125-2, Q&A 7(b)(3)] (See chapter 11 for a discussion of midyear enrollments.)

Before publication of Treasury Regulations Section 1.125-4, it was important for the insurance policy's enrollment period to coincide with the premium conversion plan year. For example, if a premium conversion plan was on a calendar basis but the health insurance plan had an effective enrollment date of July 1, changes made by employees with the July 1 effective date might have led to undesirable results. Employees might have been prevented from changing to their coverage in the middle of the premium conversion plan year. Treasury Regulations Section 1.125-4 clarifies that a change in cost or coverage can be a qualified reason to change an election under the plan, even in the middle of the plan year. (See chapter 11 for a detailed description of permitted changes to elections in a Section 125 plan.)

Q 5:23 Must an employee make an election to participate in a premium conversion plan?

Yes. One way or another, an employee must make an election to participate in or to waive participation in the plan before the period of coverage for a premium conversion plan has begun. [Prop Treas Reg § 1.125-1, Q&A 8] Such an election is usually made in writing by means of a salary reduction agreement.

Many plan documents provide for a default enrollment in years other than an eligible employee's first year of participation. If an eligible employee never submits a salary reduction agreement, most plans are designed so that such an individual will pay any premium contribution on an after-tax basis. In enrollment periods that follow the initial eligibility period, any employee who does not return a salary reduction agreement is defaulted to the salary reduction agreement most recently submitted.

Often, a plan administrator will use default language to ease the communications and administrative effort each enrollment period entails. Rather than sending out new enrollment forms and requiring their return, a plan administrator will send a notice to all participants stating that the enrollment period permits changes to election, if desired, by a given deadline, and that employees who do not want to make any changes may disregard the notice.

Some employers deem employees who do not return completed salary reduction agreements to be participants in the premium conversion plan that is in place. Many practitioners had believed that such an "automatic enrollment" approach might not represent a binding agreement between employer and employee. In light of the fact that the Office of Personnel Management implemented a premium conversion plan with automatic enrollment for federal employees, it seems that such a process for plan implementation is acceptable to the federal government. Federal employees did have an option to waive participation in the pretax premium conversion plan, but inaction resulted in participation in the plan. Automatic enrollment may, however, violate certain states' garnishment of wage laws, which prohibit restrictions on employees' paychecks without authorization.

Note. At the 1997 Midstates Benefits Conference, IRS Cafeteria Plan Study Industry Specialist Abba Rabbani answered questions about negative elections in a cafeteria (i.e., Section 125) plan. Under negative election procedures, an employee is assumed to elect pretax contributions unless he or she affirmatively tells the employer that he or she wants to make after-tax contributions. No express salary reduction agreements are used in conjunction with negative elections. Rabbani stated that negative elections are permissible, as long as participants understand their "inaction of making a positive election" to make pretax contributions to the plan and they are permitted to make a choice for each plan year. [See Prop Treas Reg §§ 1.125-1, Q&A-8, 1.125-2, Q&A-6].

Rabbani also advised that although negative elections are permissible, a plan administrator should require participants to take some affirmative action, such as a waiver of coverage where no benefits are elected, to ensure that the benefits are properly communicated to employees.

Practice Pointer. The IRS clearly prefers that employers require some form of written instrument, at least once, to reflect an employee's decision regarding an election to participate in a premium conversion plan. It seems that even "negative elections" require nearly the same amount of notification and paperwork as a positive enrollment process.

Q 5:24 If an employee's premium contributions are subject to a collective bargaining agreement, must the employee make an election to participate in a premium conversion plan?

Probably. Neither Code Section 125 nor the Treasury regulations issued under that section of the Code expressly address the issue. Nonetheless, it appears that the existence of a collective bargaining agreement provision requiring employees to participate in a premium conversion plan on a pretax basis would not supersede Code requirements pertaining to employee elections under a Section 125 plan. Specifically, Proposed Treasury Regulations Section 1.125-1, Q&A 15, says that an employee must make an election to participate before any taxable benefits under the plan becoming currently available (usually before the beginning of the plan year).

Q 5:25 May a participant revoke an election once it becomes effective?

Generally, no. Elections are irrevocable once the period of coverage has begun, except under special circumstances. In January, 2001, the IRS released final regulations describing permitted reasons to revoke or change an election to a cafeteria plan. [Treas Reg § 1.125-4] If a plan permits participants to revoke their elections (not in accordance with the Treasury regulations) once the period of coverage has begun, taxable benefits are considered to be currently available and thus subject to taxation, regardless of whether participants in fact revoke their choices and even if the revocation relates only to the remaining portion of the coverage period. (See chapter 11 for a detailed discussion of the revocation of participants' elections.)

Q 5:26 May a cafeteria plan ever automatically change the amount of a participant's health plan premium contributions?

Yes. If the terms of a Section 125 cafeteria plan state that when the cost of a health plan under the cafeteria plan increases or decreases during a plan year, employees are required to make a corresponding change in their premium payments, the cafeteria plan may, on a reasonable and consistent basis, automatically increase or decrease (as the case may be) all affected participants' elective contributions or after-tax employee contributions for the health plan. In previous years, the increase in cost had to be initiated by an "independent third party provider." Under Treasury Regulations Section 1.125-4, this condition is no longer required.

Q 5:27 May a participant in a cafeteria plan revoke an existing election and make a new election as the result of significant cost changes?

It depends on the plan document. If a health plan premium amount significantly increases, a Section 125 cafeteria plan may permit participants either to make a corresponding change in their premium payments or to revoke their elections and instead receive, on a prospective basis, coverage under another health plan with similar coverage. [Treas Reg § 1.125-4(f)(2)]

Q 5:28 May a participant in a cafeteria plan revoke an existing election and make a new election following significant changes in coverage?

Yes, if the plan document so permits. If coverage under a health plan is significantly curtailed or ceases during a period of coverage, a Section 125 cafeteria plan may permit all affected participants to revoke their elections under the health plan and instead receive coverage under another health plan with similar coverage on a prospective basis. [Treas Reg § 1.125-4(f)(3)]

Note. Previously, Proposed Treasury Regulations Section 1.125-2 permitted such a revocation and new election only if the coverage was implemented by an "independent third party provider." Treasury Regulations Section 1.125-4 merely refers to change in coverage. Thus, the change in coverage might be initiated by the participant's employer, or even the employee's spouse's employer—if the participant has coverage under his or her spouse's plan.

Q 5:29 When the cost or coverage under a self-insured health plan changes during a plan year, may employees' elections change?

Yes. Employees may change their elections under a self-insured health plan when the cost or coverage under the plan changes during a plan year—if the plan document permits such a change (see Note at Q 5:28).

Q 5:30 What are the consequences if an employee fails to make required premium payments?

A Section 125 cafeteria plan may stipulate that a benefit will cease to be provided if an employee fails to make the required premium payments. [Prop Treas Reg § 1.125-2, Q&A 6(b)] Informal discussions with the IRS have indicated that this provision was intended to address certain states' garnishment of wage laws. Some states do not allow employees to irrevocably agree to have amounts withheld from their wages. In such states, a participant in a cafeteria plan can stop making the required premium payments to have full wages restored. Previously, proposed Treasury regulations stated that in such a case, the plan was required to prohibit the employee from making a new benefits election for the remaining portion of the period of coverage. Treasury Regulations Section 1.125-4, Example 8, indicates that, except for a deliberate attempt by a plan participant (in collusion with his or her employer) to make an impermissible midyear change, a participant who terminates employment and is reinstated during the plan year may make a new election if the plan so allows (see chapter 11).

Q 5:31 May a participant revoke an existing health or accident plan election and make a new election using the special enrollment rights provided in HIPAA?

Yes. Treasury Regulations Section 1.125-4(b) confirms that a participant may revoke an existing health or accident plan election and make a new election to the extent permitted by the Health Insurance Portability and Accountability Act of 1996 (HIPAA).

HIPAA provides that a group health plan must permit an employee (or dependent of the employee) who is eligible (but not enrolled) for coverage under the terms of the plan to enroll for coverage if each of the following conditions is met:

1. The employee (or dependent) was either covered under a group health plan or had health insurance coverage at the time coverage was previously offered to the employee (or dependent).
2. The employee stated in writing at the time that coverage under a group health plan (or health insurance coverage) was the reason for declining enrollment because the plan sponsor (or health insurance issuer offering health insurance coverage in connection with the plan) required such a

statement at that time and provided the employee with notice of the requirement (and the consequences of the requirement) at that time.

3. The employee (or dependent) who lost coverage was either (a) under a COBRA continuation coverage provision and such coverage was exhausted or (b) not under a COBRA continuation coverage provision and had coverage terminated because of loss of eligibility for coverage (i.e., as a result of termination of employment, reduction in the number of hours of employment, legal separation, divorce, or death) or because the employer had terminated contributions toward such coverage.
4. Under the terms of the plan, the employee requested enrollment not later than 30 days after the exhaustion of COBRA coverage or the termination of employer contributions.

Under HIPAA, if an employee is a participant under the plan or the employee satisfied the waiting period for becoming a participant under the plan and is eligible to be enrolled under the plan but failed to enroll during a previous employment period, and a person becomes a dependent of the employee through marriage, birth, adoption, or placement for adoption, the group health plan must provide for a special enrollment period during which that person may be enrolled under the plan as a dependent of the employee. In the case of the birth or adoption of a child, the employee's spouse may be enrolled as a dependent of the employee if the spouse is otherwise eligible for coverage.

The special enrollment period for dependents must not be less than 30 days and must begin on the later of (1) the date dependent coverage is made available or (2) the date of marriage, birth, adoption, or placement for adoption.

If coverage for a dependent is sought during the first 30 days of the special enrollment period for dependents, coverage of the dependent must become effective as follows:

1. In the case of marriage, not later than the first day of the first month following the date the completed request for enrollment is received;
2. In the case of a dependent's birth, as of the date of such birth; and
3. In the case of a dependent's adoption or placement for adoption, as of the date of adoption or placement for adoption.

[IRC § 9801(f)]

Q 5:32 May a participant revoke an existing health or accident plan election and make a new election upon entitlement to Medicare or Medicaid?

Yes. Treasury Regulations Section 1.125-4(e) confirms that if a participant, or the spouse or dependent of a participant, becomes entitled to coverage under either Part A or Part B of Title XVIII of the Social Security Act (Medicare) or Title XIX of the Social Security Act (Medicaid), other than coverage consisting solely of benefits under Section 1928 of the Social Security Act (the program for distribution of pediatric vaccines), the participant may revoke an existing health or accident plan election to cancel his or her coverage or the coverage of the spouse or dependent under that accident or health plan.

Plan design may not offer a financial incentive to a participant otherwise eligible for Medicare to elect to waive or drop the employer-sponsored coverage in favor of coverage by Medicare. Each violation carries a penalty of up to $5,000. [HCFA Reg § 411.103]

> **Note.** The loss of Medicare or Medicaid entitlement on the part of the participant, the spouse, or a dependent allows the participant to add accident or health coverage.

Chapter 6

Flexible Spending Accounts

No longer limited to the plans of the largest employers, flexible spending accounts (FSAs) have become a common element in flexible benefits plan design. Section 125 plans may include FSAs for qualified medical expenses, eligible dependent care expenses, and adoption expenses. Through an FSA, a plan participant may be reimbursed on a tax-free basis for qualified expenses. For the participant to be reimbursed, the participant and the plan sponsor must abide by a strict set of rules.

This chapter will provide knowledge of how FSAs operate within a Section 125 cafeteria plan. Specifics on medical reimbursement accounts, dependent care assistance, and adoption assistance are found in Chapters 8 and 9.

Overview

Q 6:1 What is a flexible spending account?

A *flexible spending account (FSA)*, also referred to as a reimbursement account, is an account of funds used to reimburse plan participants for specified incurred expenses, subject to reimbursement maximums and other conditions. The FSA may (but need not) be a segregated bank account of the employer. In some cases, the employer sets up a bookkeeping account and the funds remain in general assets until paid out in claims. Records are maintained to show each FSA participant's account activity and account balance.

When an FSA is funded by a participant's pretax dollars, the participant has, in effect, exercised a choice between two or more benefits consisting of cash and qualified benefits. Therefore, an FSA qualifies as a type of cafeteria plan and must follow all the rules of Section 125 of the Internal Revenue Code (Code) that apply to spending accounts. FSAs may also be embedded in a larger cafeteria plan structure.

FSAs under a Section 125 plan are not to be confused with medical savings accounts (MSAs) under Code Section 220 (see chapter 16).

Q 6:2 What types of FSAs are available?

The Code permits three types of FSAs: medical, dependent care assistance, and adoption assistance. The details of each of these types of benefit are described more fully in Chapters 8 and 9.

A *medical FSA*reimburses an employee for medical expenses not reimbursed through any other means and not claimed on the employee's federal income tax return. Generally, eligible expenses are defined in Code Section 213; examples include medical plan deductibles and copayments, prescription drugs, dental care, hearing care, routine physical exams, and vision care (see Q 9:39). However, some items listed in Code Section 213 are NOT reimbursable under a Medical FSA. Code Section 213 is intended to inform taxpayers of possible itemized deductions for personal tax returns. Items listed for individual deduction, but not allowed in a Medical FSA include insurance premium payments, including premiums fcr long term care insurance.

A *dependent care FSA*reimburses an employee for certain dependent care expenses (e.g., babysitting and child care services or adult care programs) that are necessary so that the employee (and his or her spouse if applicable) can work or look for work or attend school full time. The dependent care expenses must be for the care of a qualifying person (see Q 10:2).

An *adoption assistance FSA* reimburses an employee for qualified adoption expenses, up to a maximum of $10,000 per adopted child. For plan years beginning before January 1, 2002, the maximum reimbursement was $5,000 per adopted child ($6,000 for a child defined as one with "special needs". Beginning January 1, 2002, the adoption assistance benefit was increased to $10,000. Adoption assistance through Section 125 plans became available for plan years beginning after December 31, 1996. (See Qs 10:20–10:34.)

Q 6:3 May an employer offer group legal services FSAs?

No. The tax exclusion for group legal services benefits under Code Section 120 expired on June 30, 1992, and, to date, it has not been reinstated. Employees may be allowed to purchase group legal services benefits with after-tax contributions only.

Q 6:4 Must an FSA plan be in writing?

Yes. As a type of cafeteria plan, an FSA must follow the rules of Code Section 125, including the requirement that there be a written plan document.

The written plan document must include the following information:

1. A specific description of each of the benefits available under the plan, including the periods during which the benefits are provided (the period of coverage).

   Note. Benefits established under other separate written plans may be incorporated by reference; that is, in certain circumstances the document need not be self-contained.

2. The plan's eligibility rules governing participation, including the period during which elections may be made, the extent to which elections are irrevocable, and the periods with respect to which elections are effective.
3. The manner in which contributions may be made under the plan (e.g., by a salary reduction agreement between the participant and the employer or by nonelective employer contributions to the plan).
4. The maximum amount of contributions permitted to be made by any participant under the plan.
5. The plan year for which the plan operates.

[Prop Treas Reg § 1.125-1, Q&A 3]

Q 6:5 Are FSAs subject to ERISA?

It depends. A medical FSA is subject to ERISA (Employee Retirement Income Security Act of 1974) because it qualifies as a self-insured medical reimbursement plan under Code Section 105(h). Any plan of an employer under which an employee is reimbursed for medical expenses for which reimbursement is not provided under a health or accident insurance policy is considered to be such a plan. Because medical FSAs qualify under Code Section 105(h), they must meet the reporting and disclosure requirements of ERISA. (See chapter 11.)

A dependent care FSA is not subject to ERISA. Nevertheless, certain reporting and disclosure requirements apply to such a plan under Code Sections 129. The former requirements of Code Section 6039D are now removed, effective April 2002.

Q 6:6 Who may participate in an FSA?

All employees of an employer may participate in an FSA. It should be noted, however, that because an FSA funded by an employee is a type of cafeteria plan, the Code rules and Treasury regulations that apply to participation in a cafeteria plan (see chapter 2) also apply to participation in an FSA. Those rules and regulations extend to the coverage of an employee's dependents, the coverage of a former employee (including a retiree), and the coverage of a partner, sole proprietor, or shareholder of a Subchapter S corporation.

Q 6:7 What is the period of coverage for an FSA?

The period of coverage for an FSA is 12 months, except when a short plan year is permissible (i.e., for a first plan year or when a plan year is being changed). That means that an employee's election to participate in the plan must be in effect for the entire plan year. Proposed Treasury regulations state that coverage may not be purchased on a month-by-month or expense-by-expense basis. [Prop Treas Reg §§ 1.125-1, Q&As 17, 18, 1.125-2, Q&A 7(b)(3)] (See Q 13:6 for a discussion of midyear enrollments.)

Q 6:8 May a participant revoke an election for coverage once it becomes effective?

Generally, elections are irrevocable once the period of coverage has begun. Treasury regulations do, however, permit a few changes to elections during a plan year if the covered individual has experienced a qualifying event and the change made to an election is consistent with that event. Permitted election changes are described completely in Treasury Regulations Section 1.125-4. Most of these final regulations were effective for plan years beginning on or after January 1, 2001, but some are effective for plan years beginning on or after January 1, 2002.

For plan years beginning on or after January 1, 2002, the circumstances under which a participant in an FSA may make a change to an election during the plan year are as follows:

1. A change in the participant's marital status (marriage, death of spouse, legal separation, or annulment);
2. A change in the number of the participant's dependents (as the result of birth, death, adoption, or placement for adoption);
3. A change in the participant's employment status (commencement or termination of employment, strike or lockout, commencement of or return from unpaid leave of absence, change in worksite, or change in eligibility status for the plan);
4. Dependent ceasing to satisfy eligibility requirements;
5. A change in residence of the participant or the participant's spouse or dependent;
6. For adoption assistance FSAs, commencement or termination of an adoption proceeding;
7. Conforming to a judgment, decree, or order resulting from a divorce, legal separation, annulment, or change in legal custody for a dependent child or foster child;

8. Entitlement of the participant or the participant's spouse or dependent child to coverage under Medicaid or Medicare, or loss of such coverage;
9. For dependent care FSAs only, a significant change in the cost of coverage for care provided by a dependent care provider who is not a relative of the participant; and
10. Leave of absence under the Family and Medical Leave Act (applicable to medical plans only).

Note. As has always been the case, any election changes must be on account of and consistent with the qualifying change in status.

Q 6:9 How are FSAs funded?

FSAs are typically funded from an employee's salary reduction contributions, although they may be funded solely from employer contributions or from a combination of the two sources. Each plan year, each employee decides whether to participate in the plan, up to the maximum reimbursement amount allowed by the sponsoring employer.

For salary reduction contributions, the employee agrees to set aside an amount of salary on an annual basis to cover anticipated eligible expenses. The employer calculates the appropriate amount to be deducted from each of the employee's paychecks and deducts it before calculating taxes on the earnings. The employee will thus pay less taxes because the amount on which he or she is taxed has been reduced by the amount of his or her contribution. The employer then establishes a bookkeeping account to hold the employee's contributions, which, in addition to the employee's salary reduction contributions, would include any contributions made by the employer.

Q 6:10 Must FSA contributions be held in trust and must an FSA plan be audited by a certified public accountant?

In August 1993, the Department of Labor (DOL) generally extended cafeteria plans' relief from the trust and audit requirements of ERISA until final regulations addressing trust and reporting requirements for contributory welfare plans are issued.

Previously, in May 1988, the DOL had announced that participants' contributions to a cafeteria plan are plan assets within the meaning of ERISA Section 403(a), which means that they must be held in trust. In August 1988, however, the DOL announced a delayed enforcement policy for the trust requirement, although it did not exempt cafeteria plans from the requirement that plan assets held in trust be audited by an independent accountant. In 1992 the DOL extended cafeteria plans' relief from the trust requirement and announced a nonenforcement policy for the audit requirement. (See Q 6:9 for a more detailed summary of the DOL's positions.)

Q 6:11 Where does an employer keep FSA salary reduction amounts?

Once employees' salary reduction contributions begin, the employer creates individual accounts for its employees by means of individual bookkeeping entries. Thus, for each employee, the election amount is entered, payroll deposits are made, and claims are entered, and once approved, paid to the employee. The employees' salary reduction contributions may be combined with the employer's general assets. Salary reduction amounts are not required to be segregated from the employer's general assets and are not required to be deposited into a trust. Cafeteria plans are generally exempt from the trust and audit requirements of ERISA until final regulations addressing trust and reporting requirements for contributory welfare plans are issued.

Note. Under ERISA Technical Release 92-01, the trust and reporting requirements of ERISA will *not* be enforced against a cafeteria plan. Treatment of COBRA (Consolidated Omnibus Budget Reconciliation Act of 1985) contributions to a cafeteria plan is not clearly articulated in Technical Release 92-01 and in unofficial opinions DOL representatives have differed on the issue. Nevertheless, Technical Release 92-01 is generally being interpreted to provide that the nonenforcement policy be applied to COBRA contributions to a cafeteria plan as well as to regular cafeteria plan contributions.

Practice Pointer. Employees who elect to fund a reimbursement account have opted to reduce taxable income in return for nontaxable benefits. Therefore, until paid out as benefits, the salary reduction amounts belong to the employer. If reimbursement account contributions are not segregated in a separate trust, funds available for payment of benefits are part of the employer's general assets. Unless the employer has a compelling reason to create a trust for such amounts, it should avoid setting up such a trust, thereby avoiding the additional reporting required, as well as accounting for the separate entity created by the trust. That may be especially true of small to medium-sized employers. Of course, the salary reduction amounts (i.e., the contributions to the FSAs) and account balances must be recorded separately as bookkeeping accounts.

Note. On occasion, a plan participant will withdraw more from a medical FSA than he or she has contributed to that point. The employer is presumed to have funded the difference, although, in practice, the overall plan will often have enough funds from other contributions to pay out amounts to individuals who are withdrawing more than they have contributed to date. This issue does not apply to FSAs for dependent care assistance or adoption assistance.

Q 6:12 How does an FSA pay claims?

Typically, in order to receive reimbursement from an FSA, a plan participant submits a claim for eligible expenses incurred during the period of coverage, and the plan makes reimbursement on a periodic basis.

Many plans reimburse on the same schedule as payroll processing. According to Proposed Treasury Regulations Section 1.125-2, reimbursement must be made at least monthly, or when claims reach a certain reasonable minimum (e.g., $50).

Although it is possible for a plan to make payment directly to the provider of qualified services, most FSAs make payment to the plan participant. In most cases, the plan does not have direct contact with the provider of services. See Q 6:16 for a discussion on plan debit cards.

Note. Some insurance carriers and third party administrators (TPAs) of medical claims have set up an arrangement whereby a participant's medical insurance claim will automatically be forwarded for payment by the medical FSA (also administered by the TPA) after review and payment by the health plan. Although convenient for the participant, such an arrangement may inadvertently run afoul of the requirement that reimbursements from an FSA not be paid by any other plan. Such an automatic arrangement (i.e., the participant does not specifically claim the qualified expense) may cause the participant to receive reimbursement for an expense that was already reimbursed by other coverage, such as a spouse's plan.

Q 6:13 When must expenses reimbursed under an FSA be incurred?

Expenses reimbursed under an FSA must be incurred during the participant's period of coverage under that FSA. Expenses are treated as having been incurred when the participant is provided with the care or service that gives rise to the expenses—not when the participant is formally billed or charged or pays for the care or service. Expenses are not treated as incurred during a period of coverage if such expenses are incurred before the later of the following: (1) the date the FSA is first in existence or (2) the date the participant first becomes enrolled in the FSA. [Prop Treas Reg §§ 1.125-1, Q 17, 1.125-2, Q 7(b)(6)] In general practice, a participant in a medical FSA is considered to be a participant if he or she is contributing to the plan.

Q 6:14 May reimbursements made under FSAs be limited to amounts that have actually been paid into the plan?

It depends on the type of FSA. Medical reimbursement FSAs operate under a rule that is not applied to dependent care or adoption assistance FSAs. In any event, expenses reimbursed under any of the three types of FSA must be incurred during the participant's period of coverage under the FSA. (See Q 6:13.)

Medical FSA

A medical FSA must adhere to the "uniform coverage" requirements of Proposed Treasury Regulations Section 1.125-2, Q 7 (b)(2). That section states that the maximum amount of reimbursement under a medical FSA must be available at all times during the period of coverage (properly reduced as of any particular time for prior reimbursements for the same period of coverage). A participant will have access to the entire plan year amount from the very first day of participation during the plan year. The maximum amount of reimbursement at any given time during the period of coverage cannot relate to the extent that the account has been funded.

The payment schedule for the required premiums for coverage under a medical FSA may not be based on the rate or amount of covered claims incurred during the coverage period. That is, a plan cannot relate contributions to a medical FSA to the amount of qualified claims received. (That concept was in use approximately 20 years ago and was referred to as a "zero-balance" reimbursement account, or ZEBRA. It is no longer permitted.)

Note. It will occur to readers that if an employer were to limit reimbursements to amounts that have actually been paid, it could mitigate the potential financial risk presented by the uniform coverage rules (Q 8:49); however, as noted above, such an approach is prohibited by the Treasury regulations.

Example. Maureen, a medical FSA participant, has elected to contribute $50 from pay for each of the 12 months of the plan year, for a total annual election of $600. The plan operates on a calendar year. After the first month, Maureen has contributed $50. On February 2, Maureen turns in a qualified claim for $400. The entire claim is payable. The claim paid is not related to the fact that Maureen has contributed only $50 to date. The plan may not schedule payments for a medical FSA related to the amount of "cash on hand." In fact, the entire annual election of $600 is available to Maureen from the first day of the plan year and is only reduced by claims paid out.

Dependent Care and Adoption Assistance FSAs

Dependent care FSAs are expressly exempt from the operating requirement outlined in Proposed Treasury Regulations Section 1.125-2, Q 7(b)(2). [See Prop Treas Reg § 1.125-2, Q 7(b)(8)] Although adoption assistance FSAs are not discussed in Proposed Treasury Regulations Section 1.125-2, the requirements for uniform coverage clearly relate only to medical FSAs. [See Prop Treas Reg § 1.125-2, Q 7(a)] Thus, a dependent care FSA and an adoption assistance FSA may operate to pay out claims limited to the amount that has been deposited to the account.

Example. Diego, a dependent care FSA participant, elected to contribute $400 per month for the 12-month plan year for dependent care reimbursement. By July 1, Diego had incurred and submitted $5,000 in qualified dependent care claims. Because Diego had contributed only $2,400 to date, the plan will reimburse him in the amount of $2,400. The remaining amount will be considered a qualified claim, pending payment. Diego may be entitled to reimbursement for up to $400 per month, to the extent that he actually contributes to the plan from month to month. (In most cases, the payment of a preapproved claim will be automatic to the participant each time the account is "funded" by a contribution.) Although adoption assistance expenses are not as routine as dependent care expenses, payment operates in a similar fashion.

Q 6:15 May contributions to a medical FSA be used to pay for incurred dependent care or adoption assistance FSA expenses or vice versa?

No. A participant may use his or her FSA to reimburse only those types of expenses for which the account was initiated. In other words, a medical FSA cannot reimburse dependent care or adoption assistance expenses, a dependent care FSA cannot reimburse medical or adoption assistance expenses, and an adoption assistance FSA cannot reimburse medical or dependent care expenses. Within the realm of a given type of account, however, a participant may submit a claim for any qualified expense.

Example. Eli, a new participant in a plan, believes that he will spend $600 on eyeglasses during the plan year. Instead, he incurs medical expenses on unexpected dental work. Eli is not required to limit his claim to vision care just because his intention in setting aside the contribution was to purchase eyeglasses. Vision care expenses and dental care expenses both qualify as eligible medical FSA expenses

Q 6:16 May credit card arrangements be used to expedite the processing of medical and dependent care claims?

Yes. This relatively new option offered by some FSA administrators, credit card companies and banking institutions can expedite the processing of medical and dependent care claims, but may not meet all of the requirements of Proposed Treasury Regulations Section 1.125-2.

Here is one method of processing claims with a credit card:

1. The participant charges eligible expenses for services received on a special credit card.
2. The credit card company posts the expenses on the participant's credit card.
3. The service provider faxes the expense information to the FSA administrator, which verifies the eligibility of the expenses.
4. The FSA administrator deducts the expenses from the participant's FSA and credits the amount of the FSA reimbursement, offsetting the charges.

Thus, the participant does not have to submit the claim to the FSA administrator; instead, the claim is submitted by the service provider directly to the administrator. As a result, the time it takes to receive the FSA reimbursement is typically shortened. The medical FSA participant can give consent beforehand to the provider to file medical claims directly with the insurance company so that the participant does not have to file his or her own claims.

Proposed Treasury Regulations Section 1.125-2, Q&A 7(b)(5) requires that certain items accompany each claim to substantiate it. In addition to a written statement from an independent third party explaining the expense, the participant must provide a written statement that the expense has not been reimbursed or is not reimbursable under any other coverage. The automatic method of credit card payment may, in many cases, circumvent the participant's providing a statement that the expense has not been reimbursed or is not reimbursable by other coverage.

Some credit card arrangements require that the participant follow up the claim documents with a claim form or request for payment form. Such a form would include the required statement. The benefit of this arrangement is nearly instant payment to the service provider. If a participant does not follow up with the required documentation and the claim form statement, however, repayment to the plan may be required.

In another scenario, participants hold "debit cards" attached to their medical FSAs. In order to pay for medical or prescription services, the card holder merely swipes the debit card for payment to the provider. Then, the participant follows up later with claim documentation to the third party administrator.

The benefit of this debit card method is faster reimbursement to the plan participant. However, this method has a few drawbacks. For example, while in a drug store, the participant might pay for a prescription and a pack of gum. The gum is a non-qualified expense that must be denied, and paid back to the plan. Retrieving unqualified amounts for reimbursement to the plan may prove difficult.

Credit card arrangements are gaining popularity, but many plan sponsors and TPAs remain wary. Although one might think that automatic payment via credit card would streamline the claims process, some TPAs who have implemented this service find that they are spending more time in the claims process and documentation than before.

Q 6:17 Should the maximum annual reimbursement amounts of employees who are hired at midyear be prorated?

Under an FSA program, the sponsoring employer sets a maximum amount of reimbursement available to the participant for the plan year. In most cases, that amount is the "total premium" (the sum of employee pretax contributions and any employer contributions). Neither the Code nor the Treasury regulations prohibit extending the full reimbursement to employees who are hired midyear.

The maximum contribution allowed under the Code to a dependent care FSA is $5,000 ($2,500 if the participant is married and filing a separate income tax return), but no more than the lesser of the earned income of the employee or his or her spouse [IRC §§ 129(a)(2), 129(b)] Because dependent care reimbursement is typically only paid out as the "cash" is available, a plan sponsor has no downside financial risk in permitting a participant to fund up to the IRS maximum—even in less than 12 months. The participant must ensure, however, that he or she does not exceed $5,000 in dependent care benefits in a given tax year.

Example. Lucy, a participant in a dependent care FSA, sets aside $2,500 with Employer A in the first six months of the year. She then works for Employer B, which permits midyear plan entrants to contribute up to the full IRS maximum. If Lucy sets aside $5,000 in Employer B's plan, she will create tax concerns for herself and her employer (which will have underwithheld for FICA as well as other possible taxes).

Practice Pointer. Plan sponsors that permit midplan year entrants to contribute up to the IRS maximum will want to clearly explain the annual limitations to participants.

Adoption assistance reimbursements, like those for dependent care assistance, are paid out only as the cash is available. The plan sponsor has no particular financial risk in permitting a participant to fund up to the IRS maximum in a short period of coverage.

Because of the different treatment for medical FSAs (see below), many plans prorate the maximum annual reimbursement amount for midplan year entrants, basing the maximum amount on the length of time the employee actually participates in the plan during the year.

Example. Plan Y's maximum annual calendar year reimbursement amount is $1,200. William joins the plan on September 1. He would have an annual maximum reimbursement amount available to him in the amount of $400 (based on his participation in the plan during September, October, November, and December).

When an employer that sponsors a medical FSA program extends the full reimbursement amount to employees who are hired midyear, its potential financial risk is increased. Under the uniform coverage rules (see Q 8:48), the maximum amount of reimbursement at any time during the period of coverage cannot relate to the extent to which the participant has paid the premiums (contributions) for the coverage period. An employee may submit claims exceeding his or her year-to-date contributions and then terminate employment and discontinue plan participation before contributing the full salary reduction amount for the year. If the employee had the opportunity to receive a full year's reimbursement amount rather than a prorated amount, obviously a greater amount of money is at stake.

Note. When new employees have the opportunity to receive a full year's reimbursement amount, the Section 125 nondiscrimination rules may inadvertently be violated, especially if a relatively large number of key or highly compensated employees join the plan midyear (see chapter 14).

Use-It-or-Lose-It Rule

Q 6:18 What is the use-it-or-lose-it rule, and why does it exist?

In general, a cafeteria plan may not allow employees to defer compensation that is earned in one year to the next year. Therefore, employees may not carry over unused elective contributions or plan benefits from one plan year to another. This rule is often referred to as the use-it-or-lose-it rule. Its consequences are that contributions or benefits not used by the end of the plan year are forfeited by the employee. A notable exception is contributions to a 401(k) plan, through which contributions for benefits are made now for benefits received at a future date. [See Prop Treas Reg § 1.125-1, Q&A 7]

> **Example.** Gina elects to allocate $2,000 to a medical FSA for a plan year. She incurs $1,400 in eligible expenses during the year. Gina forfeits the unused $600; it may not be carried over to the next plan year.

A cafeteria plan cannot be used to defer compensation by indirect means. The use-it-or-lose-it rule applies regardless of how the contributions or benefits are used in the subsequent plan year. For example, the rule applies whether the contributions or benefits are automatically or electively converted into another taxable or nontaxable benefit or are used to provide additional benefits of the same type. In addition, if a plan allows participants to use contributions for one plan year to purchase benefits that will be provided in a subsequent plan year, the purchase is considered a deferral of compensation, which is not permitted. [Prop Treas Reg §§ 1.125-1, Q&A 7, 1.125-2, Q&A 5(a)]

> **Example.** Plan Z offers participants the opportunity to purchase vacation days (or to receive cash in lieu of vacation days). Plan Z is not a cafeteria plan if participants who purchase vacation days for one plan year are allowed to use any of the vacation days purchased through the plan in a subsequent plan year.

Other examples of deferral of benefits not allowed within a cafeteria plan include the purchase of whole life insurance (which can accumulate a "cash value") and certain supplemental medical policies with a "return of premium" rider.

Q 6:19 Does the use-it-or-lose-it rule apply to employer-funded FSAs?

It is not entirely clear whether the use-it-or-lose-it rule applies to employer-funded FSAs. If an FSA is funded *entirely* by the employer, it is possible that unspent amounts can be carried over to subsequent plan years. The matter is under discussion at the IRS.

Fully employer funded medical reimbursement accounts with the possibility of rolling over unspent amounts from year to year operate under lack of clear guidance as to whether or not the practice is permitted. However, Code and Regulations do not specifically disallow such a practice, either, for fully-employer funded reimbursement accounts.

> **Caution.** When employee pretax contributions enter the picture, the guidance is quite clear—no rollover from year to year is permitted!)

Q 6:20 What happens to amounts forfeited from FSAs, and what happens if an FSA has an experience gain with respect to a period of coverage?

Amounts forfeited from FSAs revert to the employer and, in general, are used by the employer to help defray the administrative costs of the plan.

An FSA has an experience gain with respect to a period of coverage if the sum of the premiums paid to the FSA plus the income of the FSA exceeds the FSA's total claims reimbursements plus reasonable administrative costs for the year. The term *premiums paid* refers to any contributions to the account—salary reduction contributions made by employees and any employer contributions, as well as after-tax employee contributions.

The experience gain may be used by the employer to reduce required premiums for the following year. Here, the term*premiums* means amounts contributed to an FSA or premium account for receipt of benefits.

> **Example.** A medical reimbursement account plan sponsored by Sam's Motors Inc. has 100 participants. At the end of the first plan, participants forfeit a total of $1,800 to the plan. In the next plan year, Sam's Motors "seeds" each participant's account with $18. A participant who in the second plan year elects to set aside $400 will have access to $418 in benefits, while paying only $400 in premiums.

Alternatively, the experience gain may be returned to the premium payers as dividends or as premium refunds. The experience gain must be allocated among premium payers as taxable income on a reasonable and uniform basis. It is permissible to allocate an experience gain based on the different coverage levels received by the FSA premium payers; however, the experience gain must not be directly or indirectly allocated among premium payers based on their individual claims experience. [Prop Treas Reg § 1.125-2, Q&A 7(b)(7)]

> **Example.** A medical reimbursement account has five participants. Adam elected to contribute $100 last year. Bob contributed $300, Colin contributed $500, Doris contributed $700, and Edgar contributed $900. Total contributions to the plan thus amounted to $2,500, but claims paid out amounted to only $2,000. If the forfeiture is distributed on a per capita basis, each person would receive a forfeiture distribution of $100. It is possible, however, to structure a forfeiture payout so that Adam would receive $20 of the forfeitures while Edgar would receive $180. Adam contributed 4 percent of the total to the plan and is entitled to 4 percent of the forfeited amount; Bob contributed 12 percent and is entitled to 12 percent; and so on for the other participants.

The forfeiture contribution to a participant's account is determined by calculating the ratio of the participant's plan year contribution (for the same year as the forfeiture) to the total contribution to the plan by all participants and applying the ratio to the total forfeiture to be distributed.

Q 6:21 Are there limits on how an employer may use amounts forfeited by employees under the use-it-or-lose-it rule?

Yes. ERISA Technical Release 92-01, issued in June 1992, detailed how employer discretion can be exercised over the use of forfeited employee contributions to FSAs. Because such funds are considered plan assets, they are to be used only for the payment of benefits and reasonable administrative expenses, as follows.

Forfeited funds may be used by the employer to help defray the administrative costs of the plan, such as costs for PC-based plan administrative software or fees for outside recordkeeping services.

Forfeited funds may be used to protect the underwriting integrity of the plan from unforeseen adverse selection costs or from unexpected costs associated with the uniform coverage rule. The uniform coverage rule requires that the maximum amount of reimbursement cannot depend on the amount of premium dollars (contributions) paid.

Forfeited funds may be reallocated on a per capita basis to participants and treated as additional contributions for the following year. That means that each participant would receive the same amount of "leftover" contributions in the subsequent year. Allocation of forfeitures to participants based on amounts individually forfeited is prohibited.

Donating forfeitures to charity or having forfeitures revert to the company for general business expenses is not permitted. Utilization of participant contributions for any purpose other than those set forth above may result not only in civil sanctions under Title I of ERISA, but also criminal sanctions.

Tax Implications

Q 6:22 What are the tax implications for an employee who participates in an FSA?

An employee who participates in an FSA sets aside an amount with which to reimburse eligible expenses. That amount is not subject to federal or, in most cases, state and local taxes (see Appendix A). For employees who earn less than the Social Security wage base (for 2002, $84,900), the amount of the salary reduction contribution to a medical or dependent care FSA is not subject to FICA (Federal Insurance Contributions Act) taxes (see Q 1:17). Thus, by making pretax premium contributions, an employee reduces his or her taxable income and increases spendable income.

> **Example.** Chris is an unmarried employee who earns $21,600 a year ($1,800 a month) and incurs $125 of uninsured medical expenses (new eyeglasses, dental work, and other expenses) per month. She wants to make salary reduction contributions to a medical FSA to cover those expenses. The

following table shows the effect of an FSA on Chris's income after taxes and payment of her uninsured medical expenses.

	Without Section 125 tax advantage		*With Section 125 tax advantage (under medical FSA)*	
Gross monthly salary	$1,800		$1,800	
Less monthly reduction	(0)		(125)	
Taxable income for FICA	$1,800		$1,675	
Standard deduction	$ 346		$ 346	
Personal exemption	$ 221		$ 221	
Taxable income for federal tax	$1,233		$1,108	
Less federal tax		(185)		(166)
Less FICA (Social Security)		(138)		(128)
				(294)
Less total taxes of		(323)		
NET PAYCHECK		$ 910		$ 814
Less monthly after-tax expense		(125)		(0)
MONTHLY SPENDABLE INCOME		$ 785		$ 814
MONTHLY INCREASE IN TAKE-HOME PAY				$ 29
ANNUAL INCREASE IN TAKE-HOME PAY				$348

This comparison is based on a federal income tax rate of 15 percent and a FICA tax rate of 7.65 percent. State income tax savings are not shown. If Chris also has state tax savings, the increase in spendable income would be even greater.

Q 6:23 Does an employee ever pay taxes on amounts contributed to FSAs?

Certain taxes may be calculated before a contribution to an FSA is made. Contributions to medical and dependent care FSAs are made before federal income taxes and Social Security (FICA) taxes are withheld. In addition, in most cases contributions to medical and dependent care FSAs are made before state and local income taxes are withheld. Adoption assistance FSAs, however, allow participants to avoid only federal and state income taxes. Contributions to an adoption assistance FSA are made after FICA and federal unemployment taxes are withheld. (See Appendix A for information on how state and municipal governments treat pretax salary reductions under Code Section 125.)

On the other hand, moneys received from FSAs to reimburse eligible medical, dependent care, and adoption expenses are not subject to taxation. For example, if an employee were to receive $500 in reimbursement for eligible medical expenses, that $500 is not included in the employee's taxable income for federal (and most state) income tax purposes. Taxation by localities may vary.

> **Note.** Although amounts received from qualified claims are generally not subject to later taxation, adoption assistance and dependent care benefits are reported on an employee's W-2 form as a matter of information for the IRS.

Q 6:24 What are the tax implications for an employer that sponsors an FSA plan?

For employees earning less than the Social Security wage base (for 2002, $84,900), neither the employee nor the employer is generally subject to the old age, survivors, and disability insurance (OASDI) portion of the FICA tax. The rate for the OASDI portion of the FICA tax is 6.2 percent for 1993 and thereafter. (Employees earning in excess of the Social Security wage base are not subject to the OASDI portion of the FICA tax on those earnings in any event.)

For all employees, neither the employee nor the employer is generally subject to the Medicare portion of the FICA tax on the pretax amounts an employee sets aside. The rate for the Medicare portion of the FICA tax is 1.45 percent for 1993 and thereafter. (As of 1994, as a result of the Omnibus Budget Reconciliation Act of 1993, there is no dollar limit on wages subject to the Medicare portion of the FICA tax. [IRC § 3121(a)] Before 1994, the Medicare portion of the FICA tax was imposed only on wages up to a specified dollar threshold (for 1993, $135,000).)

Form 5500

Q 6:25 Must an employer file a Form 5500 for an FSA plan?

A Medical FSA is actually a welfare benefit plan under ERISA. If the medical FSA is exempted from filing Form 5500 (less than 100 participants in the plan), an employer will not have a filing requirement. If the medical FSA does not meet the requirements for a welfare benefit plan exemption from filing, an employer will be required to file a Form 5500.

In April, 2002, IRS announced that plans filing Form 5500 and Schedule F because of the requirement of IRS Code Section 6039D were exempted from future filing requirements. But this announcement did not affect plans the are required to file because of the welfare benefit plan filing requirements.

Dependent care assistance FSAs and adoption assistance FSAs have no Form 5500 filing requirement.

(See chapter 11 for a discussion of whether separate Form 5500s must be filed for the underlying ERISA benefits provided under the plan.)

Chapter 7

Fully Flexible Benefits Plans and Total Compensation

Fully flexible benefits plans are generally designed to comply with the requirements of Section 125 of the Internal Revenue Code (Code); when a plan is so designed, it is a type of cafeteria plan. When a fully flexible plan includes components that are not permitted in a Section 125 cafeteria plan, they must be identified as elements that are not part of the Section 125 plan, although they are options within the employee benefit plan. This chapter will define fully flexible benefit plans and explore the components of such plans that are not part of a Section 125 cafeteria plan.

Overview

Q 7:1 What does a fully flexible benefits plan offer employees, and how does such a plan qualify as a cafeteria plan under Code Section 125?

A fully flexible benefits plan offers employees significant choices in types and levels of coverage. From an array of options, each employee selects the benefits package that best meets his or her needs, based on his or her lifestyle and ability to contribute to the cost of desired options. Often, a fully flexible plan is intended to qualify as a tax preferred Section 125 plan. However, it is possible to also include options within a fully flexible plan that are not permitted within a Section 125 plan. (See chapter 3 for a discussion of nonqualified benefits that might be included in an employee benefit program.)

For a plan to qualify under Code Section 125 as a cafeteria plan, its participants must be able to choose from two or more benefits consisting of qualified benefits and cash. Qualified benefits include the following:

- Health and accident coverage, including medical, vision, prescription drug, dental, long- and short-term disability, and accidental death and dismemberment plans. [IRC §§ 105, 106]
- Group term life insurance coverage up to and in excess of $50,000 (the amount excludable from taxable income under Code Section 79).
- Dependent care assistance plans, which reimburse employees for certain dependent care expenses that are necessary so that the employee and the employee's spouse can work or look for work or attend school full time. [IRC § 129]
- Adoption assistance plans that reimburse employees for qualified adoption expenses. [IRC § 137]
- Cash or deferred arrangements. [IRC § 401(k)]

(See chapter 3 for a discussion of what constitutes cash (or taxable benefits) under a Section 125 plan.)

Plan Design

Q 7:2 What approaches might a plan sponsor take when designing a fully flexible benefits plan?

There are various ways in which a plan sponsor can design a fully flexible benefits plan. Such "models" or "characterizations" include the following approaches:

- *Modular.* Employees are offered choices among comprehensive benefits packages. The packages are usually presented as clustered benefits and no substitution between modules is allowed.
- *Core-plus.* Employees are offered a basic level of employer-provided benefits, typically at additional cost.
- *Net or traditional.* Employees are offered a baseline benefits program. Depending on the choices employees make, they may receive cash back because they selected a lower net benefit (a less costly benefit) or they may pay more because they selected a higher net benefit requiring an additional salary reduction.

- *Full credit-based.* Employees are offered credits to spend as they choose on health and welfare, vacation, or retirement benefits. Full credit-based arrangements can provide an employer with a"total compensation" approach to wages and benefits. An employee might be offered a base wage, and a benefits allowance from which to select among taxable and non-taxable options offered by the employer. If the allowance is not exhausted, an unused credit converts to taxable income.
- *Partial credit-based.* Employees are offered credits to spend as they choose on health and welfare benefits only. Unused credits may, in some plans, be converted to cash (which is taxable income to the employee). Partial credit-based plans offer a participant the option to purchase those benefits that best suit his or her circumstances. This approach stops short of a total compensation approach, however, in that it does not include the opportunity to truly redefine the proportions of wage compensation and benefits on an individual basis.

Q 7:3 Why would an employer want to offer a fully flexible benefits plan?

From an employer's vantage point, there are both cost management and employee relations reasons for offering a fully flexible benefits plan. The economic value of a fully flexible benefits plan is that it can be used to control or to contain the cost of employee benefits programs. By separating the levels of protection defined in the benefit from the cost of the benefit, employers can define the level of contribution they are willing or able to make and accomplish the following objectives:

1. Fix their annual benefits costs contribution as either a flat dollar rate or a percentage of payroll;
2. Relate benefits expenditure costs to organizational productivity or profits;
3. Introduce new benefits at no cost to the company;
4. Control the benefits options available; and
5. Manage employees' selection of benefits by controlling the price of each benefit being offered.

Although it is impossible to place an exact dollar value on the employee relations effect of implementing a fully flexible benefits plan, it is evident that such plans are highly regarded by the employees who are given the opportunity to participate in them. (Most Americans indicate that having a choice in the employee benefits offered by prospective employers would influence their decision to work for a given employer.) Two main reasons for the popularity of flexible benefits plans are as follows:

- Fully flexible benefits plans provide options and choices to employees that they would not otherwise have, and these are of considerable value in attracting and retaining high-quality employees; and

- Fully flexible benefits plans are considered by many to be an enlightened benefits delivery vehicle that is of considerable value in attracting and retaining high-quality employees for organizations that view themselves as providing progressive benefits programs.

Q 7:4 Are fully flexible benefits plans effective in controlling health care costs and in meeting the diverse needs of employees?

Yes. Recent evidence indicates that fully flexible benefits plans can be an effective and successful health care cost management tool. The following findings were documented in an EBRI Issue Brief on flexible benefits, choice, and work force diversity:

1. *Controlling health expenditures:* 72 percent of the employers who cited controlling health expenditures as a major program objective felt that flexible benefits plans had helped them to meet this goal.
2. *Cost effectiveness:* 60 percent of companies surveyed felt their programs were worth the cost.
3. *Meeting diverse employee needs:* 99 percent of employers with choice-making plans reported that they had achieved their major program objective of meeting diverse employee needs.

Q 7:5 How is a fully flexible benefits plan different from other types of flexible plans?

Fully flexible benefits plans offer employees the most flexibility and choice. These plans are also the most complex type of flexible plan to administer for several reasons. Through fully flexible benefits plans, employees are allowed to select from various types of health and welfare benefits coverages. The administrative complexity of the plan increases in direct proportion to the number of different options offered by the plan, since the employer must provide a method for tracking employees' elections. (See chapter 13 for a discussion of software developments and the growth of external administrative services that have eased the recordkeeping requirements of fully flexible benefits plans.) In addition, a fully flexible plan requires the development of a credit methodology to define the exchange rates among the various options.

In comparison with fully flexible benefits plans, the three types of less complex flexible benefits plans—choice-only plans; premium conversion plans; and flexible spending accounts—allow plan sponsors a narrower range of objectives, resulting in fewer employee elections to maintain. Choice-only plans allow employees to choose from a limited set of health and welfare benefits options. Premium conversion plans allow employees to pay for premiums for certain qualified benefits, typically medical benefits, on a pretax basis. Spending accounts allow employees to be reimbursed for specified, incurred medical and dependent care expenses, subject to reimbursement maximums and other conditions. (See chapters 3, 6, 8, and 9 for a discussion of spending accounts.)

Q 7:6 What benefits are specifically excluded from a fully flexible benefits plan?

Code Section 125(f) specifically excludes several tax-favored employee benefits plans from being components of a cafeteria plan. Among them are the following:

- Medical savings accounts [IRC § 106(b)]
- Scholarships and fellowships [IRC § 117]
- Meals and lodging [IRC § 119]
- Long-term care insurance [IRC § 106(c)]
- Educational assistance programs [IRC § 127]
- Fringe benefits plans (e.g., qualified employee discounts); qualified mass transit and parking subsidies; working condition fringe benefits (e.g., subsidized cafeteria-style employee restaurants); and *de minimis* fringe benefits. [IRC § 132]

Other items may approved as tax-preferred in Federal or State tax code, and yet not be permitted in a Section 125 plan. A recent example is a Code Section 529 College Savings Account.

Note. Congress has been revisiting benefits that may be included in a Section 125 cafeteria plan. Specifically, there have been recent attempts to include long-term care insurance premiums as a permitted expense under a Section 125 plan. Plan sponsors and designers should therefore verify the items in the list above at the time of plan implementation to determine if the list has been expanded.

Q 7:7 What Code and Treasury regulations sections apply to fully flexible benefits plans?

A fully flexible benefits plan is typically operated as a cafeteria plan under Code Section 125 and related regulations. Section 125 plans must adhere to the requirements of the following Code Sections and Treasury Regulations Sections:

- Proposed Treasury Regulations Section 1.125-1
- Proposed Treasury Regulations Section 1.125-2
- Temporary Treasury Regulations Section 1.125-2T (application is rare)
- Final Treasury Regulations Section 1.125-3
- Final Treasury Regulations Section 1.125-4

In addition, a fully flexible benefit plan might also include benefits that are described elsewhere in the Code. Many—but not all—of these Code Sections have related regulations. Benefits that might reasonably be included in a fully flexible benefit plan are governed by the following Code sections and regulations:

- Group Term Life Insurance: Code Section 79, and Treasury Regulations Sections 1.79-0, 1.79-1, 1.79-2, 1-79-3, and 1.79-4T.
- Health and Disability Plans: Code Sections 105 and 106, and Treasury Regulations Sections 1.105-1, 1.105-2, 1.105-3, 1.105-4, 1.105-5, and 1.105-11. Medical Reimbursement FSAs fall under this category. (Treasury Regulations Section 1.105-11 has applications to Medical Reimbursement FSAs, as well as other self-funded medical plans.)
- Dependent Care Assistance: Code Sections 21 and 129.
- Adoption Assistance: Code Sections 127 and 137.
- 401(k) Deferral to Retirement: Code Section 401(k) and related Code Sections and Treasury Regulations.

Q 7:8 How are fully flexible benefits plans funded?

A fully flexible benefits plan may be funded by:

1. Nonelective employer contributions;
2. Pretax employee contributions;
3. After-tax employee contributions; or
4. Any combination of the above (see Q 7:48).

One of the keys to understanding the funding principles of a flexible benefits plan is knowing where the money comes from (see Q 7:48). At the highest level, it would seem easy enough to identify whether dollars flow from the employer or from the employee. Also, differentiating employee pretax contributions from employee after-tax contributions seems straightforward.

However, there are subtleties to even these notions. For example, suppose the cost of a benefit goes down (perhaps the group insurance package is renegotiated and the employer gets a better deal). If the employer elects to share that savings with employees by increasing employer-provided credits, this becomes an employer contribution. On the other hand, if the employer elects to share that savings with employees by reducing the cost of purchasing these insurance coverages, then it may not be perceived as an employer contribution.

Another subtlety of funding occurs when subsidizations change between groups. Typically, within every employee benefits program there are cross subsidies between divisions (within an organization), younger and older workers, part-time and full-time employees, and single and married workers. When funding principles change, so do these subsidy relationships, and knowing which employees are ending up with a greater subsidy and which are ending up with a lesser subsidy is central to understanding the financial workings of a flexible benefits plan.

Q 7:9 Does the fully flexible model selected affect the cost of the options available under the plan?

Not directly. The cost of each option is determined by an insurance carrier, a third-party administrator, or in some instances by the employer. The cost of an option is not a function of the model selected by the employer to present a flexible benefits program to employees. After determining the amount of employer contributions that it can afford to make, the employer will typically try to find an acceptable balance between the amount of employer and employee contributions necessary to support each benefits option within a flexible benefits plan. Such contributions are based on the option's premium cost or working rates. These decisions are entirely separate and independent from choosing the best method for presenting the fully flexible program to employees. It should be noted, however, that the flexible benefits model chosen will affect migration patterns, which will in turn have an indirect impact on the long-term costs of an option.

Q 7:10 How may an employer manage adverse selection in a fully flexible benefits plan?

Adverse selection means that plan participants select against a benefits program by choosing only benefits that they are likely to use or exchanging the benefits they are least likely to use for cash or other benefits. For example, an employee who has had heart attacks will tend to buy more life insurance than one who has not, speculating that he or she is likely to need it; employees who have impaired vision tend to select vision coverage and employees who need braces (or whose children need braces) tend to select orthodontia coverage.

If left unchecked, adverse selection increases the cost of a fully flexible benefits plan. Adverse selection may be dealt with through design or pricing solutions (see chapter 2).

One way to manage adverse selection is to group certain benefits together in modules or clusters so that, for example, an employee who chooses health coverage will also receive coverage for orthodontia. (Permitting specialty benefits such as orthodontia or prescription drug coverage to stand alone will almost certainly lead to adverse selection.) Another way to manage adverse selection is to limit benefits paid by the plan for a period of time. For example, a plan sponsor can provide dental coverage with a one-year waiting period before major restorative dental care is covered. Of course, the latter approach works best with ancillary benefits (e.g., dental and vision care); it is not recommended for basic health coverage.

Q 7:11 How does an employer decide which model or characterization best suits its needs?

An employer must understand the advantages and disadvantages of each approach in order to make an informed decision about the best one for that particular employer's unique set of circumstances. For example, the modular approach is the most effective in controlling adverse selection; the credit-based and net-benefits approaches are the most effective vehicles for achieving a nonpaternalistic benefits program.

Q 7:12 In developing a fully flexible plan, what does the plan sponsor do after selecting the appropriate mix of underlying benefits that will be offered under the plan?

The plan sponsor must determine the model or characterization that the employer will use to present the program to employees. Any one of the following five models (characterizations) may be used:

1. *Modular approach.* Provides choices among comprehensive benefits packages.
2. *Core-plus approach.* Consists of a basic level of employer-provided benefits and enables employees to select additional benefits, typically at additional cost.
3. *Net or traditional approach.* Consists of specific plans.
4. *Full credit-based approach.* Employees receive credits to spend as they choose. Unused credits may, in some plans, be converted to cash, which is taxable income to the employee.
5. *Partial credit-based approach.* Employees receive credits to spend as they choose on health and welfare benefits only. Unused credits may, in some plans, be converted to cash, which is taxable income to the employee.

Modular Plans

Q 7:13 What is a modular plan?

A modular plan creates specific packages (modules) from which participants may choose. An employee selects the package he or she believes will best satisfy his or her personal benefits needs. Employees may not select from all available types and levels of coverage.

Each module is typically designed to appeal to a specific demographic group and can be structured to feature different benefits at similar overall total costs. If the benefits costs are so structured and an employee's contribution would be about the same for one module as for another, employees may be allowed to purchase additional options using pretax or after-tax dollars.

Example. A modular plan might offer the following choices:

Module 1

1. Comprehensive medical plan ($500 individual deductible/$1,000 family deductible).
2. Preventive dental plan ($500 annual benefit per person).
3. Group term life insurance benefit of $20,000.

4. 40 percent long-term disability coverage with 180-day elimination period.

Module 2

1. Point of service medical plan (extensive in-network benefits and more modest out-of-network benefits).
2. Preventive, basic, and restorative dental plan ($750 maximum annual benefit per person).
3. Group term life insurance benefit of two-times salary.
4. 60 percent long-term disability coverage with 90-day elimination period.

Module 3

1. Comprehensive medical plan ($500 individual deductible/$1,000 family deductible).
2. Group term life insurance benefit of $5,000.
3. Financial planning benefits.
4. Homeowner's insurance benefits.

Module 1 is geared toward younger employees without children by providing basic levels of health and life insurance, and long-term disability coverage.

Module 2 is geared toward employees with families. The medical and dental plans provide "more than basic" health benefits, while the life insurance and long-term disability benefits offer greater financial protection.

Module 3 is geared toward older employees without children. It offers basic medical and life insurance benefits, financial planning, and homeowner's insurance benefits. This module might also appeal to married employees whose spouses cover their children on their own plans.

Q 7:14 What are the key features of modular plans?

Three key features of modular plans are as follows:

1. *Greater control of adverse selection.* The hallmark of a modular plan is that, because it does not give employees access to all the individual benefits that they typically desire, it is the most successful model for minimizing adverse selection. Because benefits options are packaged in modules (i.e., clusters), employees cannot select against the program by choosing only those benefits that they are most likely to use or by exchanging the benefits they are least likely to use for cash or other benefits.

   Modular plans tend to be effective cost management tools because they do not offer employees easy choices. To obtain one benefit—for example, a generous medical plan—the employee may be required to receive another benefit that the employee and his or her family would not use—for example, a high level of life insurance. The savings that will be derived from the less frequently used—or unused—benefits may be applied to offset the costs of more frequently used benefits. In effect, modular plans force minimum participation requirements in each underlying benefit. An employee must receive all the benefits in the module he or she selects; this inability to opt out means that a significant number of employees will receive each benefits plan.

2. *Administrative simplicity.* Modular plans are relatively easy to administer because each employee selects only one complete package, rather than every specific type and level of coverage the employee wants. Modular plans do not require sophisticated administrative systems.
3. *A balance of paternalism and employee choice.* The employer exercises the greatest possible amount of control over the benefits offered to and received by employees. The employee cannot freely choose from an array of benefits options, although a well-designed program could offer various modules that at least partially satisfy the needs of many employees.

Core-Plus Plans

Q 7:15 What is a core-plus plan?

A core-plus plan provides basic or minimum levels of coverage to all eligible employees. The basic levels of coverage are typically provided by the employer and are mandatory (i.e., employees may not opt out of core benefits coverage). However, employees may elect additional types and levels of coverage, which may be funded by employer contributions, employee pretax contributions, and/or employer after-tax contributions. The following example shows what the basic and elective coverage levels of a core-plus plan might consist of.

Example. A core-plus plan might offer the following levels of coverage:

Basic Coverage

1. Comprehensive medical plan with a $500 individual deductible and a $1,000 family deductible.
2. Dental plan providing 80-percent coverage for diagnostic and preventive services and 50-percent coverage for basic restorative services (annual per person maximum of $500).
3. $5,000 group term life insurance benefit.

Elective Coverage

- A richer medical plan, for example, a plan with a $200 individual deductible and a $400 family deductible.
- Dental plan providing 100-percent coverage for diagnostic and preventive services, 80-percent coverage for basic restorative services, and 50-percent coverage for major restorative services (annual per person maximum of $1,000).
- Group term life insurance coverage in multiples of pay (one-, two-, or three-times salary).

- Long-term disability plan with 60-percent coverage and 90-day elimination period.
- After-tax benefits, such as financial planning and homeowner's insurance.

Q 7:16 What are the advantages and disadvantages of a core-plus plan from an employer's point of view?

From an employer's point of view, the advantages of a core-plus plan are as follows:

Adverse Selection. Core-plus plans are characterized by a moderate amount of adverse selection. Because a required basic level of coverage is provided to all employees, core-plus plans in effect require minimum levels of participation in every underlying benefits option. Despite the core of required benefits, employees may still select against the program by choosing additional benefits they are likely to use. To the extent that occurs, adverse selection takes place. (See Q 2:28 for a discussion of methods for avoiding or mitigating the effects of adverse selection.)

Paternalism and Limits on Employee Choice. Because basic levels of coverage must be received by all eligible employees, the employer is exercising some control over the benefits program. Further, the employer may wish to protect employees against their own inability to choose wisely. That protection arises from an inherent plan design that stipulates that, although employees have the ability to select additional types and levels of coverage (which may be paid by the employer or by the employee), they may not opt out of a core coverage and be without a minimum level of protection.

Insurance Carrier Limitations. Especially in a smaller employer environment, the insurance carriers require coverage of a high percentage of the employee population. In some cases, insurance carriers require that 50 percent, 75 percent, or even 100 percent of all eligible employees be covered by their insurance coverage.

The disadvantage of a core-plus plan is as follows:

Administrative Needs. For each underlying benefits option, a required selection parameter must be followed and verified. Core-plus plans are more complex to administer than modular plans, but less difficult to administer than the net-benefits and credit-based plans.

Net Benefits Plans

Q 7:17 What is a net-benefits plan?

In a net-benefits plan, employees choose from among various benefits plans, which are themselves the options. For example, the employee may choose to participate in a health maintenance organization (HMO), indemnity, or preferred provider organization (PPO) medical offering. The structure of a net-benefits plan places more emphasis on the benefits options than on the underlying cost and required employee contributions, if any, for each plan. Employer contributions are established on the basis of a baseline benefits program. Depending on his or her choice, the employee may receive cash back in lieu of a certain benefit or may be required to pay additional dollars for a more costly benefit. This is the traditional approach employers have used to present their benefits programs to employees. Generally, in a net-benefits model, the employee is given a package of benefits that may be traded or kept, depending on the specific needs of the employee.

The key to understanding the net-benefits model is that employees may select whichever benefits they want; however, if the cost of the benefits options selected exceeds the value of the employer-provided benefit, the employee must contribute the difference. If the cost of the benefits options selected by the employee is less than the value of the employer-provided benefit, the employee receives a cash return.

A net-benefits model may offer any of the following options:

Medical Plan Options

- Point-of-service plan (100-percent coverage for in-network services and 80-percent coverage for out-of-network services)—employer-provided benefit
- Several HMOs
- No medical plan, provided proof of other medical coverage is furnished by the employee

Dental Plan Options

- Plan providing 100-percent coverage for diagnostic and preventive services, 80-percent coverage for basic restorative services, and 50-percent coverage for major restorative services (annual per person maximum of $750)—employer-provided benefit
- No dental plan

Vision Plan Options

- Plan featuring network of PPO providers
- No vision plan

Group Term Life Insurance and AD&D Options

- One-times salary, maximum of $50,000 benefit—employer-provided benefit
- $5,000 group term life insurance benefit
- Additional one-, two-, or three-times salary benefit, subject to insurance underwriting requirements

- Portable life insurance policies, including dependent life insurance (paid for with after-tax dollars, outside of the Section 125 plan)

Long-Term Disability Options

- 60-percent coverage, 90-day elimination period with a benefit maximum of $5,000 per month
- 40-percent coverage, 180-day elimination period with a benefit maximum of $2,500 per month—employer-provided benefit

Short-Term Disability Options

- 60 percent coverage, with 60-day qualifying period with a benefit maximum of $350 per week; maximum benefit period of 60 days for any one disability
- No short-term disability insurance

After-Tax Options

- Financial planning
- Homeowner's insurance

Full Credit Plans

Q 7:18 What is a full-credit plan?

In a full-credit plan, employees are given credits to spend on the benefits they wish to receive. The total number of credits an employee receives is the sum of the credits received under each type of coverage; for example, a single employee may receive, each month, 30 credits for health insurance, 15 credits for disability, 8 credits for life insurance, and 40 credits for the purchase of one week's vacation coverage. The number of credits provided for each type of coverage may vary from one employee to another, depending on the employee's marital status, scheduled hours, family status, and age, or it could be a set dollar amount with hidden subsidies.

Full-credit plans typically include many of the qualified benefits identified in Code Section 125, such as:

1. Health benefits (medical, dental, hearing, vision, and medical flexible spending account);
2. Long- and short-term disability;
3. Group term life insurance up to the $50,000 gross income exclusion and accidental death and dismemberment benefits;
4. Dependent care assistance benefits; and
5. Retirement benefits under a 401(k) plan.

The inclusion of vacation or retirement benefits (or both) differentiates a full-credit plan from a partial-credit plan (see Q 7:19). In a full-credit plan, employees could be offered all the benefits typically provided through a net-benefits plan (see Q 7:20) with the addition of vacation or retirement benefits (or both). For example, a plan could allow employees to sell one week of vacation for a 2 percent-of-pay "credit" increase or elect a 401(k) (salary reduction) retirement contribution with an employer match (an employer match in a 401(k) plan is not paid with benefit credits in a Section 125 plan).

Under a full-credit plan, an employee typically does not receive enough credits to enable him or her to obtain every type of coverage available under the plan without making an additional contribution. Some benefits, such as vision or short-term disability coverage, may be totally employee-paid.

A plan sponsor should exercise caution in offering Section 401(k) benefits as part of any cafeteria plan, including a full-credit plan, for several reasons:

1. Doing so may make it difficult to pass the Section 125 nondiscrimination tests, specifically the key employee concentration test (see chapter 14). The relatively large salary reduction amounts that employees may annually set aside in a 401(k) plan may cause key employees to receive more than 25 percent of the total nontaxable benefits, resulting in the plan's failure of the key employee concentration test.
2. It is unclear whether the failing of the 401(k) nondiscrimination tests disqualifies the entire cafeteria plan. [Former IRC § 125(e); IRC § 125(f)]
3. Including 401(k) benefits in a cafeteria plan complicates the administration of the Section 125 plan. Section 125 salary reduction amounts used to purchase qualified benefits are not subject to federal unemployment taxes; furthermore, the amounts of the salary reductions of employees who earn less than the Social Security wage base are not subject to FICA taxes. Section 401(k) salary reduction amounts, however, are subject to FICA taxes and federal unemployment taxes.

A plan administrator also should be concerned with state and local municipality rules concerning income tax treatment of Section 401(k) and Section 125 salary reduction contributions. The amount of a Section 125 salary reduction is in most cases not subject to state or local taxes. (See Appendix A for how state governments treat pretax salary reduction under Code Section 125. Most states do not require tax on elective contributions to a 401(k) plan. Pennsylvania is the only state that requires the withholding and payment of income taxes on elective contributions to a 401(k) plan. On the other hand, a number of municipalities impose taxes and require income tax withholding on elective contributions to a 401(k) plan.

Partial Credit Plans

Q 7:19 What is a partial-credit plan?

In a partial-credit plan, as in a full-credit plan, employees are given credits to spend on the benefits they wish to receive. The total number of credits that the employee receives is the sum of the credits received under each type of coverage.

A partial-credit plan includes many of the "qualified benefits" defined under Code Section 125, as does a full-credit plan. Unlike a full-credit plan, vacation and/or retirement benefits under a 401(k) plan are not included in a partial-credit plan.

Net Benefit vs. Credit-Based Plans

Q 7:20 How does a net-benefits fully flexible plan compare with a credit-based fully flexible benefits plan?

Both models allow employees to choose freely from various types and levels of coverage. These models are not paternalistic, since employees have access to each of the available benefits and may select what they wish. In designing and pricing these plans, employers should be attentive to the potential for adverse selection: since a wide range of benefits is made available, employees will tend to choose the benefits they believe they will use and are likely to opt out of or opt down from coverages they will not use.

Both net-benefits plans and credit-based plans require sophisticated administrative systems. Depending on the nature of the plan and on the employer's staff, these plans can be administered internally with the assistance of computer software. Alternatively, an external recordkeeper may be hired to administer the plan.

Net-benefits plans and credit-based plans differ primarily in how they are presented to employees. In a net-benefits model, employees are given an array of benefits plans; then the employee selects the actual benefits options that he or she desires from the universe of choices. In credit-based plans, employees are given a number of credits to spend on the benefits they wish to receive. The focus may be on either benefits plans or credits to be spent. In both models, employees may receive cash back in lieu of a particular benefit, and employees are required to pay more for a more costly group of benefits options.

Opt-Out Benefit

Q 7:21 What is an opt-out benefit?

In fully flexible benefits plans, employees are often given the opportunity to opt out of certain coverages, such as medical and/or dental benefits. The rationale is that an employee may have coverage available to him elsewhere, perhaps through a spouse's employer plan. An employee may decide that it is in his or her best interest to waive the employer's coverage, after considering the following factors:

1. The type and cost of coverage available through a spouse's employer plan;
2. The health care expenses incurred by the employee (and the employee's family) in the previous plan year; and
3. The health care expenses expected to be incurred by the employee (and the employee's family) in the coming plan year.

If an employee decides to waive coverage, the employee does not receive the full employer contribution that he or she would have received had he or she elected coverage. For example, the opt-out amount for a medical plan reflects the realization that individuals who waive coverage are unlikely to incur the average per capita medical plan claims and that the plan must pay the opt-out amount to all employees who may have already opted out. Therefore, the risk absorbed by the plan is not diminished by the exact amount of premiums that are not paid. Since the plan still carries the risk of the remaining plan participants and may incur an up-front cost for existing opt outs, underwriters have determined that the value of any employee waiving coverage is significantly less than the actual plan cost per employee.

Q 7:22 How can offering an opt-out benefit be advantageous to an employee?

An important reason for implementing a flexible benefits program is to allow employees to elect options that are advantageous to them, based on personal and family needs. Fully flexible benefits plans with opt-out choices allow employees to eliminate duplicative or undesirable benefits. By opting out of coverage, the employee can have more credits to spend on other benefits, or if the employee does not spend the credits on benefits, he can have additional take-home pay. In this way an employee can select the menu of options that best suits his needs.

An employee may have a specific type of coverage available to him elsewhere, such as through a plan sponsored by a spouse's employer. The credits provided to an employee for waiving coverage might be substantial enough to fund a good portion of the cost of family coverage under the spouse's plan. Employees often make this comparison in deciding whether to opt out of benefits, particularly medical benefits, where relatively large amounts of money are at stake.

A particular benefit may not be deemed valuable to a particular employee based on his or her family status; for example, an unmarried employee may not value group term life insurance coverage. If the employee waives this coverage, he or she could spend the opt-out credits on other benefits or receive the opt-out amount as additional take-home pay.

Of course, opt-out amounts for group term life insurance coverage typically do not match amounts payable for opting out of more costly coverages, such as medical insurance.

Q 7:23 How much cash should an employee receive for opting out of a benefit option?

The notion of driving or "incenting" employees out of a benefit option (especially an organization's medical plan) is predicated on the simple concept that eliminating participants from the company's benefits plan will cost the company less money. This belief is based on one of three rationales:

1. If the plan is experience rated, the employee who drops the benefit will save the plan money because he or she would have incurred more in claims than the cost of the premium. This rationale is probably incorrect.
2. If the plan is capitated (for example, in a medical plan HMO), then the employee who drops the plan will save the company money because it will pay the employee less in cash than the capitated cost of the program. This is always true.
3. Regardless of whether the benefits plan is experience rated or capitated, dependents of employees are a costly group, and to the extent the company can get them onto another organization's medical plan, the cost of benefits, especially medical benefits, will go down (or will not go up so fast). This is generally true.

The basic goal of an opt-out offering, therefore, should be to induce employees who take capitated benefits, such as an HMO, to opt out.

In addition, married employees with two incomes who have children should be a primary target group for opt-out benefits for two reasons. First, one spouse may have coverage protection elsewhere (i.e., through the other's employment) and can therefore afford to opt out; and second, as a group, they make more use of employee benefits generally and of medical care specifically. In effect, by shunting dependent spouses and children onto another company's plan—a strategy sometimes known as "dependent dumping"—an employer is likely to realize an economic benefit.

Employers are protecting themselves from dependent dumping with provisions that do not allow a spouse with access to coverage elsewhere to be on their plans, or by specifying that if one spouse receives cash for not taking benefits, the premium cost of the other spouse will be increased by the amount of the cash received. Taking this type of defensive position can save an organization significant amounts of money.

With regard to pricing the opt-out benefit, there are two basic underwriting/actuarial issues to consider:

1. If the employee is already contributing to some portion of the cost of benefits, how much of the cost does the employee pay?
2. How many employees have opted out of their benefits because they do not want to pay their portion of the premium?

In terms of basic underwriting, if employees pay more than one third of the cost, it is generally not prudent to advocate any opt-out cash incentive—because anyone paying 33 percent or more of a medical plan's cost has already been given enough incentive to drop out of the plan. Remember, there is no difference between a dollar of an employee's salary not spent on benefits and giving the employee an additional dollar in salary for not taking benefits; the dollar produces the same behavior in the employee.

> **Example.** Companies ABC and XYZ both offer benefits plans to their employees; neither company requires its employees to pay for any portion of their premiums, and neither company offers an opt-out incentive.
>
> At some point, ABC requires its employees to pay $45 per month ($540 per year) for medical insurance. The payment of these premiums represents a salary decrease for ABC's employees. Meanwhile, Company XYZ permits employees who opt out of medical benefits to receive an increase in their take-home pay of $540 (the amount of the employee's share of the insurance premiums).
>
> The economic position of an employee from Company ABC who does not take medical coverage and therefore does not spend the $540 through salary reduction is not comparable to that of the XYZ employee who is given an extra $540 in compensation in exchange for opting out. From an employee's point of view, it is advantageous to have the XYZ option; however, from an underwriter's perspective, there is no difference between the two alternatives (whether or not the employee receives an increase in take-home pay, fewer individuals are being covered by the plan).
>
> Further, both companies eventually institute a 25 percent medical insurance contribution ($750 per year) by employees. Now the economics of the situation change. Suppose that as a result of XYZ's initial opt-out program, 8 percent of its eligible employee population has already opted out of medical insurance coverage. When the 25 percent contribution requirement goes into effect, shifting an additional $210 of premium from the employer to the employee, XYZ will not be able to afford to deliver this increased amount as an opt-out incentive to its employees, because the employees who were the best candidates for dropping health insurance (those who have lower claims experience) already did so when the initial opt-out incentive was offered.

Because part-time employees generally pay so much for their medical plan coverage, they are very infrequently offered opt-out incentives; it is not generally economical for the employer to do this. The higher cost of premium payment, relative to a lower pay for a part-time employee, provides an incentive in and of itself for such an employee to waive coverage, if possible.

In light of this discussion and the possible adverse cost impact of offering an opt-out option, it is generally recommended that the plan sponsor reduce the amount payable when an employee opts out accordingly. Therefore, if the actuarially correct amount for opting out of medical benefits is $900, perhaps the opt-out incentive should pay only $600. The $300 difference in effect covers some (but not all) of the risk associated with offering cash in lieu of benefits coverage.

Some employees will ask why they receive only $600 annually, yet the cost of medical care is over $3,000 per year. The answer to this question relies on the fact that the underwriting cash equivalent of opting out of medical benefits is predicated on the expected incurred claims cost for the group of employees who opt out, not on the entire eligible population for medical benefits at an organization.

For example, consider a company of two employees. Employee A incurs $0 in medical costs while Employee B incurs $4,000 a year. If we ignore all the incidental costs associated with insurance and divide the claims by two to get the composite annual premium rate, we would pay $2,000 on behalf of each employee to cover expenses of $4,000. If Employee A opts out of medical coverage and receives his $2,000 in cash, the company still must pay $4,000 in medical costs for Employee B, along with an opt-out payment of $2,000 to Employee A. This brings the total cost to $6,000, an increase of 50 percent over the prior year's expenses. That is why the opt-out payment tends to begin at around 15 percent to 25 percent of the base benefits plan cost for individual coverage.

Although it is generally expected that employees will appreciate an opt-out incentive, sometimes, because the amount being offered is perceived as small in relation to the actual plan cost, the anticipated good will is lost to a perception that the plan sponsor is being "cheap."

Q 7:24 What sort of restrictions are placed on subsequent reenrollments following the election of an opt-out benefit by an employee?

Employers' policies on rescinding waivers tend to vary according to the type of benefit. It is not uncommon for employers to develop rules governing employees' reenrollments to help control adverse selection. Adverse selection in this context means that participants will select against the program by choosing benefits when they are most likely to use them.

Example. For dental coverage, a two-year "lock-in" rule may be instituted in order to prevent adverse selection. Under such a rule, whatever dental option an employee elects (regardless of whether the employee waives or selects dental coverage) will remain in effect for a two-year period. Such a rule tends to prohibit employees from enrolling in a dental plan only when they can anticipate and plan for usage under the plan (prime examples are root canal therapy and crown construction). A two-year lock-in rule makes it more difficult for an employee to join the plan so that he can receive treatment and then opt out when treatment is completed.

Example. For group term life insurance coverage and long-term disability coverage, the ability to opt back into coverage may be contingent upon (1) the employee's demonstrating that he or she is in good health and/or (2) a waiting period of up to a year. Such rules help to protect the plan from employees who may be bad risks; that is, those whose health condition may present a risk to utilization under the plan.

Of course, adopting such rules must be weighed against the possibility that their existence may lessen the appeal of opt-out choices for employees.

Q 7:25 Should proof of coverage be required for opt-out benefits?

Most employers require proof of coverage before permitting an employee to opt out of medical benefits, while most do not require proof of coverage for opting out of other benefits, such as dental or long-term disability coverage. The reason for this is that many employers feel responsible for ensuring that employees have access to medical care, particularly if employees are provided with a monetary incentive in exchange for declining the employer's medical coverage. An employer may regard the element of paternalism in this as conflicting with the basic principles of flexible benefits; however, it is also true that these restrictions on opting out can help limit adverse selection.

Proof of coverage may be obtained by requiring the employee to complete a certification form that furnishes both the name of the insurance carrier providing the coverage and the employee's signature attesting to the existence of the other coverage.

Some plan sponsors are concerned that employees may falsify the proof of coverage requirements in order to receive cash in lieu of medical benefits. If this is a concern, the plan sponsor may require the employee to furnish a notarized certificate or an affidavit. In most cases, however, employers do not wish to assume the role of "health care police" and take the position that employees are generally honest and that since this protection is for their benefit, a simple certification should suffice.

Operational Issues

Q 7:26 May new benefit options be offered midyear in a fully flexible benefits plan?

The question of whether new benefit options may be offered midyear in a fully flexible benefits plan is specifically answered in Treasury Regulations Section 1.125-4(f)(3), which is effective for plan years beginning on or after January 1, 2002.

If during a period of coverage a cafeteria plan adds a new benefits package option or other coverage option (or eliminates an existing benefits package option or other coverage option), the plan may permit affected employees to elect the newly added option (or elect another option if an option has been eliminated) prospectively on a pretax basis and make corresponding election changes with respect to other benefits package options providing similar coverage.

The provisions of the final regulations relating to changes in cost or coverage do not apply to health FSA elections. A health FSA election may not be changed during the year based on a change in coverage, even if new coverage makes the health FSA redundant, or makes funding it more desirable.

Example. Sally, an employee at the Sweet Bakery Co., plans to set aside $900 over the course of the plan year in a health FSA for anticipated dental work. Three months after the beginning of the plan year, Sweet Bakery's cafeteria plan offers dental insurance coverage. Sally is permitted to elect to participate in the dental plan; however, she may not cease participation in her health FSA, even though the expenses she sought to pay through her FSA —dental expenses—are now covered by another plan.

Example. Holly is a participant in a cafeteria plan. She selected health insurance coverage with a $200 individual deductible. During the plan year, the health plan's deductible increases to $500. Holly may not increase contributions to her health FSA during the middle of the plan year to cover the additional expected out-of-pocket cost.

Q 7:27 Do most organizations cover all employees under the same fully flexible benefits plan?

Yes, in general. Such an approach minimizes the costs and administrative efforts involved in operating a fully flexible benefits plan because it is not necessary to plan for and provide different plans of benefits to different groups of employees.

Fully flexible benefits plans provide a mechanism for consolidating benefits programs of merged companies. Instead of continuing to offer separate programs to different groups of employees, or continuing to offer all existing programs to all employees, a flexible benefits approach allows the employer to offer only the desired benefits. The remaining benefits may not duplicate all the current choices but could offer a range of choices that would be satisfactory to most employees.

Whereas the same benefits options may be offered to all employees, different credits may be given to different groups of employees covered under a flexible benefits program, such as employees in different geographic locations or lines of business. For example, an employer may decide to provide higher credit levels to employees in competitive industries. Of course, under this approach, attention should be paid to compliance with all applicable nondiscrimination testing requirements. (See chapter 14 for information concerning nondiscrimination testing.)

In certain situations, separate benefits plans may be maintained for business reasons, such as for groups of collectively bargained employees.

Credit Methodology

Q 7:28 Does every fully flexible benefits plan have an underlying credit methodology?

Yes. In developing the model or characterization that the employer will use to present the program to the employees, the employer should be aware that every fully flexible benefits plan has an underlying credit methodology. Fully flexible design models, whether characterized as modular, core-plus, net benefits, or credit based, all have credit methodologies. The word "credit" is used only in the full and partial credit based approaches; however, all these models have an economic system of exchange that allows plan participants to assign specific values to various benefits so that they can be bought and sold.

Q 7:29 What is the importance of a credit methodology to a fully flexible benefits plan?

The importance of a credit methodology to a fully flexible benefits plan lies in the fact that it constitutes a common economic system under which benefits that are vastly different from one another in kind and in monetary value can be related. That is, a credit methodology is an economic system of exchange that allows plan participants to assign specific values to various benefits so that they can be bought and sold. The inclusion of a credit methodology in a fully flexible benefits plan differentiates such a plan from other flexible benefits plan designs, such as premium conversion plans or flexible spending accounts.

Setting up a credit methodology in a flexible benefits plan to mediate the exchange rates among the various benefits options is analogous to setting up a currency exchange for world travelers. Without some kind of pricing structure (currency exchange rates), an employee (traveler) would have no way of measuring the value of one plan (currency) against another or the cost of trading one kind of benefit (currency) for another. Without a pricing structure, a plan sponsor would be unable to separate the true cost of a benefit from the price that will be charged for the benefit under the flexible benefits plan. Like travelers with no currency exchange rate to refer to, employees without a credit methodology to look to would be left to barter for the best deal they can cut. To add to the potential chaos, at any given point in time an infinite number of relationships (exchange rates) between currencies (benefits) may exist.

Setting up a pricing structure for the benefits in a flexible benefits plan is more complex than exchanging dollars for other currencies, however, because exchange rates between the benefits options vary, depending on whether the plan participant is buying or selling the benefits option. It is as if (referring again to the travel analogy) each country is willing to subsidize its currency to a greater or lesser extent against the other currencies, so that instead of having six currency relationships that must be tracked and understood, there are 12.

If each benefits option in a flexible benefits plan represents a different country, then four medical options, two dental options, three life insurance options, three accidental death and dismemberment options, two long-term disability options, and four 401(k) options represent a great many currency exchanges to keep track of (over 300), assuming that the exchange between options is not the same for a participant buying more of a benefit or selling an option to buy more of another benefit. That is, if a plan participant sells a vacation day for cash, it is quite likely that the participant will receive a bit less than one day's pay. On the other hand, if the participant buys a vacation day, it is probable that the participant will pay a bit more than one day's pay.

All fully flexible benefits plans, regardless of how they are characterized, have credit methodologies. A plan sponsor or plan designer should not assume that credit-based models for fully flexible benefits plans are the only ones to have a credit methodology.

Q 7:30 How does a plan sponsor develop a credit methodology?

The key to developing a credit methodology is knowing the answers to the following eight pricing questions (or parameters):

1. What is the projected cost of each underlying benefit (the actual premium or working rate amount)?
2. What portion of the purchase price of any specific benefits option is the employer willing to pay?
3. How much can the employer afford to pay in total?
4. How much should employees pay for a particular benefits option?
5. Are the cost relationships between employee groupings well defined? Examples of employee groupings are—
    - Individual coverage and family coverage,
    - Full-time employees and part-time employees,
    - Current employees and future hires,
    - Union employees and nonunion employees,
    - Corporate office employees and plant employees,
    - Location A employees and location B employees 6.
6. Has the cost of any potential adverse selection been identified and taken into consideration?
7. Is there a well-articulated strategy to subsidize one plan or another or to overcharge for a particular plan?
8. Is there likely to be employee migration, and if so, have the cost consequences of this movement between the plans been examined?

Once these questions have been definitively answered, the next step in the developmental process is to create a pricing matrix for each cafeteria plan option.

Pricing Methodology and Models

Q 7:31 What is a pricing matrix, and how is it used in a fully flexible benefits plan?

A pricing matrix is a grid or chart that takes into consideration, for each and every option under the fully flexible benefits plan, the following elements:

1. The number of credits a plan participant will be given toward the purchase of that benefit;
2. The employee contribution amount;
3. The number of participants who have selected, or are expected to select, a benefit (in plans that distinguish among "employee only," "employee plus one," and "family" coverage, it is necessary to determine how many participants fall into each category of coverage);
4. The number of cash out or cash back credits the participant will receive for selecting a particular benefits option;
5. The purchase price of a benefits option;
6. The hidden employer subsidy credits; and
7. The total premium cost or budgeted expense of the plan.

Note that all the strategic pricing parameters must be identified (see Q 7:30) before attempting to build the matrix.

Q 7:32 Does every fully flexible benefits plan have a credit methodology?

Yes. All fully flexible plans are based on a credit methodology. However, although every type of fully flexible plan has a credit methodology (see Q 7:28), the credit methodology need not be complex. For example, deciding what to pay an employee who opts out of health insurance coverage represents a simple credit methodology (see Q 8:23).

Q 7:33 Why deal in credits rather than in dollars?

The reasons why a credit methodology is not framed or characterized in dollars, even if one credit is worth $1, are as follows:

1. The premium cost or budgeted expense of a benefits option is often not what the plan sponsor pays, and the plan sponsor may not want plan participants to know the true premium cost or budgeted expense.
2. There are inequities in every benefits program, even before converting to flexible benefits. The most common inequity exists in the pricing between "employee only" and "family" coverage. To the extent that a plan sponsor wants to eliminate or maintain these inequities in the flexible benefits plan, it is easier to handle these sensitive issues by using credits.

3. It is quite rare to give a plan participant who opts out of a benefits option the full value of the benefit. The use of credits and the credit methodology will draw less attention to this fact.
4. In order to protect the plan against adverse selection, the plan sponsor generally prices the cost of taking a benefit differently from the cost of not taking a benefit. By using credits instead of dollars, the sponsor can avoid the perceived inequity of this necessity in the pricing structure.
5. The credit methodology may reward or benefit one group of employees and not another. A credit approach can be used to minimize the potential human resources concerns that this imbalance may create.

Q 7:34 How does the plan sponsor determine how much money it wants to spend and how much money it wants employees to spend on a specific benefits option?

The plan sponsor must apportion costs in a way that reflects the employer's strategic benefits objectives, regardless of whether it uses a traditional or a flexible benefits delivery vehicle. The employer must strike a balance between what it can afford and what employees can be asked to contribute, and it is this balance that the benefits professional attempts to establish and maintain.

Two methods frequently used by employers to divide an insurance premium or working rate between itself and its employees are to:

1. Establish a percentage split; or
2. Set a fixed dollar amount for the employee and/or the employer.

Example. In a percentage split, the plan sponsor decides that it will pay 75 percent and employees will pay 25 percent of the cost of each medical plan that is offered. The employer offers three medical plans: Plan A costs $3,000; Plan B costs $4,000; and Plan C costs $6,000. In this case, the percentage split between costs paid by the employer and the employee is as follows:

	Plan A	*Plan B*	*Plan C*
Employer (75%)	$2,250	$3,000	$4,500
Employee (25%)	$ 750	$1,000	$1,500

Example. If the employer wanted to use the fixed dollar system, it would establish a spending level for itself that it will not exceed regardless which plan an employee selects. Suppose that the employer chooses to spend $2,250 per employee. In this case, if the employer is offering the same three medical plans as in the above example (Plan A costs $3,000; Plan B costs $4,000; and Plan C costs $6,000), the employer and employee costs are as follows:

	Plan A	*Plan B*	*Plan C*
Employer	$2,250	$2,250	$2,250
Employee	$ 750	$1,750	$3,750

Q 7:35 How does a plan sponsor assign credits?

There is no single correct way to assign credits to plan participants. The most common way is to allocate credits based on the opt-out amounts. For example, if the flexible benefits plan wants to give everyone who opts out of medical, life, and disability insurance $520 annually, then (using the weekly payroll as the basis for the calculation) each plan participant receives ten credits per week. Another common way to set and assign credits is by using the employer's full cost. Consider the following example:

1. Monthly cost breakdown of an organization's medical, dental, life insurance, and disability plans.

	Individual Coverage	*Two-Person Coverage*	*Family Coverage*
Employer's cost	$140	$200	$245
Employee's cost	$ 50	$ 80	$125
Total cost	$190	$280	$370

2. Set value of flexible credits equal to employer's average cost.

$140 + $200 + $245 = $585 ÷ 3 = $195

The value of the credit is set at $195.

Note. Typically this average calculation would be a weighted average. For simplicity, assume we have the same number of employees in individual, two-person, and family coverage.

3. Set the purchase price tags equal to the value of the credit plus the employee's cost.

	Individual Coverage	*Two-Person Coverage*	*Family Coverage*
Value of flexible plan credits	$195	$195	$195
Current employee's cost	$ 50	$ 80	$125
Purchase price tags	$245	$275	$320

This simple example shows only the mechanics of establishing and assigning credits. In order to make it easy to visualize, it is assumed that the employee cost is to remain the same as it was before the flexible benefits plan was implemented. However, this is not a complete credit methodology. First, there is no consideration for adverse selection in this pricing illustration. Second, the effect of employee selection and migration is not dealt with at all. Third, one would expect because of subsidies and overcharges that the purchase price tags would support the organization's long-term strategy. In this simplified example, no pricing strategy is employed.

Q 7:36 Why would a plan sponsor establish credits at the full price amount?

In the example shown in Q 7:35, the value of the credits represents the average full amount paid by the employer. Plan sponsors often establish credits on the basis of the full cost so that they can communicate to the employee just how expensive these programs really are. The difficulty with using the full cost to establish the credit rate is that when a participant opts out of a benefits option, the participant rarely receives the full amount that the plan sponsor would have spent. Specifically, in the Q 7:35 illustration, each participant receives credits worth $195 per month (a value of $2,340 annually); however, if the individual opts out of benefits coverage, he or she might receive only $700 annually. To be sure, there are several ways this dichotomy can be presented to employees. The employer must decide whether the positive features associated with demonstrating the costliness of these employee benefits is worth the perception of inequity, when employees who opt out of benefits have to return some of these credits.

Q 7:37 Why set credits to the opt-out amount?

Question 7:36 explains why flexible benefits plan sponsors use the full cost of benefits options to set credit values. The major problem with using a full-cost credit methodology is that when plan participants opt out of a benefits option they receive fewer credits than the purchase of the benefits option would indicate. The solution to this dilemma is to base the credit methodology on what the opt-out amount will be. If the average annual per capita expense is $2,340 but the plan provides only $700 in cash for opting out, then using the cash-out figure of $700 for the basis of the credit methodology means a participant receives monthly credits worth approximately $58 instead of the $195 worth of monthly credits the participant would have received in the example described in Q 7:35. One possible objection to this approach is that now employees cannot fully appreciate the true cost of the benefits program sponsored by employer.

Q 7:38 Should an employer apportion the number of flexible credits allowed to each employee based on the employee's family size or on the level of coverage an employee selects?

In health care programs like medical, dental, vision, and prescription drugs, it is common to distinguish among various levels of coverage such as employee only or individual, employee-plus-one/two/three, employee and spouse, employee and child(ren), and family. In a typical preflexible benefits program it is also quite common for the employer to assign its costs according to these levels. Generally the employer pays significantly greater amounts to the categories that have larger numbers of dependents.

> **Example.** Assume that the plan sponsor pays 80 percent of individual coverage, 75 percent of employee-plus-one coverage, and 70 percent of family coverage. The cost of each coverage is as follows:

- Individual coverage = $1,200
- Employee-plus-one coverage = $3,600
- Family coverage = $6,400

The employer is paying $960 per year for individual coverage (80 percent), $2,700 for employee-plus-one coverage (75 percent), and $4,480 for family coverage (70 percent).

Although it may seem both logical and appropriate to apportion the number of flexible plan credits to employees on the basis of an employee's actual family status, it would be quite unusual to do so for two reasons:

1. It is extremely difficult (next to impossible) to ascertain whether a person is married or has children.
2. There are likely to be unintended windfalls for those employees who receive family credits on the basis of their real life situations but who select less costly levels of coverage, such as individual. (In a flexible benefits plan it is quite common for an employee to select a lower level of coverage than his or her actual family status might suggest the employee needs, because the employee has a working spouse who receives health insurance protection through his or her employer's medical plan.)

Instead, it is more common to create a link in a flexible benefits plan's credit methodology between credits received and the coverage level of benefits selected. For example, assume that all employees receive $960 worth of credits in our theoretical credit methodology. In addition, employees who select employee-plus-one coverage receive an additional $1,740 worth of credits, and those who select family coverage get an additional $3,520 worth of credits.

This credit methodology can be presented in several ways on a flexible benefits plan enrollment form. Perhaps the most straightforward approach is shown in Table 7-1.

Table 7-1. Benefits Credits

1. Dollar value of annual credits paid by employer:	(1) $960
2. Dollar value of supplemental medical plan credits for participants who select two-person or family medical coverage.	
Two-person coverage = $1,740	
Family medical coverage = $3,520	
Enter dollar value of additional credits on line 2:	(2) ______
3. Dollar value of supplemental dental plan credits for participants who select two-person or family dental coverage.	
Two-person coverage = $158	
Family dental coverage = $205	
Enter dollar value of additional credits on line 3:	(3) ______
4. Total dollar value of available credits (1 + 2 + 3):	(4) ______

This particular approach is often referred to as a multiple-tier credit methodology. Although this multiple-tier approach is not uncommon, it is more typical to see a single-tier credit methodology. Multiple tiers often are used when the plan sponsor wants to present a more accurate picture of the full price and point out to families of employees how much they are receiving in subsidies. In contrast, a single-tier approach tends to hide the family subsidy. Neither approach is superior; plan sponsors must select and use an approach and a presentation strategy that they believe will work well in their own organizational structure.

Q 7:39 How should the plan sponsor resolve existing pricing inequities that become apparent when the employer develops a credit methodology?

Two issues concerning pricing inequities must be considered prior to the implementation of a flexible plan:

1. Does the plan sponsor intend to eliminate, begin to eliminate, maintain, or exacerbate these so-called inequities as part of the pricing strategy?
2. How should the employer present these differences to plan participants?

The most common inequity is the family subsidy. As discussed in Q 7:38, there are several ways to handle current pricing inequities that are to be maintained in the flexible benefits plan credit methodology; the fundamental issue is to decide early in the planning stage whether such differences are to be visible to or hidden from plan participants. If the differences are to be visible, they can be displayed as part of the credit methodology; if they are to be hidden, they can be included in hidden subsidies.

Q 7:40 What are purchase price tags?

The term "purchase price tag" refers to the dollar value of the credits, cash outs, and/or employee contributions that a plan participant must use to buy a benefits option under the flexible benefits plan (see Q 7:41). Table 7-2 contains a portion of a flexible benefits plan enrollment form that illustrates the purchase price tag concept.

Table 7-2. Sample Flexible Benefits Plan Enrollment Form

Benefits Credits

1. Dollar value of annual credits paid by employer: (1) $960

2. Dollar value of supplemental medical plan credits for participants who select two-person or family medical coverage.

Two-person coverage = $1,740

Family medical coverage = $3,520

Enter dollar value of additional credits on line 2: (2) _______

3. Dollar value of supplemental dental plan credits for participants who select two-person or family dental coverage.

Table 7-2. Sample Flexible Benefits Plan Enrollment Form (*cont'd*)

Two-person coverage = $158

Family dental coverage = $205

Enter dollar value of additional credits on line 3: (3) ______

4. Total dollar value of available credits (1 + 2 + 3): (4) ______

Purchase Price Tags

Medical	*Individual Coverage*	*Two-Person Coverage*	*Family Coverage*
M1. High-option plan	$1,200	$3,600	$6,400
M2. Low-option plan	$ 960	$2,900	$5,550
M3. HMO A	$ 960	$2,700	$4,950

M1. ______

Dental	*Individual Coverage*	*Two-Person Coverage*	*Family Coverage*
D1. High-option plan	$250	$380	$565
D2. Low-option plan	$130	$210	$380
D3. HMO A	$ 95	$160	$275

D1. ______

Q 7:41 How does an employer establish purchase price tags?

An employer can calculate a purchase price tag in a flexible benefits plan by means of the following formula:

Employer Credits + Cash Outs + Employee Contributions = Purchase Price Tag

In this formula, the term "employer credits" refers to the dollar value of the overt credits the employer gives to a plan participant toward the purchase of a particular benefit. The term "cash outs" represents the dollar value of the credits an employee gets to keep if he or she selects that option. A cash out is always a negative number. For example, if a plan sponsor wants to give an employee who has selected individual coverage in a medical health maintenance organization (HMO) (M3 in Table 7-2) a $200 value cash return annually, the employee's purchase price tag would drop from $960 to $760:

$960 (Employer Credits)	+	(–$200) (Cash Out)	+	$0 (Employee Contribution)	=	$760 (Purchase Price Tag)

This represents a significant benefit for the employee because the lower purchase price means that the employee spends less for coverage and has more credits to spend elsewhere or to take as cash. The term "employee contributions" defines the true amount that an employee pays to select a particular benefit.

Q 7:42 Why does the employer subsidize one benefit and not another, or overcharge for a particular benefit in a credit methodology?

The only reason a plan sponsor subsidizes a particular benefit or asks employees to pay more for a benefit than is necessary is to make a specific benefits option more attractive or less attractive to employees. The sponsor's objective is to encourage employees to migrate to or from a particular benefit. There can be many reasons a flexible benefits plan sponsor wants to encourage a migratory pattern. The most common reason is cost management. For example, the plan sponsor may develop a credit methodology to encourage all employees to try managed care options, especially HMOs. Or the sponsor may give employees an incentive to move from a high-option coverage dental, life insurance, or disability plan to a more cost-efficient lower-option plan. In very sophisticated credit methodologies, the sponsor may provide healthier employees with incentives to gravitate toward one plan, while less healthy employees are encouraged to gravitate toward another plan. Another sophisticated distinction in a credit methodology is sometimes made among families, married couples, and single workers. When such a distinction is made, pricing mechanisms may encourage families with children to select one benefits option (perhaps the more cost-efficient HMO), while couples are given an incentive to select a different option, and single employees are encouraged to select yet a third benefits plan (perhaps a low-coverage indemnity plan).

Q 7:43 What are one-, two-, and three-tier credit systems, and what is the difference between them?

The primary reason for using a one-tier credit system is to make the credit methodology less complex. The other important reason is to hide the fact that the plan sponsor provided a much larger subsidy to family units than it did to employee-only units. In a multiple-tier credit system, the plan sponsor always differentiates the credit according to which coverage level the employee selected within a particular benefits option (see Q 7:38).

A one-tier credit methodology results in all employees receiving the same number of credits, regardless of their actual family status or the level of coverage they select within a benefits plan (that is, there is never a credit differential based upon an employee selecting "individual," "two-person," or "family" coverage). Generally in a one-tier credit methodology the sponsor uses an average (opt-out) cost (see Qs 7:35–7:37). Plan sponsors use multiple-tier credit methodologies so that the two-person family or the three-or-more-person family to see (and presumably appreciate) the full extent of the program's cost.

Q 7:44 What is a hidden subsidy, and why is it important?

In every flexible benefits plan credit methodology there are two ways for an employer to give money to an employee. When the employer provides the money as employee credits, the employee receives overt benefits dollars that are available to buy any benefit being offered through the flexible benefits plan. The second way for an employer to make contributions is through a hidden subsidy. These employer dollars supplement the overt credits but are hidden and are tied to a single, specific benefit. For example, assume that the price of medical plan A is $1,500, and the employer gives each employee $1,000 worth of medical credits. An employee who chooses this medical plan is told that he or she must pay $200. There is a $300 cost difference between the $1,500 price of medical plan A and the accounted for dollars [$1,000 (employer credits) + $200 (employee contribution)]. That $300 differential is a hidden subsidy that is contributed by the employer and is used only when this plan is elected.

An important distinction between a flexible benefits plan credit and a flexible benefits plan hidden subsidy is that credit dollars, once given to a plan participant, can be used to buy any benefit, but a subsidy can be applied to only one particular benefit and comes into play only when that benefit is chosen. There are three basic reasons plan sponsors use hidden subsidies:

1. Overt credit dollars, together with employee contributions, will not cover the total expense of an underlying benefit within the flexible benefits plan.
2. To encourage employees to participate in a particular plan, the plan sponsor wants to charge less for that plan. The plan sponsor therefore needs to subsidize it heavily but may not want all employees to know the extent of the subsidy.
3. There are benefits subsidies between groups of employees (the most common being between employees who select single coverage versus family coverage), and the plan sponsor wishes to maintain these differences in the flexible benefits plan but does not want to disclose the extent of these subsidies.

The concept of a hidden subsidy also can be expressed in these related pricing matrix equations:

Employer Credits + Cash Outs + Employee Contributions = Purchase Price Tags

Purchase Price Tag + Hidden Subsidy = Total Expense

From the second equation it is apparent that the hidden subsidy is the factor that accounts for the difference between the employee's purchase price tag (what the employee pays using the value of the employer credits and employee pre- or post-tax contributions) and the total expense figure. As the amount of the employer's overt credit goes up, or as employee's contribution goes up, the hidden subsidy goes down. Pushed to an extreme, this can result in a negative hidden subsidy—in other words, an overcharge.

Example. An employer gives each employee credits valued at $750 annually. There is no cash out for this benefits option. The employee who selects this benefits option must contribute an additional $350 worth of credits annually. The insurance carrier premium for this benefit is $1,250 for the year.

To calculate the purchase price tag for this benefits option add the credits ($750), cash outs ($0), and employee contributions ($350):

$750 + $350 = $1,100 (purchase price tag)

The hidden subsidy is calculated by subtracting the purchase price tag ($1,100) from the total expense of this benefit ($1,250):

$1,250 – $1,100 = $150 (hidden subsidy)

Example. An employer gives each employee credits valued at $750 annually. There is a credit cash out for this benefits option valued at $50. The employee who selects this benefits option makes no contribution. The insurance carrier premium for this benefit is $1,250 for the year.

As in the previous example, the purchase price tag for this benefits option is calculated by adding the credits ($750), the cash out (which is always articulated as a negative amount: - $50), and the employee contribution ($0):

$750 + (–$50) = $700 (purchase price tag)

Again, subtracting the purchase price tag ($700) from the total expense of this benefit ($1,250) will reveal the hidden subsidy ($550):

$1,250 – $700 = $550 (hidden subsidy)

Example. An employer gives each employee employer credits valued at $750 annually. There is no cash out for this benefits option. The employee who selects this benefits option must contribute an additional $350 worth of credits annually. The insurance carrier premium for this benefit is $1,000 for the year.

Adding the credits ($750), the cash out ($0), and the employee contribution ($350) gives the purchase price tag of $1,100 ($750 + $350). The hidden subsidy in this example is negative because the difference between the purchase price tag ($1,100) and the total expense ($1,000) is –$100. Thus, the hidden subsidy becomes an employee hidden cost, or surcharge. The overcharge for this plan is $100 ($1,000 – $1,100).

Q 7:45 What is total expense, and how does it differ from an employer's cost?

The total expense is what an employer expects to pay to the insurance carrier in premiums under the contract. If a plan sponsor is self-insured, this expense figure is the budgeted amount that is paid over to the trust fund or to the third-party administrator, or maintained as a booked expense on the plan sponsor's income statement. A plan sponsor's total expense may differ from the plan sponsor's total cost for three reasons:

1. The budgeted expense of many insurance arrangements, and of all self-funded arrangements, will not equal the actual total cost, which can be determined only at the close of the final plan year, after the plan's year-end accounting;
2. Employee contributions may be used to fund part of the benefit's total cost; and
3. If cash outs to the employee are permitted, employees' choices to take or reject the cash out may give rise to cost consequences for the employer that have no bearing whatsoever on the total expense.

The following three examples use the same situations given in the examples of the preceding question (see Q 7:44). The reader should review those prior calculations before examining the calculations given here for the total employer cost.

Example. An employer gives each employee benefits credits valued at $750 annually. There is no cash out for this benefits option. The employee who selects this benefits option must contribute an additional $350 worth of credits annually. The insurance carrier premium for this benefit is $1,250 for the year.

The total expense equals the insurance carrier premium and is $1,250. The hidden subsidy has been calculated to be $150 (see Q 7:44).

The purchase price tag is the credits given ($750), plus the employer's hidden subsidy of $150, or $900:

$750 + $150 = $900 (purchase price tag)

Example. An employer gives each employee benefits credits valued at $750 annually. There is a credit cash out for this benefits option valued at $50. The employee who selects this benefits option makes no contribution. The insurance carrier premium for this benefit is $1,250 for the year.

The total expense equals the insurance carrier premium and is $1,250. The hidden subsidy is $550 (see Q 7:44).

The purchase price tag is determined by adding employer credits ($750) and the hidden subsidy ($550):

$750 + $550 = $1,300 (purchase price tag)

Example. An employer gives each employee benefits credits valued at $750 annually. No cash out is available for this benefits option. The employee who selects this benefits option must contribute $350 worth of credits annually. The insurance carrier premium for this benefit is $1,000 for the year.

The total expense equals the insurance carrier premium and is $1,000, and the hidden subsidy is a negative amount (-$100), which constitutes an overcharge (see calculation in Q 7:44).

The purchase price tag is determined by adding employer credits ($750) and the hidden subsidy (-$100):

$750 + (–$100) = $650 (purchase price tag)

Q 7:46 How much should employees pay for benefits options in a flexible benefits plan?

There is no single correct answer to this question; the amount that employees will pay will differ from one employer to the next depending upon an employer's pricing strategy, human resources concerns, and budgetary constraints. The important concern to keep in mind is that once an employee contribution schedule has been determined, it must be properly reflected in the credit methodology.

Q 7:47 Where is the bulk of funds usually located in a flexible benefits plan?

In almost every employee benefits program, the bulk of funds is dedicated to medical benefits, retirement benefits, and paid time-off programs. When designing their credit methodologies, plan sponsors are usually advised to include at least two of these three benefits categories as options because employees find flexible programs more valuable if they have some discretionary funds at their disposal.

In an example of a plan design frequently used by flexible benefits plans, employees may choose among health options, life insurance, AD&D, and disability insurance options; the plan does not offer any retirement options. In a plan of this type, the sponsor should consider including the option to buy or sell vacation time, because without such an option, an employee's choices will be limited by the lack of flexible credits.

A common design problem that arises when employees have an inadequate number of discretionary credits is that after the conversion to the flexible benefits plan, employees are able to purchase only a piece of a medical plan before they run out of credits and must start dipping into their own pockets to purchase other benefits.

Example. Before introducing the flexible benefits plan, the division of benefits costs between employee and employer may have looked like this:

Benefits	*Employee Paid*	*Employer Paid*
Medical	$600	$1,500
Dental	$100	$ 300
Life insurance	$ 0	$ 90
Disability	$ 0	$ 150

After introducing the flexible benefits plan, the division of costs may look more like this:

Dollar value of employer credits:	$2,040
Purchase price tags:	
Medical:	$2,100
Dental:	$ 400
Life insurance:	$ 90
Disability:	$ 150

The flexible design in this example runs the risk of a serious public relations problem: employees may feel that they had a better deal before the flexible plan was introduced. Before the flexible plan, almost 75 percent of medical, 75 percent of dental, and 100 percent of life and disability insurance were paid for by the employer. With the implementation of the flexible plan, employees do not have enough credits to buy the medical plan and must pay 100 percent of the dental, life insurance, and disability plans as well. Of course, in either scenario, the employee pays $700 for the plans:

Before flexible benefits:

$600 medical cost + $100 dental cost = $700 (total employee cost)

After flexible benefits:

$2,100 + $400 + $90 + $150 = $2,740 (purchase price tag)

$2,740 - $2,040 = $700 (total employee cost)

One design solution to this credit methodology problem is for the employer to augment the plan with vacation and/or retirement options that can be purchased with available (not additional) credits so that employees do not have the perception that the plan sponsor is being cheap or that there is a reduction of choices.

Another way of handling this problem is to offer less expensive options—for example, a $1,600 medical plan, a $270 dental plan, a $70 life insurance plan, and a $100 disability plan—and to inform employees that if they take the first flexible benefits plan, it will cost them the same $700, but if they choose the less expensive options, they will actually pay nothing ($1,600 + $270 + $70 + $100 = $2,040, which equals the employer credits, leaving no charge to the employee).

There is always more than one way to solve a problem in a flexible benefits plan environment. The key is to know which solution can be communicated most easily and which solutions employees will find most acceptable. Also, whenever there is a reallocation of dollars (in the above example there was no reallocation of dollars), the plan sponsor must be sensitive to who wins and who loses. In a flexible benefits plan framework, the concept of winning and losing must be defined in terms of who will have to pay more out of his own pocket for benefits and who will have more to spend on buying benefits.

Q 7:48 Why is it extremely important in a flexible benefits pricing model to know where the money comes from and where the money goes?

As a general rule, employers who introduce a flexible benefits plan do not want this plan to cost them more money than a traditional benefits program. For example, if the current year's total expenditure for benefits is $1 million and the next year's expenditure is projected to be $1,100,000 (a 10 percent increase), the introduction of a flexible plan should not cause the projected expenditure to exceed the projected $1,100,000 amount. To be sure that the plan does not exceed the projected budget, the plan sponsor must be aware of how design and pricing changes in a flexible benefits plan environment affect aggregate costs and must be able to differentiate and balance changes that represent cost increases against changes that represent cost savings. The best and most common example of this trade-off is the opt-out feature in a flexible benefits plan.

Q 7:49 How does the opt-out feature affect the aggregate cost?

Giving a person cash for not selecting a benefit such as medical, life, or disability insurance can have adverse selection consequences, as discussed in chapter 2 (see Qs 2:26–2:28). To help compensate for the effect of adverse selection, plan sponsors give employees who opt out of a benefit less (in the case of medical, dental, and vision plans, significantly less) than the cost of the benefit itself.

Another cost of opting out of plan benefits that cannot be overlooked involves giving cash to employees who dropped out of the plan prior to implementation of the flexible plan and who have been receiving nothing.

> **Example.** A company has a medical plan that was charging full-time employees $25 a month for individual coverage and $100 a month for family coverage. Fifty full-time employees dropped coverage rather than pay the required employee contribution. The employer has 1,000 full-time employees, so the 50 who do not take coverage represent 5 percent of the employee population. This company also charges part-time employees three times what it charges full-time employees to purchase medical insurance. Of 350 part-time employees, 150 do not take medical coverage, because of the cost. When the company introduces the flexible benefits plan, if it gives all these employees who have opted out $1,000 each, the cost of the medical plan increases by $200,000 [(50 FTEs + 150 PTEs) $1,000 = $200,000]. If the company does not want medical costs to jump by $200,000, it must find ways to offset this amount with either real or projected savings (or a lower payment for the opt-out privilege).
>
> Further, assume that for each new employee who drops coverage, the plan sponsor expects medical costs to be reduced by $2,000; if the sponsor was hoping that new opt-out employees would cover the $200,000 cost increase in the plan, it would need 100 additional employees to drop medical cov-

erage. It is highly unlikely that a plan sponsor would get this many new opt outs. Empirical data might indicate that 20 to 30 is a likelier range for new opt outs.

The most common solution to this dilemma is to reduce the amount of the opt-out payment, especially for the part-time employees. If the plan sponsor gives part-time employees $250 (not $1,000), the cost of providing the opt-out payments is $87,500 [(50 FTEs × $1,000) + (150 PTEs × $250)]. If the sponsor gives part-time employees nothing for opting out, the cost is reduced to $50,000 [(50 FTEs × $1,000) + (150 PTEs × $0)]. Now the sponsor needs only 25 additional employees to opt out in order to meet the projected new expense (25 × $2,000 = $50,000), which, according to our empirical data, is reasonable. It is also predictable that by refraining from paying part-time employees, the projected number of additional employees who choose to opt out will drop. Now the critical questions are: How many opt outs is the sponsor likely to get? How much is it going to cost if the sponsor gets only five, ten, or 15 new opt outs? In other words, can the potential dollar risk of this design be measured, and is the employer willing to accept it?

The risk certainly can be measured, but each plan sponsor will need to decide what constitutes an acceptable trade-off between risks and rewards. In this example, minimal risk is incurred, because giving part-time employees less or even no money will not affect the number of opt outs by very much. We know that most part-time employees are working for one of two reasons:

1. To increase their cash compensation; or
2. To obtain access to group health and welfare benefits.

The part-time employees who are working to supplement their families' incomes have already dropped out of the plan (this is the group of 150 individuals who have no reason to pay $900 per year for individual coverage or $3,600 per year for family coverage). The part-time employees who enroll in the medical benefit and who pay a lot for that privilege would not drop it regardless of what the opt-out incentive was—this group needs and wants this benefit and assigns an extremely high personal value to it. Given this perspective of the part-time worker, the employer is not really incurring much risk; the employer can expect virtually 100 percent of all employees who opt out to come from the ranks of full-time employees, and the likelihood of getting the necessary 20 to 30 to opt out is great because full-time employees still receive the full $1,000 opt-out amount.

There are other solutions to this problem. The employer may decide to charge employees more money to cover the cost of providing the opt-out payments. Some employers may experience decreases in the cost of a benefit, either because the competitive bidding process for insured benefits results in less expensive benefits or because the plan sponsor anticipates that employee migration in the flexible plan results in employees selecting more cost-effective plans—a possibility that will save the employer money. If an employer decides to shift the opt-out cost to employees, the employer should be cognizant of any potential reallocation of dollars among employees. This knowledge is important because it allows the employer to anticipate employees' reactions, prepare responses, identify winners and losers, and develop communication materials. In addition, it prevents unanticipated or accidental enrollment migration among the various benefits options.

Example. An employer gives full-time employees $1,000 for opting out; part-time employees receive nothing. This creates an additional cost of $50,000 [(50 FTEs × $1,000) + (150 PTEs × $0)]. The employer does not want to depend on any new opt outs to cover this cost, so the employer charges employees a bit more in contributions for medical benefits. In effect, employees who enroll in the medical plan are paying for those who opt out of it. The employee could charge all full-time employees $5 a month extra to cover the projected additional cost ($60 per year × 950 full-time employees who enroll in medical benefits = $57,000), but this means reallocating funds away from full-time employees who enroll in medical benefits and giving these dollars to full-time employees who do not take medical benefits.

Whether or not this approach makes good sense depends upon the employer's strategy and ability to accept risk as opposed to transfer cost. As seen in the above example, a key to successful pricing in a flexible benefits plan environment is the plan sponsor's awareness of any reallocation of funds between employee groups. Is there a reallocation from families to individuals? From full-time to part-time employees? From divisions to locations? From older to younger employees?

Finally, the employer may decide to reduce benefits costs by finding carriers and providers who will insure or administer the program more economically than previously. Rebidding the insurances (and any other vendor-provided services) very often results in significant cost savings that may adequately cover additional cash outlays in other parts of the flexible benefits plan. A more subtle way to reduce the cost of benefits is to encourage employee migration to more cost-effective benefits.

Example. An employer gives away $50,000 to 50 full-time employees who have opted out. Each employee who drops the medical high-option plan and selects the less expensive managed care medical option generates a $700 savings for the employer. In this case, the flexible benefits plan could offer the following:

Dollar value of employer credits:	$2,040
Purchase price tags:	
Medical, high option:	$2,100
Medical, low option:	$1,400
Dental:	$ 400
Life insurance:	$ 90
Disability:	$ 150

Under this pricing structure the employer may get 600 or more full-time employees to move to the low-option medical plan. However, the employer receives no benefit from any employee migration to the low-option medical plan. The employee who selects the low-option plan receives the entire economic benefit of his or her selection.

If the employer adds $300 to the price of the low-option medical plan, the credits and price tags look like this:

Dollar value of employer credits:	$2,040
Purchase price tags:	
Medical, high option:	$2,100
Medical, low option:	$1,700
Dental:	$ 400
Life insurance:	$ 90
Disability:	$ 150

The negative aspect of this strategy is that the employer may get only 170 full-time employees to move to the low-option medical plan. On the other hand, the employer now shares—in the amount of $300 per employee—in the cost savings of that migration. The funds generated by this strategy (170 × $300 = $51,000) will cover the additional cost associated with introducing a flexible benefits plan.

Q 7:50 Should an employer tie the flexible benefits plan's credit methodology to a budget?

Yes. The notion that a flexible benefits design operates as a defined contribution plan is an important cost savings concept (see Q 1:22), and tying the annual aggregate sum that the plan sponsor can spend on employee benefits to the budget is in keeping with the defined contribution concept. The budget provides a target amount that the credit methodology must aim for. If the chief financial officer indicates that this year's benefit budget of $3 million cannot grow by more than 10 percent and will become $3,300,000 next year, then the sum of each individual component of the flexible benefits plan may not exceed this amount.

Example. The employer's annual cost for the benefits program is as follows:

	Individual Coverage	*Employee-plus-one Coverage*	*Family Coverage*
Medical, high option	$1,500	$3,500	$5,000
Medical, low option	$1,100	$2,750	$4,000
Dental	$ 300	$ 450	$ 600
Life	$90 average cost per employee		
Disability	$150 average cost per employee		

And if the number of employees in each group or cell is as follows:

	Individual Coverage	*Employee-plus-one Coverage*	*Family Coverage*
Medical, high option	245	130	320
Medical, low option	70	35	40
Dental	315	170	410
Life	950 (total number of benefit-eligible employees)		
Disability	950 (total number of benefit-eligible employees)		

The cost of the benefits program is:

	Individual Coverage	*Employee-plus-one Coverage*	*Family Coverage*	
Medical, high option	$367,500	$455,000	$1,600,000	$2,422,500
Medical, low option	$ 77,000	$ 96,250	$ 160,000	$ 333,250
Dental	$ 94,500	$ 76,500	$ 246,000	$ 417,000
Life				$ 85,000
Disability				$ 142,500
TOTAL				$3,400,750

In this example, the projected cost is expected to exceed the budgetary limit by $100,750 [$3,300,000 - $3,400,750]. Assuming this is unacceptable to the plan sponsor, there must be a change to the credit methodology (akin to the types of changes described in Qs 7:48, 7:49) in order to reduce the budgetary shortfall from $100,750 to zero.

By making benefits costs responsive to budgetary restrictions, the employer is able to regulate (and presumably, control) benefits costs in the same way as he or she would regulate any other cost of doing business. The strength of a flexible benefits plan is that it is ready-made for this type of budgetary analysis, and what is more, it allows those managers who are responsible for maintaining benefits costs to see and model different solutions.

Chapter 8

Welfare Benefit Plan Options: Health/Life/Disability

An employer that initiates a flexible benefits plan needs to decide which health care options to make available to its employees. It may seek input from its employees by surveying them, or engaging them in focus group discussions to discover which benefits are most desirable. Above all, however, an employer must remember that the purpose of a flexible benefits plan is to provide employees with needed benefits in a way that makes those benefits more valuable than additional cash. This chapter focuses on which welfare benefit plan choices an employer needs to make available in order to provide employees with meaningful choices that approximate their needs.

Q 8:1 What is a "welfare benefit plan"?

ERISA Section 3.1 defines "welfare benefit plan" as any plan, fund, or program which was heretofore or is hereafter established or maintained by an employer or by an employee organization, or by both, to the extent that such plan, fund, or program was established or is maintained for the purpose of providing for its participants or their beneficiaries, through the purchase of insurance or otherwise, (A) medical, surgical, or hospital care or benefits, or benefits in the event of sickness, accident, disability, death or unemployment, or vacation benefits, apprenticeship or other training programs, or day care centers, scholarship funds, or prepaid legal services.

Health benefits, life insurance, and disability plans can be important choices within a flexible benefit arrangement—either within a Section 125 plan or outside of one. Vacation benefits can also play a part in a flexible environment.

> **Note.** Not all welfare benefit plans are permitted in a Section 125 plan. In fact, not all welfare benefits listed in ERISA have widespread application. For example, although included in the original definition of a welfare benefit plan, pre-paid legal services benefits are severely limited in operation and applicability.

Medical Plans

Q 8:2 Should an employer offer more than one type of medical plan under a flexible benefits plan?

If the plan sponsor of a flexible benefits plan (i.e., the employer) provides an array of medical plan choices that segment the health insurance market by premium coverage, the amount of required employee contribution, the level of managed care, the extent of coverage, and the freedom to select a particular doctor, the employer should provide enough options to satisfy a range of employees' needs, including the need to obtain quality care at an affordable cost.

> **Note.** Even small employers might find an insurance carrier that offers several options, including a traditional plan, a preferred provider organization (PPO), and a health maintenance organization (HMO). Such a carrier might permit employees to choose among options, as long as all choices are with that same carrier.

Q 8:3 What choices do an employer and its employees need to make when developing a health care program for a flexible benefits plan?

An employer must determine which medical plans to offer under a flexible benefits plan and how much money to ask employees to contribute toward the cost of medical benefits. Sometimes, employees who are not contributing toward the cost of their health care benefits are in reality paying for those benefits by receiving lower salaries than they might otherwise receive. On the other hand, sometimes the employees are receiving a market rate of pay, plus fully paid benefits, and the employer is less profitable. It is common practice for employees who wish to acquire medical insurance to help pay for it under contributory medical plans. The employer may require employees to make contributions for individual coverage, family coverage, or both. If the health care program includes a multiple-option medical plan, the employer may offer different levels of benefits coverage that parallel the different levels of contribution. In any case, each employee must decide whether or not to elect coverage for which a contribution is required.

The next level of decision making relates to the specific design elements of each medical plan. For example, in the implementation of an indemnity plan, the size of the plan's deductibles is an important consideration. The employer must decide whether it can afford a "first-dollar" approach to health care or whether a comprehensive approach is needed. A first-dollar approach is one in which hospital and surgical costs are insured or covered from the very first dollar of expense that an employee incurs. A comprehensive approach is one in which all costs—including hospital, surgical, and major medical—are covered only after a deductible is met. Another approach is a hybrid plan—typically with a network of "preferred providers"—which might offer 100 percent (or "first dollar") coverage when choosing to use a network provider, but require payment of deductible or co-pay when seeking services outside of the network. When choosing between the three approaches, the needs of the employees also must be considered. Thus, the employer must strike a balance between how much it can afford to pay and how much it can reasonably ask its employees to contribute toward the cost of health care.

A few decades ago, first-dollar coverage was the norm. Today, such coverage is becoming increasingly rare.

Decisions regarding any of the following can affect the cost of a health care program:

1. *Offering managed care network plans.* Under one of the most common types of managed care health plans—a point-of-service (POS) plan—the insured may choose to use a doctor inside or outside an approved network. That choice may be made at any point in the process of receiving medical services (hence its name). If the employee or the employee's covered dependents go outside the network for medical care, however, the employee's costs will be higher than if medical care is obtained within the network.
2. *Adjusting the out-of-pocket limit.* The employer can adjust the trigger point beyond which the employee's total cost does not increase and the plan provides 100 percent reimbursement coverage.
3. *Imposing limitations and caps.* Medical plans may impose a variety of limitations and maximums. For instance, limits may be placed on the amounts that a plan will reimburse for particular kinds of services. Alternatively, the plan may establish a total lifetime ceiling (cap) on the amount of money it will spend on any one employee over the course of his or her life.
4. *Setting employee rates.* A plan designer must sometimes make the difficult choice to set employee rates that accurately reflect the risk associated with a given group of employees. For instance, a designer must frequently decide whether a plan should charge a flat contribution rate for employees with at least one covered dependent or vary the contribution rate according to the number and type of dependents. Polling employees to see if they are truly interested in coverage for their depen-

dents, or if they can enroll a spouse or child in another employer's plan, can help with such a decision.

5. *Making multiple options available.* The cost of an employer's health care program also depends on the number and type of medical plan options it offers to employees. Choosing the right mix of medical plans and the insurance carrier (if the employer is not self-insuring the program) are basic decisions. HMOs, PPOs, traditional fee-for-service indemnity medical plans, and POS plans are all options that can be mixed and matched.

Perhaps even more important are the employer's decisions concerning how to finance the plan and which kind of administrator to use. If, for example, the employer offers an HMO, should the HMO's cost be capitated at a fixed rate, or should it use an adjusted community rated system? Or perhaps the employer should use a self-insured HMO. Should the HMO be a staff model or an individual physician practice model HMO? There are no absolute answers to such questions. Whenever an employer has a strategy for its medical program, however, the answers to such questions should support that strategy.

It should be noted that a small employer may not have the clout to choose among an array of options and determine whether or not those options fit within the flexible benefits plan's strategy. Such an employer might belong to an association that offers medical plan options to its members. This is one way to offer an array of options usually reserved for larger employers. Without such resources, however, a smaller employer will most likely depend on its outside advisors, such as its insurance broker, accountant, or a benefits consultant, to determine the best choice among available medical options.

Q 8:4 What are the primary employer considerations in developing medical plan options to coordinate with a fully flexible benefits plan?

The most significant issues that typically arise for an employer seeking to coordinate medical plan options with a fully flexible benefits plan are as follows:

1. *Whether or not to keep the current medical plan(s).* Having decided on a fully flexible benefits plan, it is sometimes easier for an employer to start from scratch and design a completely new package, retaining only those features of the existing program that are working well. Some employers, however, find it preferable to supplement the existing plan with a few flexible features. (See Q 8:12.)
2. *Determining which benefits configurations will best attract and retain the types of employees that the employer needs.* Primary attention should be given to those employees whose employment decisions will be affected by the health care benefits offering. For example, if a part-time workforce is an important component of an employer's staff, the employer must include several options that are designed to meet the special health insurance needs of part-time employees.

3. *Satisfying the needs of different family situations.* As many as seven different family groups are likely to emerge:
   a. Single employee with no dependents,
   b. Single employee with dependent parents,
   c. Single parent with child or children,
   d. Couple with no dependent children,
   e. Working couple with one child,
   f. Working couple with two or more children, and
   g. Married employee with a nonworking spouse and children.

Q 8:5 What common considerations come into play when structuring medical plan options under a flexible benefits plan?

Large employers may offer several coverage levels in a traditional fee-for-service indemnity plan, in which all the plan options may cover the same type of medical expenses (e.g., in-hospital room and board) but each option is priced differently to reflect the provision of different levels of service (e.g., 90 or 300 days of room and board). Another variable in indemnity plan coverage is the annual deductible; that is, how much the employee must pay before the insurance reimbursements begin.

The type of medical plan options provided under a flexible benefits plan are often described simply as high-, medium-, and low-option. The high-option plan provides the greatest amount of coverage and will appeal to employees who incur high medical expenses or who feel compelled to carry as much coverage as they can. The high-option plan is also the most expensive option. The medium option typically provides adequate coverage and may be represented as being a good value option. The low-option plan appeals to employees who have few medical expenses or who may be covered under another plan.

As a rule, the low-option indemnity plan is a comprehensive program that has a substantial up-front deductible for all medical expenditures. If the deductibles are high enough, such a low-option design becomes a safety net or catastrophic plan. Offering employees a choice between indemnity plans provides a useful grouping of alternatives for a flexible benefits plan. Whether it makes as much sense to offer a similar high-, medium-, and low-option array within managed care programs that offer high levels of coverage—in exchange for limited provider access—is questionable.

An HMO provides health care services under the managed care concept by a group of physicians, hospitals, and other delivery providers for a set monthly fee. An HMO is an alternative to an employer indemnity plan. An HMO can offer potential savings, in part because it often requires that a gatekeeper physician be in place. A gatekeeper physician is generally a primary care doctor (internist, family practitioner, pediatrician, or obstetrician) who controls and monitors a patient's access to any medical care received within the health care delivery system.

A few years ago, many flexible benefits plans offered HMOs at low cost to employees; however, as all health care costs have escalated, that practice has fallen off. Today, employees who enroll in an HMO may be given two or more coverage options that differ in the amount of (1) first-dollar cost sharing and (2) coinsurance with the HMO administrator. Furthermore, many HMO offerings differ in the buying service area covered; thus, more than one HMO may be needed to ensure that all employees who desire access to an HMO product will receive it.

A PPO offers an optional network of health care providers that deliver medical services and benefits at high levels of coverage within a specific geographic service area. PPOs often are designed to be comparable to high-option indemnity plans. Employees may elect coverage either within the network (a high-coverage, low-cost option) or outside the network (lower protection at a higher cost). Most employers provide incentives in the form of reduced deductibles and coinsurance (different benefits payment) levels to encourage employees to use the network services, because the network will ultimately save money for both the employee and employer. Some employers also penalize employees who use out-of-network services by charging employees higher premiums for all such medical care.

A flexible benefits plan does not usually offer more than one PPO because making more PPOs available would probably not significantly increase the choices available to the employee. Most PPOs already strive to include a comprehensive array of physicians, services, and specialties within their networks. Nevertheless, sometimes it becomes necessary to offer more than one PPO to meet a wide geographic disbursement of the employee group.

> **Practice Pointer.** Plan sponsors and designers should bear in mind that the introduction of numerous managed-care options (e.g., several PPOs) will complicate communication with employees and render the overall plan design more difficult to comprehend. Nevertheless, in some cases, the size and geographic spread of an employer may make such complexity a necessary part of a flexible benefits plan.

Q 8:6 How many different medical plan options are generally held to be appropriate in a health care benefit program?

Even in the absence of a flexible benefits plan, many large employers offer a considerable array of medical plan options, including traditional fee-for-service indemnity plans, PPOs, POS plans, and HMOs. Typically, employees also have the choice to waive medical coverage, presumably to avoid paying medical premiums, but some health benefit programs require that employees be covered by at least a minimum coverage plan, or show proof of adequate coverage elsewhere in order to opt out of the employer-provided plan.

While small employers might have the luxury of offering multiple options, typically the only choice for employees is the level of coverage (i.e., employee-only, employee plus one, or family) and possibly dental or other supplemental coverage.

In any event, offering more than three indemnity plans (i.e., high-, medium-, and low-option plans) and more than three HMOs or PPOs is excessive. Such an abundance of options may be difficult for the employer to explain, and may make it difficult for employees to distinguish among options.

Q 8:7 How does a flexible benefits plan make employees more sensitive to the high cost of health care and its effect on an employer?

A successful flexible benefits plan brings about a partnership between employer and employees in which the employees come to understand the employer's difficulty in allocating limited resources. A flexible benefits plan takes the search for trade-offs among cost, quality, case management, provider choice, and coverage level and places it squarely within the purview of the employee.

By enabling employees, through a flexible benefits plan, to make decisions about their health care that are personally relevant, the employer can help employees become better consumers of health care who will spend their money and the employer's money on the options that are of greatest importance and value to them. In addition, a flexible benefits plan augments the value of an employee's earnings by offering the employee tax savings through income tax deductions for salary reductions, extension of tax-free medical benefits, and reduction of Social Security and (possibly) other taxes.

A well-designed flexible benefits plan can also help reduce employees' resistance to medical plan contribution increases. When rising medical plan costs cannot be absorbed by the employer and some of the cost increases must be shifted to employees, the employees can exercise more control over their employee contributions by selecting options that reflect both their needs and their ability to pay more.

Q 8:8 In periods of high medical cost inflation, how can an employer maintain a health care program within the range of its budgetary constraints?

An employer can use many techniques to limit its health care costs; the techniques can be applied to both flexible benefits plans and other benefit plans. They include limiting coverage; increasing deductibles; increasing coinsurance requirements; and raising the rates of employees' contributions. When such techniques are used in the context of a traditional benefit plan, however, they are often interpreted by employees as cutbacks. In contrast, the more elaborate and systematic communications approach used by a flexible benefit plan tends to be more successful at educating employees so that they will more quickly comprehend and perhaps even accept cost increases.

Also, because a flexible benefits plan excels at identifying the causes of cost increases, it can become a constructive part of solving the problems—whether attributable to inflation, overutilization, or demographics. A flexible benefits plan enables employees to personally control (to some degree) the amount and quality of the health care they want, either by making additional contributions or by adjusting their benefits with the realization that uncontrolled cost increases could jeopardize the future of their benefits generally.

Over the long term, the ability to control or contain costs during periods of high medical cost inflation rests upon moving employees into managed care environments and reducing excessive, unnecessary utilization of medical services.

Q 8:9 In periods of low medical cost inflation, what should an employer do?

Most benefits professionals agree that, over the long term, the ability to control or contain medical plan costs is dependent upon changing employee behaviors when purchasing medical care. Indeed, the specific objective of moving employees into managed care environments is to make them more active partners in the health care delivery system. Periods of low medical cost inflation provide a great opportunity to increase employees' involvement in a health care program, be it part of a flexible benefits plan or not.

During times of low medical cost inflation an employer has the luxury to thoughtfully and deliberately:

- Offer new options;
- Reprice options to support desired migration of participants to the most cost-effective health plan option; and
- Redesign existing options to correct problems and support the desired migration.

Best of all, without the pressure of needing to respond to economic pressures, such changes can be implemented slowly. Employee input can be obtained and transitions can be handled more easily. When changes are implemented slowly, an employer can mitigate the of disruption for employees and thus reduce the negative feedback that often ensues when changes are made to a health care program.

Q 8:10 How does a health care program affect the design of a flexible benefits plans?

Historically, the health care program has been the most significant component of a flexible benefits plan. Other components, such as retirement income, life insurance, disability coverage, dependent care, and vacation days, are important, but they tend to shrink in stature when compared with the medical plan options.

The health care program is the dominant benefit in a flexible benefits plan for a number of reasons:

1. It is the most expensive benefit, and its costliness is increasing more rapidly than any other.
2. It is a benefit that generates a great deal of concern and interest among employees—with good cause. One serious medical event can easily cost tens of thousands of dollars.
3. It is a benefit in demand by retirees and other individuals who have been laid off through the restructuring of major corporations.

Inflation affects the provision of health care in profound ways. For many of the past 25 years, health care costs have been increasing at twice the cost of living. Most employees' experiences with other benefits are quite the reverse: life insurance costs have tended to go down as life expectancy has improved; disability insurance costs have remained constant as the result of improved rehabilitation and an overall healthy economy; and 401(k) benefits are favorably affected by more knowledgeable investment choice procedures. In contrast, health care costs are controlled by providers that can inadvertently (or intentionally) create the demand for services that drives health care cost inflation.

Q 8:11 Should employees be allowed to opt out of a health care program, or should a minimum amount of coverage be made mandatory?

The question of whether employees should be permitted to opt out of a health care program can arise in both flexible benefits plans and traditional benefit plans. There is no single easy answer. Whether to allow an opt-out option depends on the philosophy of the employer, the strategy of the flexible benefits plan, and the cost of the option. The matter tends to surface in flexible benefits plans because employees may be offered a monetary incentive to drop health coverage, and the "opt-outs" (if properly priced) generate a cost savings for the employer.

The most significant negative implications of unrestrained opt-outs are that (1) the employee can be left financially vulnerable in the event of a medical emergency and (2) the employer may suffer significant public relations damage if an employee who needs medical coverage cannot get it because he or she opted out of the medical plan. In light of such negative implications, some employers require employees to submit a sworn affidavit or other proof verifying other health care coverage, although most employers do not wish to assume the role of health care police.

In lieu of an opt-out option, a flexible benefits plan can be designed to provide relatively inexpensive basic health care options capable of providing employees with protection in the event of major injury or illness (e.g., a catastrophic-only coverage with a very high deductible: $2,500 and up). Another alternative is to make the opt-out option available only to those employees who can demonstrate that they have adequate medical coverage from sources other than their employer's health care program.

If an employer decides to encourage employees to enroll in a basic medical plan rather than to opt out, the employer can price the minimal health care coverage so favorably that few employees will reject it. If the difference in cost between a catastrophic plan and opting out is relatively insignificant, most employees will elect the catastrophic plan.

An employer that offers opt-out provisions must establish what conditions will apply to those employees who wish to reenter the health care program after having opted out. Flexible benefits plans generally allow mid-plan-year reentry if it occurs under one of the permitted rules discussed in the final Treasury regulations. [Treas Reg § 1.125-4] For example, the loss of a spouse's health insurance as the result of job loss would be an acceptable reason to permit reentry.

Reenrollment on an anniversary date generally coincides with the right of any participant to change elections once a year; however, some plans try to protect themselves against adverse selection caused by employees who have opted out and then seek to reenter the plan. Some plans limit the options from which a reentering employee may choose. In the past, plans introduced preexisting condition restrictions and proof of insurability requirements to counter adverse selection. Preexisting conditions may still be effective in limited situations. The Health Insurance Portability and Accountability Act of 1996 (HIPAA) has removed the preexisting condition clause as a reason to deny coverage to an employee who can show proof of recent prior coverage. An employer's concern about adverse selection caused by employees who seek to reenter a health care program may be a factor in the decision to require that some minimum or "core" coverage be maintained.

Q 8:12 Should the medical plan options that an employer had in place continue after a flexible benefits plan is introduced?

Whether existing medical plan options should continue after a flexible benefits plan is introduced depends on what the employer is trying to accomplish with the new flexible benefits plan. If, for example, the employer is trying to eliminate an outdated medical plan, the flexible benefits plan should not keep that plan as an option.

The arguments in favor of keeping the same medical plan options that were in place before the introduction of the flexible benefits plan are as follows:

1. Continuity of medical coverage for employees;
2. Employee satisfaction (they are less likely to perceive a loss of benefits); and

3. Less up-front administrative work as the flexible benefits plan is implemented.

The arguments against keeping the same medical plan options that were in effect before the introduction of the flexible benefits plan are as follows:

1. The existing medical plans may not be consistent with the objectives of the flexible benefits plan;
2. Many employees will stay with their existing benefits rather than evaluate the new options;
3. To encourage employees to switch to a medical plan of choice, a radical pricing of outdated medical plans may be necessary; and
4. Keeping health care choices that do not work well together can undermine the long-term financial integrity of the flexible benefits plan by promoting adverse selection among the options.

Q 8:13 What is the relationship between strategic pricing under a flexible benefits plan and an employee's decision to elect coverage for dependents?

By making dependent coverage quite expensive, an employer encourages employees to let their dependents be covered under another plan, assuming such an alternative is available to them. It is difficult to vary the price of dependent coverage according to whether the dependent waived the group insurance of another employer. Some employers charge an elevated rate to cover dependent spouses—or bar them from participating in the plan altogether—if they have opted out of the coverage offered by their own employers.

The other dependent coverage strategic pricing issue is whether to introduce *tier pricing*. Tier pricing refers to assigning a specific price for specific family configurations such as employee only; employee and spouse; employee and child; employee, spouse, and one child; employee, spouse, and two or more children; and employee and two or more children. The importance of tier pricing is that each familial configuration picks up the true cost (or something close to the true cost) of being provided with medical insurance, and the employer moves away from the kinds of subsidies that characterized benefits plans before flexible plans, in which one group heavily subsidized another.

Q 8:14 How does the packaging and pricing of flexible medical plan options encourage employees to choose a health care benefits package that provides adequate coverage and controls costs?

In the long term, the only way an employer can counter medical cost inflation is to reduce its employees' utilization of medical procedures. (Building a credit methodology that encourages employees to choose one medical plan over another is discussed elsewhere in this book.) What is important to note here is that the fundamental objective is to encourage those employees whose medical needs are greatest to join the most closely managed plan.

By subsidizing the managed care plan option, an employer can package and price that option so attractively that employees are compelled to consider the option an excellent value. Even with the subsidy, the premium cost of a managed care plan is likely to be considerably less than the premium cost of a traditional indemnity plan. Another way to encourage employees to try a managed care plan is to package it with another insurance coverage (e.g., dental, vision, or prescription drugs). Sometimes the higher levels of coverage offered by the managed care plan ($5 or $10 copayments for office visits and almost 100 percent coverage for hospitalization) are sufficient incentives to attract participants. A bonus contribution to a medical flexible spending account (FSA) by the employer for an employee who selects a particular medical option is yet another way to encourage employees to try a managed health care option. (See chapter 6 for a detailed discussion of medical FSAs.)

An employer also can make a managed care plan seem more attractive by making the other medical plan options appear less attractive. That is, the employer can use economic disincentives (instead of the economic incentives described above). An employer's ability to control the attractiveness of various medical plan options by means of plan design is significant and should not be underestimated.

> **Example.** Marley & Co. offers two medical plan options. Both plans have a $500 annual per person deductible. The plan to which Marley & Co. wants families to migrate has a maximum $1,000 family deductible for three or more dependents in the family. The other plan has no such cap; thus, for instance, a family of five will incur a $2,500 deductible. Clearly, most larger families with three or more dependents will need to consider the economic advantage of the first plan.

The type of design solution described in the example above is valuable because family maximums on deductibles (and on out-of-pocket copayments) may add very little cost to a medical plan but hold considerable appeal for employees.

Q 8:15 What health care benefits may be included in a flexible benefits plan?

A flexible benefits plan can generally provide the same health care benefits that traditional benefit plans offer. Whatever is permitted under Section 105 of the Internal Revenue Code (Code) can be included under a Code Section 125 flexible benefit plan. Generally, the most significant differences between flexible benefits plans and traditional benefit plans can be seen in the choices of levels of coinsurance, deductibles, caps, and other limitations on benefits, rather than any restrictions on the benefits themselves. Also, a flexible benefits plan might offer employees more choices regarding other coverage, such as dental, vision, and prescription drug.

Medical FSAs may also be included in a flexible benefits plan. Items submitted for reimbursement under such an account, it should be noted, must not have been reimbursable from another source and must not have been claimed on the employee's income tax return. It should further be noted that some medical expenses are not subject to reimbursement under a medical FSA. (See Qs 6:12–6:15 for a detailed discussion of reimbursements under medical FSAs.)

Q 8:16 Can a catastrophic health plan that is offered in conjunction with a medical savings account be included in a flexible benefits plan?

Yes. A catastrophic health plan offered in conjunction with a medical savings account (MSA) can be included in a flexible benefits plan. MSAs became available as a health care option as a result of the Health Insurance Portability and Accountability Act of 1996 (HIPAA). It should be noted that MSAs are not the same as medical FSAs.

An MSA is a type of tax-qualified individual savings account that is used exclusively for the payment of medical expenses incurred by a covered employee, a spouse, or a dependent. To be eligible for participation in an MSA, the covered employee also must be covered by an employer-sponsored, high deductible health plan, also known as a catastrophic health insurance plan (see Q 6:14).

A catastrophic health plan may be included in a flexible benefits plan because such a plan is an accident or health plan under Code Sections 105 and 106. Yet, the MSA itself cannot be included in flexible benefits plan because HIPAA amended Code Section 125 to forbid offering an MSA under such a plan.

Q 8:17 What health care benefits should be excluded from a Section 125 flexible benefits plan?

Any health care benefit that meets the requirements of Code Section 105—and does not include a feature that defers compensation—can be offered by a Code Section 125 flexible benefits plan.

Notwithstanding the fact that Code Section 105 permits a wide selection of health benefits in a Section 125 plan, an employer needs to consider whether it should exclude certain benefits options from its flexible benefits plan. In order to avoid adverse selection, for instance, an employer must offer enough compelling choices so that all similarly situated employees will not choose the same plan. That is, if the choices are not attractive and one option easily can be identified as the superior alternative, it may result in adverse selection, which in turn will undermine the integrity of the plan. Thus, for example, offering two medical plans that are identical in every respect, except that one plan reimburses for prescription drugs and the other does not, is poor plan design that results in adverse selection. Everyone who uses (or contemplates using) prescription drugs will choose the plan that offers that coverage, which in turn drives up the cost of that plan.

Q 8:18 What must be done to mitigate the effects of adverse selection on the medical plan options being offered under a flexible benefits plan?

The effect of adverse selection is a fundamental concern that is best handled through carefully designed options and a well-reviewed pricing policy. Although the matter is discussed in some detail elsewhere in this book (see Qs 2:27, 2:28), it bears repeating that adverse selection of medical plan options under a flexible benefits plan can be controlled by offering options that:

1. Do not force employees with a particular medical condition into a particular plan;
2. Make the selection process include a series of choices in which the participant must weigh the benefits among a variety of options; and
3. Tie or link medical design elements in a thoughtful way (e.g., link prescription drug coverage to high levels of managed care).

In addition, adverse selection can be paid for by pricing medical plans appropriately. To the extent an employer does not mitigate adverse selection through plan design, it can estimate the cost of adverse selection and add it to the cost of the medical plan options being offered (i.e., account for the cost). The cost of adverse selection can be added to the price of:

1. Only those medical plans that cost less because they are selected by the healthier employees/families (this is a subsidy of the less healthy employees);
2. Only those medical plans that cost more because they are selected by the less healthy employees/families (this drives up the cost of such plans so as to make them prohibitive); or
3. To all the medical plans in the flexible benefits plan.

Q 8:19 Should dental benefits be included in a flexible benefits plan's health care program or be kept separate?

Many employers have traditionally viewed medical and dental coverage as parts of a single program. Some plans have even used a common deductible for both, although that is no longer a common practice. Yet medical expenses are in many instances unpredictable and variable while dental care is highly predictable both in its frequency and cost. In addition, dentistry is considered to be a budgetable medical expenditure over which an individual has substantial control. Thus, for example, employees who are given the choice of electing or rejecting dental coverage under a flexible benefits plan often choose dental coverage in the year in which dental work is planned. In contrast, the choice of medical insurance is likely to be based on a much broader perspective; an employee tries to plan for a variety of possible needs over an extended period of time.

Another fundamental difference between medical insurance and dental insurance is how managed care treats each. The managed care elements of dental coverage tend to focus on provider network discounts. The case management of dental care is not as cost-effective as the case management of medical care, because in dentistry there is little disparity between treatment methodologies and their costs. The major reason for combining dental coverage with medical coverage is to use dental protection to induce employees to select a particular medical option.

A secondary reason to link the two types of plan into one option would be to limit the adverse selection potential to the dental plan. Participants who choose the medical option with dental, will do so because they need the medical plan, regardless of their plans for upcoming dental work.

Q 8:20 Should a medical FSA with a nonelective employer contribution be offered when an employer shifts to a medical plan that will result in greater out-of-pocket expenses for the employee?

Depending on the employer's objectives, this approach might be a very good idea. As an employer assumes a smaller percentage of an employee's medical expenses, the employee may be able to use a medical FSA to be reimbursed, on a tax-free basis, for the expected coinsurance, deductibles, and medical expenses that will not be covered under the medical plan that year.

The concept of using a medical FSA to mitigate the effect of a shift in medical costs to employees is one of the more common techniques used in a flexible benefits plan. Indeed, many employers take the dollar savings associated with the shift in costs in the first year and give it back to employees by funding a medical FSA vehicle. Others take a "matching" approach to funding a medical FSA. That is, to encourage employee participation in the medical FSA, the employer will make funds available only to those individuals who set aside, through salary reduction, some of their own compensation. It is not uncommon for the employer to have a matching formula under which, for example, every dollar put into a medical FSA by an employee is matched by the employer at the rate of 50 percent, up to a maximum employer contribution of $500.

Q 8:21 Should the health care portion of a flexible benefits plan be underwritten by self-insurance, insurance from an outside carrier, or a combination of the two?

The implementation of a flexible benefits plan should not require a change from the pattern of insurance funding that had been followed or was intended to be followed. Note, however, that an employer that had been self-insured may find the transition to flexible benefits easier than one that has not. Although most of the large insurance companies have by now adjusted to flexible benefits plans, their concerns have caused them to formulate underwriting guidelines that, in turn, affect plan design. Particularly in the areas of pricing, adverse selection, and company benefits philosophy, some carriers, because of their underwriting constraints, impose significant restrictions to protect plan integrity. On the other hand, the premium amount and therefore assignment of a portion of that amount to employees—is a simple matter with a fully insured plan. In contrast, in a self-insured environment, assigning a cost to employees, especially based on a percentage of the total expense, can be tricky.

It is well documented that the transition from one medical plan to another is fraught with problems when some medical plan options are self-insured or experience-rated and others are fully insured and costs are capitated. Generally, as employees move out of one medical plan and into another, the claims incurred by the migrating employees do not match the premium costs or projected working rates of the medical plan to which they are migrating. In addition, the premium costs or working rates for the group of employees who choose not to migrate no longer match claims incurred for the plan that they have chosen to stay with.

Transitional economics are created when employees migrate from one plan to another. However, the negative or positive implications of the transitional economics become the employer's concern when one or more of the medical plans being offered are not fully insured. The following example describes the most common transitional problem.

Example. Trey Inc. offers three medical plans: a traditional indemnity plan that is self-insured and two HMOs. Both HMOs are fully insured, and Trey pays capitated rates regardless of actual claims incurred. As is often the case in such situations, Trey's younger, healthier employees who have no strong physician commitments move to the capitated HMO because of its high coverage and low cost features. In fact, only the healthy young employees, whose annual medical expenses average approximately $1,000 annually, choose the capitated HMO costing $2,400 per year. Trey should try to get those employees out of that HMO and into an experience-rated plan or self-insured plan for two reasons:

1. By paying a capitated community rate of $2,400, Trey loses $1,400 per enrolled employee if the average employee indeed incurs only $1,000 of medical costs.
2. Because Trey offers other medical insurance that is experience-rated or self-insured, it is left with older, less healthy employees driving up the cost of the traditional medical indemnity plan as the younger, healthy individuals migrate to the capitated HMO plan.

Because of the dilemma illustrated in the preceding example, in addition to pricing and packaging incentives, very often an employer will work with its HMO carriers to create a self-insured HMO and thereby solve the transitional problem. Although the economic effect on the employer associated with employee migration will always exist, it need not be problematic. Plans will eventually come back into balance (i.e., claims incurred will reflect the cost of the medical plan) once the migration ends or there is underwriting parity among the medical plans being offered.

Q 8:22 What are the implications of self-insuring an HMO?

From a flexible benefits plan viewpoint, self-insuring an HMO is no different from self-insuring a traditional indemnity plan, a POS plan, or a PPO. Fundamentally, to insure and accept the risk of positive or negative claims experience is a risk management decision. It should reflect the employer's tolerance for risk and its economic capacity to absorb claims fluctuations.

Some benefits professionals believe it is *never* appropriate to self-insure an HMO because the HMO is responsible for managing the medical care of its members and should accept responsibility for its own success or failure. That is, they believe HMOs must take a primary economic interest in medical care costs and should be rewarded when they do well in managing care (which, in turn, means controlling costs) and should experience the economic consequences of failing to control health care costs.

From the vantage point of most employers, however, the objective should be to have HMOs adopt the same underwriting method used in the rest of the medical plan options offered. As noted above (see Q 8:21), underwriting parity among medical plans is an extremely important tool for managing the transition of employees between health care options.

Q 8:23 What is the relationship between the nondiscrimination rules under Code Section 105 and the special medical plan nondiscrimination rules of Code Section 125?

An insured medical plan does not need to satisfy any nondiscrimination rules other than those (if any) that are required as an underwriting issue by the carrier. A self-insured medical plan, on the other hand, must meet the Internal Revenue Code's nondiscrimination rules, which are defined in Code Section 105(h), and further described in Regulation 1.105-11. Those rules include a general facts-and-circumstances test as well as a detailed numerical test.

A medical plan that is part of a flexible benefits plan, however, must satisfy the Code Section 125 nondiscrimination rules. That is true for both insured and self-insured medical plans. Moreover, the integration of a flexible benefits plan with a self-insured medical plan does not mean that the Section 105 nondiscrimination rules are replaced by those under Code Section 125. Indeed, it means that both Code Sections 105 and 125 nondiscrimination rules must be satisfied.

Dental Plans

Q 8:24 What factors must be taken into account when designing a dental plan?

Coverage of dental care began to be added to group health insurance plans in the 1970s, with some employers including dental care as part of their medical plans and others offering separate dental plans. In the years since then, an increase in the use of dental care services among employees and their dependents has created a significant demand for a dental benefit that provides a basic level of care.

Although dental treatment is not nearly as expensive as most medical care, certain kinds of services have the potential for generating major expenses, prompting plan designers to divide dental benefits into broad categories of care that can be made subject to different minimums and caps to control costs.

Generally, the broad categories of care are defined as follows:

1. *Diagnostic and preventive care.* Basic diagnostic and preventive services that include cleaning and X-rays usually are provided without coinsurance payments, up to a specified dollar limit.
2. *Minor restorative services.* Basic restoration usually includes routine fillings, extractions, root canal work (endodontics), and oral surgery. These treatments generally require coinsurance payments from the employee, typically at the level of 20 percent.
3. *Major restorative services.* Treatments such as crowns, bridges, inlays and onlays, and periodontics are included in this group. These services are frequently coinsured, requiring payments of up to 50 percent from employees. In addition, many dental plans impose caps on the annual liability that the plan assumes for each insured individual.
4. *Orthodontics.* Primarily consisting of cosmetic dentistry, plans that offer any kind of orthodontic services generally also maintain very conservative annual and lifetime caps or limits.

Because employees often can control and plan their use of dental care—to a much greater extent than is possible with the consumption of health care—an employer must rely on annual dollar limits and caps to control the effects of adverse selection on the use of dental benefits, as follows:

1. *Caps on annual coverage.* By imposing a cap on the dollar amount of dental services for which the plan covers each insured individual per year, the plan discourages employees from enrolling in the dental benefit for only those years in which the employee requires significant amounts of dental treatment. The annual limit on covered treatment encourages the employees to participate in—and contribute to—the plan every year, which in turn reduces adverse selection.
2. *Coinsurance limits.* The division of dental care into various categories of care enables a plan designer to pinpoint precisely where and to what degree the plan assumes responsibility for coverage. Thus, a plan designer may choose to require higher coinsurance payments from employees to pay for the more expensive procedures associated with major reconstruction and orthodontia; indeed, many plans concentrate their benefits on preventive and restorative work.

3. *Preexisting condition limitations.* Most plans impose preexisting condition limitations that exempt the plan from any obligation to cover employees for major conditions incurred before the employee enrolled in the plan. (Limited scope dental plans are exempt from the requirements of HIPAA.)
4. *Limited services in first year enrollment.* As variation on preexisting condition limitations, some dental plans do not permit coverage for major restorative services in the first year of coverage under the plan. This is different from preexisting condition limitations outlined above in that a plan participant might have had no indication of the need for major restorative services before enrolling in the plan, and yet be excluded from coverage for certain services in the first year.

   Reasonable and customary charges. Another type of limit that may be imposed by an insurer is a limit on the amount of reimbursement that it will pay for specific procedures for which it has determinded a reasonable charge.

Q 8:25 What is a traditional fee-for-service dental plan?

In a traditional fee-for-service dental plan, employees are free to receive dental care from any licensed dentist. There are two basic types of fee-for-service dental plans: comprehensive plans and schedule of benefits plans.

Under a comprehensive plan, employees receive reimbursement for dental care based on the payment of deductibles and specified coinsurance limits (certain percentages of dentists' fees), as well as maximum per person annual coverage amounts. This is, by far, the most common arrangement today.

A relatively common dental plan would have the following percentages paid by the plan: 100 percent of diagnostic and preventive care; 80 percent of minor restorative services, such as fillings, extractions, and root canals; and 50 percent of major restorative work, such as crowns and bridges. Orthodontia may be covered up to a lifetime maximum or may not be covered at all. Often, orthodontia is covered only for dependent children up to age 19. Annual per person deductibles are typically $50 per person and $100 or more per family. Annual per person maximums commonly range from $500 to $1,500.

Under a schedule of benefits plan, employees receive reimbursements for specific dental services at a set dollar amount. The dental carrier pays the dentist according to the schedule, and the employee pays any additional fees. There is generally a per person maximum for certain types of procedures; for example, a plan may have a lifetime orthodontia maximum of $1,500 per eligible person. When dental costs exceed those paid by the plan, the employee picks up the additional costs (unless the schedule is increased). Therefore, schedule of benefits plans are seen as anti-inflationary from an employer's perspective.

Fee-for-service plans generally have less ability to control dental costs than do managed care plans.

Q 8:26 What is a managed dental plan?

In general, under a managed dental plan, providers of dental coverage contract with private practice dentists who agree to provide treatment to employees who sign up for the plan. The dentists agree to provide care to plan members at set fees or rates that are usually less than the fees charged in a traditional fee-for-service plan, and they typically must also agree to certain quality assurance standards. Dentists benefit by having access to an expanded patient base.

Employees agree to use a network of providers instead of selecting any licensed dentist, as in a traditional fee-for-service plan. In exchange for using a network of providers, employees pay low deductibles and copayments, if any, and typically receive high levels of coverage.

Employers usually decide to contract with managed dental plans to control costs while attempting to provide a level of benefits desired by employees.

Examples of managed dental plans are dental HMOs (see Q 8:27) and dental PPOs (see Q 8:28).

Q 8:27 What is a dental HMO?

A dental HMO agrees to provide a specified range of dental services for a set fee (commonly called a capitation fee) to employees who join the plan. As with medical HMOs, employees must receive care from a participating provider. Dentists receive a set fee each month per participant, regardless of the care received by the participant.

Dental HMOs often cover 100 percent of diagnostic and preventive care, and cover most other dental procedures, usually with copayments. Annual or lifetime maximums typically do not apply to dental HMOs. It should also be noted that annual premiums for dental HMOs can be less than premiums for traditional fee-for-service plans.

Q 8:28 What is a dental PPO?

A dental PPO pays participating dentists on a discounted fee-for-service basis. Employees who receive care from participating dentists receive the plan's "full coverage," usually 100 percent coverage for diagnostic and preventive care. Employees are responsible to pay for other services at varying percentages of the cost. Benefit amounts are lower for an employee who selects a non-network provider.

Dental PPOs typically have annual per person benefits maximums and, in the case of orthodontia, lifetime maximums. It should be noted that annual premiums for dental PPOs can be less than premiums for traditional fee-for-service plans.

Q 8:29 How does dental care fit into a flexible benefits plan?

Dental care is generally low cost and easy to manage for an employer and yet is considered a necessity in the eyes of most employees, making it a very valuable addition to a flexible benefits plan. Furthermore, because dental care typically is offered on a contributory basis, it is easily absorbed into a flexible benefits plan: the plan may supply a purchase price tag to which the employee assigns the appropriate number of credits or, depending on the employee's other choices within the plan, the employee may choose to supplement the employer's credits with his or her own contribution.

Planning Pointer. It is extremely important to note that when dental plans are put under the flexible benefits plan umbrella, the dental benefit becomes subject to high levels of adverse selection. Therefore, care must be taken in both the design and pricing of such a benefit to ensure that adverse selection between competing dental options is eliminated. From the perspective of plan design, the dental benefit can be linked to a medical option. That is, to receive a dental benefit, a plan participant would have to select a medical option. To further control dental costs and mitigate adverse selection, a flexible benefits plan could introduce a managed care networked dental maintenance organization (DMO) or a preferred dental provider network. A third design option is to limit the upside risk of the dental plan through the imposition of caps and maximum limits. Unlike the risks incurred by medical benefit plans, the possibility of incurring catastrophic dental bills is negligible because most plans use caps and limits to control their risk.

Q 8:30 How many levels of coverage should a designer build into a dental plan?

Many flexible benefits plans offer only a single dental program, and only a few plans offer more than two dental options. There is a high level of adverse selection in and between dental options. For that reason, the general rule is to offer only one or two dental options and to differentiate those options in a nonobvious way. If two dental options are available and the only difference between them is that one provides orthodontia coverage, adverse selection is guaranteed, unless the associated cost for the plan with orthodontia coverage is proportionately high enough to cover the adverse selection. Having two dental options, one of which emphasizes preventive care and the other catastrophic care, is a much better plan design.

Q 8:31 Is an FSA a viable alternative to a dental plan?

Yes. An FSA can be a viable alternative for an employer that wants to respond to employees' desire for dental coverage without having to make the financial commitment involved in making premium contributions to an insured dental program. If a medical FSA is offered to employees, employees can pay for dental expenses (including amounts for such costly treatments as root canals, crowns, and orthodontics) on a pretax basis, unless the medical FSA is designed to be more restrictive than Code Section 213 allows. Alternatively, employees can use the account to pay for other reimbursable medical expenses on a pretax basis. Or a separate dental FSA can be established for interested employees, possibly with an employer contribution at a flat dollar level or as a match for employee pretax contributions.

Example. In lieu of offering an insured basic dental program that provides only diagnostic and preventive services, Floss & Floss, Inc. offers a dental FSA program intended to appeal to employees with minimal dental needs. Employees may contribute as much as $200 a year to the special dental FSA. Floss & Floss will make a matching contribution to the account, up to a maximum of $200 per year per family.

Q 8:32 What are the most common methods of protecting the dental benefit in a flexible benefits plan against the effects of adverse selection?

Dental options in a flexible benefits plan are particularly susceptible to adverse selection because, unlike most kinds of health care, many types of dental treatment can be delayed and rescheduled once plan coverage becomes effective. For such reason, the provision of a dental benefit requires a plan designer to pay special attention to protecting the dental options against the effects of adverse selection.

The most common methods of protecting dental options against the effects of adverse selection are as follows:

1. Linking the dental options to specific medical plans.
2. Requiring a 12-month waiting period for enrollment in the high-option dental plan.
3. Permitting enrollment in the high-option dental plan (at a high-option price) but providing a lower maximum cap on annual benefits than afforded by the high-option plan to original enrollees.
4. Charging a risk premium for high-option coverage, either for a specified period of time or permanently.

Q 8:33 Should employees be allowed to waive dental coverage under a flexible benefits plan and use their credits to purchase other benefits?

Most flexible benefits plans allow participants to opt out of dental coverage. That is an easier choice for an employer to make than the opt-out decision regarding medical benefits for two reasons:

1. It is unlikely that the decision to opt out of dental coverage will cause the employee economic ruin in the event of a catastrophic dental problem; and

2. Employees who have access to dental coverage elsewhere or who see little need for dental benefits assign a very low value to the benefit and feel strongly about being able to opt out for cash.

Even in light of the foregoing, some employers, in an effort to reduce the effects of adverse selection, may insist that a good portion of an employee's benefit credits be applied toward an availability charge for dental coverage, whether or not an employee actually enrolls in the benefit. In other words, when a plan participant opts out of dental coverage, the employee may take only one third or one quarter of the total credits made available by the employer for the purchase of the dental benefit. The employer leaves the remaining credits with the plan to protect it.

For some small employers, the dental carrier may protect itself against adverse selection by requiring 100 percent participation. A benefit requiring 100 percent enrollment may not be included in a flexible benefits plan. It is possible, however, to include other dental options for participants, such as an upgrade to a more extensive dental plan, or dental coverage for dependents in a flexible benefits plan.

Vision Plans

Q 8:34 How does a vision plan fit into a flexible benefits environment?

Traditionally, employers did not regard vision care as an essential part of a basic health care package; however, the popularity of the benefit continues to increase among employees. For that reason, vision care is an ideal benefit for any employer that wishes to expand its menu of flexible benefits beyond the basics and compete in the labor market. Vision care is neither unduly expensive nor administratively complex to maintain. The cost to the employer of adding vision care to its flexible benefits menu may be as minimal as adding an administrative cost to an existing benefits package. There are two reasons for such an economy:

1. Vision care benefits are well defined and very limited in their scope (thus keeping the cost down); and
2. The employer's true contribution consists of the strength of its purchasing power and the time it takes to select a superior vendor of vision services.

In the final analysis, employees will pay for the cost of the vision benefit—either through contributions or by directly paying for the cost of the services. The difference is that by providing vision care as a flexible option, an employer uses its weight to lower costs and make the benefit affordable for more people. Deductibles, copayments, and other expenses not covered by the vision plan may be reimbursed through FSAs.

Note. Some employers that offer vision care within a flexible benefits plan make it available to all plan participants—both full- and part-time employees. Generally, that policy works in favor of the employees. The larger the number of eligible employees, the greater the employer's negotiating power and the lower the cost of the benefit.

Q 8:35 What levels of care should a vision plan provide?

In general, diseases of or injury to the eye are treatable under an employer's medical care plan; however, eye examinations and corrective lenses (either eyeglasses or contact lenses) are usually covered under a separate plan that sets a fixed-dollar limit for such expenditures.

A vision plan typically is quite simple: participants may receive discounts on the retail cost of frames, lenses, and contact lenses that are negotiated with providers by the employer (see Q 8:34). Alternatively, a plan may use fixed-fee schedules to determine reimbursable costs for basic services. Under a fixed-fee schedule, each covered procedure is assigned a dollar amount that represents the reimbursement that a provider may receive for services rendered. If the provider charges more than the reimbursement amount, the employee has to make up the difference. Therefore, it is incumbent on the employee to find providers who accept the fee schedule as payment in full. It should be noted, however, that differences in costs across wide geographical areas may make the fee-schedule approach inequitable for an employer that has a number of widely scattered locations.

A plan designer must account for the occurrence of adverse selection in a vision plan because of the likelihood of employees delaying their use of services and selecting coverage only for the year in which extensive care is anticipated. To counteract adverse selection, many plans require employees to make a two-year commitment to the option they elect. Alternatively, many vision plans are priced to reflect the fact that only those with vision problems will join the plan; in that case, vision benefits are not really an insurance but a budgetable monthly payment that is somewhat discounted.

Q 8:36 Is a flexible spending account a viable alternative to a vision plan?

Yes, a flexible spending account (FSA) can be a viable alternative for an employer who wants to respond to employees' desires for a vision care plan without having to make the financial commitment involved in making premium contributions to an insured vision care program. If a medical FSA is offered to employees, they can pay for vision care expenses, including amounts for eye exams, eyeglasses, contact lenses, and even contact lens solutions, on a pretax basis. Alternatively employees can use the account to pay for other reimbursable medical expenses on a pretax basis (see chapter 6).

Adverse selection may be especially significant when a plan offers both vision care insurance and a medical FSA. Those employees who expect to spend more in vision care than the total cost of premiums will elect the insurance coverage, while those who expect to spend less than the total cost of premiums will opt instead to fund a medical FSA for their expected vision care needs. A flexible benefit program offering both a vision care insurance option and a medical FSA will want to monitor employee elections to determine whether or not adverse selection is occurring within the program.

Medical Flexible Spending Accounts

Q 8:37 How do medical flexible spending accounts qualify as accident or health plans?

Proposed Treasury Regulations Section 1.125-2, Q&A 7, indicates that, in order for medical flexible spending accounts (FSAs) to qualify for favorable tax treatment, they must conform to the generally applicable rules under Code Sections 105 and 106 (accident and health plans).

To qualify as accident or health plans, a medical FSA must conform to the following standards:

1. Although medical coverage need not be provided through a commercial insurance contract, the medical FSA must exhibit the risk-shifting and risk-distribution characteristics of insurance.
2. The medical FSA's participants must be reimbursed specifically for medical expenses they have already incurred during the period of coverage.
3. The medical FSA cannot operate in a manner that allows participants to receive coverage only for periods in which the participants expect to incur medical expenses, if such periods constitute less than a plan year.
4. To receive reimbursement, the medical FSA's participants cannot be entitled to the medical expense amount in the form of cash or any other taxable or nontaxable benefit (including coverage for an additional period), unless the participants incur medical expenses during the period of coverage.
5. The medical FSA cannot eliminate all, or substantially all, risk of loss to the employer maintaining the plan.

[Prop Treas Reg § 1.125-2, Q&A 7]

Q 8:38 What is the maximum amount a participant may contribute to or be reimbursed from a medical FSA?

The question of maximum contribution and reimbursement amounts is more complex than it seems. Neither the Code nor the Treasury regulations set a specific maximum limit for contributions to medical FSAs. The plan document should, however indicate a maximum annual contribution limit to the FSA. In some cases, it might also be advisable to express the limit as a monthly or "per-pay" amount. A maximum benefit is imposed to minimize cash flow risk to the employer. Typically, plans set the medical FSA contribution at a maximum between $1,000 and $5,000 per year. The top limit for pretax contributions could, in theory, be 100 percent of a participant's pay. (While theoretically possible, a limit of 100 percent of pay may not be practical or compliant with nondiscrimination rules.)

In addition to a participant's contributions, the employer might make contributions to the plan on behalf of its employees, or the plan might experience gains (forfeitures; see Q 6:19) that could cause individual account balances to be funded by other than participant contributions.

As for maximum reimbursement amounts, Proposed Treasury Regulations Section 1.125-2, Q&A 7(c) states that the maximum amount of reimbursement available to a participant for a period of coverage must not be substantially in excess of the total premiums (employee plus employer contributions) paid for such coverage. The proposed regulation goes on to say that a maximum amount of reimbursement will not be considered substantially in excess of the total premium if such reimbursement is less than 500 percent (or five times) the premium.

The law is concerned with a reimbursement maximum for FSAs because, even though FSAs are considered to be like an insurance product (and like an insurance product, the potential exists for claims made to exceed the premium the policyholder paid), FSAs can be manipulated more easily in terms of their payouts. The government is concerned that if the relationship between FSA claims and FSA premiums is permitted to exceed a 5:1 ratio, employers and employees might misuse the accounts either to circumvent IRS discrimination rules or to provide a tax break to employees that the government did not intend, or both.

Q 8:39 What expenditures are eligible for reimbursement under medical FSAs?

Generally, a medical FSA may reimburse only medical expenses that are defined in Code Section 213. [Prop Treas Reg § 1.125-2, Q&A 7(b)(4)] Most of the health care expenses that may be deducted on an employee's federal income tax return are eligible for reimbursement under medical FSAs.

In 2002, the IRS recognized obesity as a qualifying medical condition. Previously, only the other conditions possibly caused in relation to obesity (i.e., heart disease, high blood pressure, high cholesterol) were recognized as qualifying medical conditions. This means that, with a medical provider's diagnosis of obesity, it may be possible to receive reimbursement for treatment. Examples of qualifying expenses include weekly meeting expenses, but do not include the cost for food replacements or supplements. Membership to a health club for general wellness remains a non-qualified medical expense.

Note. In a very few cases, the IRS has made a specific allowance for a medical expense that did not clearly fall under Code Section 213 or has reversed an earlier position. Examples include allowances for contact lens cleaning solutions (to clean medically necessary contact lenses) and prescription smoking cessation products (not permitted before 1999).

Services that are eligible for reimbursement from a medical FSA include the following:

- Acupuncture
- Alcoholism and drug abuse treatment
- Chiropractic services
- Christian Science practitioner services
- Dental services, including preventive, diagnostic, restorative, and orthodontic care
- Medical services or supplies not covered, or only partly covered, by the employee's or dependent's health plan
- Hearing aids and batteries to operate them
- Medical services provided by physicians, surgeons, specialists, or other medical practitioners
- Medical care provided by a nursing home or home for the aged for the employee, the employee's spouse, or the employee's dependents (includes the cost of meals and lodging in the home if the main reason for being there is to obtain medical care)
- Medical conferences for information about a chronic illness relating to the participant or the participant's spouse or child (including transportation and admission but not meals or lodging while attending the conference)
- Services to treat a preexisting condition not covered because of a plan's preexisting condition clause
- Prescribed medicines and drugs
- Psychiatric care, psychoanalysis, and psychologist's services
- Routine physical exams
- Transportation primarily for and essential to medical care (12 cents per mile)
- Vision care, including eye exams and frames, lenses, and contact lenses needed for medical reasons (including equipment and materials required for using contact lenses needed for medical reasons, such as saline solution and enzyme cleaner)
- Vitamins prescribed by a physician to treat a specific medical condition and available only by prescription

- X-rays

[IRS Pub 502, Medical and Dental Expenses (2000)]

Note. In no case may a participant use a medical FSA to pay premiums, even though premiums are allowable under Code Section 213 as a personal medical expense.

In addition, a medical FSA must reimburse only expenses that are *incurred* during the plan year, regardless of when the expenses are actually paid. Taxpayers reading IRS Publication 502 will see guidance relating to the date an expense is paid these instructions do not apply to medical FSAs.

Q 8:40 Generally, when must expenses reimbursed under a medical FSA be incurred?

The general rule is that expenses reimbursed under a medical (or dependent care) FSA must be incurred during the participant's period of coverage under the FSA. Expenses are treated as having been incurred when the participant is provided with the care that gives rise to the expenses—not when the participant is formally billed or charged or pays for the care. Expenses are not treated as incurred during a period of coverage if the expenses are incurred before the later of (1) the date the FSA is first in existence or (2) the date the participant first becomes enrolled in the FSA. [Prop Treas Reg §§ 1.125-1, Q&A 17, 1.125-2, Q&A 7(b)(6)]

Q 8:41 Do orthodontic expenses have to have been incurred to be eligible for reimbursement from a medical FSA?

Any medical expense must be incurred before it can be reimbursed. [Treas Reg § 1.125-2] Orthodontic treatment is unique in its handling, however, in that orthodontic expenses may not need to be specifically incurred in a given period within the plan year to be eligible for reimbursement from a medical FSA. However, the patient must be receiving a course of orthodontic treatment related to the expenses. Orthodontic expenses are typically payable at the onset of treatment or through an installment-based treatment plan. The IRS informally recognizes the billing practice specific to orthodontic treatment, and informal IRS opinions indicate that orthodontic expenses may be reimbursed when payments have been made, even if the services have not been rendered. That position is an exception to the general rule that pertains to FSAs.

Example. Jane, a participant in an FSA, is required to pay $100 each month to her orthodontist for ongoing treatment. Jane was unable to keep an appointment during the month of June. She was, however, required to pay $100 for June. The $100 Jane paid for June is reimbursable.

Q 8:42 Which expenditures may not be reimbursed from medical FSAs?

The following expenditures may not be reimbursed from medical FSAs:

1. Expenses for cosmetic surgery not deductible under Code Section 213(d). Cosmetic surgery is defined as any procedure that is directed at improving appearance and does not meaningfully promote the proper function of the body or prevent or treat illness or disease.
2. Premiums paid for other health plan coverage, including coverage provided by another employer to the participant in a medical FSA, his or her spouse, or any of the participant's dependents. This prohibition does not prevent premiums for current health coverage from being paid on a salary reduction basis through the operation of the cafeteria plan. [Prop Treas Reg § 1.125-2, Q&A 7(b)(4)] (See Q 5:16 regarding conditions that must be met for an employee to be able to pay for the premium of an individual health plan policy through his or her premium conversion plan.)

Per the Health Insurance Portability and Accountability Act (HIPAA), long-term care insurance contracts may not be offered under a medical FSA or a Section 125 plan.

Q 8:43 What is a dependent under a medical FSA program for purposes of reimbursement?

The definition of *dependent* for purposes of reimbursement of eligible expenses under a medical FSA program follows the definition of *dependent* for purposes of a federal income tax deduction for medical expense.

IRS Publication 502 (2000) outlines eligible deductions for medical expenses and describes persons for whom medical expenses may be claimed. Such persons include the following:

1. *Self.* A plan participant may deduct medical expenses paid for himself or herself.
2. *Spouse.* A plan participant may deduct medical expenses paid for his or her spouse. To claim these expenses, the participant must have been married either at the time his or her spouse received the medical services or at the time the participant paid the medical expenses.
3. *Dependents.* A plan participant may deduct medical expenses he or she paid for a person who was a dependent at the time the medical services were provided or at the time the participant paid the expenses. A person generally qualifies as a dependent for purposes of the medical expense deduction if:
   a. That person lived with the participant for the entire year as a member of his or her household or is related to the employee;
   b. That person was a U.S. citizen or resident or a resident of Canada or Mexico for some part of the calendar year in which the tax year began; and
   c. The participant provided over half of that person's total support for the calendar year.

The participant may deduct the medical expenses of any person who is the employee's dependent, even if the employee cannot claim an exemption for that person on the employee's federal income tax return because the dependent received gross income of more than the standard deduction amount or filed a joint return.

4. *Adopted child.* A plan participant may deduct medical expenses paid for a child before adoption if the child qualified as a dependent when the medical services were provided or when the expenses were paid. If the participant pays back an adoption agency or other persons for medical expenses it or they paid under an agreement with the participant, the participant is treated as having paid those expenses, provided that he or she clearly substantiates that the payment is directly attributable to the medical care of the child. If, however, the participant pays for medical expenses incurred and paid before adoption negotiations began, he or she may not include them as medical expenses.
5. *Child of divorced or separated parents.* If either parent can claim a child as a dependent under the rules for divorced or separated parents, each parent (either of which may be the plan participant) may include the medical expenses he or she pays for the child, even if an exemption for the child is claimed by the other parent.
6. *Support claimed under a multiple support agreement.* A multiple support agreement is used when two or more people provide more than half of a person's support but no one alone provides more than half of a person's support. If the plan participant is considered to have provided more than half of a person's support under a multiple support agreement, the participant may include medical expenses he or she pays, even if the participant cannot claim the person because the participant had gross income of more than the standard deduction amount or filed a joint return.

Q 8:44 What constitutes acceptable claims substantiation for a medical FSA reimbursement?

A medical FSA may reimburse a medical expense only if:

1. The participant provides a written statement from an independent third party confirming that the medical expense has been incurred and citing the amount of the expense; and
2. The participant provides a written statement that the medical expense has not been reimbursed or is not reimbursable under any other health plan coverage.

[Prop Treas Reg § 1.125-2, Q&A 7(b)(5)]

The written statement referred to in item 1 above could be the medical services statement produced by the medical services provider. A billing statement (merely showing, for example, "balance due") or a canceled check is not considered adequate documentation. The billing statement most often does not include all necessary elements of a claim, and a canceled check (or a credit card receipt or a personal computer print-out) is not provided by an independent third party. The written statement referred to in item 2 above is often included on the reimbursement request claim form, which is then signed by the plan participant.

Note. A medical FSA may not make reimbursements in advance for projected expenses. [Prop Treas Reg § 1.125-2, Q&A 7(b)(5)]

Q 8:45 What nondiscrimination rules must medical FSAs follow?

Medical FSAs must satisfy the nondiscrimination standards of Code Section 125 and of Code Section 105(h) because they are self-funded medical plans. That is, the nondiscrimination requirements of Code Section 125 apply to any Section 125 benefit and so encompass medical FSAs. Further, the nondiscrimination requirements of Code Section 105 are specific to self-funded medical plans—and thus medical FSAs within a Section 125 plan.

Section 125 requirements. A Section 125 plan may not discriminate in favor of highly compensated employees as to eligibility or contributions and benefits. Qualified (nontaxable) benefits under the plan, as well as total benefits, may not discriminate in favor of highly compensated participants. That restriction applies to any employer contributions allocable to total nontaxable benefits or total benefits. Generally, a determination of discrimination is made on a facts-and-circumstances basis. [Code §§125(b)(1)(A), 125(b)(1)(B), 125(c)]

A more quantitative test is required by Code Section 125(b)(2). Key employees may not enjoy more than 25 percent of the aggregate of all nontaxable benefits provided under the plan. The 25 percent test considers all the nontaxable benefits under the plan and is not applied individually to the medical FSA as a standalone benefit.

Code Section 125(g)(3) provides guidelines for nondiscriminatory eligibility. A plan will meet the requirements of Code Section 125(b)(1)(A) for eligibility if the plan provides benefits to a group of employees described in Code Section 410(b)(2)(A)(i) and requires no more than three years of service before entering the plan on the first day of the plan year after satisfaction of the service requirement. That provision is intended to be applied to the entire Section 125 plan, not to the medical FSA individually.

Further discussion of nondiscrimination in a medical FSA is found in Proposed Treasury Regulations Section 1.125-1, Q&A 19, which states that cafeteria plans may not discriminate in favor of highly compensated participants as to benefits and contributions (echoing Code Section 125(c)). The determination is generally made on a facts-and-circumstances basis.

Further guidance for medical FSAs is offered in Proposed Treasury Regulations Section 1.125-1, Q&A 17, which states that medical FSAs (self-insured medical plans) under a cafeteria plan must satisfy the rules of Code Section 105 in order not to be considered a discriminatory plan.

Code Section 125(g)(2) offers specific guidance for health benefits offered under a Section 125 plan. Although the wording of that section can be confusing, in reality, almost all typical plans pass the requirement. In any event, contributions under the cafeteria plan on behalf of each participant must be at least:

1. 100 percent of the cost of the health coverage provided under the cafeteria plan for the majority of the similarly situated highly compensated participants, or
2. 75 percent of the cost of the health coverage of the similarly situated participant having the highest cost health coverage under the cafeteria plan.

Any cafeteria plan contributions in excess of the minimum levels described above must be made as a uniform percentage of pay. (See chapter 14 for a broad discussion of nondiscrimination requirements under a Section 125 plan.)

Section 105 requirements. Code Section 105 and the related regulations define operation of a self-insured accident and health plan. Those rules apply to a medical FSA. Such a plan may not discriminate in favor of highly compensated employees as to eligibility or in favor of highly compensated participants as to benefits. [Code §§ 105(h)(2)(A), 105(h)(2)(B)]

A self-insured medical reimbursement plan is nondiscriminatory regarding eligibility if it satisfies one of three tests. For the tests, the term *benefits* can mean either that employees have the opportunity to participate, whether or not they actually choose to do so, or that employees actually participate by making contributions to an FSA. In the list that follows, the meaning that practitioners generally accept in each case is indicated in parentheses:

1. The plan benefits (opportunity) 70 percent or more of all nonexcludable employees;
2. The plan benefits (actual) 80 percent or more of all employees who are eligible to benefit (opportunity) under the plan, if at least 70 percent of all nonexcludable employees are eligible to benefit (opportunity) under the plan; or
3. The plan benefits (opportunity) a classification of employees not discriminatory in favor of highly compensated individuals.

In addition to the foregoing eligibility rules, a self-insured medical reimbursement plan must provide benefits that do not discriminate in favor of highly compensated participants. All benefits provided to such individuals must also be provided to all other individuals.

Further, a plan may not discriminate in actual operation. That determination is made based on all facts and circumstances.

Q 8:46 Are medical FSAs subject to COBRA?

COBRA continuation requirements are intended to ensure that a qualified beneficiary has guaranteed access to coverage under a group health plan and that the cost of that coverage is no greater than 102 percent of the applicable premium.

In 2001, final regulations were released for both COBRA and Section 125 plans. Both of these sets of final regulations provide guidance on the interaction between COBRA and Section 125 plans, most notably, medical FSAs. [Treas Reg §§ 1.125-4, 54.4980B]

Most medical FSAs satisfy the definition of group health plan in Code Section 4980B(g)(2) and, accordingly, are generally subject to the COBRA continuation coverage requirements. The final COBRA regulations have not changed the applicability of COBRA to medical FSAs; however, employers offering medical FSAs are not required to provide COBRA continuation coverage for those FSAs in certain circumstances (see below), effective for plan years beginning on or after January 1, 2000. Until January 1, 2000, however, plans had to operate in good faith compliance with the 1987 and 1998 proposed regulations.

The proposed Section 125 regulations published by the IRS in 1989 provided employees with certain advantages in electing to continue medical FSA coverage through COBRA. Under the uniform coverage rules, the maximum amount of reimbursement under a medical FSA must be available at all times during a period of coverage, regardless of the level of contribution. Thus, an employee could commence paying COBRA premiums, obtain the maximum reimbursement, and then discontinue paying COBRA premiums. The advantages provided to the employee by the proposed Section 125 regulations increased the employer's potential financial exposure in sponsoring a medical FSA program. Some aspects of that financial exposure may be decreased by the final COBRA regulations. (See chapter 15 for a discussion of how the COBRA continuation coverage rules affect cafeteria plans in general and medical FSAs in particular.)

For plan years beginning on or after January 1, 2000, a medical FSA need not offer COBRA continuation coverage to a participant if, as of the date of the qualifying event, the maximum benefit available to the qualified beneficiary under the medical FSA for the remainder of the plan year is not more than the maximum amount that the plan could require as payment for the remainder of that year to maintain coverage under the medical FSA.

> **Example.** Each of three employees, Ruth, Sam, and Theresa, elects to contribute $100 per month to a medical FSA for the 2003 calendar plan year and each has a COBRA qualifying event on June 30. For the first six months of the plan year, each of the three participants has contributed $600 to the plan. Ruth has received benefits of $1,000 from the plan by June 30; Sam has received benefits of $600; and Theresa has received benefits of $200. The

COBRA premium for the remaining six months of the plan year is $612, which is $100 for each of the remaining six months of the year, plus 2 percent.

The plan does not need to extend COBRA coverage to Ruth. The maximum remaining benefit available to her ($200) is less than the premium she would be required to pay for the remainder of the plan year ($612). Similarly, Sam would need to pay $612 for the remainder of the plan year for $600 in benefits. Therefore, the plan need not offer COBRA coverage to Sam. Theresa, however, may be entitled to COBRA continuation coverage. She would need to pay $612 for the remainder of the plan year for a possible COBRA benefit during the six-month period of $1,000.

Also beginning January 1,2000, most medical FSAs that are required to offer COBRA continuation coverage in the year of a COBRA beneficiary's qualifying event do not need to extend that coverage beyond the end of the plan year in which the qualifying event occurs. To terminate COBRA continuation coverage for a medical FSA at the end of the plan year of the qualifying event, the FSA must satisfy two conditions. The first condition is that the medical FSA must be classified as an "excepted benefit" not subject to HIPAA portability provisions; the second is that the maximum amount a COBRA beneficiary could be required to pay for a full plan year of COBRA must be equal to or exceed the maximum benefit available under the health FSA for the year. It is contemplated that this second condition will be satisfied in most cases. (See chapter 15 for a more complete description of the impact of COBRA on cafeteria plans.)

Q 8:47 Can an employee claim a tax deduction for the expenses reimbursed through a medical FSA?

No. An employee may not claim a tax deduction for the expenses reimbursed through a medical FSA. Under current IRS rules, only that part of an employee's medical and dental expenses that is more than 7.5 percent of adjusted gross income may be deducted from income taxes. Most individuals' out-of-pocket medical and dental expenses are not so large that they are entitled to take a tax deduction for them. For that reason, it is advantageous for most individuals who expect to incur uninsured medical expenses to contribute to a medical FSA.

Q 8:48 Must the maximum amount of reimbursement under a medical FSA be available at all times during the period of coverage?

Yes. Under applicable uniform coverage rules, the maximum amount of reimbursement from a medical FSA at any time during the period of coverage cannot relate to the extent to which the participant has paid the premiums (contributions) for the coverage period. Furthermore, the payment schedule for the required premiums may not be based on the rate or amount of covered claims incurred during the coverage period. Reimbursements must be paid at least monthly or until the submitted claims total a specified, reasonable minimum amount; for example, $50. [Prop Treas Reg § 1.125-2, Q 7(b)(2)]

Thus, under the uniform coverage rules, an employee may submit claims exceeding his or her year-to-date contributions and then terminate employment before contributing the full salary reduction amount. (See Q 8:46 regarding COBRA and the uniform coverage rules.) As a result, the employer assumes some potential financial risk in sponsoring a medical FSA program.

Q 8:49 Can an employer that sponsors a medical FSA program minimize the potential financial risk?

Yes. An employer may design its medical FSA program to include certain rules to mitigate its potential financial risk, such as the following:

1. A waiting period for eligibility may be instituted (as long as it does not exceed three years of employment, and the employment requirement for each employee is the same). Such a waiting period is often applied in situations where a significant turnover in the first months or years of employment is common.
2. A maximum annual reimbursement amount may be set (e.g., $2,000 a year).
3. Eligible types of reimbursements may be limited by excluding costly services and benefits options (e.g., experimental surgery) or otherwise limiting the benefits payable under the medical FSA to, for example, insurance deductibles and copayments only.

Some plans provide that by electing to join the medical FSA program, the employee agrees to participate in the plan for a full plan year, even if he or she subsequently terminates employment in the course of the year. In continuing coverage under the plan, the employee may agree to having a lump-sum, before-tax payment taken from his or her final paycheck to cover the balance of the annual contribution amount that would have been deducted from the employee's pay during the course of the year had he or she not terminated employment. If the employee's final paycheck does not cover the entire balance, the excess amount owed may be paid by check, using after-tax dollars. Alternatively, the employee may continue the coverage by making contributions solely on an after-tax basis.

Practice Pointer. COBRA entitlement applies under both approaches just discussed, and the arrangement that calls for full-year participation may be construed as forced COBRA continuation, which is a violation of the COBRA provisions. A plan sponsor should review such an arrangement with legal counsel before implementation.

Q 8:50 May an employer use a reinsurance product to minimize the potential financial risk in sponsoring a medical FSA?

The reinsurance product approach is not addressed by the Code or Section 125 regulations, but, according to informal opinions obtained from the IRS, it is an acceptable approach.

Through a reinsurance product, an employer pays a premium to an insurance carrier for reinsurance coverage that would be used to help defray the cost of any employer losses that may occur as a result of the uniform coverage rules (see Q 8:46).

If an employer purchases such reinsurance coverage, the question arises whether the cost of the reinsurance product can be passed on to the employees who elect to participate in the program. Like accident and health plans, medical FSAs must exhibit the risk-shifting and risk distribution characteristics of insurance. In an informal opinion, the IRS has responded negatively to the idea of the employee's making pretax contributions to provide a benefit for the employer (i.e., eliminating or substantially eliminating the employer's financial risk in sponsoring a medical FSA program).

Q 8:51 Has the financial risk of employers that sponsor medical FSA programs in fact increased as a result of the uniform coverage rules?

No. Although the introduction of the uniform reimbursement rules in 1989 generated fears that employees would take advantage of the system and submit claims exceeding year-to-date contributions before terminating employment, those fears are not being borne out.

The risk of financial loss for employers has been mitigated for several key reasons:

1. Many employers have designed their medical FSA programs to include certain features that minimize their potential financial risk. Such design approaches include instituting waiting periods, setting maximum reimbursement amounts, and limiting eligible types of expenses (see Q 8:49).
2. Even if a few employees take out more than they contribute, there will be other employees who forfeit account balances as a result of the "use-it-or-lose-it" rules (see Qs 6:18–6:21).

A Hewitt Associates' 1997 survey indicated that forfeitures for the 1996 plan year occurred in 91 percent of medical FSAs. The average amount forfeited from 1996 medical FSAs was $136 per employee.

Q 8:52 What funds are used to cover the availability of full reimbursement under the uniform coverage rules?

Under the uniform coverage rules (see Q 6:14), an employee may submit claims exceeding his or her year-to-date contributions and then terminate employment before contributing the full salary reduction amount. The employer is, in effect, required to "front" the money to cover the cost of amounts that employees are entitled to receive as a result of the uniform coverage rules. Those advanced amounts are drawn from the employer's general assets.

Note. In most instances, employees will remain employed throughout the entire plan year so that if an employee submits claims exceeding his or her year-to-date contributions, the employee will contribute the full salary reduction amount by year-end. As a result, the employer will not ultimately incur a financial loss for most employees and may not incur a financial loss for the plan as a whole.

Life Insurance

Q 8:53 What basic plan design choices must an employer make when developing a life insurance program, regardless of whether it operates in a flexible benefits plan environment?

An employer must consider a number of life insurance plan design choices, regardless of whether it is operating in a flexible benefits plan environment. Those choices include the following:

1. Whether to have employees make contributions in order to participate in basic life insurance protection.
2. Whether to provide free basic life insurance protection (a core benefit) to employees but require them to pay the full amount of any supplemental benefit (which would be based on the amount of their contribution).
3. Whether the basic life insurance protection benefit should be something that an employee can opt out of in exchange for cash—in which case the coverage is not mandatory. When cash is the alternative option, the election to pay for benefits on a tax-preferred basis must be part of a cafeteria plan.
4. How much life insurance is sufficient for a particular individual.
5. Whether to base life insurance benefits on flat dollar amounts.
6. Whether to base life insurance benefits on the compensation of the employee (i.e., some multiple of annual salary).
7. If a compensation-based formula is used, how compensation should be defined (e.g., should the definition cover all deferred compensation, including flexible benefits and 401(k) salary reductions).
8. Whether to have different insurance benefit formulas at different ages or have a single blended rate that applies to younger and older employees alike.
9. Whether to offer life insurance as a group policy (a non-portable policy written for a group of employees, the price of which is determined by the condition of eligible employees in the group) or as an individual policy (usually portable) with premium rates that reflect the individual's specific circumstances.
10. Whether the insurance policy should be a term-based policy, which generally lasts for one year and is renewable each year at a slightly

higher cost, or a cash value policy, which tends to have level premiums throughout the life of the policy.

Note. Some of the plan design alternatives listed above may be offered on an after-tax basis in a flexible benefits environment, but not in a Code Section 125 (cafeteria) plan.

Q 8:54 When developing a life insurance program, what are the reasons for using different benefits formulas for different ages rather than a single blended rate that applies to all employees?

Hand in hand with offering employees the choice as to whether or not to purchase life insurance, an employer generally selects age-related rates because they bear a relationship to the actual cost of coverage for a particular employee. The rates for younger employees are less costly than those for older employees because younger employees are less likely to experience a claim. Under a single blended rate approach, older employees would be more likely to participate, younger employees less likely—which could cause adverse selection to affect the life insurance program.

It should be noted that when the employer is purchasing life insurance for all eligible employees (e.g., without a requirement for the employees to contribute to the cost), it is often administratively easier to select a single rate insurance, even though premiums paid on behalf of younger employees will be subsidizing those paid on behalf of older employees.

Table 8-1 shows a representative chart of the different rates that might be paid by employees at different ages for supplemental group term life insurance under a hypothetical fully flexible benefits program.

Table 8-1. Age and Life Insurance Rates

Employee age as of 1/1/02	*Life insurance rate per $1,000 of coverage*
< 25	.07
25 to 29	.12
30 to 34	.17
35 to 39	.23
40 to 44	.28
45 to 49	.48
50 to 54	.87
55 to 59	1.41
60 to 64	1.61
65 to 69	2.66
70 +	7.23

Q 8:55 What should an employer's primary objective be in developing a life insurance program under a flexible benefits plan?

An employer's primary objective when developing a life insurance program under a flexible benefits plan should be to offer an array of options that meet most of its employees' coverage needs. Of all the group health and welfare coverages, life insurance is the benefit most likely to be under- or overvalued by employees because the importance of life insurance to an individual depends so much on the individual's lifestyle, age, health, and perspective. For example, a young single employee with no mortgage, no dependents, and no need to leave a death benefit to anyone may see life insurance as a waste of money. Such an employee would nearly always rather have the cash. In contrast, to a 50-year-old employee who is married and has children and a large mortgage, the employer's provision of the life insurance option is a significant benefit. Such an employee may even wish to trade other benefits in exchange for additional life insurance protection.

Setting aside the fact that life insurance is a valuable benefit for some and perceived as an unnecessary benefit for others, a life insurance program is an important benefit to include in a flexible benefits plan because of the security it provides and because life insurance is an eminently tradable commodity. In addition, life insurance is a benefit an employer may easily provide: it is not very costly, and adverse selection in life insurance is very low. An employer that is developing a life insurance program under a program of flexible benefits should provide as wide an array of options as possible. Some options will necessarily be offered outside of a Section 125 plan. Options that could be offered within a flexible benefits program may range from a $5,000 burial benefit to a multiple-of-salary option up to, for example, $1 million. They may include individual cash value and portable policies as well as group term life insurance and policies that require no medical underwriting as well as those that require health risk evaluations.

> **Note**. Only group term life insurance may be offered as a qualified benefit in a cafeteria plan as defined by Section 125 of the Internal Revenue Code (Code). Also, life insurance offered in multiples of salary can be problematic within a Section 125 plan.

> **Practice Pointer.** An employer should refrain from offering so many life insurance options that plan participants become confused about what the options actually offer.

Q 8:56 When employees are offered various types of life or disability insurance options, does adverse selection become a problem?

Not really. Allowing employees to pick and choose from an array of life or disability insurance options (or waive such coverage entirely) increases the risk that employees with poor health histories will enroll in maximum coverage while healthy employees will enroll in reduced coverage or opt out of coverage altogether. The result is adverse selection. Yet the effect of adverse selection on the life or disability insurance portion of a flexible benefits program is minimal in contrast to other types of insurance protection and may be dealt with quite easily.

Adverse selection tends not to be a serious problem with regard to life and disability insurance because very few people can predict with any accuracy when they will die or become disabled. Even high-risk employees who have had heart attacks are unable to predict when they will die or, should they become disabled, the length and severity of the disability. That degree of uncertainty may be compared to an employee's ability to predict the need for, plan, and schedule dentistry.

A greater concern for insurance companies in regard to the high payout coverages for life and disability insurance is the possibility of fraud by covered employees or dependents. Although feigning disability or death to defraud a carrier is not uncommon in the general population, it occurs infrequently in employee benefits group insurance programs.

Q 8:57 How may an employer control adverse selection when offering employees a choice of life or disability insurance options?

The following are two prevalent methods for controlling adverse selection in life and disability insurance options:

1. Use plan design to reduce or eliminate adverse selection; or
2. Calculate the price of adverse selection and make it part of the insurance premiums cost.

More specifically, one method commonly used to control adverse selection is to require employees who initially waive either life or disability insurance (or both) to provide medical evidence of insurability if they subsequently decide to enroll. The concept of medical insurability is common among individual income replacement insurance policies—an individual who purchases a whole life policy typically completes a medical questionnaire or provides a medical history to a nurse who performs some basic medical tests. In a group benefits insurance market, however, the insurance usually is a guaranteed issue (i.e., it is not subject to any medical underwriting). Nevertheless, even for group insurance, the insurance carrier requires evidence of medical insurability when the dollar payout from such income replacement insurances becomes significant.

Another method of controlling adverse selection in life and disability insurance options is to limit the amount of increased (or decreased) coverage an employee may elect. That is to say, an employee who wishes to upgrade his or her life or disability benefits generally is allowed to do so, provided the benefits increase is not extreme. An employee who decides to increase his or her life insurance from a one-times-salary option to a three-times-salary option may, however, be required to select the two-times salary option for one plan year before choosing the three-times-salary option. Generally, the insurance carrier requires some kind of protection against dramatic coverage swings, and many employers consider an incremental approach to be a more satisfactory solution than requiring employees to provide medical evidence of insurability.

Q 8:58 What administrative issues pertain to the design of a life insurance policy?

One of the important issues that arises in the administration of life insurance is the form of payout—that is, how the beneficiary receives his or her money. In the absence of specific instructions to the contrary, the insurance company pays the death benefit to the designated beneficiary in a lump sum; if the insured employee has not designated a beneficiary, the insurance company pays the lump sum to the employee's estate. Many alternative forms of payout are available, however, including a life annuity, a life annuity with a guaranteed minimum period of payments, and installments for fixed periods.

Practice Pointer. Whether or not an employer has a flexible benefits plan in place, it might be useful to offer employees a choice of payout elections. That way, an employee and his or her beneficiary can review optional payout alternatives in conjunction with other aspects of family or estate planning.

In addition to the form of a payout, an employer can provide options to employees by offering different methods of paying out the benefits. Many insurance carriers now offer a check access approach under which a beneficiary may take a portion of the payout amount by writing a check that is drawn against the death benefit. Another option is an accelerated death benefit (ADB), which pays out the death benefit before the actual death of the insured (generally to help defray medical costs) as long as the insured is terminally ill or, in some cases, chronically ill.

Under the Health Insurance Portability and Accountability Act of 1996 (HIPAA), an ADB to a terminally or chronically ill individual will not be included in gross income, whether payment is made to the insured or assigned or sold to a viatical settlement provider. The exclusion applies to amounts received after December 31, 1996.

A *terminally ill individual* is an individual who has been certified by a physician as having an illness or physical condition that can reasonably be expected to result in death within 24 months or less after the date of certification.

A *viatical settlement provider* is anyone engaged in the business of purchasing or taking assignments of life insurance contracts on the lives of terminally or chronically ill individuals, provided that person is licensed for such purpose in the state in which the insured resides. If a state does not require such licensure, the person must meet the requirements of sections 8 and 9 of the Viatical Settlements Model Act of the National Association of Insurance Commissioners (NAIC) and other applicable regulations or standards of the NAIC.

The definition of a *chronically ill individual* is the same as that used in connection with long-term care services. (A terminally ill individual, it should be noted, is not considered chronically ill.) In order to be excluded from income, payments to a chronically ill individual must conform to the following requirements:

1. The payments must be received under a rider or other provision of a contract that is treated as a qualified long-term care contract; and
2. The payments must be for actual costs incurred for qualified long-term care services that are not paid for or reimbursed by insurance or otherwise.

In addition, the following provisions apply to the contract under which such payments are made:

1. The contract must not pay or reimburse expenses reimbursable under Medicare, except if Medicare is the secondary payer or if the contract pays on a per diem basis (or on some other type of periodic payment basis) without regard to the actual cost of the long-term care services; and
2. The contract must satisfy the consumer protection provisions added by HIPAA (or, in certain circumstances, analogous standards adopted by the NAIC).

The income exclusion limit for payments made on a per diem or other periodic basis is the same as that for long-term care. It should be noted, however, that such an exclusion for an ADB does not apply to business-related policies. Therefore, such an amount paid to anyone other than the insured is not excluded from income if that person has an insurable interest with respect to the insured because the insured is a director, officer, or employee of that person or because the insured has a financial interest in the person's business.

Still another payout option is a survivor income program, which provides a stated monthly income for a particular person over a certain period of time following the insured employee's death. Very often a survivor income program is used to pay benefits to a spouse or child who has little financial expertise and who would find a sizable lump sum death benefit overwhelming. The benefit should be designed to cease after there is no longer a surviving spouse or children (e.g., if the spouse or children predecease the employee). An employee who ceases to have such dependents should be given an opportunity to change not only the designation of beneficiary but also the type of benefit.

Q 8:59 How many different life insurance options might be appropriate in a flexible benefits plan?

It is not uncommon to see as many as seven life insurance options offered in a flexible benefits plan of a large employer. Included in those options is a basic amount (core benefit) stated either as a flat dollar amount or a salary multiple.

Generally, a core benefit does not exceed two times salary under a salary multiple system or $25,000 to $50,000 under a flat life insurance benefit system.

To increase an employee's total life insurance coverage beyond those limits, additional options could be made available, up to four times an employee's salary. Such additional levels of life insurance protection are known as voluntary or supplemental life insurance and generally are purchased entirely with the employee's funds on an after-tax basis.

The salary multiple approach is more generous than a flat dollar amount and has the advantage of being automatically increased each time a change in salary occurs. That avoids the administrative inconvenience of periodically updating life insurance amounts. There is a certain logic about tying life insurance to the amount of an employee's salary; flat dollar amounts, on the other hand, are easy to grasp because there are no automatic increases to alter them and create odd amounts. Furthermore, flat dollar amounts can be assigned to special needs; for example, a $5,000 benefit can be linked to the cost of a burial, and a $50,000 benefit can be linked to the maximum tax-free benefit available to employees under Code Section 79.

Q 8:60 Is a life insurance benefit a catalyst for installing a flexible benefits plan?

No. It is medical benefits that create the most complexity and cost for an employer—not life insurance. While flexible benefits plans have earned a reputation for their ability to bring health care benefit costs under control, the cost of providing life insurance is much lower and the issues less complicated than those associated with medical benefits. It is therefore unlikely that a life insurance benefit alone would create the need for a flexible benefits plan. Still, all income replacement insurances, including life insurance, are important aspects of a flexible benefits approach, and such types of insurance function better within a flexible environment than in a nonflexible one. Indeed, an employer may impart versatility and responsiveness to a flexible benefits plan by endowing it with an array of life insurance options.

Q 8:61 Should a life insurance policy include a premium waiver provision, and should it include a conversion right in the event an employee terminates?

A premium waiver provision and a conversion privilege can be useful add-on options to a life insurance policy. A premium waiver provision allows employees who become disabled to maintain their life insurance coverage throughout the disability period without having to pay premiums during that period. A group term life insurance policy that has a conversion privilege enables an employee to convert the group coverage into an individual life insurance policy that is portable when the employee terminates employment. Although such policy options can be expensive, they are valuable to employees who have occasion to use them.

An employer must weigh the cost of providing a premium waiver and a conversion privilege as options against the benefit of having those features included in a basic life insurance program. Companies with more than 500 employees also should consider whether or not to self-insure a premium waiver if the life insurance policy has such a clause. Employers often find that having such features self-insured in the employer-paid basic coverage is both sensible and cost-efficient. Nonetheless, an employer may choose to make the waiving of premiums and conversion rights under the employee-paid supplemental life insurance protection provisions optional. Because employees are going to pay for the benefit, they can decide whether or not the additional cost is warranted.

Q 8:62 Is it good plan design to include an accidental death and dismemberment income replacement benefit under a flexible benefits plan?

Yes. Accidental death and dismemberment (AD&D) has traditionally been closely tied to the life insurance benefit and is often included in a flexible benefits plan. An employer may choose to create a separate AD&D program with coverage amounts that are entirely separate from the coverage level taken under the group life insurance plan. AD&D premiums may be deducted either on a pretax or after-tax contribution basis.

It is important to note that disability income generating benefits and AD&D benefits are entirely different from one another in the manner in which the benefits are paid out and taxed. On an AD&D payout, both the death proceeds and payments related to dismemberment are excludable from income, regardless of how premiums were paid (see Q 8:74). [IRC §105(c); Treas Reg § 1.106-1]

> **Practice Pointer.** Because AD&D policies do not act like disability income benefits, it is usually better for the employee to pay for them with pretax dollars.

Q 8:63 Is it good plan design to include dependent group life insurance under a flexible benefits plan?

No. An employer that wants to offer dependent group life insurance *must* offer that benefit outside a flexible benefits plan on an after-tax basis. If dependent life insurance is offered outside the flexible benefits plan, up to $2,000 of coverage can be considered to be a Section 132 *de minimis* fringe benefit, and the benefit will not be subject to imputed income. [Notice 89-110, 1989-2 CB 447] If the value of the coverage is more than $2,000, the benefit may be subject to imputed income. The employer must calculate the value of the entire coverage (including the first $2,000) at the uniform premium rates for $1,000 of group term life insurance protection as described in Table I under Paragraph (d)(2) of Treasury Regulations Section 1.79-3 (see Q 8:64), subtract any after-tax employee contributions, and determine whether the remaining amount is *de minimis*.

Dependent group life insurance, which may be for the employee's spouse and children, generally is not linked to the employee's own life insurance election. An employer may want to consider offering age-related rates, as opposed to a flat rate, so that the amount of imputed income paid is linked to the actual age of the covered individual.

Q 8:64 What are the consequences of offering employees the option of electing more than $50,000 of death protection under a group term life insurance policy?

A flexible benefits plan may include group life insurance in any amount. If the amount of coverage exceeds $50,000, however, the imputed tax that would have resulted under Code Section 79 applies. While a flexible benefits plan preserves tax-free benefits, it does not make otherwise taxable benefits become tax free. In general, therefore, the design decision to offer group term life insurance in excess of $50,000 is not affected by the introduction of a flexible benefits plan. The plan sponsor may find it advantageous, considering overall plan design, to permit employees to purchase in excess of $50,000 in group term life insurance. At issue will be whether to permit employees to use pretax dollars when purchasing group term life insurance. In most cases, group term life insurance in excess of a $50,000 death benefit is best purchased with after-tax dollars.

It is extremely important for the designer of a flexible benefits plan to fully understand (1) how life insurance coverage in excess of $50,000 is imputed for purposes of taxable income and (2) the relationship between imputed income rates for life insurance and the actual cost of the life insurance. There are a number of different ways to structure the life insurance design to respond to the issue of imputed income (see Q 8:65). All the designs reflect the uniform costs assigned per age group (see Table 8-2), which is how imputed income is calculated.

Table 8-2. Uniform Premiums for $1,000 of Group Term Life Insurance Protection

Five-year age bracket	*Cost per $1,000 of protection for one-month period*
<25	$0.05
25–29	.06
30–34	.08
35–39	.09
40–44	.10
45–49	.15
50–54	.23
55–59	.43

Table 8-2. Uniform Premiums for $1,000 of Group Term Life Insurance Protection (*cont'd*)

Five-year age bracket	*Cost per $1,000 of protection for one-month period*
60–64	.66
65–69	1.27
70 +	2.06

The calculation for imputing group term life insurance costs to an employee's taxable income is described in Treasury Regulations Section 1.79-3. The calculation defines an employee's taxable imputed income generated by employer-paid group term life insurance coverage in excess of $50,000, regardless of the actual cost of the life insurance.

Example. Moshe, a 45-year-old employee of Fine Fabrics, Inc., receives $70,000 of employer-paid group term life insurance (this includes any amounts paid for by Moshe with pretax salary reduction dollars). The $20,000 amount of the group term life insurance in excess of $50,000 (i.e., $70,000–$50,000) results in taxable income. To determine the imputed taxable income, $20,000 is divided by $1,000 and the result is multiplied by the Table I rates, which are based upon the employee's age. Thus,

$$(\$20{,}000 \div 1{,}000) \times \$0.15 = \$20 \times \$0.15 = \$3.00 \text{ per month}$$

If Moshe was covered at the $70,000 group term life insurance amount for the entire year, the additional taxable income he would receive for the year would be $36 ($3 × 12). Assuming Moshe is in the 30 percent tax bracket, the resulting tax from this $36 of additional income is $10.80.

Practice Pointer. If employees pay for group term life insurance with their own money and the cost of such insurance is more than the Table I cost of such insurance, the employees should consider paying for such coverage with pretax dollars. In such instances the tax savings associated with buying the group term life insurance is greater than the imputed income generated by Table I rates.

Q 8:65 In light of the imputed income caused by group term life insurance coverage in excess of $50,000, what is the best way to structure such a benefit under a flexible benefits plan?

The primary objective of a group term life insurance option under a flexible benefits plan is to devise a program that allows each employee to maximize his or her tax-free benefit under Code Section 79. To accomplish that objective within the framework of a single plan, however, the employer must give some employees different benefits than originally intended or complicate the administration of the life insurance program to an unacceptable degree.

Example. Fa La La, Inc. wants to purchase and implement a core benefit of group term life insurance for its employees in the amount of one-times-salary. In addition, Fa La La wants to make available to employees the option of purchasing additional supplemental insurance of up to two-times-salary. (Total available life insurance is therefore three-times-salary.)

Possible Outcomes:

1. If Fa La La gives all employees a core benefit of one-times-salary, the benefit may cause employees who earn more than $50,000 per year to be credited with unwanted imputed income on an undervalued benefit.
2. If Fa La La gives all employees a core benefit of one-times-salary up to a maximum of $50,000, employees who earn more than $50,000 do not receive the full benefit of one-times-salary.
3. If Fa La La makes supplemental life insurance benefits available on a pretax basis, employees who purchase the supplemental two-times-salary benefit and earn more than $16,667 will cross the $50,000 threshold and incur imputed income.
4. If Fa La La makes supplemental life insurance benefits available on a pretax basis, employees who purchase the supplemental one-times-salary benefit and earn more than $25,000 will cross the $50,000 threshold and incur imputed income.
5. If Fa La La makes supplemental life insurance benefits available on an after-tax basis, employees who purchase the supplemental two-times-salary benefit and earn less than $16,667 will not be able to take advantage of the tax-qualified benefit on amounts up to $50,000.
6. If Fa La La makes supplemental life insurance benefits available on an after-tax basis, employees who purchase the supplemental one-times-salary benefit and earn less than $25,000 will not be able to take advantage of the tax-qualified benefit on amounts up to $50,000.

There are several ways to let those Fa La La employees who can maximize contributions on a pretax basis do so without hurting those employees to whom a pretax contribution brings unwanted imputed income. Individually, none of the solutions provides a perfect answer; however, they are not mutually exclusive and may be combined to provide acceptable solutions for many organizations.

Solutions:

1. Provide employer-paid core life insurance coverage up to $50,000. Require all supplemental life insurance to be purchased with after-tax employee contributions.
2. Give employees flexible benefits plan credits equal to whatever Fa La La would have paid toward life insurance before implementing the flexible benefits plan. Then allow employees to buy only the first $50,000 of life insurance with pretax funds.

3. Offer Section 79 group term life insurance policies that write coverage levels based on multiples of salary—but only up to $50,000. Then offer after-tax group term or group universal coverage for amounts in excess of $50,000.
4. Provide all life insurance on a pretax basis and make whole any employee who has taxable income because of that decision. Fa La La can do that by compensating employees with additional cash or credits. Fa La La must decide whether or not to gross up the employee's compensation to account for the effects of taxation. To compensate an employee who is taxed at the 30 percent tax bracket, Fa La La needs to pay $1.43 for every $1 of imputed income. It should be noted that an employee who paid imputed income taxes before the introduction of the flexible benefits plan will be getting too much money if Fa La La grosses up by the full $1.43. In fact, to account for the imputed taxes the employee had already paid, Fa La La should offset those taxes against the gross-up amount.

Q 8:66 If an employer is able to self-insure its life insurance benefit, should it?

Given the risk attributes of life insurance—the mortality frequency is highly stable and measurable, but a very high level of payout is possible at any time—self-insuring is advisable only if an employer has sufficient cash reserves to pay out at least twice what is actuarially expected and if the risk is spread over a large group. As a practical matter, only large companies self-insure life insurance. The cost of obtaining group life insurance through an insurance company is generally considered a good buy relative to the risk the employer thereby avoids; however, large companies may be able to save on the premiums charged by insurance companies if they underwrite their own risk.

Even when a plan is self-insured, the benefit may be administered by an outside insurance company to provide ease of delivery and to ensure that the $50,000 tax exclusion provided for group life insurance is not somehow compromised. A self-insured approach usually involves a special financial arrangement between the employer and the insurer under which the underwriting risk of an insurance company is minimized or limited to an administrative charge and, if appropriate, a premium tax.

Q 8:67 Should employees be allowed to opt out of all life insurance benefits, or should an employer impose a mandatory core level of benefits?

Most employers feel that because the cost of group life insurance is so low, it makes sense to require all employees to be covered, if only for a nominal amount. By doing so, the employer avoids having to contend with irate and possibly destitute survivors who receive no death benefits. Sometimes in a flexible benefits plan environment, employees object to having an automatic employer-provided life insurance requirement, even if it is only a small burial benefit. One design compromise is to allow employees to opt out of life insurance but to require a spouse's signature. That strategy avoids the embarrassment of an uninsured employee's death leading to a visit from an aggrieved spouse.

Q 8:68 What are the nondiscrimination rules of Code Section 79 and the special nondiscrimination rules of Code Section 125?

Code Section 79 requires that group term life insurance plans meet one of several eligibility tests and a benefits test in order to avoid nondiscrimination penalties. The Section 79 nondiscrimination rules apply regardless of whether or not a flexible benefits plan is in effect.

Code Section 79(d) prohibits discrimination in favor of key employees in a group term life insurance plan. A *key employee* is defined as someone who, in the current plan year or in the four preceding plan years is (or was) either:

1. An officer who earned more than 50 percent of the Section 415(b) limit; or
2. A partial owner of the company who earned more than a certain dollar limit.

Code Section 79(d) has a coverage test that requires the total amount of employer-paid coverage provided to key employees also be provided to at least 70 percent of all employees, or to a group of employees of whom at least 85 percent are not key employees, or to a classification of employees that does not discriminate in favor of key employees.

In addition, a group term life insurance plan that meets the nondiscrimination rules of Code Section 125 will be considered nondiscriminatory with respect to coverage. Optional employee-paid supplemental life insurance is nondiscriminatory if it is available to a nondiscriminatory group, and group term life insurance elected under a Section 125 plan is treated as paid for with employee contributions.

Disability Coverage

Q 8:69 What basic plan design choices must an employer make when developing a disability program?

A well-integrated disability program includes salary continuation programs such as sick leave, as well as more expensive and protracted benefits such as short- and long-term disability. Short-term salary continuation is provided when an employee is absent from work because of accident or sickness, and the entire benefit may be as much as 100 percent of an employee's salary. In contrast, short- and long-term disability benefits are always less than 100 percent of an employee's salary. The cause of the absence generally must be unrelated to the employee's occupation and hence not covered by workers' compensation.

An employer must make a number of basic plan design choices when developing a disability program, including the following:

- Who is eligible
- When coverage begins
- How much the employee will be paid (i.e., a dollar limit)
- How much replacement income will be provided (as a percentage of salary)
- How long the income replacement will last
- What coverage exclusions, if any, will apply

Q 8:70 How do sick leave, short-term disability, and long-term disability work in a disability program?

Generally, a true salary continuation program, such as a sick leave plan, is the result of a personnel policy that provides a salary continuance for only one to two weeks of absence each year. (In the case of executives, sick leave is rarely defined as a specified number of days. In effect, an indefinite period of sick time is given to executives, ending when short- or long-term disability becomes activated.) In general, sick leave is provided at 100 percent of an employee's regular salary.

A short-term disability plan usually commences after an employee exhausts available sick leave. Some employers combine the two phases administratively. The critical differences between short-term disability and salary continuation sick leave is that short-term disability does not pay out at 100 percent of salary and its duration period, which typically begins after one, two, or three weeks, usually ends after 26 weeks. It is possible, however, to have a short-term disability plan with a shorter (or longer) duration of coverage. If an employer provides a long-term disability plan, it should become effective after the short-term disability plan ends so that the short-term disability benefit dovetails with the long-term disability benefit, and benefit coverage protection is not lost.

Typically, a long-term disability plan allows for a six-month elimination period (i.e., the 180 days of coverage under the short-term disability plan). Shorter elimination periods significantly increase the cost of the long-term disability plan. Nevertheless, shorter elimination periods (e.g., three months) are sometimes used, especially when dovetailing a short-term disability plan with a short duration of coverage (e.g., three months). The percentage of salary continued under a long-term disability plan will typically be between 50 percent and 60 percent of gross compensation; however, plans are most often written so that the gross amount upon which benefits are calculated is reduced by Social Security disability benefits when payable. The Social Security offset generally includes all payments, including those to family members, that result from the disability. Social Security, it should be noted, rarely comes into the picture before the onset of long-term disability benefits.

A total long-term disability income replacement of 50 percent to 60 percent of pay generally is less than the total provided during a short-term disability: the percentage of coverage protection in a short-term disability plan is 70 percent to 80 percent. Neither short- nor long-term disability plans replace 100 percent of compensation because of the expense, and because the design of a disability plan should encourage an employee to return to work.

Practice Pointer. It is a common practice in employee-paid disability plans to include a minimum benefit. Doing so prevents the Social Security benefit offset from making the disability benefit too small. In contrast, if the employer pays the premium, a minimum benefit is not considered necessary.

Disability defined. To receive short-term disability benefits, an employee needs to establish only that he or she is temporarily unable to perform his or her job. Long-term disability benefits, however, may last a few years or for the remainder of an employee's career. Therefore, it is necessary for the employee to establish that the disability is likely to be total and permanent and that it will prevent the employee from working in either his or her own occupation or in any occupation that would require similar education and training. A related consideration are the rules outlined in the insurance policy regarding rehabilitative employment and how they affect the employee's continuation of benefits.

Q 8:71 Do salary continuation plans fit in with a flexible benefits plan?

Salary continuation plans (e.g., a sick leave policy) are generally regarded as an adjunct to payroll. As such, they fit easily into the context of a fully flexible benefits plan. Although Treasury regulations do not describe sick leave time (for example) as a benefit that may be traded for cash or benefits in a Section 125 plan and thus an employer must keep sick leave separate from the such a plan, the employer may tie salary continuation plans into the concept of choice provided under the broader flexible benefits plan, outside of the qualified benefits of a Section 125 plan.

Practice Pointer. State labor laws occasionally prevent benefit plans from offering trades of paid leave for other benefits. For example, Hawaii, New Jersey, New York, and Rhode Island have enacted statutes requiring employers to provide short-term disability benefits.

Q 8:72 What are the positive and negative aspects for an employee of choosing either pretax or after-tax premium payments?

The taxation of disability benefits payments, when received, depends on whether the benefits resulted from employee after-tax contributions or whether the benefits were funded by employer contributions.

When the employee pays for the contributions on a pretax basis, as occurs in a flexible benefits plan, the benefits are taxed as if the employer made the contributions. Benefits resulting from employer contributions are taxable to the employee. Those received from a plan where after-tax contributions were made by the employee to cover the full cost of the plan are tax free.

When the contributions are made partly by the employee on an after-tax basis and partly by or on behalf of the employer, the benefits payments will be partly taxable. In other words, when a disability payment is made, the portion of that payment that is taxable and the portion that is nontaxable are prorated according to the proportion of the cost originally paid by the employer and employee, respectively. For example, if an employee pays 40 percent of a long-term disability premium with after-tax dollars and subsequently receives a disability payment of $1,100 per month, $440 (40% of $1,100) would be tax free and $660 of the benefit would be taxable income.

Given a choice, some employees prefer to avoid the taxation of their benefits at a time of great need; others prefer to save the cost of the premiums because they believe it is likely that the benefits will never be paid. The second group also believes that medical deductions at a time of disability will help push the employee into a low tax bracket that would preclude the taxation of their income replacement benefit.

The best approach is to allow employees to decide whether they wish to purchase long-term disability benefits with pretax or after-tax dollars. A flexible benefits plan permits either type of contribution, so, in addition to selecting the desired option level, employees would also select the payment method (pretax or after-tax). If such a choice is offered, the employer must take care to communicate the issue of disability taxation clearly to employees.

Another approach to the employee's tax problem is to provide a lump-sum flat dollar amount for total and permanent disability that is unrelated to salary indemnification. If the disability involves dismemberment, a benefits payment such as AD&D coverage will be totally tax free. Such a benefit generally is supplemental to the regular long-term disability income; however, the supplemental benefit is tax free even though the disability income might not be tax free.

Long-term Disability

Q 8:73 What are the primary objectives of the employer in developing a fully flexible benefits plan to coordinate with or superimpose on a long-term disability program?

When developing a fully flexible benefits plan together with a long-term disability program, an employer typically has two main objectives: (1) to be insulated from the sense of responsibility for providing long-term benefits for an employee who becomes disabled for causes not directly related to occupational hazards and (2) to provide the fullest possible menu for the flexible benefits plan.

Note. In the absence of a flexible benefits plan, an employer may be willing to incur the nominal cost of long-term disability to avoid any further obligation. Generally, the value of such protection is greater than its cost to the employer. Alternatively, an employer may share the cost with employees and strongly urge them to join the long-term disability plan.

As for the second main objective, the long-term disability benefit is another item that an employee might elect in lieu of a more costly medical benefit. As many options as possible are needed to encourage the selection of lower cost health care options by employees. Unlike health care costs, the inflation rate for long-term disability benefits has been controlled by the better recovery rates resulting from improved medical care. Another positive aspect of the inclusion of long-term disability benefits in the flexible benefits menu is that it will increase participation in the long-term disability benefit—the employer's first objective.

To increase participation in the long-term disability benefit and to minimize the risk of employees dropping the benefit after it is added to the flexible benefits plan, an employer should consider the following flexible design features for the long-term disability option:

- Maintaining a low price
- Making the long-term disability benefit free if a favored medical option is chosen
- Requiring that the long-term disability benefit be elected for no less than two years
- Charging for the long-term disability benefit even if it is not elected
- Requiring a core long-term disability election (i.e., do not permit employees to opt out and the core level is fully employer-paid)

Note. Denying employees the choice of opting out of long-term disability coverage is an underwriting requirement imposed by many insurance companies.

Q 8:74 How many levels of long-term disability coverage should an employer offer?

When an employer is large enough to sustain several levels of long-term disability coverage, either two or three percentage reimbursement levels should be offered within a range of 40 percent to 70 percent. Small employers may offer only one level of long-term disability coverage.

The objective is to provide the employee receiving disability benefits with an adequate standard of living; however, the benefit should not be so great that it deprives the employee of the incentive to return to work. It is common practice to keep the range of choices narrow so that the choice of the smallest benefit is not a serious risk and the choice of the largest benefit does not represent a wasteful cost. A narrow range of alternatives also limits the risk of adverse selection.

In addition to differentiating long-term disability benefits by their percentage reimbursement levels, a plan designer may also differentiate high- and low-option plans by their elimination periods. For example, a low-option plan might have a 210-day waiting period, while a high-option plan might have a 90-day waiting period. As a further twist, an employer could offer a single group long-term disability plan with a 60 percent salary reimbursement level and a 180-day elimination period, but allow employees to "buy down" the 180 days to 150 or 120 or "buy up" the 60 percent to 65 percent or 70 percent.

Q 8:75 What are the advantages to the employer and the employees of administering a long-term disability benefit through a flexible benefits plan?

As discussed in Q 8:72, a critical design issue is whether disability coverage should be purchased with employee after-tax dollars (a choice that preserves the tax-free status of any disability payments that the employee may receive). Under a flexible benefits plan, the employer may allow employees to choose between pretax and after-tax treatment. The employee who wishes to pay for the disability benefit may do so outside the flexible benefits plan. The employee receives a new source of funds from which to make such payments by taking cash out of the flexible benefits plan that was made available because the employee did not use up all of his or her flexible credits. The cash distribution is taxable; the net amount after tax can be used to pay the cost of long-term disability. The cash withdrawal can even be increased enough so that after withholding it equals the employee's contribution requirement.

On the other hand, the employer is giving the employee a choice: if the credits are used to make the employee's long-term disability contribution, it is treated as a pretax contribution and as an employer's contribution. The resulting benefit (i.e., the portion of the cost financed in such a manner) is taxable to the employee when received in benefits.

Q 8:76 When is it advisable to self-insure a long-term disabiity program, and how can it be done?

Although sick leave and short-term disability benefits frequently are not insured, most employers prefer to insure the long-term disability benefit. Unless the group is very large and the employer has the administrative capability to handle self-insurance, the carrier relieves the employer of a risk that could be considerable. Long-term disability is rated on the assumption that only a small portion of the participants will ever receive benefits. If other conditions develop, the financial risk can be considerable. That is why only the largest employers are interested in self-insurance.

Any employer that self-insures may impose a cap on the number of years for which benefits are paid. The typical insured plan covers benefits all the way to retirement age, but not later than age 65.

Q 8:77 Should employees be allowed to opt out of all long-term disability benefits, or should a core level of coverage be mandatory?

The decision regarding making the long-term disability benefit a core benefit should be made independently of the decision to implement a flexible benefits plan. Such a plan, however, makes it possible for the employer to insist on such coverage and to charge for it by using up flexible credits that would otherwise have to be applied to other benefits or be returned to the employee in cash. Indeed, the employer may provide the benefit free of contributions by the employee and take that into account when deciding the number of credits to be made available for other benefits. The result is that, rather than requiring all employees to elect long-term disability coverage and spend a mandatory level of benefit credits (which is not a permitted arrangement under a Section 125 plan), the employer merely reduces the amount of benefit credits available for all covered employees and provides the benefit universally.

Q 8:78 Is there a nondiscrimination issue with long-term disability other than the nondiscrimination rules of Code Section 125?

Yes. Code Sections 105 and 106 do not contain any special nondiscrimination rules relating to long-term disability; however, disability plans are fringe benefits and as such are part of the terms and conditions of employment, which makes such plans subject to the compliance provisions of Title VII of the Age Discrimination in Employment Act (ADEA). The ADEA specifies the administrative and drafting requirements of disability plans. In addition, the Equal Employment Opportunity Commission (EEOC) has some jurisdiction over such programs. For example, a long-term disability plan may neither discriminate on the basis of gender nor condition disability coverage on an employee's status as head of household or as primary wage earner in the family unit. The EEOC also oversees allegations of age discrimination; as in the case of life insurance ineligibility, severe cutbacks in long-term disability coverage for older workers can result in violations of the ADEA or the Older Workers Benefit Protection Act (OWBPA).

> **Practice Pointer.** Although disability plans are ERISA plans and are therefore subject to the rules and requirements of that act, ERISA excludes plans intended solely to comply with a state's disability insurance laws. That is, a state's disability insurance laws are not preempted by ERISA; therefore, a plan designer must check state rules and requirements regarding nondiscrimination.

Chapter 9

Fringe Benefits

In addition to the welfare benefits typically provided in a flexible benefit arrangement, a plan may also offer certain fringe benefits on a tax-preferred basis. This chapter will describe the fringe benefit options that may be offered under a Section 125 cafeteria plan. In addition to the welfare benefit options described in chapter 8, the fringe benefits permitted in a Section 125 plan are dependent care assistance, adoption assistance, and the purchase or sale of vacation days.

Q 9:1 What is a qualified fringe benefit?

For purposes of a Section 125 plan, a qualified "fringe benefit" is a dependent care assistance program, adoption assistance program, or vacation time purchase or sale option, provided in conjunction with the overall ability to pay toward the cost of welfare or fringe benefits on a pretax basis.

Although certain other fringe benefits are defined in the Internal Revenue Code—notably in Code Section 132—these fringe benefits are not permitted to be offered within a Section 125 plan. (It is interesting to note that under Code Section 132, a benefit offering pretax benefits for parking and mass transit is offered. However, such fringe benefits are not permitted to be offered within a Section 125 plan.)

Dependent Care Assistance Programs

Q 9:2 Who is a qualifying dependent for purposes of a dependent care assistance program?

Within a dependent care assistance program, the expenses covered are only those incurred by a qualified dependent. A qualified dependent is defined as any of the following:

1. A dependent under age 13 who qualifies as a dependent for income tax purposes;
2. A spouse who is physically or mentally unable to care for himself or herself; or
3. A dependent who is unable to care for himself or herself and who qualifies as a dependent for income tax purposes.

[IRC § 21(b)(1); Family Support Act of 1988, PL 485 § 703]

Note. If the qualifying person is age 13 or older and incapable of self-care, dependent care expenses incurred outside the home can be reimbursed only if the qualifying person regularly spends at least eight hours a day in the employee's household. [IRC § 21(b)(2)(B)]

Q 9:3 If an employee's spouse does not work, is not incapacitated, and is not a full-time student, may the employee participate in a dependent care assistance program?

No. If an employee has a spouse who does not work, is not incapacitated, and is not a full-time student, no benefits are available under a dependent care assistance program.

Q 9:4 Are there certain circumstances under which an employee's spouse is treated as if he or she is working even though the spouse is not employed?

Yes. If an employee's spouse is a full-time student or is physically or mentally incapable of self-care, he or she is treated as a working spouse, and is determined to have "deemed" income for purposes of this benefit.

A spouse is considered incapable of self-care if he or she is not able to dress, clean, or feed himself or herself because of physical or mental problems. A person who requires constant attention to prevent self-injury or injury to others is not considered capable of self-care.

A spouse is a full-time student if he or she is enrolled at and attends a school for the number of hours or classes that the school considers full time. The spouse must have been a student for some part of each of five calendar months during the year. [IRS Pub 503, Child and Dependent Care Expenses (1998); IRC §§ 21(b)(1), 21(e)(7)] Note that, even though a part-time student might have a need for dependent care assistance, the Code describes only full-time students as eligible for tax-preferred dependent care assistance.

Q 9:5 Do documentation and disclosure rules apply to dependent care assistance plans?

Yes. The terms of a dependent care assistance plan must be described in a written plan document. [IRC § 129(d)(1)]

Two disclosure requirements apply:

1. The employer must provide eligible employees with a notification of the availability and terms of the dependent care assistance plan. [IRC § 129(d)(6)]
2. On or before each January 31, the expenses incurred by the employee for dependent care assistance benefits in the preceding calendar year must be reported on the employee's Form W-2. [IRC § 129(d)(7)] This reporting requirement is a calendar requirement, regardless of the plan year of the dependent care assistance plan.

Q 9:6 Must dependent care assistance plans be for the exclusive benefit of employees?

Yes. An employer-provided dependent care assistance program must be provided for the exclusive benefit of employees. [IRC § 129(d)(1)]

Q 9:7 Must an employer help an employee determine if a dependent care assistance plan or a tax credit is more advantageous based on the employee's circumstances?

No. Current law does not require that an employer help employees weigh a dependent care assistance plan against a tax credit. Nonetheless, many employers choose to provide employees with worksheets to help them make that comparison.

Of course, without consulting a tax advisor, it is difficult to be certain which option would be better for an employee. Table 9-1 provides some general guidelines.

Factors affecting the choice between a tax credit and a dependent care assistance plan include state tax savings and the fact that for a taxpayer with only one dependent child, the tax credit provides benefits up to a maximum dependent care expense of $3,000 per year, whereas a dependent care assistance plan will very often provide benefits up to a maximum of $5,000 per year. An employee with one dependent in dependent care who is spending well over $3,000 in dependent care expense may therefore find the dependent care assistance plan to be more advantageous than the tax credit. On the other hand, an employee with two or more children will want to carefully weigh the tax benefit between using the tax credit for up to $6,000, versus a company-provided dependent care assistance account with a maximum benefit of up to $5,000.

Table 9-1. Tax Credit vs. Dependent Care FSA

	Employee should consult with a tax advisor if his or her combined taxable income is LESS than	*Dependent care FSA generally better if employee's combined taxable income is MORE than*
Married: One child	$23,000	$23,000
Two or more children	$25,000	$25,000
Single parent—head of household: One child	$21,000	$21,000
Two or more children	$22,000	$22,000

Note. For plan years beginning after December 31, 2002, the maximum tax credit for individual taxpayers is $3,000 for one child and $6,000 for two or more children. Before the increase, the dependent care tax credit maximum was $2,400 for one child in dependent care, and $4,800 for two or more children. The maximum benefit available under an employer-sponsored dependent care assistance account has not increased beyond $5,000.

Q 9:8 What expenditures are eligible for reimbursement from dependent care assistance accounts?

Eligible expenses under a dependent care assistance account are defined as those that enable the participant and the participant's spouse to work or to look for work. They include the following:

1. Child care centers that care for six or more children and that meet the IRS's definition of a qualified day care center;
2. Caregivers for a disabled spouse or dependent who lives with the participant;
3. Babysitters;
4. Nursery schools;
5. Day camps; and
6. Household expenses, provided that a portion of such expenses are incurred to ensure a qualifying dependent's well-being and protection.

Note. A stipulation imposed by the IRS is that the service provider cannot be an individual for whom a personal tax exemption may be claimed and, if a child of the participant or spouse, cannot be under the age of 19. [IRC § 21(e)(6)] For example, a plan participant could not submit for dependent care expense the value of his spouse's caring for their children.

Q 9:9 What household expenses may be reimbursable from a dependent care assistance account?

Household expenses are eligible expenses under a dependent care assistance plan if some of the expenses are incurred to ensure a qualifying dependent's well-being and protection.

Household services are ordinary and usual services performed in and around the home that are necessary to run a home. They include the services of a housekeeper, maid, or cook; they do not include the services of a chauffeur, bartender, or gardener.

If a portion of an expense is work related (i.e., is for either household services or the care of a qualifying person) and another portion is for other purposes, only the portion that is work related counts as an eligible expense. The expense need not be divided, however, if only a small portion of it is for other purposes.

> **Example.** Mary Beth, an employee, pays a dependent care provider (Jan) to care for 9-year-old Sean and 15-year-old Libby so that Mary Beth can work. Jan spends most of the time doing normal household work and spends 30 minutes a day driving Mary Beth to and from work. Mary Beth may treat the entire amount paid to Jan as work related because the time spent driving is minimal. The amount does not have to be divided between the two children, because the expense is partly for the care of 9-year-old Sean, who is a qualifying person.

If a participant must pay for food consumed by the dependent care provider while the provider is working, that expense may be counted as work related. If the employee has extra expenses for a housekeeper's lodging, those expenses may also be counted as work related. [IRS Pub 503, Child and Dependent Care Expenses (2000)]

Q 9:10 What expenditures may not be reimbursed from a dependent care assistance account?

Expenditures that may not be reimbursed from a dependent care assistance account include the following:

- Babysitting needed to attend social events (not in order to be able to work)
- Educational expenses
- Charges for overnight camp
- Expenses that the participant will take as a child care tax credit on his or her income tax return

[See IRS Pub 503, Child and Dependent Care Expenses (2001).]

Q 9:11 What is the maximum dependent care assistance benefit available for a plan participant?

The IRS stipulates maximum dependent care assistance benefits based on a participant's tax year. In most cases, a participant's tax year is the calendar year. Therefore, the dependent care assistance maximum (most often $5,000 per year) is a calendar year maximum, even if the dependent care assistance plan operates on other than a calendar year.

The maximum aggregate dollar amount of excludable employer-provided dependent care assistance benefits under Code Section 129 is $5,000 ($2,500 if the participant is married and files a separate income tax return) but no more than the lesser of the earned income of the participant or his or her spouse (if applicable). [IRC § 129(a)(2), 129(b)]

A spouse who is incapacitated or who is a full-time student for at least five calendar months during the year is treated as having earned income of $200 per month if there is one qualifying dependent; the same individual is treated as having earned income of $400 per month if there are two or more qualifying dependents. [IRC §§ 21(d), 129(b)(2), 129(e)(2)]

> **Note.** It is easy to confuse the employer-provided dependent care assistance limit ($5,000 per year) with the newly increased tax credit limit for individual taxpayers ($3,000 or $6,000). These two types of taxpayer assistance are mutually exclusive.

Q 9:12 What constitutes acceptable claims substantiation for dependent care assistance reimbursement under a flexible spending account (FSA)?

Under Proposed Treasury Regulations Section 1.125-2, Q&A 7(b)(5) and 7(b)(8), a dependent care FSA may reimburse qualified dependent care expenses only if:

1. The participant provides a written statement signed by an independent third party confirming that the dependent care expense has been incurred and citing the amount of the expense; and
2. The participant provides a written statement that the expense has not been reimbursed or is not reimbursable under any other coverage.

Proof of expenses having been incurred is an important element of a dependent care FSA claim. A participant may not merely submit a contract for services at the beginning of the plan year and receive "automatic" reimbursement without additional evidence that services are in fact being incurred throughout the plan year (see Q 9:15).

> **Note.** A dependent care FSA may not make reimbursements in advance for projected expenses.

Q 9:13 What nondiscrimination rules must dependent care assistance programs satisfy?

A dependent care assistance program must satisfy four nondiscrimination tests under Code Section 129—an eligibility test, a contributions and benefits test, a 25 percent benefits test, and a 55 percent average benefits test as follows:

1. The plan must be available to a classification of employees that does not discriminate in favor of highly compensated employees or their dependents. An objective test provides a safe harbor, an unsafe harbor, and a facts-and-circumstances test for the evaluation of this requirement.
2. The contributions and benefits under the plan must not discriminate in favor of highly compensated employees.
3. No more than 25 percent of the amounts paid or incurred by the employer for dependent care assistance may be provided for 5 percent shareholders or owners (or their spouses or dependents). Unlike the medical reimbursement FSA nondiscrimination rules, this 25 percent concentration test must be applied separately to dependent care benefits.
4. The average benefits received by non-highly compensated employees must be at least 55 percent of the average benefits received by highly compensated employees. Average benefits include the "zero" benefit elected by those who do not participate in dependent care assistance. This test can be extremely difficult to pass with even one highly compensated participant.

In addition, dependent care flexible spending account contributions must be included in the Section 125 nondiscrimination testing (see chapter 14).

Q 9:14 Must an employee provide any information about the employee's dependent care service provider on his or her federal income tax return?

Yes. An employee must provide the name, address, and taxpayer identification number of the person performing dependent care services on his or her federal income tax return filed for the year in which the services were performed. If the service provider is a tax-exempt organization, its name and address must be provided on the employee's tax return. If the preceding information is not provided, the tax exclusion can be maintained if the employee demonstrates to the IRS that the employee exercised due diligence in trying to obtain the information. The employee may demonstrate the exercise of due diligence by furnishing a copy of the service provider's driver's license or Social Security card. [IRC §§ 21(e)(9),129(e)(9), 6109(a)(3)]

Q 9:15 If an employee who participates in a dependent care assistance account receives a contract from a day care provider indicating that a specified amount will be payable every month during the plan year, can such expense be reimbursed on a monthly basis even though the participant does not submit claims showing that services have been incurred?

No. The participant must provide a written statement from the dependent care provider stating that the dependent care expense has been incurred and citing the amount of such expense. The participant must also provide a written statement that the expense has not been reimbursed or is not reimbursable from any other source. [Prop Treas Reg § 1.125-2, Q 7(b)(5), Q 7(b)(8)]

Expenses reimbursed using a dependent care assistance account must be incurred during the participant's period of coverage under the assistance account. Expenses are treated as having been incurred when the participant is provided with the care that gives rise to the expenses—not when the participant is formally billed or charged or pays for the care. [Prop Treas Reg §§ 1.125-1, Q 17, 1.125-2, Q 7(b)(6)]

Note. One concern with automatically reimbursing, based on a beginning-of-the-year contract, is that there is no proof that the service has continued throughout the entire plan year.

Change in Status

Q 9:16 If a dependent becomes disabled during a plan year and therefore cannot continue to attend a qualified day care center, does that constitute a change in status for a dependent care assistance account, thereby permitting a change to the contribution rate by the participant?

Treasury Regulations Section 1.125-4(c)(2)(iv), effective for plan years beginning on or after January 1, 2002, states that events that cause an employee's dependent to satisfy or cease to satisfy eligibility requirements for coverage on account of attainment of age, student status, or any similar circumstance constitute change in status events. Severe disability that would affect eligibility to attend day care may qualify as a similar circumstance.

Q 9:17 Does a change made by a dependent care provider to the cost of providing services constitute a change in status for a dependent care assistance account, thereby permitting a change to the contribution rate by the participant?

Yes. According to Treasury Regulations Section 1.125-4(f)(2), effective for plan years beginning on or after January 1, 2002, if a dependent care provider significantly increases or decreases the cost of providing services, that would be a permitted change in status. Like all election changes, the new election for the remaining portion of the period must be attributable to and consistent with the change in status.

Q 9:18 Does a dependent care provider's cessation of business constitute a change in status for a dependent care assistance account?

Yes. According to Treasury Regulations Section 1.125-4(f)(3), effective for plan years beginning on or after January 1, 2002, if coverage under a dependent care FSA is significantly curtailed or ceases during a period of coverage, the plan may permit affected employees to revoke elections and make new elections on a prospective basis.

Form 5500

Q 9:19 Must a Form 5500 be filed for a dependent care assistance account?

No. The IRS removed the Form 5500 and Schedule F reporting requirement for Section 125 plans that do not have an ERISA component. Dependent care assistance plans are exempt from filing. See Appendix J for a copy of the IRS Announcement published in April 2002 removing the Form 5500 and Schedule F filing requirement.

Adoption Assistance Programs

Q 9:20 What may an employer offer through an adoption assistance program?

An adoption assistance program may be offered as a flexible spending account (FSA) through a cafeteria plan. It may also be an employer-sponsored and employer-funded plan outside of a cafeteria plan. An adoption assistance FSA may be funded by the employer, by the employee, or by both on a pretax basis. Through an adoption assistance program, employees may exclude from gross income reimbursements made for their expenses relating to adopting a child. [See IRC § 23(adoption expenses), and § 137(adoption assistance programs)]

Q 9:21 What are the requirements for an employer that sponsors an adoption assistance program?

An employer that sponsors an adoption assistance program must ensure that the following requirements are met:

1. The program must be described in a separate written plan of the employer;

2. Although the employer may establish eligibility rules, the plan may not favor highly compensated employees or their dependents (see Q 9:29);
3. The plan must be for the exclusive benefit of employees;
4. The plan may not pay more than 5 percent of its payments during the year for shareholders or owners (or their spouses or dependents). (A shareholder or owner is someone who owns—on any day of the year—more than 5 percent of the stock or of the capital or profits interest of the employer.) In a Section 125 plan, only shareholders in a C corporation may participate; that is, shareholders or owners in other types of companies such as S corporations, partnerships, and LLCs taxed as partnerships are excluded from participation; and
5. The employer must give reasonable notice of the plan to eligible employees.

Q 9:22 For which years may an adoption assistance reimbursement program be offered?

Employer-sponsored programs for reimbursement of qualifying adoption expenses have been available since January 1, 1997. These programs were scheduled to expire on December 31, 2001, but were extended and expanded by the Economic Growth and Tax Relief Reconciliation Act of 2001. New limits on adoption assistance benefits are effective for plan years beginning on or after January 1, 2002.

Q 9:23 What are qualifying adoption expenses?

Qualifying adoption expenses are reasonable and necessary adoption fees, court costs, attorneys' fees, traveling expenses (including amounts spent for meals and lodging while away from home), and other expenses directly related to, and whose principal purpose is for, the legal adoption of an eligible child. [IRC § 23(d)(1)]

Q 9:24 Who is an eligible adopted child?

For purposes of reimbursement of qualifying adoption expenses or the receipt of a tax credit (see Qs 9:30, 9:31), an eligible adopted child must be (1) under 18 years of age or (2) physically or mentally incapable of caring for himself or herself. [IRC § 23(d)(2)]

Q 9:25 Who is an eligible adopted child with special needs?

A child with special needs is defined by Code Section 23 (referred to in Code Section 137) as any child for whom:

1. A state has determined that the child cannot or should not be returned to the home of his parents;

2. Such state has determined that there exists with respect to the child a specific factor or condition such as his ethnic background, age, or membership in a minority or sibling group, or the presence of factors such as medical conditions or physical, mental, or emotional handicaps, because of which it is reasonable to conclude that such child cannot be placed with adoptive parents without providing adoption assistance; and
3. Citizenship or residence in the United States has been established.

Note. If a participant's state determined that the child being adopted was a child with special needs, the participant should keep evidence of that fact for his or her records. [IRC § 23(d)(3)]

Q 9:26 How much could an employee receive in adoption expense reimbursement for plan years beginning before January 1, 2002?

For plan years beginning before January 1, 2002, up to $5,000 per adopted child could be reimbursed to an employee for qualifying adoption expenses; for adopting a child with special needs, the maximum was $6,000. These limits applied per adopted child; they were not annual limits.

Note. The definition of a child with special needs changed in 2002.

These benefits were subject to an income limit. Beginning at an adjusted gross income (AGI) of $75,000, the maximum available benefit was reduced. The reduction continued until AGI reached $115,000, at which point no benefit remained.

The formula for determining the adoption expense benefit limit was set out in Code Section 137(b)(2). The amount excludable from gross income for any taxable year had to be reduced (but not below zero) by the amount that bore the same ratio to the amount so excludable as the amount (if any) by which the taxpayer's AGI exceeded $75,000 bore to $40,000.

Example. A participant has an AGI of $105,000 for 2001. The amount exceeding $75,000 is $30,000. The ratio of $30,000 to $40,000 is three-fourths. The participant's adoption expense reimbursement must be reduced by 75 percent. If the participant has qualified adoption expenses of $5,000, he is entitled to only $1,250 of excludable benefits.

The $5,000 (or $6,000) amount was the maximum amount of qualifying expenses taken into account over all taxable years for a given adopted child. Therefore, it had to be reduced by the amount of qualifying expenses taken into account in previous years for the same adoption effort.

Example. Alex is adopting Stephen, an eligible child who is not a child with special needs. Alex's qualifying adoption expenses, before he applies the dollar limit, are $1,000 for 1998 and $6,000 for 1999. The maximum amount of expenses Alex can take into account for the total adoption effort is $5,000. If Alex takes the $1,000 into account for 1998, the maximum amount of expenses he can take into account for 1999 must be reduced by the expenses he took into account for 1998. Therefore, Alex's maximum benefit for 1999 is $4,000 ($5,000 – $1,000).

Example. In 2001, Brenda adopts two sisters, Katherine and Valerie, neither of whom is a child with special needs. Brenda's qualifying adoption expenses, before she applies the dollar limit, are $7,500 for Katherine and $7,500 for Valerie. Under the dollar limit, the maximum amount of expenses Brenda can take into account for both adoptions is $10,000 ($5,000 for each child).

Example. In 2001, Carol pays $3,000 of qualifying adoption expenses in an effort to adopt an eligible child in the United States. The adoption is not successful. Carol then pays an additional $4,000 of qualifying adoption expenses for the successful domestic adoption of a different eligible child, Henry. For the dollar limit, Carol must treat the $7,000 of expenses as paid in one adoption effort. Thus, the maximum amount of expenses Carol can take into account is $5,000 ($6,000 if Henry is a child with special needs).

Q 9:27 How much may an employee receive in adoption expense reimbursement after 2001?

After 2001, up to $10,000 per adopted child may be reimbursed to an employee for qualifying adoption expenses. The limit applies per adopted child; it is not an annual limit.

In the case of adoption of a child with special needs, the adoption assistance benefit is $10,000, regardless of actual cost of adoption. [IRC § 137(a)(2)]

This benefit is subject to an income limit. Beginning at an AGI of $150,000, the maximum available benefit is reduced. The reduction continues until AGI reaches $190,000, at which point no benefit remains.

The formula for determining the adoption expense benefit limit is set out in Code Section 137(b)(2). The amount excludable from gross income for any taxable year must be reduced (but not below zero) by the amount that bears the same ratio to the amount so excludable as the amount (if any) by which the taxpayer's AGI exceeds $150,000 bears to $40,000.

Example. Jennifer, a participant in an adoption assistance plan, has an AGI of $180,000. The amount exceeding $150,000 is $30,000. The ratio of $30,000 to $40,000 is three-fourths. Jennifer's adoption expense reimbursement must be reduced by 75 percent. If Jennifer has qualified adoption expenses of $10,000, she is entitled to only $2,500 of excludable benefits.

The $10,000 amount is the maximum amount of qualifying expenses taken into account over all taxable years for a given adopted child. Therefore, it must be reduced by the amount of qualifying expenses taken into account in previous years for the same adoption effort.

Example. Alex is adopting Stephen. Alex's qualifying adoption expenses, before he applies the dollar limit, are $8,000 for 2002 and $6,000 for 2003. The maximum amount of expenses Alex can take into account for the total adoption effort is $10,000. If Alex takes the $8,000 into account for 2002, the maximum amount of expenses he can take into account for 2003 must be reduced by the expenses he took into account for 2002. Therefore, Alex's maximum benefit for 2003 is $2,000 ($10,000 – $8,000).

Example. Brenda adopts two sisters, Katherine and Valerie. Brenda's qualifying adoption expenses, before she applies the dollar limit, are $12,500 for Katherine and $12,500 for Valerie. Under the dollar limit, the maximum amount of expenses Brenda can take into account for both adoptions is $20,000 ($10,000 for each child).

Example. Carol pays $7,000 of qualifying adoption expenses in an effort to adopt an eligible child in the United States. The adoption is not successful. Carol then pays an additional $4,000 of qualifying adoption expenses for the successful domestic adoption of a different eligible child, Henry. For the dollar limit, Carol must treat the $11,000 of expenses as paid in one adoption effort. Thus, the maximum amount of expenses Carol can take into account is $10,000.

Q 9:28 What adoption-related expenses may not be reimbursed by an adoption assistance program?

Adoption-related expenses that are not qualifying adoption expenses (and thus may not be reimbursed) include those:

- That violate state or federal law
- For carrying out any surrogate parenting arrangement
- For the adoption of the participant's spouse's child
- Paid using funds received from any federal, state, or local program
- Allowed as a credit or deduction under any other federal income tax rule
- Paid or reimbursed by any other program

Q 9:29 What nondiscrimination requirements must an employer-sponsored adoption assistance program meet?

Employer-sponsored adoption assistance programs must meet an eligibility test and a concentration test.

Eligibility. An adoption assistance program must benefit employees who qualify under a classification set up by the employer that is not discriminatory in favor of employees who are highly compensated employees (within the meaning of Code Section 414(q)) or their dependents. Members of a collective bargaining unit may be excluded from the plan and the eligibility test if the adoption assistance program was the subject of good faith bargaining between the employer and employee representatives.

A highly compensated employee for 2002 is an employee who:

1. Was a 5 percent owner at any time during the current year or the preceding year; or
2. Received more than $85,000 in pay for the preceding year (2002 limit). This part of the definition may be further limited by imposing the requirement that the employee fall within the top 20 percent of employees ranked by pay for the preceding year.

Concentration. Shareholders or owners (or their spouses or dependents) may receive no more than 5 percent of all the adoption assistance reimbursements or expenses paid by the employer during the year. For this purpose, a shareholder or owner is someone who owns (on any day of the year) more than 5 percent of the stock or capital or profits interest of the employer. An adoption assistance program offered through a Section 125 plan may not include partners, sole proprietors, or shareholders of 2 percent or more of an S corporation.

Tax Implications

Q 9:30 Which taxes are avoided by employee contributions to an adoption assistance FSA?

Amounts paid into or received from an adoption assistance program are not subject to federal income tax withholding. Most (but not all) states follow the federal guidelines on income tax exclusion. It should be noted, however, that such amounts are subject to Social Security, Medicare, and federal unemployment taxes. That is a significant deviation from most other benefits in a Section 125 plan, including medical and dependent care FSAs.

Q 9:31 Is there any tax benefit available to adoptive parents for qualified adoption expenses other than the exclusion from income offered through an employer's plan?

Yes. From 1997 through 2001, a tax credit of up to $5,000 was available to adoptive parents for qualifying expenses paid to adopt an eligible child. The credit could be as much as $6,000 if the expenses were for the adoption of an eligible child with special needs. After 2001, the adoption tax credit is $10,000 for any qualifying adoption. The credit is an amount subtracted from a taxpayer's tax liability.

An employee who participates in an employer's adoption assistance program may be able to claim both a credit on his or her personal income tax return and an exclusion through the employer's adoption assistance program. For example, a plan participant who has at least $20,000 in qualifying expenses may be able to claim a tax credit of up to $10,000 and exclude up to $10,000 from his or her income through an employer-sponsored reimbursement plan. The participant cannot claim both a credit and an exclusion *for the same expense.*

Q 9:32 If an adoption effort spans more than one plan year, when may the participant take a credit or exclude adoption expenses from income?

When a participant may take an adoption credit or exclude adoption expenses from income depends on whether the eligible child is a citizen or resident of the United States (including U.S. possessions) at the time the adoption effort begins.

If the eligible child is a U.S. citizen or resident, a participant may take the adoption tax credit or exclude adoption expenses from income even if the adoption never becomes final. A participant in an adoption assistance FSA receives reimbursement of qualifying adoption expenses in the year in which the expenses are incurred.

If the eligible child is not a U.S. citizen or resident, the adoption assistance expenses may not be reimbursed until the adoption becomes final. That is, expenses relating to the adoption of a foreign child that are incurred in the year the adoption becomes final are submitted during the year they are incurred. Further, expenses incurred in the year after the adoption becomes final are submitted in the year they are incurred. Expenses incurred in the year before the adoption becomes final, however, are not eligible for reimbursement until the year in which the adoption becomes final. These rules differ significantly from other FSA rules.

Note. If a sponsoring employer makes adoption assistance reimbursements to a participant in a year before the adoption of a foreign child becomes final, the participant will be required to make an adjustment on his or her federal income tax return for the earlier year to include the payments in income. Then, on the participant's federal income tax return for the year the adoption becomes final, the participant can make an adjustment to take the exclusion. [See Instructions to Form 8839.]

Practice Pointer. An employer's communications materials must clearly outline the tax planning considerations for adoptions, especially for foreign adoptions.

Q 9:33 Must a participant take any special action regarding his or her personal income tax return if he or she receives reimbursement from an employer's adoption assistance plan?

Yes. When a participant receives an exclusion from income through an employer's adoption assistance plan (or earns a tax credit), the participant must file Form 8839 (Qualified Adoption Expenses).

A participant who is married must file a joint return to take the adoption credit or exclusion. A participant who is legally separated under a decree of divorce or separate maintenance, or who is living apart from his or her spouse for the last six months of the tax year, may take the exclusion on a separate return if the participant's home is the eligible child's home for more than half the year and the participant pays more than half the cost of keeping up the home for the year.

Adoption assistance payments made by the employer's plan will be shown in box 13 for Form W-2, identified with the letter "T." Those reimbursements will not be included in taxable wages of box 1. If any of the payments do not qualify for the exclusion, the participant will need to make an adjustment on his or her return to include non-excludable payments. [See Instructions to Form 8839.]

Reporting

Q 9:34 What are a sponsoring employer's reporting obligations for an adoption assistance program?

An employer that sponsors an adoption assistance program must report adoption expenses or reimbursements for each participant for the year in box 13 of the employee's Form W-2. Code "T" identifies the amount on the Form W-2. Also included in the amount are the totals for Social Security wages in box 3 and Medicare wages in box 5. Adoption benefits paid or reimbursed from pretax contributions made by the employee to a cafeteria plan should also be included, but adoption benefits forfeited from a cafeteria plan should not. Total benefits paid or reimbursed, including any benefits exceeding the $5,000/$6,000 exclusion for 2001, should be reported in box 13. (The exclusion beginning in 2002 is $10,000.) Adoption assistance contributions or reimbursements are not included in the participant's wages in box 1 of Form W-2. [See Instructions for Forms W-2 and W-3.]

Buying and Selling Vacation Time

Q 9:35 How can the purchase or sale of vacation paid time off be an element in a Section 125 cafeteria plan?

Included in the concept of flexible benefits is the buying or selling (or trading) of paid time off (PTO). A qualified benefit that may be offered in a Code Section 125 cafeteria plan is the purchase or sale of vacation days by participants. Sometimes, a participant may want to sell some accrued vacation time to increase the funds available for purchase of other benefits. Other times, a participant may want to forgo certain benefits in favor of purchasing additional vacation time—in some cases even contributing to the cost of vacation days from pay as a pretax deduction.

Q 9:36 What issues relate to the buying and selling of vacation days in a cafeteria plan?

A number of issues arise when an employer tries to blend paid time off (PTO) policies with a Section 125 cafeteria plan.

First, both the Internal Revenue Code (Code) and the Treasury regulations pertaining to Code Section 125 specify that only *vacation* time may be included as a benefit in a cafeteria plan. Other forms of PTO are not specified in the Code or the regulations as a permitted benefit in a cafeteria plan. Therefore, buying and selling of PTO within a cafeteria plan should be limited to, or defined as, vacation time.

Second, an employer may feel it risks losing control over aspects of a PTO policy that is tailored to satisfy the requirements of Code Section 125. Problems that typically arise when an employer ceases to control the taking of leave time include the following:

1. Too many employees wish to take time off concurrently, leaving too many positions unstaffed; and
2. Increased costs result from the need to bring in temporary workers to staff essential positions.

Practice Pointer. Companies must be prepared to modify PTO rules that prove unworkable within a flexible benefits framework. Still, certain challenges—such as making sure that positions are covered—can be met the same way they would be addressed under any circumstances. For instance, a company's policy might require that vacation of more than two days must be approved in advance.

A third issue is the cost of buying and selling vacation time. Whether an employer makes or loses money on such a transaction depends on who is buying, who is selling, and the exchange rate. If, for example, only executives are permitted to sell a week of vacation—and that week represents time that the executives never got to take off and was generally lost to them—then no matter what an executive is paid, the employer loses money. (In addition, this example demonstrates questionable plan design for other reasons!) In contrast, if an employee sells a week of vacation for a fair price and is consequently available to perform one additional week of service during the year, the employer will likely save money as a result of not having to pay overtime (because of the extra week of work that is now available) or because it will not be necessary to hire temporary help to replace the employee for a week.

An employee who sells PTO is being paid twice: wages for time now worked plus the money received for selling the vacation days. An employee who buys vacation time may appreciate that he or she was able to purchase additional time off. Such a buyer of time off may be able to perform the same amount of work in a year, even though he or she has taken an additional week away from the workplace.

Q 9:37 How is a typical paid time off program structured under a cafeteria plan?

Holidays, personal days, wellness days, and sick days—which may include a salary continuation program or a short-term disability program (or both)—are all examples of PTO. The only permitted PTO program under a Section 125 cafeteria plan includes either buying or selling vacation time (or both).

Adding vacation PTO options to a cafeteria plan may have particular appeal for employees with short service and those who have little accrued vacation or sick time. Also, employees from two-income households may find that the opportunity to take additional days during the course of their year presents an attractive benefit to purchase with their flexible benefits credits. Senior employees may wish to purchase additional leave time before retirement.

Practice Pointer. If a plan is designed such that the employer is buying vacation days at one price and selling them at another, higher price, the employer should be prepared to explain to employees that the price differential is governed by adverse selection. Otherwise, employees may find the difference in pricing to be unfair. Of course, a cafeteria plan that prices the purchase and sale of vacation days at the same relative rate has no employee relations concern in such instance.

Q 9:38 How are buy-and-sell choices for paid time off designed under a cafeteria plan?

Specific design issues for a vacation PTO program within a Section 125 cafeteria plan revolve around the amount of time an employee may buy or sell within the program (usually a number of days or a week at a time) and the price of the time off.

A typical limit on a vacation time option may be a five-day unit to be purchased at a set price. There is a trend to cap the amount of days to be bought and sold to a manageable number that will not unfavorably impact business requirements. Furthermore, the privilege of buying may be limited to those whose vacation time is no more than a stated number of weeks.

Many employers allow vacation days to be sold only if deemed to be extra days; that is, above a minimum vacation the employer requires every employee to take. Minimum vacations, it may be noted, are often required for an employee's general health or as a type of accounting control (i.e., to see what happens when the employee is away).

It is important to note that the plan must be designed to satisfy rules imposed by the Internal Revenue Service (IRS) that require that nonelective (i.e., employer-provided) vacation days be taken before any elective (purchased) vacation.

The price for selling vacation days can be set lower than the price for buying vacation days. That is done in an effort to dissuade highly compensated employees from selling a day or two of vacation and in that way buying out the entire benefits package. On the other hand, the buying price might be kept low so that non-highly compensated employees could afford to buy additional vacation.

Another consideration for the employer centers on accounting issues. Should the proceeds from buying vacation days be credited to reduce salary costs or be credited against the cost of the cafeteria plan? Similarly, should the selling costs be charged to payroll or debited to the cafeteria plan? Practices vary and may be affected by whether the plan is being used here as a cash-out or cash-in vehicle.

Practice Pointer. An employer must always be aware of and comply with any state laws regarding the vesting of vacation accruals.

Q 9:39 Are there any restrictions on a paid time off program?

Employers should not include sick leave programs, leaves of absence, and any PTO programs other than vacation as part of a Section 125 plan (i.e., cafeteria plan).

Q 9:40 How may controls be imposed on a PTO program within a cafeteria plan?

One of the problems associated with the option to buy and sell vacation days is that uncontrolled usage could prove detrimental to an employer's functioning. Thus, a Section 125 cafeteria plan must protect against unexpected costs through conservative pricing and design controls.

Controls similar to those in a nonflexible environment may be incorporated into a cafeteria plan, including the following:

1. Limiting the number of vacation days that may be bought or sold to five or fewer days each year;
2. Allowing an election only in alternate years;
3. Requiring the proceeds of the sale to be invested in other benefits on the benefit menu or to be discounted if the employee wants to exchange the benefit for cash; and
4. Imposing a maximum price on the sale of vacation time.

Example. Smith Consulting Group permits employees to sell five days of vacation at 1.8 percent of pay up to a maximum payment of $630 per week. As a result, employees who are paid $35,000 or less receive the full 1.8 percent, but employees who earn in excess of $35,000 do not. The more an employee earns in excess of $35,000, the more uneven the exchange becomes. Hillary, an employee of Smith Consulting Group, earns $80,000. Her vacation time is therefore valued at over $1,400 ($80,000 × 1.8%). Hillary can receive no more than the maximum of $630, or approximately 0.8 percent.

Q 9:41 May vacation days be carried forward under a cafeteria plan?

Under Section 125 cafeteria plan rules, the use of vacation time purchased within the plan beyond the flexible benefit plan year is prohibited. There is no such restriction, however, on unused regular (i.e., employer-provided non-elective) vacation time.

To avoid the possibility of carrying forward either elective days (i.e., all the days in excess of a minimum and over which the employee may exercise some choice) or nonelective days (i.e., those provided under the general employment provisions), most companies encourage employees to use all vacation days in the current year. IRS rules seem to require such an approach.

Purchased vacation days can be used only after nonelective vacation days are used and must be used in the year for which they were elected. When vacation days are sold, a plan may permit those days to be repurchased in the following year.

To avoid loss of unused vacation time, some employers will cash out any unused elective days before the end of the year. By doing so, employees are not in the position of having been allowed to defer compensation to a subsequent year. [Treas Reg § 1.125-2, Q&A 5(c)(3)]

Other employers prefer not to become involved with cash-outs because they tend to be an end-of-year problem, creating difficulties with payroll. The remedy within a Section 125 plan is to consider any elective vacation time not taken by year-end as forfeited.

Q 9:42 What is vacation trading?

Some benefit plans broaden the concept of vacation buying and selling to include transfers of vacation time between employees; that is, vacation trading. *Vacation trading, as defined here, is not permitted under a Section 125 plan.* The IRS has clarified the tax status of donor and donee in instances where employees transfer unused vacation time to other employees or to a leave bank from which employees with emergencies may draw supplemental leave time. [Rev Rul 90-29, 1990-15 IRB 5] Amounts paid to an employee under such a leave-sharing plan are treated as compensation received from the employer and are therefore taxable. Employees who surrender leave to the employer or to the leave bank realize no income either on the occasion of the surrender or at the time it is used by the other worker.

Employee Participation

Q 9:43 Which employees tend to be most interested in buying additional vacation time under a Section 125 cafeteria plan?

Buying vacation time under a Section 125 cafeteria plan tends to appeal to the following types of employees:

1. New hires who have relatively few years of work with the employer may want additional vacation time, especially in their first year, because

vacation allotments tend to be graded and linked to an employee's years of service.

2. Employees who have working spouses may be willing to opt out of other coverages (e.g., medical coverage) because such coverage can be obtained through the spouse's employer. Such employees can then use the opt-out amount provided by the employer to purchase additional vacation time. Often, employees value the ability to match, as much as possible, the vacation time available to their spouse and children. An employee who has two weeks of vacation compared to a spouse's three or four weeks now has a way to match his or her spouse's time off.

3. Younger, lower-paid employees who may find it easier to leave work and take vacation time, resulting in a greater desire for additional vacation time off.

4. Older employees who may desire to make less of a commitment to work and who may have the economic resources to enjoy more vacation time off.

Practice Pointer. It is important to identify which types of employees may elect to buy additional time off in an organization because the purchase price tag of buying an additional vacation day must be based on who is the likely purchaser, which, in turn, defines possible adverse selection.

Q 9:44 Which employees tend to be most interested in selling vacation time under a cafeteria plan?

Selling vacation time under a Section 125 cafeteria plan tends to appeal to the following types of employees:

1. Employees with more years of service who typically have more vacation time available to them. If they also have greater job responsibilities, they may not be able to take all the available time and may even have to forfeit days that cannot be carried over from one year to the next because of the use-it-or-lose-it rule implemented by many employers. Selling days that they would not necessarily use thus becomes appealing to such employees because they would not be penalized for being responsive to job demands.

2. More highly paid employees who wish to spend the opt-out credits on coverage for other relatively expensive benefits (either pretax or after-tax) available through a flexible benefit plan, such as supplementary life insurance coverage or high levels of long-term disability coverage.

State Laws

Q 9:45 May state laws affect flexible paid time off plans?

Yes. Some states have recently passed legislation regarding employee pay for accrued vacation time. California, for example, is one state that treats vacation time as a form of wages that must be cashed out during the course of a year. In addition, in California any unused vacation at the time of termination must be paid to the employee.

Practice Pointer. It is advisable to check with legal counsel regarding any state provisions regarding vacation time.

Chapter 10

Cash and 401(k) Deferrals

Implied in every Section 125 plan transaction is the choice between "cash" and "benefits." Even the most basic premium conversion plan, offering only the opportunity to pay for premiums on a pretax basis, includes an implied "cash" alternative. This chapter will explain how this sometimes confusing concept works.

Also permitted in a Section 125 plan is the opportunity to defer compensation to a 401(k) plan. When such a feature is offered in a Section 125 plan, it is most often because participants are permitted to reduce other benefits to their cash value, and then convert that value to a 401(k) deferral. This chapter will explore the rules pertaining to cash and 401(k) deferrals within a Section 125 cafeteria plan.

Cash as a Plan Benefit

Q 10:1 Why is "cash" always an element in a Section 125 cafeteria plan?

The very definition of a cafeteria plan in Code Section 125(d) states that a cafeteria plan is a plan under which participants may choose among two or more benefits consisting of cash and qualified benefits. [IRC § 125(d)(1)(B)]

The choice offered to participants is a choice between cash (or a "cash equivalent") or benefits on a tax-preferred basis. A plan that offers choice merely between two or more tax-preferred benefits is not required to be offered to participants within the protection of a Section 125 plan (see Chapter 4). For example, a plan that offers employees fully employer paid health insurance, with a choice between various PPO and HMO options, is not required to be offered within a Section 125 plan. However, if employees must contribute from pay toward the cost of benefits, the only way to do so on a pretax basis is under a Section 125 plan.

Q 10:2 Is a Section 125 cafeteria plan *required* to offer a "cash" benefits allowance for purchase of benefits?

The short answer is "no." This can be a point of some confusion. A cafeteria plan is not required to offer a benefits allowance, per se. However, a cafeteria plan does, by definition, have a cash option. The following examples help illustrate the difference:

Example. Bob offers his employees health insurance. Employees are required to pay a contribution from pay toward the cost of the health insurance premium. Employees have the following options:

a. To be covered by a health plan, and pay the contribution on a pretax basis;

b. To be covered by a health plan, and pay the contribution on an after-tax basis; or

c. Reject coverage, and take full compensation—not reduced by health insurance contributions.

Option (a) above can be offered only within a Section 125 cafeteria plan. Under options (b) and (c), the choice the participant is electing is "cash." With option (b), the participant elects to receive cash as taxable income, and then pays the insurance premium contribution on an after-tax basis. With option (c), the participant elects to receive cash as taxable income, and rejects coverage by the health insurance plan.

Options (b) and (c) do not require a cafeteria plan. However, any cafeteria plan has a "cash" option, such as (b) and (c), within it.

Example. Hollyhock Nursery offers employees health insurance. Employees who elect single coverage pay $50 per month toward the cost of premium, and those who elect the family level of coverage pay $125 per month. Employees may pay this premium on a pretax basis through a Section 125 plan, or on an after-tax basis.

Nancy has a need for single coverage. Nancy's base pay (before any reductions) is $2,000 per month. Nancy may elect to pay the $50 per month premium contribution before taxes are calculated, or afterwards. Nancy elects to pay the $50 contribution on a pretax basis. Therefore, her taxable income will become $1,950. The $50 contribution will be removed from pay before certain taxes are calculated.

Maria wishes to elect family coverage. On the advice of her accountant, Maria elects to pay toward coverage with after-tax dollars. (Note: There are very few reasons that an informed individual would elect to pay for qualified benefits with aftertax dollars when pretax payment is an available choice.)

Maria's base pay before any reductions is $2,000 per month. Maria is taxed on the $2,000, and then makes her premium contribution of $150. In this scenario, Maria is considered to have chosen the cash option. She has permitted her entire pay to be considered taxable income. After taxation, Maria chooses to pay premiums, but for Section 125 plan purposes, she has chosen the cash option within the plan.

Alan does not require health insurance coverage, as he is covered through his spouse. Alan's base monthly pay is $2,000. Alan will be taxed on the $2,000, and receive the remainder as cash. Because Alan did not choose pretax premium contribution toward health insurance, he has chosen the "cash" option within the plan.

Q 10:3 What is a "cash allowance" or "benefits allowance"?

Although not a requirement of a Section 125 plan, it is possible for the plan sponsor to state a specific dollar amount "benefits allowance" to be used toward the cost of benefits. The benefits allowance is offered to employees on a nondiscriminatory basis. The allowance is used toward the cost of benefits within the plan. Any unspent amounts are often converted to cash (taxable income), sometimes at discounted value.

If a plan offers benefits that may be paid on an after-tax basis (for example, long term disability coverage), a benefits allowance amount might first convert to taxable income and, after reduction by taxes, be used toward the cost of the benefit.

Offering a benefits allowance toward the purchase of benefits can provide employees with more choice as to how to allocate their total compensation.

Example. Sperry Foods provides employees a flexible benefits plan under Code Section 125, with a benefits allowance amounting to $190 per month, and a menu of options from which to choose. Employees may elect single health insurance at its full cost of $187 per month, or family coverage at $400 per month. They may also elect dental coverage at $30 per month for single, or $65 per month for family coverage. This plan also includes a medical reimbursement account and a dependent care flexible spending account (FSA). Any cash that is unspent can be deferred to the 401(k) plan at full value, or taken as taxable income at 50% of its value within the plan.

Ben elects to be covered by the single health insurance coverage. Because he has $3 per month still unallocated, Ben assigns that amount to his medical reimbursement account. His take-home pay is not reduced for benefits. He used the benefits allowance toward all of his benefits.

Jessica has health insurance coverage through a spouse. She elects to participate in the dependent care FSA, and elects coverage of $400 per month. Jessica's election will be partially funded by the $190 monthly allowance offered by the company. An additional $210 will be deducted from her monthly pay on a pretax basis.

Dan does not wish to be covered by any of the benefits offered. However, after some consideration, Dan determines that placing the full value of $190 per month in his 401(k) plan is better than taking one-half of his allowance as taxable income. Therefore, Dan defers the $190 monthly allowance to his 401(k) plan.

Kate likewise does not wish to be covered by any of the benefits offered, including the 401(k) plan. Kate will be receiving the discounted value of the benefits allowance as taxable income. The allowance that had been $190 per month within the plan will now show up in Kate's pay as approximately $50–$70 in after-tax income. Often, choosing after-tax income is not the best financial decision if any of the tax-preferred choices within the plan are useful or desirable.

When a participant chooses to convert all or a portion of the company provided benefits allowance to taxable income—or to defer it to the 401(k) plan —the employer must be aware of the fact that the employer provided benefits allowance has become taxable income for payroll taxes, including FICA tax, state and federal unemployment tax, and possibly others.

401(k) Plan Deferrals

Q 10:4 How does a Code Section 125 treat 401(k) plan deferrals?

Internal Revenue Code Section 125 and the related regulations do not permit a cafeteria plan to operate in a manner that enables employees to defer the receipt of compensation to a future plan year. A plan that permits employees to carry over unused benefits or contributions beyond the plan year will generally not qualify as a cafeteria plan under Code Section 125. There is, however, a significant exception to that rule: employee deferrals to a 401(k) plan may be made through a cafeteria plan, even though the benefit is typically received in a future plan year.

Furthermore, while cafeteria plans are required to be very restrictive regarding when and for what reason participants may change an election during the plan year, deferral levels under a 401(k) plan may be changed during the plan year in accordance with the 401(k) plan document.

Q 10:5 How does a Section 401(k) cash or deferred arrangement work in the context of a cafeteria plan?

In a cafeteria plan an employee may select among various tax-free benefit alternatives, including health care, a limited amount of life insurance, and long-term disability insurance, or may elect to take flexible benefits dollars in the form of a taxable benefit such as cash. In addition, a cafeteria plan may offer one type of tax-deferred benefit through a 401(k) retirement plan. In many respects the 401(k) option does not differ from any other tax-qualified benefit option under a cafeteria plan.

Before a plan year begins, an employee may elect to allocate a certain amount of flexible benefits dollars (contributed by the employer) or a certain amount of the employee's salary reduction dollars to a 401(k) plan. (Alternatively, the employee may elect to spend these funds on other available benefits or take cash.) By choosing a 401(k) option, however, the employee defers tax on the money contributed under the plan. From the standpoint of taxation, when an employee defers money into a 401(k) plan it does not matter whether the contribution is made under a cafeteria plan or directly to a stand-alone 401(k) plan. It is important, however, for a cafeteria plan sponsor to assign tax avoidance correctly to various benefits in the plan. Most notably, a plan participant's pay must be taxed for Social Security and Medicare before the 401(k) deferral is made. This is different from the tax treatment of most other benefits under a cafeteria plan.

Under a stand-alone 401(k) plan, an employee may not need to reelect to participate each year—the plan document is often written to permit the election to continue in force unless it is amended by the plan participant. In contrast, the 401(k) option under a cafeteria plan often requires a new election each year, principally because the 401(k) plan is only one of a number of options receiving annual reconsideration.

> **Practice Pointer.** It is possible to design a cafeteria plan so that certain options (including the 401(k) option) remain in effect from year to year. Under a plan with such a "default" provision, a participant who wants to make a change to an election needs to actively elect to make that change before the beginning of the plan year.

Q 10:6 How does incorporating a 401(k) option into a cafeteria plan compare with maintaining a separate 401(k) plan?

The primary design advantage of offering a 401(k) option through a cafeteria plan is that doing so enables employees to make direct exchanges between group health and welfare benefits and retirement benefits. An employer can bundle the retirement, group health and welfare, and cash compensation options together and package them all in a single, well-constructed total compensation program presented as a cafeteria plan. The added advantage to the employer of presenting the entire benefits package as one program is increased efficiency, ease of communications, and possibly decreased cost.

The primary disadvantage of presenting a 401(k) option under a cafeteria plan is the resulting administrative complexity. For example, the nondiscrimination testing requirements of a cafeteria plan do not dovetail with the 401(k) plan election requirements or discrimination rules. If nondiscrimination testing reveals that a cafeteria plan has violated the nondiscrimination rules, it is not entirely clear whether highly compensated employees (HCEs) must then change their salary reduction contributions to the 401(k) plan or whether the 401(k) plan is tainted by the failure of the cafeteria plan to meet the nondiscrimination rules.

Another example of the administrative complexity is that taxes imposed under the Federal Insurance Contributions Act (FICA) are treated differently under a cafeteria plan than under a 401(k) plan: FICA taxes must be paid on salary reduction dollars put into a 401(k) plan, but not on salary reduction dollars used for tax-preferred welfare and fringe benefit plans. The employer that entertains the idea of introducing a 401(k) option under a cafeteria plan must have the administrative capacity to track every dollar of salary reduction to every employee's selected deferral. The systems in place must prioritize when dollars are spent so that FICA taxation is consistently handled for all employees. To reduce FICA liability, the systems need to specify that expenses for health and welfare benefits are deducted first and 401(k) deferrals last. These calculations can be further complicated by specific taxation requirements of certain localities. Some municipal governments require that local tax be calculated on an employee's "base" pay, before any deductions or contributions (see Appendix A).

Example. Lieder Inc. offers participants a monthly equivalent of $250 to spend on benefits in its cafeteria plan. Melody decides to purchase health insurance at a cost of $300; she also wants to put $100 per month into her 401(k) plan. In addition to Lieder's benefits credit of $250, Melody will be spending some of her pay on a pretax basis for benefits. Frank has health insurance coverage elsewhere. He therefore elects to make a contribution of $250 per month to his 401(k) plan using the benefits credit provided by Lieder.

If the cafeteria plan and its administrative procedures are set up so that non-FICA taxable payments are deducted first, Melody and Frank would see the following effects:

1. Melody's $250 monthly benefits credit would be used entirely to help fund her health insurance premium contribution. She would have an additional $50 taken from her pay on a pretax basis for the remainder of the health insurance contribution and $100 taken for her 401(k) deferral before federal and state taxes but not before FICA tax.
2. Frank's $250 benefits credit is used to fund his 401(k) plan. First, the $250 credit must be taxed for FICA—both the employee and employer portions of FICA. Then, the $250 may be used to fund the 401(k) plan before state and federal taxes are calculated and deducted.

Generally, an employer would not want to set up a procedure under which 401(k) contributions are deducted first, that is, before health and welfare benefits. Such a procedure would cause both the employee and employer to pay more in FICA tax than they would when health and welfare benefits are deducted from pay first.

Example. The facts are the same as those in the preceding example, except that 401(k) contributions are considered first in the payroll process. Melody's

$250 benefits credit would be spent first on her 401(k) plan. Because Melody elected to contribute only $100 per month to the 401(k) plan, $100 of her benefits credit becomes taxable for FICA. The remaining $150 of the benefits credit can be used to offset Melody's $300 health plan contribution. Any amount not paid by the benefits credit is taken from Melody's pay on a pretax basis.

The different outcomes illustrated in the two examples above—one using employer contributions first for health and welfare benefits, the other using employer contributions first for 401(k) contributions—are significant. The timing and order of contributions can make a difference of $7.65 per month for both Melody and Lieder, amounting to over $90 per year in FICA tax for each. Depending on the number of employees at issue and the total contributions to a 401(k) plan made through a cafeteria plan, the amount of FICA tax that can be avoided merely by changing the order in which benefit dollars are processed can be large.

Q 10:7 Should an employer that offers a 401(k) option under a cafeteria plan also permit contributions to be made separately to its 401(k) plan?

Yes. Because of the complexities of administration and compliance, most employers will want to retain the stand-alone status of their 401(k) plans, even if the option to defer to a 401(k) plan is also offered as a cafeteria plan option (see Q 10:6). Employers will want to have the option for deferrals directly to the 401(k) plan, in addition to participation through the cafeteria plan.

An employer may choose to communicate the appearance of a unified program when a 401(k) plan and a cafeteria plan are, in reality, separately administered. If an employer uses a communications campaign to forge a link between a 401(k) plan and a cafeteria plan, in the minds of its employees the employer may be seen as offering a single benefits package. In such a manner, the employer avoids the administrative concerns of combining the 401(k) plan and the cafeteria plan by, in reality, running two parallel programs.

Q 10:8 How can the addition of a 401(k) option help an employer satisfy its objectives for a cafeteria plan?

The addition of a 401(k) plan as an option under a cafeteria plan encourages employees to set aside savings for retirement. That can reduce pressures for retiree health benefits and pension benefits. Although the same objective may be accomplished through a 401(k) plan without making it part of a cafeteria plan, the existence of a cafeteria plan—and the communications efforts that usually accompany it—tend to increase employees' interest in saving for retirement through the 401(k) plan and thus increase the total amount of funds deferred under the 401(k) plan.

Further, the offer of a 401(k) plan as a cafeteria plan option can help advertise and sell the cafeteria plan. Employees appreciate 401(k) plans, and that positive regard can carry over to the cafeteria plan. A 401(k) plan also supports several of the main themes associated with cafeteria plans: tax-efficient benefits; employee responsibility and partnership; and choice.

Q 10:9 How does an employer offer a matching 401(k) contribution under a cafeteria plan?

Neither a stand-alone 401(k) plan nor a 401(k) option under a cafeteria plan is required to contain any provision for a matching contribution by the employer. Nevertheless, the vast majority of 401(k) plans have provisions allowing for employer matching contributions, in part because matching contributions encourage employees to participate. Such matching formulas range from a matching amount equal to 25 percent of the employee deferral to an amount equaling 100 percent of the employee deferral or more.

The employer match is typically based on the employee deferral, and is usually capped at some dollar amount or at some percentage of the employee's contribution. Even if a stand-alone 401(k) plan contains a provision for matching contributions through regular deferrals to the 401(k) plan, the employer is not required to offer a match on a 401(k) contribution made through a cafeteria plan's 401(k) option.

Under no circumstance may an employer use benefits credits, offered to all eligible employees under a cafeteria plan, as the source for matching contributions to a 401(k) plan. Benefits credits are made available to employees to choose among qualified options. In other words, although an employer may choose to match 401(k) deferrals, it may not require that a portion of the allocated benefits credit be spent to make that matching contribution.

Q 10:10 Should an employer incorporate a profit sharing contribution feature incorporate under its cafeteria plan's 401(k) option?

It is generally not advisable to incorporate a profit sharing contribution feature in a cafeteria plan; for a stand-alone retirement plan, such a feature is common. Employers may choose to award an extra employer contribution under a stand-alone 401(k) plan because of exceptional company performance. In a stand-alone 401(k) plan, a plan sponsor might have the option (based on the plan design and document) to determine annually (or more frequently) whether a profit sharing contribution is warranted and what the amount of such a contribution should be. It would be unusual, however, to make a profit sharing contribution only to the 401(k) option of the cafeteria plan. A more likely scenario is for the employer to make its profit sharing contribution to the entire flexible benefits plan so that plan participants can use the funds to buy any of the benefits provided for under the cafeteria plan, not just 401(k) benefits.

Q 10:11 May an employee change his or her 401(k) elections during the plan year?

It depends on the cafeteria plan document and 401(k) plan document. In general, employees must make their benefit elections under a cafeteria plan upon eligibility or before the beginning of a plan year. The only provision for changing elections during the plan year applies to a qualified change in status (see chapter 15). Participants in a 401(k) plan, however, may be permitted to make changes during the plan year. Further, Treasury Regulations Section 1.125-4(h) states that a cafeteria plan may permit an employee to modify or revoke elections in accordance with Sections 401(k) and 401(m) of the Internal Revenue Code (Code) and the regulations thereunder. An employee may only make participation changes that are permitted by the 401(k) plan document.

Q 10:12 May an employee divert contributions that might otherwise have gone into a 401(k) plan to defray the employee's portion of increased health care costs?

Yes, if the cafeteria plan has a 401(k) deferral option. The reason for linking a 401(k) plan to a cafeteria plan is to allow employees the opportunity to divert deferrals from a 401(k) plan to other benefits, including healthcare benefits, or vice versa. As in other cafeteria plan trade-offs, the employee is given the option of reducing one benefit to pay for inflation in another. Alternatives are an inherent part of flexible compensation.

Of course, even if the cafeteria plan is not linked directly to the employer's 401(k) plan, there is a way for employees to "divert" 401(k) contributions to other tax-preferred benefits. The employee would merely defer less to the 401(k) plan and contribute more on a pretax basis to the cafeteria plan.

Example. Charles has determined that his health insurance premium contribution will soon increase by $100 per month. Charles could opt to decrease his 401(k) deferral in order to have the funds to pay for the health insurance increase—even if the cafeteria plan and 401(k) plan are not linked. Incidentally, because Charles is trading 401(k) dollars for tax-preferred health and welfare benefits, his pay may increase slightly. He will not be paying FICA tax of $7.65 on the $100 monthly deferral to the cafeteria plan. On the other hand, 401(k) deferrals are FICA taxable.

Q 10:13 May a 401(k) option be used in lieu of allowing employees to take their unused flexible benefits as cash?

Some plan sponsors want to eliminate taxable income ("cash") as an option when a plan offers employer-provided benefits credits. Plans have been drafted to permit unallocated benefits credits to be diverted to a 401(k) plan rather than converted to cash. The Internal Revenue Service (IRS) has taken a position in Private Letter Ruling 9635002 that a 401(k) plan is a qualified, nontaxable benefit and should not be viewed as a cash equivalent benefit. In the facts given for the letter ruling, employees could choose among vacation time, a contribution to a 401(k) plan, or forfeiture of vacation time. The IRS stated that there was no constructive receipt in part because the employees' election choices did not include cash or a cash equivalent. Although a letter ruling issued to another plan sponsor cannot be relied upon by anyone other than the addressee to support a particular action or interpretation, knowing how the IRS responds to a certain set of facts and circumstances provides a better understanding of how it views certain issues. In this instance, neither vacation time nor a contribution to a 401(k) plan was viewed as cash.

The true purpose of this answer is to discuss the plan design practice of channeling unused cafeteria plan credits directly into a 401(k) plan and to consider its legality. For some time now, some cafeteria plan sponsors have used a design feature that automatically rolls unused employer credits into a 401(k) option. The practice is used when a plan sponsor does not want to offer the option to receive taxable income from unused benefit allowances or credits. By having unused flexible benefit allowancess flow directly into the 401(k) option, the plan sponsor has a palatable default option that produces two possible side benefits: (1) such moneys, once they are diverted to the 401(k) plan, are used to assist the 401(k) plan to meet its nondiscrimination tests, and (2) the practice clearly helps employees to save for their retirement.

There are basically two viewpoints regarding such a practice:

1. It can be done, and the moneys that are rolled over to the 401(k) plan should be viewed as nonelective employer contributions.
2. It cannot be done.

Clearly, the more defensible position is the more conservative one: that is, it cannot be done. The facts underlying the conservative viewpoint follow:

Fact 1. Code Section 125(d)(2)(B) will allow a deferred compensation arrangement, which is generally not permitted in a cafeteria plan, provided it includes a cash or deferred arrangement (CODA) (as defined in Code Section 401(k)(2)) to the extent that a covered employee may elect to have the employer pay such contributions to the 401(k) trust.

Fact 2. Code Section 401(k)(2) states that a qualified CODA is a CODA under which an employee may elect to have the plan sponsor make contributions directly to the 401(k) plan as deferred compensation or to the employee directly in cash.

Fact 3. Treasury Regulations Section 1.401(k)-1(a)(3) clearly states that a CODA is any election by an employee to have the employer either (1) provide an amount to the employee in the form of cash *or some other taxable benefit* that is not currently available or (2) contribute an amount to a 401(k) plan that defers the receipt of compensation. In the case at hand, however, the default contribution is really an employee election between a cash equivalent benefit and a 401(k) deferral. That situation is described elsewhere in Treasury Regulations Section 1.401(k)-1, which states that for a plan to meet the requirements of a CODA, it must satisfy the following additional condition: The amount that employees are allowed to defer as an elective contribution under a qualified CODA must be available to the employees in cash. Furthermore, if an eligible employee is given an option to receive a taxable benefit other than cash or have the employer contribute, on the employee's behalf, an amount equal to the value of the taxable benefit, the arrangement is not a qualified CODA. [Treas Reg § 1.401(k)-1(e)(2)] That portion of the Treasury Regulation ends by indicating that the cash availability requirement applies even if the CODA is part of a cafeteria plan within the meaning of Code Section 125.

The argument against the practice of directing unused credits to a 401(k) plan in effect takes the position that when the cafeteria plan regulations are combined with the Section 401(k) regulations, cafeteria plan sponsors do not appear to have the latitude to roll unused employer credits *directly* to a 401(k) plan. Employees would need to have a cash option for there to be a bona fide employee election; a cash equivalent option does not appear to satisfy the Section 401(k) regulations associated with employee elective contributions.

The argument just set forth is difficult to refute—except that it presumes that a default or flexible benefits rollover contribution is an employee elective contribution. Why the focus on employee elective contributions? As already noted, cafeteria plans do not permit deferred compensation arrangements generally, but do permit 401(k) plan deferrals. In turn, retirement plans with a 401(k) option may permit several types of contributions, including the following:

- Employee elective contributions;
- After-tax employee elective contributions;
- Matching employer contributions based on employee elective contributions; and
- Employer contributions (other than elective contributions).

Employee elective contributions are discussed further in the cafeteria plan regulations, which offer the following two more important facts relating to permissible types of 401(k) contributions in a cafeteria plan:

1. Proposed Treasury Regulations Section 1.125-1, Q&A 7, states that employer contributions made at the participant's election to a profit sharing plan containing a qualified CODA (as defined in Code Section 401(k)) will be treated as nontaxable benefits.
2. Proposed Treasury Regulations Section 1.125-2, Q&A 4(c), indicates that (1) elective contributions to a qualified CODA, (2) after-tax employee contributions, subject to Section 401(m) testing, under a qualified plan, and (3) employer matching contributions that are made with respect to elective or after-tax employee contributions are *each* specifically permitted under a cafeteria plan.

The three contribution types set forth in item two above are permissible exceptions to the general cafeteria plan rule that says a cafeteria plan may not include benefits that defer the receipt of compensation. [Prop Treas Reg § 1.125-2, Q&A 5(b)]

Thus, an employer wanting to take the more aggressive stance in support of the position that rollover flexible benefits contributions are nonelective employer contributions must be willing to make the following arguments:

1. It is clear that a 401(k) plan can receive nonelective employer contributions under Treasury Regulations Section 1.401(k)-1(g)(10).
2. Even though nonelective employer contributions are not specifically identified as a permissible contribution, they are also not specifically listed as an impermissible contribution. It should be noted that the cafeteria plan regulations provide a list of other benefits that are specifically excluded from a Section 125 plan.
3. Proposed Treasury Regulations Section 1.125-2, Q&A 5(b), focuses on contributions arising from employee elections because the IRS is most concerned with employees being able to "manipulate" their tax burdens between periods of time. In the case of nonelective employer contributions, the employee has no ability to control the timing of taxes paid because he or she has no election opportunity.

Note. It is difficult to imagine that the IRS intended to have two classes of 401(k) plans—one that permits a nonelective employer contribution and one that does not.

Based on the arguments presented above, some practitioners are prepared to contend that as long as there is no employer 401(k) or cash election in the cafeteria plan (i.e., there is a series of options such as medical, life insurance, group legal, dental, and long-term disability, but no 401(k) or cash option) and the plan mandates that any flexible benefits credits not spent on medical, life insurance, group legal, dental, or long-term disability will go into the 401(k) plan as a nonelective employer contribution, the automatic rollover is permissible.

This discussion is made even more complex by having a 401(k) option in the array of benefits being offered but not having a cash option for unused flexible benefits credits.

The enrollment form (see example below) is somewhat problematic. An employee who spends $700 on B1 through B5 will have a salary reduction of $400 ($700 - $300), and there truly will be a cash option in the program. Yet an employee who spends only $200 of benefits credits on B1 through B4 and is forced by design to put the remaining $100 of credits into B5 will not have had a "cash" alternative in the cafeteria plan—possibly in violation of the requirements of Code Section 125.

Although diverting unallocated benefits credits to a 401(k) plan might help increase enrollment in the retirement plan, and help employees to save more for retirement than they would have otherwise, diverting those unallocated credits only to a 401(k) plan, without having the option of receiving cash, seems to be an aggressive interpretation of Code Section 125 and the regulations thereunder.

Example. The following is an enrollment form for the Complex Computer Co.

A	Credits .... (Any unused credits will be allocated to your 401(k) account)			$300
		Plan	*Cost*	$ _______
B1	Medical	A	$100	
		B	200	
		C	300	
B2	Life Insurance	A	$ 5	$ _______
		B	10	
		C	15	
		D	20	
B3	Dental	A	$ 30	$ _______
		B	40	
B4	Long-Term Disability	A	$ 15	$ _______
		B	30	
B5	401(k)	Fill in desired amount		$ _______

Add B1 through B5. If this total amount exceeds A, there will be a salary reduction of the excess amount.

To discourage employees from electing to receive cash for unallocated benefits credits, a cafeteria plan that includes a provision for discounting unspent benefits credits may be a safer plan design. An employee who elects to receive $50 in cash for unallocated benefits credits each month might experience a discount of, for example, 50 percent, so the unallocated benefits credits actually become $25 in taxable pay. After being taxed, the $50 benefits credit is further reduced, so the plan participant might receive only $15-$19 in pay—a true discouragement to taking cash when compared to $50 in benefits credits.

Administrative Considerations

Q 10:14 What administrative complications is an employer likely to encounter when attaching a 401(k) plan to a Section 125 cafeteria plan?

It is likely that some language changes may be needed in the 401(k) plan document when a 401(k) plan is attached to a Section 125 cafeteria plan. Certain administrative concerns must also be considered when combining the two plans.

First, if employees are allowed to make 401(k) plan contributions through an option in a cafeteria plan as well as through salary deferral to the stand-alone 401(k) plan, the employer must be sure to combine the employee and employer contributions to both plans for plan testing.

Second, there may be eligibility provisions in the cafeteria plan that do not correspond to the 401(k) plan eligibility rules. These discrepancies can be resolved by changing the provisions of the cafeteria plan, the 401(k) plan, or both plans to accommodate the need for parallel language or language that bridges the eligibility rules of the two plan documents. It should be noted, however, that synchronizing eligibility rules may not meet other objectives of the employer.

When a cafeteria plan has eligibility requirements that are different from those for a 401(k) plan, employees may need to make choices as to how to best use employer-provided benefits credits. That will most likely be the case when an employee is eligible to spend benefits credits in the cafeteria plan but has not yet met the eligibility requirements of the 401(k) plan. Although an employee might be able to make changes to elections for the 401(k) plan during the year, he or she may not change other cafeteria plan elections. Those conflicting rules can be confusing to plan participants.

> **Example.** Kim is a new hire with Computers R Us. The company's cafeteria plan requires only one month of service before an employee can enter the plan, but the 401(k) plan requires six months of service. Kim has an employer-provided benefits credit allocation of $200 per month. She has no interest in the health and welfare benefits offered under the plan. Instead, she wants to spend the credit entirely on the 401(k) plan. Kim has two choices. She can decide to spend the $200 per month on welfare benefits in the plan, and when she becomes eligible for the 401(k) plan in the middle of the plan year, she can begin deferrals from her pay to the 401(k) plan. By doing so, she will make use of the entire $2,400 credit, but will spend it on benefits that are not appealing to her. In addition, she will spend an amount from her pay, reducing it while making inefficient use of the employer-provided benefits credit. Kim can instead decide to allocate all of the benefits credit to the 401(k) plan. Because she is not eligible for the plan until her fifth month of participation in the cafeteria plan, she will forfeit $1,000 of the employer-provided benefits credit—the $200 per month for the first five months of participation in the plan. Fortunately for Kim (and other employees) this eligibility dilemma occurs only in the year in which the employee is first eligible for the 401(k) plan.

Third, appropriate contribution limits may be required by the cafeteria plan to accommodate the 401(k) plan option. Such funding limits help maintain a balance between the amount of money flowing into the cafeteria plan and the amount of money flowing into the 401(k) plan. A balance is necessary to ensure that the 401(k) plan remains in compliance with nondiscrimination rules and contribution limits under the Code.

Under a combined 401(k) and cafeteria plan, the 401(k) plan is an ERISA-qualified profit sharing plan subject to one set of rules and regulations, while the cafeteria plan, which is not an ERISA (Employee Retirement Income Security Act of 1974) plan, is subject to its own set of comprehensive requirements. That complexity alone can create a variety of issues. For example, the Department of Labor (DOL) regulations under ERISA require timely deposit of Section 401(k) salary reduction contributions by the 401(k) plan trustee and impose strict audit and accounting requirements on the trust. Cafeteria plan salary reduction contributions have been exempted from such rules by the DOL. [DOL Tech Rel 92-01]

Although employees may perceive the 401(k) plan and the cafeteria plan as one integrated program, the linkage between the two must be clearly understood by the plan administrator. To that end it may help to have the payroll and recordkeeping systems track the 401(k) option separately from other options under the cafeteria plan.

Q 10:15 What payroll issues must an employer consider when offering a 401(k) option within a cafeteria plan?

An employer must keep the following points in mind regarding payroll when offering a 401(k) option within a cafeteria plan:

1. It must allocate a sufficient number of pretax salary reduction cells in the payroll system to accommodate contributions to both the 401(k) and cafeteria plans.

2. Timing difficulties may occur in relation to when employees make contributions, when employees may change their investments, and when the 401(k) plan administrator issues account balance reports.

3. The payroll system must be properly coded to correctly handle the different tax implications of salary reduction 401(k) money and cafeteria plan money. It is important to recognize that 401(k) deferrals *must* first be taxed for FICA, which is paid equally by both the employer and the employee.

4. As noted earlier (see Q 10:6), an employer (and participating employees) can save a considerable amount of FICA tax if the payroll system is set up to calculate 401(k) deferrals after using employer-provided dollars for other benefits.

An employer should keep separate records detailing the various salary reduction amounts being contributed by each employee so that it can reconcile the sources of contributions to the cafeteria plan and properly account for tax treatment.

Q 10:16 Do salary reduction contributions under a cafeteria plan, including 401(k) deferrals, affect the calculation of the Section 415 limits?

Not any more. Code Section 415 places a limit on the amount of benefits employees may accrue in a plan year under a qualified retirement plan, including a 401(k) plan. The Section 415 limit for a 401(k) plan is a percentage of compensation (100 percent) up to a maximum amount of $40,000. Before 2002, the Section 415 limit for a 401(k) plan was 25 percent of compensation up to a maximum amount of $30,000.

The Section 415 limits were increased by the Economic Growth and Tax Relief Reconciliation Act of 2001 (EGTRRA) and are scheduled to increase each year. Because the first part of the Section 415 limit calculation is based on an amount of compensation, the more compensation earned, the greater the limit.

Before 1998, salary reduction contributions to any 401(k) account—regardless of whether the account was part of a stand-alone plan or was an option under a cafeteria plan—as well as salary reduction contributions to a cafeteria plan resulted in lowering the compensation limit for the Section 415 test. That is, testing under Code Section 415 was performed on net compensation after salary reduction contributions. For years beginning after 1997, however, salary reduction contributions to a 401(k) plan, a 403(b) annuity, or a cafeteria plan (as well as to a Section 457 plan of a tax-exempt organization or a state or local government) are included in compensation for purposes of calculating the Section 415 limit. [IRC § 415(c)(3)(D), as added by the Small Business Job Protection Act of 1996 (SBJPA)]

> **Example.** George, an employee of Ultra Upholstering, earned $30,000 in plan year 1994. George is credited with a contribution made on a salary reduction basis of only $6,000, not $7,500, if by virtue of its being a pretax salary reduction, the $6,000 has the effect of reducing covered compensation. In effect, the $6,000 contribution reduces George's $30,000 salary to $24,000. Although $6,000 represents only 20 percent of $30,000, it represents 25 percent of $24,000—the new salary level.
>
> **Example.** Sandra, an employee of Perfect Plumbing Co., earned $30,000 in 2000. Sandra is credited with a contribution made on a salary reduction basis of $7,500, which represents 25 percent of $30,000—the compensation amount used for determining her Section 415 limit.
>
> Sandra earns $38,000 in 2002. Sandra is not in need of current income and wants to defer as much as possible to the company's 401(k) plan. Sandra uses $2,000 in pretax dollars toward cafeteria plan options (not including a 401(k) option). Her remaining income of $36,000 is available to be deferred to the 401(k) plan (up to the 2002 year maximum of $11,000) under the changes made by EGTRRA.

Q 10:17 How does the annual limit imposed by Code Section 402(g) apportion contributions made to a 401(k) option that is part of a cafeteria plan and contributions made directly to a stand-alone 401(k) plan?

Code Section 402(g) imposes a flat dollar limit specifically on 401(k) plans. Under this limit, annual salary reductions under all 401(k) plans in which an individual participates may not exceed a fixed amount: $7,000, indexed to compensate for inflation. The 2002 limit, $11,000, will increase by $1,000 each year until 2006.

Under Code Section 402(g), contributions are measured by the total 401(k) elective pretax contributions made by an employee to all the 401(k) plans to which the employee belongs, including elective pretax contributions either to a stand-alone 401(k) plan or to any 401(k) account under a cafeteria plan. It is thus necessary to ensure that the total amount of employee elective pretax contributions to both plans stays within the Section 402(g) dollar limit.

If contributions do not stay within the Section 402(g) limit, the employer must make a corrective distribution to the employee. With that in mind, it is important to prescribe in the plan document which part of the 401(k) contribution is to be affected or whether the adjustment will be made proportionately. Generally, such administrative alterations are more disruptive to a cafeteria plan than to a stand-alone 401(k) plan. This is why most employers take initial corrective actions through the stand-alone 401(k) plan. The best approach is never to be in violation of the Section 402(g) limit.

One way a company can protect against violating the Section 402(g) limit is to coordinate the use of contribution caps when the employer permits contributions to the 401(k) plan through multiple avenues (i.e., when there is both a stand-alone 401(k) plan and a 401(k) option under a cafeteria plan).

> **Practice Pointer.** Whereas the contribution cap in effect under the 401(k) plan might be stated either in dollars or as a percentage of pay (perhaps through the contribution formula itself), the cap in the cafeteria plan is better set as a dollar limit only. When both the stand-alone 401(k) and the 401(k) option under a cafeteria plan employ dollar limits, the interplay of caps must be handled with great care, and it may require adjustment from time to time by an administrative committee. Violations of Code limits and dollar caps generally can be avoided if the proper language and administrative checks are incorporated into both the plan documents and the administrative process.

Q 10:18 What happens if a 401(k) plan that is offered under a cafeteria plan becomes discriminatory and requires elective deferral adjustments for HCEs?

The amount of contributions made to a 401(k) option under a cafeteria plan must be carefully balanced between highly-compensated employees (HCEs) and non-highly compensated employees (NHCEs). If the Section 401(k) nondiscrimination tests indicate that the plan is discriminatory, the 401(k) plan could be disqualified unless certain deferrals are returned to HCEs. The calculations are complex, and the adjustments can cause income that was previously reported as nontaxable by HCEs to become taxable. Effective for years beginning after 1996, however, the Section 401(k) nondiscrimination tests—the actual deferral percentage (ADP) test and the actual contribution percentage (ACP) test —are performed using the current year's deferrals for HCEs and the prior year's deferrals for NHCEs. That means that an employer is able to determine the acceptable level of deferrals for HCEs early in the plan year, thereby decreasing the possibility that deferrals will have to be returned to them. An employer may elect to perform the ADP and ACP tests using the current year's deferrals for NHCEs; once made, such an election may be changed only as provided by the IRS. [IRC §§ 401(k)(3)(A), 401(m)(2)(A), as amended by SBJPA]

Generally, cafeteria plan administrators regard 401(k) nondiscrimination testing with trepidation. They realize that a cafeteria plan could be compromised if one of its qualified options becomes nonqualified under its own section of the Code. In other words, it is not enough to satisfy only the Section 125 cafeteria plan nondiscrimination tests—the Section 401(k) nondiscrimination rules also must be met each year.

The employer must predict (as accurately as possible) how the 401(k) option will affect both the 401(k) plan and the cafeteria plan, and the cafeteria plan administration needs to be structured to allow the plan administrator sufficient time to take corrective measures if necessary. A serious concern is that if employees put their funds into a 401(k) option under a cafeteria plan, those funds may consist disproportionately of contributions from HCEs. Organizations with many young employees or NHCEs may have difficulty passing the nondiscrimination tests. Often, retirement savings is a lower priority for such groups of employees.

The employer must be sure to include a provision in both the stand-alone 401(k) plan and the cafeteria plan to address the failure of a 401(k) option existing within a cafeteria plan to satisfy the nondiscrimination rules. It is generally best to adjust contributions to the stand-alone 401(k) plan. Indeed, the 401(k) plan should already be geared to handle the matter of discrimination. With proper planning, the entire adjustment to discriminatory deferrals can most effectively be handled without affecting the 401(k) allocations made through the cafeteria plan.

Q 10:19 May a Section 403(b) arrangement or a Section 457 plan be incorporated into a cafeteria plan?

No. A 401(k) arrangement is the only type of retirement income program specifically allowed to be included in a cafeteria plan. [Prop Treas Reg § 1.125-2, Q&A 4(c)] Code Section 125 does not specifically allow Section 403(b) arrangements or Section 457 plans to be included in a cafeteria plan.

Planning Pointer. SBJPA provided that tax-exempt organizations and Indian tribal governments (but not state or local governments) may establish 401(k) plans for their employees. This provision is effective for plan years beginning after 1996. Therefore, most employers may now offer a 401(k) deferral option through a Section 125 plan.

A Section 403(b) arrangement, commonly referred to as a tax-sheltered annuity, is a form of defined contribution plan available only to employees of educational and charitable organizations. Subject to various limitations and restrictions, Code Section 403(b) allows tax-deferred contributions to be made for such employees through either an employer-funded plan or voluntary salary reduction contributions by employees. Section 403(b) contributions must be invested in annuity contracts issued by life insurance companies (Section 403(b)(1) annuity contracts), shares of regulated investment companies held in custodial accounts (Section 403(b)(7) custodial accounts), life insurance contracts (subject to further limitations), and retirement income accounts maintained for employees of certain church-affiliated organizations.

A Section 457 plan is a nonqualified deferred compensation arrangement between a state or local government or a nongovernmental, nonchurch, tax-exempt organization and an individual who performs services for such an entity.

Planning Pointer. Although it is not possible to include a Section 403(b) arrangement or a Section 457 plan in a cafeteria plan, unused Section 125 credits may, in effect, be contributed to such plans by an indirect process. An employee could receive unused Section 125 credits as cash, and then contribute the same amount to the Section 403(b) arrangement or Section 457 plan through salary reduction, as long as contribution requirements that apply to these plans are met.

Chapter 11

Rules For Cafeteria Plan Operation

Cafeteria plans must operate in accordance with the requirements of Internal Revenue Code Section 125, and the regulations promulgated thereunder (Treasury Regulations Sections 1.125-1, 1.125-2, 1.125-3, and 1.125-4). Other laws may also affect the operation of a Section 125 plan, or the benefits offered within such a plan.

For example, the reporting and disclosure requirements mandated by the Employee Retirement Income Security Act of 1974 (ERISA) do not specifically apply to cafeteria plans; however, they do apply to many of the benefits that may be offered through cafeteria plans, such as health and accident plans, group term life insurance, vacation benefits, and 401(k) plans. ERISA requirements have an impact on the operation and communications of portions of a Section 125 plan.

This chapter describes some of the operational rules required of a cafeteria plan. In some cases, the rules are described briefly in this chapter, and discussed in detail elsewhere in the book.

ERISA

Q 11:1 What objectives does ERISA aim to fulfill?

ERISA instituted requirements that employee benefits plans must meet in order to achieve and maintain their tax-favored status. It imposes various qualification standards and fiduciary responsibilities on both welfare plans and retirement plans and provides enforcement procedures. Among the standards that ERISA established are rules pertaining to reporting and disclosure, funding, fiscal responsibility, eligibility, plan coverage and participation, forms of benefits payment, and maximum contributions and benefits.

ERISA's reporting and disclosure requirements reflect the belief that communications to plan participants enable employees to better understand their benefits and that reporting to the federal government assists the monitoring of plans' compliance with the statute. "Reporting" refers here to the requirement that employers offering employee benefits plans must supply certain information to government agencies. Disclosure refers to the requirement that plan administrators must distribute certain information to plan participants and that certain documents must be available for inspection by participants and copies must be provided upon request. (See Q 11:2.)

A cafeteria plan (which is to say, the delivery system for employee benefits) is not typically an ERISA plan. However, the various benefits offered within the cafeteria plan may very well be ERISA plans. Often, an entire cafeteria plan, with all of the benefits offered within it, is considered as one plan, and reported as if the entire plan were subject to ERISA.

Q 11:2 What are the reporting and disclosure requirements of ERISA?

Generally, an employee benefits plan subject to ERISA must satisfy certain reporting and disclosure requirements, including the following provisions:

Summary plan description (SPD). A summary of certain plan provisions must be provided to participants and, upon request, to the Department of Labor (DOL). [ERISA § 101(a), 101(b)] The required information includes such provisions as the plan requirements pertaining to eligibility for participation and benefits; the circumstances that may result in disqualification, ineligibility or denial, loss, forfeiture, or suspension of any benefits; procedures for applying for benefits and the remedies available for claims that are denied in whole or in part; and the type of pension or welfare plan, along with the name, business address, and business telephone number of the plan's administrator and the agent for service of process and the persons performing such functions for the plan.

An SPD should be written so as to be understood by the average participant, and it must be sufficiently accurate and detailed so that participants and beneficiaries are reasonably informed of their rights and obligations.

An SPD must be provided to participants within 90 days of eligibility. If a material modification is made to the SPD during the five-year period that follows its distribution, a revised SPD must be distributed to participants within 210 days after the end of the fifth plan year. If no material modifications are made, the SPD must be redistributed within 210 days after every tenth plan year. An initial SPD must be distributed within 120 days after the plan becomes subject to ERISA (i.e., within 120 days after the date of the adoption of the plan) for plans adopted after January 1, 1975.

It is important to ensure that an SPD is written with current requirements. For example, the Health Insurance Portability and Accountability Act of 1996 (HIPAA) and the Newborns' and Mothers' Health Protection Act of 1996 (NMHPA) added certain requirements to SPDs. More recently, SPDs are required to describe changes to claims procedures and deadlines. Under an amendment by the PWBA to ERISA Regulation 2560.503-1, the regulation contains separate applicability dates for group health claims and all other claims. Under the regulation as amended on July 9, 2001, the applicability date for group health claims is the first day of the first plan year that begins on or after July 1, 2002, but not later than January 1, 2003. This means that group health plans must comply with the regulation beginning with new claims filed on or after the first day of the first plan year beginning on or after July 1, 2002, but not later than January 1, 2003. For all calendar year group health plans, the applicability date will be January 1, 2003.

Summary of material modifications (SMM). A summary of changes in any information required in the SPD and certain items in discontinued Form EBS-1 must be provided to participants and the DOL. [ERISA §§ 102(b)(2), 104(a)(1)(D)] The DOL has not issued regulations stating what constitutes a material modification. It may be noted, however, that in the discontinued Form EBS-1, the DOL characterized a material modification as being a change that is most important to plan participants, such as the following:

- The name and address of the plan sponsor or administrator
- The structure, name, and type of plan
- The agent for service of process and the persons performing such functions for the plan
- The plan requirements
- The disposition of employee contributions

The DOL has stated that a document providing notification of a change in plan trustees, or of a trustee's change in name, is a material modification that must be furnished to participants. [ERISA Op 80-32A (May 23, 1980)]

An SMM is due within 210 days after the end of the plan year in which the modification is adopted (unless a revised SPD is distributed with the modification). Effective as of the first day of the first plan year beginning after June 30, 1997, HIPAA amended that requirement when there is a "modification or change that is a material reduction in covered services or benefits provided under a group health plan." In such a case, the SMM must be furnished to participants covered under the plan and beneficiaries receiving benefits no later than 60 days after the adoption of the modification or change. It should be noted that if the plan administrator maintains a system of communication (e.g., an employee newsletter or union publication) that provides information concerning the plan, including modifications and changes, at regular intervals of not more than 90 days, and such communication otherwise meets the disclosure requirements of DOL Regulations Section 2520.104b-1, the summary does not have to be sent to any participant or beneficiary who would reasonably be expected to receive that communication. Individual notices of material reductions would still have to be sent to retirees, employees on leave, and others who are not likely to receive the communication. [Treasury Proposed Regulation (Apr 8, 1997) amending DOL Reg § 2520.104b-3]

Form 5500. Annual reporting on certain employee benefits plans is required by the IRS. Form 5500, Annual Return/Report of Employee Benefit Plan, is used for such reporting to the IRS, the DOL, and, upon written request, to participants. Form 5500 includes detailed information about an employee benefits plan, such as the number of plan participants and amounts of plan distributions to participants and beneficiaries; financial, actuarial, and insurance information; and the amount and composition of plan assets.

A Form 5500 and applicable schedules are due within seven months after the end of the plan year, unless the plan sponsor receives an extension. A plan sponsor may obtain a two and one-half month extension by filing Form 5558 (Application for Extension of Time to File Certain Employee Plan Returns) before the due date of the Form 5500.

Although ERISA requires annual reporting on Form 5500 for certain welfare and retirement benefit plans, it is important to note that cafeteria plans and certain other plans have no Form 5500 reporting requirement, effective April 2002 (see Q 11:3).

Summary annual report (SAR). When a Form 5500 filing is required for certain employee benefit plans, an abbreviated report must be distributed to employees. A narrative SAR (a summary of the information found on Form 5500) in prescribed format must be provided to participants. [ERISA §§ 101(a)(2), 104(b)(3)] The SAR must include financial information indicating plan assets and liabilities, as well as receipts and disbursements during the previous year. It must also include other specified information required to summarize the latest annual report. The DOL has issued model language to be used for SARs for welfare benefits and pension plans.

Plan sponsors must provide an SAR two months after the Form 5500 is due to the IRS (including any extension).

Form 5500

Cafeteria Plans

Q 11:3 Must a plan sponsor file a Form 5500 and any other schedule to maintain a cafeteria plan?

Until Spring of 2002, the answer to this question was yes. However, on April 4, 2002, the IRS released Notice 2002-24. Effective on the date of the Notice and *retroactively,* IRS has eliminated the requirement for a cafeteria plan (or other fringe benefit plan) to file a Form 5500 and Schedule F, if the Form 5500 filing was entirely due to the requirement of Code Section 6039D. (See Appendix J for a copy of the IRS Notice and the accompanying News Bulletin.)

It is no longer necessary to file Form 5500 and Schedule F in order to maintain a cafeteria plan. However, it is important to note that certain underlying benefits may continue to have a Form 5500 reporting requirement by virtue of being ERISA plans. For example, a medical plan (including a medical reimbursement account) with 100 or more participants will have a stand-alone requirement to file Form 5500 and related schedules. This filing may have been incorporated into a larger "cafeteria plan" filing in the past. While the need to file an annual report on the cafeteria plan is gone, the underlying benefits may continue to have a reporting requirement. A welfare benefit plan is required to file a Form 5500. However, welfare benefit plans are exempted from filing if the plan covers fewer than 100 participants as of the beginning of the plan year and is unfunded, fully insured, or a combination of insured and unfunded.

Q 11:4 When is Form 5500 due for ERISA plans?

Form 5500 (with the required Schedules) is due within seven months after the end of the plan year, unless the plan sponsor receives an extension. A plan sponsor may obtain a two-and-one-half month extension by filing Form 5558 before the due date of the Form 5500.

Often, welfare benefit plans (such as health, life, and disability programs) report on the same 12-month basis as the underlying insurance contract. However, it is not required for the plan year to coincide with the policy year.

Q 11:5 If a cafeteria plan had in the past filed one Form 5500 with several underlying benefits, what is the correct way to file now that there is no filing requirement for the cafeteria plan?

This can be confusing. While the requirement for reporting on the cafeteria plan *per se* has been eliminated, the underlying welfare benefit plans may continue to have a reporting requirement under ERISA. In many cases, a plan sponsor may have used a single Form 5500 to report on all of the benefits offered within the cafeteria plan.

It is still possible to file a single Form 5500 for the overall employee benefit plan offered by the plan sponsor. The employee benefit plan might include various welfare benefits, fringe benefits, and possibly even retirement benefits. The difference now will be the schedules required to accompany the Form 5500.

There is no longer any requirement for any plan to attach Schedule F to a Form 5500. Fringe benefit plans that had, in the past, been required to file an annual report (Form 5500) with IRS because of the requirements of Code Section 6039D will no longer have any reporting requirement.

> **Example.** Beautiful Paint Co. offers a premium conversion plan with two medical plan choices. The traditional indemnity plan has 132 participants and the high level indemnity plan has 77 participants. The plan operates on a calendar year. The policies are also calendar-year based.
>
> In the past, Beautiful Paint filed one Form 5500 for the employee benefit plan (Plan Number 501) that consisted of a premium conversion feature under Code Section 125, and the two medical plans. The Form 5500 had Schedule F and two Schedules A attached. (Actually, whether or not the high level plan should have been reported is debatable, but for purposes of this example, the company included both medical plans in the past Form 5500 filing.)
>
> Effective for the 2002 plan year, Beautiful Paint may continue to file for the two medical plans as Plan Number 501.
>
> Alternatively, Beautiful Paint might decide to eliminate Plan Number 501, and merely file for the Welfare benefit plan with more than 100 participants as a new Plan Number 502. The high level plan would have no ERISA reporting requirement at this time, based on the number of plan participants.

In all other circumstances, when a plan number is going to be discontinued, it is necessary to file a final Form 5500 in order to let IRS/DOL know that no future Forms 5500 will be forthcoming. However, in this unique situation, IRS no longer wants any filing related to Code Section 6039D. No final report is required or expected.

401(k) Plans

Q 11:6 When an employee benefits program includes welfare benefits and a 401(k) plan, must separate Forms 5500 be filed?

The instructions for the 2001 Form 5500 do not explicitly allow a joint filing for welfare benefit plans and 401(k) benefits provided under a plan sponsor's employee benefit arrangement. In the absence of such guidance and considering the different information that would apply to the cafeteria plan and the 401(k) plan, it appears that separate Form 5500s should be filed. It is important to note that welfare benefit plans are identified by the IRS and the DOL by a plan number beginning with 501, while pension and retirement plans are identified by a plan number beginning with 001. It would be impossible to report both of these plan numbers on a single Form 5500.

Dependent Care FSAs

Q 11:7 Must a Form 5500 be filed for a dependent care FSA?

No (see Q 11:3 and Appendix J). The reporting requirement for dependent care assistance plans has been eliminated.

Adoption Assistance FSAs

Q 11:8 Must a Form 5500 be filed for an adoption assistance FSA?

No (see Q 11:3 and Appendix J). The reporting requirement for adoption assistance programs has been eliminated.

Q 11:9 Do any special disclosure rules apply to adoption assistance FSAs or employer-funded adoption programs?

Yes. An adoption assistance FSA (see chapter 9) or an employer-funded adoption program must be communicated to employees.

Also, the employer must show adoption assistance payments in box 12 of the employee's Form W-2, with the letter "T" identifying the amount as an adoption assistance reimbursement. Such a reimbursement should not be included in taxable wages of box 1. However, adoption assistance benefits are included as Social Security and Medicare wages in boxes 3 and 5. It is generally the responsibility of the plan participant to make adjustments to taxable income, as necessary, for any nonexcludable payments. [See IRS Pub 968, *Tax Benefits for Adoption* (2002)]

Q 11:10 Must an employee provide any special information regarding adoption assistance benefits on his or her federal income tax return?

Yes. To take advantage of the adoption assistance exclusion from income, a participant must complete Form 8839, Qualified Adoption Expenses, and attach it to his or her Form 1040 or Form 1040A. The amount of the adoption assistance benefit is entered on line 45 of Form 1040 or line 30 of Form 1040A. [See IRS Pub 968, *Tax Benefits for Adoption* (2002)]

Compliance

Q 11:11 Who is eligible to participate in a Section 125 cafeteria plan?

In general, a cafeteria plan may cover employees and by virtue of the employee's participation, dependents of employees. Owners of 2 percent or more in an S-corporation, partners in a partnership, and sole proprietors may not participate in a Section 125 plan, although those employers may offer such a plan to employees. (See Qs 2:9 through 2:11 for a detailed discussion of eligibility).

The Internal Revenue Code permits classification of certain employees as ineligible for a Section 125 plan without adverse consequence.

Q 11:12 What are the requirements for aggregating employees of a controlled group of employers?

Code Section 125(g)(4) states that all employees who are treated as employed by a single employer under Code Section 414(b), (c), or (m) are also treated as employed by a single employer for purposes of Code Section 125.

Q 11:13 What are the nondiscrimination requirements of a Section 125 plan?

Overall, a Section 125 cafeteria plan may not discriminate in favor of highly compensated employees or in favor of key employees. Both terms "highly compensated" and "key" have specific definitions based on the Internal Revenue Code and the Treasury Regulations. In addition to the overall requirement of a Section 125 plan not to discriminate, each underlying plan may also have independent nondiscrimination requirements. (See Chapter 14 for an in-depth discussion of nondiscrimination requirements.)

Changes to Elections

Q 11:14 What is the history pertaining to changes in participant elections in a Section 125 cafeteria plan?

Changes to cafeteria plan elections during the plan year have always been restricted. The first set of proposed Treasury regulations guiding cafeteria plans, published in 1984, stated that a participant could revoke an election during the plan year only if he or she experienced a "change in family status." The examples of a change in family status given in the proposed regulations were marriage, divorce, death of a spouse or child, birth or adoption of a child, and termination of a spouse's employment.

Further guidance was offered by Proposed Treasury Regulations Section 1.125-2, issued in 1989. These proposed regulations provided examples and new permitted reasons for making a change to a cafeteria plan election during the plan year.

For nearly ten years, cafeteria plans operated with only these two sets of proposed regulations for guidance as to what constituted a qualified reason for a participant to make a midyear change to a cafeteria plan election.

In 1997, the IRS issued Temporary Treasury Regulations Section 1.125-4T to further define a change in status. (Note the change from the term "change in family status.") The temporary regulations were to become effective for plan years beginning on or after January 1, 1999. In December 1998, however, the IRS issued an announcement stating that the temporary regulations would not be effective before plan years beginning at least 120 days after further guidance was issued. [Ann 98-105, 1998-2 CB 714] In the absence of further guidance, the IRS announcement stated that plans could rely on the change in election provisions of the 1997 temporary regulations or the change in election provisions of Proposed Treasury Regulations Section 1.125-2. Either alternative was available, regardless of whether the plan document had been amended to conform to the 1997 temporary regulations.

In March 2000, the IRS issued (final) Treasury Regulations Section 1.125-4, effective for plan years beginning on or after January 1, 2001. (This was the first time final regulations had been issued for cafeteria plans.) At the same time, the IRS published Proposed Treasury Regulations Section 1.125-4 to complement the final regulations. Concurrently, the temporary regulations expired for plan years beginning after November 6, 2000. In January 2001, the IRS finalized Proposed Treasury Regulations Section 1.125-4, so that all regulations numbered 1.125-4 are now final regulations (see Appendix M).

Q 11:15 Under what circumstances may a participant in a cafeteria plan revoke an existing election and make a new one?

Effective for plan years beginning on or after January 1, 2001, a participant in a cafeteria plan may revoke an existing election and make a new one only as provided under the final Treasury regulations describing permitted election changes. Some of the final regulations were issued in March 2000, and some were issued in early 2001. Some provisions are effective for plan years beginning on or after January 1, 2002, but most of the provisions apply to plan years beginning on or after January 1, 2001.

For plan years beginning *before* January 1, 2001, the change in election provisions of the 1997 temporary regulations [Temp Treas Reg § 1.125-4T] or the change in election provisions of pre-1990 Proposed Treasury Regulations Section 1.125-2 could be relied on. [Ann 98-105, 1998-2 CB 714]

Treasury Regulations Section 1.125-4 permits the following reasons for making mid-plan-year changes to elections under certain conditions:

- Special enrollment status under the Health Insurance Portability and Accountability Act of 1996 (HIPAA) (See Qs 11:33, 11:34)
- Certain changes in status (see Q 11:16)
  —Change in marital status
  —Change in number of dependents
  —Change in employment status
  —Dependent satisfying or ceasing to satisfy eligibility requirements
  —Change in residence,
  —Commencement or termination of adoption proceedings

- A judgment, decree, or order in the context of a divorce, legal separation, annulment, or change in legal custody (see Q 11:36)
- Entitlement to Medicare or Medicaid (see Q 11:35)
- Significant cost or coverage changes (see Qs 11:26–11:30)
- Family and medical leave under the Family and Medical Leave Act (FMLA)

A plan is not required to permit midyear changes due to changes in status, even though the changes in status are described in Treasury Regulations Section 1.125-4 (see Appendix M).

Q 11:16 What changes in status are permitted under Treasury regulations?

Final Treasury Regulations Section 1.125-4 permits an employee to revoke an election during a period of coverage and make a new election for the remaining portion of the period if, under the facts and circumstances, a change in status (as defined in the regulations) occurs and the election change satisfies the consistency rule outlined in the regulations. Such changes in status are applicable not only for health and group term life insurance plans, but also for other qualified benefits under Code Section 125, including dependent care assistance plans and adoption assistance programs.

The permitted change in status events identified in Final Treasury Regulations Section 1.125-4(c)(2) are:

- Change in legal marital status; that is, marriage, death of spouse, divorce, legal separation, and annulment.
- Change in number of dependents as the result of birth, death, adoption, and placement for adoption.
- Change in employment status affecting the employee, the employee's spouse, or the employee's dependent; that is, termination or commencement of employment, a strike or lockout, a commencement or return from an unpaid leave of absence, and change in worksite. Also includes a change in eligibility status such that the individual becomes or ceases to be eligible for the plan; for example, if a plan covers salaried employees only and a salaried employee becomes an hourly employee.
- Dependent satisfies or ceases to satisfy eligibility requirements because of attainment of limiting age (e.g., 19), student status, or any similar circumstance.
- Change in residence for the employee, spouse, or dependent (primarily a factor for participants participating in HMOs but could also affect day-care provider use).
- Commencement or termination of adoption proceedings (a qualified reason for change in status only with respect to an adoption assistance program within a cafeteria plan).

The foregoing list of change in status events is inclusive. No events, other than these identified by the final regulations issued in 2000, may be considered a permitted change in status for making a mid-plan-year change

Q 11:17 When did the final regulations became effective?

The portions of the final regulations that were published as final in March 2000 are effective for plan years beginning on or after January 1, 2001. The portions of the final regulations that were proposed in March 2000 but finalized in January 2001 are effective for plan years beginning on or after January 1, 2002.

Q 11:18 May a participant in a cafeteria plan revoke an existing election and make a new election for accident or health and group term life insurance plans?

Yes. Furthermore, Treasury Regulations Section 1.125-4 describes changing cafeteria plan elections for other benefits as well. It is important to note, however, that a plan sponsor is not *required* to permit revocations or mid-plan-year changes of existing elections.

Q 11:19 Can COBRA eligibility affect the ability to make a midyear change to coverage under the final Treasury regulations?

Yes If a participating employee or his or her spouse or dependent becomes eligible for continuation coverage under the group health plan of the employee's employer as provided under Section 4980B of the Consolidated Omnibus Budget Reconciliation Act of 1985 (COBRA) or any similar state law, a cafeteria plan may permit the employee to increase payments under the employer's cafeteria plan in order to pay for the continuation coverage. [Treas Reg § 1.125-4(c)(3)(iv)]

Note. An employee may not have a pretax amount deducted from his or her pay for COBRA continuation coverage under a different employer. This limitation includes COBRA coverage of a spouse (for health insurance provided by a different employer) and COBRA coverage of the employee (for health insurance provided by a former employer).

Example. Jane, an employee at Quality Toys, is covered by the company's health plan, along with her daughter, Ellen. Ellen is about to turn age 19, and will become ineligible as a dependent under the health plan. When Ellen has the COBRA qualifying event causing her to lose coverage under Jane's health plan, Jane may opt to increase her pretax premium contribution to pay for Ellen's COBRA continuation.

Q 11:20 How are the consistency rules applied under the final Treasury regulations?

Under the final Treasury regulations, the change in election made because of a change in status has to correspond with the change in status that affected eligibility for coverage under an employer's health plan. Furthermore, if the change in status is due to the employee's divorce, annulment, or legal separation, the death of the employee's spouse or dependent, or the employee's dependent ceasing to satisfy the eligibility requirements for coverage, the employee's election to cancel coverage for anyone other than his or her ex-spouse, deceased spouse or dependent, or ineligible dependent fails to correspond with that change in status.

Example. Triform Co. offers three levels of coverage: employee-only, employee plus one, and family coverage. Doug, who had a wife and child, originally elected family coverage. In 2001 Doug divorced his wife. He is permitted to drop her from coverage (and thus change to the employee plus one level of coverage). He is not, however, permitted to switch to employee-only or to drop health coverage altogether because of the divorce.

In a significant change from the temporary regulations issued in 1997, a change in status attributable to a change in marital status or a change in the employment status of a *spouse or dependent* qualified a participant to elect an increase or decrease in group term life insurance or disability income coverage consistent with the change in status.

For accident or health and group term life insurance, a change in status that affects eligibility under an employer's plan includes a change in status that results in an increase or decrease in the number of an employee's family members or dependents who may benefit from coverage under the plan.

Changes to dependent care expenses and adoption expenses are specifically recognized as permitted changes if the change in election is consistent with the change in expense.

Q 11:21 Does a change in status occur when the spouse of an employee covered under a cafeteria plan becomes eligible for a less costly health plan?

Yes. Treasury regulations list examples of changes in status for which a benefits election may be permitted under a cafeteria plan. One of the examples listed in the Final Treasury Regulations Section 1.125-4 is a significant change in the health coverage of the employee or the employee's spouse attributable to the spouse's employment.

If a spouse continues to be employed by the same employer and there is a change in the cost of health coverage attributable to the spouse's employment that is not a significant change, that would not be considered a qualified change in status. Previously, the Treasury regulations did not list a change in the cost of health coverage attributable to the spouse's employment as a change in status. Treasury Regulations Section 1.125-4, however, indicates that a cafeteria plan may permit an employee to make a prospective election change that is on account of and corresponds with a change made under the plan of the spouse's (or former spouse's or dependent's) employer. Of course, for the spouse to make a mid-plan-year change to his or her election, the spouse's plan must be designed to allow mid-plan-year changes as permitted by the regulations. [Treas Reg § 1.125-4(f)]

Q 11:22 May an employee who has not elected any qualified benefits under a cafeteria plan experience a change in status?

Yes. A participant in a cafeteria plan by definition chooses among two or more benefits consisting of cash (or a cash equivalent benefit) and qualified benefits. A participant who has not elected any qualified benefits has necessarily elected cash (in the form of salary) or a cash equivalent benefit (such as group term life insurance coverage in excess of $50,000).

If a cafeteria plan recognizes changes in status and does not limit those changes to participants who elected qualified benefits at the start of the plan year, a participant may opt for qualified benefits midyear upon the occurrence of a change in status, even if the participant initially opted for cash rather than benefits under the plan.

Q 11:23 How soon after the occurrence of a change in status should an employee be required to notify his or her employer?

Neither Code Section 125 nor the Treasury regulations issued under that section expressly address when an employee should notify his or her employer of a change in status. Most plans require that employees provide notification of a change in status within 30 days. A period of 30 days is generally considered sufficient time for an employee to provide notification of a change and for the plan to verify that the new election is consistent with the change.

A change to an election can be made only prospectively, unless the reason for the change corresponds with special enrollment rights under HIPAA. [IRC § 9801(f)] For example, an employee adding coverage because of marriage can do so only prospectively, but an employee adding coverage because of the birth or adoption of a child can add coverage retroactively, as provided by HIPAA.

Q 11:24 Should an employer design a cafeteria plan so as to allow employees to change elections for changes in status?

There is no simple answer to this question. Employers tend to be concerned about allowing changes in elections under a cafeteria plan because of changes in status for several reasons. First, permitting a participant to revoke an election during a period of coverage and to make a new election for the remaining portion of the period may complicate the plan's communications with participants, since the employer must make extra efforts to communicate to participants the special circumstances under which election changes are allowed. Second, plan administration becomes more challenging because qualified changes in status may result in new, prospective employee contribution amounts and plan selections. The most compelling reason not to permit midyear changes, however, has to do with medical FSAs. There can be significant confusion as to how much reimbursement a participant is entitled to, and during what period of time claims must be incurred, when a participant makes a mid-plan-year change.

The most conservative approach is not to allow changes to elections during a period of coverage. This approach is easy to communicate and administer. Of course, employees tend to be less enthusiastic about participating in a cafeteria plan that does not allow midyear changes following a significant life event.

Another approach is to allow changes for only some change in status events, such as divorce or the death of a spouse or dependent. Although limited, such an approach is responsive to employees' special needs at a time of personal loss.

A third approach is to permit mid-plan-year changes only if the change is to increase coverage. This approach limits the employer's potential risk of loss in a medical FSA.

Despite the drawbacks, most employers allow all changes in status permitted by the Treasury regulations.

Q 11:25 Do the change in status rules apply to 401(k) plans and Section 401(m) plans?

No. The final regulations indicate that the change of status rules in those regulations do not apply to employees' elective contributions under a qualified cash or deferred arrangement within the meaning of Code Section 401(k) or to employee contributions subject to Code Section 401(m). [Treas Reg § 1.125-4(h)] Employees may modify or revoke existing elections in accordance with Code Sections 401(k) and 401(m) and the regulations thereunder.

Q 11:26 May a cafeteria plan ever automatically change the amount of a participant's health plan premium contributions?

Yes. Regulations issued before 1990 [Prop Treas Reg § 1.125-2] stated that when the cost of a health plan provided by an independent third-party provider under a cafeteria plan increased or decreased during a plan year, the cafeteria plan could, on a reasonable and consistent basis, automatically increase or decrease (as the case might be) all affected participants' elective pretax contributions or after-tax employee contributions for the health plan.

Under Treasury Regulations Section 1.125-4(f), which is effective for plan years beginning on or after January 1, 2002, if the cost of a qualified benefits plan increases or decreases during a period of coverage and, under the terms of the cafeteria plan, employees are required to make a corresponding change in their payments, the cafeteria plan may, on a reasonable and consistent basis, automatically make a prospective increase or decrease in affected employees' elective contributions for the plan. Treasury Regulations Section 1.125-4(f) does not restrict such a change to cost changes made by an independent third-party insurance carrier. Changes to cost or coverage may be initiated by an independent third-party provider by the employer, or even by the spouse's employer. In the case of a dependent care FSA, the change in cost or coverage can even be initiated by the participant.

Q 11:27 May a participant in a cafeteria plan revoke an existing election and make a new election as the result of significant cost changes?

If the cost of a benefit package option significantly increases during a period of coverage, the cafeteria plan may permit employees either to make a corresponding prospective increase in their payments or to revoke their elections and, in lieu thereof, receive on a prospective basis coverage under another benefit package option providing similiar coverage. For example, if the cost of an indemnity option under an accident or health plan significantly increases during a period of coverage, employees who are covered by the option may either make a corresponding prospective increase in their payments or elect to revoke their election for the indemnity option and, in lieu thereof, elect coverage under an HMO option. [Treas Reg § 1.125-4(f)(2)(ii)]

Application to Dependent Care. If the cost change is imposed by a dependent care provider (who is not a relative of the employee), a corresponding change in election is permitted. [Treas Reg § 1.125-4(f)(2)(iv)] A relative of the employee includes lineal ascendants and descendants, brothers, sisters, nieces, nephews, aunts, uncles, and in-laws. Step-relations are included in the definition, as are half-brothers and half-sisters. [IRC § 152]

Q 11:28 May a participant in a cafeteria plan revoke an existing election and make a new election following changes in coverage?

If the coverage under a plan is significantly curtailed or ceases during a period of coverage, the cafeteria plan may permit affected employees to revoke their elections under the plan. In such case, each affected employee may make a new election on a prospective basis for coverage under another benefit package option providing similar coverage. Treas Reg § 1.125-4(f)(3)]

Q 11:29 If the cost or coverage under a self-insured health plan changes during a plan year, may employees' elections change?

Current Treasury Regulations Section 1.125-4(f) does not specify that the change in cost or coverage must be initiated by an independent third-party provider. This is an important difference between the previous guidance and the final regulations, which are effective for plan years beginning on or after January 1, 2002. Under the previous guidance found in Proposed Treasury Regulations Section 1.125-2, the answer was clearly no.

Q 11:30 What qualifies as a change in cost or in coverage?

A change in cost is a change in the amount of elective contributions under the cafeteria plan, whether the change results from an action taken by the employee or by an employer. [Treas Reg § 1.125-4(f)(2)(iii)]

A change in coverage includes, among other changes, a significant curtailment of coverage under a plan, with or without loss of coverage. Coverage under a plan is significantly curtailed only if there is an overall reduction in coverage to participants under the plan so as to constitute reduced coverage to participants generally. Thus, for example, if a given participant's physician is dropped from a preferred provider organization (PPO) network, the participant may not have experienced a significant curtailment of coverage. If, however, a major hospital network is dropped from the PPO, affecting many participants, a significant curtailment of coverage may have occurred. [Treas Reg § 1.125-4(f)(3)]

Note. Health FSA elections may not be changed because of a change in cost or coverage. [Final Treas Reg § 1.125-4(f)(1)]

Example. Juan is planning to make use of his health FSA for vision care expenses. In the middle of the plan year, Juan's employer adds a very generous vison care package at no cost to employees. Juan cannot—because of his "change in coverage"—change the amount he is setting aside in his health FSA. He can, however, use the health FSA for other types of qualified medical expenses.

Q 11:31 May a participant revoke an existing election and make a new election because of a separation from service?

Change of employment has been and continues to be considered a qualified change in status. [Treas Reg § 1.125-4(c)(2)(iii)] Proposed Treasury Regulations Section 1.125-2, Q&A 6(d) (now withdrawn), indicated that an employee who separated from service could revoke his or her existing elections and terminate receipt of benefits for the remaining portion of the coverage period. The plan was prohibited, however, from permitting the employee to make new benefit elections if he or she was rehired during the plan year.

Treasury Regulations Section 1.125-(c)(4), Example 8, points out that collusion between an employer and a participant to "create" a change in status does not, in fact, cause a change in status. If, by prior understanding, the employee terminates employment so as to revoke his or her elections, and returns to employment within the same plan year, the employee will be compelled to continue the elections that were in effect before the termination of employment.

If the termination and rehire during the plan year are not done by previous arrangement to create a change in status, the plan may offer a few options to rehired employees. If the rehire occurs within 30 days after termination, the participant can return to his or her previous elections. If the rehire occurs more than 30 days after termination but within the same plan year, the cafeteria plan may permit the rehired participant the option of returning to the elections in effect before termination of employment, or of making new elections under the plan. Alternatively, the cafeteria plan may prohibit the rehired employee from returning to the plan during that plan year.

Q 11:32 What are the consequences when an employee fails to make required premium payments?

A cafeteria plan may stipulate that a benefit will cease to be provided to an employee when the employee fails to make the required premium payments. [Prop Treas Reg § 1.125-2, Q&A 6(b)] Informal discussions with the IRS have indicated that this provision was intended to address certain states' garnishment of wages laws. Some states do not allow employees to irrevocably agree to have amounts withheld from their wages. In such states, a participant in a cafeteria plan could stop making the required premium payments and thus have full wages restored. Proposed Treasury Regulations Section 1.125-2 states that in such a case, the plan must prohibit the employee from making a new benefits election for the remaining portion of the period of coverage.

> **Note.** The final Treasury regulations do not identify cessation of required contributions as a qualified reason for revoking an election under a cafeteria plan. However, Proposed Regulations, Section 1.125-2, Q&A 6(b) appears to provide guidance in this area.

Q 11:33 May a participant revoke an existing health or accident plan election and make a new election using the special enrollment rights provided in HIPAA?

Yes. Treasury Regulations Section 1.125-4 confirms that a participant (or dependent of the employee) who is eligible (but not enrolled) for coverage under the terms of a plan may enroll for coverage if each of the following conditions is met:

1. The employee (or dependent) was either covered under a group health plan or had health insurance coverage at the time coverage was previously offered to the employee (or dependent).
2. The employee stated in writing at the time that coverage under a group health plan (or health insurance coverage) was the reason for declining enrollment because the plan sponsor (or health insurance issuer offering health insurance coverage in connection with the plan) required such a statement at that time and provided the employee with notice of the requirement (and the consequences of such requirement) at that time.

3. The employee (or dependent) who lost coverage was either under a COBRA continuation coverage provision and such coverage was exhausted or was not under a COBRA continuation coverage provision and had coverage terminated because of loss of eligibility for coverage (e.g., as a result of termination of employment, reduction in the number of hours of employment, legal separation, divorce, or death) or because the employer had terminated contributions toward such coverage.
4. Under the terms of the plan, the employee requested enrollment not later than 30 days after the exhaustion of COBRA coverage or the termination of employer contributions.

Under HIPAA, if an employee is a participant under the plan or the employee satisfied the waiting period for becoming a participant under the plan and is eligible to be enrolled under the plan but failed to enroll during a previous employment period, and a person becomes a dependent of the employee through marriage, birth, adoption, or placement for adoption, the group health plan must provide for a special enrollment period during which that person may be enrolled under the plan as a dependent of the employee. In the case of a birth or adoption of a child, the employee's spouse may be enrolled as a dependent of the employee if the spouse is otherwise eligible for coverage.

The special enrollment period for dependents must not be less than 30 days and must begin on the later of (1) the date dependent coverage is made available or (2) the date of marriage, birth, adoption, or placement for adoption.

If coverage for a dependent is sought during the first 30 days of the special enrollment period for dependents, coverage of the dependent must become effective as follows:

1. In the case of marriage, not later than the first day of the first month following the date the completed request for enrollment is received.
2. In the case of a dependent's birth, as of the date of the birth.
3. In the case of a dependent's adoption or placement for adoption, as of the date of the adoption or placement for adoption.

[IRC § 9801(f); Treas Reg § 1.125-4(b)]

Q 11:34 Under Treasury Regulations Section 1.125-4, are cafeteria plan election changes that correspond with the special enrollment rights of HIPAA permitted?

Yes. Under the final Treasury regulations issued in 2001, a cafeteria plan may permit a participant to revoke an election for coverage under a group health plan during a period of coverage and make a new election corresponding with the special enrollment rights provided in Code Section 9801(f) (i.e., the special enrollment rights detailed in HIPAA).

Example. Greg, an employee of Honey Hams, Inc., has employee-only health coverage through a cafeteria plan offered by Honey Hams. Greg adopts a child. He may—within 30 days—revoke his election for employee-only coverage and prospectively add family coverage as of the date of adoption. The increased salary reduction is permitted to reflect the cost of family coverage from the date of adoption.

Example. Harry and Sally, two unmarried individuals, are employed by different employers. Both carry employee-only coverage. In 2001 Harry and Sally marry each other. The marriage results in special enrollment rights under Code Section 9801(f), so either Harry or Sally has the option of revoking employee-only coverage and electing family coverage under one employer's group health plan. The election of family coverage would be effective no later than the first day of the first calendar month beginning after the completed request for enrollment is received by the plan. [Treas Reg § 1.125-4(b)]

Q 11:35 May entitlement to Medicare or Medicaid qualify a participant to make a change in election under the final Treasury regulations?

Yes. If an employee, spouse, or dependent who is enrolled in an accident or health plan of an employer under a cafeteria plan becomes entitled to coverage (i.e., becomes enrolled) under Part A or Part B of Title XVIII of the Social Security Act (Medicare) or Title XIX of the Social Security Act (Medicaid), other than coverage consisting solely of benefits under the program for distribution for pediatric vaccines, the cafeteria plan may permit the employee to make a prospective election change to cancel or reduce coverage of the employee, spouse, or dependent under the accident or health plan.

In addition, if an employee, spouse, or dependent who has been entitled to coverage under Medicare or Medicaid loses eligibility for such coverage, the cafeteria plan may permit the employee to make a prospective election to commence or increase coverage of the employee, spouse, or dependent under the accident or health plan. The provision to add or increase coverage under the cafeteria plan in case of loss of Medicare or Medicaid eligibility is described in Treasury Regulations Section 1.125-4; it was not part of Temporary Treasury Regulations Section 1.125-4T, issued in 1997.

Q 11:36 May a participant revoke an existing health or accident plan election and make a new election as a result of a judgment, decree, or order in the context of a divorce, legal separation, annulment, or change in legal custody?

Yes. Treasury Regulations Section 1.125-4 indicates that if a judgment, decree, or order resulting from a divorce, legal separation, annulment, or change in legal custody (including a qualified medical child support order as defined in ERISA Section 609) requires accident or health coverage for an employee's child or for a foster child who is a dependent of the employee, the plan may do one of the following:

1. Change the employee's election to provide coverage for the child if the order requires coverage under the employee's plan; or
2. Permit the employee to change his or her election to revoke coverage for the child if the order requires that the employee's spouse or former spouse or other individual provide such coverage.

[Treas Reg § 1.125-4(d)]

Q 11:37 Does a legal document or order requiring health coverage for a child qualify as a permitted change in status under the final Treasury regulations?

Yes. If a judgment, decree, or order resulting from a divorce, legal separation, annulment, or change in legal custody—including a qualified medical child support order—requires accident or health coverage for an employee's child or foster child who is a dependent of the employee, the employee may elect to provide coverage for the child under the final Treasury regulations. Conversely, if the judgment, decree, or order requires the employee's spouse, former spouse, or other individual to provide coverage for the child, the employee may make an election to cancel coverage for the child.

COBRA

Q 11:38 How does COBRA impact options in a Section 125 plan?

A Section 125 plan participant (or a beneficiary of such a participant) who has a COBRA eligible qualifying event may elect coverage under a Section 125 plan in certain circumstances. For example, an employee may opt to pay for the COBRA coverage provided by his or her employer on a pretax basis under a Section 125 plan. (See Q 11.19.) Or, a former employee might opt to remain in a medical FSA after experiencing a COBRA qualifying event. COBRA continuation is discussed in Chapter 15.

Family and Medical Leave Act (FMLA)

Q 11:39 How does the Family and Medical Leave Act (FMLA) impact participation in a Section 125 plan?

The interaction of the FMLA and Section 125 plans is the subject of an entire set of Final Regulations. A copy of Final Regulations 1.125-3 is included as Appendix K. The application of Section 125 and the ability to change elections or remain a participant while on FMLA leave is described in Chapter 15.

Chapter 12

Communicating To Employees

Informing employees of the benefits available under a flexible plan and enrolling them into a plan can be time-consuming and expensive. Because the character of the employer's communications about the program directly affects both the enrollment and the ultimate success of the program, it is important for the employer to develop a strong message that accurately reflects both the philosophy and intent of the plan and the business conditions of the employer. Furthermore, it is essential to convey a flexible benefits program accurately if employees are to achieve a clear understanding of the choices available to them under the plan. This chapter highlights the importance of having a good communications strategy and describes methods of building effective communications plans. The first portion of this chapter will focus on developing a communications program for a new or changed flexible benefit plan, while the remainder of the chapter will discuss continuing communications approaches for an existing flexible benefit plan.

Q 12:1 What is a communications strategy?

A communications strategy is a statement of principles that describes in general terms—rather than in specific details—how concepts will be communicated from an employer to its employees. The communications strategy must be consistent with the overall business strategy that guides the employer. It outlines the corporate values that allow a company to position, within a broader context, specific flexible benefits messages effectively and correctly. In short, a communications strategy provides the blueprint an employer will use when making communications decisions.

An effective communications strategy for implementing a flexible benefits plan must address the concerns of both employees and employer. Employees must perceive the plan as being fair to them as well as being an intelligent business choice for the employer. A well-conceived communications strategy helps convince employees that the employer is looking out for their best interests and eases their natural reluctance to try something new.

To develop an effective communications strategy, the employer must also address the following considerations:

1. The need to deliver the message in an upbeat fashion, characterizing change as a positive development;
2. The need to show how the flexible benefits plan is compatible with the current economic climate; and
3. The need to fully disclose the reasons for implementing the change.

It is important to keep in mind that a communications strategy is *not* a communications plan. A strategy articulates a philosophical overview, whereas a plan requires detail. The specific details of a communications plan are developed from the overview of a communications strategy. The communications strategy is always a broad statement, as demonstrated by the following sample:

> The Company recognizes that competitive employee benefits are necessary to attract, retain, and motivate an intelligent, diverse workforce. The benefits must be comprehensive, flexible, and affordable for both the Company and employees. The Company will offer only those benefits that provide value for the employee and for the Company.
>
> The Company believes that well-informed employees with accurate information can make good decisions for themselves and their families. Employees must take control of the planning and selection of their own benefits.

The flexible benefits being offered must be communicated in a way that promotes employee involvement in decision making, and proper utilization of benefits based on understanding of the provisions of the plan.

The communications program should stress the idea of partnership between the employer and employees, cost effectiveness, and the flexibility offered by the plan. The communications materials should also help guide reluctant employees through the process of change when the plan is introducing new benefits or new concepts in the election or delivery of benefits.

Q 12:2 Why is a communications strategy important?

A communications strategy is a compass for those individuals charged with explaining a flexible benefits plan to employees. It provides both short-and long-term direction so that communicators do not lose the message or the focus of the employer's intent. A well-defined strategy keeps the message from being scattered or vague, and it avoids conflicting elements.

A communications strategy helps build employees' confidence in the company by allowing them to participate in setting the company's direction and to feel that that direction makes sense. Relating benefits communications to general business communications by means of the company's business strategy is essential—it focuses everyone on common goals.

A communication strategy helps communicators do the following:

1. *Deliver a consistent message.* A good communicator strives to create a consensus on issues that compete for attention, such as cost and quality.
2. *Repeat the message.* Consistent repetition familiarizes employees with the message and helps build understanding and a sense of trust.
3. *Reinforce the message with action.* Explanation followed by clear, visible activity helps build trust by communicating a sense of partnership between employer and employees.

For example, the strategy may require regular use of the word "cost" to reinforce delivery of "value" to the employees. If a communications strategy addresses the partnership of employer and employees in providing job and financial security, sharing benefits costs, and attaining value, a communicator must also discuss costs in the context of a partnership, cost sharing, and obtaining value—which serves as an outline for the discussion of costs.

Q 12:3 What must a communications strategy accomplish?

A communications strategy must accomplish two equally important objectives:

1. It must establish the context in which the flexible benefits plan will be discussed; and
2. It must define the values that underlie the flexible benefits plan.

Context. Messages are not delivered in a vacuum; a communications strategy helps to create and define the expectations of the employees who will eventually listen to the core message. Establishing the context must include the delivery of information about the external environment, such as escalating health care costs.

Frequently, the primary goal of a flexible benefits program is to spend the same amount of money spent formerly under the plan, but to allocate it differently. The concept of *smarter spending* targets the escalating rate of benefits plan costs and leads toward price stability. A communications strategy can support the concepts of cost-effectiveness and affordability in a flexible benefits plan. Employees do not want to pay for inefficiencies; they want their money spent wisely. Before employees readily agree to cost increases or additional coverage, they must believe the employer is doing everything it can to control costs. An essential component of affordability—in any discussion—is mutual cost sharing by both the employee and the employer.

Values. Benefits plans usually are based on the values that define the corporate culture (e.g., establishing the employees' right to affordable health care, a fair hearing, and a safe working environment). Corporate culture also dictates such things as whether employees wear jeans or suits to work and whether on-site day care is offered to working parents. An employer's values not only embody its identity, they also provide important clues for the style of communication it should use to present information to its employees. Corporate values guide the manner in which an organization directs its short-range operations and long-range actions. A communications strategy that promotes an open attitude about establishing a candid dialogue between employer and employees establishes a valuable forum in which change is treated as part of the normal course of events.

A typical communications strategy could include the following concepts and values:

1. The employer and its employees are partners in providing competitive benefits that create security and distribute costs fairly. As a partner, the employer provides its employees with information and assistance so that the employees can understand how to select and use the flexible benefits plan properly.
2. The benefits must be cost-effective and tax-efficient. They must be affordable for both the employer and the employees. They must provide real value. Employees must determine how to use their benefits wisely in a cost-effective manner and communications should reinforce that behavior.
3. The plan must be flexible enough to recognize the diverse needs of all employees; that flexibility, in turn, promotes broader communications on a range of issues. Such information is sometimes complex and may require some study and effort to understand it.
4. Employees must be given pertinent information in a style and format that will allow them to make informed, timely decisions for themselves and their families.

Q 12:4 Why should a communications strategy be conveyed to managers before it is revealed to employees?

A communications strategy should be conveyed to managers before it is revealed to employees for many reasons, chief of which are the following:

1. The employer wants managers to understand the strategy so they can support the initiative. More often than not, if managers find reason to support the flexible benefits plan, the plan also will gain rank-and-file acceptance. As organizations continue to downsize, managers may be the only contact most employees have with employer's policy; thus, convincing managers of the plan's validity is especially important.
2. Managers must be able to respond to employee inquiries regarding the organization's policy objectives. Unless managers are provided with reliable information, a flexible benefits plan is left defenseless against criticism and misinformation generated by the office grapevine. The job of the designated spokesperson for the plan becomes much more diffi-

cult when an employee who asks a manager whether the plan is a good deal is told: "I don't know; it looks like another cost-cutting move to me."

3. Managers also can serve as a valuable test group. An employer can "test" its communications strategy on managers before trying it out on employees in the form of group meetings or expensive newsletters. Managers will know immediately if the spokesperson is moving in the right direction or if employees are likely to scoff at the presentation.

Another practical value of managerial communications is that managers can advise communicators on how to most effectively employ buzzwords, which may be used somewhat differently by different employers, while avoiding terms that may be misunderstood or misinterpreted. For example, the word "affordable" may convey reasonable quality and cost by one employer, but it may carry the connotation of being cheap and worthless by another.

Q 12:5 When and how should a communications strategy be presented to managers?

The best time to present a communications strategy to managers is six to eight weeks before the general employee population receives information packets. The best way to reach management is by developing a white paper, or position paper, in which a communicator provides greater detail about the circumstances and content of the plan than that normally communicated to the average employee. The communicator includes all the appropriate details, thus allaying the suspicion that facts have been left out or obscured. In addition, the white paper may include a communications survey that invites managers to provide feedback on the strategy. (See Appendix F for a Sample Background Report for Management.) The white paper may be delivered to managers in print format or, as is increasingly the case, via electronic media such as e-mail, the Internet, or an intranet.

Q 12:6 What are the elements of a successful flexible benefits communications strategy?

The best flexible benefits communications strategy stresses responsibility and partnership. If the flexible benefits program is new, the communications strategy will want to approach the introduction of a flexible benefits plan as an effective way to change a benefits program that has been in place for a long time. The communications strategy should address the following issues:

- How the employer considers and makes a commitment to a given selection of employee benefits.
- What the employee can expect to be told by the employer.
- What the employer expects from the employee.
- What the roles of dependents and family members are.

- Why employee input and employee satisfaction are important measures of success.
- Which principles guide the operation of the plan; for example, benefits are cost-effective, benefits are a part of compensation, benefits are competitive.

Q 12:7 What roles do employees and the human resources staff play in developing a communications strategy?

For a communications strategy to be effective, it must be responsive to the concerns of the participants, who are, after all, the main audience. Employees play an important role in the development of a flexible benefits plan: they must be able to tell management which options work and which ones do not—and what they think and feel about the plan's implementation. The employees communicate feedback through surveys or focus groups.

Employee input is especially valuable during a period of transition in delivery of employee benefits. Often at such a time, employees' sense of entitlement is challenged, and that unease can motivate employees to resist reductions or changes in benefits. A communicator must be aware of such perceptions.

The human resources staff can be especially helpful in developing a communications strategy because of its experience disseminating information to employees. The staff should review the communications strategy to be sure it conforms to human resources initiatives in total compensation planning, recruiting, and quality management.

Part of the role of the human resources staff is to provide the communicator with the following information:

1. Demographic data, including age, sex, marital status, length of service, and salary data, about the employee population, to help the communicator develop an appropriate strategy; and
2. Competing issues that have the potential to consume employee efforts and direct attention away from implementation of the flexible benefits plan. For example, a reduction in workforce or a new job evaluation system can distract managers from concentrating productively on flexible benefits communications.

Q 12:8 How does a communications strategy give rise to a communications plan?

A communications *plan* is a detailed outline of what will be accomplished, what specific messages will be conveyed, who will be responsible for each task, how much the communications effort will cost, and when the implementation will be complete. It is a highly detailed tactical program.

A communications *strategy* provides an outline of how those activities will occur. For example, a strategy may call for a senior executive to announce the plan so as to give the implementation effort credibility and to assure employees that the effort is receiving support and authority. Furthermore, the strategy outlines the key words and concepts that the announcement will use (e.g., "partnership," "informed choice," "cost sharing," "value"). The plan specifies which executive will sign the announcement letter, when the letter will be sent, and how it will be distributed. The strategy provides the overall guidelines; the plan provides the operational details.

The communications plan may contain provisions for using some or all of the following resources in the communications effort:

- Focus groups to meet with the human resources, administration, and communications departments within the organization, as well as with outside advisors
- Position papers to be sent to the management group
- Newsletters announcing the new plan details (available in print or electronic format)
- Management training sessions
- Employee enrollment materials
- Employee meetings with question-and-answer sessions
- Visual aids
- Confirmation statements and follow-up newsletters

Q 12:9 How long does it take to develop a communications strategy and a communications plan?

The concepts underlying a communications strategy can be created in several hours, but considerable time is required for discussion and refinement. Discussion meetings may take place over several days or over weeks.

A communications plan usually takes more time to develop than does a communications strategy because a communications plan requires exhaustive detail. An estimate of the hours required to develop an overall plan is as follows:

Strategy Development	*Hours*
Research	15–20
Write outline	3–4
Review with management and update	6–8
Total	24–32

Plan Development		*Hours*
Research into flexible benefits plan details		20–30
Outline messages for	Newsletters (3)	6–8

Plan Development	*Hours*
Enrollment kit	6–8
Schedules	4–5
Total	36–51

Q 12:10 What are the steps to building a communications plan?

There is no single correct way to construct a communications plan, although the following steps are recommended:

1. Establish communications objectives.
2. Identify audiences.
3. Develop specific messages.
4. Conduct fact-finding and research.
5. Select media.
6. Identify tone.
7. Set time frames.
8. Establish a project team.
9. Determine feasibility of the plan.

Q 12:11 How does a communications plan define and establish communications objectives?

A communications plan must take into account both organizational and communications objectives. It is important to keep these objectives focused and specific. Ideally, there should be no more than six organizational objectives and no more than five communications objectives.

Organizational objectives. An organization's objectives form the core communications on which its specific benefits message may be layered. It is usually appropriate to include specific corporate values and objectives with the benefits messages, especially those that relate to market position and current financial challenges. Where possible, an employer's objectives should echo and even amplify the external themes, initiatives, and positions by which it is driven. Typical organizational objectives include the following:

- Increasing employees' awareness of the extent and cost of benefits.
- Promoting the perception that benefits are a significant part of a total compensation package.
- Encouraging employees to use benefits judiciously and economically.
- Involving employees in the selection and use of flexible benefits options.
- Becoming an "employer of choice."
- Responding to diverse employee needs.

Communications objectives. The communications objectives established by the communications plan include specific applications of at least one, and usually all three, of the following basic objectives: to inform; to educate; and to persuade.

Inform. Details and information in the form of announcements and brief introductions should be provided. "How-to-do-it" or "how-to-use-it" instructions should not be included. Informing is usually a one-step process using a single communications medium.

The following ideas are common to most flexible benefits plans and usually need to be made clear to employees:

1. Benefits are expensive.
2. The concept of one-size-fits-all does not work for benefits.
3. Personal responsibility replaces paternalism.
4. Benefits selection requires the active involvement of the employee.

Educate. More detailed materials that will help employees understand important and complex subject matter should be introduced. Employees should be shown how to use the data provided to make decisions and take actions. Messages should be reinforced through repetition, using two or more communications media.

Educational objectives can be developed by asking: "What basic concepts or rules must an employee understand to make the most intelligent and effective use of the flexible benefits plan?" The answers usually fall into the following categories:

1. *Determination of needs.* The employee determines his or her personal needs. It is essential to give the employee guidelines for choosing which medical plan is appropriate, how much life insurance is enough, and so on.
2. *Credit methodology.* An employee must understand how credits can be used.
3. *Pretax concept.* The employee must be able to measure the effect of pretax benefits elections.
4. *Dynamics and restrictions of benefits selection.* Elections in cafeteria plans are generally irrevocable once the period of coverage has begun, except under special circumstances allowed under the law (see Qs 11:14–11:37).

Persuade. A specific attitude should be created or encouraged that will modify existing behaviors. Employees should be convinced that the intended attitude or behavior is logical, desirable, and correct. When introducing a flexible benefit plan as a new concept, this is the most difficult communications objective to achieve because it requires people to change.

Attitude objectives can be isolated by asking, "What behaviors do we wish to see employees exhibit regarding this plan?" Some typical responses are as follows:

1. *Diligence and responsibility.* With work and study, employees will improve their finances and health, life, and disability income protection coverage.
2. *Involvement.* Employees will become smart consumers and work with the company to hold down costs.

Persuasion requires a communications approach that starts with a broad generalization and progresses toward a specific required action or desired behavior. The following examples of "broad" and "specific" statements illustrates this progression:

Broad

America is facing a health care crisis.

Health care costs are rising out of control.

Medical costs are growing much faster than all other benefits costs.

In order to remain competitive, our company must reduce benefits costs.

Employees want access to high-quality, affordable health care.

When employees have a financial interest in managing their health benefits, unnecessary health care costs will be reduced.

Specific

The company is replacing the traditional medical insurance plan with a higher deductible plan. At the same time, the company will fund a personal health care account for each employee, which will help subsidize uninsured medical expenses such as deductibles. When medical care is necessary, the insurance plan and health care account will help provide the funds necessary. However, if health care is not a necessary expenditure, the balance in the compny-funded health care account will roll over from year to year, until used on medical expenses, as necessary.

In this way, the available balance in the health care account may accumulate over time, and remain ready to cover uninsured qualified medical expenses as they arise.

Q 12:12 How does an employer identify the audiences for a communications plan?

Typically, a benefits communication has several primary and secondary audiences. Primary audiences may consist of the following groups:

- All active employees
- Non-English-speaking employees
- Illiterate or subliterate employees
- Exempt employees
- Nonexempt employees
- Retirees

- Line supervisors and managers
- Spouses of active employees.

Secondary audiences may consist of any of the preceding groups plus any of the following groups:

- Union employees who are not included in the new program
- Employees who do not participate in the existing program
- Employees who are not yet eligible for the program
- Employees who are approaching retirement

It is important to identify and target appropriate messages for each distinct audience in the communications plan. When listing each audience, identify all work-related, social, or demographic factors that could affect the audience's interpretation of the messages, such as education level or language. Indicate the primary purpose of each objective—whether it is to inform, educate, or persuade each primary and secondary audience.

Q 12:13 How should an employer develop specific messages in a communications plan?

The employer must develop a series of short, direct statements that connect its organizational objectives with corresponding communication objectives. The messages, adapted for each primary audience, should be benefit-specific and will become the core of each communication.

Key messages should provide answers to the following questions:

1. Why is the plan being offered?
2. What are the major advantages or features of the plan?
3. What activities are required of the employee?
4. When is the plan available?
5. What are the deadlines for enrolling?

Q 12:14 What advance research must an employer conduct in order to develop a communications plan?

Before creating a communications plan, an employer should analyze any successes and failures it has already experienced in communicating similar messages to employees. A review of past projects can reveal which measures work well for a particular audience and which presentation styles the employer should avoid. First hand knowledge is invaluable in this kind of research, which also should include a review of all available expense information for earlier projects. This review and analysis will help substantiate the feasibility of the current effort.

The employer should also compile a preliminary list of available human, financial, and administrative resources needed to support the communications effort.

Human resources.

- *Technical resources* include both employees and consultants who can provide the benefit, legal, financial, systems, and administrative support to develop and execute the plan.
- *Operational resources* include both employees and consultants who can provide media planning, writing, editing, design, training, and project management support to implement a communications plan.
- *Approval resources* include all individuals whose approval is needed to implement any phase of a plan.

Financial resources. Identify the range of financial support available for the project before establishing a budget. It may be helpful to determine the staff time and out-of-pocket expenses committed to similar projects. The goal of each communications plan is to maximize all time and expenses, so analyzing comparable past projects provides a yardstick for measuring the relative value offered by the current plan.

Administrative resources. Identify conflicting projects, meetings, or conferences that may compete for the attention and availability of the administrative resources required for the communications effort.

Q 12:15 How should an employer select the media that will be used to implement a communications plan?

The communications plan should identify and sequence every communications medium and event that will be used to implement the plan. Each medium or event can address one or more communications objectives. The following checklist includes events that frequently figure in major communications plans.

Note. Introducing a flexible benefit plan in a smaller organization, or communicating a plan that is not a radical departure from the existing approach will not require such an extensive selection of media.

Media Checklist

1. Notification

❒ Memorandum at office
❒ Letter at office
❒ Letter at home
❒ Newsletter at office
❒ Newsletter at home
❒ E-mail at office

2. Public announcement

❒ Posters
❒ E-mail
❒ Articles in the company newspaper
❒ Broadcast voice-mail messages

3. Management support

Media Checklist (*cont'd*)

- ❒ Paycheck inserts
- ❒ Training booklets/manuals
- ❒ Q&As for employees
- ❒ Q&As for managers and supervisors
- ❒ Q&As for trainers/HR personnel

4. Enrollment materials

- ❒ Train-the-trainer meetings
- ❒ Personalized benefits statements
- ❒ Personalized enrollment/benefits statements
- ❒ Employee telephone hotline
- ❒ Internet/intranet enrollment
- ❒ Video presentations
- ❒ Highlight brochure
- ❒ Employee general attendance meetings
- ❒ Slides/overhead presentations
- ❒ Employee workbooks/Web applications
- ❒ General enrollment booklets/Web publications
- ❒ Personalized enrollment booklets
- ❒ Telephone voice response

5. Compliance

- ❒ Summary plan descriptions for underlying ERISA plans
- ❒ Summary of material modifications for underlying ERISA plans

Although particular media may lend themselves to certain phases of the benefits communications campaign—for example, newsletters and e-mail can be particularly effective in notifying employees about an upcoming enrollment—it is important to consider carefully the use of one medium over another. Selection of specific media will depend on a variety of factors, including the following:

- Specific organizational/communications plan objectives
- Company flexibility and openness to change
- Time frame and complexity of the communications plan
- Experience with communications delivery systems and knowledge of what works well for a particular company
- Technical and operational resources available in-house or through other providers
- Available administrative resources and the preferences of administrative executives/decision makers
- Available financial resources
- Size and composition of the plan's audience
- Employee comfort level with technology
- Consistency of communications media selected with the tone of the messages

Extra care in media selection helps ensure a smooth and effective communications campaign and flexible benefits enrollment.

Q 12:16 How should the communications plan's tone be determined and implemented?

The communications plan should identify the tone of each message. The strategy, objectives, and audiences will determine this tone.

The tone of a communication is derived from its design and writing style. Tone signals the image, attitude, and message a plan projects. When well-planned and controlled, tone contributes enormously to the overall effectiveness of the plan when ignored or poorly conceived, it can undermine or even destroy the message's effectiveness. For instance, a slick, four-color, high-quality annual report is not appropriate for introducing a benefits reduction or cost-sharing plan, because it establishes a contradiction between the employer's stated message and the employees' perception of the message (tone), which could damage the plan's objectives.

Writing style, selection of vocabulary, and graphics primarily establish the tone of a communications plan. The overall communications plan should indicate in advance how serious or light-hearted the writing style should be. Also, graphic elements such as cartoon illustrations, photographs, pie charts, etc., should be consistent with plan objectives. Just as a communications plan should avoid light-hearted cartoons to illustrate a major cost-shifting of benefits cost to employees, a formal, all-text approach to a significant improvement in the benefits package might under emphasize the positive aspects of the change, or may even be misconstrued by employees as a negative change.

Q 12:17 What time frames must a communications plan establish?

Timing can determine the success or failure of a communications effort. The importance of timing to the success of the effort increases in proportion to the size and complexity of the communications plan. An employer cannot condense a six-month benefits communications plan into six weeks and expect to achieve acceptable results.

The communications plan should break large projects down into four phases: (1) introduction and training; (2) education; (3) enrollment and installation; and (4) follow-up and review. Each phase can then be organized as a small project and presented in weekly intervals.

The communications plan designates the planning, preparation, production, and distribution of each communication element.

Q 12:18 How does an employer establish a project team for a communications plan?

The communications plan should identify a project team. Team members can be drawn from the list of human resources staff and consultants (see Q 12:14). Generally, the following disciplines are required:

- *Plan design expert.* This person must have a strong background in the specifics of the benefits program. The plan design expert provides information on eligibility, cost, and other plan details.
- *Legal advisor.* This person monitors the employer's compliance with various federal and state laws and regulations regarding communications with employees regarding their benefits.
- *Administrative/payroll staffer.* This person plays an essential role from the beginning of the effort because so much of the implementation is payroll-driven.
- *Vendor representative.* Insurance carriers and outside administrators should be available to define and clarify their roles and information needs.

Q 12:19 How does the employer determine the feasibility of the communications plan?

An effective way to test the feasibility of the communications plan is to have a preliminary project team meeting to review the plan, step by step. The primary purpose of this meeting is to garner each team member's point of view and opinion. The project team's comments are incorporated into the final communications plan, and this revised plan is circulated to the team. The preliminary review helps to ensure that each member both supports the strategy and accepts his or her responsibilities. Obtaining the concurrence and commitment of the project team is a good indication of the plan's feasibility.

Q 12:20 What is audience assessment, and why is it important?

Audience assessment is the research process that communicators use to determine how an audience will react to a certain set of conditions or messages. When introducing or significantly changing a flexible benefits program, it is essential to include employees in the decision making process. Not only would it seem odd to tell employees that the plan was designed for them without asking for their input, but the plan would have less chance of success without that input. Often, input from employees can prevent catastrophes later. The process of gathering feedback allows concepts to be developed openly while confidence grows within the communications group that its message will be well received.

Q 12:21 How is audience assessment done?

Communicators rely on employee surveys and focused discussion groups and/or one-on-one interviews conducted with both managers and employees to assess their audience. Such proven research techniques are more widely accepted than anecdotal information that, at best, is unreliable and, at worst, is inaccurate.

Employee surveys. Employee surveys play an important role in defining and reaching an audience, and their importance is not confined to employee benefits and compensation. Such surveys can probe employees' perceptions of a company's top management, supervisory relationships, communication effectiveness, working conditions, career development, and job opportunities. Specifically, effective use of employee surveys accomplishes the following goals:

- Determining the overall health of a company's morale at a given time
- Helping establish priorities for benefits changes
- Providing baseline data for measuring the success of benefits plans and programs and their effect on employees' attitudes and needs
- Acting as safety valves for employees, allowing them to vent frustrations in a constructive manner
- Assuring employees that their opinions are important, valued, and taken into account in decision making
- Making it clear to employees that difficult choices must be made
- Helping to predict (and evaluate) the reaction to a new program or changes to an existing benefit
- Eliciting suggestions for improving benefits offerings and administration

Employee surveys can examine four types of information that are useful to employers:

1. Attitudes and perceptions—how employees feel about certain benefits.
2. Knowledge—how much employees know about specific benefits.
3. Behavior—what employees actually do in relation to a benefit program.
4. Demographics—how various subgroups of employees compare in terms of their attitudes, levels of knowledge, and behavior.

Combining such types of information can be revealing. For instance, by looking at employee attitudes and knowledge together, it is possible to determine whether employees' perceptions about their benefits are based on fact or misconception. Further, the survey data can help direct remedial efforts. As a result, instead of spending more money to improve benefits, an employer may be able to spend less and achieve better results by directing efforts at improving employees' understanding and appreciation of existing benefits.

A survey is more than a tool to help an employer focus on specific attitudes of its audience; it is also a communications device in its own right that can be used to present important background information to employees. When administering a survey, an employer should explain to employees what is being done and why. The employer should use the survey as an opportunity to create a positive impression about trust and respect between the company and employees by promising feedback to employees after the results are consolidated and analyzed.

When administering employee surveys, special care should be taken to:

1. *Acknowledge the special concerns of managers and supervisors.* These individuals may feel threatened by a survey and could undermine the

process if they do not understand its intent or how the results will be used.

2. *Guarantee confidentiality.* Employees will be more likely to participate and give honest responses if their anonymity is assured.
3. *Set realistic expectations.* A survey is an opportunity to explain the facts that management must consider before making decisions. Employees' preferences, budgetary constraints, legal considerations, and regulations all must be considered. It is important that the employer tell the employees how information gleaned from the survey will be used, and that employees be given sufficient time to complete the survey.

Focused discussion groups and one-on-one interviews. Focused discussion groups and one-on-one interviews may be conducted when an employee survey is not feasible (e.g., because of time constraints) as alternative vehicles for gathering information and assessing opinion.

Q 12:22 What issues must an employer consider before conducting an employee benefits survey?

A series of preliminary questions includes the following:

- Who should design the survey?
- Should the employer survey all employees, get a random sample, or examine a select group?
- Should the employer administer the questions on site during work hours, or mail it to employees' homes?
- Which benefits should the survey cover?
- What type of questions should the survey contain?

There is no single correct answer for any of these questions. Each employer's unique situation helps to determine the right answers for that employer.

Q 12:23 What is the importance of feedback to the employer?

There are four fundamental ways to review survey data:

1. On a stand-alone basis;
2. In comparison to other companies;
3. In terms of the relative importance of various issues; and
4. Over time, by comparing the data to earlier survey responses.

All four methods of analysis can provide useful information about the audience and the need for benefits communications. However, the last two are probably the most meaningful. Analyzing the number or percentage of employees who respond one way or another to a battery of questions provides statistics—but not context. Comparative data can be interesting and helpful, but they can also be misleading.

Q 12:24 What is the importance of feedback to the employee?

Employees take surveys seriously and are usually pleased that their opinions are sought. If no feedback is given, however, they will assume their input is not valued or was discarded. That can severely damage an employere's credibility. The employer can take proactive measures to prevent the problem by making the survey the beginning of a process of examination, not an isolated event. The employer should be prepared to act on the results and should make its intention clear to employees when the surveys are distributed.

In addition, focus should be on positive as well as negative results. Surveys usually reveal areas of strengths, as well as weaknesses that need improvement. The employer should use the feedback process to capitalize on those strengths, and consider an action plan to minimize weaknesses.

Q 12:25 What communications are needed to inform employees about special features that have been built into the plan design for their protection?

While choice-driven plans place responsibility on employees to analyze their needs and make sound benefits selections, choice-driven plans cannot prevent an employee from making a poor decision. Thus, employees are understandably nervous about making the complex decisions that flexible plans require. To help employees avoid making a potentially serious mistake, it is important to inform them about whatever safeguards the plan will contain. For example, some plans offer a default basic health insurance coverage that all employees receive, even if they do not actively make any elections within the plan.

Q 12:26 What is the message phase of a communications plan, and why is it important?

A clear and compelling message enables employees to grasp program elements and act upon the choices available to them. The perceptions and facts concerning the flexible benefits plan that remain with employees as a result of the communications program are—for better or worse—the messages they have to work with. The cumulative effect of the individual messages usually builds until enrollment, by which time all messages are delivered.

Some messages are not readily accepted. Messages can fail to be convincing for a number of reasons, including the following:

1. *Lack of authority*. Unless the new changes obviously have the approval of upper management, employees will not take them seriously.
2. *Lack of supervisory support*. Supervisors who do not support benefits communications can be a barrier to acceptance. A supervisor's opinion can color employees' impressions of a plan—either favorably or unfavorably.

Q 12:27 How does an employer develop and convey a message?

Developing a message is the result of a logical question-and-answer process. The following questions may be helpful in creating a comprehensive message:

- Why change to a flexible benefits plan? Include three key issues—
    1. *Flexibility*. Employees will have a choice of benefits options.
    2. *Cost*. Does the company expect to increase, maintain, or reduce its costs?
    3. *Diversity*. The company wishes to provide options that will address the diverse needs of the workforce.
- What other solutions did the employer investigate?
- Why is change necessary at this time?
- How were the changes determined?
- How much input came from employees?
- How do the changes compare with the current plan?
- How will the cost of the new benefits compare with those of the current plan?
- Who will the changes affect?
- When will the changes become effective?
- Will employees be able to keep their current coverage?
- Are there any elements or features in the flexible benefits plan that will affect employees' tax liabilities?
- How will the plan compare with those offered by other employers?
- What are the major improvements to the plan?
- Is it necessary for employees to enroll?
- What is the enrollment process?

Q 12:28 What basic concepts must employees understand about flexible benefits plans to use them effectively?

Employees must understand several concepts to use flexible plans effectively. For example, employees must understand that a flexible benefits plan is based on employees choosing what they need and that pretax contributions for benefits result in tax savings for the employee. Furthermore, some flexible plans make use of credits to purchase benefits; if the benefits cost more than the credits, employees must make up the shortfall.

Q 12:29 What is the importance of a "theme" in conveying a message?

A theme helps capture the main elements of the new plan. For example, a theme entitled "Benefits by Design" establishes the concept that employees design their own coverage. A theme entitled "Flex Choice" ties the element of choice to the concept of flexibility.

As a matter of fact, the flexible benefits program often becomes known as "flex"—no matter what name is selected. However, a theme can be helpful in focusing attention on a new plan and in creating a positive identity for it.

Q 12:30 Why should the flexible benefits communicators develop different messages?

Different messages are important because they address the needs of different components of the employee population. Some employees may not be covered by the flexible design; others may be members of a group that participates in a different plan design; and some employees may not yet be eligible for the flexible plan.

These differences may occur because of special staffing needs or collective bargaining agreements. Employers need to reach ineligible groups with special messages explaining why they are not covered by a particular effort.

Because a new flexible benefits program is often touted as an "improved delivery system for benefits," communicators must be careful not to alienate groups not yet covered by the plan. If some employees are not covered by the flexible benefits plan, the details of that group's coverage should be communicated to the group as the details of the flexible benefits plan are explained to the group eligible for flexible benefits. Both groups must be treated as parts of a broad-based communications process that is all-inclusive.

This strategy of inclusion also applies to a collective bargaining agreement. An employer that wishes to send information to covered employees, perhaps with the objective of including them in a flexible plan, should check with the industrial relations and legal staff to make sure such an action would not create a technical violation of an existing contract.

In general, only those benefits aimed at a particular group should be explained to that group in detail. An exception occurs if certain benefits, such as a health maintenance organization (HMO) or other medical coverage, are offered specifically to one group and not to another. In such an instance, the employer should explain why its benefits offerings were limited—or different—for certain groups.

Q 12:31 What are the barriers to message acceptance?

A number of situations, such as lack of time, information overload, excessive loss of benefits, and complexity of benefits options, present clear and certain difficulties for the individual or team charged with bringing the message to the employees. In some instances such difficulties will prove so overwhelming as to entirely prevent the employees from being receptive to or accepting of the content.

Lack of time. If there is not enough time for employees to become accustomed to the new concept, they may reject the notion that change is necessary. If there is not enough time for employees to make an educated choice, they may not feel confident about their selections, and that may cause them to resent the plan. The plan sponsor should establish a realistic time frame for implementing a flexible benefits plan (see Q 2:19).

Information overload. Another barrier to acceptance is having too much change occur at one time. When flexible plans are implemented, employers tend to improve all plans at the same time. That entails changes to existing plans and the addition of new plans. The entire process, which also may include the use of credits, may be overwhelming and can leave employees feeling that the plan is too difficult to understand or to accept. Under such circumstances, a communicator must break the message down into bite-size portions and explain each element of the new plan individually. A series of newsletters or other announcements can be sent to employees until they become conversant with all parts of the plan. Such an approach can be difficult because the communicator must attract and hold employees' attention for several months.

Excessive loss of benefits. If benefit modifications appear to be reducing the number of available benefits or passing along higher costs than employees are accustomed to paying, employees will believe that the flexible benefits plan is a mechanism for shifting costs to them. The best response is to emphasize that being able to elect the specific benefits required will result, in the long run, in lower costs for employees.

Complexity of benefits options. The benefits options and the implementation of a credit/cost formula system can be difficult to explain. Two approaches can be used to handle this problem:

1. The time and energy necessary to explain how the credits were calculated should be expanded. That may entail explaining the distinctions between benefits provided for younger and older employees and the salary-based structure of the credits. For clarity, the employer may also need to explain the so-called subsidy for family coverage—the inherent subsidy provided for those who elect family medical coverage that keeps this coverage affordable to the average employee.

   The family subsidy can be explained as the company's attempt to provide benefits during a complete "range of employment"; that is, to offer benefits plans to employees who are at different stages in their careers. The idea is that for some periods in an employee's career the company makes extra contributions, but the company will amortize its costs over the length of an employee's career.

2. Some employers contend that it is not possible to explain all the benefit option concepts. They believe the employees will understand how the credit formulas affect them only after they elect coverage and authorize deductions from their paychecks. Such belief can result in a tendency to gloss over the details of how credits are calculated. Companies may provide worksheets to help employees work it out for themselves. (See Appendixes B and G for sample calculation sheets.)

Q 12:32 What is a communications environment?

Communications are always delivered within the cultural environment of a specific company. This environment is a composite of the following:

1. Business climate;
2. Profitability;
3. How the company finds, hires, treats, and develops employees; and
4. Management's credibility with employees.

A communicator must have a good understanding of the cultural environment to correctly position the message. For example, if the company is attempting to cut costs and wishes to encourage frugality among employees, it would not be appropriate nor consistent to generate expensive communications materials.

If the company culture endorses face-to-face communications in meetings, that method should be applied to communicating a flexible benefits program. If management has enormous credibility with its employees, management should explain the flexible benefits program to employees. Conversely, if management keeps a low profile, and first-line supervisors or human resources staff typically communicate effectively with employees, those individuals should present the plan.

The communicator also must realize that the communications environment normally reflects the fear of change that most people have concerning anything as important as their benefits plans. To help counteract that fear, the communications should be presented in a concerned, nonconfrontational way that offers reassurance during the period of change.

Employees, for their part, must be aware that employers are becoming less paternal. Instead of picking and paying for benefits, employers are implementing systems that compel employees to accept personal responsibility for their selections. Such a shift is occurring throughout the workplace, and benefits programs are no exception. The communicator must emphasize that a paternal system does not permit employees the range of choices required by a workforce that increasingly consists not only of traditional family groups, but also of one-parent families, spouse-only families, and individuals. By implementing flexible systems that provide a choice of desirable benefits options, employers hope employees will find it worthwhile to help pay for the benefits they really need.

Q 12:33 How can a communicator determine an employer's communications environment?

Conducting surveys and interviews with employees and managers will provide the primary means of determining an employer's communications environment. Interviews with the designers of the flexible benefits plan, upper management, and those who will deliver the benefits, such as the human resources, benefits, and payroll groups, can be quite helpful. The important task for the communicator is to obtain a composite picture of the views of upper management, designers, and line managers, so that the communications, when disseminated, will transmit information effectively to each of the various constituent groups.

For example, when the concept of a flexible plan is presented to various constituencies, different aspects of the plan will naturally and spontaneously draw the interest and attention of different groups. The finance group may tend to focus on financial concerns, whereas the human resources group may find the concepts of flexibility and diversity most intriguing. Curiously, both focal points of interest can exist within the message simultaneously without being contradictory. If well communicated, they can even reinforce each other.

The plan's design team also analyzes the communications environment. It discusses the external environment, including factors such as significant increases in health care costs and difficulty in locating insurance carriers and other vendors to provide necessary oversight services (e.g., cost management and monitoring quality of service). First-line managers frequently express the opinion that employees are pleased with their benefits plan but need more information to use it more effectively.

A sample message containing many underlying themes that will appeal to many different constituencies within an employee population appears in the Sample Background Report for Management in Appendix F.

Q 12:34 What is the role of the communicator?

In a flexible benefits plan implementation, the communicator identifies the message sender and resolves competing interests and formats the material so that it presents a unified view to the group receiving the message.

Identify the message sender. The communicator must determine how closely the employer wishes to be connected to the development of the flexible benefit plan. For example, when the employer is clearly sending the message, the material may state, "We have developed a flexible benefits plan for your use." If the employer does not wish to be identified as at the center of plan design (and thus the sender of the message), the material may state, "The flexible benefits plan has been developed to help you select your own benefits program."

The second format is written in the passive voice to avoid identifying the subject of the sentence—in this case, the developer of the plan. Communication plans that employ the passive voice frequently encounter difficulties when the need for subsequent communications arises. Because it is less direct, that form of address disguises the employer's commitment to, belief in, and support for the plan. For those reasons, most communicators opt for a declarative form of announcement using the active voice that clearly identifies the employer as the message sender.

The communicator must also determine the advisability of having the message emanate from senior management or from the benefits and human resources staff. Those decisions usually are dictated by company culture.

Resolve competing interests. By surveying the different constituencies, the communicator discovers various rationales for plan implementation. In order to explain those convictions to employees, communicators must invent a universal solution containing arguments that are appealing and even compelling to many diverse groups. That involves understanding the motivations and objectives of each group.

Q 12:35 Is it advisable to isolate "good" and "bad" news messages?

No. The communicator must strive to present information in a balanced format that conveys good and bad news simultaneously in a balanced outline of facts.

To be effective, the issues should be derived from the same time frame: there is no point in recycling last year's good news to counterbalance this year's bad news. Fortunately for those communicating and implementing flexible benefits plans, what is perceived as bad news may apply to only a small number of employees. It is also helpful to keep in mind that negative news for one group may be neutral for another.

Q 12:36 Should "bad" news be minimized or slanted differently to seem not so bad?

Usually, employees will figure out the real message. There is a credibility risk if bad news is disguised or minimized. A balanced approach is usually better. For example, if an employer is raising health insurance plan deductibles in order to save money, it should not state that the new health plan is being implemented to help employees become better consumers. However, if the new high deductible plan will also save employees money, that fact should be included in the communications materials to employees.

Q 12:37 What specific rules should a communicator follow in the presentation of a message?

The objective is to keep the communications as clear and simple as possible so that there will be no artificial barriers to comprehension. By applying the following simple rules, the communicator can achieve that objective:

1. Avoid complex mathematical examples that are difficult to apply and understand. Pie charts and bar graphs may be used to compare numbers and costs because they are relatively simple, have clear visual impact, and are understood intuitively by most employees.
2. Be careful when writing in the second person. Use of terms such as *we* and *you* may highlight an already adversarial relationship between the employer and the employees receiving the benefits. In the right setting,

however, writing in the second person can be inviting, warm, and friendly.

3. Avoid using a tone that is either too formal or too sophisticated. Sounding too formal can be disturbing and may even have a dehumanizing effect on the benefits program. Formal language also tends to make employees suspicious of the employer's intentions, and it may send them searching for a hidden agenda. A friendly, conversational tone is much better than a formal tone for explaining benefits issues.

4. Use a simple question-and-answer format that allows the employee to enter into a real-life situation. It may be advisable to distribute a series of questions and answers separately from the communications materials or to give it to supervisors. Because supervisors often are queried about plans, they should receive the questions and appropriate answers before the general employee population.

5. Write at the seventh- or eighth-grade level rather than at high school or college level. An example of an appropriate reading level is the level used by most newspapers.

6. Include examples with anecdotal information that draws a useful conclusion. One scenario might describe someone in good health, requiring little or no medical care, who opts for a higher deductible or a higher coinsurance limit. The conclusion of the scenario is that the person described saves money regularly by not paying the high cost of a coverage that she probably will not use.

Q 12:38 Do special rules apply to the use of electronic media to communicate with employees?

There are no special rules that apply solely to the use of electronic media to communicate with employees. The rules customarily applied to any medium should be followed when using an interactive voice response (IVR) system, e-mail, the Internet, or an intranet. An employer should, as always, be tuned in to and considerate of the audience being targeted. It should make sure its messages are not only upbeat and appropriate for that audience, but also consistent with the communications strategy that defines the employer's values. It is important to keep in mind that employees need to receive pertinent information in a style and format that will allow them to make educated, timely decisions for themselves, their dependents, and their beneficiaries. With electronic media, as with all types of media used to communicate flexible benefits plans, the hallmark of effective communication is *clarity*. In that respect, special care must be taken in the design and use of an IVR system—essentially a nonvisual communications vehicle (although some type of printed worksheet is normally used with IVR benefits enrollment).

Q 12:39 What communications efforts need to be initiated?

A flexible benefits plan is actually a delivery vehicle; its underlying plans covered by ERISA are subject to ERISA disclosure requirements (see Q 11:2). A summary of material modifications (SMM) must be provided to employees as changes occur in information required to be in the summary plan description (SPD) and in certain other items. The SPDs for the plans must be made available to the employees upon enrollment or shortly thereafter.

Other appropriate administrative procedures include having employees who opt for no medical coverage provide the name of the plan under which they are covered to ensure they are not going without medical coverage just to receive a cash reimbursement.

The employer should provide each employee with a confirmation of the employee's selected options. The confirmation should also state the conditions under which changes to coverage can occur. For cafeteria plans, the frequency and conditions under which changes may take place are dictated by law.

Coordinating the implementation date of the plan with the appearance of a short article or memorandum in the company newsletter that alerts employees to the implementation is a good idea and a practical communication device. The memorandum should remind employees to check their paystubs for the deduction amounts and, in flexible plans, to check the amount being returned to them for accuracy.

Q 12:40 What elements does a typical flexible benefits plan campaign include?

A typical flexible benefits plan campaign begins with a letter from the president or another high-ranking officer of the company that introduces the plan. The letter is followed by a series of newsletters that state the following:

1. The reasons for the changes in the benefits plan;
2. The rationale for providing choice within a plan;
3. Major benefits options available under the new plan;
4. An outline of the timetable projected for implementation; and
5. A listing of opportunities the employer will provide for employees to ask questions or review other communications materials.

The newsletters are followed by an enrollment kit that contains detailed information about each specific option, including eligibility, cost, major benefit descriptions, and significant plan exclusions. It is important to provide employees with the opportunity to attend small group meetings to allow them to ask specific questions about their particular situations. If such meetings prove impractical, the employer should make an effort to educate supervisors about how various situations might be handled.

Many companies produce either a video or a slide show that explains the details of the flexible benefits plan. Video presentations may range from simple explanations given by benefit managers to elaborate productions. The advantage of a video or other visual format is that it holds employees' interest and delivers a consistent, upbeat message to everyone. Meetings led by supervisors or human resources staff tend to run out of steam over time, and employees who attend later presentations may see a less impressive, more lackluster presentation that does not truly represent the effort that went into creating the flexible benefits program. (Conversely, sometimes presenters get better with each presentation, and thus, the first presentations are more "wooden.")

Certain aspects of the plan will provoke questions from employees. With regard to health care, for example, employees will want to know how certain situations will affect them, such as coverage of spouse and children under more than one plan, choice of physicians within a network, out-of-town medical services, and scheduling of surgical procedures.

If supervisors are unavailable or unable to respond to such queries, the organization paying the claims or providing the coverage (such as an insurance carrier) can become the source of information, and employees can be given a telephone number or web site to contact for specific answers. After enrollment, employees should receive written confirmation of the coverage they have elected or have received by default. The administrative staff may allow employees to alter their selections at that point if their selections were incorrectly recorded or if employees have changed their minds.

An Interactive Voice Response (IVR) system, an outgrowth of the voice-mail system, allows employees to select the benefits they want by telephone. By using such a self-enrollment system, employees have immediate access to their benefits information and can change their elections, update dependent information, and correct inaccurate data—all without delays. An IVR system not only reduces paperwork and allows employees to enroll at their convenience (during open enrollment periods), it also gives supervisors and human resources staff more time to resolve problem situations.

Growing at an even faster pace is enrollment to a benefit plan via the Internet, or a company's intranet. Often, an outside third party administrator will maintain participant balances in FSAs and other pertinent information that can be accessed on a secure site by use of a log-in and password. In some cases, employees may even submit their own request for change in coverage, based on a change in status.

Enrollment via the Internet has many of the advantages of IVR, with the added advantage of being an appealing, somewhat speedier and more visual enrollment process.

As the communications process comes to a close, each employee should receive a newsletter or other memorandum that proclaims the entire effort a great success, highlights the diversity of the benefits chosen, and notes the company's continued interest in examining other ways to provide employee benefits on an efficient, tax-effective basis.

Q 12:41 What features distinguish the various media used to communicate flexible benefits plans?

Table 12-1 provides an overview of various methods of communicating that experienced professionals use effectively. Communications campaigns often achieve excellent results by combining different media.

Table 12-1. Comparison of Communication Methods

Media Type	*Definition*	*Objectives*	*Pros*	*Cons*	*Information*
Announcement postcards	Colorful postcards sent to home or office	Notify employee about an upcoming benefit event	Inexpensive	Limited to brief facts	Minimal
Audiovisual/video	Slide, tape, or video presentations	Convey corporate objectives, strategies, philosophy	An audiovisual supplemented by a printed piece results in a 90% retention factor	Modifications can be difficult; viewing equipment required	Varies with application
Bulletin board notices	Short, simple descriptions of plan changes and updates	Inform, advertise	Inexpensive	Can be overlooked	Minimal
Confirmation of benefit election statements	Personalized statement following completion of an open enrollment process	Allows employee to correct errors	Ensures employee satisfaction with benefit elections	May encourage changes to benefit elections, creating additional work	Minimal
E-mail	Inter- and intra-office computer-generated communications	Notify employee about an upcoming benefits event	If system already in place (many companies rely on e-mail), not expensive; speedy way to communicate with employees	Some employees may be uncomfortable with its use; if system is down, communications may be delayed	Minimal
Employee handbooks/guidebooks	A reference containing policies,	Educate	Can help to maintain employee sat-	Amount of information can over-	Medium

Table 12-1. Comparison of Communication Methods (*cont'd*)

Media Type	*Definition*	*Objectives*	*Pros*	*Cons*	*Information*
	procedures, and benefits program		isfaction with programs	whelm and intimidate	
Employee meetings	A forum for explaining benefits and clarifying programs	Educate	Effective	Employees may vent unrelated concerns	Maximum
Enrollment brochure	Comprehensive overview of plans giving instructions for enrollment; sent to employees during new-hire orientation and annual enrollment periods	Call to action	Effective educational/reference tool	Amount of information can overwhelm and intimidate	Medium
Enrollment form	Means by which employees join benefits plan	Call to action	Standardized forms may facilitate enrollment	Must comply with legal and data entry requirements	Minimal
Focus groups	Meetings at which employees discuss proposed changes, current programs, communication efforts	Fact-finding	An effective survey mechanism	May require staffing investment and/or outside consultant	Varies
Highlight brochures	Overview of plan; may support audiovisual or video presentation or	Educate new employees; inform existing employees; recruit pro-	Informative	Lack depth; may raise questions; need supportive materials	Minimal

Table 12-1. Comparison of Communication Methods (*cont'd*)

Media Type	*Definition*	*Objectives*	*Pros*	*Cons*	*Information*
	summarize a reference brochure or SPD	spective employees			
Interactive modeling software	Personalized "what if" scenarios for employees	Educate, inform, create excitement	Allows employees to determine and compare economic benefits of a variety of benefit choices	May be expensive; effectiveness varies depending on employees' comfort with computers	Varies
Internet enrollment	A Web-based, online, self-enrollment system	Facilitate enrollment or benefit changes	Visual, speedy, paperless, easily accessible method for employees to enroll themselves	May be expensive; some employees may be uncomfortable with computers; security issues	Minimal
Internet-based publications/applications	Online, computer-generated newsletters and enrollment-related information	Inform, educate employees about benefits and enrollment procedures	Convenient, speedy means of reaching many employees, who can access at their convenience	May be expensive; everyone may not have Internet access	Medium
Invitations	Requests for attendance at an event include date, time, location	Create awareness of important benefit events	Gives employee sense of importance—the VIP approach	Throwaway communications piece (no shelf life)	Minimal
Letters to home or office	Explain a plan feature or illustrate tax advantages;	Inform; letters sent to employee's home may reach	Likely to be read; can convey that employee is a val-	May be lost among junk mail	Varies

Table 12-1. Comparison of Communication Methods (*cont'd*)

Media Type	*Definition*	*Objectives*	*Pros*	*Cons*	*Information*
	may target specific events such as retirement, disability, or layoff	employee's family	uable asset to company		
Memorandum at office	Nonpersonalized memo describing benefit changes, updates	Inform	People generally read their office mail	May be lost in an overflowing in-box	Varies
Newsletter articles	Announce benefit changes or highlight plan features; contain benefit news, Q&As, interviews, puzzles, contests, cartoons	Create general awareness	Keep employees aware of the existence of company benefits	Employees may not remember specifics of newsletter articles	Varies
Overhead presentation	Overhead slide presentation usually followed by a Q&A period	Inform and educate	Talking is an effective form of communication	May create a forum for discussion of unrelated issues; may require a significant investment of staff hours	Varies
Payroll stuffer	Notice of changes to benefits plans accompanies paycheck	Effective, inexpensive method of communicating brief benefit information	Reinforces the idea that benefits are part of compensation	Overuse makes them less effective	Minimal

Table 12-1. Comparison of Communication Methods (*cont'd*)

Media Type	*Definition*	*Objectives*	*Pros*	*Cons*	*Information*
Personalized enrollment materials	Personalized materials that publish the benefit choices available to an individual employee	Inform and educate	An especially effective method of communicating where benefits/rates vary for different groups	Difficult to produce (collate)	Varies
Personalized illustration	Can show the specific advantages of a plan feature	Educate	Aimed at employee's personal situation; effective	If more than a single sheet is personalized, the illustrations can be difficult to produce (collate)	Varies
Posters	Large, colorful announcements attract employees' attention	Make a public statement about benefits plans	High visibility; can create excitement and remind employees of current benefit information	Cannot accommodate too much information (one topic per poster)	Minimal
Q&As	Sample Q&As distributed to managers and communicators to help them respond to employees' questions	Reference tool; acquaint audience with new program; prepare expert to respond to questions	Provide experts with an idea of the types of questions to expect	Sample questions may not be exactly like the ones raised by employees	Medium
Summary annual report	A synopsis of financial, accounting, and general	Comply with federal regulations (inform); ERISA	Required by law for underlying ERISA plans	Required format may not be understood by some	Minimal

Table 12-1. Comparison of Communication Methods (*cont'd*)

Media Type	*Definition*	*Objectives*	*Pros*	*Cons*	*Information*
	plan information; must be provided to plan participants in a specified format, without regard to general readability	guidelines		plan participants	
Summary of material plan modifications	A synopsis of certain changes to an ERISA plan; has no prescribed format; must be comprehensible to average plan participant	Comply with federal regulations (inform); ERISA guidelines	Required by law for underlying ERISA plans	Where plan changes are extensive, reissue SPDs instead	Varies
Summary plan description	Fully explains provisions, limitations, exclusions of benefits plan to participants; has no prescribed format but must be generally understandable	Comply with federal regulations (inform); ERISA guidelines	Required by law for underlying ERISA plans. SPDs can be coordinated with past communications efforts or may be used to initiate the communications process	Amount of information provided may be overwhelming to employees	Maximum
Supervisor/meeting leader guide	Contains information and materials for presenting an	Educate and orient supervisors	Reference tool containing answers to fre-	Experienced meeting leaders may ignore it	Varies

Table 12-1. Comparison of Communication Methods (*cont'd*)

Media Type	*Definition*	*Objectives*	*Pros*	*Cons*	*Information*
	effective program		quently asked questions		
Tabletop tents	Freestanding cardboard fliers placed on cafeteria tables	Disseminate benefits information; create excitement	Fairly inexpensive to produce and highly visible to most employees	This approach will not reach all employees	Minimal
Telephone hotline	A telephone number answered by benefits experts or by machine, with experts returning employees' calls	Educate and inform	Benefits experts will provide useful and pertinent information	A busy hotline or slow return of calls is frustrating; benefits staff may provide different responses to questions	Varies
Telephone voice response	An automated enrollment system using Touch-Tone technology	Facilitate enrollment or benefit changes	Employees enroll themselves with little or no intervention from human resources	May intimidate some employees; may not be available in some telephone exchanges	Minimal
Train-the-trainer meetings	Orientation for supervisors and trainers	Educate	Raise the comfort level and confidence of trainers	May represent a significant staff investment	Maximum
Video	Taped presentation or story explaining employee benefits	Educate, inform, create excitement	Excellent for overview purposes; less effective for detail	Expensive; difficult to update	Varies
Voice-mail broadcast messages	Inter- and intraoffice automated	Announce/notify employees about	Speedy, personalized method of	Employees may forget messages if	Minimal

Table 12-1. Comparison of Communication Methods (*cont'd*)

Media Type	*Definition*	*Objectives*	*Pros*	*Cons*	*Information*
	method of communications	an upcoming benefits event, enrollment deadlines	delivering messages	they do not mark calendars; system may be expensive to install	
Worksheets	Short exercises for employee showing how a plan affects that person	Educate	Fairly inexpensive to develop and can produce compelling results	Complex worksheets may intimidate employees and prevent completion	Varies

Q 12:42 What makes ongoing, follow-up communications different from the kind of communications used during the actual flexible benefits campaign?

A significant number of communications needs to be made to employees even after the initial communications effort regarding a flexible benefits program is complete—a need often overlooked by communicators. An initial flexible benefits campaign must provide a rationale for change and devote time and effort to creating informational materials with which to educate employees on the use of the new benefits plans. During the campaign, new concepts, such as the use of flexible benefits credits, are introduced and explained. In subsequent months and years, the focus shifts away from the enrollment function because most employees, already familiar with the available options, are making fewer changes than they were during and immediately after the implementation of the plan.

After the vigorous implementation effort, employees may appreciate a low-key, more restrained communications effort in following years. Consequently, ongoing communications about flexible benefits can be less demonstrative and more concise. Frequently, the default insurance plan coverage (i.e., the coverage that employees receive if they make no benefits elections) will be the same as the coverage the employees elected in prior years. The following situations involving subsequent elections require that communicators exercise particular caution:

1. In almost all plans, failure to submit a new plan year enrollment for flexible spending accounts will cause FSA election to reset (default) to zero. Communications materials must call attention to this fact so that account participants are not inadvertently misled into believing their accounts will continue indefinitely on the basis of a single election.
2. Significant cost increases in a plan or in an option merit special communications and advance warning to participants.
3. Age-banded life insurance rates constitute a sensitive issue that requires clear communications. When an employee reaches a specified age (e.g., age 50), the rates increase dramatically for the coverage the employee has chosen. Employees should be notified as they approach the specified age so that they can make appropriate financial arrangements.

One important reason for continuing the communications effort and making it part of maintaining the flexible benefits program is to eliminate unwelcome surprises; employees must not be caught off guard by cost increases or left unprepared to deal with important deadlines or events.

Q 12:43 What does a continuing communications effort entail?

A communicator must consider whether plan enrollment will be positive or negative. A positive enrollment approach requires all employees to reelect the benefit coverages they want to have for the coming year. Failure to do so results in the waiver of any benefits not reelected for the plan year. A negative or default enrollment approach includes as its most significant feature a default option that enables employees to keep most of the same coverage elections made in the previous year. Under this approach, participants are not required to reelect benefits each year to remain in the plan.

Except in the case of FSAs covered under Section 125 of the Internal Revenue Code (Code), many plans permit default enrollments. The primary reasons for doing so are that (1) it is much easier for employees not to have to make enrollment choices again, and (2) the plan sponsor's administrative staff does not have to reenter the information, much of which is repeated from year to year.

If an employer permits default plan enrollment, the plan's communicator should generate the following documents to help explain various aspects of the enrollment to employees:

1. *A concise list of changes that will affect plan benefits for the coming year.* An explanation of how the changes will affect the portion of the cost that is deducted from the employees' paychecks should accompany the list.
2. *Enrollment instructions.* The explanation of how and when employees can enroll in the plan should be accompanied by an explanation of available default options. This communication is intended to make employees aware of which coverages are automatically available to them without taking any direct action. The communication should also include pertinent enrollment deadlines and a list of individuals who can provide additional information or assistance.
3. *Individualized enrollment form.* A personalized form outlines the coverages in which an employee is currently enrolled and shows all available benefits choices and their costs. It provides all the information that an employee needs to make an informed decision. (See Appendix G for a sample individualized enrollment form.)

Q 12:44 How should an employer enroll new employees who are hired after the initial flexible benefits communications campaign?

Because new employees are not covered under the old plan, the employer is not required to explain the differences between prior and current plans. The employer should focus on the current offering.

Generally, the materials used for the second year of flexible benefits enrollment are adequate to inform new employees of their choices under the plan. These materials should inform new employees of any specific eligibility requirements or portions of the plan that are not currently available to them, and of any special conditions that may apply to them, as for example, the prorating of their new credits, and the effect that a shortened plan year will have on their election to participate in flexible spending accounts.

Many new employees may already be familiar with the concept of flexible benefits and therefore will need only a brief explanation of how the employer's plan operates.

For administrative purposes and to streamline communication, some employers make available to their new employees a basic benefits package containing a number of mid-level options, such as health insurance, life insurance, and disability insurance. Spending accounts are generally excluded. This basic package becomes available to the employee immediately, allowing the employee to obtain basic coverage under the benefits program without having to make detailed and time-consuming examinations of the coverage. The employee passes the interim period between the date of hire and the date of the next scheduled plan reenrollment covered by the basic plan; during this time he or she evaluates the full array of plan options that will become available to him or her at the next regularly scheduled company-wide reenrollment.

It is efficient to enroll all new employees at the same time—usually the first of the month of or after the date of hire. This allows the administrative staff to calculate costs on a monthly basis instead of having to prorate credits for fractions of months.

Q 12:45 How should a plan sponsor inform employees of midyear changes in cost, coverage, and plan design?

A cafeteria plan can automatically change the amount of a participant's health plan contributions and a participant can revoke an existing election and make a new one only under special circumstances (see chapter 11).

If a change meets the requirements of Code Section 125, the manner in which information about the change is communicated depends on the nature and extent of the change. Changes of a significant nature may make it possible for employees to make new elections under the plan.

> **Example.** The premium of a health plan offered under O. Twist Co.'s cafeteria plan significantly increases. The cafeteria plan can permit participants either to make a corresponding change in their premium payments or to revoke their elections and instead receive, on a prospective basis, coverage under another health plan with similar coverage.

It is evident from the example that reenrollment for a portion of the benefit options may be required at midyear, while other enrollments remain in effect. Although such a procedure flies in the face of the notion that an employee should be able to choose from a full array of benefit options, in the case of a midyear change, a limited choice may be necessary.

In other circumstances, employees should be informed about automatic changes allowed under the terms of a cafeteria plan.

> **Example.** The terms of the cafeteria plan offered by W. Sikes Inc. state that when the cost of a health plan increases or decreases during a plan year,

participants are required to make a corresponding change in their premium payments. The cost of the health plan does increase during the plan year. The cafeteria plan, on a reasonable and consistent basis, automatically increases all affected participants' elective contributions or after-tax employee contributions for the health plan. Employees should be informed about the automatic change; a memorandum or letter is the likely communications vehicle.

Example. A Section 125 cafeteria plan is altered mid-year to include flexible spending accounts (FSAs). The plan must communicate the addition of this new benefit feature within the plan.

Practice Pointer. The plan sponsor should seek the advice of legal counsel regarding the wording required to be used in midyear change materials.

Caution. A plan sponsor may have to issue a summary of material modifications (SMM) regarding midyear changes to plan design for underlying ERISA plans to comply with the Employee Retirement Income Security Act of 1974 (ERISA).

Q 12:46 How should the employer inform employees of changes in the allocation of flexible benefits credits within the plan?

There are a number of reasons that may compel a company to change the manner in which it calculates flexible benefits credits after the initial introduction of a flexible benefits plan. Sometimes the old method causes unforeseen administrative burdens, or perhaps the company can no longer afford the subsidies it originally created for the plan. Whatever the reason, any change to the method by which employee benefit credits are determined must be fully communicated to employees. The employer must provide communications materials that explain in detail how the new credit formula applies and how it will affect the amount of employees' contributions by means of their payroll deductions.

Another concern with equally serious implications for the employee has to do with communicating significant cost increases in coverage that are scheduled to be introduced in subsequent years. Because the employer controls both costs and credits, it may not be immediately obvious that a significant cost increase has occurred until the employees complete a worksheet that outlines their coverages, the employer's credits provided, and the costs of their benefits options.

Employers often debate whether or not to tell employees how much the cost of their coverage is increasing. There is no doubt that keeping employees fully informed of cost increases that affect the availability of benefits coverage is the wiser option. In the early days of flexible benefits plans, many communicators let employees calculate their own cost increases. As flexible benefits plans have matured and become more commonplace, covering more employees, most employers provide their employees with a statement that tells them exactly how much last year's options will cost to renew for the coming year and how much of a cost increase this represents.

This procedure details the history and progress of the employees' benefits costs and eliminates the possibility of their being unaware of a cost increase until they receive the first paycheck that reflects the new increases. To use this method, the employer must be capable of generating an individualized personalized report for each employee. (See Appendix G for a sample of such a report.)

Q 12:47 How should an employer transmit information about a flexible benefits plan that is certain to have a negative or depressing effect on employees' opinions and morale?

The way to communicate bad news successfully is to present it in a balanced fashion. The employer must explain the reasons for the negative impact this change in benefits will have and simultaneously acknowledge that although the employer is aware of the effects, this alternative is the best of many investigated.

Apart from a written communication that describes the reasons for the change, the employer may choose to have a person with significant authority and visibility in the corporation deliver the message. This communicates to employees that the decision process was thorough and considered by the highest echelons of management, rather than an arbitrary decision made on the spur of the moment. It also conveys a certain resistance on the part of management to having to resort to an obviously unpopular but necessary action. Taking a forthright approach in transmitting displeasing information produces the best results among employees.

Q 12:48 What information must an employer communicate to terminated employees and employees who are not "actively at work"?

In most cases, there is no difference between the information required to be provided to terminated employees in a flexible benefits environment and that required in any other benefits environment. An employer may nevertheless want to inform former employees that they are ineligible for the employer's flexible benefits plan.

Employers subject to the Consolidated Omnibus Budget Reconciliation Act of 1985 (COBRA) must provide any employees who experience a "qualifying event" with the health insurance coverage continuity information required by the Act. COBRA coverage requirements for health FSAs changed as of January 1, 2000. In some cases, COBRA information must address participation in a health FSA, a requirement often overlooked in COBRA communications. (See chapter 15 for a discussion of the COBRA continuation coverage rules.)

Under a flexible benefits plan, employees who are not "actively at work" but who are not terminated (e.g., employees on medical leave) can continue to make choices similar to the choices active employees can make. (See chapter 15 for a discussion of how the Family and Medical Leave Act of 1993 (FMLA) affects employees.) An employer must be particularly careful not to overstate the types of benefits available to nonactive employees under the plan. In many cases, health insurance, life insurance, and disability benefits require that an employee be actively at work for any changes to be made to his or her coverage. It is wise to communicate separately with nonactive employees, notifying them that their coverage will remain the same, that any requests to change their coverage must be made in writing, and that such requests are subject to the final approval of the appropriate benefits committees or insurance carriers.

Employers must consider several crucial points in connection with the FMLA provisions, including the following:

1. Health insurance coverage for employees on FMLA leave under a group health plan must be maintained at the same level and conditions of coverage that would have been provided had the employees not taken the leave.
2. Employees who take FMLA leave cannot lose any other employment benefits that they accrued before the leave during the time they are on the leave (e.g., forfeiture of pension eligibility).
3. The employee's responsibility for payment of insurance premiums during FMLA leave depends on the leave policy that the employer has established. In general, the policy must be no different for FMLA leave than for any other unpaid leave. (See Qs 15:18–15:32.)
4. The employer should examine the requirements of its group life insurance and disability plans. Although the FMLA does not mandate that the employer pay for any benefits coverage other than health care benefits during the employee's leave, it does require that all fringe benefits be reinstated on the employee's return.
5. Regulations issued by the Department of Labor (DOL) allow the employer to institute a practice permitting all premium payments made during the leave to be recovered from the employee after he or she has returned to work; however, notice of this practice must be in writing.

Practice Pointer. It is extremely important that all applicable plan rules and regulations, as well as the employer's policies, are communicated fairly and accurately to all active and nonactive employees. The employer may also have to communicate with the beneficiaries and dependents of employees; similar caution should be exercised with those individuals.

Q 12:49 What communications must be made to the beneficiaries of a deceased plan member?

Under a flexible benefits plan, several benefits may become available to the beneficiaries of a deceased employee. As noted above, the COBRA requirements for medical, vision, and dental insurance will be in effect and should be extended to these beneficiaries, who are COBRA "qualified beneficiaries." Aside from COBRA, there are no specific requirements to communicate to beneficiaries under a flexible benefits plan. (See chapter 15 for a discussion of the COBRA continuation coverage rules.)

Often, a flexible benefits plan will permit the spouse or dependent of a deceased participant to submit claims for FSA reimbursement, especially if incurred while the deceased was an active participant in the plan. In such circumstances, it is helpful for the plan administrator to provide the spouse and/or dependents of the deceased with claim forms.

Q 12:50 What are the most commonly occurring situations that require the delivery of continuing communications?

Many communications problems arise in connection with an employee's need to change elections under a flexible benefits plan. During the initial communications campaign for such a plan, it may not be possible to cover all the situations that may arise once the plan goes into operation. Those situations typically involve changes in an employee's status or eligibility for certain benefits programs that require the employee to make new selections, including the following:

1. *Buying and Selling Vacation Time.* Employees who buy and sell vacation time may discover that unforeseen restrictions—not outlined in the initial flexible benefits material—apply to their use of the time. For those who purchase additional vacation time, those restrictions may range from having to obtain a supervisor's approval to not being permitted to use the vacation time during certain periods. Employees who sell their vacation time may find themselves unable to take an unpaid leave when time off from work becomes necessary.
2. *Taking a Leave of Absence.* An employee on a leave of absence draws no salary during the period of the leave; therefore, there is no source of funds from which the employer can make the necessary salary reductions to pay for the employee's share of elected benefits. (See chapter 15 for a discussion of the payment options available to employees on a leave of absence covered by the FMLA.) Employee contributions could be made on an after-tax basis. Alternatively, Treasury regulations under Code Section 125 allow employees to change their salary reduction elections when they take unpaid leave. The regulations allow employees to either prepay their health coverage by making extra pretax contributions in the period before a scheduled leave, or where timing permits, to make up any missing contributions on a pretax basis when they return from leave. If the latter approach is taken, the salary reduction contributions should be made in the same plan year as the employee's leave. To do otherwise would enable the employee to defer receipt of compensation by carrying forward plan contributions—a violation of the Section 125 rules.

The communications created for the enrollment process should include examples of the conditions under which participants can change their coverages. If an employee's coverage premiums are paid for on a pretax basis, the changes in family and employment status, as well as the cost of coverage changes that may trigger reenrollment, are quite specific. The conditions should be explained in detail, not only in the enrollment materials but also in the document that confirms the employee's benefits selections. Many employers put the applicable change requirements on all claims forms—from health care to dependent care reimbursement accounts.

Note. In addition to continuing communications to active employees about coverage change decisions, the appropriate COBRA notification and election materials must be furnished on a timely basis to a covered employee (or retiree) and his or her family members. (See chapter 15 for a discussion of the COBRA continuation coverage rules.)

Q 12:51 What is the single most important element of the flexible benefits communications campaign?

The enrollment—the employee's selection of the benefits coverages for the coming year—is generally considered the single most important element of the entire communications campaign. The enrollment is the high point for which all the other communications of the campaign—explanatory, educational, motivational, or inspirational—have been preparing the employee. If the communications campaign is successful, it provides employees with enough information to make an informed decision about which benefits they require. (See Appendix I for a sample telephone enrollment form; see Appendix G for a sample confirmation statement.)

Q 12:52 What communications requirements does ERISA impose on flexible benefits plans?

ERISA contains no special requirements for flexible benefits plans. As has been noted earlier, a flexible benefits plan is not an ERISA plan and therefore is not subject to ERISA's reporting and disclosure requirements; however, the underlying benefits contained in a flexible benefits plan may in fact be ERISA benefits if they qualify. Underlying plans that are subject to ERISA must satisfy ERISA's three major disclosure requirements:

1. Summary plan description (SPD)
2. Summary of material modifications (SMM)
3. Summary annual report (SAR)

Note. An SAR is a summary of the Form 5500 filed for the plan. While it is a disclosure document, it is not typically thought of as part of an employee benefits communications program. Welfare benefit plans with fewer than 100 participants are exempt from Form 5500 filing. Therefore, such plans have no obligation to distribute an SAR.

Q 12:53 When must an employer distribute the materials required under ERISA?

Table 12-2 summarizes the distribution timetable for ERISA-required communications materials.

Table 12-2. The Distribution Schedule of ERISA-Required Communications

Required Report	*Due*	*Recipient*
Summary plan description (SPD)	*New plans:* 120 days after later of effective date or adoption date	Employer must provide SPD to new participant within 90 days of eligibility
	Revised plans: 210 days after the end of the fifth plan year following distribution of current SPD, if material modification in SPD was made during that period	Employer must provide new SPD to participants
Summary of material modification (SMM)	210 days after the end of the plan year in which modification is made (unless a revised SPD is distributed that includes the modification)	Employer must provide SMM to participants
Summary annual report (SAR)	Two months after the Form 5500 is due to the IRS (including any extension)	Employer must provide SAR to participants

Q 12:54 How must employers and plan administrators distribute ERISA-required materials to plan participants?

Employers and plan administrators must "use measures reasonably calculated to ensure actual receipt of" materials that are requested by plan participants and beneficiaries. [DOL Reg § 2520.104b-1(b)] Materials such as SPDs and SARs, which must be distributed to all plan participants and beneficiaries who are receiving benefits, "must be sent by a method or methods of delivery likely to result in full distribution." [DOL Reg § 2520.104b-1(b)]

The following methods of delivering ERISA-required communications materials generally are considered to be acceptable:

1. Desktop or internal mail distribution at the work site if certain safeguards are adhered to, as outlined in ERISA Section 2520.1046-11;
2. Hand delivery;
3. A special insert in a periodical such as a company newsletter or newspaper, if a prominent notice is displayed on the front page advising readers of the important information. If some participants and beneficiaries are not on the publication's mailing list, other methods of distri-

bution must be used in conjunction with it, so that, taken together, the methods are reasonably calculated to ensure receipt. [DOL Reg § 2520.104b-1(b)]

4. Required materials also may be distributed to participants at home by first-, second-, or third-class mail. However, distribution by second- or third-class mail is acceptable only if return and forwarding postage is guaranteed by the sender and an address correction is requested. All material that is returned to the employer or plan sponsor with a corrected address must be either remailed by first-class mail or delivered in person at the employee's work site. [DOL Reg § 2520.104b-1(b)]

5. Delivery through electronic media such as e-mail, if the plan administrator is reasonably sure that the documents will actually be delivered, or will be notified if they are not. Notification could consist of return of undelivered e-mail, and periodic reviews or surveys to confirm receipt of electronically transmitted information. It is necessary to protect the confidentiality of personal information, including controls to ensure that only the intended recipient receives plan benefit and account balance information.

Electronic delivery of plan information (as described in item 5) brings with it some special requirements. Before electronic delivery of important plan information (such as a summary plan description), an advance notice must be provided in electronic or non-electronic form, apprising plan participants of the significance of the plan's descriptive materials (e.g., "The attached document describes changes in your flexible benefit plan.").

Recipients must have the right to request and receive a paper version of any electronically delivered document.

Intended recipients must be those individuals who have the ability to effectively access documents in electronic form at any location where the participant is reasonably expected to perform his or her duties as an employee, and for whom access to the employer's electronic information system (i.e., e-mail or intranet) is an integral part of the participant's duties.

Furthermore, the participant must affirmatively consent to receiving documents in electronic form. If documents are furnished through the Internet, the participant must affirmatively consent electronically in a manner that demonstrates the individual's ability to access information via e-mail (or in the same electronic form that will be used to provide information that is the subject of his or her consent), and must have provided an e-mail address.

Before consenting to receipt of electronic communications, the participant must be provided with a clear and conspicuous statement indicating: 1) the types of documents to which consent would apply; 2) that consent may be withdrawn at any time; 3) the procedures for withdrawing consent and for updating the participant's, beneficiary's, or other individual's address for receipt of electronically furnished documents or other information; 4) statement of the right to request and obtain a paper version of an electronically furnished document and guidance as to whether the paper version will be provided free of charge); and 5) any hardware and software requirements for accessing and retaining documents sent by electronic means.

If, following consent, a change in hardware or software requirements needed to access or retain electronic documents creates a material risk that the participant will be unable to access or retain electronically furnished documents, the participant must be furnished with a statement of the revised hardware or software requirements for access to and retention of the documents; be given the right to withdraw consent without charge, and without the imposition of any condition or consequence that was not disclosed at the time of initial consent; and again consent to receipt of plan documents through electronic media. [ERISA § 2520.104b-1]

Chapter 13

Enrollment and Related Administrative Issues

Certain issues arise in connection with the enrollment (and reenrollment) process of a cafeteria plan as defined by Section 125 of the Internal Revenue Code (Code). This chapter identifies likely trouble spots and focuses on ambiguous aspects of plan design that could cause problems for an employer. It also reviews technologies that can be used to streamline data input and discusses several related administrative concerns, including whether to outsource or retain internal control of the administration of a cafeteria plan.

Enrollment

Q 13:1 What are the enrollment requirements for a cafeteria plan?

One of the basic requirements of a cafeteria plan as defined by Section 125 of the Internal Revenue Code (Code) is that the participant must enroll in the plan by making his or her benefit elections from the various choices that the plan provides. Further, such elections are prospective in nature and irrevocable until the end of the coverage period (usually the plan year). Those requirements are imposed by the Internal Revenue Service (IRS), which exercises particular oversight to prevent plan participants from manipulating their compensation through a flexible benefits plan.

Q 13:2 Are negative elections permitted in a cafeteria plan?

Yes, if certain guidelines are followed. Eligible employees must have the opportunity to elect out of the plan, and receive cash rather than contribute to the plan. Also, the plan sponsor should confirm that the proposed automatic salary deduction is permitted under state law.

When the federal government implemented a premium conversion plan in 2000, it used negative elections. Employees who were required to contribute toward the cost of health insurance premiums were automatically signed up to do so on a pretax basis, unless they opted out of the pretax payment option.

It is important for employees to clearly understand their choices under a cafeteria plan. Often, rather than negative elections or automatic enrollment, an employer will require an active election at least once and then allow further inaction by the employee to result in a default to the enrollment choice most recently elected for insured (including employer's self-insured) benefits.

Under negative election procedures, employees are assumed to elect pretax contributions (most likely for payment of premiums) unless they affirmatively tell the employer that they want to make after-tax contributions (or no contributions at all). No express salary reduction agreements are used in conjunction with negative elections, also referred to as automatic enrollment.

> **Note.** Negative elections are most likely to be used for pretax payment of premiums, or for a default package of benefits if a participant does not submit his or her enrollment form on time. Participation in a flexible spending account (FSA) does not usually remain at a given level of participation on a default basis from year to year. A participant should actively elect the amount to contribute to the FSA each year.

IRS officials answered questions about negative elections at the Midstates Benefits Conference held in April 1997. They stated that negative elections to make pretax salary deferrals to a Section 125 cafeteria plan are permitted, as long as participants understand their "inaction of making a positive election" to make pretax contributions to the plan and they are permitted to make a choice for each plan year. (See Prop Treas Reg §§ 1.125-1, Q&A 8 and 15, 1.125-2, Q&A 6.)

> **Practice Pointer.** Although negative elections are permitted in a cafeteria plan, a plan administrator should require participants to take some affirmative action, such as a waiver of coverage where no benefits are elected, to ensure that the benefits are properly communicated to employees.

> **Practice Pointer.** When an employer uses an interactive voice response system for plan enrollment, it should provide plan participants with confirmation statements before the beginning of the plan year so that participants can make any necessary corrections. The employer should retain copies of such confirmation statements for its records.

Q 13:3 Are the enrollment requirements different for a premium conversion plan, an FSA, and a fully flexible benefits plan?

Proposed Treasury Regulations Section 1.125-1, Q&A 8, specifically addresses the enrollment and election requirements relating to cafeteria plans.

The regulation makes no distinction whatsoever between different cafeteria plan designs. It therefore seems reasonable to assume that the enrollment and election rules for premium conversion programs and FSAs are the same as those for fully flexible benefits plans.

Q 13:4 What are the eligibility rules of a cafeteria plan?

The nondiscrimination rules that apply to a Section 125 cafeteria plan dictate the eligibility requirements. A cafeteria plan cannot discriminate in favor of highly compensated employees (HCEs) as to their eligibility to participate in the plan. Thus, for example, allowing only employees earning more than $85,000 to participate in a cafeteria plan constitutes de facto discrimination. Similarly, allowing HCEs to enroll in a cafeteria plan from their first day of employment and making all other employees wait one year is discriminatory.

Under the nondiscrimination rules pertaining to eligibility, a cafeteria plan is not discriminatory if it meets all the following conditions:

1. The group of employees that benefits under the plan satisfies the Section 125(g)(3)(A) nondiscrimination classification test, which cross-references Code Section 410(b)(2) (see chapter 14).
2. The length of the required period of employment for eligibility is the same for all employees, and no employee is made to wait for more than three years as a condition of plan participation.
3. An employee who satisfies the plan's required period of employment eligibility begins plan participation by the first day of the first plan year following the date on which the employee satisfied the plan's eligibility requirement.

[IRC §§ 125(g)(3)(A), 125(g)(3)(B)]

Note. The cafeteria plan nondiscrimination eligibility rules focus on the availability of coverage among groups of employees rather than on whether employees in fact participate. For example, if a cafeteria plan's eligibility requirements favor HCEs, the fact that some of the HCEs do not elect coverage under the cafeteria plan does not matter—the plan is still held to be discriminatory.

For purposes of classifying employees into groups for the Section 410(b) classification test, the regulations indicate that an employee classification must be reasonable and based on rational business criteria. [Treas Reg § 1.410(b)-4(b)] Classifying employees by division, location, or job category is considered to be reasonable classification; classifying employees by title or by name does not constitute reasonable classification.

Q 13:5 What are the main issues relevant to a cafeteria plan allowing participants to change or to revoke their elections?

The specific rules concerning revocations and changes in a participant's elections are discussed in chapter 11. As noted there, a Section 125 cafeteria plan can, under well-defined circumstances, allow plan participants to make the following changes to their elections:

1. Midyear elections of new benefits that an employer makes available when the new benefits represent a change in cost or coverage of benefits. [Treas Reg § 1.125-4] A participant cannot, however, change a health FSA election as a result of change in cost or coverage in benefits in the middle of the plan year.

   Example. At the beginning of the plan year, the MesoLink Co. offers a cafeteria plan with medical coverage and a health FSA. At midyear, MesoLink introduces a vision care plan. Candace, a MesoLink employee, chose medical and health FSA coverage at the beginning of the plan year. She cannot drop the medical or health FSA coverage at midyear and replace them with participation in the vision care plan. Candace can, however, add the vision care plan to her overall benefits package. Candace cannot drop the health FSA because such a change is not permitted, even if Candace was funding the health FSA specifically for vision care expenses. Candace cannot drop the medical coverage because vision care coverage does not replace medical coverage and Candace has not had any other qualifying change in status permitting a change to that election.

2. Revocations of benefits elections by not making required contributions, provided the plan permits such revocations. Generally, participants who revoke their benefits elections should not be allowed to make new elections for the remaining portion of the coverage period unless (a) the cessation of required contributions occurs during an absence under the Family and Medical Leave Act (FMLA) and the employee returns to work, or (b) the benefit elections are revoked under the permitted election change rules described in item 3 below.

3. Modifications of an election, provided that the new election is consistent with one of the following reasons:
   - Change in health coverage or in the cost of health coverage
   - Change in legal marital status
   - Change in number of dependents
   - Change in employment status
   - Dependent satisfying or ceasing to satisfy eligibility requirements
   - Change in residence (affecting delivery of benefits)
   - Failure to make the required premium payments
   - Excess contributions to the 401(k) plan

- Having special enrollment rights as provided in the Health Insurance Portability and Accountability Act of 1996 (HIPAA)
- Entitlement to Medicare or Medicaid
- A judgment, decree, or order in the context of a divorce, legal separation, annulment, or change in legal custody

A cafeteria plan can automatically increase or decrease a participant's required contribution—provided such changes are implemented consistently—to cover changes in health care coverage or the cost of health care coverage.

When an election change becomes permissible as a consequence of a significant increase in cost, employers frequently permit plan participants to decide whether they want to retain their current choices and pay the new amount or to revoke their current election and select another medical plan option for the remainder of the plan year.

Separation from service may cause other election-related problems. Before final Treasury Regulations Section 1.125-4 was issued in March 2000, a revoked election that resulted from separation from service was not permitted to be changed during the same plan year if the employee was rehired. Effective January 1, 2001, however, a plan sponsor can permit a rehired participant to reinstate a prior election—or even make a new election—upon rehire (see chapter 11).

> **Note.** An employer and a participant are not permitted to collude to terminate and reinstate employment merely to avoid the change in election restrictions and to effect a midyear change in election when no other qualifying event has taken place.

When cafeteria plan election changes become permissible as a result of a participant making elective contributions to a 401(k) plan, the cafeteria plan can permit employees to change or revoke their elective contributions to the 401(k) cash or deferred arrangement in accordance with the rules of the 401(k) plan, even though such provisions do not meet the election change requirements of the cafeteria plan. That is so for both the employee's pretax and after-tax 401(k) contributions.

Q 13:6 How should a cafeteria plan handle midyear enrollments?

An employer must, in the design of a Section 125 cafeteria plan, decide whether to allow employees to join the cafeteria plan during a plan year or instead to make eligible employees who are not yet participants wait until the next open enrollment period. Either approach is perfectly acceptable.

The singular advantage of having all eligible employees enroll at the same time is ease of administration. As for new hires, they may be given a package of benefits framed as a traditional nonflexible benefits plan to provide basic coverage until they become eligible to enroll in the flexible benefits plan. In such a scenario, enrollment in the cafeteria plan would come on the first day of the plan year following attainment of the eligibility criteria. The disadvantage of such an approach is that employees may be unhappy about having to wait so long before becoming a cafeteria plan participant, and the employer's payroll department might prefer not to have an array of pretax and after-tax contributions if it is avoidable.

Allowing newly eligible employees to join a cafeteria plan at any time during the plan year creates good public relations with employees, particularly with new hires; however, it also creates a steady stream of enrollment forms that must be processed. When midyear entrants are highly compensated or key employees, nondiscrimination testing may need to be performed more frequently to ensure that the addition of the midyear entrants did not cause a nondiscriminatory plan to become discriminatory.

Another major issue related to midyear enrollment is whether to prorate benefits levels for midyear entrants. For example, if a cafeteria plan year runs from January 1 to December 31 and a midyear entrant becomes a plan participant on October 1, how should the plan apply a $1,200 cap in the health FSA with regard to the entrant? The plan could permit the new participant to sign up for a $300 FSA (3/12 of the $1,200 annual maximum because the employee is a plan participant for only 3/12 of the plan year). Alternatively, the plan could permit the new participant to elect a health FSA up to the full annual maximum.

Similarly, a cafeteria plan might encounter a participant who wants to set aside up to the plan maximum for dependent care assistance, even if the participant is joining the plan at midyear. The participant will need to be informed that the IRS sets an annual maximum of $5,000 per year per taxpayer. (A married couple filing jointly has one $5,000 maximum between them; a married person filing separately has an annual dependent care assistance maximum of $2,500.) If a participant joins the plan at midyear, but has already received dependent care assistance benefits from another employer's plan, the amount available for benefits must be offset by other dependent care benefits received during the year. If, on the other hand, a midyear participant has not received other dependent care benefits during the year, and the plan does not require prorating the benefit amount, the participant may contribute up to the maximum, even if it is late in the plan year.

> **Example.** Sally, an employee of Super Sudz Inc., pays $1,000 per month in child care expenses. She joins Super Sudz's cafeteria plan effective July 1, when the plan year has six months remaining. Sally may contribute up to $5,000 for the remaining six months of the plan year and thereby take advantage of the full annual maximum set by the IRS.

Thus, an employer has two approaches from which to choose: (1) permit all participants, including those joining the plan at midyear, to elect up to the same annual benefit amount, or (2) prorate the amount permitted to be elected so that the maximum contribution is expressed as a maximum per month (or per pay period) rather than per year.

The first approach offers the employer the administrative advantage of maintaining only one set of benefits limits under the plan; when prorated midyear enrollment is permitted, the employer must keep track of different plan limits for every midyear entrant. This approach, however, also presents the employer with a serious administrative disadvantage: it is more likely to inadvertently violate the nondiscrimination rules. In addition, when an employer maintains only one annual plan limit, the employer's potential financial risk under the health FSA uniform coverage rules is increased.

Practice Pointer. There are no universally correct solutions for the issues raised by midyear enrollment and prorating benefits. The key to making the correct decision is to be aware of both sides of every issue and to balance the administrative complexities with goodwill toward employees.

Q 13:7 How should a flexible benefits plan handle changes in a plan participant's age, compensation, employment status, or any other participant-specific item that occur during the plan year and have direct consequences on the administration of the flexible benefits plan?

The employer must strike a balance between employee relations and administrative ease. From a recordkeeping vantage point, the objective regarding any participant-specific item that may change during the year would be to maintain, for example, a plan participant's age and compensation constant throughout the plan year. Thus, an employee who enters the flexible benefits plan year at 39 years of age and $41,000 of earnings will keep this demographic and compensation profile for the entire year, even when the employee reaches age 40 in a month or when the employee receives a salary increase of 4 percent. In a very large organization, or one that is unable to handle administrative complexities with ease, this once-per-year change in data may be appropriate. The problem with the purely administrative perspective is that, as compensation increases, so could compensation-related benefits such as life and disability insurance. This creates a loss of potential benefits for a portion of the plan year.

For an employer that is able to easily process data, or one that uses an outside recordkeeper for administrative issues, a change in age or compensation is not such a problem. If, for example, an employee crosses an "age-band" by turning 40 years old, and thus must pay a higher premium contribution for health, life, or disability insurance, it is a relatively simple matter to share that information from the cafeteria plan records to the payroll system. As an aside, regulations permit an increase in premium contribution to be automatic, as long as the increase is not "significant." [Treas Reg § 1.125-4(f)] The employee need not reapprove the new premium amount due to a change in age or salary.

Regardless of the administrative sophistication (or lack thereof) of a plan sponsor, changes in employment status must be administered as soon as feasible. For example, when an employee goes from full-time to part-time or from part-time to full-time, the benefits changes are usually dramatic, and accordingly, the cost of benefits changes significantly. In some flexible benefits plans, the benefits that are made available to full-time employees differ from those that a part-time employee may elect. With these types of dramatic differences, the plan administrator has no choice but to account for shifts in employment status during an employee's career. During a plan year, many of the changes that are processed by the plan administrator will involve changes in the employment status of individuals. These types of changes are especially important to the plan administrator when it comes to preparing the list bills for the insurance carriers and collecting the correct amount of employee premium dollars.

New Technologies

Q 13:8 How does a traditional enrollment process compare to a reengineered, high-technology enrollment process?

It is quite common for an employer that is conducting plan enrollment in a traditional manner to establish a highly centralized paper flow with ten or more steps. For a larger employer, the steps to traditional enrollment can be time and labor intensive. While a smaller employer may be able to eliminate or combine some of the steps below, the overall process will be similar. The steps to a traditional enrollment may include the following:

1. Employer disseminates plan information through a workbook.
2. Employee determines personal needs and estimates cost impact.
3. Employee completes the paper enrollment form.
4. Employee submits completed enrollment form to the benefits department.
5. Benefits services personnel log and verify receipt of the enrollment form.
6. Benefits services personnel do an initial check of the form for accuracy and availability.
7. If benefits services personnel have no questions regarding the enrollment form, they send it to data entry clerks, who enter the data into the system.
8. Benefits services personnel check a sample of enrollment forms for data entry accuracy.
9. The system processes the data.
10. Employee receives a paper confirmation form and reviews it for accuracy.
11. Once all errors have been corrected, a computer printout for payroll salary reductions or deductions is sent to the payroll department.

Under a reengineered cafeteria plan enrollment process that uses new technologies, several important changes occur. First, employees enroll themselves;

the process therefore becomes decentralized and has fewer errors. Second, the enrollment process becomes less paper intensive and, in turn, more streamlined. Third, there is a shift of resources from human resources (fewer benefits services personnel and data entry clerks) toward technology resources (greater need for new hardware and software).

Using a high-technology approach to cafeteria plan enrollment, the process can be reduced to five steps, as follows:

1. Employee receives enrollment information disk or visits plan intranet pages to learn about the plan, and creates "what if" scenarios to distinguish between choices. Employee models different enrollment selections until he or she is satisfied.
2. Employee enrolls via the Internet or by use of a telephone voice response system so that log-in and enrollment verification are immediate.
3. The system processes the data.
4. Employee receives a confirmation form (data input is significantly reduced compared to the all-paper method outlined above).
5. Throughout the process, the payroll salary reductions or deductions are constantly and automatically being updated within the payroll department.

The end result of a reengineered cafeteria plan enrollment is a more efficient process. Whether the more streamlined enrollment process is cost-effective depends on the size of the employer and resources already in place. For example, an employer with 175 employees and with moderate computer technology but no voice response system may not want to invest in more technology to "improve" the enrollment process. In such a scenario, both the costs and the structures that must be put into place will not be worth the apparent benefit of more efficient enrollment.

Q 13:9 What new technologies can a plan administrator use to reengineer the enrollment process and make it more efficient?

A variety of computer tools can assist a cafeteria plan administrator in improving the efficiency of the enrollment process. They include enrollment form software; bar coding and scanning devices; interactive telephone voice response systems (or units); and internet enrollment and data access.

Enrollment Form Software. One measure of the adequacy of a cafeteria plan recordkeeping system is an enrollment form package that allows the plan administrator to develop customized enrollment forms. A customized enrollment form is essential for two reasons:

1. It documents the features of the plans being offered and the comparative cost relationships of those features.
2. It is a personal statement for each plan participant that describes in detail the cost of benefits for that individual.

Interactive Modeling Software. A basic tool for comparing benefits options, interactive modeling software gives plan participants a means of assessing the costs of different groupings of benefits selections. Not only do participants have the opportunity to compare and contrast options, they can also compare in-network and out-of-network costs. They can construct hypothetical scenarios to determine the economic benefit of having a spending account. Take-home pay and any imputed income can also be calculated quickly. This technology can be used on-site or at home on the employee's personal computer.

Bar Coding and Scanning Devices. Elections submitted on paper enrollment forms can be efficiently processed by the benefits administrator by means of bar code technology. Whether such a tool is appropriate for a particular employer depends on size and availability of funds. Bar coding and scanning technology is less expensive than other automated techniques, is easy to learn and easy to use, and can reduce data input errors to very low levels. The main drawback is that an operator or data entry clerk must take each enrollment form and use the light wand to read every choice the plan participant marks on his or her form. Still, bar coding is superior to standard keypunching in every way. Although less automated than interactive telephone response systems, bar coding is considerably less expensive and therefore better suited for medium-sized organizations (under 2,000 employees) and companies of any size that operate under cost constraints but want to use the most efficient technology available within their cost constraints.

Interactive Telephone Voice Response Systems. An interactive telephone voice response system enables employees to enroll by telephone. Election confirmation is immediate, so input data errors are nearly nonexistent, and, except for the confirmation form, there is almost no paper flow. An interactive telephone voice response system can also be used to respond to ongoing coverage inquiries. It can operate as a stand-alone system, or it can be completely integrated with a cafeteria plan's administrative system.

Several factors should be kept in mind when considering an interactive telephone voice response system:

1. Such a system is costly to buy or to rent. Very large companies can justify the cost on a per capita basis; however, small companies may find the cost difficult to support.
2. Such a system may be used on either a mandatory or voluntary basis. If it is used voluntarily, it will not eliminate all paper submissions.
3. Such a system requires touch-tone service; in some areas, some employees may not have ready access to a touch-tone system.
4. Such a system can be used purely for rapid enrollment or for both enrollment and communication purposes.

Practice Pointer. An interactive telephone response system is not a good communications tool for an employer that wants to provide employees with a great deal of descriptive information about a plan or for discussions of hypothetical situations; participants will tend to stay on the telephone too long. The cost of using an enrollment tool for such purposes is quite high.

Internet Enrollment and Data Access. Many plan participants now have access to the Internet, either through work or home. When a plan sponsor can guarantee Internet access—either through individual employee access or placement of temporary kiosks on the worksite—enrollment and later data access through the Internet may be an appealing alternative.

Internet-based systems have many of the same pros and cons as interactive voice response systems. The initial development is expensive, some employees may be frustrated by the lack of interactive contact with someone who can help answer questions, and some employees may either not have access to the Internet, or prefer not to use it. In addition, the plan sponsor will want to be absolutely sure that the Web site is secure, and cannot be compromised.

Q 13:10 What are the advantages and disadvantages of using newer technologies to enroll employees in a Section 125 cafeteria plan?

The advantages of using newer technologies to enroll plan participants in a Section 125 cafeteria plan are as follows:

- Specialty software designed with one purpose in mind
- Speed and accuracy of enrollment
- No paperwork
- Experienced support available and contractually guaranteed
- Wide range of options at a wide range of costs
- Cost-effective technology

The disadvantages of using newer technologies to enroll employees in a Section 125 cafeteria plan are as follows:

- Some employees may prefer working with paper enrollment forms
- Costs can still be too high
- New training may be required
- Technology may have limited use
- Mistakes can happen, requiring the employer to spend time and money to correct
- Software may not be adequately customized, especially when purchased as a prepared package

Q 13:11 How does the plan administrator of a cafeteria plan meet the documentation requirements for a Section 125 plan when using an electronic enrollment system to enroll employees?

A conservative interpretation of the documentation requirements for a Section 125 cafeteria plan is that the plan administrator should receive an affirmative election form from a plan participant. That is especially true for an initial employee enrollment. [Treas Reg § 1.125-1, Q&A 8]

If a traditional enrollment form is used, the positive election should be in writing and include an employee signature. If an electronic enrollment system—for example, floppy disk, Internet response, or interactive telephone voice response system—is used, the employer should offer an electronic signature mechanism such as a personal identification number (PIN) code. The issue of whether such a code is a bona fide signature has been tested from a legal aspect, and it is generally felt that the plan administrator can use an electronic signature as documentation that a plan participant has made an affirmative election.

Q 13:12 How important are enrollment meetings to the enrollment process?

Enrollment meetings are an extremely important aspect of the enrollment process for a Section 125 cafeteria plan for a variety of reasons, including the following:

1. To ensure that employees be given the information they need to make informed decisions, because a cafeteria plan places a lot more responsibility on employees.
2. To ensure that employees understand and value the plan and its programs, they must have an opportunity to interact with the human resources or benefits department staff as questions arise during the enrollment process.
3. To ensure that minimum participation guarantees are being attained because, very often, the cafeteria plan design contains voluntary employee programs that may require a minimum level of participation.

Practice Pointer. Enrollment meetings are fundamentally part of the communications process. They should be a part of every open enrollment period, not just the first one. For more discussion on communicating a flexible benefit plan, see chapter 12.

Q 13:13 How is the enrollment form the bridge between communications and administration?

The enrollment form is the document that marks the end of the communications enrollment process. After all the meetings have been held and published materials distributed, after all the "what ifs" and questions have been considered, the employee must make his or her selections and enroll. The enrollment form is the document that permits the employee to take that step. In some instances, the enrollment form functions as a worksheet that establishes the format for a telephone voice response or Internet enrollment.

However, whether the enrollment is done on the form itself or by another method, the form is the pivotal document that visually helps the plan participants to understand the relationship between credits and purchase price tags. When employees submit their enrollment forms, they begin the administrative process of implementation. The enrollment form, after its data is input into the system, leads to the confirmation form, which in turn establishes some measure of accountability that the plan participant is receiving the benefits that he or she has selected. (See Appendix G for a sample individualized enrollment form; see Appendix I for a sample telephone enrollment form.)

Q 13:14 What is a confirmation form?

A *confirmation form* is the document that an employee receives from the Section 125 cafeteria plan administrator confirming the enrollment choices made on the enrollment form. As a general rule, the confirmation form is automatically produced by the cafeteria plan's recordkeeping system. If a telephone voice response enrollment is used, it is common for the voice response unit to produce the confirmation form automatically. The confirmation form serves three very important functions:

1. It acknowledges that the plan participant's enrollment form was received;
2. It verifies that the selections made by the plan participant were in fact entered correctly into the plan's recordkeeping system; and
3. It provides the plan participant with a final check on the cost of the options that were selected and gives the employee one last opportunity to make a change in enrollment.

Q 13:15 Are plan participants required to complete forms specific to an insurance carrier in addition to the enrollment form?

Plan participants are frequently required to complete a carrier-specific form, in addition to the general enrollment form, for the following reasons:

1. Some insurers require their own paper documentation.
2. Some coverages require data not always captured on the cafeteria plan enrollment form, such as beneficiary information on a life insurance policy.
3. These forms can be used to identify issues related to HIPAA requirements and prior coverage.

The cafeteria plan administrator needs to be aware of the insurance carrier's requirements concerning these forms so they can be distributed at the enrollment meetings or as part of the enrollment package. Alternatively, the flexible benefits plan administrator may wish to raise the issue of carrier-specific forms during its negotiations with the carrier, to see if they can be eliminated from the enrollment process.

Practice Pointer. By including all information required by various benefit providers on the general enrollment form, a plan administrator can reduce or entirely eliminate the insurance carrier-specific forms, thus reducing inefficiencies and streamlining the enrollment process. However, the trade-off is that the enrollment form may become very complex, because it will become the single source for all information required for a variety of plans.

Q 13:16 How much time should the enrollment process take?

An important consideration when determining the length of the enrollment process in a Section 125 cafeteria plan is the size of the employer and the ability of its administrative departments to respond. Also, the complexity of the cafeteria plan is a factor. In a very large organization, a plan administrator should leave at least eight to twelve weeks for the initial enrollment process; that is, from the time that the enrollment form is developed and available for distribution until the time that the confirmation forms are verified by the plan participants and the data is available to go to payroll. Subsequent enrollment periods may well require less time, perhaps four to six weeks.

Smaller organizations may require only four to six weeks for the initial enrollment of a full-flex plan, and less than a month for subsequent enrollment periods.

A plan comprised only of a premium conversion feature may require less than a month in the initial enrollment, and only a few weeks in ongoing years.

Outsourcing

Q 13:17 What must be considered when deciding whether to administer flexible benefits claims internally or to outsource the claims process?

A plan administrator of a Section 125 cafeteria plan should consider three essential issues relative to the assignment of any plan administration function, as follows.

1. *Human Resources.* Available human resources include not only the benefits or human resources staff and the investment of time they will make in implementing and administering the cafeteria plan but also the appropriate technical support staff, such as the management information systems, electronic data processing, and systems personnel.

   It should also be noted that availability presumes capability. An employer that has human resources, benefits, and systems staff that are poorly equipped or not properly trained to handle the task is not really prepared to administer a cafeteria plan internally.

2. *Systems Resources*. The term *systems resources* refers to an employer's computer resources. The plan administrator must determine whether the employer possesses the equipment necessary to perform administrative functions internally. Large organizations that have a mainframe or miniframe may have sufficient systems capacity—in terms of both memory and processing speed—to conduct plan administration internally. Alternatively, a microcomputer may be sufficient to perform all administrative functions necessary, especially in small and medium-sized organizations.

3. *Organizational Environment*. If an employer decides to administer its cafeteria plan internally, the entire organization must commit itself to the effort. Programming support from systems personnel is essential even for an employer that purchases flexible benefits recordkeeping systems because, at a minimum, the payroll function and the flexible benefits system will require interface documentation and programming.

   Another significant aspect of an organization's environment that the implementation team must be aware of is the way in which the organization defines its business interests. Some employers will want to administer their plans internally because they believe they know their own idiosyncrasies better than an outside agent ever could; others will want to define their interests more narrowly and will state that benefits recordkeeping is not part of their business. It is essential for the implementation team to know with what type of employer it is dealing.

A plan administrator must also take timing and fiscal constraints into account when considering outsourcing. No matter how much an employer may want to conduct flexible benefits recordkeeping internally, if it cannot allow enough time to design and test systems properly, the recordkeeping must be outsourced—at least for the short term. Of course, the bottom line is that financial considerations usually determine whether a cafeteria plan should be administered internally or outsourced. Nevertheless, the employer that premises its decision solely on financial data, disregarding nonfiscal issues, risks making an incorrect choice.

Table 13-1 shows a cost comparison of internal and outsourced plan administration. It reveals a cost differential in Year 1 that favors outsourcing; however, by Year 3 the cost differential in favor of internal administration is $23,600, and by Year 5, it is more than $58,000.

Before a plan administrator decides whether a cafeteria plan should be administered internally or outsourced, it is essential that the plan implementation team conduct a cost comparison along the lines of the one shown in Table 13-1. Changes in the original assumptions will produce entirely different results. Because each employer's situation is unique, such analysis is well worth the effort.

Table 13-1 Administration/Recordkeeping Cost Comparison Chart (Assumes 800 employees)

	Year 1	*Year 2*	*Year 3*	*Year 4*	*Year 5*	*5-Year Total*
		Internal Administration				
Software licensing	$10,000	$ 1,750	$ 1,750	$ 1,750	$ 1,750	$17,000
Meetings, design, setup	$25,000	$ 12,500	$ 6,250	$ 6,250	$ 6,250	$56,250
Staff time[a]	$ 4,375	$ 4,375	$ 4,375	$ 4,375	$ 4,375	$21,875
1-Year Total:		$ 39,375				
3-Year Cumulative Total:		$ 70,375				
5-Year Cumulative Total:		$ 95,125				
Average 3-year cost per employee per month		$ 2.44	Average 5-year cost per employee per month			$ 1.98
		Outsourced Administration				
Set-up fee ($10,000 + $6.25 per employee)	$15,000	$0	$0	$0	$0	$15,000
Monthly recordkeeping ($1.75 + $3.00/FSA)[b]	$19,680	$ 19,680	$19,680	$19,680	$19,680	$98,400
Annual renewal fee ($5,000 + $6.25 per employee)	$0	$ 10,000	$10,000	$10,000	$10,000	$40,000
Miscellaneous fees ($70–$100/hr)	$0	$0	$0	$0	$0	$0
1-Year Total:		$ 34,680				
3-Year Cumulative Total:		$ 94,400				
5-Year Cumulative Total:		$153,400				
Average 3-year cost per employee per month		$ 3.27	Average 5-year cost per employee per month			$ 3.20

[a]Assumes a current human resources staff member earning $35,000 will attribute 1/8th of his or her workday to flexible plan administration.
[b]Assumes 5 percent of all employees will elect to participate in both a health care and dependent care spending account.

Q 13:18 Can employees be charged for the cost of outsourcing the administration of a cafeteria plan?

Yes. Although neither the Code nor its supporting regulations specifically allow an employee to be charged for the outsourcing of a Section 125 cafeteria plan, employers are not specifically prohibited from doing so.

Particularly with regard to FSAs, some employers charge employees a fee to cover the cost of outside recordkeeping and claims processing fees. Despite this fee, it is often still advantageous for employees to participate in an FSA, because of the tax savings that FSAs produce. A plan participant who is subsidizing the cost of administration should contribute to the plan at least the amount that will produce enough tax savings to pay for the administrative cost.

> **Example.** Martha is taxed at the 15 percent federal tax bracket and pays state tax of 4 percent and FICA tax of 7.65 percent. Martha's overall tax rate is 26.65 percent. If Martha's employer selects a claims administrator that charges $5 per participant per month ($60 annually) for claims administration and Martha, as a participant in the plan, is required to have that $5 deducted from pay in addition to her FSA contribution, Martha needs to contribute at least $225 to the FSA for the year just to break even. At an overall tax rate of 26.65 percent, a $225 contribution produces a tax savings of nearly $60. Of course, Martha should plan to participate if she is to do better than break even. A participant in this plan would have to contribute no less than $225, and probably significantly more, for this plan to make financial sense.

Chapter 14

Nondiscrimination Rules and Testing

Qualified plans—those for which the cost may be expensed by an employer or paid by an employee on a pretax basis—must comply with nondiscrimination requirements. Broadly stated, such plans may not discriminate in favor of either highly compensated employees or owners of the company. A cafeteria plan must meet the nondiscrimination requirements of Section 125 of the Internal Revenue Code, and each of the underlying benefits offered within the Section 125 plan must meet the nondiscrimination requirements for that type of benefit. For example, Section 105(h) includes nondiscrimination tests for self-insured medical reimbursement plans, Section 129 rules apply to dependent care assistance plans, Section 79 standards are in place for group term life insurance plans, and 401(k) plans are subject to their own nondiscrimination tests. In general, nondiscrimination rules are in place to ensure that non-highly paid individuals are eligible for, and actually receive, their fair share of benefits. This chapter discusses the nondiscrimination rules pertaining to Section 125 cafeteria plans. (Nondiscrimination testing for the underlying benefits is covered in the chapters of this book relating to those specific benefits.)

Q 14:1 To what extent is testing required to ensure that a Section 125 cafeteria plan is nondiscriminatory?

A Section 125 plan has overall tests it must pass in order to ensure that the plan does not discriminate in favor of either key employees or highly compensated individuals. The plan must be tested in terms of its eligibility, contributions, and benefits.

The underlying benefits offered within the plan may also be subject to independent testing. For example, a dependent care assistance FSA will have a stand-alone test to ensure that such a benefit does not discriminate in favor of either key or highly compensated individuals.

A Section 125 plan must ensure that it passes the overall Section 125 nondiscrimination tests, as well as any required tests for underlying benefits offered within the plan.

Q 14:2 What are the nondiscrimination rules and testing requirements for a cafeteria plan?

Section 125 of the Internal Revenue Code (Code) contains several sets of nondiscrimination rules with which cafeteria plans must comply. The rules are intended to ensure that such plans do not discriminate in favor of highly compensated individuals or owners or officers of the company. Specifically, the code provides that benefits become taxable as income for a highly compensated participant or key employee during a plan year in which the plan discriminates in favor of highly compensated individuals as to eligibility to participate and as to benefits and contributions, or in favor of key employees in the concentration of benefits provided under the plan. (Highly compensated individuals and participants are discussed in Q 14:7, and key employees are defined in Q 14:8.)

In other words, the nondiscrimination rules set forth in Code Section 125 include an eligibility test, a contributions and benefits test, and a key employee concentration test (see Exhibit 14-1), as follows:

1. The *eligibility test* measures whether or not the plan discriminates in favor of highly compensated individuals or their dependents with regard to their ability to participate in the plan. Included in this test is a classification test, as well as a length-of-service test and a participation test. (See Q 14:11.)
2. The *contributions and benefits test* requires that the plan not discriminate in favor of highly compensated participants regarding contributions made to or benefits received under the cafeteria plan. Included in this test is a facts-and-circumstances test, as well as a test that analyzes the actual operation of the plan. There is a special contributions test for health coverage under a cafeteria plan. (See Q 14:13.)
3. The *key employee concentration test* mandates that the aggregate nontaxable benefits provided to key employees may not exceed 25 percent of the aggregate nontaxable benefits provided to all employees. (See Qs 14:14, 14:15.)

Exhibit 14-1. Process for Cafeteria Plan Nondiscrimination Testing

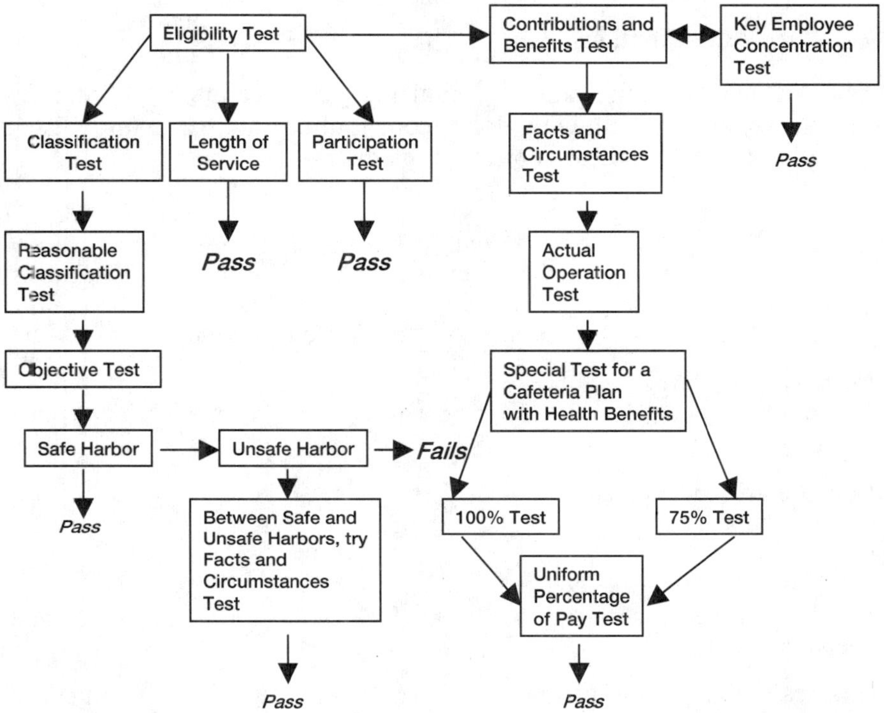

Q 14:3 How are salary reduction amounts treated for nondiscrimination testing purposes?

Salary reduction amounts are treated as cafeteria plan contributions for purposes of Section 125 nondiscrimination testing. Under Code Section 125, the employer may make contributions pursuant to salary reduction agreements under which participants elect to reduce their compensation or to forgo increases in compensation and to have such amounts contributed, as employer contributions, by the employer on their behalf. [Prop Treas Reg § 1.125-1, Q&A 6]

Example. Boffo Breads, Inc. is performing the contributions and benefits test that applies because its cafeteria plan offers health benefits (see Q 14:13). In this example, "nonelective employer" contributions are amounts used by the employee for benefits within the plan. Under the cafeteria plan, the following contributions for health benefits are provided:

Monthly Nonelective Employer Contributions	+	Monthly Employee Salary Reduction Contributions	=	Monthly Total Cafeteria Plan Contributions

An HMO medical plan and a dental plan are available to Boffo Breads employees, and the following dollar contributions are made under the cafeteria plan for the medical and dental plans:

	Monthly Nonelective Employer Contributions	+	*Monthly Employee Salary Reduction Contributions*	=	*Monthly Total Cafeteria Plan Contributions*
Medical Plan (HMO)					
Individual coverage	$152.28	+	$38.13	=	$190.41
Family coverage	$391.45	+	$97.76	=	$489.21
Dental Plan (covers diagnostic and preventive, basic restorative and major restorative services)					
Individual coverage	$ 19.50	+	$ 4.87	=	$ 24.37
Family coverage	$ 48.97	+	$12.24	=	$ 61.21

Total cafeteria plan contributions for each participant are counted. Thus, when Benjamin, a participant in the Boffo Breads cafeteria plan, elects family medical and individual dental, the annual contributions made under the cafeteria plan on his behalf are $5,870.52 ($489.21 x 12 months for medical coverage) plus $292.44 ($24.37 x 12 months for dental coverage).

Q 14:4 Are employees of a controlled group or an affiliated service group treated as employed by a single employer for purposes of nondiscrimination testing?

Yes. Employees of businesses under common control are treated as if they are employed by a single employer. Therefore, employees of a controlled group of corporations are treated as employed by a single employer, and employees of an affiliated service group are treated as employed by a single employer as well. [IRC § 125(g)(4)]

Q 14:5 Must collectively bargained cafeteria plans comply with the Section 125 nondiscrimination rules?

No. Code Section 125(g)(1) states that "a plan shall not be treated as discriminatory if the plan is maintained under an agreement which the Secretary [of Labor] finds to be a collective bargaining agreement between employee representatives and one or more employers."

Q 14:6 If just a premium conversion plan is provided, must nondiscrimination testing be performed?

Yes. Section 125 nondiscrimination testing must be performed for all types of cafeteria plans, including the following:

1. Premium conversion plans (see chapter 5);
2. Flexible spending accounts (see chapter 6); and
3. Fully flexible plans that provide a benefits allowance (see chapter 7).

All the foregoing types of plans constitute cafeteria plans because they offer participants a choice among two or more benefits consisting of cash and qualified benefits.

Definitions

Q 14:7 Who are highly compensated individuals, as defined by the Internal Revenue Code and Treasury Regulations?

For the purpose of Section 125 nondiscrimination testing, *highly compensated individuals* are:

1. Officers;
2. More than 5 percent shareholders;
3. Individuals who are, based on facts and circumstances, highly compensated; and
4. Spouses or dependents of any of the individuals described in items 1, 2, and 3.

A *highly compensated participant* is a plan participant who fits into any of the above categories. [IRC § 125(e)]

> **Note.** It may seem redundant to discuss highly compensated individuals as a separate group from highly compensated participants. Oftentimes, the individuals fitting both of those descriptions within a company are one and the same. However, a highly compensated individual may or may not be a plan participant. It is important to consider the group of highly compensated individuals when reviewing plan eligibility guidelines. Highly compensated participants are important when testing a plan's contributions and benefits provided to participants.

Practitioners may wonder how to apply the facts-and-circumstances standard referenced in item 3 above to define *highly compensated*. In the absence of specific guidance, many plan sponsors use the Code Section 414(q) definition of *highly compensated employee*, but that is not required by law.

The Small Business Job Protection Act of 1996 (SBJPA) simplified the definition of *highly compensated employee* under Code Section 414(q). For plan years beginning after December 31, 1996, an employee is considered to be highly compensated under Code Section 414(q) if he or she:

1. Was a 5 percent owner during the current or preceding plan year; or
2. For the preceding year had compensation from the employer in excess of $80,000 (indexed for cost of living) and, if the employer so elects, for the preceding plan year was in the top-paid group of employees, defined as the top 20 percent of employees ranked by compensation for the plan year.

The $80,000 figure in item 2 is subject to cost-of-living adjustments like those made under Code Section 415(d). For 2001, the compensation limit for defining a highly compensated individual was $85,000; for 2002, it was increased to $90,000.

Note. The term *highly compensated individual* (or employee) is defined differently in other sections of the Code. For example, self-insured medical reimbursement plans under Code Section 105(h) and dependent care assistance plans under Code Section 129 are subject to their own definitions of highly compensated individuals (or employee) for purposes of nondiscrimination testing for those benefits. [IRC §§ 105(h)(5), 129(d)(2)]

Q 14:8 Who are key employees, as defined by the Internal Revenue Code and Treasury Regulations?

A key employee is an individual who, at any time during the plan year, is:

1. An officer of the employer whose annual compensation exceeds $130,000;
2. An owner of more than 5 percent of the company; or
3. An owner of more than 1 percent of the company, with annual compensation from the employer for a plan year in excess of $150,000.

[IRC § 416(i)(1)]

Tax Treatment

Q 14:9 What tax treatment does the IRS impose on participants in a discriminatory cafeteria plan?

If a cafeteria plan fails any of the Section 125 nondiscrimination tests, the employer is not penalized if the discrimination is detected in a timely manner. Instead, the benefits received by highly compensated participants and key employees become taxable to those employees. The highly compensated participant or key employee is taxed as if he or she selected the taxable benefits under the cafeteria plan that produced the greatest aggregate value, whether or not that amount was in fact selected. (Highly compensated participants are taxed if the eligibility or contributions and benefits test is failed, and key employees are taxed if the concentration test is failed.) There are no adverse tax consequences for the other employees.

If a plan is determined to be discriminatory after the close of a tax period (e.g., the employee's tax year or the employer's fiscal year), however, the employer could have some difficulties related to underwithholding of taxes.

Q 14:10 If a cafeteria plan is found to be discriminatory, how should the plan administrator allocate taxable income to highly compensated participants and key employees?

In a discriminatory cafeteria plan, a highly compensated participant or key employee is taxed as if he or she had selected the taxable benefit under the cafeteria plan that produced the greatest aggregate value, whether or not that benefit was in fact selected. The value is first allocated to the taxable benefits actually selected and then on a pro rata basis to the nontaxable benefits actually selected by the individual.

Example. Good Gravy Co.'s cafeteria plan provides Theresa, a highly compensated participant, with the opportunity to select plan year benefits costing $1,500 from among the following: up to $300 in cash, coverage under a health plan providing medical expense reimbursement (cost of $900), or coverage under a disability plan (cost of $300).

For the 2002 plan year, Theresa elects to receive $100 in cash, coverage under the health plans ($900), and coverage under the disability plan ($300). If the cafeteria plan is discriminatory for the plan year, Theresa will be taxed on the $100 cash benefit actually selected and on the $200 cash benefit that she could have selected. Income taxes, as well as Social Security and unemployment taxes, are payable on that $300 of income.

Under these facts (and in similar situations), the taxability of amounts received under the other plans may be affected. The $300 will be allocated first to the taxable benefits actually selected by Theresa and second, on a pro rata basis, to the nontaxable benefits actually selected by her. Thus, $100 is allocated to the $100 cash benefit actually received and the $200 is allocated as after-tax employee contributions among the nontaxable benefits actually selected as follows: $150 ($200/$1,200 x $900) to coverage under the health plan, and $50 ($200/$1,200 x $300) to the coverage under the disability plan. Such an allocation will not affect the nontaxable status of any of these benefits—that is, the purchase of coverage under any of these plans with employee contributions would not trigger taxable income—but it might affect the taxability of amounts received under any of the plans. Thus if Theresa becomes disabled during the year of coverage, benefits provided under her disability plan would be nontaxable to her to the extent that the benefits were attributable to the portion of the coverage purchased with her after-tax contributions. Benefits attributable to premium amounts paid with pre-tax dollars will be taxable when received. [Prop Treas Reg § 1.125-1,

Q&As 10, 11] This could be a potentially serious consequence of a discriminatory Section 125 cafeteria plan.

Note. Amounts that an individual must include in gross income because a cafeteria plan is discriminatory are treated as received or accrued in the individual's taxable year within which ends the plan year for which an election was or could have been made. [Prop Treas Reg § 1.125-1, Q&A 12]

There are no adverse tax consequences for non-highly compensated participants or non-key employees who participate in a discriminatory cafeteria plan. [Prop Treas Reg § 1.125-1, Q&A 10]

Eligibility Test

Q 14:11 What are the various components of the test regarding the conditions an employer may impose on the eligibility of its employees to participate in its cafeteria plan?

Code Section 125(b)(1)(A) indicates that a cafeteria plan cannot discriminate in favor of highly compensated individuals as to eligibility to participate in the plan. There are three components of the eligibility test: classification, length of service, and participation.

Classification Test. The classification test includes both a reasonable classification test and an objective test.

1. *Reasonable classification test.* The program must benefit employees who qualify under a classification set up by the employer and found by the Secretary of the Treasury not to discriminate in favor of highly compensated individuals or their dependents. Under this test, the classification of employees eligible to participate in the plan must represent a "bona fide business classification"; (for example, limiting the plan to all salaried employees and not offering the plan to hourly employees would be considered a reasonable classification of employees).
2. *Objective test.* The classification test also incorporates the objective test used for qualified pension and profit-sharing plans under Code Section 410(b). This test may be considered a safe harbor, described below, for satisfying the objective test component of the classification test.

Safe Harbor. Generally, the *percentage* of highly compensated individuals eligible under the plan cannot exceed two times the *percentage* of non-highly compensated individuals eligible under the plan.

If the percentage of the employer's workforce that is non-highly compensated is greater than 60 percent, the safe harbor percentage may be modified according to the Objective Test Table (see Table 14-1). If a classification falls within the safe harbor and passes the reasonable classification test, it satisfies the requirements of Code Section 410(b).

Unsafe Harbor. Generally, if the *percentage* of highly compensated individuals eligible under the plan exceeds two and one-half times the *percentage* of non-highly compensated individuals eligible under the plan, the plan falls into the unsafe harbor and fails the objective test.

If the percentage of the employer's workforce that is non-highly compensated is greater than 60 percent, the unsafe harbor percentage may be modified according to the Objective Test Table (see Table 14-1). If a classification falls within the objective unsafe harbor, it automatically fails the Section 410(b) test, regardless of whether or not it passes the reasonable classification test.

Facts and Circumstances. If the cafeteria plan's percentages fall between the safe and unsafe harbor amounts, the plan will pass or fail the objective test based on all the facts and circumstances. The following facts and circumstances are relevant in determining whether a classification is discriminatory:

1. The underlying business reason for the classification;
2. The percentage of employees that are eligible under the plan;
3. Whether the number of employees eligible for the plan in each salary range is representative of the number of employees in each salary range of the employer's workforce; and
4. The extent to which the eligibility classification is close to satisfying the safe harbor rule.

Table 14-1. IRC Section 125—Objective Test Table

Non-Highly Compensated Individual Concentration Percentage	*Safe Harbor Percentage*	*Unsafe Harbor Percentage*
0–60	50.00	40.00
61	49.25	39.25
62	48.50	38.50
63	47.75	37.75
64	47.00	37.00
65	46.25	36.25
66	45.50	35.50
67	44.75	34.75
68	44.00	34.00
69	43.25	33.25
70	42.50	32.50
71	41.75	31.75
72	41.00	31.00
73	40.25	30.25
74	39.50	29.50
75	38.75	28.75

Table 14-1. IRC Section 125—Objective Test Table (*cont'd*)

Non-Highly Compensated Individual Concentration Percentage	*Safe Harbor Percentage*	*Unsafe Harbor Percentage*
76	38.00	28.00
77	37.25	27.25
78	36.50	26.50
79	35.75	25.75
80	35.00	25.00
81	34.25	24.25
82	33.50	23.50
83	32.75	22.75
84	32.00	22.00
85	31.25	21.25
86	30.50	20.50
87	29.75	20.00
88	29.00	20.00
89	28.25	20.00
90	27.50	20.00
91	26.75	20.00
92	26.00	20.00
93	25.25	20.00
94	24.50	20.00
95	23.75	20.00
96	23.00	20.00
97	22.25	20.00
98	21.50	20.00
99	20.75	20.00

If a classification does not fall within the safe or unsafe harbors and passes the facts and circumstances and reasonable classification tests, it satisfies the Section 410(b) test. To help employers pass the tests, certain groups of employees may be excluded from the total number of employees upon which the classification test for nondiscrimination is based, including the following:

- Individuals who are subject to specific age or service requirements under the plan, as long as the service requirement does not exceed one year and the age requirement does not exceed age 21.
- Collectively bargained employees, as long as the benefits were the subject of good-faith bargaining (any benefits received by collectively bargained employees are tested on a bargaining unit basis).

- Nonresident aliens, provided they receive no earned income from United States sources.

Example. Acme Meat Co. has 480 employees, 400 of which are nonexcludable for purposes of 410(b) testing. Of those 400, 240 are non-highly compensated and 160 are highly compensated. Of the 240 non-highly compensated employees, 120 are eligible to participate in the Acme Meat plan; of the 160 highly compensated employees, 144 are eligible to participate in the plan. Acme Meat can determine whether it passes the classification test as follows:

1. *Determine the non-highly compensated employee concentration percentage.* Determine the percentage of nonexcludable employees who are non-highly compensated by dividing the number of nonexcludable, non-highly compensated employees by the total number of nonexcludable employees.

   240 (nonexcludable, non-highly compensated employees)/400 (nonexcludable employees)

   Result = 60%

2. *Determine the safe harbor and unsafe harbor percentages.* For the non-highly compensated employee concentration percentage determined in step 1, determine the applicable safe harbor and unsafe harbor percentages.

   For a 60 percent non-highly compensated employee concentration percentage, the safe harbor is 50 percent and the unsafe harbor is 40 percent (see Table 14-1).

3. *Calculate the highly compensated employee benefiting percentage.* Divide the number of highly compensated employees who are eligible by the total number of nonexcludable employees who are highly compensated.

   144 (highly compensated employees who are eligible)/160 (nonexcludable employees who are highly compensated)

   Result = 90%

4. *Apply the safe harbor percentage.*

   a. Multiply the safe harbor percentage (a result in step 2) by the highly compensated employee benefiting percentage.

      50% (safe harbor percentage) x 90% (highly compensated employee benefiting percentage)

      Result = 45%

   b. Multiply the number of nonexcludable non-highly compensated employees by the result above.

      240 (nonexcludable non-highly compensated employees) x 45%

      Result = 108 non-highly compensated employees must be eligible

5. *Determine if the plan passes the safe harbor test.* The plan passes the safe harbor test because at least 108 non-highly compensated employees are eligible (120 non-highly compensated employees are, in fact, eligible).

Length of Service Test. No employee can be required to complete more than three years of employment as a condition of participation in the plan, and the employment requirement must be the same for all employees.

Participation Test. Any employee who satisfies the length of service requirement (see above) and is otherwise entitled to participate in the plan must participate no later than the first day of the first plan year following completion of the employment requirement, unless the employee was separated from service before the first day of that plan year.

Q 14:12 Is the eligibility test for cafeteria plans a safe harbor test?

It appears that the eligibility test that applies to cafeteria plans (which includes the classification, length of service, and participation tests; see Q 14:11) is a safe harbor test. If a cafeteria plan can otherwise demonstrate that the plan does not discriminate in favor of highly compensated individuals with respect to eligibility to participate in the plan, it appears that the plan can be considered nondiscriminatory for purposes of eligibility. [IRC § 125(g)(3)]

Contributions and Benefits Test

Q 14:13 What is the contributions and benefits test?

The second test that a cafeteria plan must satisfy under the nondiscrimination rules of Code Section 125 is that it not favor highly compensated participants with respect to contributions and benefits. [IRC § 125(b)(1)(B)] That is, a cafeteria plan is not considered discriminatory with regard to contributions and benefits if qualified benefits and total benefits (or the employer's contributions allocable to each) do not discriminate in favor of highly compensated participants. [IRC § 125(c)]

According to congressional committee reports, a plan will not be discriminatory regarding benefits if total benefits or nontaxable benefits attributable to highly compensated participants, measured as a percentage of compensation, are not significantly greater or less than total benefits or nontaxable benefits attributable to other participants (measured on the same basis), provided the plan is not otherwise discriminatory. [H Rep No 95-1445 (Revenue Act of 1978), *reprinted in* 1978-3 CB 238; Sen Rep No 95-1263 (Revenue Act of 1978), *reprinted in* 1978-3 CB 373] The Internal Revenue Service (IRS) has not released a testing method, nor is any direct support for this approach found in the Internal Revenue Code or related regulations.

The Section 125 proposed regulations issued in 1984 indicate that whether or not a plan is found to be nondiscriminatory is based on the facts and circumstances of each particular situation. [Prop Treas Reg § 1.125-1] The proposed regulations state that each participant must be given an equal opportunity to select nontaxable benefits and that the actual utilization of nontaxable benefits must not be discriminatory. Highly compensated participants must not disproportionately select nontaxable benefits while other participants elect taxable benefits.

In addition to not discriminating with regard to benefit availability or benefit selection, a cafeteria plan must not discriminate in favor of highly compensated participants in actual operation. A plan may be discriminatory in actual operation if the duration of the plan (or of a particular nontaxable benefit offered under the plan) coincides with the period during which highly compensated participants use the plan (or the benefit). [Prop Treas Reg § 1.125-1, Q&A 19]

Special test for health coverage. If a cafeteria plan offers health benefits, the plan is not discriminatory with regard to contributions or benefits provided contributions under the cafeteria plan on behalf of each participant are at least:

1. 100 percent of the cost of health coverage provided under the cafeteria plan for the majority of the similarly situated highly compensated participants; or
2. 75 percent of the cost of health coverage of the similarly situated participant having the highest-cost health coverage under the cafeteria plan, and cafeteria plan contributions or benefits above those levels must be made as a uniform percentage of pay. [IRC § 125(g)(2)]

There are no Treasury regulations that definitively interpret the two-part test for health benefits, and there are numerous ways of understanding it. Generally, "cost" is considered to be the premium or premium equivalent. Most practitioners take the position that the Section 125(g)(2) test was enacted before the contemplation of salary reduction cafeteria plans. Therefore, the principles upon which Code Section 125(g)(2) are based appear to be no longer applicable and make testing under the section somewhat illogical. Another interpretation is that, although the test offers a safe harbor, a plan may not necessarily be discriminatory when it does not pass the test. It does not appear that the IRS will cause a plan to be considered discriminatory merely because it may fail to comply with Code Section 125(g)(2).

Key Employee Concentration Test

Q 14:14 What is the key employee concentration test?

The key employee concentration test demands that nontaxable benefits provided to key employees not exceed 25 percent of the aggregate nontaxable benefits provided to all employees. That is, the testing procedure for key employee concentration consists of comparing the nontaxable benefits provided to key employees to the nontaxable benefits provided to all employees with the caveat that nontaxable benefits provided to key employees may not exceed 25 percent of the aggregate. [IRC § 125(b)(2)]

Example. Tasty Taters Inc. has 300 employees, of whom 10 are key employees and 290 are non-key employees. Tasty Taters provides $5,000 in total nontaxable benefits annually to its key employees and $150,000 in total nontaxable benefits to all employees, both key and non-key. Because the nontaxable benefits paid to key employees ($5,000) is less than 25 percent of the nontaxable benefits paid to all employees (25% x $150,000 = $37,500), Tasty Taters passes the concentration test.

Q 14:15 Does the key employee concentration test apply to coverage received by employees or to the benefits actually received?

In determining whether the nontaxable benefits provided to key employees exceed 25 percent of the aggregate nontaxable benefits provided to all employees, *coverage* received by employees (rather than the benefits or reimbursement actually received) should be taken into account. Generally, coverage is considered to be the premium or premium equivalent. Note that employee contributions to flexible spending accounts are also considered to be "premiums" for purposes of testing.

Example. Darryl, an employee of the Fly Fish Co., elects to be covered by Fly Fish's family medical coverage at a premium contribution expense to him of $250 per month. That amount is paid by Darryl on a pretax basis. Darryl and his family incur $8,000 in covered medical claims throughout the year. Notwithstanding the amount of claims (benefits received), the amount used in testing for the key employee concentration test is the $3,000 paid over the course of the year for the coverage.

Example. Grace contributes $600 over the course of the year to a medical flexible spending account, but she claims out only $450 and forfeits $150. The amount used for the key employee concentration test is the $600 paid for coverage, not the $450 actually received in benefits.

Q 14:16 May the former pretax benefit elections of key employees be reinstated if the discrimination statistics of the cafeteria plan change during the plan year?

Apparently not. Informally, the IRS has indicated that where key employees have been required to reduce pretax elections at the beginning of the plan year to meet nondiscrimination requirements, they may not later in the year reinstate their full benefit elections if more non-key participants join the plan. Such an event is not a qualified change in status.

Timing of Testing

Q 14:17 When should a cafeteria plan perform nondiscrimination testing?

Nondiscrimination testing is best performed after the open enrollment period, but before the plan year actually begins. By commencing testing at such time, the plan administrator may take action to change the elections of highly compensated participants or key employees before the start of the plan year if the administrator should find that the plan is discriminatory. A cafeteria plan must be nondiscriminatory every day of the plan year.

It is also possible, however, to address unfavorable testing results once the plan year has commenced. The legislative history of the Technical and Miscellaneous Revenue Act of 1988 (TAMRA) authorizes a method by which the plan administrator may intervene in the plan during the year and reduce the contributions of highly compensated participants or key employees or both so that the plan may pass the discrimination test. Generally, the administrator's intervention is limited by the following restrictions:

1. The reduction must be done in a consistent manner;
2. The procedure for adjustment of the contributions of highly compensated participants or key employees must not avoid the "use-it-or-lose-it" requirements of the Code [see Prop Treas Reg §§ 1.125-1, Q&A 7, 1.125-2, Q&A 5];
3. The employer must not exercise discretion on how to limit elections in the year in which elections are adjusted; and
4. For plan years after 1989, the method of limiting elections must be stated in the plan document before the start of the plan year for which that method will apply.

Example. The Virtuous Veggies Co.'s nondiscrimination testing results in the failure of the key employee concentration test. The company has 600 employees, of whom 20 are key employees and 580 are non-key employees. Virtuous Veggies provides $200,000 in total nontaxable benefits annually to its key employees and $400,000 in total nontaxable benefits to all employees, both key and non-key. Because the nontaxable benefits paid to key employees ($200,000) is more than 25 percent of the aggregate benefits ($100,000), Virtuous Veggies fails the key employee concentration test. Elections must be limited in the manner stated in the plan document before the start of the plan year. For instance, if the plan document so provides, the plan administrator may reduce the contributions of the key employee who elected to contribute the highest amount to the plan until the contributions reach the level where the plan passes the nondiscrimination test or until the amount reaches the same amount as the key employee who elected to contribute the second highest amount to the plan. Then, the contributions of both key employees are reduced until the plan satisfies the test or until their contributions reach the amount elected by the key employee with the third highest contribution amount. That process continues until Virtuous Veggies passes the test.

Q 14:18 Is there ever a need to perform discrimination testing during the plan year?

Yes. Discrimination testing may need to be performed again after initial testing if participants' elections materially change midyear as a result of their ability to revoke existing elections and make new elections, as the result of significant cost or coverage changes, or if the plan has a significant change in enrollment (gain or loss of participants.) Such election changes may affect the outcome of the Section 125 discrimination tests. (See chapter 11 for a discussion of circumstances under which participants may revoke existing elections on a prospective basis following significant cost or coverage changes.)

Other Nondiscrimination Rules

Q 14:19 With what nondiscrimination rules other than those of Code Section 125 must a cafeteria plan comply?

A cafeteria plan must, in addition to complying with Code Section 125, meet the nondiscrimination standards of the underlying plans, which could include the following:

1. Self-insured medical reimbursement plans, including medical FSAs (see IRC § 105(h));
2. Dependent care assistance plans, including dependent care FSAs (see IRC § 129);
3. Adoption assistance programs, including adoption assistance FSAs (see IRC § 137);
4. Group term life insurance plans(see IRC § 79);
5. 401(k) plans (see IRC § 401(k)); and
6. Voluntary employees' beneficiary association (VEBA) trusts (see IRC § 505(b)).

Q 14:20 What are the consequences when a benefit that is qualified under Code Section 125 fails a nondiscrimination test under another section of the Code?

If a Section 125 qualified benefit fails a nondiscrimination test under another section of the Code (e.g., if the nondiscrimination tests that apply to group term life insurance coverage under Code Section 79 are failed), it is unclear if the cafeteria plan is disqualified. Plan disqualification would mean that the employer must include all qualified benefits as taxable income to employees who received the benefits, so that those benefits would be subject to income tax withholding and Federal Insurance Contribution Act (FICA) taxes. In addition, if the plan were disqualified, the employer would have to pay FICA and Federal Unemployment Tax Act (FUTA) taxes on the qualified benefits that were received by employees.

Formerly, maintaining qualified benefit status under Code Section 125 was not linked to satisfying any other Code section's nondiscrimination tests. When former Code Section 89 was repealed, however, the statutory authority that had been included in that section to disregard the benefit's discriminatory status under another Code section was repealed. [Former IRC § 125(e); IRC § 125(f)]

> **Note.** A discriminatory self-insured medical reimbursement plan that is included in a cafeteria plan will *not* cause the cafeteria plan to be disqualified. Treasury Regulations Section 1.105-11(k)(1) offers a special rule for taxation of discriminatory self-insured medical benefits provided through a cafeteria plan.

Chapter 15

Other Laws Affecting Flexible Benefits Plans

In addition to the rules issued under Section 125 of the Internal Revenue Code (Code), other federal laws affect the operation of flexible benefits plans, including the Consolidated Omnibus Budget Reconciliation Act of 1985 (COBRA), the Family and Medical Leave Act of 1993 (FMLA), and the Health Insurance Portability and Accountability Act of 1996 (HIPAA).

On February 3, 1999, the Internal Revenue Service (IRS) issued final regulations on COBRA continuation coverage, and new proposed regulations to help provide further guidance and interpretation of the law. The proposed regulations were finalized on January 10, 2001. The 1999 final regulations adopt a U.S. Supreme Court decision on the application of COBRA rights, provide baseline rules for determining the COBRA liabilities of buyers and sellers, give employers flexibility in determining the number of group health plans they maintain, and limit the application of COBRA for most health flexible spending accounts (FSAs). The final regulations published in January 2001 simplify the small group exception and the determination of the number of group health plans maintained by an employer. The proposed regulations offered a rule limiting the application of COBRA continuation coverage in the case of health FSAs and revised the rules relating to the duration of COBRA continuation coverage. The final and proposed regulations issued in 1999 applied to qualifying events occurring in plan years beginning on or after January 1, 2000. Some of the clarifying aspects of Treasury Regulations Section 54.4980B-1 are effective for plan years beginning on or after January 1, 2001.

This chapter outlines the objectives that these laws seek to achieve with regard to flexible benefits plans. Because this chapter focuses on flexible benefits plans, not all of the changes to COBRA are discussed in these questions. Similarly, some of the requirements of HIPAA are discussed in this chapter, since

HIPAA relates to Section 125 plan administration and maintenance, but HIPAA is not discussed in its entirety.

Consolidated Omnibus Budget Reconciliation Act of 1985 (COBRA)

Q 15:1 What is the Consolidated Omnibus Budget Reconciliation Act of 1985 (COBRA)?

COBRA, which was enacted into law on April 7, 1986, generally gives certain employees, former employees, and/or their spouses and dependent children the right to temporary continuation of health coverage at group rates. Coverage for these "qualified beneficiaries" is available only in specified instances. To be entitled to elect COBRA coverage, the qualified beneficiary (the covered individual who loses coverage) must experience a loss of coverage as a result of one of the following specified qualifying events:

1. Termination (including retirement) of a covered employee's employment (for reasons other than gross misconduct);
2. Reduction in hours of a covered employee's employment;
3. Death of a covered employee;
4. Divorce or legal separation of a covered employee;
5. Covered employee's entitlement to Medicare, which is a qualifying event for the spouse and dependents;
6. Covered dependent child's ceasing to be a dependent child of the covered employee under the terms of the applicable plan; or
7. Employer's commencement of a bankruptcy proceeding under Title 11 of the United States Code.

The following chart indicates the qualified beneficiaries and maximum required coverage period for each of the first six qualifying events.

Qualifying Events	*Qualified Beneficiaries*	*Coverage Period*
Termination of employment Reduction in hours of employment	Employee, spouse, dependent child	18 months
Death of covered employee Divorce or legal separation	Spouse, dependent child	36 months

Qualifying Events	*Qualified Beneficiaries*	*Coverage Period*
Employee's entitlement to Medicare		
Loss of dependent-child status	Dependent child	36 months

If the qualifying event is the employer's filing of a bankruptcy petition under Title 11 of the United States Code, the maximum applicable COBRA continuation period is as follows:

1. The coverage of employees who retired on or before the date of a substantial elimination of coverage continues until their dates of death. In other words, retirees receive lifetime coverage.
2. The coverage of individuals who are widows or widowers of such retirees on the day before the petition is filed continues until the earlier of such surviving spouse's dates of death or 36 months after the death of the retired covered employee.
3. The coverage of the spouse and dependent children of a retiree continues until the earlier of the death of such spouse or dependent child, or 36 months after the retiree's date of death.

Qualified beneficiaries who are entitled to COBRA coverage because of an employer's bankruptcy are only those individuals who experienced a substantial elimination of coverage within one year before or after the commencement of the bankruptcy proceeding.

Example. Susan is a dependent child covered under her father's medical plan sponsored by Alright Metals. Under the terms of the plan, Susan loses dependent status (i.e., she no longer satisfies the plan's eligibility rules for dependent children when she attains age 19, the age limit specified in the plan, and she is not a full-time student). Susan is entitled to COBRA coverage for a maximum of 36 months. She may elect coverage under her father's medical plan at the COBRA premium rate. (See Q 15:17 for information about pretax payment of Susan's COBRA premium.)

Example. Rick has coverage through his wife's health plan sponsored by her employer, CDE Industries. Rick loses health coverage when he and his wife divorce. Rick may purchase health coverage through the plan of his former wife's employer. Since divorce is the qualifying event, Rick is entitled to a maximum of 36 months of coverage at the COBRA premium rate. (See Q 15:17 for information about pretax payment of Rick's COBRA premium.)

Q 15:2 Which types of plans must comply with the requirements of COBRA?

Only group health plans that are maintained by an employer or employee organization to provide health care to covered participants are required to provide continuation coverage through COBRA. An employer maintains a plan if the employer contributes to the plan directly or indirectly. Even employee-pay-all plans qualify, as long as coverage would not be available at the same cost to an employee who does not work for the employer.

Covered plans include plans provided through insurance, direct reimbursement, or self-funding under a flexible benefits plan or an on-site facility. A plan maintained by an employee representative is not "maintained by an employer" if the employer does not contribute to the plan and has no involvement in the operation of the plan.

A plan is a group health plan subject to COBRA if it provides "health care" to the employer's employees, former employees, or such employees' family members. Health FSAs satisfy the definition of group health plan in Code Section 5000(b)(1) and so are generally subject to COBRA; however, the regulations stipulate that COBRA continuation for health FSAs need not be offered in all circumstances, or for the entire COBRA period of coverage (see Q 15:3).

A plan provides coverage to a group if it is an arrangement providing health care to two or more employees. For this purpose, employees include common-law employees, whether full-time or part-time, as well as certain self-employed individuals. Effective for plan years beginning on or after January 1, 1990, a group health plan covering only non-common-law employees constitutes a group health plan for COBRA purposes. For prior plan years, such a plan did not constitute a COBRA-covered group health plan unless that plan, or another plan maintained by the employer, covered at least one common-law employee.

The final regulations clarify that *health care* has the same meaning as *medical care* under Code Section 213. [Treas Reg § 54.4980B-2, Q&A 1(b)] Medical care under Code Section 213 includes the diagnosis, cure, mitigation, treatment, or prevention of disease, and any other undertaking for the purpose of affecting any structure or function of the body. It includes transportation primarily for, and essential to, medical care. Benefits that are provided merely for general well-being, however, are not medical care for COBRA purposes. In addition, a plan under which substantially all of the coverage is for qualified long-term care (as defined in Code Section 7702(c)) does not qualify as a health plan for COBRA purposes. [Treas Reg § 54.4980B-2, Q&A 1(e)]

Besides those mentioned here, many other rules govern the operation of group health plans under COBRA, including the following aspects of operation:

1. *Exempt employers.* Small-employer plans are exempt. A group health plan maintained by an employer that normally employed fewer than 20 employees during the preceding calendar year qualifies as an exempt plan. The regulations clarify that, in determining the number of employees of an employer, each full-time employee is counted as one employee and each part-time employee is counted as a fraction of an employee.[Prop Treas Reg § 54.4980B-2, Q&A 5(d)–(f)]

   Certain church plans are exempt from COBRA. Federal, state, and local government employers are also exempt from COBRA; however, state and local governments are subject to the continuation coverage provisions of the Public Health Service Act (PHSA), and continuation coverage rules apply to the federal government under the Federal Employees Health Benefits Amendments Act of 1988.

2. *Offering of core-only and core-and-non-core coverage.* The final regulations eliminate the requirement that group health plans offer qualified beneficiaries the option to elect only core (health) coverage under a group health plan that otherwise provides both core and non-core (vision and dental) coverage.
3. Various circumstances may extend the maximum COBRA continuation period: second qualifying events, a determination that an individual is disabled under Title II or XVI of the Social Security Act, and the employee's entitlement to Medicare benefits.

Q 15:3 How does COBRA affect cafeteria plans?

Treasury Regulations Section 54.4980B-2, Q&A 8, details how COBRA continuation requirements apply to cafeteria plans and other flexible benefits arrangements. (For the text of Q&A 8 from the final regulations, see Appendix O.)

COBRA continuation coverage requirements apply only to the type and level of coverage under the cafeteria plan or other flexible benefits arrangement that a qualified beneficiary is actually receiving on the day before the qualifying event. Under the regulations, COBRA continuation in an FSA may be limited.

According to the regulations, if a health FSA satisfies the following two conditions, the COBRA obligation can be limited to continuation during the year of the qualifying event only:

1. The benefits of the health FSA are excepted benefits within the meaning of Code Sections 9831 and 9832 (excepted benefits).
2. The maximum amount that the health FSA can require to be paid for a year of COBRA continuation coverage equals or exceeds the benefit available under the health FSA for the year.

Almost all health FSA benefits will qualify as excepted benefits under Code Sections 9831 and 9832. The second condition will also apply to almost every case. The maximum amount for a year's COBRA continuation coverage will equal or exceed (by 2 percent) the maximum benefit payable by the plan for a year.

Furthermore, no COBRA continuation need be offered for a health FSA if the two conditions above are satisfied, *and* if, as of the date of the qualifying event, the maximum benefit available to the qualified beneficiary under the health FSA for the remainder of the plan year is equal to or less than the maximum amount that the plan could require as payment to maintain COBRA coverage.

Example. Assume that the two conditions listed above apply. Nancy elected to contribute $100 per month to her health FSA, for total calendar plan year coverage of $1,200. Nancy terminated employment on June 30. As of the date of her qualifying event, she had been reimbursed $800 from her health FSA. The employer need not offer COBRA continuation coverage to Nancy. Her premium amount for the remainder of the plan year would be $102 per month, multiplied by six months ($612), but the amount she could be reimbursed for the remainder of the plan year is only $400.

Example. Assume that the two conditions listed above apply. Charles elected to contribute $100 per month to his health FSA, for total calendar plan year coverage of $1,200. Charles terminated employment on June 30. As of the date of his qualifying event, he had been reimbursed $50 from his health FSA. The employer must offer Charles COBRA continuation coverage for the remainder of the plan year. The amount that Charles would be required to pay in premiums ($102 × 6 = $612) is less than the benefit available to Charles for the rest of the year ($1,150). (For an explanation of the calculation of COBRA premiums, see Q 15:5.)

Q 15:4 Why would a former employee want to elect COBRA continuation of a health FSA?

Generally, Section 125 plans—and in particular, health FSAs—permit only plan *participants* (and their spouses and children) to incur expenses for reimbursement from the plan. A participant who is, for example, terminating employment with a company might want to elect COBRA coverage if he or she expects to incur medical expenses after the date of termination and money is available in the health FSA that might otherwise be forfeited.

Example. Assume that Lena has contributed $50 per month to her employer's health FSA for the first three months of the plan year. At the end of the third month, Lena experiences a qualifying COBRA event such as termination of employment. Lena has not incurred any medical expenses in the first three months of the plan year. The only way for Lena to recover the $150 contributed to the plan is to submit qualified claims. Since Lena has not incurred any medical expenses to date, she must extend her participation in the plan—via COBRA continuation—to submit and be reimbursed for expenses incurred after her date of termination and during her COBRA continuation period. Lena's COBRA payment would be $51 per month, probably paid on an after-tax basis. (It might be possible for Lena and her employer to arrange for pretax payment from her final paycheck.)

Note. A COBRA continuant may waive COBRA continuation at any time during the COBRA continuation period. If Lena incurs qualified expenses several weeks after termination (but while she is still a plan participant on COBRA), she may submit her claims for up to her expected annual election to the plan. Lena might want to waive further COBRA coverage once she has recovered her $150 pretax contribution. Unlike regular plan participants, Lena is not obligated to remain in the plan for the entire plan year.

Q 15:5 How is the applicable premium calculated for insured health plans, for the purpose of calculating COBRA premiums?

Under COBRA, employers are expressly permitted to charge employees 100 percent of the cost of the group health plan coverage, plus an additional 2 percent, for a total premium of 102 percent. For each 12-month determination period, the applicable premium for insured plans is "the cost to the plan for such period of the coverage for similarly situated beneficiaries with respect to whom a qualified event has not occurred (disregarding whether any portion of such cost is paid by the employer)," plus an additional 2 percent. The cost of coverage generally will be the monthly premium paid to the insurance company for active employees and their covered family members. [IRC § 4980B(f)(4)(A)] See Q 15:7 for a discussion of actual cost of premium versus a "price tag" communicated in a flexible benefit plan for purchase of benefits.

Q 15:6 How is the applicable premium calculated for self-insured health plans, for the purpose of calculating COBRA premiums?

COBRA provides that the applicable premium for self-insured plans must be calculated using either of two methods specified in the statute.

Under the first method, the applicable premium for the 12-month determination period is equal to a "reasonable estimate of the cost of providing coverage for such period for similarly situated beneficiaries" (i.e., active employees under the group health plan who have not experienced a qualifying event). This reasonable estimate must:

1. Be determined on an actuarial basis; and
2. Take into account such factors as the Secretary of the Treasury may prescribe in regulations. The COBRA regulations, however, do not provide any guidance on how to calculate the applicable premium under COBRA.

The second method for calculating premiums for a self-insured plan is a safe harbor, but this method permits less flexibility. A plan administrator cannot elect to use this method for a determination period if either of the following events has occurred:

1. A significant change in coverage under the group health plan between that determination period and the preceding determination period; or
2. A significant change in the number of employees covered by the group health plan between that determination period and the preceding determination period.

Under this method, the applicable premium is equal to the cost to the plan for providing coverage to similarly situated beneficiaries for the same period during the preceding determination period, adjusted by the percentage increase or decrease in the implicit price deflator of the gross national product (calculated by the Department of Commerce and published in the Survey of Current

Business) for the 12-month period ending on the last day of the sixth month of the preceding determination period. [IRC § 4980B(f)(4)(B)]

Q 15:7 What ramification does an employer's subsidizing or overcharging for a particular benefit in a credit methodology have for the calculation of premiums for COBRA continuation coverage?

As discussed in Q 15:5, for the calculation of COBRA premiums, the cost of coverage for an insured plan will generally be the monthly premium paid to the insurance company for active employees and their covered family members. Thus, to the extent that an employer subsidizes or overcharges for a particular benefit in a flexible benefits credit methodology (i.e., it charges less or more than the premium charged by the insurance company), it appears that the employer has to live with the potential employee realization that the rates reflected in the flexible benefits pricing strategy differ from the rates charged via COBRA premiums.

Also, as discussed in Q 15:6, there are two alternative methods for calculating the applicable premium for self-insured plans: the reasonable estimate method and the safe harbor method. To the extent that a pricing strategy causes the employer to subsidize or overcharge for a particular benefit, it appears that such subsidization or overcharging would not be allowable under either calculation method specified in COBRA.

The reasonable estimate method requires that a "reasonable estimate of the cost of providing coverage for such period for similarly situated beneficiaries" be determined on an actuarial basis and that the estimate take into account such factors as the Secretary of the Treasury may prescribe in regulations. Two points are worth noting: it would be difficult to justify the incorporation of an employer's pricing strategies in an actuarial cost calculation, and, to date, no factors for cost estimations have been prescribed in regulations.

Under the safe harbor method, the applicable premium is equal to the cost to the plan for providing coverage to similarly situated beneficiaries for the same period during the preceding determination period, adjusted by the percentage increase or decrease in the implicit price deflator of the gross national product (calculated by the Department of Commerce and published in the Survey of Current Business) for the 12-month period ending on the last day of the sixth month of such preceding determination period.

Neither of these methods provides for the flexibility necessary to allow for the incorporation of overcharging or subsidization under a pricing strategy in COBRA rate calculations. For self-insured plans, as with insured plans, it appears that the employer has to live with the potential employee realization that the rates reflected in the flexible benefits pricing strategy differ from the rates charged under COBRA premiums.

Q 15:8 What events trigger COBRA benefits for medical flexible spending accounts?

The same qualifying events (events that cause "qualified beneficiaries" to lose coverage) that trigger COBRA benefits for an employer's other group health plans also trigger COBRA benefits for medical FSAs:

1. Termination of a covered employee's employment (for reasons other than gross misconduct);
2. Reduction in the hours of a covered employee's employment;
3. Death of the covered employee;
4. Divorce or legal separation of the covered employee;
5. Covered employee's entitlement to Medicare;
6. Covered dependent child's ceasing to be a dependent child under the terms of the plan; or
7. Employer's commencement of a bankruptcy proceeding under Title 11 of the United States Code.

Q 15:9 Who are the qualified beneficiaries who have the right to continue medical flexible spending account coverage under COBRA?

The same individuals who are qualified beneficiaries under an employer's other group health plans are qualified beneficiaries under a medical FSA and may continue their coverage under COBRA.

In general, a qualified beneficiary is an individual who is covered under the group health plan on the day before the qualifying event. Mere eligibility for coverage is not sufficient to be a qualified beneficiary, regardless of the reason that the individual is not covered under the plan. The individual must actually be covered under the group health plan on that date.

Based on their status on the day before the qualifying event, three classes of individuals may be qualified beneficiaries:

1. Covered employees under a group health plan;
2. Covered spouses of covered employees; and
3. Covered dependent children of covered employees.

In bankruptcy situations, special rules apply that create a fourth class of qualified beneficiaries that includes certain retirees, their spouses, surviving spouses, and dependent children. [IRC § 4980B (g)(1)(D)]

Effective January 1, 1997, as a result of HIPAA, the definition of a "qualified beneficiary" is modified to include a child born to or placed for adoption with the employee during the COBRA continuation coverage period. Thus, a child born or placed for adoption while the employee is on COBRA can be added to that coverage immediately and becomes a "qualified beneficiary."

Under certain circumstances, individuals who are not qualified beneficiaries may be enrolled in COBRA coverage. For example, a qualified beneficiary receiving COBRA may be permitted to enroll his or her new family member, who is not a qualified beneficiary, in the plan; however, it is important to note that such individuals generally do not then become qualified beneficiaries with respect to future qualifying events.

Q 15:10 Does COBRA permit qualified beneficiaries to elect higher or lower maximum annual reimbursement amounts for health FSAs at the time of the qualifying event?

No. COBRA continuation coverage for any group health plan of an employer must generally be the same as the group health plan coverage enjoyed by the qualified beneficiary immediately before the qualifying event. [Treas Reg § 54.4980B-5, Q&A 4] Therefore, a qualified beneficiary can elect only an annual reimbursement amount under COBRA that matches the level he or she enjoyed immediately before the qualifying event.

Generally, if the continuation coverage that the employer makes available differs in any way from the coverage that the qualified beneficiary received from the employer immediately before the qualifying event, the group health plan is not in compliance with COBRA. This does not mean, however, that the qualified beneficiary "vests" in or is guaranteed the level of benefits the plan offered on the day before the qualifying event. Instead, the qualified beneficiary's right to receive continuation coverage is at all times subject to the plan's amendment provisions. COBRA expressly provides that continuation coverage must be identical to the coverage provided to similarly situated active employees who have not experienced a qualifying event, and if coverage is modified for active employees, COBRA coverage must be similarly modified. [IRC § 4980B(f)(2)(A)]

(See Q 15:12 for a discussion of circumstances under which qualified beneficiaries can change their elections during the COBRA continuation coverage period.)

Q 15:11 Do qualified beneficiaries have open enrollment rights for health FSAs?

Before publication of the 1999 proposed regulations, COBRA participants in a health FSA could make new elections at open enrollment in the same manner as other similarly situated participants. Now, in most cases, if the FSA participant has a COBRA right at all (see Q 15:3), COBRA participation in a health FSA terminates at the end of the plan year.

> **Example.** James participates in his employer's medical FSA, contributing $50 per month. The FSA plan operates on a calendar year. On November 30, James terminates employment. If James meets the requirements for COBRA continuation eligibility (i.e., the company must comply with COBRA require-

ments, and James has contributed more to the FSA than he has received in disbursements), James will be entitled to COBRA FSA continuation for the month of December. After December 31, James loses eligibility to participate in his former employer's FSA plan under COBRA.

Q 15:12 Can qualified beneficiaries experience changes in status?

Yes. COBRA continuation coverage for any group health plan of an employer must generally be the same as the group health plan coverage enjoyed by the qualified beneficiary immediately before the qualifying event.

A cafeteria plan may permit a participant to revoke an election during a period of coverage and make a new election for the remaining portion of the period if both the revocation and the new election are on account of and consistent with a change in status that satisfies the requirements of Treasury Regulations Section 1.125-4. If a cafeteria plan recognizes changes in status for similarly situated active employees, it must recognize the same changes in status for qualified beneficiaries.

Q 15:13 If the participant does not elect to continue coverage through COBRA for a medical flexible spending account, may the participant be reimbursed for expenses incurred after the "period of coverage"?

No. Expenses reimbursed under a medical FSA must be incurred during the participant's period of coverage under the FSA. Typically, the period of coverage is determined as the period of time for which the employee is funding (or receiving funding for) a medical FSA. Expenses are treated as having been incurred when the participant is provided with the care that gives rise to the expenses, and not when the participant is formally billed or charged or pays for the care. [Prop Treas Reg §§ 1.125-1, Q&A 17, 1.125-2, Q&A 7(b)(6)]

If the participant does not elect COBRA within the election period prescribed in the COBRA law, his or her period of coverage under the medical FSA comes to an end, and claims incurred thereafter are not reimbursable.

Some medical FSA plans have been designed to require any participant to commit to coverage for the entire plan year, regardless of whether or not the participant terminates employment during the year. Such a plan design intends for the participant to continue to contribute to the plan after termination (or to have a deferral from the final paycheck for the remainder of the plan year). The only way such a plan design might be permitted is if the plan requires such annual participation from all participants, regardless of their status in the plan as of date of termination. In other words, a participant who has been paid out more than he has contributed to the plan will be required to defer the balance of the expected contributions to the plan—but so will a participant who had not yet claimed out even as much as he or she had deferred while employed.

Such a plan design is intended to help mitigate an employer's risk of loss due to the risk-shifting rules of health FSAs. However, there is a question as to whether such a plan design and requirement is valid, since COBRA continuation may not be forced.

Q 15:14 What are the advantages available to employees who elect to continue medical flexible spending account coverage under COBRA?

The proposed Section 125 regulations published by the IRS in 1989 contain "uniform coverage rules" that provide employees with certain advantages in electing to continue medical FSA coverage with COBRA. These rules dictate that under a medical FSA, the maximum amount of reimbursement must be available at all times during a period of coverage, regardless of the level of contribution. Thus, a terminated employee could commence paying COBRA premiums, obtain up to the maximum reimbursement, and then discontinue paying COBRA premiums before making all of the plan contributions. The advantages provided to the employee by the Section 125 regulations increase the potential financial risk of employers who sponsor medical FSA programs. (See Qs 8:49–8:51 for a discussion of ways to design medical FSA programs to mitigate the employer's potential financial risk.) [Prop Treas Reg § 1.125-2, Q&A 7]

Q 15:15 Can each qualified beneficiary make separate elections for health FSAs?

Under the final regulations, each qualified beneficiary must be offered the opportunity to make an independent election to receive COBRA continuation coverage. [Treas Reg § 54.4980B-3, Q&A 1] Treasury Regulations Section 54.4980B-2, Q&A 8, (reproduced in Appendix O) indicates that health FSAs are subject to COBRA. Therefore, each qualified beneficiary, including a divorced spouse and a former dependent child, has the right to make an independent COBRA election. Thus, each has access, either together or independently, to the maximum health FSA amount. Informal discussions with the IRS have confirmed this interpretation.

> **Example.** Howard decides to set aside $1,200 of his salary per year ($100 per month) in a health FSA to cover anticipated eligible expenses. At the end of nine months, he has made $900 in salary reduction contributions and has incurred and claimed $700 in eligible expenses.
>
> At this point Howard terminates employment and therefore experiences a COBRA qualifying event. Through COBRA, Howard contributes $300 for himself. At the same time, Howard's wife, Marie, also contributes $300 for the remainder of the year for herself, making a total of $600 for the remainder of the year for Howard and Marie combined. Howard and his wife together are entitled to reimbursement of $800 of eligible expenses incurred during the remainder of the year. The $800 represents the $1,200 annual election

amount funded by Howard, plus Marie's $300, minus the $700 in eligible expenses already reimbursed.

Upon careful consideration of the example above, most qualifying COBRA beneficiaries will determine that only one person should continue coverage in a health FSA under COBRA. There is no financial benefit for multiple qualifying beneficiaries to each continue COBRA under a single health FSA when such premium payment is made on an after-tax basis.

Example. Shirley decides to set aside $1,200 of her salary per year ($100 per month) in a health FSA to cover anticipated eligible expenses. At the end of nine months, she has made $900 in salary reduction contributions and has incurred no eligible expenses.

At this point Shirley terminates employment and therefore experiences a COBRA qualifying event. Through COBRA, Shirley is given the opportunity to make a pretax contribution of $300 for herself and $300 for her husband (a total of $600) from her last paycheck. Shirley and her husband together are entitled to reimbursement of $1,500 of eligible expenses incurred during the remainder of the year. This $1,500 is made up of the $900 already contributed to the plan during Shirley's employment, plus the $600 deferred from Shirley's final pay on a pretax basis for COBRA continuation.

Q 15:16 Are dependent care FSAs subject to COBRA?

No. According to the Treasury regulations, COBRA continuation coverage requirements apply to the medical benefits that a covered employee has actually chosen to receive, if any. Because dependent care benefits do not constitute medical benefits as defined under the Treasury regulations, they are not subject to COBRA. Sometimes, however, dependent care assistance plans are designed so that former employees may continue to participate for the remainder of the plan year. This presents no financial risk to the employer, since dependent care assistance accounts only pay as the cash becomes available. They are not subject to the uniform coverage rules of health FSAs. [Prop Treas Reg § 1.125-2, Q&A 7(b)(2) and 7(b)(8)]

Q 15:17 Can an employee pay for COBRA premiums on a pretax basis for former spouses and former dependent children?

Yes. Treasury Regulations Section 1.125-4(c)(3)(iv) makes clear that an employee may elect to make pretax COBRA continuation payments for qualifying beneficiaries, including him- or herself, a spouse, and/or dependents. It is important to note that the COBRA continuation must be under the group health plan of "the employee's employer." It *is* permissible for a participant in a Section 125 premium conversion plan to pay COBRA premiums on behalf of himself, his spouse, or his child when the premium is for the employer's health plan. But it is *not* permissible to pay the COBRA premium on a pretax basis for the plan of another employer.

Example. Linda is covered by her employer's group health plan at a level of Employee + 1, in order to cover herself and her 18-year-old daughter, who has just graduated high school. When Linda's daughter turns 19, she will experience a qualifying event, as the health plan carrier will wish to drop her from Linda's coverage. Linda may pay for her daughter's COBRA premium on a pretax basis through her company's Section 125 plan's premium conversion feature. [Final Regulations 1.125-4(c)(3)(iv)]

Example. Jack is hired by Colorful Paints. Colorful Paints offers a health plan after 6 months of employment. Jack would like to be on the COBRA coverage of his former employer during the waiting period. Jack asked his employer if they would merely reduce his pay on a pretax basis under their Section 125 plan, and pay his COBRA premium for him. This is *not* a permitted method of paying COBRA under a Section 125 plan. An employee may not reduce pay for the premium expense of a different employer.

Family and Medical Leave Act of 1993 (FMLA)

Q 15:18 What is the Family and Medical Leave Act (FMLA) and why does it affect flexible benefits plans?

FMLA provides that employers with 50 or more employees must grant eligible employees up to 12 weeks of unpaid leave in the following circumstances:

1. The birth, adoption, or foster care placement of a child, if the leave is taken within 12 months of the birth, adoption, or placement;
2. The serious medical condition of a parent, spouse, or child (under age 18, or an adult child who cannot care for himself or herself); or
3. The worker's own serious medical condition that prevents him or her from performing the functions of his or her job.

Eligible employees could take as much as 12 weeks of family or medical leave in each 12-month period.

While on leave, employees must continue to receive the same group health benefits they had while employed. Employers must pay for this continued group health coverage to the same extent that they paid for the coverage that each employee had before beginning his or her leave. This is a continuation of active-employee coverage, not COBRA coverage.

Employees on leave may not lose any other employment benefits that they had accrued before going on leave. Aside from health coverage, however, the law does not require that employees accrue any additional benefits while on family or medical leave. The law specifies that these "employment benefits" include pensions, disability benefits, sick leave, annual leave, group life insurance, and paid vacation.

At times, FMLA leave may appear to conflict with the requirements of a Section 125 flexible benefit plan. To help plan sponsors properly administer FMLA in the presence of a Section 125 plan, Treasury released a set of regulations—finalized in November of 2001—describing the interaction between FMLA events and Section 125 plan rules. A copy of the final regulations is included as Appendix K.

Q 15:19 What are the special rules under FMLA that affect health insurance payments and contributions to health FSAs?

An employee taking FMLA leave must be permitted to:

1. Continue coverage under a health plan or health FSA while on FMLA leave;
2. Revoke an existing health plan or health FSA election under the cafeteria plan for the remainder of the coverage period; or
3. Revoke an existing health plan or health FSA election under the cafeteria plan and reinstate the coverage upon return from FMLA leave.

The uniform coverage rules of a health FSA apply during FMLA leave regardless of the payment option selected (see Q 15:23) for as long as the employee continues coverage (or for as long as the employer continues the coverage of an employee who fails to make the required contributions). Therefore, the full amount of the elected coverage, less any prior reimbursements, must be available to the employee at all times, including during the FMLA leave period of a plan participant who has elected to continue participation in the health FSA during FMLA leave.

An employee whose coverage under the health FSA terminates while he or she is on FMLA leave is not entitled to receive reimbursements for claims incurred during the period when the coverage is terminated. If, upon the employee's return from FMLA leave, the employee subsequently elects to be reinstated in the health FSA for the remainder of the plan year, he or she may not retroactively elect health FSA coverage for claims incurred during the period when the coverage was terminated. Further, the employee is not entitled to greater health FSA benefits relative to premiums paid than an employee who has been working continuously throughout the plan year. Therefore, if an employee elects to be reinstated in a health FSA upon return from FMLA leave, his or her coverage for the remainder of the plan year is equal to his or her election for the plan year (or if applicable, the short plan year), prorated for the period during the FMLA leave for which no premiums were paid, and reduced by prior reimbursements.

An employee on FMLA leave has the right to revoke or change elections (e.g., because of changes in status) under the same terms and conditions that apply to employees participating in the cafeteria plan who are not on FMLA leave. Thus, notwithstanding the rules described in the preceding paragraph, an employee who returns from FMLA leave may make a new health FSA election for the remainder of the plan year if return from leave without pay constitutes a change in status under the employer's cafeteria plan.

Example. Jane elects $1,200 worth of coverage under a calendar-year health FSA provided under a cafeteria plan, with an annual premium of $1,200. She is permitted to pay the $1,200 through pretax salary reduction amounts of $100 per month throughout the 12-month period of coverage. She incurs no medical expenses before April 1. On April 1, Jane takes FMLA leave after making three months' worth of contributions totaling $300 (3 months × $100 = $300). Pursuant to her rights under FMLA, she elects to terminate coverage upon going on FMLA leave. Consequently, Jane makes no premium payments for the months of April, May, and June, and she is not entitled to submit claims or receive reimbursements for expenses incurred during those months. Jane returns from FMLA leave and elects to be reinstated in the health FSA on July 1.

Under FMLA, Jane has no greater right to benefits upon reinstatement than she would have if she had been continuously working during the plan year. Therefore, she is reinstated to her annual election ($1,200) prorated for the period during the FMLA leave for which no premiums were paid (i.e., reduced for three months or one quarter of the plan year) less prior reimbursements ($0). Consequently, Jane's coverage for the remainder of the plan year equals $900. She must make premium payments of $100 per month for the remainder of the plan year. [Treas Reg § 1.125-3, Q&A 6]

Q 15:20 How is an employee's entitlement to non-health benefits determined when the employee is on an FMLA leave?

FMLA does not require an employer to maintain an employee's non-health benefits, such as life insurance, during FMLA leave. An employee's entitlement to any non-health benefits under a cafeteria plan while he or she is on FMLA leave is determined by the employer's established policy for providing such benefits when the employee is on non-FMLA leave, whether paid or unpaid. Therefore, an employee who takes FMLA leave is entitled to revoke an election of non-health benefits under a cafeteria plan to the same extent as an employee taking non-FMLA leave (for example, due to changes of family status or upon enrollment for a new plan year).

The FMLA regulations provide, however, that in certain cases, an employer may continue an employee's non-health benefits under the cafeteria plan while the employee is on FMLA leave to ensure that the employer can meet its responsibility to provide equivalent benefits to the employee upon his or her return from unpaid FMLA leave. If the employer continues an employee's non-health benefits during FMLA leave, the employer is entitled to recoup the costs incurred for paying the employee's share of the premiums during the FMLA leave period. In addition, a cafeteria plan must, as required by FMLA, permit an employee whose coverage terminated while on FMLA leave (either by revocation or nonpayment of premiums) to be reinstated in the cafeteria plan upon return from FMLA leave. [Treas Reg § 1.125-3, Q&A 7]

Q 15:21 What do the regulations under the FMLA indicate regarding flexible benefits plans?

The FMLA regulations describe the ways in which the employer may require employees to pay their share of premium payments. The regulations describe a voluntary agreement between the employer and the employee, which may include prepayment of premiums (e.g., through increased pretax payroll deductions) when the need for the FMLA leave is foreseeable.

Depending on the reason for the family or medical leave, it may not be possible to make increased pretax contributions in the period before the leave, such as in the case of a leave due to an unscheduled event—for example, a serious health condition. (See Q 15:22 for a discussion of alternative ways of making contributions for health benefits while an employee is on leave.)

Q 15:22 Can health benefits under a flexible benefits plan be continued on a pretax or after-tax basis while an employee is on leave?

Salary reduction participation in a cafeteria plan is feasible only if the employee is receiving some taxable pay from the employer. Whatever arrangements or accommodations employers make for COBRA enrollees or employees who take other kinds of unpaid absences could presumably be applied to absences taken under the FMLA, so that employee contributions could be made on an after-tax basis.

Final Regulations. 125-3 regulations allow employees to change their salary reduction elections when they take unpaid leave. This would presumably allow employers to permit employees to prepay for their health coverage by making extra pretax contributions in the period before a scheduled family or medical leave or, where the timing permits, to make up any missed contributions on a pretax basis when the employee returns. If the latter approach is taken, the salary reduction contributions should be made in the same plan year as the employee's leave. To do otherwise would enable employees to defer the receipt of compensation by carrying plan contributions forward, and therefore would violate the Section 125 rules.

In the case of a self-insured health plan, any special arrangements for employees on leave should be offered on a nondiscriminatory basis.

Note. The "catch-up" provision outlined above is available for health coverage plans, but not available to a health FSA participant on a retroactive basis. It may be possible, however, for the participant going out on FMLA leave to elect at the time leave begins to catch up on contributions to the plan upon the participant's return to the company, thereby making a prospective election rather than a retroactive election.

Q 15:23 What payment options for health benefits may a cafeteria plan offer when an employee is on an unpaid FMLA leave?

A cafeteria plan may, on a nondiscriminatory basis, offer one or more of the following payment options, subject to certain restrictions (see Q 15:27), to an employee who continues health benefits (including a medical FSA) while on unpaid FMLA leave:

- Prepayment (see Q 15:24)
- Pay-as-you-go (see Q 15:25)
- Catch-up (see Q 15:26)

An employer also has the option of voluntarily waiving, on a nondiscriminatory basis, the requirement that an employee who elects to continue health coverage while on FMLA leave pay the amounts that the employee would otherwise be required to pay for the leave period. [Treas Reg § 1.125-3, Q 3]

Q 15:24 What are the terms of the prepayment option for unpaid FMLA leave?

Under the prepayment option, a cafeteria plan may permit an employee to pay, prior to commencement of the FMLA leave period, the amounts due for the FMLA leave period; however, under no circumstances may the employer require an employee to prepay the amounts due for the leave period. [FMLA Reg § 825.210(c)(3), 825.210(c)(4)] Contributions under the prepayment option may be made on a pretax salary reduction basis from any taxable compensation (including the cashing out of unused sick days or vacation days). These contributions will not be included in the employee's gross income, provided that all cafeteria plan requirements are satisfied. Contributions under the prepayment option may also be made on an after-tax basis. [Treas Reg § 1.125-3, Q&A 3(a)(1)]

Q 15:25 What are the terms of the pay-as-you-go option for unpaid FMLA leave?

Under the pay-as-you-go option, employees may pay their share of the premium payments on the same schedule as payments would be made if the employee were not on leave or under any other payment schedule permitted by FMLA Regulations Section 825.210(c) (including but not limited to the employer's payroll deduction schedule or the schedule used for COBRA payments). Contributions under this option are generally made by the employee on an after-tax basis; however, contributions may be made on a pretax basis to the extent that the contributions are made from taxable compensation (such as cashouts of unused sick or vacation days) that is due the employee during the leave period and provided that all cafeteria plan requirements are satisfied.

An employer is not required to continue the health coverage of an employee who fails to make required premium payments while on FMLA leave; however, if the employer chooses to continue the health coverage of such an employee, the employer is entitled to recoup those payments using the catch-up option (see Q 15:26). [Treas Reg § 1.125-3, Q&A 3(a)(2)]

Q 15:26 What are the terms of the catch-up option for unpaid FMLA leave?

An employer that continues providing group health coverage to an employee who does not pay premiums while on FMLA leave is permitted to utilize the catch-up option to recoup the employee's share of premium payments. Where an employee is electing to use the catch-up option, the employer and the employee must agree in advance of the coverage period that:

1. The employee elects to continue health coverage while on FMLA leave;
2. The employer will assume responsibility for advancing payment of the premiums on the employee's behalf during the FMLA leave; and
3. The advance amounts must be paid by the employee when the employee returns from FMLA leave.

Contributions under the catch-up option may be made on a pretax salary reduction basis when the employee returns from FMLA leave from any available taxable compensation (including cashouts of unused sick days and vacation days). These contributions will not be included in the employee's gross income, provided that all cafeteria plan requirements are satisfied. Contributions under the catch-up option may also be made on an after-tax basis. [Treas Reg § 1.125-3, Q&A 3(a)(3)]

Q 15:27 Are there any restrictions on the payment options that a cafeteria plan offers to an employee on unpaid FMLA leave?

Yes. There are three restrictions on payment options, as follows:

1. The prepayment option cannot be the sole option offered to employees on FMLA leave; however, the cafeteria plan may include prepayment as an option for employees on FMLA leave even if such option is not offered to employees on non-FMLA leave without pay. [Treas Reg § 1.125-3, Q&A 3(b)(1)]
2. The catch-up option can be the sole option offered to employees on FMLA leave if and only if the catch-up option is the sole option offered to employees on non-FMLA leave. [Treas Reg § 1.125-3, Q&A 3(b)(2)]
3. A cafeteria plan cannot offer employees on FMLA leave a choice of either the prepayment option or the catch-up option without also offering the pay-as-you-go option, if the pay-as-you-go option is offered to employees on non-FMLA unpaid leave. [Treas Reg § 1.125-3, Q&A 3(b)(3)]

Q 15:28 Do the payment options differ if an FMLA leave is *paid*, rather than *unpaid*?

Yes. If an employee is on paid FMLA leave and the employee continues health coverage while on FMLA leave, the employee's share of the premiums must be paid by the method normally used during any paid leave (presumably salary reduction). [Treas Reg § 1.125-3, Q&A 4]

Q 15:29 If an employee's FMLA leave spans two plan years, what restrictions apply to contributions made to the cafeteria plan?

Contributions to a cafeteria plan during FMLA leave will not be included in an employee's gross income, provided that the plan complies with all cafeteria plan requirements. Among other requirements, a plan may not operate in a manner that enables employees on FMLA leave to defer compensation from one cafeteria plan year to a subsequent cafeteria plan year. [Treas Reg § 1.125-3, Q&A 5]

Example. Patrick elects health coverage under a calendar year cafeteria plan. His premium for health coverage is $100 per month throughout the 12-month period of coverage. He takes FMLA leave for 12 weeks beginning on October 31 after making 10 months' worth of premium payments totaling $1,000 (10 months × $100 = $1,000). He maintains health coverage while on FMLA leave, using the prepayment option by cashing out his unused sick days in order to make the required premium payments due while he is on FMLA leave. Because he cannot defer compensation from one plan year to a subsequent plan year, Patrick may prepay the premiums due in November and December ($100 per month) on a pretax basis, but he cannot prepay the premium payment due in January on a pretax basis. If Patrick participates in the cafeteria plan in the subsequent plan year, he must use another option (pay-as-you-go or catch-up) to make the January premium payment.

Q 15:30 When an employee takes a leave and returns from it, may the employee revoke his or her election and make a new election for the remainder of the period of coverage?

Yes. Treasury Regulations Section 1.125-4(c)(2)(iii) includes the commencement of or return from an unpaid leave of absence as an acceptable change in status. Of course, the consistency rule described in Treasury Regulations Section 1.125-4(c)(3) applies to any midyear change in status.

Q 15:31 If an employee ceases to make contributions to his or her flexible benefits plan while on FMLA leave and therefore loses coverage, may that employee reelect to receive benefits under the flexible benefits plan upon returning to work?

Yes. The FMLA final regulations state that even in these circumstances, the employer must restore coverage to the employee, if the employee so requests, and pays as appropriate. [FMLA Reg § 825.212(c)]

Q 15:32 How does health coverage extended during a period of family or medical leave relate to coverage under COBRA?

An employee who takes FMLA leave does not experience a COBRA qualifying event, because the reduction in hours will not lead to a loss of health coverage. [IRS Notice 94-103, Q&A 1, 1994-2 CB 569]

The legislative history notes that a COBRA qualifying event does occur when it becomes clear that the employee will not be returning. Under IRS Notice 94-103 [1994-2 CB 569], a COBRA qualifying event occurs on the last day of FMLA leave when an employee does not return from leave. In the case of an employee who notifies the employer that he or she is not returning to work, the last day of leave is the date of that notice. [FMLA Reg § 825.209] If, however, health coverage under the plan is lost at a later date and the plan provides for the extension of the required periods, as permitted under Code Section 4980B(f)(8), the maximum coverage period is measured from the date when coverage is lost. [IRS Notice 94-103 Q&As 1, 2, 1994-2 CB 569]

> **Example.** Carol, an employee covered under the employer's group health plan, takes FMLA leave on August 16. She informs her employer on September 28 (less than seven weeks later) that she will not be returning to work. Under FMLA Regulations Section 825, Carol's last day of FMLA leave is September 28, and under IRS Notice 94-103, she has a qualifying event on that date. Carol's maximum coverage period will therefore be measured from September 28.

> **Note.** Because the COBRA period will begin once an employee on leave gives the employer notice that he or she will not be coming back, employees might have an incentive to avoid giving employers notice of their intent in order to delay the beginning of the COBRA period. Such a delay would lengthen the period of time a former employee (or other qualified beneficiary) is covered by the employer's group health plan.

Health Insurance Portability and Accountability Act (HIPAA)

Q 15:33 What are the HIPAA privacy rules?

Privacy of individually identifiable health information is protected by law. On December 20, 2000, the Department of Health and Human Services issued final regulations under HIPAA to protect the privacy of medical records and other personal health information maintained by health care providers, health plans, and others.

Q 15:34 Who must comply with the HIPAA privacy rules?

The rules give guidance as to who is a "covered entity." For purposes of this book, those who must be concerned with compliance are employers who self-administer a health plan and third party administrators. An employer who administers a medical FSA in-house would be a covered entity.

Group health plans provided solely through insurance company products and HMOs are specifically exempted, as long as the employer does not handle or have access to any individually identifiable health information.

Q 15:35 What is required of an employer who is subject to the privacy rules?

No individually identifiable heath information may be used for any employment purpose. Therefore, it is best to appoint a person (or persons) to be responsible for the group health function, separately from the human resource function. (Note that HIPAA regulations do not require that these be separate individuals, but such separation will help ensure compliance with the rules.)

Also, the computer system used for managing group health plan data should be accessible only to the person(s) designated as responsible for such data.

Q 15:36 How do the HIPAA privacy rules impact a cafeteria plan?

Administration of medical FSAs is impacted by the HIPAA privacy rules. Employers who administer health FSAs in-house will become a covered entity under HIPAA, even if all other group health plans are exempted. For this reason, employers may wish to outsource the FSA administration. Third party administrators will also need to comply with the HIPAA privacy rules to protect health information of plan participants. Processes and requirements are still in development. Third party administrators who have not considered the HIPAA privacy rules should review them now, and plan for compliance. The effective date for compliance is in 2003.

Chapter 16

Other Benefits: Employer-Funded Health Reimbursement Arrangements, Parking and Mass Transit Benefits, and Archer Medical Savings Accounts

Health reimbursement arrangements (HRAs), parking and mass transit benefits, and Archer medical savings accounts (MSAs) are benefits often found in flexible benefit plans. This chapters covers the specific regulatory and operatonal requirements of each of these benefits, and discusses their appropriate use within a flexible benefits program.

Health Reimbursement Arrangements

In June 2002, the IRS published Internal Revenue Notice 2002-45 outlining a type of employer-funded health reimbursement arrangement. Revenue Ruling 2002-41 provides guidance on how to properly design and administer a health reimbursement arrangement.

Q 16:1 What is a health reimbursement arrangement?

A health reimbursement arrangement (HRA) is an arrangement that:

1. Is paid for solely by the employer and *not* provided pursuant to salary reduction or otherwise under a Section 125 cafeteria plan;
2. Reimburses the employee for medical care expenses (as defined by Code Section 213) incurred by the employee and the employee's spouse and dependents (as defined by Code Section 152); and

3. Provides reimbursements up to a maximum dollar amount for a coverage period. Any unused portion of the maximum dollar amount at the end of a coverage period is carried forward to increase the maximum reimbursement amount in subsequent coverage periods.

To the extent that an HRA is an employer-provided accident or health plan, coverage and reimbursements of medical care expenses of an employee and the employee's spouse and dependents are generally excludable from the employee's gross income under Code Sections 105 and 106.

Generally, an HRA will be considered to be a flexible spending arrangement (FSA) as defined in Code Section 106(c)(2). In order to qualify as an FSA, the maximum amount of reimbursement available to a participant must be less than 500 percent of the value of the coverage. Under most circumstances, this requirement is a non-issue. However, an HRA will want to ensure that the amount of available benefit is not more than 500 percent of the annual contribution. This could happen if, for example, a participant in an HRA with identical contributions for each year does not submit any claim for at least five years. In the sixth year, the amount available would exceed 500 percent of the coverage for that sixth year.

Q 16:2 What benefits may an HRA provide?

To qualify for the exclusions under Code Sections 105 and 106, an HRA may only provide benefits that reimburse expenses for medical care as defined in Code Section 213(d). Each claim for reimbursement must be substantiated.

An HRA may reimburse a participant for qualified medical services, as well as for the cost of premiums that are defined in Code Section 213(d)(1)(D) as medical care. Note that the definition of premiums for medical care could include premiums for accident or health coverage for current employees, retirees, and COBRA continuants.

In general, an HRA *may* reimburse a participant for premiums related to long-term care insurance coverage. (This is different from the rules for a medical FSA.) However, an HRA may *not* reimburse a participant for the cost of long-term care *services*. In other words, the premium cost would be a qualified expense, but reimbursement for the actual cost of services would not be reimbursable. [IRC §§ 106(c), 213(d)(1)(C)]

Q 16:3 Are there limitations on how an HRA may provide benefits?

Yes. The first limitation is related to the date the medical service is incurred. An HRA may not reimburse a participant for any medical expense attributable to a deduction taken by the participant that was allowed by Code Section 213 for any prior taxable year. Also, an HRA may not reimburse a medical expense that was incurred before the effective date of the HRA, or incurred before the participant first became enrolled in the HRA.

The second limitation has more to do with HRA plan design. The HRA does not qualify for the exclusion under Code Section 105(b) if any person has the right to receive cash or any other taxable or non-taxable benefit under the HRA other than the reimbursement of medical care expenses. If any person has such a right under an HRA currently or in any future year, *all* distributions to *all* persons made from the arrangement in the current tax year are included in gross income—even those amounts used to reimburse medical expenses.

For example, if an HRA pays a death benefit to beneficiaries without regard to medical expenses, no amounts paid under the HRA to *any* person are excludable from income under Code Section 105(b).

Unlike the rules for an Archer MSA that permit a payout upon retirement, an HRA is intended strictly for reimbursement of qualified medical expenses.

Q 16:4 Are there ways around the requirement that an HRA pay out only for medical expenses?

No. IRS Notice 2002-45 notes that arrangements formally outside the HRA that provide for adjustment of an employee's compensation or receipt of any other benefit will be considered in determining whether the arrangement is an HRA. For example, if upon retirement the retiring employee is given a bonus equal to the amount remaining in his HRA, no amounts paid under the HRA for any participant are reimbursements qualified under Code Section 105(b). Similarly, if an employer provides a severance pay amount to exiting employees equal to the amount remaining in that employee's HRA, no amounts paid under the HRA for any participant is considered to be a reimbursement of medical care under Code Section 105(b). [Notice 2002-45, 2002-28 IRB 93]

Attempting to give unspent amounts to exiting or retiring employees (or any other method to give benefits for other than medical expenses) will result in the entire HRA becoming disqualified, and taxable income for all participants.

Q 16:5 Who may participate in an HRA?

An HRA may cover current and former employees (including retired employees), their spouses and dependents, and the spouses and dependents of deceased employees. "Dependents" are those defined in Code Section 152, with the added clarification that, for purposes of an HRA, a child of divorced parents is treated as a dependent of both parents.

The term "employee" does not include self-employed individuals as defined in Code Section 401(c). Self-employed individuals include sole proprietors and partners in a partnership. However, owners in an S corporation are not considered to be self-employed individuals under this section of the Code.

There is some question as to whether an owner in an S corporation may participate in an HRA. A literal reading of IRS Notice 2002-45 would indicate (by its silence on the matter) that an S corporation owner may participate in an

HRA. However, informal discussions with the IRS indicate that it may have intended to exclude S corporation owners. It is important to note that S corporation owners are excluded from similar benefits such as participation in a health FSA under Code Section 125. However, this is because, under Code Section 1372(a), 2 percent shareholders of S corporations are treated as partners for fringe benefit purposes.

Shareholders in an S corporation may participate in a health benefit plan provided by the employer—although Code Section 162(l)(1) requires that, for the remainder of 2002, a portion (30 percent) of the premium paid for healthcare benefits be included in taxable income of the S corporation shareholder. Beginning in 2003, 100 percent of the cost for insurance for medical care will be considered to be deductible by the employer, and not reportable by the employee. (See IRC § 162(l).)

If S corporation shareholders participate in an HRA offered by the employer, the HRA will want to carefully follow rules stipulated for self-funded health plans, including the nondiscrimination requirements.

Q 16:6 May an HRA reimburse participants who are former employees?

Yes, an HRA may continue to reimburse former employees or retired employees for medical care expenses after termination of employment or date of retirement. The former employee is not required to have selected COBRA continuation in order to continue to receive reimbursements.

The HRA may provide that the maximum reimbursement amount available after retirement or termination of employment be reduced for any administrative costs of continuing such coverage.

An HRA has the option of increasing the amount available for reimbursement of medical care expenses after the employee retires or otherwise terminates employment—even if the employee does not elect COBRA continuation coverage.

Q 16:7 How is an HRA funded?

In order to qualify as an HRA, the only funding source is employer contribution. No employee contributions may be made to the HRA, either directly or indirectly.

Employees may not use pretax dollars under a Section 125 plan to fund an HRA. Also, an HRA may not be indirectly funded by use of employer-provided credits in a Section 125 cafeteria plan. If an HRA is funded with employee dollars, it ceases to be an HRA, and instead becomes subject to the rules under Code Section 125.

Q 16:8 Could an employer require a cafeteria plan election in excess of the premium cost of health insurance, in order to help fund an HRA?

No. Because no employee money may be used to fund an HRA, an employer may not require that a participant in a combined medical plan and HRA pay more than the premium cost of the medical plan in order to participate. The maximum premium amount that may be charged in such a situation is the COBRA applicable premium for the medical plan.

Q 16:9 Could a cafeteria plan be structured so that a participant's choice included funding for the HRA?

No. If there is a correlation between the maximum reimbursement amount available under the HRA for the coverage period and the amount of salary reduction election for the health plan, then the salary reduction will be attributed to the reimbursement arrangement, and will not be an HRA.

The following is an example of an impermissible approach when attempting to offer an HRA: An employer offers employees health coverage at 50 percent of the total premium cost. An employee who also wishes to receive up to $600 in HRA benefits pays an additional $50 per month from the cafeteria plan.

Even though the employee is not paying more than the total COBRA applicable premium for the health benefit (see Q 16:8), the impermissible approach outlined above violates the requirement that an employee not fund the HRA directly or indirectly.

When an employee has funded the HRA directly or indirectly, it is not an HRA, but it is subject to Section 125 FSA rules. (This means, among other things, no rollover option and no S corporation shareholder participants.)

Q 16:10 Could a participant in an HRA use those funds to pay the employee portion of employer-provided health insurance premiums?

While health insurance premiums might be a covered expense in an HRA, there is one set of circumstances that plan sponsors must avoid. When an employee has a choice of paying toward the cost of employer sponsored health insurance premium on a pretax basis from pay, or paying that premium amount from the HRA, the HRA is considered to be indirectly funded pursuant to salary reduction. This is true even when the HRA does not reimburse employees who contribute from pay on a pretax basis to pay for health insurance sponsored by the employer.

The attempted HRA does not meet the definition of an HRA because it is funded by salary reduction and it is subject to the rules under Code Section 125. Here's why: Assume that an employee must pay $100 per month toward the cost of health insurance. The employer (impermissibly) sets up an arrangement whereby the employee may reduce pay on a pretax basis by $100 for the premium contribution, or the employee opts to have the HRA pay the $100 expense, thereby keeping his or her pay intact.

The impermissible arrangement outlined above would cause those employees who have the premium paid by the HRA to have swapped payment by the HRA for pretax reduction of pay. This is an indirect funding of the HRA by the employee, which makes the arrangement subject ot the rules of Code Section 125, rather than the HRA rules.

Q 16:11 Can the HRA be funded with cafeteria plan forfeitures?

No. If an HRA is funded by amounts forfeited under a cafeteria plan, it will be considered to have been funded by salary reduction, and will not qualify as an HRA.

Q 16:12 How does an HRA compare to a medical flexible spending arrangement (FSA) permitted under Code Section 125?

An HRA is funded solely by the employer, and not pursuant to salary reduction by the employee. An HRA is not restricted in the same ways as a medical FSA under Code Section 125. Following are the differences:

1. An HRA may permit participants to carry over unused amounts from one year to the next. A medical FSA under Section 125 may not include a carry-over feature.
2. An HRA may be designed to pay out only amounts funded to date. A medical FSA must pay out up to the annual maximum amount, regardless of when the claim is submitted. For example, if both an HRA and an FSA are funded at the rate of $100 per month, the HRA may be permitted to pay out only the amount funded to date, while the FSA would be required to pay out up to $1,200, regardless of the date the claim is submitted during the plan year.
3. A medical FSA must operate under a mandatory 12-month period of coverage (with the exception of a short plan year as necessary). An HRA does not have the 12-month period-of-coverage requirement, and may specify a coverage period of less than one year.
4. A medical FSA must require that medical expenses be incurred during the period of coverage; an HRA (with certain exceptions) does not have such a requirement. Claims may be incurred during one period of coverage (while the claimant is an HRA participant) and reimbursed in a later coverage period.
5. The maximum reimbursement amount credited under the HRA in the future may be increased or decreased without regard to the qualified reasons required by a medical FSA under Code Section 125. However, before increasing benefits, it is important to keep in mind the nondiscrimination requirements of Regulations Section 1.105-11(c)(3)(ii)

regarding highly compensated individuals as defined in Code Section 105(h).

Q 16:13 Must a medical expense be reimbursed by an HRA before it may be reimbursed by an FSA?

In general, yes. A medical care expense may not be reimbursed from a Section 125 medical FSA if the expense has been reimbursed or is reimbursable under any accident or health plan. If coverage is provided under both an HRA and a Section 125 medical FSA for the same medical care expenses, amounts available under an HRA must be exhausted before reimbursements may be made from the FSA. However, see Question 16:14 for a plan design method to change the ordering of payment of claims.

However, when an employee is covered by both an FSA and an HRA, the FSA may reimburse the employee for expenses that are not covered by the HRA. In no event may the employee be reimbursed for the same medical expense by both an HRA and a Section 125 medical FSA.

Q 16:14 May an HRA be designed to pay claims only after an FSA is exhausted?

Yes. An HRA plan document may specify that coverage under the HRA is available only after expenses exceeding the dollar amount of the Section 125 FSA have been paid. The document must include this provision before the medical FSA plan year begins.

Example. Acme Floor Film sponsors a Section 125 medical FSA and an HRA, both of which provide coverage for the same medical expenses. The HRA plan document includes a provision that the HRA is not available for reimbursements of medical expenses that are covered by the Section 125 medical FSA. When the FSA is exhausted, the HRA may begin paying eligible expenses.

In this manner, an HRA may be designed to be second to a medical FSA in reimbursement ordering.

Q 16:15 May a participant choose from which arrangement (HRA or FSA) to reimburse a claim when both are available?

Apparently not. In general, an HRA will be required to reimburse eligible claims first, before an FSA may provide reimbursement. If the HRA plan is designed to pay claims only after the FSA is exhausted, a participant may not receive payment from the HRA if the FSA is available to make payment on the claim. IRS Notice 2002-45 does not identify any other ordering rules when a claim could be submitted to an HRA or an FSA.

Q 16:16 What nondiscrimination requirements are there for HRAs?

HRAs are intended to operate as self-insured medical plans. To the extent that an HRA is a self-insured medical expense reimbursement plan, the nondiscrimination rules under Code Section 105(h) apply to the HRA. [Treasury Regulations § 1.105-11.]

Q 16:17 How does COBRA affect an HRA?

An HRA is a group health plan generally subject to COBRA continuation of coverage requirements. Premiums for COBRA continuation are determined under the existing rules in Code Section 4980B. COBRA continuants must be treated in the same manner as similarly situated non-COBRA beneficiaries of the plan. For example, if the maximum benefit amount is increased for participants who are active employees, it must also be increased for COBRA beneficiaries.

Of course, when a plan sponsor notifies a qualified beneficiary of COBRA rights, an HRA should be included in the list of COBRA eligible benefits.

It is possible for an HRA, by plan design, to provide for continued reimbursements after a COBRA qualifying event regardless of whether a qualified beneficiary elects continuation coverage. For example, an HRA might allow reimbursements up to the unused maximum reimbursement amount following termination of employment. In this situation, an HRA subject to COBRA must still comply with the COBRA continuation coverage requirements. If a qualified beneficiary elects COBRA continuation coverage in addition to the continued reimbursement amount already available, an HRA complies with COBRA requirements by increasing the maximum reimbursement amount at the same time and by the same increment that it is increased for similarly situated non-COBRA beneficiaries (and by decreasing it for claims reimbursed).

Q 16:18 What filing and documentation requirements are there for an HRA?

Most often, an HRA will be a welfare benefit plan under Title I of ERISA. Such plans have a Form 5500 reporting requirement under Department of Labor rules. However, if the HRA is an unfunded plan, it will be exempt from Form 5500 filing as long as it has less than 100 participants. [DOL Reg. § 2520.104-20] A *funded* HRA that pays benefits from plan assets would not be exempt from Form 5500 filing.

If the HRA is a self-insured medical plan, it will need to be described in a plan document, per the requirements of Code Section 105(h). Such a plan will also need a summary plan description (SPD), including new language for claims review and payment.

Parking and Mass Transit Benefits

Q 16:19 Can an employer offer paid parking or mass transit benefits to its employees?

Yes. An employer has the ability to pay for mass transit and/or parking expenses for employees as a fringe benefit. The employer may consider these as business expenses, up to the exclusion limit (see Q 16:29). Cash reimbursements for transit passes qualify only if a voucher or a similar item that the employee can exchange only for a transit pass is not readily available for direct distribution by the employer to its employees.

Q 16:20 Can an employee request that his or her pay be reduced on a pretax basis for payment of parking and/or mass transit expenses when the employer does not otherwise offer paid parking and/or mass transit as a paid fringe benefit?

Yes. Effective January 1, 1998, it is possible to have one's pay reduced on a pretax basis and to receive reimbursement for qualified parking and/or mass transit expenses. Code Section 132(f) describes such arrangements. Monthly pay can be reduced on a pretax basis up to the exclusion limit (see Q 16:29).

Note. Pretax contributions toward the cost of qualified transportation expenses cannot be included in a Section 125 plan.

Q 16:21 What is a qualified transportation benefit?

An employer that offers a *qualified transportation benefit* provides employees with the right to elect to receive either a fixed amount of cash compensation at a specified future date or a fixed amount of qualified transportation fringe benefits for a specified future period—for example, qualified parking to be used during a future calendar month.

For an employee to elect the qualified transportation benefit, the employee's election must be in writing or in some other form (e.g., electronic) that is permanent and verifiable and must include the following:

1. The date of the election;
2. The amount of compensation to be reduced; and
3. The period for which the benefit will be provided.

Furthermore, the election must be for a fixed dollar amount or a fixed percentage of compensation.

Note. An election to reduce compensation for a period can be automatically renewed for subsequent periods.

Q 16:22 Is a negative election permitted for a qualified transportation benefit plan?

Yes. An employer is permitted to deem that an election to participate in a qualified transportation plan has been made if an employee does not elect to receive cash compensation in lieu of the qualified transportation benefit. The employer must, however, provide adequate notice that a compensation reduction will be made, and the employee must have the opportunity to choose to receive the cash compensation instead of the fringe benefit.

Q 16:23 When must an employee make a compensation reduction election to receive a qualified transportation benefit?

An employee who wants to make a compensation reduction election in order to receive a qualified transportation benefit must do so before he or she is currently able to receive the cash (i.e., his or her pay). The determination of whether an employee is currently able to receive the cash does *not* depend on whether it has been constructively received for purposes of Code Section 451.

The compensation reduction election must specify that the period for which the qualified transportation benefit will be provided (e.g., a calendar month) must not begin before the election is made; in other words, the compensation reduction election must relate to qualified transportation fringes that are provided only after the election. For this purpose, the date a qualified transportation benefit is provided is:

1. The date the employee receives a voucher or similar item; or
2. In any other case, the date the employee uses the qualified transporation benefit.

Q 16:24 Are compensation reduction elections irrevocable?

A compensation reduction election (made to receive a qualified transportation benefit) is irrevocable—but only for the period for which the fringe benefit will be provided (generally a month).

According to Final Treasury Regulations Section 1.132-9, Q&A 14, an employee cannot revoke a compensation reduction election after the employee is currently able to receive the cash (or other taxable amount). In addition, the election cannot be revoked after the beginning of the period for which the qualified transportation fringe benefit will be provided. An employee can, however, make a prospective change to a compensation reduction election to be effective at the beginning of a new benefit period—generally each month.

Q 16:25 Are unspent amounts contributed to a qualified transportation benefit plan refundable?

No. Any amount contributed to a qualified transportation fringe benefit plan must be spent on qualified expenses and thus is not refundable. Unspent amounts can, however, be carried forward, even into new plan years (an option *not* available under a Section 125 plan). [Treas Reg § 1.132-9, Q&A 15]

Q 16:26 If less than the statutory monthly limit is reimbursed in one month, can the leftover amount be used to increase the limit in another month?

No. The statutory monthly limit is absolute. It is reestablished each month, and the amount reimbursed over the course of a year is *not* a factor in its calculation.

Example. Mary Ann pays $8.50 per day for parking. She has her compensation reduced by $170 per month to cover her parking expense. A few months of the year, Mary Ann pays only $161.50 for parking. She will have to set aside $8.50 more than she can claim in those months. The unspent balance will be available to her in her account. In four months of the year, Mary Ann's parking expense is $187. If Mary Ann has unspent dollars remaining in her account, she can use those unspent dollars—up to $185—for reimbursement of her parking expense. Because of the monthly limit on reimbursement, Mary Ann cannot, however, use unspent dollars for reimbursement up to the full $187. If Mary Ann does receive reimbursement of $187 in September, $2 of that reimbursement will be taxable for employment and income tax purposes.

Q 16:27 Can an employer reimburse an employee more than one month's worth of qualified transportation expenses at one time?

Yes, an employer can reimburse an employee more than one month's worth of qualified transportation expenses at one time. All expenses, however, must have been elected prospectively. Each month's expenses must be calculated separately and cannot exceed the statutory monthly limit.

Example. Alex is hired by Golly G Co. in January. He pays $150 per month for parking. On February 27, Alex submits his compensation reduction election. At the end of March, Alex submits a claim for $750 for all of his parking expenses since his date of hire. Only $150 (March expense) can be reimbursed through the plan because Alex did not prospectively elect to receive reimbursement for January and February. If Alex waits until July to submit another batch of receipts, he can receive reimbursement for months in which he was a participant in the plan.

Q 16:28 What are "qualified" transportation expenses?

In general, in order to qualify, a parking and/or mass transit expense must be incurred in order for the employee to be able to work. The expense must be the employee's. (For example, an employee may not submit "gas/parking money" reimbursement requests because he or she shares some of the cost of commuting with another driver.)

A qualified transportation fringe benefit is:

1. Transportation in a commuter highway vehicle (such as a van) between the employee's home and work place;
2. A transit pass; or
3. Qualified parking.

A commuter highway vehicle is any highway vehicle that seats at least six adults (not including the driver), provided by the employer for its employees. The employer must reasonably expect that at least 80 percent of the vehicle mileage will be for transporting employees between their homes and the work place, and that the company's employees will occupy at least one half of the vehicle's seats (not including the driver's).

A transit pass is any pass, token, farecard, voucher, or similar item entitling a person, free of charge or at a reduced rate, to ride:

- Mass transit; or
- In a vehicle that seats at least six adults (not including the driver), if a person in the business of transporting persons for pay or hire operates it.

Qualified mass transit may be publicly or privately operated and includes bus, rail, or ferry.

Qualified parking is parking used by employees on or near the site of employment. It also includes parking on or near the location from which employees commute to work using mass transit, commuter highway vehicles, or carpools. It does not include parking at or near the employee's home.

Q 16:29 What is the exclusion limit on parking and mass transit benefits?

The following benefits may be provided in any combination (not exceeding the limits) and so are not mutually exclusive:

- A ride in a commuter highway vehicle if the ride is between the employee's home and work place;
- A transit pass; and/or
- Qualified parking.

For 2002, the monthly exclusion limit for the aggregate of commuter highway vehicle transportation and transit pass fringe benefits is $100 per month, regardless of the total value of both benefits.

The monthly exclusion limit for the qualified parking fringe benefit is $185 a month, regardless of its actual value. [IRC § 132(f)(2)]

A monthly exclusion limit is the maximum amount that may be reimbursed for that expense, even if the actual expense was greater, and even if the account has funds available exceeding the exclusion limit for the month.

If the employer provides parking and/or mass transit benefits that have a value exceeding these limits, the excess must be included in the employee's income.

Q 16:30 What amount is includible in an employee's wages for income and employment tax purposes if the value of the qualified transportation benefit exceeds the monthly limit?

If an employer provides an employee with a qualified transportation benefit that exceeds the applicable statutory monthly limit, the value of the benefit that is in excess of the monthly limit is included in the employee's wages for income and employment tax purposes. The excess benefit payment is, however, reduced by any after-tax payment the employee may have made to the employer toward the cost of benefits.

> **Example.** Alloys Inc. provides parking valued at $200 per month to Karl. Karl does not contribute toward the cost of that parking. The fair market value of the parking benefit exceeds the statutory monthly limit by $15. Over a year, Karl will have $180 included in his wages for income and employment tax purposes.

> **Example.** Boffins.com provides parking valued at $210 per month to Lizette. The company charges employees $25 per month (on an after-tax basis) for parking expenses. Lizette will not have an additional amount attributable to qualified parking expenses included in her wages for income and employment tax purposes, because $185 ($210 minus the $25 payment made by her) does not exceed the statutory monthly limit.

> **Example.** ChemCo permits employees to contribute toward the cost of qualified transportation expenses. Martin pays $200 per month for parking and requests a pretax contribution level of $200 per month. Because the current limit is $185 per month, however, Martin can contribute only $185 per month on a pretax basis. If Martin inadvertently contributes more than $185 per month, the excess amount must be returned as taxable income for income and employment tax purposes.

Q 16:31 Can an employee receive qualified transportation benefits from more than one employer?

Yes. Although the statutory monthly limits outlined above (see Q 16:29) apply to an employee of any employer or employers treated as a single employer under Code Section 414(b), (c), (m), or (o) and qualified transportation benefits paid by entities under common control are combined for purposes of applying the applicable statutory limit, an individual who is an employee of two *unrelated* employers can receive up to the monthly limit in such fringe benefits from *each* employer.

> **Example.** Sam works downtown for Ace Attorneys during the day. Ace Attorneys offers a parking expense reimbursement of up to $150 and Sam takes advantage of the full amount. In the evening, Sam works uptown for

We Compute, an unrelated employer. Sam's parking expense of $50 per month is paid by We Compute. Although, when added together, Sam's parking benefits ($200) exceed the statutory monthly limit ($185), neither unrelated employer provided in excess of the limit. Sam is therefore permitted to keep the reimbursements without incurring employment and income tax on any part of those amounts.

Q 16:32 How do the qualified transportation benefit rules apply to van pools?

Employer- and employee-operated van pools, as well as private or public transit van pools, can qualify as qualified transportation benefits. Expenses for employer- and employee-operated vehicles qualifying as "commuter highway vehicles" under Code Section 132(f)(5)(B) are considered to be qualified expenses.

The value of qualified van pool benefits can be excluded from an employee's income up to the applicable statutory monthly limit for transportation in a commuter highway vehicle and transit passes, less the value of any transit passes provided by the employer for the month.

If an employee obtains a qualified parking space as a result of membership in a car pool or van pool, the monthly limit for qualified parking applies to the individual to whom the parking space is assigned. This individual is described in Proposed Treasury Regulations Section 1.132-9, Q&A 21(f), as the "prime member." The monthly limit amounts of each car pool member cannot be combined. If the employer provides access to the space and the space is not assigned to a particular individual, the employer must designate one of its employees as the prime member. The employer cannot designate more than one prime member for a car pool or van pool during a month. The employer of the prime member is responsible for including the value of the qualified parking in excess of the statutory monthly limit in the prime member's wages for income and employment tax purposes.

Q 16:33 What are the substantiation requirements for employee expense reimbursement?

An employer that makes cash reimbursements for qualified transportation expenses must establish a bona fide reimbursement arrangement to substantiate that its employees have in fact incurred expenses for transportation in a commuter highway vehicle, for transit passes, or for qualified parking. That is, the employer must implement reasonable procedures to ensure that an amount equal to the reimbursement amount was incurred for the transportation benefit. The expense must be substantiated within a reasonable period of time. An expense substantiated to the reimbursement program payor within 180 days after it has been paid by the employee will be treated as having been substantiated within a reasonable period of time. An employee certification at the time of reimbursement in either written or electronic form may be a reasonable reimbursement procedure depending on the facts and circumstances.

[See Prop Treas Reg § 1.132-9, Q&A 16(c)]

Note. It may be possible for an employee to certify expenses incurred, even when no receipt is provided—for example, in the case of metered parking. If the employer has no reason to doubt the employee's certification, an employee-certified expense could be considered to be substantiated.

Q 16:34 What are the substantiation requirements for an employer that distributes transit passes?

There are no substantiation requirements for an employer that distributes transit passes.

Q 16:35 Can an employer impose substantiation requirements in addition to those outlined in the proposed Treasury regulations?

Yes. An employer can impose substantiation requirements in addition to those outlined in the proposed Treasury regulations, such as a signed receipt from a parking vendor or proof of purchase of a mass transit voucher. Such substantiation requirements may cause certain arrangements (e.g., parking at meters) to become an ineligible expense of the employer's plan.

Archer Medical Savings Accounts (MSAs)

Q 16:36 Why were Archer Medical Savings Accounts created?

Congress passed the Health Insurance Portability and Accountability Act of 1996 (HIPAA) after months of political wrangling that nearly derailed the bill on several occasions. HIPAA—the result of a bipartisan effort led by Senators Nancy Kassebaum (R-Kan.) and Ted Kennedy (D-Mass.)—should be viewed as an incremental health insurance reform; its passage was made possible in part because of a compromise on a provision now known as the Archer medical savings account (Archer MSA). The Republicans sought an individual account similar to an individual retirement account (IRA) that would become a funding vehicle for individual health care. It was envisioned that an Archer MSA owner could self-insure his or her unexpected medical expenses and, because the balance in an Archer MSA can be rolled over from year to year and earns interest, use the account to fund postretirement medical benefits.

Supporters of Archer MSAs believe they encourage people to be more responsible consumers of health care. The insurance industry has generally been supportive of Archer MSAs. Those who did not support Archer MSAs in 1996 tended to believe they would result in a significant loss of tax revenues and threaten the stability of the traditional insurance marketplace. Detractors were concerned that only well-off individuals will establish Archer MSAs, that such adverse selection will prove a serious problem for the insurance industry, and that, overall, Archer MSAs are a poor substitute for a broad-based federal government response to the health care crisis.

The reality is, Archer MSAs have not had much of an impact at all. Many consumers have found them to be unwieldy, limiting, and not particularly cost-effective.

At the time of this writing, Archer MSAs are scheduled to expire on December 31, 2002. While existing Archer MSAs may remain intact, no new Archer MSAs may be opened after the cut-off date.

Q 16:37 What is an Archer medical savings account?

An Archer medical savings account (Archer MSA) is a type of tax-qualified individual savings account that is used exclusively for the payment of medical expenses incurred by the covered individual, a spouse, or a dependent. Medical savings accounts were introduced with the Health Insurance Portability and Accountability Act (HIPAA). The name was changed to *Archer* MSA late in 2000.

Note. Archer MSAs are scheduled to expire on December 31, 2002. While existing Archer MSAs may remain intact, no new Archer MSAs may be opened after the cut-off date.

Generally speaking, Archer MSAs can be adopted only by people who participate in catastrophic health insurance coverage plans, also known as "high deductible" health care plans (see Q 16:44). Archer MSAs are intended to require the participants to assume direct responsibility for paying a greater share of their medical expenditures. Because it is believed that employees who pay for a higher proportion of their own medical expenses act more diligently and carefully as consumers than those who do not, Archer MSAs are being proposed as a vehicle for cost management as well as an employee empowerment tool to complement high deductible indemnity programs. It is hoped that these plans will have a strong appeal for employers, especially small employers that have been reluctant to establish health insurance programs because of cost or unwillingness to become involved in their employees' health care choices.

After being established, an Archer MSA is owned by the individual employee. Penalties will be applied if withdrawals are made from the Archer MSA for expenditures other than health care.

Monies can be contributed by either the employer or the employee and can accumulate on a tax-qualified basis. Most important is the fact that the Archer MSA will roll over from year to year and may be accumulated. Thus, use-it-or-lose-it rules do not apply to Archer MSAs.

Q 16:38 How does a medical flexible spending account differ from an Archer medical savings account?

Medical flexible spending accounts (FSAs) differ from Archer MSAs in a number of essential aspects, as follows:

1. A medical FSA may not under any circumstances carry forward the account balance: it operates strictly on a use-it-or-lose-it basis. In contrast, an Archer MSA permits funds to be carried forward and will operate more like an IRA.
2. A medical FSA is designed and permitted under the rules and regulations associated with a Code Section 125 cafeteria plan. In contrast, an Archer MSA is not permitted to be in or operate under a Code Section 125 cafeteria plan.
3. A medical FSA can be adopted by any individual provided that the person works for an employer who has adopted a cafeteria plan permitting medical FSAs. In contrast, Archer MSAs can be adopted only by those individuals who elect catastrophic health coverage: that is, a high-deductible healthcare plan offered by an employer.
4. A medical FSA may or may not stipulate an upper limit for annual contribution amounts. In contrast, an Archer MSA has well-defined annual contribution limitations based on a percentage of the annual deductible of the high deductible health plan.
5. A medical FSA does not operate under rules or requirements mandating tax penalties for early withdrawal of funds. In contrast, tax penalties are mandated for early withdrawal from an Archer MSA.

Medical FSAs and Archer MSAs are more dissimilar than similar. In fact, an Archer MSA is much closer to an IRA than to a medical FSA. Indeed, the strongest point of similarity between a medical FSA and an Archer MSA is that both are sources of funds (i.e., both are accounts) through which unreimbursed medical expenses can be paid.

Q 16:39 Can an Archer MSA be included in a Section 125 cafeteria plan or a flexible benefits plan?

No. Under no circumstances may an Archer MSA be included in a cafeteria plan. [HIPAA § 301 (d)] HIPAA specifically modifies Code Section 125(f) by inserting a new cross reference [HIPAA § 106(b)] to stipulate that an Archer MSA that is discussed in Section 106(b) of HIPAA becomes a benefit that is not permitted under a cafeteria plan.

Q 16:40 How did the notion of an individual medical savings account arise?

Archer MSAs are intended to be a means of reducing and controlling medical care expenditures. The concept underlying this expectation is that the Archer

MSA must be paired with a high deductible indemnity plan. When this pairing takes place, each individual consumer assumes an increasingly larger responsibility for deciding how much medical insurance to purchase. Combining a high deductible plan with the Archer MSA concept presumably promotes more responsible consumerism and potential savings for future medical care. Prototype programs have dovetailed a high-deductible/catastrophic medical or health care insurance program with medical FSAs through cafeteria plans (because prior to the passage of HIPAA, Archer MSAs were not permitted). These prototypes revealed that although the plan design promoted responsible consumerism, the use-it-or-lose-it aspect of the medical FSAs encouraged the account owners to spend all monies in the account prior to the close of the plan year. This attitude was contrary to the savings mentality that was targeted for this model. Because the Archer MSA can roll over from year to year and build up a large balance on a tax-deferred basis, the health care consumer gains a very powerful health care funding vehicle.

> **Note.** See Qs 16:1–16:18 on Health Reimbursement Arrangements (HRAs). HRAs provide many of the same benefits as Archer MSAs. While Archer MSAs and HRAs operate in much the same manner, they are not identical. Caution must be exercised if converting from an Archer MSA environment to an HRA application.

Prior to the passage of HIPAA, a study performed by the American Academy of Actuaries tried to estimate how people might behave if a high-deductible indemnity program was offered together with a savings account for medical expenses. The results indicated that increases in the amount the employee needs to pay for his or her health insurance will result in savings in the cost of health care. As people become more involved in the financial aspects of their health care, they become more cost-conscious consumers.

Notwithstanding this result, the monograph suggests that Archer MSAs will not receive overwhelming support. The greatest opportunity for savings will be associated with employees who have few health care expenses; employees who have high medical expenditures will have, according to this study, little or no interest in a health insurance program that couples a catastrophic indemnity plan with an Archer MSA.

Q 16:41 How did the Archer MSA pilot program work?

A number of fairly complex operating rules governed the pilot program initiated by HIPAA; however, there were four basic rules:

1. Archer MSAs were allowed during the pilot period (from 1997 through 2002).
2. Archer MSAs were made available to a maximum of 750,000 individuals.
3. Individuals could be either self-employed or employed by small employers. In the Code, a small employer is defined as any employer who employed an average of 50 or fewer employees during either of the

two preceding calendar years. A new employer (one who wasn't in existence in any preceding year) may determine headcount for purposes of this benefit based on the average number of employees it is reasonably expected to employ during the current calendar year.

4. The Archer MSA pilot program was available on a first-come, first-served basis.

Not surprisingly, the term *employer*was defined on a controlled-group basis. A small employer that adopted an Archer MSA plan did not have to drop it if the company's work force grew beyond the 50-person limitation. In fact, employers that were growing could continue to make contributions to an Archer MSA until the first year in which the employer had an average of 200 employees for the year. At that point, plan participants could assume control over the contributions for their own accounts as long as they remained employed by the plan's sponsor. After an employer's work force exceeded 200, the employer could not make additional contributions, and an individual who had not yet begun participation in the plan could not thereafter do so.

An Archer MSA could be established beginning in the taxable year after December 31, 1996. After the pilot period, people who were participants or employees of employers that sponsored an Archer MSA program can continue their participation. After 2002, however, regardless of how many Archer MSAs were actually established during the pilot period, no new accounts are allowed unless, of course, Congress decides to authorize expansion of the program.

A detailed set of rules required the number of Archer MSAs to be reported so that the IRS could announce cutoff dates as the number of Archer MSAs in the pilot program increased. A penalty of $25 per employee Archer MSA account was imposed on each trustee that failed to file an Archer MSA report.

At the time of this writing, the Archer MSA pilot program is scheduled to expire on December 31, 2002. Various proposals in Congress have suggested extending the date (and even the scope of eligible individuals).

Note, however, that in June 2002, the IRS provided guidance for a different type of healthcare reimbursement arrangement. These arrangements are discussed in Qs 16:1–16:18.

Q 16:42 Who is eligible to contribute to a medical savings account and what tax advantages does it offer?

An Archer MSA is intended to create a long-term account for the payment of unanticipated and unreimbursed medical expenditures. To the extent that an Archer MSA helps an individual to defray medical expenditures, it will be done on a tax-favored basis: monies that are put into an Archer MSA will not be deemed income for federal income tax purposes. Contributions to the Archer MSA may be made by the individual, in which case they would be deductible from his or her adjusted gross income. In addition, a "participating employer" can also make contributions to employees' Archer MSA accounts, in which case the employer contributions are excluded from income.

It appears that an employer that incorrectly contributes to an employee's Archer MSA through a cafeteria plan will create a situation where such contributions are included in the taxable income of the employee.

Contributions to an Archer MSA (whether they are made by the participating employers or by the employees) may be made for a tax year at any time before the due date of the return for that year. Employers' contributions would appear (like other forms of deferred compensation) on the W-2 form; however, as noted earlier, this amount will not be included as taxable income for the employee. Furthermore, earnings on the monies in the Archer MSA are not included in taxable income when they are earned.

Q 16:43 How are distributions from an Archer medical savings account taxed?

Monies withdrawn from an Archer MSA are not taxed, provided that the reason for the withdrawal is a qualified medical expense (i.e., a medical expense that is unreimbursed and is an otherwise eligible medical expenditure under Code Section 213). In addition, the medical expenditure must be for the benefit of the individual, his or her spouse, or eligible dependent. HIPAA specifies that distributions from an Archer MSA may not be used to purchase health insurance except for (1) "continuation coverage" as required by federal law, (2) qualified long-term care insurance, or (3) a medical plan that was purchased while the individual was receiving unemployment compensation.

If an individual establishes an Archer MSA and uses the funds that are accrued in that Archer MSA for purposes other than medical expenditures, these funds will be subject to both taxation and a penalty. An additional 15 percent penalty will be imposed unless the distribution is made on the employee's attainment of age 65 or the death or disability of the employee. Subtitle A, Section 301(a) of HIPAA contains a provision (Section 220(f)(4)(c)) allowing for an exception for distributions after the Medicare eligibility age (currently age 65). Should Medicare eligibility age change, so shall this requirement.

Q 16:44 What is a high-deductible plan?

HIPAA defined the limits of a high-deductible health plan. The limits have risen over the past few years. It is important to review high-deductible health plan provisions from year to year, to ensure that they meet the definition required for Archer MSAs. At time of creation of Archer MSAs (1996), the definition of a high-deductible health plan was a health plan:

1. That in the case of self-only coverage has an annual deductible that is not less than $1,500 and not more than $2,250;
2. That in the case of family coverage has an annual deductible that is not less than $3,000 and not more than $4,500; and

3. Under which the annual out-of-pocket expenses required to be paid for covered benefits (but not for premiums) does not exceed either $3,000 for self-only coverage or $5,500 for family coverage.

Beginning in 1999, the amounts of the deductibles were indexed for inflation. For 2000, for individual coverage, the deductible had to range from $1,550 to $2,350, with an out-of-pocket maximum of $3,100, and for family coverage, the deductible range was $3,100 to $4,650, with an out-of-pocket maximum of $5,700.

Effective for 2001, the individual coverage deductible limit was $1,600 to $2,400 for individual coverage, with an individual out-of-pocket limit of $3,200. The family deductible limit for 2001 was $3,200 to $4,800, with an out-of-pocket limit of $5,850.

In 2002, the limits defining a high-deductible health plan are as follows:

- The individual deductible can range from $1,650 to $2,500. The individual out-of-pocket limit is $3,300.
- The family deductible can range from $3,300 to $4,950. The family out-of-pocket limit is $6,050.

A high-deductible plan does not include a health plan (regardless of its deductible) if the health plan substantially covers accidents, disability, dental care, vision care, or long-term care. Finally, notwithstanding any of these rules, a health plan does not fail to qualify as a high-deductible health plan under these Archer MSA provisions if it provides no deductible or a very small deductible for preventive care, provided that no deductible provisions are required by state law.

Q 16:45 What is the limit on contributions to an Archer medical savings account?

A description of monthly limitations on contributions to an Archer MSA is outlined under Code Section 220. The Code limits annual contributions—when computed as an aggregate of the monthly limitations—to less than a specified percentage of the deductible that is required in the high-deductible plan. For individual coverage—the annual contribution limit is 65 percent of the deductible in the high-deductible plan and for family coverage the limit is 75 percent of such deductible. In the case of a married couple, if either spouse has family coverage both the husband and the wife must come under the 75 percent limit. In these instances the husband and wife must divide the amount of the annual contribution limitation equally between them if they fail to reach agreement on an alternate division. No deduction is allowed for an excess contribution to an Archer MSA that the individual or his or her spouse has received.

The statute also specifies that when an employer contributes to an Archer MSA, its contribution must be made on behalf of all employees and will be subject to comparability rules that require either that the same dollar amount be contributed on behalf of each employee, or that the same percentage of the deductible be contributed on behalf of each employee. Because controlled group rules are in effect for Archer MSAs, employers under common control, brother/sister corporations, and parent/child corporations will be aggregated for purposes of these comparability rules and treated as single employers.

Q 16:46 How does an Archer MSA compare to an individual retirement account?

An Archer MSA is intended to help individuals meet uninsured health expenses on a tax-favored basis, whereas an IRA helps individuals meet their pension income needs on a tax-favored basis. The tax advantages of an Archer MSA mirror the tax advantages of an IRA, especially when money is flowing into the actual account. Contributions made to an Archer MSA, like contributions made to an IRA, are deductible from an individual's adjusted gross income, and therefore, these employee contributions may be made on a salary reduction basis.

In the event the contributions are being made by an employer, they can be excluded from the individual's income (see Q 16:42). Archer MSAs are similar to IRAs because they accumulate and accrue from year to year with an ultimate objective of building up a sizeable account to provide either pension income or post-retirement medical protection.

Another similarity between Archer MSAs and IRAs concerns the penalty that the employee must pay if withdrawals are premature and if the employee does not follow the specific rules and requirements associated with premature withdrawals. In the case of an Archer MSA, an early withdrawal of monies that are not used to pay uninsured medical expenses results in a penalty of 15 percent, whereas in the case of an IRA the comparable penalty is 10 percent.

A final similarity between Archer MSAs and IRAs lies in how these plans are administered. Per the statute, the IRS is going to monitor the extent of usage (at least throughout this pilot program), based on periodic reports required from Archer MSA custodians. Clearly, a need will exist for custodial services. An Archer MSA custodian, like an IRA custodian, would include a bank, insurance company and/or mutual fund company. Thus, both products, because of their similarities, are being serviced by the same vendor group.

The similarities between IRAs and Archer MSAs disappear when considering taxation of distributions. Distributions for qualified medical expenditures are generally excludable from the individual's gross income provided that such distribution was made for a bona fide health care expense (as defined in Code Section 213) and that such medical expenditures were made for the employee, the spouse, or dependents of the employee. Under an IRA, the distribution of pension income is a taxable event, and such income does become part of the taxable income incurred by the employee during the year in which such distribution was made.

Q 16:47 Are there any variations on Archer MSAs?

Yes. A test program called Medicare + Choice MSAs became available in 1999. Medicare + Choice MSAs are defined by Internal Revenue Code Section 138.

A Medicare + Choice MSA permits the Medicare program to deposit money for qualified medical expenses to an emplyees's account. The money is not taxed if it is used for qualified medical expenses. Operating under Archer MSA rules, participants in a Medicare + Choice MSA must be insured only by a high-deductible health plan. The high deductible health plan must be a policy approved by the Medicare program. *As of this writing, no high deductible health plan has been approved by Medicare. Therefore, no Medicare + Choice MSAs have been established to date.*

Only certain Medicare-eligible individuals can participate in the pilot program. Individuals suffering from end-stage renal disease could not enroll in an Archer MSA plan and therefore cannot establish a Medicare + Choice MSA. Individuals who develop end-stage renal disease while enrolled in an Archer MSA plan can, however, continue to participate in that plan.

Distributions for qualified medical expenses (which would exclude payments for insurance premiums, other than premiums for (1) long-term care insurance, (2) COBRA continuation coverage, or (3) coverage while an individual is receiving unemployment compensation) incurred for the benefit of the account holder are excluded from income. Distributions are deductible regardless of whether the account holder is enrolled in the MSA plan at the time of the distribution. The value of a Medicare + Choice MSA must, however, be included in the account holder's gross estate for estate tax purposes. Distributions for other purposes are includible in taxable income and may even be subject to an additional penalty if they exceed a certain amount.

Contributions are subject to an annual limitation, which is 75 percent of the deductible for the individual's required MSA health plan. For example, the yearly contribution for an account holder that has an MSA health plan with an annual deductible of $6,000 cannot exceed $4,500.

This pilot program is scheduled to expire on December 31, 2002. It is available on a first-come, first-served basis to the first 390,000 eligible seniors who want to participate.

Appendix A

Exclusions from Income Under State Law: Benefits and Other Payments

Note: In 2001, each state was sent a survey to determine current treatment of benefits and state income taxation. Not all states responded. The table below therefore indicates the date its information was last updated or confirmed. Some states do not have an income tax. Since this information is subject to change at any time, readers are strongly urged to verify current information with the appropriate state's department of revenue before relying on it.

Most states conform to the definition of income in the Internal Revenue Code (Code, I.R.C.), with certain modifications. If a state's statute does not mention any modification relevant to flexible benefits, that state uses the same definition of income as the Code for the issues under discussion in this book. In many states, local governments follow the state's treatment of income and taxation. Some states, however, permit localities to define taxable income independently. In those states, it is imperative to understand the tax rules of the local jurisdictions when implementing a Section 125 plan, or producing W-2s showing taxable income at the local level. The table below includes comments when a state is known to permit localities to define taxable income.

Table Legend

A dash (—) indicates that the state provides no specific statutory exclusion. Excludable items may be subject to change, by statute or regulation. *SAF* (same as federal) means that the state generally follows the federal rule as to whether the item is considered taxable income. Most states adhere to the federal guidelines for the majority of the items listed in the table.

The "Benefits" column refers to contributions made by the employer (including contributions by the employee on a pretax basis) to cafeteria plan benefits, educational assistance programs, dependent care programs, fringe benefits, and meals and lodging provided by the employer. The scope of this table does not include retirement plans.

The acronym *AGI* refers to adjusted gross income under state law. Unless otherwise specified, the state law generally conforms to federal tax provisions relating to the definition of income, with certain modifications.

Specific Exclusions from Income Under State Law

State	*Benefits*	*Other*	*Citations to Authority*
AL	Sick pay per I.R.C. §§ 104, 105; payments for cafeteria plans excluded from federal income taxes under I.R.C. § 125; employer's dependent care payments for employees if excludable under I.R.C. § 129.	Localities can define taxable compensation independently of the state.	Ala. Code § 40-18-1 *et seq.* This information was last confirmed prior to 1999.
AK	—	—	— This information was last confirmed prior to 1999.
AZ	SAF.	Contributions by employers to employees' individual medical savings accounts to extent not deductible under I.R.C.; employee's deposits into individual medical savings account to extent excluded in taxpayer's federal AGI.	Ariz. Rev. Stat. Ann. §§ 42-101, 43-104, 43-1041. This information was last confirmed prior to 1999.
AR	Amounts received through accident/health insurance; workers' compensation for injuries (plus damages); amounts received by employees under cafeteria plans and dependent care assistance and disability/health plan payments. Educa-	—	Ark. Code Ann. §§ 15-4-801 *et seq.*, 26-51-101 *et seq.*, 26-51-403, 26-51-404. (*Note:* Arkansas law conforms to federal tax provisions relating to the definition of income, with certain modifications. Arkansas specifically adopts

Specific Exclusions from Income Under State Law (*cont'd*)

State	*Benefits*	*Other*	*Citations to Authority*
	tional assistance programs, fringe benefits, meals, and lodging are SAF.		I.R.C. §§ 82, 119, and 132. Ark. Code Ann. § 26-51-404.) This information was last confirmed prior to 1999.
CA	SAF.	Reimbursed expenses in connection with employment are excluded.	Cal. Rev. & Tax. Code §§ 17041, 17071, 17271. (*Note:* California law conforms to federal tax provisions relating to the definition of income, with certain modifications, and specifically provides for the same treatment regarding deductions as allowed under federal law.) This information was confirmed in 2001.
CO	SAF.	Contributions to medical expense accounts to extent included in federal AGI are excluded from Colorado AGI.	Colo. Rev. Stat. Ann. § 39-22-104 *et seq.* This information was last confirmed prior to 1999.
CT	SAF.	—	Conn. Gen. Stat. Ann. § 12-701. This information was updated in 2001.
DE	SAF.	Excludes certain employer payments to totally disabled employees and certain employer pension payments and other retirement benefits.	Del. Code Ann. tit. 30, §§ 1105, 1106. This information was updated in 2001.
DC	SAF. Educational assistance programs are not excluded.	—	D.C. Code Ann. §§ 47-1801, 47-1803.2. Conforms to federal tax provisions relating to the definition of income, with certain modifications. This information was

Specific Exclusions from Income Under State Law (*cont'd*)

State	*Benefits*	*Other*	*Citations to Authority*
			last confirmed prior to 1999.
FL	—	—	— This information was confirmed in 2001.
GA	Excludes from gross income amounts paid by employer for individual employee's dependent care assistance if they were excluded from federal gross income of employee. Other benefits are SAF.	—	Ga. Code Ann. §§ 48-7-1 *et seq.*, 48-7-27(a), 48-7-27(b). This information was confirmed in 2001.
HI	SAF.	Prepaid legal services, including employer contributions to plan, are excluded from gross income.	Haw. Rev. Stat. §§ 235.1, 235-2.3. (*Note:* Hawaii law conforms to federal tax provisions relating to the definition of income, with certain modifications; in determining taxable income, Hawaii uses the I.R.C. in effect 12-31-99.) This information was updated in 2001.
ID	SAF.	Expenses for dependent children (using federal guidelines) and contributions to an Idaho medical assistance account are subtracted from federal AGI to arrive at Idaho AGI. Income of American Indians from employment on reservation (if they live and work on reservation) is subtracted from federal AGI to arrive at Idaho AGI.	Idaho Code §§ 63-3001, 63-3004, 63-3022. This information was confirmed in 2001.
IL	SAF.	Withdrawals from medical savings account	35 Ill. Comp. Stat. Ann. 5/203.

Specific Exclusions from Income Under State Law (*cont'd*)

State	*Benefits*	*Other*	*Citations to Authority*
		established under the Medical Care Savings Account Act to the extent deducted from federal tax are added to federal AGI to arrive at state AGI. Employer contributions are excluded.	This information was last confirmed prior to 1999.
IN	SAF.	Amount equal to federal Social Security and railroad retirement benefits included in federal gross income per I.R.C. § 86 is subtracted to arrive at state AGI.	Ind. Code Ann. §§ 6-3-1-3.5, 6-3-1-11. This information was last confirmed prior to 1999.
IA	Sick pay is excluded subject to limitations found in I.R.C. § 105(d). Other benefits are SAF.	—	Iowa Code Ann. §§ 422.5, 422.7. This information was confirmed in 2001.
KS	SAF.	Income earned on contributions deposited to individual development account under Kansas law are subtracted from federal AGI to arrive at Kansas AGI.	Kan. Stat. Ann. § 79-32,117. This information was confirmed in 2001.
KY	Railroad retirement and railroad sick-pay benefits are subtracted from federal AGI to arrive at Kentucky AGI. Other benefits are SAF.	Taxes paid to foreign countries are deductible as an itemized deduction in arriving at Kentucky taxable income. Premiums paid (with after-tax dollars) for health insurance and long-term care insurance are deductible from federal AGI to arrive at Kentucky AGI. Localities can define taxable compensation independently of the state.	Ky. Rev. Stat. Ann. §§ 141.010, 160.593, 160.607. (*Note:* Kentucky law conforms to federal tax provisions relating to the definition of income; in determining wage and salary income, Kentucky uses the I.R.C. in effect 12-31-99.) This information was updated in 2001.

Specific Exclusions from Income Under State Law (*cont'd*)

State	*Benefits*	*Other*	*Citations to Authority*
LA	SAF.	—	La. Rev. Stat. Ann. § 47-293. This information was last confirmed prior to 1999.
ME	Amount of premiums paid for certified long-term care insurance policies are subtracted from federal AGI to arrive at Maine AGI. Other benefits are SAF.	—	Me. Rev. Stat. Ann. tit. 36, §§ 5101 *et seq.*, 5121. Taxable income is determined by reference to federal AGI, with certain modifications, under I.R.C. in effect 12-31-91. This information was confirmed in 2001.
MD	SAF.	Household dependent care expenses as defined by I.R.C. are subtracted from federal AGI in arriving at Maryland AGI. Expenses incurred by individuals and employers for providing a human or mechanical reader for the blind up to maximum of $1,000 of expenses that an employer incurs for use in employment or $5,000 of expense incurred by individual to extent that such expense is not allowed as medical expense under I.R.C. § 213 are subtracted from federal AGI.	Md. Code Ann. Tax-Gen. §§ 10-201 *et seq.*, 10-207, 10-208. This information was last confirmed prior to 1999.
MA	SAF.	Foreign earned income as defined by I.R.C. § 911 is added to federal AGI to determine Massachusetts AGI; annuity contributions excluded per I.R.C. § 403(b) are added to federal AGI to	Mass. Gen. Laws Ann. ch. 62, §§ 1, 2(a). (*Note:* Low-income taxpayers are exempt if Massachusetts AGI is not over $8,000 for single or separate filers and not over $7,600

Specific Exclusions from Income Under State Law (*cont'd*)

State	*Benefits*	*Other*	*Citations to Authority*
		determine Massachusetts AGI if by salary reduction agreement authorized by that I.R.C. section and not required by employer's retirement program.	plus personal and dependent exemption for joint filers or household heads (effective tax years starting after 12-31-94; not to exceed $12,000 for joint filers).) This information was last confirmed prior to 1999.
MI	SAF.	—	Mich. Stat. Ann. § 7.557 *et seq.* This information was confirmed in 2001.
MN	SAF.	—	Minn. Stat. Ann. § 290 *et seq.* This information was last confirmed prior to 1999.
MS	SAF.	—	Miss. Code Ann. §§ 27-7-5, 27-7-13. This information was updated in 2001.
MO	SAF.	— Localities can define taxable compensation independently of the state.	Mo. Rev. Stat. § 143.121. This information was confirmed in 2001.
MT	Benefits paid under workers' compensation laws. Health insurance premiums paid by employer for employee if attributed as income to the employee under federal law are subtracted from federal AGI to determine Montana AGI. Other benefits are SAF.	Tips from services to patrons of businesses licensed to provide food, lodgings, or beverages are subtracted from federal AGI to arrive at Montana AGI. Dependent care costs for employees to extent taken as federal deduction and Montana credit are added to federal AGI to arrive at Montana AGI.	Mont. Code Ann. §§ 15-30-101, 15-30-111. This information was last confirmed prior to 1999.
NE	SAF.	—	Neb. Rev. Stat. Ann. § 77-2714 *et seq.*

Specific Exclusions from Income Under State Law (*cont'd*)

State	*Benefits*	*Other*	*Citations to Authority*
			This information was confirmed in 2001.
NV	—	—	— This information was last confirmed prior to 1999.
NH	—	New Hampshire imposes a limited tax on interest and dividend income. Residents are taxed on income received, credited, or accumulated from stocks and bonds in preceding calendar year.	N.H. Rev. Stat. Ann. §§ 77:1, 77:4. This information was last confirmed prior to 1999.
NJ	Transportation fringe benefits excluded up to $1,145 (indexed for inflation). Benefits above the excludable amount are taxable. Exclusion applies only if the benefit is in addition to, and not in lieu of, compensation payable to the employees. Any salary reduction amounts, including any amounts paid by the employee toward an employer-provided benefit such as premium contribution toward insurance coverage or contribution toward a flexible spending account, are *not* exluded from taxable income. Payments and benefits received under any unemployment insurance law are excludable.		N.J. Stat. Ann. §§ 54A:6-13, 54A:6-23, 54A:6-24. This information was updated in 2001.
NM	Payments for hospital, dental, medical, or drug	Income earned on reservation or pueblo by	N.M. Stat. Ann. §§ 7-2-1, 7-2-2(A).

Specific Exclusions from Income Under State Law ***(cont'd)***

State	*Benefits*	*Other*	*Citations to Authority*
	expenses to or on behalf of taxpayer are excluded from gross income. Other benefits are SAF. Effective in 2000, New Mexico provides a deduction from personal income tax for uncompensated and unreimbursed medical expenses not already itemized on federal Form 1040.	Indian-enrolled member is subtracted from base income. Child day care expenses allowed if necessary for gainful employment, limited to 40% of compensation paid ($480 per dependent or $1,200 maximum), for taxpayers not exceeding income qualifications.	Enacted by a special session of the 2000 legislature of New Mexico. This information was updated in 2001.
NY	Disability income that would have been excluded under the repealed provisions of I.R.C. § 105(d) is subtracted from federal AGI to arrive at New York AGI. Other benefits are SAF, with some exceptions for cafeteria plan benefits of public employees in N.Y.C.	—	N.Y. Tax Law §§ 601 *et seq.*, 611, 612. This information was confirmed in 2001.
NC	SAF.	Credit allowed for care of dependent children: amount of federal credit allowed for employment-related expenses for care of dependent children: 7%–9% of expenses to care for over-7-year-olds not able to care for selves, 10%–13% for other qualified persons. $2,400 maximum if one dependent, $4,800 maximum if more than one.	N.C. Gen. Stat. §§ 105-130 *et seq.*, 105-134.2. This information was last confirmed prior to 1999.
ND	SAF.	Vietnam veteran adjusted compensation is exempt; American Indians residing on Indian reservations are exempt	N.D. Cent. Code §§ 57-38-01, 57-38-01.2. This information was last confirmed prior to 1999.

Specific Exclusions from Income Under State Law (*cont'd*)

State	*Benefits*	*Other*	*Citations to Authority*
		from taxes on reservation-earned income. Medical expenses disallowed by the federal limit are subtracted from federal AGI to determine North Dakota AGI.	
OH	SAF.	To extent included in federal AGI, amounts included solely as reimbursement or refund of expenses in past year are subtracted to determine Ohio AGI. School districts tax follows the state definition of taxable compensation. Localities can define taxable compensation independently of the state.	Ohio Rev. Code Ann. § 5747.02. This information was confirmed in 2001.
OK	SAF.	—	Okla. Stat. Ann. tit. 68, §§ 2355, 2538. This information was last confirmed prior to 1999.
OR	SAF. Oregon allows a tax credit for long-term care insurance premiums.	Unemployment compensation is taxable. The imputed value of health insurance benefits provided by an employer to an employee's domestic partner is exempt from state income tax.	Or. Rev. Stat. §§ 315.048, 316.01 *et seq.*, 316.680. This information was updated in 2001.
PA	Amounts contributed by employer or salary reduced by employee under a cafeteria plan for accident/health benefits (including health flexible spending account) are SAF. Pennsylvania has *no*	Localities can define taxable compensation independently of the state.	61 Pa. Cons. Stat. §§ 101.6(i), 101.7. This information was updated in 2001.

Specific Exclusions from Income Under State Law (*cont'd*)

State	*Benefits*	*Other*	*Citations to Authority*
	exclusion from state income tax for employer or employee contributions to a dependent care account. Pennsylvania applies constructive receipt to parking and mass transit benefits when a taxpayer could have chosen cash instead. Contributions by employees or employers for long-term care is not excludable from Pennsylvania income.		
RI	SAF.	Income, gain, or tax preference resulting from sale or transfer of qualifying stock options provided by a qualifying company may be excluded from income.	R.I. Gen. Laws §§ 44-30-1 *et seq.*, 44-30-12, 44-39-3, 44-43-8. This information was updated in 2001.
SC	SAF.	(1) A credit is allowed for expenses for worker's household and dependent care services (applies only to those with AGI of $10,000 or less). (2) First $5 of daily subsistence allowances earned by law enforcement officers and full-time firefighters and emergency medical service personnel is subtracted from federal AGI to arrive at South Carolina AGI.	S.C. Code Ann. §§ 12-6-1140, and 12-6-3380. This information was updated in 2001.
SD	—	—	— This information was confirmed in 2001.
TN	—	—	Tenn. Code Ann. §§ 67-2-101,

Specific Exclusions from Income Under State Law (*cont'd*)

State	*Benefits*	*Other*	*Citations to Authority*
			67-2-102. State taxes only stock dividend and investment income. This information was confirmed in 2001.
TX	—	—	— This information was last confirmed prior to 1999.
UT	SAF.	Up to $4,800 (depending on income) of qualified retirement income if under age 65 and up to $7,500 (regardless of income) if 65 or older is subtracted from federal AGI to determine Utah AGI.	Utah Code Ann. §§ 59-10-101 *et seq.*, 59-10-112. This information was last confirmed prior to 1999.
VT	SAF.	Wage expense disallowed when claiming federal targeted job credit (to extent included in federal AGI).	Vt. Stat. Ann. tit. 32, §§ 5811, 5823. This information was last confirmed prior to 1999.
VA	SAF.	—	Va. Code Ann. § 58.1-300 *et seq.* This information was last confirmed prior to 1999.
WA	—	—	— This information was confirmed in 2001.
WV	SAF.	—	W. Va. Code Ann. § 11-21-1 *et seq.* This information was last confirmed prior to 1999.
WI	To extent included in federal AGI, 100% of medical care insurance (less federal deducted amount) paid by self-employed for self, spouse, and dependents is subtracted from fed-	To extent included in federal AGI, 50% of medical care insurance (less federal deducted amount) paid by employee (employer not paying for any) for self, spouse, and	Wis. Stat. Ann. §§ 71.01 *et seq.*, 71.05(6). This information was last confirmed prior to 1999.

Specific Exclusions from Income Under State Law (*cont'd*)

State	*Benefits*	*Other*	*Citations to Authority*
	eral AGI to arrive at Wisconsin AGI. Other benefits are SAF.	dependents is subtracted from federal AGI to arrive at Wisconsin AGI.	
WY	—	—	— This information was last confirmed prior to 1999.

Appendix B

2002 Dependent Care Estimated Tax Worksheet

This worksheet will help you decide whether it is more advantageous for you to take the dependent care tax credit on your income tax return or to establish a Dependent Care Spending Account to pay for dependent care expenses.

	Tax Credit	*Spending Account*
1. **Adjusted Gross Income**—Put the amount for your household during 2002 on Line 1.	1. $ ________	$ ________
2. **Dependent Care Spending Account**—Put the amount to be reimbursed from your Account on Line 2.	2. $ 0.00	$ ________
3. **Income Sub-total**—Subtract Line 2 from Line 1. Put Answer on Line 3.	3. $ ________	$ ________

4. **Income Reductions**

   i. Estimated itemized deductions. $ ________

   ii. Standard deduction (see 2002 Tax Rate Schedule) $ ________

   Enter greater amount from Line i. or Line ii. on Line a.

   a.) $ ____________

	Tax Credit	*Spending Account*
Calculate personal exemptions below and enter result on Line b. $3,000 × _______ (number of personal exemptions) = b.) $ _____________		
c.) Add Lines a. and b. Enter amount on Line 4.	4. $ ________	$ ________
5. **Taxable Income**—Subtract Line 4 from Line 3. Put answer on Line 5.	5. $ ________	$ ________
6. **Tax**—Find the tax for the amount on Line 5 using the 2002 Tax Rate Schedule for your filing Status. Enter your tax on Line 6.	6. $ ________	$ ________
7. **Child Care Tax Credit**—For Tax Credit method only. Your total child care expenses for 2002 up to $2,400 for one child or $4,800 for more than one. (Note: Beginning in 2003 the limits will be increased to $3,000 and $6,000 respectively.) a.) $ ________ TIMES The percentage from Table A that applies to you. b.) $ ________ EQUALS Your child care credit on your income tax return. Put amount from Line c. below on Line 7. c.) $ ________	7. $ ________	$ 0.00
8. **Net Tax**—Subtract Line 7 from Line 6. Enter answer on Line 8.	8. $ ________	$ ________

The column that has the smaller number on Line 8 is the more advantageous method for you to use to pay for your dependent care expenses during 2002.

Tax Rate Schedule

2002—Married Individuals Filing Joint Returns and Surviving Spouses

If your taxable income after personal exemptions ($3,000) and deductions (the standard deduction in 2002 is $7,850) is:

Over—	*But not over—*	*The tax is:*
$ 0	$ 12,000	10% of taxable income
12,000	46,700	$1,200 + 15% of excess over $12,000
46,700	112,850	$6,405 + 27% of excess over $46,700
112,850	171,950	$24,265.50 + 30% of excess over $112,850
171,950	307,050	$41,995.50 + 35% of excess over $171,950
307,050		$89,280.50 + 38.6% of excess over $307,050

2002—Heads of Households

If your taxable income after personal exemptions ($3,000) and deductions (the standard deduction in 2002 is $6,900) is:

Over—	*But not over—*	*The tax is:*
$ 0	$ 10,000	10% of taxable income
10,000	37,450	$1,000 + 15% of excess over $10,000
37,450	96,700	$5,117.50 + 27% of excess over $37,450
96,700	156,600	$21,115 + 30% of excess over $96,700
156,600	307,050	$39,085 + 35% of excess over $156,600
307,050		$91,742 + 38.6% of excess over $307,050

2002—Single Taxpayers

If your taxable income after personal exemptions ($3,000) and deductions (the standard deduction in 2002 is $4,700) is:

Over—	*But not over—*	*The tax is:*
$ 0	$ 6,000	10% of taxable income
6,000	27,950	$600 + 15% of excess over $6,000
27,950	67,700	$3,862.50 + 27% of excess over $27,950
67,700	141,250	$14,625 + 30% of excess over $67,700
141,250	307,050	$36,690 + 35% of excess over $141,250
307,050		$94,720.50 + 38.6% of excess over $307,050

2002—Married Individuals Filing Separate Returns

If your taxable income after personal exemptions ($3,000) and deductions (the standard deduction in 2002 is $3,925) is:

Over—	*But not over—*	*The tax is:*
$ 0	$ 6,000	10% of taxable income
6,000	23,350	$600 + 15% of excess over $6,000
23,350	56,425	$3,202.50 + 27% of excess over $23,350
56,425	85,975	$12,132.75 + 30% of excess over $56,425
85,975	153,525	$20,997.75 + 35% of excess over $85,975
153,525		$44,640.25 + 38.6% of excess over $153,525

Table A

If your family's adjusted gross income is:	*The percent you can take as a tax credit is:*
$10,000 or less	30%
$10,001–$12,000	29%
$12,001–$14,000	28%
$14,001–$16,000	27%
$16,001–$18,000	26%
$18,001–$20,000	25%
$20,001–$22,000	24%
$22,001–$24,000	23%
$24,001–$26,000	22%
$26,001–$28,000	21%
$28,001 or more	20%

Appendix C

Sample Flexible Benefits Implementation Schedule

Sample Flexible Benefits Implementation Schedule 9-Month Time Line*

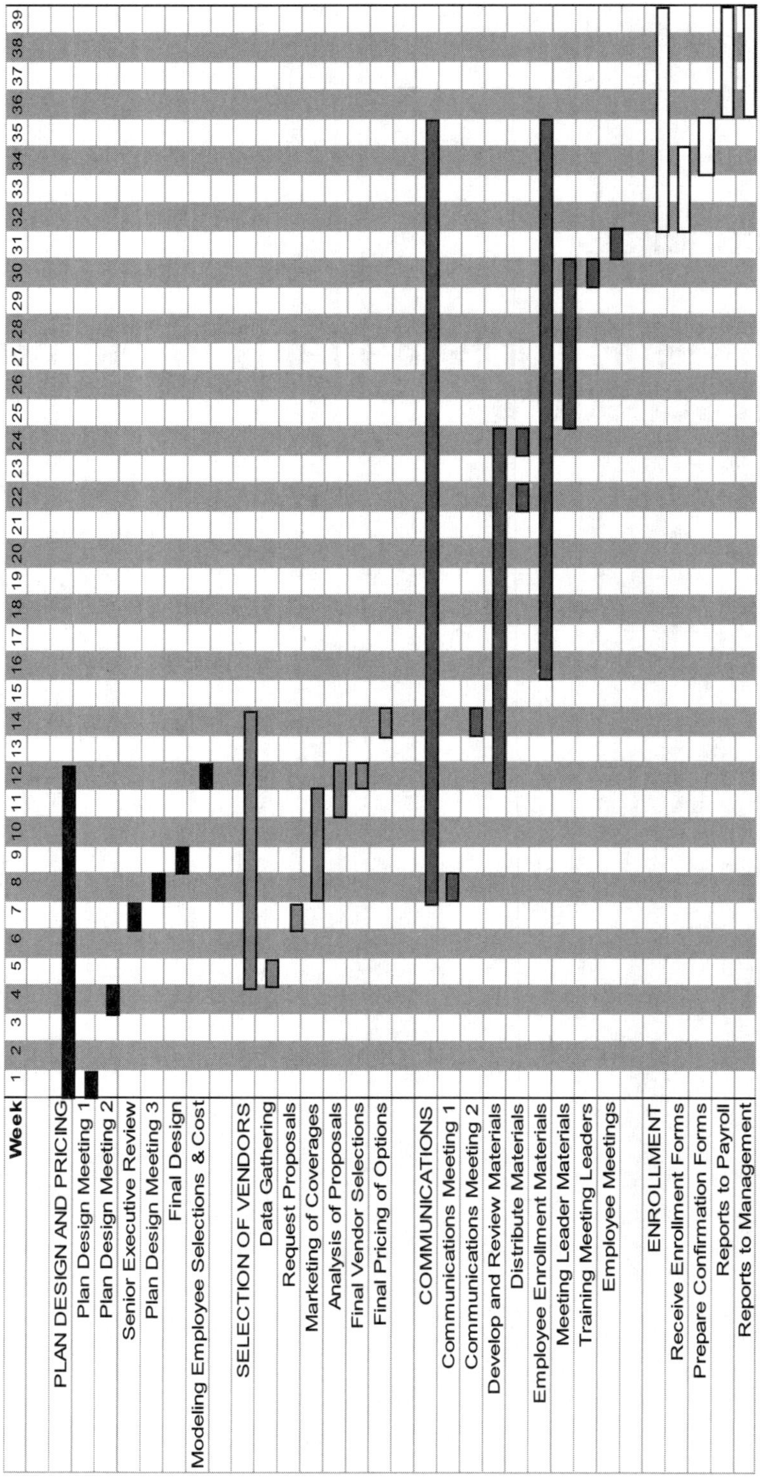

*Courtesy of The Segal Company

Plan Design and Pricing	**12 Weeks**
Plan Design Meeting 1	Week 1
•Selection of Design Components •Determination of Coverage Levels	
Plan Design Meeting 2	Week 4
•Final Design Review •Development of Credits/Pricing Strategy	
Senior Executive Review	Week 7
Plan Design Meeting 3	Week 8
•Suggested Credits/Price Tags	
Final Design	Week 9
•Eligibility Rules •Default Rules	
Modeling of Employee Selections & Costs	Week 12
Selection of Vendors (as needed)	**10 Weeks**
Data Gathering	Week 5
Request for Proposal Preparations	Week 7
Marketing of Coverages	Weeks 8 to 11
Analysis of Proposals	Weeks 11 and 12
•Recommendation of Finalists	
Final Vendor Selections	Week 12
Final Pricing of Options	Week 14

Communications	**28 Weeks**
Communications Meeting 1	Week 8
• Develop Communication Strategy	
Communications Meeting 2	Week 14
• Review Suggested Theme and Media	
Develop and Review	Weeks 12 to 24
• Preliminary Announcement/Education Materials	
Distribute Preliminary Materials	Weeks 22 and 24
Develop and Distribute	
• Employee Enrollment Materials Weeks	Weeks 16 to 35
• Meeting Leader Training Materials	Weeks 25 to 30
Training Meeting Leaders	Week 30
Employee Meetings	Week 31
Enrollment	**8 Weeks**
Receive Enrollment Forms	Weeks 32 to 34
Prepare Confirmation Forms	Weeks 34 and 35
Reports to Payroll	Weeks 36 to 39
Reports to Management	Weeks 36 to 39

Appendix D

Sample Employee Benefits Workbook

Flex System and You

On April 1, 2003, the Company is introducing Flex System—Benefits by Design. This new flexible benefits plan is designed to meet your individual needs and the varying needs of our national workforce.

Benefits Options. Here's an overview of the benefits Flex System provides:

- Medical (including prescription drug benefits)
- Dental
- Vision
- Long-Term Disability
- Life and Accidental Death and Dismemberment (AD&D) Insurance
- Flexible Spending Accounts

Each plan has different options that provide various levels of coverage. You decide which benefits make the most sense for you.

The Choice Is Yours. You are the key to making our new flexible benefits program work. Flex System allows you to custom design your own benefits package to suit your lifestyle and needs. You should read this workbook carefully and then enroll in the options that are best for you and your family.

Choose Carefully. Your benefits elections will become effective on April 1, 2003. Outside of the open enrollment period, changes are restricted. You can make changes to your benefits decisions only if you have a "qualified family status change," including

- Marriage or divorce
- Birth or adoption of a child
- Death
- Gain or loss of your spouse's employment
- Relocation outside your plan's service area

The new coverage must be requested within 31 days of the change and must be consistent with your reason for making the change in election.

Your Next Step. Read this workbook carefully; it describes the coverage provided by each plan and shows how the options differ. Then refer to Your Personal Fact Sheet for the options and costs that apply to you. When you've made your decisions, follow the telephone enrollment instructions. If you have any questions, please contact Human Resources.

Medical

Options. Today, everyone needs protection against the high cost of medical care. The Flex System medical options are designed to protect you from financial loss if you or a family member becomes ill. Flex System offers these medical options:

- No coverage
- Preferred provider organization (PPO) coverage
- Out-of-service area coverage, in areas where the PPO is not available
- XYZ health maintenance organization (HMO) coverage, in many locations

Waiving Medical Coverage. If you have coverage through another plan, you may choose "no coverage." If you choose this option, you must have other coverage. You will have another chance to join the plan during next year's enrollment, or earlier if you lose coverage. However, if you join later, you may be required to provide evidence of good health before coverage will be effective.

PPO Coverage. When you enroll in the PPO, you will receive a list of doctors and hospitals that belong to the PPO network. The network includes many fine physicians from pediatricians to family practitioners and specialists. If you're eligible for the PPO, a Provider Directory that lists participating providers in your area is included in this kit for your review.

Each time you receive care from a network provider, you will pay lower out-of-pocket costs. If you receive treatment from a doctor or a facility that does not belong to the PPO network, your expenses may still be eligible for reimbursement, but you will be responsible for more of the cost of care. Here's how the PPO works:

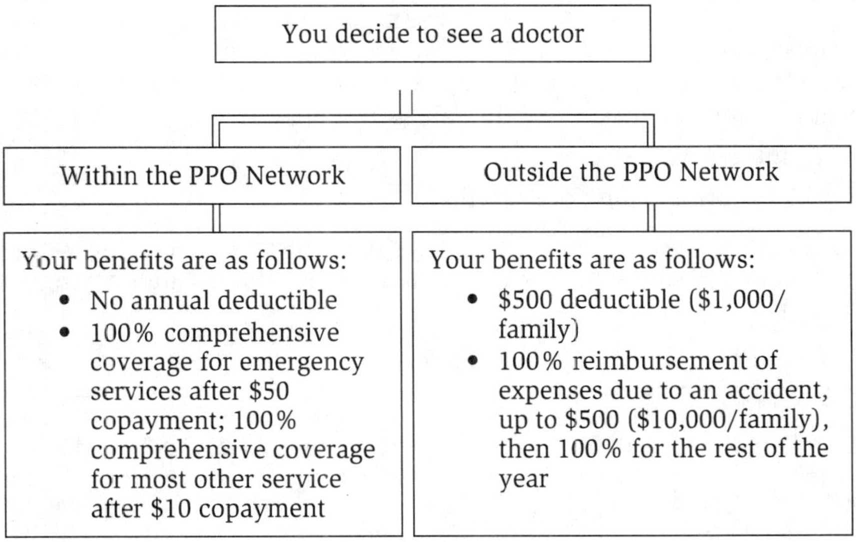

Note: Services outside the PPO network are reimbursed based on reasonable and customary charges, which are the charges made by most providers in your area for similar services.

You decide whether to go in-network or out-of-network each time you need treatment. Inside the network, depending on your doctor's policy, you may need to pay for services up front and file a claim for reimbursement. If you decide to go outside the network, you still receive coverage, you just pay more of the cost and will always have to file a claim.

Out-of-Service Area Coverage. If you live in an area where there are no PPO providers, you may choose the out-of-service area plan. Your eligible expenses are reimbursed at the out-of-network rate, except the plan covers hospitalizations in full and a lower deductible applies—$100/person ($200/family). The plan then pays 80 percent of the next $2,500 ($5,000/family) of covered expenses. After that, the plan pays 100 percent of covered expenses for the rest of that year. In addition, the plan always covers the first $500 of expenses that are due to an accident at 100 percent.

XYZ HMO Coverage. If you are eligible for the XYZ HMO, you will receive a list of doctors and facilities that belong to the XYZ HMO network included in this kit. You will need to choose a primary care physician (PCP) from this list. As long as your health care is arranged for or provided by your PCP, most of your expenses will be covered at 100 percent with no deductible. You may be required to make a $10 copayment for some services, like office visits, or a $50 copayment for emergency room care. No claim forms are required. Health care that is not arranged for or provided by your PCP will not be covered.

Prescription Coverage. No matter which medical option you choose, you will receive this prescription coverage, as follows.

Prescription Drug Card. Your prescription drug card allows you to obtain prescriptions quickly and easily from participating pharmacies. When you show a participating pharmacist your prescription drug card, you will receive 100 percent coverage after you pay the following copayments:

- $8 for generic drugs
- $20 for brand-name prescriptions

Mail-Order Service. In addition, a mail-order prescription drug service allows you to obtain a 90-day supply of maintenance prescriptions after paying a single deductible.

Wellness Benefits—All Medical Options.

Benefit	PPO	Out-of-Service Area	XYZ HMO
Routine physical Well baby care Immunizations Certain nutritional counseling Smoking cessation patch	*In-network:* 100% after $10 copayment *Out-of-network:* After deductible, plan pays 80% of next $5,000; then 100%	100% coverage, up to a maximum of $400/ calendar year	100% coverage after $10 copayment

Dental

Options. Dental coverage is designed to keep small dental problems from becoming big problems. So these plans pay 100 percent of the cost for preventive and routine care. Flex System offers you the following three dental options:

1. No coverage;
2. High-Option Dental; or
3. Low-Option Dental.

You may choose the option you want, regardless of your medical election.

Waiving Dental Coverage. If you choose "no coverage," you will not receive dental benefits from the Company this year. You can join the plan again during next year's open enrollment, or earlier if you have a qualified change in family status. However, if you join after you are first eligible, you may be required to provide evidence of good health before coverage will be effective.

High-Option Dental. High-Option Dental covers four levels of dental services as shown on the following chart. You may choose to see any dentist and still receive benefits.

<table>
<tr><th>Preventive and Diagnostic</th><th>Minor Restorative</th><th>Major Restorative and Prosthodontics</th><th>Orthodontics</th></tr>
<tr><td>No deductible applies</td><td colspan="2">$50 annual deductible/person (maximum $100/family) applies</td><td>No deductible</td></tr>
<tr><td rowspan="2">Plan Pays 100%

Covered expenses include:
• Cleanings
• Bitewing X-rays
• Emergency visits for treatment of pain</td><td>Plan Pays 80%[a]

Covered expenses include:
• Fillings
• Extractions</td><td>Plan Pays 50%[a]

Covered expenses include:
• Periodontal treatments
• Crowns, bridges
• Dentures</td><td>Plan Pays 50%[a]

Covered expenses include:
• Basic orthodontic treatments</td></tr>
<tr><td>You Pay 20%</td><td>You Pay 50%</td><td>You Pay 50%</td></tr>
<tr><td colspan="4">Plan pays an annual maximum of $2,500/person. Plan pays a separate lifetime orthodontic maximum of $2,500/person.</td></tr>
</table>

[a]Services are reimbursed based on reasonable and customary charges, which are the charges made by most providers in your area for similar services.

Low-Option Dental. Low-Option Dental is the same as high-option dental coverage, except that

1. The maximum benefit each year is limited to $1,000/person, and
2. There is no coverage for orthodontic treatment.

Vision

Options. Vision coverage is designed to help you and your family see things more clearly. The plan provides coverage for vision care expenses such as eye exams, lenses, and frames. Flex System offers you two vision care options:

1. No coverage; or
2. Vision care coverage.

Waiving Vision Coverage. If you choose "no coverage," you will not receive vision benefits from the Company this year. You can join the plan again during next year's open enrollment, or earlier if you have a qualified change in family status.

Vision Care Coverage. The vision plan is similar to an HMO. When you enroll in the vision plan, you will receive a list of participating vision care providers. If you go to one of these providers, you will receive full coverage based on the following annual schedule:

- Up to $50 for a routine eye exam
- Up to $200 for frames and lenses
- Up to $200 for contact lenses (if elected instead of eyeglasses)

If you go outside the vision network, no benefits are available. However, in addition to the network benefits described above, if you enroll in one of the Flex System medical options, you will receive full coverage for an annual eye exam, up to a maximum of $50. No other vision benefits are included in the medical options.

Long-Term Disability

Options. How would you manage financially if you became seriously ill or injured and couldn't work? Most of us would have a tough time making ends meet. That is why Flex System includes long-term disability (LTD) coverage that replaces part of your earnings if you become disabled and can't work.

If your annual base salary is $30,000 or less, Flex System automatically provides you with LTD coverage. This coverage is provided at no cost to you.

If your annual base salary is over $30,000, you pay for the full cost of LTD coverage with pretax or after-tax dollars. Therefore, Flex System offers the following LTD options for employees earning over $30,000:

- No coverage
- LTD coverage on a pretax basis
- LTD coverage on an after-tax basis

How LTD Works. You may submit a claim for LTD benefits after you have been completely disabled for 180 days. The monthly benefit would be the lesser of

1. 60 percent of your monthly salary; or
2. $21,000.

In most cases, if you are age 60 or younger at the time of your disability and your disability continues, benefits are payable until you reach age 65. If you are older than age 60 at the time of your disability, benefits are payable according to a schedule.

Plan Exclusions. The LTD plan will not pay benefits for any disability that results from the following:

- War, acts of war, or participation in a riot
- Intentionally self-inflicted injuries

Preexisting Condition Limitation. The LTD plan contains a preexisting condition limitation. This means that benefits will not be paid for disabilities that result from an injury or illness that occurred during the 24-month period before your LTD coverage originally becomes effective. This limitation no longer applies after you have been a member of the plan for 12 months and are not treated for the condition during that period. In general, this means that the preexisting condition limitation applies to employees electing the Company coverage for the first time on or after April 1, 2003. In addition, the preexisting condition limitation also applies on any amounts over $15,000.

Life and AD&D Insurance

Providing for those who depend on you is an essential part of good financial planning. And life insurance offers important financial protection. That's why Flex System includes an automatic life and accidental death and dismemberment (AD&D) insurance policy and the opportunity to purchase optional coverage.

Basic Life and AD&D Insurance. Flex System provides you with a base level of life insurance equal to two times your annual salary (plus bonus and commissions) plus an additional $10,000. You also receive a matching amount of AD&D coverage. Your Basic Life and AD&D Insurance coverage is provided at no cost to you.

Life Insurance Options. Flex System also offers you these additional life insurance options:

- An additional 1 times salary (plus bonus and commissions)
- An additional 2 times salary (plus bonus and commissions)
- An additional 3 times salary (plus bonus and commissions)
- An additional 4 times salary (plus bonus and commissions)

*Note:*Your life and AD&D insurance amounts are based on your age and salary as of January 1, 2003, plus bonus and commissions from 1999.

How Life Insurance Works. The amount of your coverage will be rounded up to the next higher $1,000, unless it is already an even multiple of $1,000. For example, if your salary is $24,750 and you elect an additional two times salary, your coverage would be $50,000 ($24,750 2 = $49,500, which rounds up to $50,000). You may not elect a total amount of coverage that exceeds $760,000. If you are age 65 or older, your coverage amount will be reduced according to the following schedule:

Your Age	*Maximum Benefit Available*
65–69	65% of the amount elected
70–74	50% of the amount elected
75 and over	35% of the amount elected

Evidence of Good Health. You may choose as much life insurance coverage as you want. If the amount you choose equals (or is less than) your current amount of the Company life insurance, no further action is required. However, if you choose more than your current amount of life insurance, you may need to provide evidence of your good health. For instance, evidence will be required if your total amount of life insurance exceeds four times your salary or $600,000.

AD&D Insurance Options. You may purchase AD&D insurance that will pay your beneficiaries a benefit if you die as a result of an accident. Under this policy, benefits are also payable for certain types of physical loss, such as loss of a hand, foot, or eye. The options available are the same as your additional life insurance options (from an additional one to four times salary).

Flexible Spending Accounts

Our Flexible Spending Accounts (FSAs) can save you money on your taxes. FSAs let you pay for health and dependent care expenses with pretax dollars.

Options. During each calendar year, you may

- Save from a minimum of $50 up to a maximum of $1,000 for health care expenses
- Save from a minimum of $50 up to a maximum of $5,000 for dependent care expenses

Note: The IRS sets the $5,000 limit on the amount you can contribute to a dependent care FSA. If you (or your spouse) will participate in another FSA in 2003, you should make sure that your total dependent care FSA contributions do not exceed $5,000.

How FSAs Work. The secret behind our FSAs is the pretax advantage. FSAs let you take part of your earnings—the part you already use to pay out-of-pocket health and dependent care expenses—and exclude it from your taxable income. As a result, you keep the money you would have used to pay taxes on this amount. Here's how your FSA makes this happen:

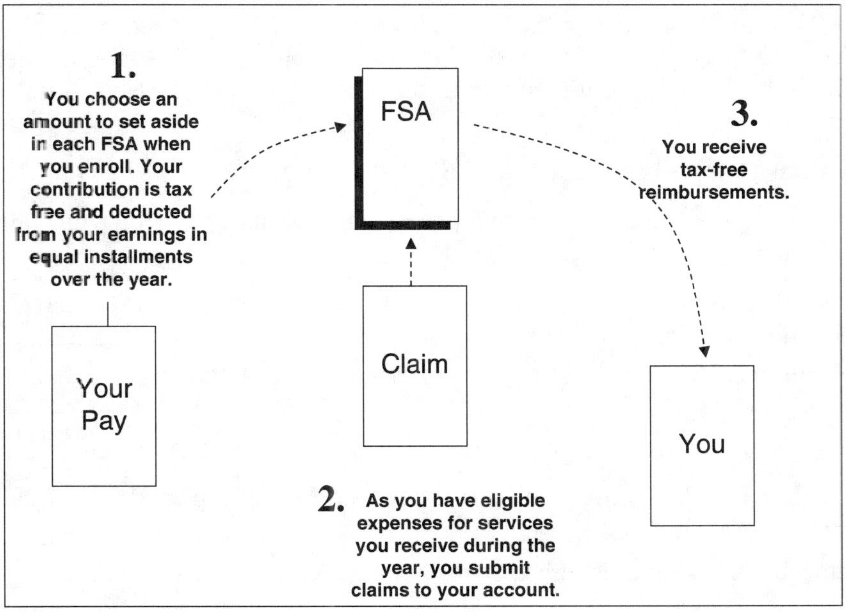

So, your contributions are not taxed as they flow into your accounts or when you receive them as reimbursement. That's how you save money.

You must make separate contributions to each account. You cannot transfer contributions back and forth between the two accounts.

IMPORTANT NOTE. When estimating the amount(s) you wish to contribute to the FSAs, do so carefully and conservatively. If you overestimate your expenses and have unclaimed money left in the account at year-end, IRS regulations prohibit the return of any excess amount to you. This is called the "use-it-or-lose-it" rule.

The Health Care FSA. Qualified expenses are outlined on the following worksheet. You can also consult IRS Publication 502 for a more detailed listing of eligible health care expenses. You can obtain this booklet by calling the IRS at 1-800-829-FORM(3676). Keep in mind, however, that the publication the IRS distributes is intended for individual taxpayers. Some very important differences between medical expense reimbursement through an FSA, and deduction of medical expense as a taxpayer are (1) expenses must be *incurred* during the plan year for the FSA, and (2) premium payments are not a reimbursable expense through an FSA.

Remember, you can't claim any expense that has been paid by your or your spouse's benefit plan.

How Much You Can Contribute. In 2003, you may save from a minimum of $50 up to a maximum of $3,000 in your Health Care FSA. The annual amount you choose will be divided and deducted equally from your remaining paychecks in 2003.

Health Care Personal Expense Worksheet. The worksheet below can help you estimate the amount you should put into your Health Care FSA. Remember you can include all unreimbursed expenses—not just for yourself but for all dependents.

A. Plan Deductibles, Copayments, and Coinsurance

List estimated health care expenses below for you and your eligible dependents:

Deductibles(s) and copayments	$________
Coinsurance (the estimated medical expenses not covered in full by the plan)	$________
TOTAL A	$________

B. Other Eligible Expenses (if not covered by your plans)

Medical, dental, and vision expenses not covered by your plans	$________
Medicine or other drugs recommended by your doctor (dietary supplements, birth control items)	$________
Ambulance service or similar transportation for medical care	$________
Counseling (psychoanalysis, psychiatric therapy, learning disability counseling, in-patient care and treatment for a handicap)	$________
Treatment for drug abuse or alcoholism (including meals and lodging if they are necessary for the treatment)	$________
Wheelchairs or other special medical equipment	$________
TOTAL B	$________
TOTAL A + B	$________

A contribution cannot exceed $1,000/year, nor can it be less than $50/year. To determine the amount of your contribution each pay period, divide the total by the number of pay periods remaining in the calendar year. Remember, there are two pay periods in each month.

*The Dependent Care FSA.*Qualified expenses are those that you (and your spouse, if you are married) must pay for the care of your dependents in order for you (and your spouse) to be able to work.

If your spouse is a full-time student at least five months out of the year or is an eligible disabled dependent, your dependent care expenses may also be eligible.

Eligible dependents include your child(ren) under age 13, your disabled spouse, or other disabled dependent (such as an elderly parent). If care is provided outside your home, the dependent must spend at least eight hours a day in your household.

Eligible expenses include dependent/child care for the upcoming year. For a more detailed listing of eligible dependent care expenses, you can consult IRS Publication 503. You can call the IRS at 1-800-829-FORM (3676) to obtain this booklet.

IMPORTANT NOTE. When you use this account, you are required to report the name, address, and Social Security number or taxpayer identification number of the day care provider(s).

How Much You Can Contribute. In 2003 you may save up to $5,000 in your Dependent Care FSA, except for the following conditions:

1. If you or your spouse earn less than $5,000, then the most you can contribute is the lesser of your or your spouse's income.
2. If you are married but file separate returns, you may save a maximum of $2,500 each year.
3. If both you and your spouse contribute to Dependent Care FSAs, the maximum you may save jointly is a *total* of $5,000.
4. If your spouse is a full-time student at least five months a year or is disabled and incapable of self-care, the IRS considers his or her income to be $2,400 if you have one dependent or $4,800 if you have two or more dependents. This is the maximum amount you could save in this account.

The annual amount you choose will be divided and deducted equally from your remaining paychecks in 2003.

Dependent Care FSA Versus Federal Tax Credit. In some situations, you may be better off using the federal tax credit on your income tax return instead of the Dependent Care FSA. Although your personal situation may vary, in general, if your total family income is less than $24,000 a year, the tax credit method will most likely be to your advantage. *Note:*The actual taxation of dependent care can be quite complicated. For more accurate information, you should consult a tax counselor.

More About Your Flex System Benefits

Who Is Eligible. All full-time Company employees who work at least 20 hours per week are eligible to participate in medical, dental, vision, long-term care, and FSAs through Flex System. Life, AD&D, and long-term disability insurance are available only to employees who work at least 30 hours per week.

Covering Your Family Members. You can cover certain family members under the medical plan, dental plan, vision plan, and dependent life insurance plan. Eligible family members include the following persons:

- Spouse
- Unmarried, dependent children under age 19
- Unmarried, dependent children age 19–25 who are full-time students
- Unmarried, dependent children age 19 and older who are not able to take care of themselves because of a physical or mental disability

The Pretax Advantage. With Flex System, you pay for most of your benefits with pretax dollars deducted from your pay. This means you make contributions before you pay federal or state taxes, as well as Social Security taxes. Lower taxes means you keep more of what you earn. Here's how it works:

	Without Flex System		**With Flex System**
When you use taxable dollars to pay for benefits, taxes are deducted first. Then your contributions are taken.	Annual Salary	When you use pretax dollars to pay for benefits, your benefit contributions are deducted from your pay first. Then your taxes are taken.	Annual Salary
	Taxes		Benefit/Costs
	Benefit/Costs		Taxes
	Take-Home Pay		Take-Home Pay

This means you are taxed on less income—you will have lower taxes and higher take-home pay than if the Company was not offering you this pretax advantage. The Company is doing its best to help keep your benefit costs as low as possible.

Other Benefits. Keep in mind that the Company provides many benefits in addition to your Flex System options. Many of these benefits are provided at no cost to you and include programs like the short-term disability plan, sick days, the Employee Assistance Plan, the 401(k) plan, vacation, and holidays.

To Enroll

Now you can make your Flex System enrollment decisions.

If You Do Not Want Any Flex System Benefits. If you do not want to take advantage of *any* Flex System benefits, then no action or response from you is necessary at this time. In a few weeks, you will receive a statement confirming that you have elected no coverage in 2003.

If You Want Flex System Benefits. If you want to take advantage of any of the Flex System coverages, you should complete Steps 1 and 2. After the end of the enrollment period, you will receive a statement confirming your Flex System coverage levels and the cost to you. In addition to the confirmation, you will receive any additional forms you need to complete.

If you have a hearing impairment and cannot use the telephone, or if you do not have access to a Touch-Tone telephone, please contact Human Resources for assistance.

IMPORTANT NOTE. Make your enrollment decisions carefully. Unless you have a qualified change in family status, you will not have another opportunity to enroll in options benefits until January 1, 2004, and each January 1 thereafter. At that time, some benefits may be limited, denied entirely, or subject to evidence of insurability.

Step 1

Enter Your Selections

Refer to Your Personal Fact Sheet for your selection choices. Enter the selection number of the benefit options you choose.

❒ Medical Plan Selection

❒ Medical Coverage Level
1 = You Only
2 = You + 1 Dependent
3 = You + Family

❒ Dental Plan Selection

❒ Dental Coverage Level
1 = You Only
2 = You + 1 Dependent
3 = You + Family

❒ Vision Plan Selection

❒ Long-Term Disability Selection

❒ Optional Life Insurance Selection

❒ Optional AD Insurance Selection

❒ Optional Dependent Life Insurance Selection

$__________ Health Care FSA—enter an annual $ amount (minimum $50; maximum $1,000)

$__________ Dependent Care FSA—enter an annual $ amount (minimum $50; maximum $5,000)

Step 2

Dial Flex System—1-800-111-1111

- Enter the Company access code __________
- Enter your Social Security number __________
- Enter the selections you made in Step 1. You will be prompted to enter each in turn until you hear "Your enrollment is complete."

Your enrollment is now complete. You can change your coverage as often as you like during the enrollment period—your last change will be the one that is effective. If you call more than once, you must reenter all your choices.

The Next Step Following the end of the enrollment period, you will receive a statement confirming your Flex System benefits elections.

Appendix E

Sample Flexible Benefits Resource Guide

Overview

Welcome to today's session. I'm _____________ from _____________. Today's presentation will give you an overview of our new flexible benefits program, called Flex System Benefits by Design. This presentation marks the beginning of our enrollment process. Don"t worry about getting all the details. Your enrollment materials contain the specifics about the enrollment process and your benefit choices.

In today's session, we'll give you an overview of the new flexible benefits program. We'll also go through some of the details of each of the benefits offered and the enrollment procedure. Finally, we'll have some time to respond to your questions. Please hold your questions until the end of our session—that way we'll be sure to get through all the material. We expect today's presentation to take about an hour.

Let's begin by looking at the objectives of this new program.

Program Objectives

- Control benefits costs
- Provide flexibility and choice

The goal of Flex System is to help the Company control benefits costs better while offering benefits choices that will continue to meet your needs. With this innovative new approach to benefits, you determine which benefit options make the most sense for you and how much coverage you should have.

If you decide that there are certain types of coverages that you don't need, you simply don't purchase those options. This way you can help control your benefits costs—as well as the Company's—because you select only the benefits that you and your family need.

Offer Opportunities for Tax Savings

- Pretax contributions
- Flexible spending accounts

In addition to controlling costs, Flex System offers two ways for you to save on taxes. If you need to contribute toward the Flex System coverages you've elected, your contributions are taken out of your paycheck before Social Security, federal, and most state income taxes are withheld. Your taxable income is reduced by the amount of your plan contributions. You also have an opportunity to save on taxes by paying for dependent care expenses and certain health care expenses through flexible spending accounts. We'll talk more about how these accounts work later in the presentation.

Benefit Choices Effective April 1, 2003

- Medical
- Dental
- Vision
- Long-term disability
- Life and AD&D insurance
- Flexible spending accounts

Flex System offers seven benefits from which to choose—medical, dental, vision, long-term disability, life and AD&D insurance, long-term care, and flexible spending accounts. Each plan has different options that provide various levels of coverage. You decide which benefits make the most sense for you. Any of the options may be paid on either a pretax or an after-tax basis. You decide which payment method is best for you.

Changes in Family Status

Your benefit elections will become effective on April 1, 2003. After the open enrollment period, changes are restricted. You can make changes to your benefit decisions only if you have a "qualified" reason to make a change as defined by the IRS. Qualified reasons to make a mid-year change to your election include the following:

- Your marriage or divorce
- The birth of or your adoption of a child
- Death of a spouse or dependent
- Gain or loss of your spouse's employment
- Relocation outside your provider's service area (medical only)

The new coverage must be requested within 31 days of the change and must be consistent with your reason for requesting the change.

Medical Plans

- Medical benefits have become increasingly expensive
- You and the Company can work together to manage medical costs
- The old medical plan will be replaced with new options

As you are probably aware, the cost of health care, which has been rising at an alarming rate for the past two decades, has yet to slow. Over the past several years, the Company has experienced significant cost increases that are not expected to stop or even slow down in the near future—unless we do something about it. That's why we are making some dramatic changes to our medical benefits—to better manage medical costs for both you and the Company.

Probably the most important change is that our old medical plan will no longer be available. Also, some new options will now be offered to Company associates:

- No coverage
- Preferred provider organization (PPO)
- Out-of-service area option
- Health maintenance organization (HMO)

Program Details. You have four categories of medical options. If you have coverage elsewhere, for instance, through a spouse's plan, a "no coverage" option is now available. In addition, the Company will offer associates across the country several medical plan choices, including health care delivery through a preferred provider organization (PPO), an indemnity medical plan called the out-of-service area option for those associates who live outside of the PPO service area, and the XYZ health maintenance organization (HMO). Your home zip code determines which of these options is available to you personally.

Let's take a minute now to go over all the options available at this location. Your Personal Fact Sheet details your options.

NO COVERAGE

- Must sign medical waiver
- If you choose a Company medical plan later, you may be subject to medical underwriting restrictions, unless you have been covered by another medical plan for at least one year, with less than a 63-day lapse in coverage

Program Details. If you have coverage through another plan—for instance, through your spouse's employer—it may make sense for you to choose "no coverage." If you choose this option, you will need to sign a waiver of medical coverage form.

When you choose "no coverage," you and your family will receive no medical benefits from the Company this year. You will have another opportunity to choose medical coverage during next year's open enrollment, or earlier if your spouse loses coverage before then.

PPO COVERAGE

- In-network
- Out-of-network

Program Details. A preferred provider organization—also called a PPO—features a network of doctors and hospitals who are committed to providing members with the highest quality care in the most cost-effective setting. This is a managed care plan, yet the PPO also offers members the freedom to go outside the network for care—and still receive benefits. When you join the PPO, you decide whether to go "in-network" or "out-of-network" each time you need treatment.

PPO COVERAGE IN-NETWORK

- No deductible
- 100 percent coverage after $50 copayment for emergency room care and a $10 copayment for all other services
- Claim forms may be required

Program Details. When you enroll, you receive a list of doctors and hospitals that belong to the PPO network. The list is included in your enrollment workbook and is called the XYZ Provider Listing.

Each time you receive care from a network provider, you will pay lower out-of-pocket costs. For instance, when you go to a network doctor, you will receive 100 percent coverage after paying a $50 copayment for emergency room care or a $10 copayment for most other services. You will not be required to pay an annual deductible. However, depending on your doctor's policy, you may need to pay for services up front and file a claim for reimbursement.

PPO COVERAGE OUT-OF-NETWORK

- $500 deductible for single coverage, $1,000 deductible for family coverage
- 80 percent reimbursement of the next $5,000, then the plan pays 100 percent
- 100 percent reimbursement of accident expenses, up to $500
- Claim forms are required

Program Details. If you decide to go outside the PPO, you will still receive benefits, but you will be responsible for more of the cost. For example, you'll need to satisfy a $500 deductible before receiving benefits for most services. Then the plan will reimburse you for 80 percent of the next $5,000. After your out-of-pocket costs reach $1,500, the plan pays 100 percent of covered expenses for the rest of the plan year. Out-of-network services are reimbursed on reasonable and customary charges, which are the charges made by most providers in your area for similar services. In addition, certain expenses—like those that result from accident—are always covered at 100 percent, up to a maximum of $500.

To receive payment from the plan for out-of-network services, you will need to file a claim for reimbursement.

OUT-OF-SERVICE AREA COVERAGE

- 100 percent reimbursement of hospital expenses
- $100 deductible
- 80 percent reimbursement of the next $2,500, then the plan pays 100 percent
- 100 percent reimbursement of accident expenses, up to $500
- Claim forms are required

Program Details. If you live in an area where the PPO network is not available, you may elect the Out-of-Service Area option. This plan covers hospitalizations in full, with no deductible. For all other expenses, you must pay a deductible of $100 per person, $200 per family. The plan then pays 80 percent of the next $2,500 of your covered expenses ($5,000 per family). Then, the plan pays 100 percent of covered expenses for the rest of that year. In addition, accident expenses are always covered at 100 percent, up to a maximum of $500.

To receive payment from the plan, you will need to file a claim for reimbursement.

XYZ HMO COVERAGE

- Full coverage for most services after $10 copayment
- No deductible
- No coverage for care not authorized by your primary care physician
- No claim forms are needed

Program Details. XYZ HMO is available in many locations. The benefits available from these HMO options are the same—but the participating providers vary. The HMO listing in your enrollment workbook is called the network listing.

When you enroll in an HMO, you will receive a list of doctors and facilities that belong to the HMO network. You will need to choose a primary care physician (PCP) from this list. As long as your health care is arranged for or provided by your PCP, most of your expenses will be covered at 100 percent with no deductible. You may be required to make a $10 copayment for some services, like office visits, or a $50 copayment for emergency room care. With the HMO options, no claim forms are required.

Note: Health care that is not arranged for or provided by your PCP will not be covered.

PRESCRIPTION DRUG BENEFITS

- Prescription drug card
  —$8 generic drugs
  —$20 brand-name drugs
- Mail-order service
  —Maintenance drugs covered in full
  —No copayment or deductible

Program Details. No matter which medical option you choose—PPO, out-of-area, or HMO coverage—you will receive prescription drug benefits through a prescription drug card and mail-order service.

Your prescription drug card allows you to obtain prescriptions quickly and easily from participating pharmacies. When you go to a participating pharmacy, simply present your card and pay $8 for a 30-day supply of a generic prescription or $20 for a 30-day supply of a brand-name prescription.

With the mail-order service, you can receive up to a 90-day supply of a maintenance prescription—such as high blood pressure medicine—while paying only one deductible. This can save you money compared to paying a monthly deductible for a new prescription every month.

WELLNESS BENEFITS

- Routine physical exams
- Medically necessary nutritional counseling

- Smoking cessation patch
- Healthy pregnancy
- Well baby care
- Immunizations

Program Details. All the medical plans also feature wellness benefits—like coverage for routine physical exams, medically necessary nutritional counseling, and the smoking cessation patch. More information about these benefits will be included in the plan materials you receive after your coverage becomes effective.

Dental Plans

- No coverage
- High-option
- Low-option

Program Details. You have three dental options—no coverage, high-option dental, or low-option dental. If you have coverage elsewhere—for instance, through a spouse's plan—a "no coverage" option is now available. If you choose no coverage, you and your family will not receive dental benefits from the Company this year. You may join the plan again during next year's open enrollment, or earlier if you have a qualified change in family status.

HIGH-OPTION DENTAL COVERAGE

- Annual deductible: $50
- Coverages
  - —100 percent for preventive care (cleanings, X-rays); no deductible
  - —80 percent for minor restorative services (fillings, extractions)
  - —50 percent for major restorative services (crowns, bridges, dentures)
  - —50 percent for orthodontics; no deductible
- Annual maximum: $2,500 per person per year
- Orthodontic lifetime maximum: $2,500 per person

Program Details. The high-option dental plan matches the old Company dental plan, except you will now be asked to contribute toward the cost of this coverage. The plan features 100 percent reimbursement, with no deductible, for preventive services; 80 percent reimbursement for minor restorative services; and 50 percent reimbursement for major restorative services after you pay a $50 annual deductible. The plan also reimburses orthodontics at 50 percent, with no deductible. Dental services are reimbursed on reasonable and customary charges, which are the charges made by most providers in your area for similar services.

Under the high-option coverage, the calendar-year maximum for dental benefits is $2,500 and the lifetime maximum for orthodontics is $2,500.

LOW-OPTION DENTAL COVERAGE

- Annual deductible: $50
- Coverages
  —100 percent for preventive care (cleanings, X-rays); no deductible
  —80 percent for minor restorative services (fillings, extractions)
  —50 percent for major restorative services (crowns, bridges, dentures)
- Annual maximum: $1,000 per person per year
- No orthodontic coverage

Program Details. The low-option dental is the same as high-option dental, except the maximum benefit each year is limited to $1,000, there is no coverage for orthodontics, and your contribution each pay period is lower.

Vision Care Plan

- No coverage (medical plan covers annual eye exam)
- Vision care coverage
  —Up to $50 for a routine eye exam
  —Up to $200 for frames and lenses
  —Up to $200 for contact lenses (if elected instead of eyeglasses)
  —No coverage for out-of-network providers

Program Details. One of the new benefits available through Flex System is the vision care plan. This program is designed to keep the cost of routine eye examinations, lenses, frames, and contacts more affordable. You may choose between two vision options—no coverage or coverage.

If you choose no coverage, you and your family will not receive vision benefits from the Company this year. However, if you enroll in one of the Flex System medical options, you will receive full coverage for an annual eye exam, up to a maximum of $50. You will have another chance to join the vision plan during next year's open enrollment, or earlier if you have a qualified change in family status.

Program Details. The vision care plan is similar to an HMO. When you enroll in the plan, you will receive a list of participating vision care providers. If you go to one of these providers, you will receive full coverage for an annual eye exam, up to a maximum of $50; full coverage for frames and lenses each year, up to a maximum of $200; and full coverage for contact lenses elected instead of eyeglasses, up to a maximum of $200 per year.

Long-Term Disability Plan

- Full coverage, at no cost, is automatically provided to employees whose annual base salary is $30,000 or less
- Employees with an annual salary over $30,000 pay full cost or may opt out of coverage
- Benefit begins after 180 days of disability
- Benefit equals 60 percent of monthly salary
- Benefit reduced by disability income from other sources
- Maximum monthly benefit $21,000
- Preexisting condition limitation

Program Details. Another feature of Flex System is long-term disability (LTD) coverage. This valuable benefit replaces part of your earnings if you become disabled and can't work for an extended period. If you pay toward the cost of premiums on a pretax basis, any benefits received will be taxable income. If you pay the cost of premiums with after-tax dollars, benefits you might receive are not taxed.

If your annual base salary is $30,000 or less, Flex System provides LTD coverage automatically, at no cost to you. If your annual salary is over $30,000, you pay the full cost of LTD coverage with either pretax or after-tax dollars. Therefore, Flex System offers you the option of waiving or electing LTD coverage on a pretax basis or an after-tax basis.

Here's how LTD coverage works. If you are disabled for longer than 180 days, the LTD benefit will replace 60 percent of your monthly salary, up to a maximum monthly benefit of $21,000. Your benefit is reduced by any disability income you receive from other sources—like workers' compensation or Social Security.

If you are age 60 or younger at the time of your disability, in most cases benefits will continue to be paid until you recover or reach age 65, whichever is sooner. If you are older than age 60 at the time of your disability, benefits will continue to be paid as long as you remain disabled, up to scheduled limits.

The LTD plan contains a preexisting condition limitation. This means that benefits will not be paid for disabilities that result from an injury or illness that occurs during the 24-month period before your LTD coverage originally became effective. This limit won't apply after you've had LTD coverage for 12 months and have not been treated for the condition.

In general, this means that the preexisting condition limitation only applies to associates electing Company coverage for the first time after April 1, 2000. In addition, this limitation also applies on benefit amounts that exceed $15,000.

Basic Life Insurance and Accidental Death and Dismemberment (AD&D)

- 2 × salary (plus bonus and commissions) + $10,000

Program Details. Another feature of Flex System is basic life and AD&D insurance. These plans provide life insurance coverage equal to two times your salary, plus $10,000 at no cost to you. At the time of enrollment, evidence of good health may be required.

The amount of your coverage will be rounded to the next higher $1,000, unless it is already an even multiple of $1,000. For example, if your salary is $24,750, your basic coverage would be $60,000 ($24,750 2 = $49,500, which rounds up to $50,000 + $10,000 = $60,000).

ADDITIONAL LIFE INSURANCE OPTIONS

Your life and AD&D insurance amounts are based on your age and salary as of January 1, 2003, plus bonus and commissions from 2002. These premiums are paid by you with after-tax dollars.

- 1 × salary (plus bonus and commissions)
- 2 × salary (plus bonus and commissions)
- 3 × salary (plus bonus and commissions)
- 4 × salary (plus bonus and commissions)

(Maximum—$760,000)

Program Details. If you want additional life insurance, you may choose coverage equaling from one to four times your annual salary.

You may choose as much additional life insurance coverage as you want, up to an overall maximum of $760,000. If the amount you choose equals (or is less than) your current amount of Company life insurance, no further action is required. However, if you choose more than your current amount of life insurance, you may need to provide evidence of your good health. For instance, evidence will be required if your total amount of life insurance exceeds four times your salary or $600,000.

ADDITIONAL AD&D INSURANCE OPTIONS

- 1 × salary (plus bonus and commissions)
- 2 × salary (plus bonus and commissions)
- 3 × salary (plus bonus and commissions)
- 4 × salary (plus bonus and commissions)

Program Details. You may also purchase additional AD&D insurance—from one to four times your annual salary—that will pay your beneficiaries a benefit if you die as a result of an accident. Under this policy, benefits are also payable for certain types of physical loss, such as loss of a hand, foot, or eye.

AD&D COVERAGE

- Loss of life—full benefit
- Loss of both hands, both feet, or sight in both eyes—full benefit
- Loss of one hand, one foot, or sight of one eye—one-half the full benefit

Program Details. For loss of life, both hands, both feet, or sight in both eyes—as a result of an accident—you (or your beneficiaries) will receive the full benefit amount. This is paid in addition to any life insurance benefit, if applicable. For loss of one hand, one foot, or sight of one eye, the plan pays you one half of your full benefit amount.

Flexible Spending Accounts (FSAs)

- Health care FSA
- Dependent care FSA

Program Details. The flexible spending accounts are another important new option available from Flex System. These accounts allow you to put aside a portion of your salary—before it is taxed—into special accounts from which you are reimbursed for qualified health care and dependent care expenses.

FSAs can help save you money on your taxes and lower your out-of-pocket costs for health and dependent care. Because the money that goes into your FSA is deducted from your pay before federal, Social Security, and most state taxes are withheld, you pay less in taxes and ultimately have more disposable income.

HEALTH CARE FSA

- Eligible expenses
  —Deductibles and copayments
  —Expenses in excess of reasonable and customary charges
  —Other expenses not covered by your medical, dental, or vision plans
- Minimum contribution: $50/year
- Maximum contribution: $3,000/year

Program Details. Most health care expenses not covered by your medical, dental, or vision care plan can be reimbursed through the health care FSA. For example, if you went to an out-of-network PPO doctor, incurred a charge of $100 for the office visit, and the PPO paid $80 of that fee, the remaining $20 would be considered an unreimbursed medical expense and could be submitted to the health care FSA for reimbursement.

Generally, any health care expenses that qualify under the Internal Revenue Code definition of deductible medical expenses for your federal tax return will qualify for reimbursement. A complete list of eligible expenses may be obtained from the IRS by calling 1-800-829-3676. Keep in mind, however, that the publication the IRS distributes is intended for individual taxpayers. Some very important differences between medical expense reimbursement through an FSA, and deduction of medical expense as a taxpayer are (1) expenses must be *incurred* during the plan year for the FSA, and (2) premium payments are not a reimbursable expense through an FSA.

You can set aside from a minimum of $50 up to a maximum of $3,000 in 2003. The annual amount you choose will be divided and deducted equally from your remaining paychecks in 2003. The only expenses that can be reimbursed from your health care FSA are those that you incur during the benefit period—from April 1 through December 31, 2003.

DEPENDENT CARE FSA

- Eligible dependents
  - —Your child(ren) under age 13
  - —Your disabled spouse or other disabled dependent (such as an elderly parent)
  - —if care is outside your home, the dependent must spend at least 8 hours/day in your home
- Eligible expenses
- Minimum contribution: $50/year
  - —Day care centers
  - —Nursery schools
  - —Baby-sitters
  - —Home care specialists
- Maximum contribution: $5,000/year

Program Details. Generally, any dependent care expense that you (and your spouse if you are married) must pay in order for you (and your spouse) to be able to work can be reimbursed through the dependent care FSA. Dependent care expenses that qualify under the Internal Revenue Code definition of deductible dependent/child care expenses for your federal tax return will qualify for reimbursement. A complete list of eligible expenses may be obtained from the IRS by calling 1-800-829-3676.

You can set aside from a minimum of $50 up to a maximum of $5,000 in 2003. The annual amount you choose will be divided and deducted equally from your remaining paychecks in 2003. The only expenses that can be reimbursed from your dependent care FSA are those that you incur during the benefit period—from April 1 through December 31, 2003.

REQUESTING REIMBURSEMENT

- Obtain claim form from Human Resources
- Return form to the FSA administrator

Program Details. To request reimbursement for an eligible FSA expense, follow these steps:

1. Obtain an FSA claim form from Human Resources. Subsequent claim forms will be sent to you along with your reimbursement checks.
2. Complete the form and return it with a copy of your invoice, explanation of benefits, or receipt to the FSA program administrator.

For dependent care expenses, requests will be paid up to the balance in your dependent care FSA. If your claim is larger than your account balance, it will be held until further contributions are made to your account. For health care expenses, if your request totals more than the balance in your account, you will be reimbursed up to the *total* amount you elected to contribute for the year, minus any amounts already reimbursed.

THINGS TO CONSIDER ABOUT FSAs

- Forfeiture of unused funds
- No transfers between accounts
- The health care or dependent care tax credit may be better

Program Details. Since FSAs offer tax advantages, the IRS imposes these restrictions on their use:

1. The IRS requires that you use all the money in your FSAs for expenses you incur during 2003. If you don't use all the money in your FSAs by the end of the year, the balance will be forfeited; this is called the "use-it-or-lose-it" rule. Because of this rule, you should carefully and conservatively estimate your health care and dependent care expenses.
2. If you enroll in both FSAs, you may not transfer money from one FSA to the other. Your health care FSA remains totally separate from your dependent care FSA.

In addition, depending on your personal situation, the health care and/or dependent care federal tax credit may be better for you. Consult a tax specialist for advice about which approach is better for you.

Enrollment Process

Now that you have a better understanding of your Flex System choices, it's time to make your enrollment decisions and join. The enrollment period runs from February 7 through February 13. You must enroll by February 13.

- Open enrollment—February 7 through February 13
- Program effective April 1, 2003

To enroll, you will use the Flex System Phone Line, our new automated enrollment system. The Flex System Phone Line will let you make your 2003 benefit choices quickly and accurately, using a Touch-Tone telephone. After the end of the enrollment period, you will receive a confirmation statement that allows you to verify your selections—before they become effective.

Complete instructions about how to use the Flex System Phone Line, including all the appropriate numbers, are included in your enrollment workbook. But take a minute to review how easy the Flex System Phone Line is to use.

First, call the Flex System Phone Line number. Enter the Company access code, and then enter *your* nine-digit Social Security number. (If your spouse makes the call for you, he or she must enter *your* Social Security number.) The system will then ask you to enter your enrollment choices, beginning with medical. The system will confirm your medical choice and then ask for your dental choice and so on until you've entered your choices for all the benefit options.

At that point, you will hear "Your enrollment is complete." After you make your enrollment telephone call, you may change your decisions by calling the Flex System Phone Line again and going through all the steps again. Your last telephone call to the system will be used to update your records and create the confirmation statement that you will receive at the end of the enrollment period.

DEFAULT PLAN

- No coverage

Enrollment Process. If you do not make an enrollment telephone call by February 13, 2003, you will receive *no* Flex System coverages. However, you will still be eligible for certain standard benefits you receive from the Company—such as the employee assistance plan, sick days, the short-term disability plan, 401(k) plan, vacations, and holidays.

TRANSITION ISSUES

- Submit claims incurred *before* April 1, 2003, to Former Administrators
- Submit claims incurred on or after April 1, 2003, to XYZ New Administrators
- Submit a copy of your last Former Administrators EOB Form to XYZ New Administrators with your first claim
- If you are on TDY, special enrollment provisions may apply—contact Human Resources
- Contact Human Resources if you were hired after January 21, 2003
- Contact Human Resources if you are receiving ongoing medical treatment (including pregnancy)

Enrollment Process. ____

____

Figure 1. Company Health Care Continuum

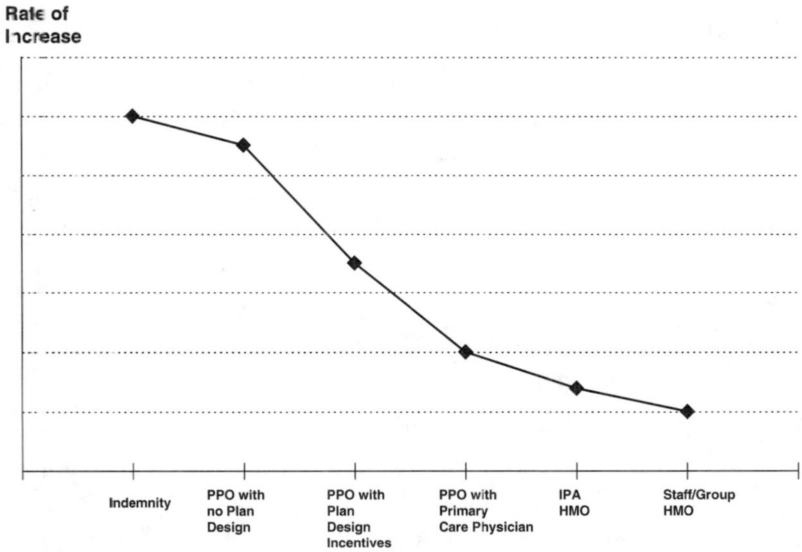

Meeting Materials and Presentation Format

These instructions are provided to help you

- Become familiar with the materials you are receiving
- Understand what equipment you will need to present the material to your audiences and
- Organize and make effective presentations

MATERIALS FOR ASSOCIATE MEETINGS

- The script and overheads for the meetings (included at the beginning of this guide)
- A copy of each of the printed communications associates have received, including
  —A series of two informational newsletters through internal mail
  —An enrollment kit and personal fact sheet at home. These were mailed to homes to involve family members in the communication process.

EQUIPMENT

For your meetings, you should arrange to have the following equipment on hand and tested:

- Overhead projector or computer and LCD projector for Power Point presentation
- Any necessary extension cords

- Blackboard or easel and chart pad for illustrating answers to employees' questions

MEETING AGENDA

Each session should run approximately one hour. Each meeting should consist of the following segments:

- A brief introduction, 3 minutes
- A description of the plan details and review of the printed materials (with overhead transparencies or Power Point presentation as a guide), 40 minutes
- Closing remarks, 2 minutes
- Employees' questions, 15 minutes

GUIDELINES FOR EFFECTIVE PRESENTATIONS

- Begin the meeting promptly at the scheduled time.
- As people enter the room, speak to them and establish contact. Be welcoming, enthusiastic, and positive.
- When you give your introductory comments, face your audience and speak to them directly. Establish eye contact and try to project your voice to the people in the rear of the room.
- Your attitude will be contagious, so be enthusiastic.
- You'll want to put the scripted comments that are in the overhead presentation into your own words. The important thing is *what* you say and *how* you say it—not necessarily the specific words you use.

RESPONDING TO QUESTIONS

The primary purpose of these enrollment meetings is to answer questions about Flex System and to encourage employees to make the best benefit selections for them personally. Employees may not fully understand the plans or their choices until they have had a chance to think them over and ask questions. Try to remain focused on what is changing and how Flex System improves on the current program.

The questions and answers session will provide an opportunity for employees to listen to other employees' questions and to clarify points that may have occurred to them during the presentation. It should be an informal gathering. Your job is to encourage questions and answer them as fully as possible.

It would be unrealistic to expect that you can answer every question that might come up in a meeting. If you can't answer a question, write it down and contact Human Resources for the answer. Then, make sure you follow up with that person later.

HINTS FOR PRESENTERS

- Center the overhead.

- Have hard copy of overheads for each employee. This will make it easier for employees to follow your presentation and take notes.
- Speak facing your audience. Do not turn your back on the audience to read the overhead screen.
- Speak slowly and distinctly. Because of the amount of information you must cover, you may have a tendency to speak too quickly. Be conscious of this and avoid rushing.
- Try not to be nervous. You are "the expert" in the sense that you probably know more about this subject than any member of your audience. If you don't know the answer to a question, make a note and let the employee know you'll get back to him or her. Remember, you are providing these information sessions as a further help to employees. Employees are attending these sessions in addition to—not instead of—reading the printed materials provided.
- If you need "crib notes," consider jotting your notes on the frame of each overhead.
- Lighten up! Although this is a serious topic, there's no reason why it can't be fun for both you and the audience.
- We've prepared a narrative for all the overheads. Without changing the content, feel free to rephrase what you don't feel comfortable with. That way, your presentation will truly be your own.

HANDLING QUESTIONS AND ANSWERS

Here are three steps to follow when a question is asked:

1. **Repeat it** to be sure you understand and the whole group has heard it.
2. **Answer it** as directly, briefly, and as clearly as possible. Do not permit the discussion—yours or someone else's—to go off on a tangent.
3. **Check** the questioner to be sure your answer was clear and satisfactory; if not, repeat the process.

If you follow this procedure, the two primary objectives of your meeting—that everyone present feels he or she understands the program and that no one leaves with questions ignored—will be accomplished:

- Many people hesitate to speak first. Be prepared to stimulate discussion if employees do not readily volunteer questions. Have a few questions to raise that are likely to begin a discussion.
- It is important to listen carefully and avoid indicating what you expect or want to hear. If you anticipate what will be said, it is difficult to listen well.
- Try to remain the focus of attention. One way to draw attention back to you is by using a blackboard or easel to illustrate an answer. Or use one of your overhead transparencies.

- When answering questions, you should talk to people—look them in the eye.

- Questions should be answered honestly. An audience is quick to spot a half-answer or half-truth. When they do, your credibility suffers. If you don't know the answer, just say so and assure the associate that you'll get back to him or her. The group will respect you if you are honest and take responsibility for getting back to them with answers. Guessing and giving the wrong answer is far worse than admitting that you don't know but that you'll find out.

- Be brief. Answer a question simply and concisely; then move on to the next one.

- If individual members of the group engage in lengthy and complex questioning, express a willingness to stay after the session or to meet with them later to discuss their concerns in greater detail.

The Questions and Answers section of this guide will give you an idea of the types of questions you may hear and includes answers that have been prepared for your review and study. Remember, these are anticipated questions and suggested answers. You"ll probably hear some questions not contained in the Questions and Answers section of the guide. If there are questions you can't answer, be sure to write them down so you can follow up later.

Meeting Questions Response Form

(For meeting leader's use in noting questions for later response. Contact Human Resources for answers to these questions.)

Q: ____

____

____

Associate name ______________________________

Location/address ______________________________

Phone ______________________________

Q: ____

____

____

Associate name ______________________________

Location/address ______________________________

Phone ______________________________

Q: ____

____

____

Associate name ______________________________

Location/address ______________________________

Phone ______________________________

Q: ____

____

____

Associate name ______________________________

Location/address ______________________________

Phone ______________________________

Q: ____

____

____

Associate name ______________________________

Location/address ______________________________

Phone ______________________________

Questions and Answers

GENERAL

1. *Why is the Company introducing the new Flex System?*

Our benefits program has been in place since the company's inception; however, benefits costs have risen at an alarming rate—especially in the health care area. After much analysis, including careful review of employees' input from the employee benefits survey, the Company developed Flex System—Benefits by Design. The Company believes that this flexible benefits program will offer more predictable costs, choices, and some new coverages for you and your family.

2. *Why are we changing our medical plan?*

As you know, the Company has grown dramatically over the past several years. In addition, health care costs have been increasing exponentially and the definition of "family" has expanded to include more two-worker and single-parent families. With all these changes, it's no wonder that our old health care plan was no longer meeting the needs of the company and associates. We are changing our medical plan to help make sure that the plan works for both you and the Company. The new PPO (preferred provider organization) approach will control costs for you and the Company, while offering you the freedom to choose the kind of care that's best for you and your family.

3. *Who was involved in making these decisions regarding the Company's benefits program?*

The Company established the Benefits Review Committee, an eight-person team, consisting of Company employees from across the country. They thoroughly reviewed the current Company benefits program and compared it to the "best practices" of other companies. They then analyzed the needs of individual employees by conducting the recent employee benefits survey. After developing the new approach, the Benefits Review Committee took their recommendations to senior management for approval. Upon reviewing the committee's recommendations, senior management gave its approval and instructions to implement the new flexible benefits program as quickly as possible.

4. *How are other companies dealing with the "health care crisis"*?

Most companies today are implementing some sort of managed care strategy. In fact, health care experts predict that by the next century almost all American companies will have switched to managed care programs. The focus on national health care reform has also caused many companies to put managed care programs in place in anticipation of more stringent federal requirements.

5. *Do many companies have PPO plans?*

Yes. More and more companies in the United States are looking for creative solutions to the problem of increasing health care costs. Preferred provider organizations are emerging as one viable alternative to the more expensive and less manageable indemnity plans.

6. *Why do we have to begin contributing toward the cost of our medical benefits?*

In 2002 the Company spent about $6 million for employee benefits. It doesn't make sense for the company to pay that kind of money for coverage that you may not need or for plans that you don't want. In addition, the responsibility for controlling the rising costs of health care must now be borne by employees as well as by the Company.

7. *Is it to the Company's advantage for me to pick one plan over another?*

No advantage or disadvantage to the Company will result from your medical plan choice.

8. *Explain what you mean by "pretax" contributions.*

Any contributions you make for medical, dental, and vision coverage will be made before federal, FICA and, in most states, state and local taxes are withheld. This results in an overall reduction in the amount of taxes deducted from your salary each week.

9. *What happens if the government changes the rules in the future and pretax contributions are no longer allowed?*

The Company offers the pretax feature based on the provisions of Section 125 of the Internal Revenue Code (IRC), which is subject to change at any time. This could result in a reduction or even a loss of this feature. If this were to happen, your payroll deduction would remain the same, but employees would lose this tax advantage. The Company currently intends to make this feature available as long as it is approved by the IRS. You will be notified of any changes in this feature.

10. *Can I change my enrollment choices at any time during the year?*

In most cases, you will not be able to change your enrollment choices during the year. This restriction is set by the IRC—not by the Company.

Exceptions to this restriction are as follows: If you are enrolled in an HMO or the PPO and you relocate away from the HMO or PPO service area, you may change your medical choice at that time. In addition, you will be able to change coverages (individual vs. family) between open enrollment periods if you have a change in family status or employment status. Other changes to your cost or coverage may permit a change in election during the plan year.

Because of these restrictions, it is important that you make the appropriate selection about your medical coverage. If you do not, you will not be allowed to make any changes until the next open enrollment period.

11. *Why are there restrictions on when I can change my coverage?*

Section 125 of the IRC, which allows pretax contributions for medical, dental, and vision premiums, imposes restrictions on how often and under what circumstances you can change your medical or dental plan or coverage level.

12. *What qualifies as a change in status?*

The following events are defined as changes in status:

- Addition of a dependent through marriage, birth, or adoption
- Loss of a dependent through death or divorce
- Gain or loss of a dependent as a result of a change in the dependent's eligibility status under the medical and dental plans
- Spouse's employment or loss of employment
- Switch from part-time to full-time status, or vice versa
- Significant change in health coverage, attributable to spouse's employment
- Unpaid leave of absence for employee or spouse
- Relocation outside your medical plan's service area

13. *Will another open enrollment period occur next year?*

Yes. Open enrollment periods generally occur on an annual basis. Next fall and each fall thereafter, you will once again be asked to evaluate your benefits choices and select the coverages that best meet your needs and the needs of your family. These choices will become effective the following January 1.

14. *How can I decide which medical choice is better for me and my family—PPO or HMO?*

You need to ask yourself the following questions:

- What kind of medical services will my family and I need over the next year?
- Will these services include hospitalization and/or surgery?
- Do I prefer the HMO structure or the in-network and out-of-network features of the PPO?

Remember, if you join an HMO, most services are covered at 100 percent after a $10 copayment. If you join the PPO and use an in-network physician, most services are covered at 100 percent after your copayment. If you choose an out-of-network provider, your benefits are a $500 deductible ($1,000/family); 100 percent reimbursement of expenses for an accident, up to $500; and 80 percent reimbursement of the next $5,000 ($10,000/family), then 100 percent for additional expenses during the rest of the year.

MEDICAL

15. *What if I join the PPO and then decide that I would rather join an HMO; when can I change my coverage choice?*

You can only change your coverage selection at open enrollment or if you have a qualified change in family status. (See Q 12 for more details.)

16. *What is the claim filing procedure for the PPO plan?*

Inside the PPO network, depending on your doctor's policy, you may need to pay for services up front and file a claim for reimbursement, or you may simply pay your copayment and your doctor will take care of filing the claim. If you go outside the network, you will always have to file a claim for reimbursement. Claim forms are available in Human Resources.

17. *Can you explain the difference between "in-network" and "out-of-network"?*

A PPO, or preferred provider organization, is a network made up of member physicians and other health care providers, usually in a geographic area, that agree to provide services at a lower cost to companies participating in the PPO.

If you choose an "in-network" provider from the PPO member list, most of your services are covered in full after a $50 copayment for emergency room services and after a $10 copayment for nonemergency services.

"Out-of-network" refers to health care providers that are not members of the PPO network. If you choose to go to a physician outside the network, after you pay a $500 deductible ($1,000/family), the plan pays 80 percent of the next $5,000 ($10,000/family), after which the plan pays 100 percent.

18 *Can I enroll my dependents in the PPO, but enroll myself in the HMO?*

No. You must choose one health care option to cover yourself and your eligible family members.

19. *Why is the PPO not available in some areas?*

At this time, the XYZ PPO is not available in all locations. As the network expands into new areas, the PPO will be offered in those locations, too.

20. *If I join the PPO, can I receive care from a doctor who is not affiliated with the network and still receive coverage?*

Yes. However, you will receive a lower benefit for treatment received outside the PPO.

21. *If I join the PPO and have an emergency, how is that handled?*

If you have an emergency and go to an in-network doctor, you will receive 100 percent coverage for emergency room care after you pay a $50 copayment. If you go to an out-of-network physician, you are covered at 100 percent, up to a maximum of $500.

22. *Can you review the differences between the PPO and the XYZ HMO?*

Through the PPO, you have the freedom to choose any doctor and still receive some level of coverage. Through the XYZ HMO, if you receive care from a doctor outside the HMO, you must pay the full cost of these services.

23. *Since I have medical coverage through my spouse's plan, I want to choose the "no coverage" option under Flex System. What kind of proof of other coverage must I provide?*

If you choose the no coverage option, you do not have to provide proof of coverage. However, you must sign a waiver, which you will receive along with written confirmation of your Flex System benefits elections. Please sign and return the waiver form promptly to Human Resources.

24. *If I waive medical coverage, is my dental coverage affected?*

No. Your dental election is totally separate from your medical plan choice. The Flex System allows you to choose from three dental coverages—no coverage, high-option, and low-option—and decide which one makes the most sense for you and your family, no matter which medical plan you choose.

25. *Can I waive medical coverage and still participate in the health care flexible spending account (FSA)?*

Yes. If you choose the no coverage option, you can still participate in the health care FSA.

26. *If I join the PPO and go out-of-network, is there medical review for hospitalization or surgery?*

Yes. In order to receive full coverage for out-of-network hospitalizations, you must contact XYZ to certify that the hospital is the most appropriate place for your care. If you do not comply with this preadmission review requirement, your benefit will be reduced by $500. In addition, the plan features a voluntary surgical opinion program that provides benefits for second opinions prior to surgery.

27. *What are "reasonable and customary" charges?*

"Reasonable and customary" charges are defined as the usual costs for comparable treatment, services, or supplies for similar medical conditions in your geographic area.

28. *Who determines which charges are reasonable and customary?*

XYZ determines what is reasonable and customary. Certain cases may warrant special consideration because of unforeseen complications or other reasons. In all cases, these charges are based on an attempt to protect the patient, while not interfering unnecessarily with the provider's right to establish his or her own fees.

29. *Does the PPO feature any "wellness" programs?*

Yes. All medical options offered to Company employees include such wellness options as the following:

- Routine physicals
- Well baby care
- Immunizations
- Healthy pregnancy
- Certain nutritional counseling
- Smoking cessation patch

30. *How are prescription drugs covered under the PPO? How about the XYZ HMO?*

Prescription drugs are covered uniformly, no matter which medical option you choose. Your prescription drug card allows you to obtain prescriptions quickly and easily from participating pharmacies. You will receive 100 percent coverage after you pay a $8 copayment for generic drugs and $20 for brand-name prescriptions when you show your prescription drug card to a participating pharmacist.

In addition, a mail-order prescription drug service allows you to obtain a 90-day supply of maintenance prescriptions after paying one $8 or $20 copayment.

31. *How will I know whether or not I live outside the PPO service area?*

Your personal fact sheet, located in the back pocket of your enrollment workbook, will indicate if you live in an area outside the PPO service area.

32. *If I live outside the PPO service area, what medical plans are available?*

You may be eligible to participate in the XYZ HMO. If you prefer, you may also choose the out-of-service medical option, which reimburses your eligible expenses at the PPO's out-of-network rate, except the plan covers hospitalizations in full, with no deductible, and features a lower annual deductible.

DENTAL

33. *How do the Flex System dental plans compare to the current dental plan?*

In the new Flex System, the high-option dental matches the old Company dental plan, except you will now be asked to contribute toward the cost of this coverage. In addition, a low coverage option—one that doesn't cover orthodontia—and a no coverage option are now available.

34. *Is coverage available for orthodontics?*

Yes. Under the high-option dental coverage, the plan reimburses orthodontics at 50 percent, with no deductible and a lifetime maximum of $2,500.

VISION

35. *How does the vision care plan work?*

The vision care plan works much the same as an HMO. When you enroll in the vision plan, you will receive a list of participating vision care providers. If you go to one of these providers, you receive full coverage for up to $50 for a routine eye exam, up to $200 for frames and lenses (combined), and up to $200 for contact lenses (elected instead of eyeglasses). If you go outside the vision plan network, no coverage is available.

36. *Are there any limits on the frequency of covered eye exams, lenses, or frames?*

Yes. The plan pays for eye exams and contact lenses or eyeglasses only once annually per covered family member.

37. *What if I go outside the vision network for care?*

If you go outside the vision network for care, no benefits are provided by the vision plan. However, if you enroll in one of the Flex System medical options, your medical plan may provide coverage for an annual eye exam, up to a maximum of $50.

LONG-TERM DISABILITY (LTD) INSURANCE

38. *What qualifies as a disability under the LTD plan?*

If you earn $50,000 or more per year, you are considered disabled if, after 180 days of disability, you remain unable to perform the essential duties of your regular job.

If you earn less than $50,000 per year, you are considered disabled if, after 180 days of disability, you remain unable to perform the essential duties of your regular job and if, after two years, you are unable to perform any other position the company identifies you are capable of performing by virtue of skill, training, and experience.

39. *If a disability starts after age 60, how long are benefits available?*

If you are disabled after age 60, your LTD benefits are payable according to this schedule:

Age When Disability Begins	*Maximum Benefits Period*
61	4 years
62	3 1/2 years
63	2 3/4 years
64	2 years
65	2 years
66	1 3/4 years
67	1 1/2 years
68	1 1/4 years
69 and over	1 year

40. *Are there limits on the payment of disability benefits?*

Yes. The LTD plan will not pay benefits for any disability that results from

- War, acts of war, participation in a riot; or
- Intentionally self-inflicted injuries.

In addition, the LTD plan contains a preexisting condition limitation. This means that benefits will not be paid for disabilities that result from an injury or illness that occurs during the 24-month period before your LTD coverage originally became effective. This limitation no longer applies after you have been a member of the plan for 12 months and are not treated for the condition during that period. In general, this means that the preexisting condition limitation applies to associates electing Company coverage for the first time on or after April 1, 2003. In addition, the preexisting condition limitation also applies on any amounts over $15,000.

LIFE AND AD&D INSURANCE

41. *In some instances, I may be required to provide evidence of good health. What does this mean?*

Evidence of good health is necessary to obtain certain amounts of excess life and LTD insurance. It provides medical certification to the insurer stating you have no preexisting medical conditions that would otherwise disqualify you from receiving coverage.

42. *Who can I name as the beneficiary of my life insurance benefit?*

You may name anyone you wish as beneficiary of your life insurance benefit.

43. *When does the AD&D plan pay a benefit?*

The AD&D plan pays a benefit if you die as a result of an accident or if you lose a hand, foot, or eye. Here's how the benefit works. For loss of life, both hands, both feet, or sight in both eyes—as the result of an accident—you (or your beneficiary) will receive the full benefit amount. For loss of one hand, one foot, or sight of one eye, the plan pays you one half of your full benefit amount.

FLEXIBLE SPENDING ACCOUNTS (FSAs)

44. *What are FSAs?*

FSAs, or flexible spending accounts, allow you to put aside a portion of your salary—before it is taxed—into special accounts from which you are reimbursed for qualified health care and dependent care expenses.

FSAs can help you save taxes and lower your out-of-pocket costs for health and dependent care because the money that goes into your account is deducted from your pay before federal, Social Security, and most state and local taxes are withheld.

45. *Can the Company use any of my FSA money?*

No.

46. *Who administers the FSAs?*

Bigest Benefit Systems.

47. *Where do I call if I have a question about a claim?*

Call Human Resources if you have a question about a claim.

48. *Can I participate in both the health care FSA and the dependent care FSA?*

Yes. However, you make separate contributions to each account. You cannot transfer contributions back and forth between the two accounts.

49. *What happens if I don't use all the money in my FSA during the year?*

The use-it-or-lose-it rule requires that you forfeit any amounts left in either your health care or dependent care FSAs at the end of the year. This rule is set by the IRS—not by the Company.

HEALTH CARE FSAs

50. *How much can I contribute to a health care FSA?*

You may set aside up to $3,000 in a health care FSA in 2003. The amount you choose will be divided and deducted in equal amounts from your remaining paychecks in 2003.

51. *What is the minimum amount I can contribute?*

The minimum amount you can contribute to a health care FSA is $50 in 2003.

52. *What kinds of expenses qualify under this program?*

Eligible expenses under the health care FSA include deductibles and copayments; expenses in excess of reasonable and customary charges; and other expenses not covered by your medical, dental, or vision plans.

53. *If I have a family, can my health care FSA be used to pay for my family members' expenses?*

Yes. However, you cannot claim any expense that has been paid by your or your spouse's benefit plan.

54. *Can I use my health care FSA to pay for eligible medical expenses and then also deduct those expenses when filing my federal tax return?*

No. Using the health care FSA is just one way in which you can receive a tax break for qualified health care expenses. The federal government also allows a tax deduction for qualified health care expenses when you file a tax return. However, you may not deduct the same expenses on your tax return as are reimbursed from your FSA.

55. *What happens if I submit a claim in excess of my account balance?*

Regardless of your account balance, you have access to the full amount of the annual contribution you've elected at any time during the benefit period. So, if you elected to contribute $50 per month ($600 for the year) to your health care FSA and you incur a $600 eligible expense in January, you would be reimbursed the full $600 immediately. Payroll deductions would then continue for the remainder of the year. Any additional claims from your health care FSA would not be reimbursed because you would have exhausted your balance in January.

DEPENDENT CARE FSAs

56. *How much can I contribute to a dependent care FSA?*

You may contribute up to $5,000 to your dependent care FSA in 2000 except for the following conditions:

- If you or your spouse earns less than $5,000, then the most you can contribute is the lesser of your or your spouse's income.
- If you are married but file a separate return, you may save a maximum of $2,500 each year.
- If both you and your spouse contribute to dependent care FSAs, the maximum you may save jointly is a total of $5,000.
- If your spouse is a full-time student at least five months a year or is disabled and incapable of self-care, the IRS considers his/her income to be $2,400 if you have one dependent or $4,800 if you have two or more dependents. This is the maximum amount you could save in this account.

57. *What is the minimum amount I can contribute?*

The minimum amount you may contribute to a dependent care FSA is $50 annually.

58. *What kinds of expenses qualify under this program?*

Eligible expenses under the dependent care FSA include:

- Day care centers
- Nursery schools
- Baby-sitters
- Home care specialists

59. *Can I use my dependent care FSA to pay for day care expenses and then also deduct those expenses when filing my federal tax return?*

No. Using the dependent care FSA is just one way to receive a tax break for qualified health care expenses. The federal government also allows a tax deduction for qualified health care expenses when filing a tax return. You can use both the dependent care FSA and take the tax deduction, provided you do not claim the same expenses for both.

60. *What happens if I submit a claim in excess of my account balance?*

You will receive reimbursement up to your account balance. As you continue contributing, you receive additional reimbursements up to the full amount of your claim.

ELIGIBILITY AND ENROLLMENT

61. *What is the deadline for enrolling in Flex System?*

The deadline for enrolling in Flex System is midnight (EST), February 13, 2003.

62. *What happens if I don't enroll? Do I receive some automatic coverage?*

No. You will receive no Flex System coverage in 2003. However, you will still be eligible for those benefits that the Company offers in addition to Flex System —such as the employee assistance plan, sick days, short-term disability, 401(k) plan, vacations, and holidays.

FLEX SYSTEM PHONE LINE

63.*What if I get a busy signal when I call the Flex System Phone Line?*

Although the Flex System Phone Line can be accessed by calling a single toll-free number, it actually uses several phone lines. If you get a busy signal when you call, simply wait a few minutes and try your call again.

64. *What should I do if I have specific questions about the Flex System Phone Line?*

Contact Human Resources for assistance.

COMMUNICATIONS PROGRAM

65. *Why are you spending so much money on communications?*

The Company spends about $6 million a year to provide benefits. Yet many employees do not understand these programs and, as a result, they do not benefit fully. Because of the organization's investment in these benefits and because of the importance of benefits to employees' security, we think that the money spent on a strong communications program is a good investment.

66. *Why didn't we receive all this information at once?*

Because the new Flex System offers many features that were never before available, we felt it was imperative that all employees understand the new program. Therefore, we designed a staged communications approach. Our strategy called for breaking the information down into easily understandable and easily remembered pieces. We believe that this balanced approach will best meet the needs of our diverse workforce.

Appendix F

Sample Background Report for Management

ABOUT THIS REPORT

This background report is part of an ongoing effort to keep our management team informed about benefits changes at the Company as well as to preview the information that will be communicated to all employees beginning in mid-September. It also provides you with an overview of the Company's benefits strategy and objectives.

As a member of management, it is important that you understand the benefits changes we are considering for 2003, and how these changes were developed. Please read this report carefully so you will be able to respond to any employee questions or concerns.

AN OVERVIEW OF THE COST OF OUR CURRENT BENEFITS

The Company provides employees with a comprehensive and competitive benefits program. The cost of providing our benefits program represents a significant business expense. Last year, the cost to the Company to provide benefits to employees and their families was over $16.7 million. This represents over 33 percent of our total 2001 compensation expense. So, it is especially important that these benefits meet our employee's needs.

The Company's goal is to update our overall benefits program so that it remains competitive and cost-effective.

Since 8 percent of our total compensation amount is consumed by medical expenses, and these expenses are expected to exceed 13 percent within five years, we have chosen to address welfare benefits initially. Retirement plans currently represent under 2 percent of compensation expenses and are not of immediate concern from a cost standpoint. Therefore, we are deferring addressing that issue until next year.

THE NEW APPROACH OFFERS MORE FLEXIBILITY AND CHOICE

The results of our recent employee survey showed a favorable reaction to choices for both new benefits options and improvements to our existing plans. The Company also wants to put in place a benefits program structure that encourages the use of cost-effective benefits, and at the same time allows for ongoing changes to all our plans in response to the changing needs of both the Company and employees.

We can achieve both these goals by offering a flexible benefits approach. A flexible benefits program (or cafeteria plan) is designed to offer flexibility and choice to better meet the diverse needs of employees. With this type of program, employees can choose the benefits that meet their personal and family needs and decline those they don't need. This may entail cost sharing when employees purchase benefits.

The Company's flexible benefits program allows employees to choose *annually* from a selection of benefits options—including medical, dental, life insurance, disability, and more—and arrange them in the combination that best suits their different needs, priorities, and lifestyles. The program has been specifically designed to complement the other Company benefits and to allow for more efficient use of benefit dollars.

THE REVIEW AND EVALUATION PROCESS

Over the past four months, a committee reviewed all of our benefits and evaluated many alternatives. Based on their research and our employees' survey input, the committee has recommended a number of new or improved benefits.

The employee survey also provided valuable input for the initial design of the new program. As a result, a preliminary flexible benefits program was developed that offers more choice, some new coverages, and improved plan designs, all aimed at meeting the varied needs of our work force. Some possible program features that are a direct result of employee preferences are as follows:

- New medical options
- A prescription drug plan
- Improved dental benefits
- Vision care benefits
- Improved and expanded life insurance options for employees and their dependents
- New flexible spending accounts for pretax payment of many health care and dependent care expenses
- Cash in lieu of benefits

Once we developed this preliminary flexible program design, we conducted a number of employee focus groups. From these discussions, we learned more about the kinds of choices that are most important to our employees. We will communicate the results of these focus groups to all employees in late September. Our final flexible design will be responsive to these employee preferences.

HOW THE NEW FLEXIBLE APPROACH WORKS

In the past, the Company made most benefits option selections for employees. This was fine when our workforce was relatively homogeneous. However, today our workforce is diverse, and our new flexible benefits approach will offer our employees an opportunity to select the benefits that best meet their personal needs and preferences. Another important goal of our new flexible program is to better control our benefits costs.

Every year, each employee receives a number of flexible credits. Using these credits, employees can then "purchase" the benefits of their choice. Under a flexible plan, each employee can create a personalized benefits package, choosing from a variety of benefits options and coverages.

Depending on the coverages employees choose, they may or may not need to contribute toward the cost of their benefits. If an employee wants a higher level of benefits than his or her credits will buy, the additional cost will be deducted from his or her pay *before taxes* are calculated. If employees have credits left over after buying the benefits options they want, they can take these credits as cash in their paychecks or put the dollars in a flexible spending account to pre-fund out-of-pocket health care and dependent care expenses or put the cash in their 401(k) plan.

The following chart shows how the new flexible approach works:

Company gives you flexible credits.

↓

You choose the benefits options you want.

↓

You add up the total cost for your choices.

↓

Then compare your total cost with your flexible credits.

↓

If your total cost is *MORE* than your flexible credits, you make up the difference through *pretax* payroll deductions. (This means that for each dollar you make up, you will have less than 85 cents reduced from your paycheck.)	If your total cost is *LESS* than your flexible credits, leftover credits are added to your paycheck as taxable income or are available for 401(k) contributions or a flexible spending account.

THE UPCOMING COMMUNICATIONS EFFORT

As we move ahead with these plans over the next several months, we will be providing all employees with information about the changes to our health and welfare plans. Our communications program is designed to educate all employees about the philosophy behind the benefits changes as well as the new flexible program details. Information will be available through many channels—newsletters, group meetings, and other printed materials. As managers, your role is *essential* to our communications effort. The timetable shows our proposed communications schedule.

Mid-November 2002	November	
• Employee Newsletter (survey results)	• Report to Management Group	• Employee Newsletter (focus group results) • First Poster

January	February	March
• Second Employee Newsletter (program details) • Second Poster	• Group Meetings • Enrollment Materials Distributed	• Enrollment Confirms

April 2003
• New Program Effective April 1, 2003

THE OUTLOOK FOR THE FUTURE

The Company will continue to focus on more cost-effective ways to provide a competitive benefits program to employees. "Buying smarter"—educating employees to make more informed, individualized, and cost-conscious benefits choices—is an important part of our approach to controlling our benefits costs.

Our efforts will be ongoing. We will continue to examine ways to keep our benefits costs under control and explore new program alternatives as time goes on. We encourage your comments and suggestions as this process continues.

Sample Communications Strategy

Component	*Audience*	*Description*	*Time Frame*
Background Report for Management	Management group	This 8-panel "white paper" will be targeted at those who would benefit from an understanding of why the Company is implementing the flexible benefits program and more detailed information about how the program will work. Many of the messages fleshed out in the position paper will also be contained in the newsletters. The newsletters, however, will be written to appeal to a wider audience.	January
Newsletters	All associates	These 4-panel, 8½'' x 11'' newsletters will be aimed at everyone in the organization and provide the rationale behind the new flexible benefits program and details about how the new program will work. We will produce a series of three newsletters: • *Newsletter #1*—Introduction of the new program and survey results • *Newsletter #2*—Program details • *Newsletter #3*—Recap of errors and success	Newsletters will be distributed according to the following schedule: • *Newsletter #1*—January • *Newsletter #2*—February • *Newsletter #3*—May

Component	Audience	Description	Time Frame
Associate Presentation	All associates	This 10–15 minute slide show will provide an overview of the flexible benefits program and will serve to kick off the implementation. The slide show will be presented to all associates during company-wide meetings.	February
Flexible Benefits Program Enrollment Brochure and Personalized Choice Report	All associates	This 16-page booklet and personalized choice report describe more details of the flexible benefits program. The booklet will also offer instructions about how to enroll by telephone and where to go for more information. The personalized Choice Report will provide each associate with a list of the benefits he or she is eligible for and their associated costs.	February
The Benefits Line—An automated telephone enrollment system	All associates	This automated enrollment system will allow associates to complete their enrollment by telephone. Associates may access the system by dialing a toll-free number and using a Touch-Tone telephone to enter their choices.	February, with enrollments complete by March 1
Confirmation Statements	All associates	This 8½'' x 11'' single-sided statement will confirm the enrollment decisions made by associates. Associates who do not complete an enrollment telephone call will receive a confirmation statement that outlines the "default coverage."	March

Appendix G

Sample Employee Enrollment Packet

Your Choice

FLEXIBLE BENEFITS

Overview

. . .

Your Choice Flexible Benefits Plan gives you the ability to choose the types of benefit plans that best meet your needs, and those of your family.

YOUR BENEFIT DOLLARS

You "buy" the benefit options you want with Benefit Dollars. The COMPANY provides you with a fixed amount of Benefit Dollars every year.

If you want a higher level of benefits than your Benefit Dollars will buy, the additional cost will be deducted from your pay on a pre-tax basis. **(Note: You must pay for Spouse and Dependent Life Insurance with after-tax dollars.)**

If you have Benefit Dollars left over after "buying" the benefit options you want, the difference (up to the maximum amount determined each year) will be added to your gross pay, subject to income taxes.

Beginning in 2003, the medical plan costs shown on the Price List reflect only *your* portion of the cost. That is because the COMPANY's contribution toward the cost of your medical coverage has already been factored into the Price List. Note: If you decline medical coverage through the COMPANY (because you have coverage elsewhere), you'll receive additional Benefit Dollars, as shown on your personalized worksheet.

CHANGING YOUR COVERAGE

The choices you make must remain in effect for the entire calendar year. (Your dental and LTD choices remain in effect for two years.)

If you experience a qualified change in status (as defined by the IRS) during the year, you are permitted to change your benefit elections in a way that is consistent with the change in status. Some examples of a qualified change are marriage; divorce; birth, death, or adoption of a dependent; a spouse's involuntary loss of medical coverage; or a change in your employment status. You have 30 days from the date of your change in status in which to make such changes, so contact your Benefits Department Representative if such a change occurs.

Medical

. . .

Coverage, choice, cost and convenience are factors each of us considers important in selecting a medical plan. That's why the COMPANY offers seven different plans. Choose the one that best meets your needs.

COVERAGE

You may elect coverage for:

- Individual--for yourself only
- Individual-Plus-One--for yourself and one eligible dependent (spouse or same sex spousal equivalent or one child)
- Family--you and all eligible dependents (spouse or same sex spousal equivalent and/or eligible children)

PLANS

You may choose coverage under the COMPANY Total Health Plan PPO or one of several Health Maintenance Organizations. This chart shows how the plans differ.

COMPANY TOTAL HEALTH PLAN PPO	HEALTH MAINTENANCE ORGANIZATIONS
• Using the TAHP Provider Network--most expenses covered in full • Using non-network provider--coverage has deductibles, co-insurance payments, and out-of-pocket maximums	• Most expenses covered in full, some may require small co-payments
• You may choose to use PPO network providers or not. This affects the amount of coverage.	• All services must be provided/arranged by your HMO's doctors, using Plan facilities
• Emergencies covered anywhere in the world	• Emergencies covered, but you must follow your Plan's procedures
Review individual plan brochures for coverage of specific items of particular importance to you such as age limit for students, mental health treatment, prescription drugs, substance abuse treatment, vision and hearing treatment, etc., as these may vary widely among plans.	

When you change plans or add dependents during Open Enrollment, there are no Pre-Existing Condition or Waiting Period requirements.

YOUR CHOICE

FLEXIBLE BENEFITS

MEDICAL continued

. .

DECLINING MEDICAL COVERAGE

You have the option to decline coverage in all of the medical plans offered by COMPANY if you are covered under some other plan. To decline, fill in Medical Option No. 12 on the Enrollment Form, sign the Waiver on the back of the Enrollment Form, and attach proof of your other coverage.

DEFAULT COVERAGE

Flex participants who do not have medical insurance and fail to return an Enrollment Form and proof of other coverage will automatically be enrolled for individual coverage in the COMPANY Total Health Plan PPO.

DENTAL

. . .

Dental care is important for good health. Your dental plan encourages preventive care and provides financial help in meeting the cost of dental work.

COVERAGE

You may elect coverage for:

- Individual--for yourself only
- Individual-Plus-One--for yourself and one eligible dependent (spouse or one child)
- Family--you and all eligible dependents (spouse and/or eligible children)

PLAN BENEFITS

If you use a Massachusetts dentist who is a Delta Dental Plan participant, the Plan will provide the following benefits:

PREVENTIVE	MINOR RESTORATIVE	MAJOR CARE
Plan Pays 100%	You Pay 20%	You Pay 50%
	Plan Pays 80%	
Coverage includes exams, cleanings, and X-rays	Coverage of basic dental treatment including fillings, extractions, root canals	Plan pays 50% coverage of bridges, crowns, inlays, dentures, etc.

- No annual deductible
- Payment maximum of $1,000 per person per year
- Orthodontia is not covered by the Plan. However, you may use your Health Care Reimbursement Account to pay for expenses on a pre-tax basis, as long as the services are medically necessary.

If you use a non-participating or out-of-state dentist, you may be responsible for additional costs. Please refer to your plan brochure for details.

ENROLLMENT PERIOD

When you decide to elect dental coverage, your election and level of coverage **must remain in effect for two years.** Each subsequent enrollment is also for a two-year period.

Dependents Over Age 19--All medical and dental plans offered by COMPANY cover unmarried dependent children up to age 19. Full-time students are covered to age 23 (or older, depending on the specific plan you have chosen).

YOUR CHOICE
FLEXIBLE BENEFITS

LIFE INSURANCE
. . .
Your life insurance needs will vary depending on your family situation. Because people's needs differ, the life insurance options available let you choose the level of coverage that's right for your situation.

GROUP LIFE INSURANCE
OPTIONS
- No coverage
- Your current amount of coverage
- $50,000
- 1/2 x your base salary*
- 1 x your base salary*
- 2 x your base salary*
- 3 x your base salary*
- 4 x your base salary*
- 5 x your base salary*

*Rounded up to next highest even multiple of $5,000.

Accelerated Benefit--This new program helps to ease the financial strain of terminal illness by providing partial payment of your life insurance *prior* to your death. If a doctor certifies that you have a life expectancy of less than a year, you could receive up to 50% of your life insurance amount ($50,000 maximum).

Evidence of Insurability--If you choose to increase your coverage by more than one times your salary (amount noted on Price List), the insurance company must approve the increased coverage. Please complete an Evidence of Insurability Form, available from the Benefits Office, if you are electing coverage in this amount or more. The increase of one times your salary becomes effective on the "Date Elections Effective" shown on your Enrollment Form. The excess amount would be effective upon approval by the insurance company.

ACCIDENTAL DEATH AND DISMEMBERMENT INSURANCE
AD&D Insurance provides benefits in addition to your Group Life coverage if your death is the result of an accident. You may select from the following options:

- No coverage
- Your current amount of coverage
- $50,000
- 1/2 x your base salary*
- 1 x your base salary*
- 2 x your base salary*
- 3 x your base salary*

*Rounded up to next highest even multiple of $ 5,000.

Maximum--The maximum amount of coverage you can choose is equal to your life insurance amount or 3 x your base salary, whichever is less.

Note: If you are adding or increasing your Group Life and/or AD&D coverage, you must be actively at work on the first work day that the new coverage is to begin for your benefits to be effective.

SPOUSE AND DEPENDENT LIFE INSURANCE
You may purchase coverage for your spouse and/or dependent child(ren). A dependent child is covered up to age 19 or, if a full-time student, up to age 23. Your options are as follows:
- Option 1--$5,000 per child
- Option--$10,000 for your spouse
- Option 3--Both Options 1 and 2
- Option 4--No coverage

Note: Your cost for Spouse and Dependent Life Insurance must be deducted from your pay on an after-tax basis, in accordance with IRS regulations.

TAX CONSIDERATIONS
You should know that IRS regulations treat the value of life insurance over $50,000 as taxable income. The amount that is added to your W-2 as a result of this law is based on a formula that considers the amount of insurance and your age. Please contact the Benefits Office for a work-sheet to calculate your estimated taxable amount.

YOUR CHOICE

FLEXIBLE BENEFITS

DISABILITY PLANS

Having Short-Term Disability (STD) and Long-Term Disability (LTD) coverage is important if you become unable to work for medical reasons. These plans provide a continuing income to you after your paychecks would otherwise stop.

If you are enrolling in either plan for the first time, you must be actively at work on the first work day that coverage is to begin for your benefits to be effective.

SHORT-TERM DISABILITY

STD provides benefits between the time your sick leave is used and the beginning of LTD coverage (if you elect it). All accrued sick leave must be used before your STD benefits.

The Plan plays 50% of your base pay, less any benefits you're eligible to receive from Social Security, Workers' Compensation or other state plans. The maximum payment is $5,000 per month. Your payments continue until you are medically able to return to work or for a maximum of 180 consecutive days from your last day actively at work, whichever is earlier.

Your STD Options--All options provide payment of 50% of base pay. The difference is how soon STD payments could begin:

Option 1--Provides benefits after **15** consecutive working days of disability
Option 2--Provides benefits after **40** consecutive working days of disability
Option 3--Provides benefits after **60** consecutive working days of disability
Option 4--No coverage

LONG-TERM DISABILITY

LTD benefits begin after 180 consecutive days of disability and continue for as long as you are unable to work. Benefits vary depending on the option you choose.

Option 1--Pays **65%** of your base pay, less any benefits you may be eligible to receive from Social Security, Workers' Compensation, or other state plans. The maximum payment is $6,000 per month.

Option 1--Pays **50%** of your base pay, less any benefits you may be eligible to receive from Social Security, Workers' Compensation, or other state plans. The maximum payment is $4,600 per month.

Option 3--No coverage

LTD Election Period--When you elect LTD coverage, your election and level of coverage must remain in effect for two years. Each subsequent enrollment is also for a two-year period. Employees who became eligible for Flexible Benefits on or after August 1, 1991 are required to maintain indefinitely at least the 50% LTD Plan (Option 2) when they enroll in Flex, unless they are covered under another plan.

YOUR CHOICE

FLEXIBLE BENEFITS

REIMBURSEMENT ACCOUNTS

. . .

By participating in a reimbursement account, you reduce your taxable income. The amount you choose is deducted from your pay before income taxes and put into your account. You are then reimbursed from this account when you submit claims for eligible expenses.

HEALTH CARE REIMBURSEMENT ACCOUNT

This can be used to pay for expenses not covered by your medical and dental insurance plans, including:

- Insurance deductibles and co-payments
- Amounts above the Reasonable and Customary limits
- HMO co-payments
- Orthodontia (if medically necessary)
- Dental expenses
- Hearing aids
- Eyeglasses/contact lenses
- Cosmetic surgery (if medically necessary)
- Other treatments not covered by your plans

DEPENDENT CARE REIMBURSEMENT ACCOUNT

If you must pay for dependent care in order for you to be able to work, you may use the Reimbursement Account to pay for expenses. Your dependents include children under 13, a disabled spouse, or some other disabled dependent, such as an elderly parent.

The government requires that all employers test dependent care plans to see that they are utilized by all levels of employees. This testing may require that the maximum contribution be reduced. Should this occur, you will be notified as early in the year as possible.

USE IT OR LOSE IT

When figuring how much to set aside in your reimbursement accounts, be sure to estimate carefully and conservatively. If you have unused amounts left over at the end of the year, government regulations do not allow the money to be returned to you.

AFTER YOU'VE MADE YOUR DECISIONS

. . .

Any questions? Your Benefits Office Representatives will be happy to help you with any questions you might have.

Please complete the Enrollment Form per the instructions. You'll need to also complete other forms if you are:

- Changing medical carriers
- Electing coverage for a same sex spousal equivalent
- Adding or dropping dependents on your current medical plan
- Electing no medical coverage (complete back of Enrollment Form)
- Enrolling in or continuing your dental insurance coverage
- Electing a new life insurance amount if your new amount is more than your current amount plus 1 x your base pay
- Changing your beneficiaries

You can get any additional forms you need by calling or visiting the Benefits Office.

After you submit your Enrollment Form, and any other forms required, your new choices will be processed and will go into effect on the effective date shown on your Enrollment Form. You will receive a Confirmation Form which will detail your new Benefits Choices and your additional cost or Benefit Dollars refund.

If you are enrolling in or changing medical plans, your new identification card(s) will be sent to you within 12 weeks **after** the effective date. **Be sure to retain your copy of your Enrollment Form as your temporary proof of coverage.**

BENEFIT DOLLARS WORKSHEET

Use this worksheet to calculate your payroll deduction or refund. After you complete your Enrollment Form, use the Pre-Tax and After-Tax boxes from the Form to complete the following:

Enter Pre-Tax Total A or B here	____________	
Enter Pre-Tax Total C here	____________	
Enter Pre-Tax Total D here	____________	
Total A or B + C + D	____________	Line 1
Enter COMPANY Benefit Dollars here	____________	Line 2
Enter After-Tax Total here	____________	Line 3

If Line 1 is greater than 2:

	____________	Line 1
—	____________	Line 2
	$	Total Pre-Tax Dollars To Be Deducted**
	$	Enter Line 3 here. This is Your Total After-Tax Dollars To Be Deducted**

OR

If Line 2 is greater than 1:

	____________	Line 2
—	____________	Line 1
	$	Unused Benefit Dollars Added to Pay*
	$	Enter Line 3 here. This is Your Total After-Tax Dollars To Be Deducted**

*This is taxable income and subject to annual maximum limit.

****Divide these amounts by 52 if you are paid weekly, 26 if you are paid bi-weekly, or 12 if you are paid monthly to find your amount per paycheck.**

YOUR CHOICE

FLEXIBLE BENEFITS

INSTRUCTIONS

. . .

1. Read the plan information in this brochure, noting any changes that may affect your choices.
2. Think about your personal needs. Have there recently been or will there be changes to your family status? These should be considered as you decide what benefit options will best meet your needs for the coming year.
3. Review your personal Price List/Enrollment Form. Review your current coverage, the options available, and the cost of the options.
4. Make your decisions and complete the Enrollment Form. Refer to the Enrollment Checklist in this package.
5. Use the worksheet above to figure your cost or refund amount. (Note that your refund amount cannot exceed the annual maximum limit specified on the Enrollment Form.)
6. Note: If you are electing coverage under the same sex spousal equivalent benefit, please contact the Benefits Office for additional information.

PRICE LIST

Flexible Benefit Salary	$21,661.25	Date of Birth	12/01/67	$2,310
Flexible Eligible Date	4/01/92			COMPANY Benefit Dollars Provided

Your Options and Prices FOR PLAN YEAR 2003

Use this price list below as a guide when making your 2003benefit plan choices and filling out the Enrollment Form. Your current selections for 2002 are indicated below with an asterisk (*) and on the Enrollment Form at right. **2003 Annual Prices**

Benefit Programs		**Options**	**Individual Coverage A**	**Individual Plus One Coverage B**	**Family Coverage C**
MEDICAL	05	**HARVARD HMO**	**$1,990**	**$2,500**	**$2,648**
	10	**TUFTS ASSOC. HMO**	***$2,069**	**$2,367**	**$2,727**
	13	**COMPANY TOTAL HEALTH PPO**	**$2,615**	**$3,556**	**$4,504**
	14	**NEIGHBORHOOD HEALTH**	**$2,063**	**$2,672**	**$2,718**
	15	**HMO BLUE**	**$2,052**	**$2,441**	**$2,718**
	XX	**TUFTS VALUE PLAN**	**$X,XXX**	**$X,XXX**	**$X,XXX**
	12	**NO COVERAGE–ADD $X,XXX TO YOUR BENEFIT DOLLAR AMOUNT**			
DENTAL	01	**DENTAL PLAN**	***$297**	**$554**	**$738**
	02	**COVERAGE**	**$0**	**$0**	**$0**

Dental Enrollment is for a 2-year period. You **ARE NOT** eligible to change your election this year.

		Options		Annual Prices	Comments
SHORT-TERM DISABILITY		Payments begin after:			
		1. 15 Consecutive Workdays		**$103**	
		2. 40 Consecutive Workdays		**$91**	
	*	3. 60 Consecutive Workdays		**$78**	
		4. 15 No Coverage		**$0**	
LONG-TERM DISABILITY		1. 65% of Pay		**$147**	LTD enrollment is for a 2-year period. You **ARE NOT** eligible to change your election this year.
	*	2. 50% of Pay		**$65**	
		3. No Coverage		**$0**	
LIFE INSURANCE		**001.** No Coverage		**$0**	Evidence of insurability is required if your new amount exceeds **$70,000.**
	*	**010.** Current Amount		**$76**	
		011. **$50,000**		**$89**	
		004. 1/2 X Salary		**$25**	Life Insurance amounts over $50,000 result in additional taxable income to you.
		006. 1 X Salary		**$42**	
		010. 2 X Salary		**$76**	
		014. 3 X Salary		**$92**	
		019. 4 X Salary	**$90,000**	**$113**	
		023. 5 X Salary	**$110,000**	**$130**	
ACCIDENTAL DEATH & DISMEMBERMENT INSURANCE		**001.** No Coverage	**$0**	**$0**	The amount of your AD&D Insurance cannot exceed the amount of your life insurance.
	*	**001.** Current Amount	**$45,000**	**$0**	
		011. **$50,000**	**$50,000**	**$21**	
		004. 1/2 X Salary	**$15,000**	**$6**	
		006. 1 X Salary	**$25,000**	**$11**	
		010. 2 X Salary	**$45,000**	**$19**	
		014. 3 X Salary	**$65,000**	**$27**	
SPOUSE & DEPENDENT LIFE INSURANCE		1. $5,000 Child		**$21.60**	Your cost for this coverage is deducted on an after-tax basis. Coverage may result in additional taxable income to you.
		2. $10,000 Spouse		**$22.44**	
		3. Spouse & Child		**$44.04**	
	*	4. No Coverage		**$0**	
REIMBURSEMENT ACCOUNTS		1. Health Care–**$2,000** maximum in 2003 2. Dependent Care–**$5,000** maximum in 2003			Estimate carefully. Unused amounts cannot be refunded to you.

ENROLLMENT FORM

		1/1/00	Date Elections Effective
		$1,500	Maximum Benefit Dollars Refund
JOHN DOE		**000-00-0002**	Social Security No.
750 WASHINGTON ST.	**0**	**0001 XYZ**	Time Sheet/Pay Group
BOSTON MA 02111		**$2,310** **COMPANY Benefit Dollars Provided**	

INSTRUCTIONS: To make changes for 2003, fill in the boxes below using information from the Price List. To make no changes to your current coverage, check the "NO CHANGE BOX." If choosing "NO COVERAGE" for medical, complete waiver on reverse side **and add $X,XXX to the Benefit Dollars Provided amount in the box shown above.**

REIMBURSEMENT ACCOUNTS--To participate in 2003 **you must make new elections here.**

HEALTH CARE REIMBURSEMENT ACCOUNT-- **$250** is your 2002 deferral amount.
Enter your 2003 election here (**$2,000** maximum) → [ ] **PRE-TAX TOTAL A**

DEPENDENT CARE REIMBURSEMENT ACCT.--
Enter your 2003 election here (**$5,000** maximum) → [ ] **PRE-TAX TOTAL B**

NO CHANGE BOX [ ] To keep all the same choices shown above for 2002 check this box. **Do not use if participating in** 2003 **Reimbursement Accounts.**

PRE-TAX BENEFITS	**Your** 2002 **Elections** Option	Coverage	**New Prices to Keep Same Elections**	**Your Choices for the Coming Year** Option	Coverage	**New Prices (from Price List)**
MEDICAL	10	A	$2,069			
DENTAL	01	A	$297			
SHORT-TERM DISABILITY			$78			
LONG-TERM DISABILITY			$65			
LIFE INSURANCE	XXX - $X,XXX,XXX		$76			
ACCIDENTAL DEATH & DISMEMBERMENT	XXX - $X,XXX,XXX		$0			
		PRE-TAX TOTAL C	$2,585		**PRE-TAX TOTAL D**	

AFTER-TAX BENEFITS	**Option**	**Your New Price**		**YOUR CHOICE FOR THE COMING YEAR Option**	**New Price**	
SPOUSE & DEPENDENT LIFE INSURANCE			**AFTER-TAX TOTAL**			**AFTER-TAX TOTAL**

I understand that in accordance with IRS regulations, my elections will remain in effect for one year* from the effective date above, provided I remain an eligible COMPANY employee. (*Refer to Brochure for exceptions.)

Signature ______________________ Date ____________

Submit top copy to the Benefits Department no later than 11/24/99.

WAIVER OF MEDICAL COVERAGE

I have chosen to have no medical coverage under the COMPANY'S flexible benefits program.

I have coverage under another plan and have attached proof of that coverage.

I understand that I will not be able to receive coverage under the COMPANY's program until the next annual enrollment period, unless I have a qualifying change (as defined by the IRS) in my family status.

I hereby release COMPANY from any financial liability for any medical, health care, or other expense which I, or any of my dependents, may incur which could be covered under any of the medical insurance options offered under the flexible benefits program.

SIGNATURE DATE

Attach proof of other coverage and return to the Benefits Department.

YOUR CHOICE

FLEXIBLE BENEFITS

ENROLLMENT CHECKLIST

Before returning your enrollment form, please check the following . . .

If you . . .	*You must . . .*
1. **Changed** from one HEALTH PLAN* to another or **changed** the number of people covered on your health insurance	**Complete** a health plan application
2. **Elected** NO COVERAGE for health insurance (because you are covered by another health plan, such as a spouse's)	**Attach** new Proof of Coverage (such as a copy of your membership card) and sign the Waiver Section on the back of the Enrollment Form. This must be done every year.
3. **Currently have** or are enrolling in the DENTAL PLAN*	**Complete** the enclosed dental application form
4. **Newly Elected** LIFE INSURANCE, ACCIDENTAL DEATH & DISMEMBERMENT, SPOUSE & DEPENDENT LIFE*	**Complete** a beneficiary form
5. **Newly Elected** or **increased** your LIFE INSURANCE coverage to more than 1 times salary over your current insurance amount	**Complete** Evidence of Insurability form (statement of your health)
6. **Contributed** to the HEALTH CARE REIMBURSEMENT ACCOUNT and/or the DEPENDENT CARE REIMBURSEMENT ACCOUNT	**Indicate** your deduction amount(s) for 2003 on the Enrollment Form if you wish to have a deduction for 2003. Your 2002 election(s) will *not* carry over to 2003.
7. **Elect** to participate in the same sex spousal equivalent benefit.	**Contact** the Benefits Office and complete the necessary forms.

*Note: Health, Dental and Dependent Life Insurance's--Dependents age 19 and older who are not full-time students are not eligible for these plans. Full-time students can be covered to the age of 23. (Some Health Plans cover full-time students past age 23--check your plan brochure for details.)

THESE ADDITIONAL FORMS ARE AVAILABLE IN THE BENEFITS OFFICE.

YOUR CHOICE CONFIRMATION FORM

FLEXIBLE BENEFITS

Date Elections Effective:

Social Security No.:

COMPANY Benefit Dollars Provided

You have elected the following Pre-Tax benefits:

	OPTION	COVERAGE		PRICE
MEDICAL				
DENTAL				
SHORT-TERM DISABILITY				
LONG-TERM DISABILITY				
LIFE INSURANCE				
ACCIDENTAL DEATH & DISMEMBERMENT				

HEALTH CARE REIMBURSEMENT ACCOUNT

DEPENDENT CARE REIMBURSEMENT ACCOUNT

REIMBURSEMENT ACCOUNT TOTAL

YOUR TOTAL PRE-TAX BENEFIT COST

COMPANY BENEFIT DOLLARS PROVIDED

You have elected the following After-Tax Benefit:

SPOUSE & DEPENDENT LIFE INSURANCE

YOUR AFTER-TAX BENEFIT COST

Please report any errors to the Benefits Office immediately.

Appendix H

Sample Communications Campaign Calendar

May 2002	June 2002	July 2002
▲ Preliminary communications plan to Committee Committee comments/approves plan	Final communications plan with Plan name, theme, logo, style, and media	Committee approves communication plan Drafting begins 
August 2002	**September 2002**	**October 2002**
1st Manager Position Paper 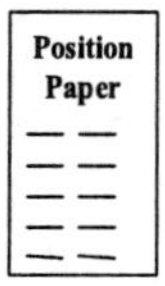 Drafting/review/approvals ---- Design/artwork ---- 	---- (Drafting/review/approvals) ---- (Design/artwork) ▲ Employee announcement  Poster #1/ tent cards 	2nd Manager Position Paper 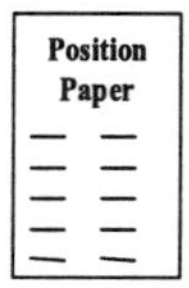 Voice Script draft/review ---- ---- (Drafting/review/approvals) ---- (Design/artwork)

November 2002	December 2002	January 2003
Voice script draft/review (con't) Drafting/review/approvals (con't) Design/art work (con't) Employee Newsletter #1 Poster #2/ tent cards	HR Rep training: -- A/V, Q&A Guide Employee Newsletter #2	Employee Newsletter # 3 Poster #3/ tent cards ▲Telephone Q&A hotline
February 2003	**March 2003**	**April 2003**
Personalized enrollment packages distributed Enrollment Form ▲ Enrollment meetings: -A/V -Q&A	Confirmations sent Confirmations	Employee Newsletter #4 on enrollment wrap-up Begin planning for reenrollment Begin SPDs for completion 7/31/03 SPDs

Appendix I

Sample Telephone Enrollment Form

COMPANY FLEX TELEPHONE ENROLLMENT INFORMATION

This booklet contains information you'll need to enroll in your COMPANY Flex benefits for 2003.

Here's your current coverage:

Medical
Harvard Pilgrim Healthcare—Single

Dental
Coverage—Single

Vision
Network Coverage

Employee Life Insurance
$10,000

Dependent Life Insurance
No coverage

Long-Term Disability
50% of salary

Spending Accounts
Health Care—Not participating
Dependent Care—Not participating

Fitness Center
Member

To keep the same coverage for 2003, do nothing. Your cost for coverage will be **$XX.XX** per pay period.
To change coverage for 2003 or to enroll or reenroll for spending accounts

OPEN

This booklet was especially prepared for:
JOHN DOE
110 MORNING GLORY DRIVE
PROVIDENCE, RI 00001

XXX-XX-XXXX
Department Number: XX XXX

Pay Period Flex Credits: Your flex credits are determined by the medical coverage category you select:

No Medical Coverage	**Single Coverage**	**Family Coverage**
10-.92	$211.58	$461.58

Medical	**Single**	**Family**
0: No Coverage	0.00	0.00
1: Ocean State Plus	$176.67	$446.67
2: Ocean State HMO	175.67	443.67
3: Prudential Plan	166.67	416.67
4: Harvard Pilgrim Healthcare	181.67	456.67
Dental		
0: No Coverage	0.00	0.00
1: Coverage	$12.00	$17.00
Vision		
0: No Coverage	0.00	0.00
1: Network Coverage	$2.50	$2.50
2: Enhanced 1 Coverage	3.50	3.50
3: Discount Plan Coverage	0.50	0.50
Employee Life Insurance		
0: $10,000	$2.75	
1: 1 x Salary	9.67	
2: 2 x Salary	19.25	
3: 3 x Salary*	28.92	
4: 4 x Salary*	38.50	
**Evidence of insurability is required to elect this option.*		
Dependent Life Insurance		
0: No Coverage	0.00	
1: $5,000 spouse/$2,500 each eligible child	$1.76	
2: $10,000 spouse/ $5,000 each eligible child	3.52	
Personal Accident Insurance		
0: No Coverage	0.00	0.00
1: 1 x Salary	$1.17	$1.75
2: 2 x Salary	2.33	3.50
3: 3 x Salary	3.50	5.25
4: 4 x Salary*	4.67	7.00
Please refer to your enrollment package for information on coverage amounts for spouse and children.		
Long-Term Disability		
1: 50% of Salary	$9.08	
2: 66-2/3% of Salary	13.17	
3: 70% of Salary	13.75	

Spending Accounts

Health Care:	Minimum:	$17.33
	Maximum:	$100.00
Dependent Care:	Minimum:	$17.33
	Maximum:	$416.67

Fitness Center
0: Do not join center
1: Join center for $10.00

HOW TO MAKE A CHANGE FOR 2003

Step 1: Enter Your Selections

Refer to the facing page for your selection choices. If you are not making a change, enter * otherwise enter the selection number

☐ **Medical Plan Selection**

☐ **Medical Coverage Level**

1 = You only
2 = You + family

☐ **Dental Plan Selection**

☐ **Dental Coverage Level**

1 = You only
2 = You + family

☐ **Vision Plan Selection**

☐ **Vision Coverage Level**

1 = You only
2 = You + family

☐ **Group Life Insurance Plan Selection**

☐ **Dependent Life Insurance Plan Selection**

☐ **Personal Accident Insurance Plan Selection**

☐ **Long-Term Disability Plan Selection**

☐ **Health Care Reimbursement Account** — Enter per pay period $ amount (minimum $17.33, maximum $100)

☐ **Dependent Care Reimbursement Account** — Enter per pay period $ amount (minimum $17.33, maximum $416.67)

☐ **Fitness Center Plan Selection**

Step 2. Dial Benefits Line

1-800-XXX-XXXX

You will first be required to enter your Social Security Number.

You will be asked if you want to

1	Hear a summary of 1998 plan changes.
2	Review your current benefit coverages.
3	Make a change or enroll in a Reimbursement Account for 1998

Select 3 to make a change or enroll in a Reimbursement Account.
Then you will be "asked" to enter the selections you made in Step 1.

Enter each in turn until you hear **"Your changes are confirmed."**
Your enrollment is now complete.

The Next Step!

Following the end of the Enrollment period, you will receive a statement confirming your 1998 benefit coverages.

Appendix J

Internal Revenue Service Notice 2002-24

In April 2002, the IRS announced that filing Schedule F would no longer be required. This change was effective immediately and retroactively. The change affects fringe benefit plans that were filing Schedule F, and plans that were filing Form 5500 merely because of the Internal Revenue Code Section 6039D requirement. The IRS Notice does not provide an exemption from filing for ERISA plans.

The IRS issued the following news release on April 4, 2002.

> WASHINGTON—Effective immediately, the Internal Revenue Service has indefinitely suspended the requirement for taxpayers to file Schedule F (Form 5500) "Fringe Benefit Plan Annual Information Return." This is part of the agency's ongoing commitment to reduce unnecessary taxpayer burden.
>
> "This IRS effort will simplify tax administration and eliminate the filing of about 200,000 forms each year," said Larry Langdon, Commissioner of the IRS's Large and Mid-Size Business Division.
>
> The suspension of the requirement to file Schedule F is outlined in Notice 2002-24. The filing suspension applies to all plan years, including years prior to 2001. During the suspension period, the IRS will review reporting requirements and electronic filing options.
>
> Before today's announcement, sponsors of certain fringe benefits were required to file the annual information return, Schedule F (Form 5500) for cafeteria plans, educational assistance programs, and adoption assistance programs.
>
> Sponsors of fringe benefit plans who have not filed required Forms 5500, Schedule F, for plan years prior to 2001 should not seek relief under the Department of Labors Delinquent Filer Voluntary Compliance

Program (DFVC). There is also no need to request relief from the IRS for failure to file these forms.

The IRS notice does not affect annual reporting requirements under Title I of ERISA, or relieve administrators of employee benefit plans from any obligation to file a Form 5500 and any required schedules (other than the Schedule F) under that title. For further information on annual reporting requirements applicable to employee benefit plans under Title I of ERISA, see the instructions for the Form 5500 Annual Return/Report and the Department of Labors regulations.

IRS Notice 2002-24 is available on the IRS Web at www.irs.gov. The announcement will be published in the Internal Revenue Bulletin 2002-16 dated April 22, 2002.

Following is the text of IRS Notice 2002-24.

Notice 2002-24, I.R.B. 2002-16, April 22, 2002, Form 5500: Schedule F: Fringe benefits: Cafeteria Plans: Educational assistance plans: Adoption assistance plans.

Part III—Administrative, Procedural, and Miscellaneous

Section 6039D Reporting Requirements

Notice 2002-24

PURPOSE

This notice suspends the filing requirement imposed on specified fringe benefit plans by section 6039D of the Internal Revenue Code and modifies and supersedes Notice 90-24, 1990-1 C. B. 335.

BACKGROUND

Section 6039D of the Code, as enacted by Pub. L. 98-611, §1, 98 Stat. 3176 (1984), required employers maintaining group legal services plans described in section 120, cafeteria plans described in section 125, and educational assistance programs described in section 127 to file an annual information return with the Internal Revenue Service. Announcement 86-20, 1986-7 I.R.B. 34, required the return for these plans to be filed on the Form 5500 Series Annual Return/Report. Section 1151(h) of the Tax Reform Act of 1986 (TRA '86), amended section 6039D and expanded the reporting requirement to group-term life insurance plans described in section 79, accident and health plans described in sections 105 and 106, and dependent care assistance programs described in section 129. Section 1601(h)(2)(D)(iii) of the Small Business Job Protection Act of 1996 added adoption assistance programs described in section 137 to the list of specified fringe benefit plans required to file annual returns under section 6039D.

Notice 90-24 suspended the filing requirement for those fringe benefit plans added to section 6039D by the TRA '86. The notice stated that, until the Service provides further guidance, employers maintaining plans under sections 79, 105 and 106, or 129, are not required to file information returns pursuant to section 6039D. However, the notice instructed employers maintaining plans under sections 120, 125 or 127 to continue to file the return for these plans on the Form 5500 Series Annual Return/Report. Current filing instructions provide that plans described in sections 125, 127 and 137 are considered fringe benefit plans and must file Schedule F attached to a completed Form 5500 to satisfy the annual return requirement of section 6039D. The IRS is evaluating whether this method of reporting the information required by section 6039D is appropriate.

RELIEF FROM FILING REQUIREMENTS AND EFFECTIVE DATE

Employers maintaining specified fringe benefit plans under sections 125, 127 or 137 are relieved from the requirement to file annual information returns (Schedule F) attached to a completed Form 5500 pursuant to section 6039D. This notice is effective upon publication and applies to all plan years for which information returns have not been filed. Any future reporting obligations under section 6039D will apply only to plan years beginning on or after the date of publication of further guidance.

This notice does not affect annual reporting requirements under Title I of the Employee Retirement Income Security Act of 1974 (ERISA), or relieve administrators of employee benefit plans from any obligation to file a Form 5500 and any required schedules (other than the Schedule F) under that title. For further information on annual reporting requirements applicable to employee benefit plans under Title I of ERISA, see the instructions for the Form 5500 Annual Return/Report and the Department of Labor's regulations. The Form 5500 instructions may be obtained by calling 1-800-TAX FORM, or may be viewed at www.efast.dol.gov or www.irs.gov.

DRAFTING INFORMATION

The principal author of this notice is Felix J. Zech of the Office of Division Counsel/ Associate Chief Counsel (Tax Exempt and Government Entities). For further information regarding this notice, please contact Mr. Zech at (202) 622-6080 (not a toll-free number).

Appendix K

Final Treasury Regulations § 1.125-3

In November 2001, Treasury Regulations Section 1.125-3 was finalized. The final regulation is substantially similar to the proposed regulation. The complete text of the final regulation follows.

§ 1.125-3 Effect of the Family and Medical Leave Act (FMLA) on the operation of cafeteria plans.

The following questions and answers provide guidance on the effect of the Family and Medical Leave Act (FMLA), 29 U.S.C. 2601 et seq., on the operation of cafeteria plans:

Q-1: May an employee revoke coverage or cease payment of his or her share of group health plan premiums when taking unpaid FMLA, 29 U.S.C. 2601 et seq., leave?

A-1: Yes. An employer must either allow an employee on unpaid FMLA leave to revoke coverage, or continue coverage but allow the employee to discontinue payment of his or her share of the premium for group health plan coverage (including a health flexible spending arrangement (FSA)) under a cafeteria plan for the period of the FMLA leave. See 29 CFR 825.209(e). FMLA does not require that an employer allow an employee to revoke coverage if the employer pays the employee's share of premiums. As discussed in Q&A-3, if the employer continues coverage during an FMLA leave, the employer may recover the employee's share of the premiums when the employee returns to work. FMLA also provides the employee a right to be reinstated in the group health plan coverage (including a health FSA) provided under a cafeteria plan upon returning from FMLA leave if the employee's group health plan coverage terminated while on FMLA leave (either by revocation or due to nonpayment of premiums). Such an employee is entitled, to the extent required under FMLA, to be reinstated on the same terms as prior to taking FMLA leave (including family or dependent coverage), subject to any changes in benefit levels that may have taken place during the period of FMLA leave as provided in 29 CFR

825.215(d)(1). See 29 CFR 825.209(e) and 825.215(d). In addition, such an employee has the right to revoke or change elections under § 1.125-4 (e.g., because of changes in status or cost or coverage changes as provided under § 1.125-4) under the same terms and conditions as are available to employees participating in the cafeteria plan who are working and not on FMLA leave.

Q-2: Who is responsible for making premium payments under a cafeteria plan when an employee on FMLA leave continues group health plan coverage?

A-2: FMLA provides that an employee is entitled to continue group health plan coverage during FMLA leave whether or not that coverage is provided under a health FSA or other component of a cafeteria plan. See 29 CFR 825.209(b). FMLA permits an employer to require an employee who chooses to continue group health plan coverage while on FMLA leave to be responsible for the share of group health premiums that would be allocable to the employee if the employee were working, and, for this purpose, treats amounts paid pursuant to a pre-tax salary reduction agreement as amounts allocable to the employee. However, FMLA requires the employer to continue to contribute the share of the cost of the employee's coverage that the employer was paying before the employee commenced FMLA leave. See 29 CFR 825.100(b) and 825.210(a).

Q-3: What payment options are required or permitted to be offered under a cafeteria plan to an employee who continues group health plan coverage while on unpaid FMLA leave, and what is the tax treatment of these payments?

A-3: (a) *In general.* Subject to the limitations described in paragraph (b) of this Q&A-3, a cafeteria plan may offer one or more of the following payment options, or a combination of these options, to an employee who continues group health plan coverage (including a health FSA) while on unpaid FMLA leave; provided that the payment options for employees on FMLA leave are offered on terms at least as favorable as those offered to employees not on FMLA leave. These options are referred to in this section as pre-pay, pay-as-you-go, and catch-up. See also the FMLA notice requirements at 29 CFR 825.301(b)(1)(iv).

(1) *Pre-pay.* (i) Under the pre-pay option, a cafeteria plan may permit an employee to pay, prior to commencement of the FMLA leave period, the amounts due for the FMLA leave period. However, FMLA provides that the employer may not mandate that an employee pre-pay the amounts due for the leave period. See 29 CFR 825.210(c)(3) and (4).

(ii) Contributions under the pre-pay option may be made on a pre- tax salary reduction basis from any taxable compensation (including from unused sick days or vacation days). However, see Q&A-5 of this section regarding additional restrictions on pre-tax salary reduction contributions when an employee's FMLA leave spans two cafeteria plan years.

(iii) Contributions under the pre-pay option may also be made on an after-tax basis.

(2) *Pay-as-you-go.* (i) Under the pay-as-you-go option, employees may pay their share of the premium payments on the same schedule as payments would have been made if the employee were not on leave or under any other payment schedule permitted by the Labor Regulations at 29 CFR 825.210(c) (e.g., on the same schedule as payments are made under section 4980B (relating to coverage under the Consolidated Omnibus Budget Reconciliation Act (COBRA), 26 U.S.C. 4980B), under the employer's existing rules for payment by employees on leave without pay, or under any other C6/ROP10-12-01 system voluntarily agreed to between the employer and the employee that is not inconsistent with this section or with 29 CFR 825.210(c)).

(ii) Contributions under the pay-as-you-go option are generally made by the employee on an after-tax basis. However, contributions may be made on a pre-tax basis to the extent that the contributions are made from taxable compensation (e.g., from unused sick days or vacation days) that is due the employee during the leave period.

(iii) An employer is not required to continue the group health coverage of an employee who fails to make required premium payments while on FMLA leave, provided that the employer follows the notice procedures required under FMLA. See 29 CFR 825.212. However, if the employer chooses to continue the health coverage of an employee who fails to pay his or her share of the premium payments while on FMLA leave, FMLA permits the employer to recoup the premiums (to the extent of the employee's share). See 29 CFR 825.212(b). Such recoupment may be made as set forth in paragraphs (a)(3)(i) and (ii) of this Q&A-3. See also Q&A-6 of this section regarding coverage under a health FSA when an employee fails to make the required premium payments while on FMLA leave.

(3) *Catch-up.* (i) Under the catch-up option, the employer and the employee may agree in advance that the group coverage will continue during the period of unpaid FMLA leave, and that the employee will not pay premiums until the employee returns from the FMLA leave. Where an employee is electing to use the catch-up option, the employer and the employee must agree in advance of the coverage period that: the employee elects to continue health coverage while on unpaid FMLA leave; the employer assumes responsibility for advancing payment of the premiums on the employee's behalf during the FMLA leave; and these advance amounts are to be paid by the employee when the employee returns from FMLA leave.

(ii) When an employee fails to make required premium payments while on FMLA leave, an employer is permitted to utilize the catch-up option to recoup the employee's share of premium payments when the employee returns from FMLA leave. See, e.g., 29 CFR 825.212(b). If the employer chooses to continue group coverage under these circumstances, the prior agreement of the employee, as set forth in paragraph (a)(3)(i) of this Q&A-3, is not required.

(iii) Contributions under the catch-up option may be made on a pre- tax salary reduction basis from any available taxable compensation (including from unused sick days and vacation days) after the employee returns from FMLA leave. The cafeteria plan may provide for the catch- up option to apply on a pre-tax salary reduction basis if premiums have not been paid on any other basis (i.e., have not been paid under the pre-pay or pay-as-you-go options or on a catch-up after-tax basis).

(iv) Contributions under the catch-up option may also be made on an after-tax basis.

(b) *Exceptions.* Whatever payment options are offered to employees on non-FMLA leave must be offered to employees on FMLA leave. In accordance with 29 CFR 825.210(c), cafeteria plans may offer one or more of the payment options described in paragraph (a) of this Q&A-3, with the following exceptions:

(1) FMLA does not permit the pre-pay option to be the sole option offered to employees on FMLA leave. However, the cafeteria plan may include pre-payment as an option for employees on FMLA leave, even if such option is not offered to employees on non-FMLA leave-without-pay.

(2) FMLA allows the catch-up option to be the sole option offered to employees on FMLA leave if and only if the catch-up option is the sole option offered to employees on non-FMLA leave-without-pay.

(3) If the pay-as-you-go option is offered to employees on non-FMLA leave-without-pay, the option must also be offered to employees on FMLA leave. The employer may also offer employees on FMLA leave the pre-pay option and/or the catch-up option.

(c) *Voluntary waiver of employee payments.* In addition to the foregoing payment options, an employer may voluntarily waive, on a nondiscriminatory basis, the requirement that employees who elect to continue group health coverage while on FMLA leave pay the amounts the employees would otherwise be required to pay for the leave period.

(d) *Example.* The following example illustrates this Q&A-3:

Example. (i) Employer Y allows employees to pay premiums for group health coverage during an FMLA leave on an after-tax basis while the employee is on unpaid FMLA leave. Under the terms of Y's cafeteria plan, if an employee elects to continue health coverage during an unpaid FMLA leave and fails to pay one or more of the after-tax premium payments due for that coverage, the employee's salary after the employee returns from FMLA leave is reduced to cover unpaid premiums (i.e. the premiums that were to be paid by the employee on an after-tax basis during the FMLA leave, but were paid by the employer instead).

(ii) In this Example, Y's cafeteria plan satisfies the conditions in this Q&A-3. Y's cafeteria plan would also satisfy the conditions in this Q&A-3 if the plan provided for coverage to cease in the event the employee fails to make a premium payment when due during an unpaid FMLA leave.

Q-4: Do the special FMLA requirements concerning payment of premiums by an employee who continues group health plan coverage under a cafeteria plan apply if the employee is on paid FMLA leave?

A-4: No. The Labor Regulations provide that, if an employee's FMLA leave is paid leave as described at 29 CFR 825.207 and the employer mandates that the employee continue group health plan coverage while on FMLA leave, the employee's share of the premiums must be paid by the method normally used during any paid leave (e.g., by pre-tax salary reduction if the employee's share of premiums were paid by pre-tax salary reduction before the FMLA leave began). See 29 CFR 825.210(b).

Q-5: What restrictions apply to contributions when an employee's FMLA leave spans two cafeteria plan years?

A-5: (a) No amount will be included in an employee's gross income due to participation in a cafeteria plan during FMLA leave, provided that the plan complies with other generally applicable cafeteria plan requirements. Among other requirements, a plan may not operate in a manner that enables employees on FMLA leave to defer compensation from one cafeteria plan year to a subsequent cafeteria plan year. See section 125(d)(2).

(b) The following example illustrates this Q&A-5:

Example. (i) Employee A elects group health coverage under a calendar year cafeteria plan maintained by Employer X. Employee A's premium for health coverage is $100 per month throughout the 12- month period of coverage. Employee A takes FMLA leave for 12 weeks beginning on October 31 after making 10 months of premium payments totaling $1,000 (10 months x $100 = $1,000). Employee A elects to continue health coverage while on FMLA leave and utilizes the pre- pay option by applying his or her unused sick days in order to make the required premium payments due while he or she is on FMLA leave.

(ii) Because A cannot defer compensation from one plan year to a subsequent plan year, A may pre-pay the premiums due in November and December (i.e., $100 per month) on a pre-tax basis, but A cannot pre-pay the premium payment due in January on a pre-tax basis. If A participates in the cafeteria plan in the subsequent plan year, A must either pre-pay for January on an after-tax basis or use another option (e.g., pay-as-you-go, catch-up, reduction in unused sick days, etc.) to make the premium payment due in January.

Q-6: Are there special rules concerning employees taking FMLA leave who participate in health FSAs offered under a cafeteria plan?

A-6: (a) *In general.* (1) A group health plan that is a flexible spending arrangement (FSA) offered under a cafeteria plan must conform to the generally applicable rules in this section concerning employees who take FMLA leave. Thus, to the extent required by FMLA (see 29 CFR 825.209(b)), an employer must—

(i) Permit an employee taking FMLA leave to continue coverage under a health FSA while on FMLA leave; and

(ii) If an employee is on unpaid FMLA leave, either—

(A) Allow the employee to revoke coverage; or

(B) Continue coverage, but allow the employee to discontinue payment of his or her share of the premium for the health FSA under the cafeteria plan during the unpaid FMLA leave period.

(2) Under FMLA, the plan must permit the employee to be reinstated in health coverage upon return from FMLA leave on the same terms as if the employee had been working throughout the leave period, without a break in coverage. See 29 CFR 825.214(a) and 825.215(d)(1) and paragraph (b)(2) of this Q&A-6. In addition, under FMLA, a plan may require an employee to be reinstated in health coverage upon return from a period of unpaid FMLA leave, provided that employees who return from a period of unpaid leave not covered by the FMLA are also required to resume participation upon return from leave.

(b) *Coverage.* (1) Regardless of the payment option selected under Q&A-3 of this section, for so long as the employee continues health FSA coverage (or for so long as the employer continues the health FSA coverage of an employee who fails to make the required contributions as described in Q&A-3(a)(2)(iii) of this section), the full amount of the elected health FSA coverage, less any prior reimbursements, must be available to the employee at all times, including the FMLA leave period.

(2) (i) If an employee's coverage under the health FSA terminates while the employee is on FMLA leave, the employee is not entitled to receive reimbursements for claims incurred during the period when the coverage is terminated. If an employee subsequently elects or the employer requires the employee to be reinstated in the health FSA upon return from FMLA leave for the remainder of the plan year, the employee may not retroactively elect health FSA coverage for claims incurred during the period when the coverage was terminated. Upon reinstatement into a health FSA upon return from FMLA leave (either because the employee elects reinstatement or because the employer requires reinstatement), the employee has the right under FMLA: to resume coverage at the level in effect before the FMLA leave and make up the unpaid premium payments, or to resume coverage at a level that is reduced and resume premium payments at the level in effect before the FMLA leave. If an employee chooses to resume health FSA coverage at a level that is reduced, the coverage is prorated for the period during the FMLA leave for which no premiums were paid. In both cases, the coverage level is reduced by prior reimbursements.

(ii) FMLA requires that an employee on FMLA leave have the right to revoke or change elections (because of events described in § 1.125- 4) under the same terms and conditions that apply to employees participating in the cafeteria plan who are not on FMLA leave. Thus, for example, if a group health plan offers an annual open enrollment period to active employees, then, under FMLA, an employee on FMLA leave when the open enrollment is offered must be offered the right to make election changes on the same basis as other employees. Similarly, if a group health plan decides to offer a new benefit package option and allows active employees to elect the new option, then, under FMLA, an employee on FMLA leave must be allowed to elect the new option on the same basis as other employees.

(3) The following examples illustrate the rules in this Q&A-6:

Example 1. (i) Employee B elects $1,200 worth of coverage under a calendar year health FSA provided under a cafeteria plan, with an annual premium of $1,200. Employee B is permitted to pay the $1,200 through pre-tax salary reduction amounts of $100 per month throughout the 12-month period of coverage. Employee B incurs no medical expenses prior to April 1. On April 1, B takes FMLA leave after making three months of contributions totaling $300 (3 months x $100 = $300). Employee B's coverage ceases during the FMLA leave. Consequently, B makes no premium payments for the months of April, May, and June, and B is not entitled to submit claims or receive reimbursements for expenses incurred during this period. Employee B returns from FMLA leave and elects to be reinstated in the health FSA on July 1.

(ii) Employee B must be given a choice of resuming coverage at the level in effect before the FMLA leave (i.e., $1,200) and making up the unpaid premium payments ($300), or resuming health FSA coverage at a level that is reduced on a prorata basis for the period during the FMLA leave for which no premiums were paid (i.e., reduced for 3 months or 1/4 of the plan year) less prior reimbursements (i.e., $0) with premium payments due in the same monthly amount payable before the leave (i.e., $100 per month). Consequently, if B chooses to resume coverage at the level in effect before the FMLA leave, B's coverage for the remainder of the plan year would equal $1,200 and B's monthly premiums would be increased to $150 per month for the remainder of the plan year, to make up the $300 in premiums missed ($100 per month plus $50 per month ($300 divided by the remaining 6 months)). If B chooses prorated coverage, B's coverage for the remainder of the plan year would equal $900, and B would resume making premium payments of $100 per month for the remainder of the plan year.

Example 2. (i) Assume the same facts as Example 1 except that B incurred medical expenses totaling $200 in February and obtained reimbursement of these expenses.

(ii) The results are the same as in Example 1, except that if B chooses to resume coverage at the level in effect before the FMLA leave, B's coverage for the remainder of the year would equal $1,000 ($1,200 reduced by $200) and the monthly payments for the remainder of the year would still equal $150. If instead B chooses prorated coverage, B's coverage for the remainder of the plan year would equal $700 ($1,200 prorated for 3 months, and then reduced by $200) and the monthly payments for the remainder of the year would still equal $100.

Example 3. (i) Assume the same facts as Example 1 except that, prior to taking FMLA leave, B elects to continue health FSA coverage during the FMLA leave. The plan permits B (and B elects) to use the catch-up payment option described in Q&A-3 of this section, and as further permitted under the plan, B chooses to repay the $300 in missed payments on a ratable basis over the remaining 6-month period of coverage (i.e., $50 per month).

(ii) Thus, B's monthly premium payments for the remainder of the plan year will be $150 ($100 + $50).

Q-7: Are employees entitled to non-health benefits while taking FMLA leave?

A-7: FMLA does not require an employer to maintain an employee's non-health benefits (e.g., life insurance) during FMLA leave. An employee's entitlement to benefits other than group health benefits under a cafeteria plan during a period of FMLA leave is to be determined by the employer's established policy for providing such benefits when the employee is on non-FMLA leave (paid or unpaid). See 29 CFR 825.209(h). Therefore, an employee who takes FMLA leave is entitled to revoke an election of non-health benefits under a cafeteria plan to the same extent as employees taking non-FMLA leave are permitted to revoke elections of non-health benefits under a cafeteria plan. For example, election changes are permitted due to changes of status or upon enrollment for a new plan year. See § 1.125-4. However, FMLA provides that, in certain cases, an employer may continue an employee's non-health benefits under the employer's cafeteria plan while the employee is on FMLA leave in order to ensure that the employer can meet its responsibility to provide equivalent benefits to the employee upon return from unpaid FMLA. If the employer continues an employee's non-health benefits during FMLA leave, the employer is entitled to recoup the costs incurred for paying the employee's share of the premiums during the FMLA leave period. See 29 CFR 825.213(b). Such recoupment may be on a pre-tax basis. A cafeteria plan must, as required by FMLA, permit an employee whose coverage terminated while on FMLA leave (either by revocation or nonpayment of premiums) to be reinstated in the cafeteria plan on return from FMLA leave. See 29 CFR 825.214(a) and 825.215(d).

Q-8: What is the applicability date of the regulations in this section?

A-8: This section is applicable for cafeteria plan years beginning on or after January 1, 2002. [Reg. § 1.125-3.]

Appendix L

Revenue Ruling 61-146

Reimbursements by an employer to his employees for his share of premiums for hospital and medical insurance for them may be considered as contributions by the employer to accident or health plans for his employees so as to result in the exclusion of such payments from the gross income of the employees under section 106 of the Internal Revenue Code of 1954.

Revenue Ruling 57-33, C.B. 1957-1, 303, distinguished.

Advice has been requested whether amounts paid by an employer, under the circumstances below, as his share of premiums for hospital and medical insurance for his employees are excludable from the gross income of the employees under section 106 of the Internal Revenue Code of 1954.

In the instant case, the employer pays a share of the premiums for hospital and medical insurance for his employees. For those employees who are covered by a group policy through their employment, the employer pays his share of the premium directly to the insurance company. For those employees who are not covered by the employer's group policy but have other types of hospital and medical insurance for which they pay the premiums directly to the insurers, the employer pays a part of such premiums upon proof that the insurance is in force and is being paid for by the employees.

To facilitate payment of his share of the premiums paid directly by the employees to the insurers, the employer uses the following methods: (1) reimburses each employee directly once or twice a year for the employer's share of the insurance premiums upon proof of prior payment of the premiums by the employee; (2) issues to each employee a check payable to the particular employee's insurance company, the employee being obligated to turn over the check to the insurance company; or (3) issues a check as in method (2) except the check is made payable jointly to the insurance company and the employee.

Section 106 of the Code provides that gross income does not include contributions by the employer to accident or health plans for compensation (through insurance or otherwise) to his employees for personal injuries or sickness.

Section 1.106-1 of the Income Tax Regulations provides that the employer may contribute to an accident or health plan either by paying the premium (or a portion of the premium) on a policy of accident or health insurance covering one or more of his employees, or by contributing to a separate trust or fund, which provides accident or health benefits directly or through insurance to one or more of his employees.

In this case it is clear that in method (2) the employer is actually paying accident or health insurance premiums directly to the insurer of the particular employee, utilizing the employee as his agent for the delivery of the checks to the insurer. Method (3) is not substantially different, inasmuch as the employee there is obligated to turn the checks over to the insurer and can in no event divert the payments to other uses. Although method (1) involves direct payment to the employee, in practical effect it does not differ from methods (2) or (3), since proof is required by the employer that hospital and medical insurance is in force for the employee and that premiums for the period involved have been paid by the employee and because the employer's payment is stated to be in reimbursement for the employe's share of the insurance premiums.

Under the circumstances of this case, it is held that the amounts paid by the employer under methods (2) or (3) above constitute payments of premiums or portions of premiums on policies of accident or health insurance covering one or more employees within the meaning of section 1.106-1 of the regulations. Similarly, the payments under method (1) constitute employer payments of accident or health insurance premiums for employees if the payments are shown to be in reimbursement of premiums actually paid by the employees to the insurers. Accordingly, amounts paid as above are excludable from the gross income of the employees under section 106 of the Code.

Revenue Ruling 57-33, C.B. 1957-1, 303, holds that certain weekly payments made by employers direct to employees, pursuant to a union contract of employment, for the purpose of purchasing individual hospitalization and surgical insurance coverage, are "wages" for Federal employment tax purposes and are includible in the gross income of the employees.

Under the facts in that case, the employers had no accident or health plan of their own in effect and, with respect to the payments which they made directly to the employees, did not require an accounting either by the employees or the employees' union that the funds were expended in the acquisition of insurance coverage. Revenue Ruling 57-33, accordingly, is distinguishable from the instant case.

Certain payments made by employers direct to employees, pursuant to a union contract of employment, for the purpose of purchasing individual hospitalization and surgical insurance coverage, constitute "wages" for purposes of the Federal employment taxes.

Advice has been requested relative to the applicability of the taxes imposed by the Federal Insurance Contributions Act, the Federal Unemployment Tax Act, and the Collection of Income Tax at Source on Wages (chapters 21, 23, and 24, respectively, subtitle C, Internal Revenue Code of 1954), to payments made by member employers of an employers' association to employees for use in the purchase of hospitalization and surgical insurance coverage.

Pursuant to the contract of employment entered into between the association on behalf of its members and the employees' union, the member employers are required to pay a stipulated sum weekly to each employee covered by the agreement for the purchase of individual hospitalization and surgical insurance coverage. Where less than a full week is worked, the agreed-upon amount is prorated on a percentage basis per shift worked. It is further agreed that in lieu of these weekly payments the member employers may provide individual hospitalization and surgical insurance benefits to their union employees under a company plan, provided written notice is given to the union.

As specifically agreed to by the parties concerned, the payment of the sum per week is for the express purpose of purchasing the hospitalization and surgical insurance benefits for covered employees. Where member employers have no existing company program to cover their employees, the union assumes the responsibility of making sure that its members spend the weekly payment for such benefits. The union has made direct arrangements with a hospital service for this purpose and in no instance are payments under the contract being made or used for a purpose other than providing the hospitalization and surgical insurance benefits.

For purposes of the Federal Insurance Contributions Act, the Federal Unemployment Tax Act, and the Collection of Income Tax at Source on Wages, "wages" consist of all remuneration for services performed by an employee for his employer, including the cash value of all remuneration paid in any medium other than cash, with certain exceptions not here material.

The payments in the instant case are required under the terms of a labor agreement governing employee relations of the employers here involved, they are directly related to the units of services performed by the employees, and they are paid directly to the employees by the employers. Thus, they constitute a basic part of the compensation of each employee involved. Accordingly, it is held that such payments which are made by the employers directly to the employees constitute "wages" for "employment" for purposes of the Federal employment taxes (chapters 21, 23, and 24, supra) and are includible in the gross income of the employees under section 61 of the 1954 Code.

The fact that the union assumes the responsibility for the disposition of such payments by the employees and the purchase of hospitalization and surgical insurance is immaterial.

In reaching these conclusions, consideration was given to S.S.T. 146, C.B. 1937-1, 443, S.S.T. 234, C.B. 1937-2, 458, and I.T. 3738, C.B. 1945, 90, which hold that the payments by the employers under the circumstances present in those rulings do not constitute wages. It is believed that the facts in the instant case are distinguishable from the facts and circumstances in those rulings and, therefore, justify the conclusions reached herein.

Appendix M

Final Treasury Regulations § 1.125-4

On January 10, 2001, the IRS released Treasury Regulations Section 1.125-4, providing further guidance for cafeteria plans on permitted election changes. [TD 8878 (Mar 22, 2000), amended by TD 8921 (Jan 9, 2001)] Most of these final regulations are effective for plan years beginning on or after January 1, 2001, and a few provisions are effective for plan years beginning on or after January 1, 2002. They replace Temporary Treasury Regulations Section 1.125-4T, which expired November 6, 2000, and Proposed Treasury Regulations Section 1.125-4, which was published in March 2000.

§ 1.125-4. Permitted election changes

(a) *Election changes.* A cafeteria plan may permit an employee to revoke an election during a period of coverage and to make a new election only as provided in paragraphs (b) through (g) of this section. Section 125 does not require a cafeteria plan to permit any of these changes. See paragraph (h) of this section for special provisions relating to qualified cash or deferred arrangements, and paragraph (i) of this section for special definitions used in this section.

(b) *Special enrollment rights*—(1) *In general.* A cafeteria plan may permit an employee to revoke an election for coverage under a group health plan during a period of coverage and make a new election that corresponds with the special enrollment rights provided in section 9801(f).

(2) *Examples.* The following examples illustrate the application of this paragraph (b):

Example 1. (i) Employer *M* provides health coverage for its employees pursuant to a plan that is subject to section 9801(f). Under the plan, employees may elect either employee-only coverage or family coverage. *M* also maintains a calendar year cafeteria plan under which qualified benefits, including health coverage, are funded through salary reduction. *M*'s employee, *A*, is married to *B* and they have a child, *C*. In accordance with *M*'s cafeteria plan, Employee *A* elects employee-only health coverage before the beginning of the calendar year. During the year, *A* and *B* adopt a child, *D*. Within 30 days thereafter, *A* wants to revoke *A*'s election for employee-only health coverage and obtain family health coverage for *A*'s spouse, *C*, and *D* as of the date of *D*'s adoption. Employee *A* satisfies the conditions for special enrollment of an employee with a new dependent under section 9801(f)(2), so that *A* may enroll in family coverage under *M*'s accident or health plan in order to provide coverage effective as of the date of *D*'s adoption.

(ii) *M*'s cafeteria plan may permit *A* to change *A*'s salary reduction election to family coverage for salary not yet currently available. The increased salary reduction is permitted to reflect the cost of family coverage from the date of adoption. (*A*'s adoption of *D* is also a change in status, and the election of family coverage is consistent with that change in status. Thus, under paragraph (c) of this section, *M*'s cafeteria plan could permit *A* to elect family coverage prospectively in order to cover *B*, *C*, and *D* for the remaining portion of the period of coverage.)

Example 2. (i) The employer plans and permissible coverage are the same as in *Example 1.* Before the beginning of the calendar year, Employee *E* elects employee-only health coverage under *M*'s cafeteria plan. Employee *E* marries *F* during the plan year. *F*'s employer, *N*, offers health coverage to *N*'s employees, and, prior to the marriage, *F* had elected employee-only coverage. Employee *E* wants to revoke the election for employee-only coverage under *M*'s cafeteria plan, and is considering electing family health coverage under *M*'s plan or obtaining family health coverage under *N*'s plan.

(ii) *M*'s cafeteria plan may permit *E* to change *E*'s salary reduction election to reflect the change to family coverage under *M*'s accident or health plan because the marriage would result in special enrollment rights under section 9801(f), pursuant to which an election of family coverage under *M*'s accident or health plan would be required to be effective no later than the first day of the first calendar month beginning after the completed request for enrollment is received by the plan. Since no retroactive coverage is required in the event of marriage under section 9801(f), *E*'s salary reduction election may only be changed on a prospective basis. (*E*'s marriage to *F* is also a change in status under paragraph (c) of this section, as illustrated in *Example 1* of paragraph (c)(4) of this section.)

(c) *Changes in status*—(1) *In general*—(i) *Change in status rule.* A cafeteria plan may permit an employee to revoke an election during a period of coverage with respect to a qualified benefits plan to which this paragraph (c) applies and make a new election for the remaining portion of the period (referred to in this section as an election change) if, under the facts and circumstances—

(A) A change in status described in paragraph (c)(2) of this section occurs; and

(B) The election change satisfies the consistency rule of paragraph (c)(3) of this section.

(ii) *Application to accident or health plans and group-term life insurance plans.* This paragraph (c) applies to plans providing accident or health coverage and plans providing group-term life insurance coverage.

(iii) *Application to other qualified benefits.* [Reserved]

(2) *Change in status events.* The following events are changes in status for purposes of this paragraph (c):

(i) *Legal marital status.* Events that change an employee's legal marital status, including the following: marriage; death of spouse; divorce; legal separation; and annulment.

(ii) *Number of dependents.* Events that change an employee's number of dependents, including the following: birth; death; adoption; and placement for adoption.

(iii) *Employment status.* Any of the following events that change the employment status of the employee, the employee's spouse, or the employee's dependent: a termination or commencement of employment; a strike or lockout; a commencement of or return from an unpaid leave of absence; and a change in worksite. In addition, if the eligibility conditions of the cafeteria plan or other employee benefit plan of the employer of the employee, spouse, or dependent depend on the employment status of that individual and there is a change in that individual's employment status with the consequence that the individual becomes (or ceases to be) eligible under the plan, then that change constitutes a change in employment under this paragraph (c) (e.g., if a plan only applies to salaried employees and an employee switches from salaried to hourly-paid with the consequence that the employee ceases to be eligible for the plan, then that change constitutes a change in employment status under this paragraph (c)(2)(iii)).

(iv) *Dependent satisfies or ceases to satisfy eligibility requirements.* Events that cause an employee's dependent to satisfy or cease to satisfy eligibility requirements for coverage on account of attainment of age, student status, or any similar circumstance.

(v) *Residence.* A change in the place of residence of the employee, spouse, or dependent.

(3) *Consistency rule*—(i) *Application to accident or health coverage and group-term life insurance.* An election change satisfies the requirements of this paragraph (c)(3) with respect to accident or health coverage or group-term life insurance only if the election change is on account of and corresponds with a change in status that affects eligibility for coverage under an employer's plan.

(ii) *Application to other qualified benefits.* [Reserved]

(iii) *Application of consistency rule.* If the change in status is the employee's divorce, annulment or legal separation from a spouse, the death of a spouse or dependent, or a dependent ceasing to satisfy the eligibility requirements for coverage, an employee's election under the cafeteria plan to cancel accident or health insurance coverage for any individual other than the spouse involved in the divorce, annulment or legal separation, the deceased spouse or dependent, or the dependent that ceased to satisfy the eligibility requirements for coverage, respectively, fails to correspond with that change in status. Thus, if a dependent dies or ceases to satisfy the eligibility requirements for coverage, the employee's election to cancel accident or health coverage for any other dependent, for the employee, or for the employee's spouse fails to correspond with that change in status. In addition, if an employee, spouse, or dependent gains eligibility for coverage under a family member plan (as defined in paragraph (i)(5) of this section) as a result of a change in marital status under paragraph (c)(2)(i) of this section or a change in employment status under paragraph (c)(2)(iii) of this section, an employee's election under the cafeteria plan to cease or decrease coverage for that individual under the cafeteria plan corresponds with that change in status only if coverage for that individual becomes applicable or is increased under the family member plan. However, if the change in status is a change in the employee's marital status under paragraph (c)(2)(i) of this section or a change in the employment status of the employee's spouse or dependents under paragraph (c)(2)(iii) of this section, an election to increase, or an election to decrease, group-term life insurance or disability income coverage corresponds with that change in status.

(iv) *Exception for COBRA.* If the employee, spouse, or dependent becomes eligible for continuation coverage under the group health plan of the employee's employer as provided in section 4980B or any similar state law, a cafeteria plan may permit the employee to elect to increase payments under the employer's cafeteria plan in order to pay for the continuation coverage.

(4) *Examples.* The following examples illustrate the application of this paragraph (c):

Example 1. (i) Employer *M* provides health coverage (including a health FSA) for its employees through its cafeteria plan. Before the beginning of the calendar year, Employee *A* elects employee-only health coverage under *M*'s cafeteria plan and elects salary reduction contributions to fund coverage under the health FSA. Employee *A* marries *B* during the year. Employee *B*'s employer, *N*, offers health coverage to *N*'s employees (but not including any health FSA), and, prior to the marriage, *B* had elected employee-only coverage. Employee *A* wants to revoke the election for employee-only coverage, and is considering electing family health coverage under *M*'s plan or obtaining family health coverage under *N*'s plan.

(ii) Employee *A*'s marriage to *B* is a change in status under paragraph (c)(2)(i) of this section, pursuant to which *B* has become eligible for coverage under *M*'s health plan under paragraph (c)(3)(i) of this section. Two possible election changes by *A* correspond with the change in status: Employee *A* may elect family health coverage under *M*'s plan to cover *A* and *B;* or *A* may cancel coverage under *M*'s plan, if *B* elects family health coverage under *N*'s plan to cover *A* and *B*. Thus, *M*'s cafeteria plan may permit *A* to make either election change.

(iii) Employee *A* may also increase salary reduction contributions to fund coverage for *B* under the health FSA.

Example 2. (i) Employee *C,* a single parent, elects family health coverage under a calendar year cafeteria plan maintained by Employer *O*. Employee *C* and *C*'s 21-year-old child, *D,* are covered under *O*'s health plan. During the year, *D* graduates from college. Under the terms of the health plan, dependents over the age of 19 must be full-time students to receive coverage. Employee *C* wants to revoke *C*'s election for family health coverage and obtain employee-only coverage under *O*'s cafeteria plan.

(ii) *D*'s loss of eligibility for coverage under the terms of the health plan is a change in status under paragraph (c)(2)(iv) of this section. A revocation of *C*'s election for family coverage and new election for employee-only coverage corresponds with the change in status. Thus, *O*'s cafeteria plan may permit *C* to elect employee-only coverage.

Example 3. (i) Employee *E* is married to *F* and they have one child, *G*. Employee *E* is employed by Employer *P,* and *P* maintains a calendar year cafeteria plan that allows employees to elect no health coverage, employee-only coverage, employee-plus-one-dependent coverage, or family coverage. Under the plan, before the beginning of the calendar year, *E* elects family health coverage for *E, F,* and *G. E* and *F* divorce during the year and *F* loses eligibility for coverage under *P*'s plan. *G* does not lose eligibility for health coverage under *P*'s plan upon the divorce. *E* now wants to revoke *E*'s election under the cafeteria plan and elect no coverage.

(ii) The divorce is a change in status under paragraph (c)(2)(i). A change in the cafeteria plan election to cancel health coverage for *F* is consistent with that change in status. However, an election change to cancel *E*'s or *G*'s health coverage does not satisfy the consistency rule under paragraph (c)(3)(iii) of this section regarding cancellation of coverage for an employee's other dependents in the event of divorce. Therefore, the cafeteria plan may not permit *E* to elect no coverage. However, an election to change to employee-plus-one-dependent health coverage would correspond with the change in status, and thus the cafeteria plan may permit *E* to elect employee-plus-one-dependent health coverage.

Example 4. (i) Employer *R* maintains a calendar year cafeteria plan under which full-time employees may elect coverage under one of three benefit package options provided under an accident or health plan: an indemnity option or either of two HMO options for employees who work in the respective service areas of the two HMOs. Employee *A,* who works in the service area of HMO #1, elects the HMO #1 option. During the year, *A* is transferred to another work location which is outside the HMO #1 service area and inside the HMO #2 service area.

(ii) The transfer is a change in status under paragraph (c)(2)(iii) of this section (relating to a change in worksite), and, under the consistency rule in paragraph (c)(3) of this section, the cafeteria plan may permit *A* to make an election change to either the indemnity option or HMO #2.

Example 5. (i) Employer *S* maintains a calendar year cafeteria plan that allows employees to elect coverage under an accident or health plan providing indemnity coverage and coverage under a health FSA. Prior to the beginning of the calendar year, Employee *B* elects employee-only indemnity coverage, and elects salary reduction contributions of $600 during the year to fund coverage under the health FSA for up to $600 of reimbursements for the year. Employee *B*'s spouse, *C*, has employee-only coverage under an accident or health plan maintained by *C*'s employer. During the year, *C* terminates employment and loses coverage under that plan. *B* now wants to elect family coverage under *S*'s accident or health plan and increase *B*'s FSA election.

(ii) *C*'s termination of employment is a change in status under paragraph (c)(2)(iii) of this section, and the election change satisfies the consistency rule of paragraph (c)(3) of this section. Therefore, the cafeteria plan may permit *B* to elect family coverage under *S*'s accident or health plan and to increase *B*'s FSA coverage.

Example 6. (i) Employer *T* provides group-term life insurance coverage as described under section 79. Under *T*'s plan, an employee may elect life insurance coverage in an amount up to $50,000. *T* also maintains a calendar year cafeteria plan under which qualified benefits, including the group-term life insurance coverage, are funded through salary reduction. Employee *D* has a spouse and a child. Before the beginning of the year, *D* elects $10,000 of group-term life insurance coverage. During the year, *D* is divorced.

(ii) The divorce is a change in status under paragraph (c)(2)(i) of this section. Under paragraph (c)(3)(iii) of this section, either an increase or a decrease in coverage is consistent with this change in status. Thus, *T*'s cafeteria plan may permit *D* to increase or to decrease *D*'s group-term life insurance coverage.

Example 7. (i) Employee *E* is married to *F* and they have one child, *G*. Employee *E*'s employer, *U*, maintains a cafeteria plan under which employees may elect no coverage, employee-only coverage, or family coverage under a group health plan maintained by *U*, and may make a separate vision coverage election under the plan. Before the beginning of the calendar year, *E* elects family health coverage and no vision coverage under *U*'s cafeteria plan. Employee *F*'s employer, *V*, maintains a cafeteria plan under which employees may elect no coverage, employee-only coverage, or family coverage under a group health plan maintained by *V*, and may make a separate vision coverage election under the plan. Before the beginning of the calendar year, *F* elects no health coverage and employee-only vision coverage under *V*'s plan. During the year, *F* terminates employment with *V* and loses vision coverage under *V*'s plan. Employee *E* now wants to elect family vision coverage under *U*'s group health plan.

(ii) *F*'s termination of employment is a change in status under paragraph (c)(2)(iii) of this section, and the election change satisfies the consistency rule of paragraph (c)(3) of this section. Therefore, *U*'s cafeteria plan may permit *E* to elect family vision coverage (covering *E* and *G* as well as *F*) under *U*'s group health plan.

Example 8. (i) Before the beginning of the year, Employee *H* elects to participate in a cafeteria plan maintained by *H*'s employer, *W*. However, in order to change the election during the year so as to cancel coverage, and by prior understanding with *W*, *H* terminates employment and resumes employment one week later.

(ii) In this *Example 8*, under the facts and circumstances, a principal purpose of the termination of employment was to alter the election, and reinstatement of employment was understood at the time of termination. Accordingly, *H* does not have a change in status under paragraph (c)(2)(iii) of this section.

(iii) However, *H*'s termination of employment would constitute a change in status, permitting a cancellation of coverage during the period of unemployment, if *H*'s original cafeteria plan election for the period of coverage was reinstated upon resumption of employment (for example, if *W*'s cafeteria plan contains a provision requiring an employee who resumes employment within 30 days, without any other intervening event that would permit a change in election, to return to the election in effect prior to termination of employment).

(iv) If, instead, *H* terminates employment and cancels coverage during a period of unemployment, and then returns to work more than 30 days following termination of employment, the cafeteria plan may permit *H* the option of returning to the election in effect prior to termination of employment or making a new election under the plan. Alternatively, the cafeteria plan may prohibit *H* from returning to the plan during that plan year.

(c) *Changes in status*—(1) *Change in status rule.* A cafeteria plan may permit an employee to revoke an election during a period of coverage with respect to a qualified benefits plan (defined in paragraph (i)(8) of this section) to which this paragraph (c) applies and make a new election for the remaining portion of the period (referred to in this section as an election change) if, under the facts and circumstances—

(i) A change in status described in paragraph (c)(2) of this section occurs; and

(ii) The election change satisfies the consistency rule of paragraph (c)(3) of this section.

(2) *Change in status events.* The following events are changes in status for purposes of this paragraph (c):

(i) *Legal marital status.* Events that change an employee's legal marital status, including the following: marriage; death of spouse; divorce; legal separation; and annulment.

(ii) *Number of dependents.* Events that change an employee's number of dependents, including the following: birth; death; adoption; and placement for adoption.

(iii) *Employment status.* Any of the following events that change the employment status of the employee, the employee's spouse, or the employee's dependent: a termination or commencement of employment; a strike or lockout; a commencement of or return from an unpaid leave of absence; and a change in worksite. In addition, if the eligibility conditions of the cafeteria plan or other employee benefit plan of the employer of the employee, spouse, or dependent depend on the employment status of that individual and there is a change in that individual's employment status with the consequence that the individual becomes (or ceases to be) eligible under the plan, then that change constitutes a change in employment under this paragraph (c) (e.g., if a plan only applies to salaried employees and an employee switches from salaried to hourly-paid with the consequence that the employee ceases to be eligible for the plan, then that change constitutes a change in employment status under this paragraph (c)(2)(iii)).

(iv) *Dependent satisfies or ceases to satisfy eligibility requirements.* Events that cause an employee's dependent to satisfy or cease to satisfy eligibility requirements for coverage on account of attainment of age, student status, or any similar circumstance.

(v) *Residence.* A change in the place of residence of the employee, spouse, or dependent.

(vi) *Adoption assistance.* For purposes of adoption assistance provided through a cafeteria plan, the commencement or termination of an adoption proceeding.

(3) *Consistency rule*—(i) *Application to accident or health coverage and group-term life insurance.* An election change satisfies the requirements of this paragraph (c)(3) with respect to accident or health coverage or group-term life insurance only if the election change is on account of and corresponds with a change in status that affects eligibility for coverage under an employer's plan. A change in status that affects eligibility under an employer's plan includes a change in status that results in an increase or decrease in the number of an employee's family members or dependents who may benefit from coverage under the plan.

(ii) *Application to other qualified benefits.* [Reserved]

(iii) *Application of consistency rule.* If the change in status is the employee's divorce, annulment or legal separation from a spouse, the death of a spouse or dependent, or a dependent ceasing to satisfy the eligibility requirements for coverage, an employee's election under the cafeteria plan to cancel accident or health insurance coverage for any individual other than the spouse involved in the divorce, annulment or legal separation, the deceased spouse or dependent, or the dependent that ceased to satisfy the eligibility requirements for coverage, respectively, fails to correspond with that change in status. Thus, if a dependent dies or ceases to satisfy the eligibility requirements for coverage, the employee's election to cancel accident or health coverage for any other dependent, for the employee, or for the employee's spouse fails to correspond with that change in status. In addition, if an employee, spouse, or dependent gains eligibility for coverage under a family member plan (as defined in paragraph (i)(5) of this section) as a result of a change in marital status under paragraph (c)(2)(i) of this section or a change in employment status under paragraph (c)(2)(iii) of this section, an employee's election under the cafeteria plan to cease or decrease coverage for that individual under the cafeteria plan corresponds with that change in status only if coverage for that individual becomes applicable or is increased under the family member plan. With respect to group-term life insurance and disability coverage (as defined in paragraph (i)(4) of this section), an election under a cafeteria plan to increase coverage (or an election to decrease coverage) in response to a change in status described in paragraph (c)(2) of this section is deemed to correspond with that change in status as required by paragraph (c)(3)(i) of this section.

(iv) *Exception for COBRA.* If the employee, spouse, or dependent becomes eligible for continuation coverage under the group health plan of the employee's employer as provided in section 4980B or any similar state law, a cafeteria plan may permit the employee to elect to increase payments under the employer's cafeteria plan in order to pay for the continuation coverage.

(4) *Examples.* The following examples illustrate the application of this paragraph (c):

Example 1. (i) Employer *M* provides health coverage (including a health FSA) for its employees through its cafeteria plan. Before the beginning of the calendar year, Employee *A* elects employee-only health coverage under *M*'s cafeteria plan and elects salary reduction contributions to fund coverage under the health FSA. Employee *A* marries *B* during the year. Employee *B*'s employer, *N*, offers health coverage to *N*'s employees (but not including any health FSA), and, prior to the marriage, *B* had elected employee-only coverage. Employee *A* wants to revoke the election for employee-only coverage, and is considering electing family health coverage under *M*'s plan or obtaining family health coverage under *N*'s plan.

(ii) Employee *A*'s marriage to *B* is a change in status under paragraph (c)(2)(i) of this section, pursuant to which *B* has become eligible for coverage under *M*'s health plan under paragraph (c)(3)(i) of this section. Two possible election changes by *A* correspond with the change in status: Employee *A* may elect family health coverage under *M*'s plan to cover *A* and *B;* or *A* may cancel coverage under *M*'s plan, if *B* elects family health coverage under *N*'s plan to cover *A* and *B*. Thus, *M*'s cafeteria plan may permit *A* to make either election change.

(iii) Employee *A* may also increase salary reduction contributions to fund coverage for *B* under the health FSA.

Example 2. (i) Employee *C*, a single parent, elects family health coverage under a calendar year cafeteria plan maintained by Employer *O*. Employee *C* and *C*'s 21-year-old child, *D*, are covered under *O*'s health plan. During the year, *D* graduates from college. Under the terms of the health plan, dependents over the age of 19 must be full-time students to receive coverage. Employee *C* wants to revoke *C*'s election for family health coverage and obtain employee-only coverage under *O*'s cafeteria plan.

(ii) *D*'s loss of eligibility for coverage under the terms of the health plan is a change in status under paragraph (c)(2)(iv) of this section. A revocation of *C*'s election for family coverage and new election for employee-only coverage corresponds with the change in status. Thus, *O*'s cafeteria plan may permit *C* to elect employee-only coverage.

Example 3. (i) Employee *E* is married to *F* and they have one child, *G*. Employee *E* is employed by Employer *P*, and *P* maintains a calendar year cafeteria plan that allows employees to elect no health coverage, employee-only coverage, employee-plus-one-dependent coverage, or family coverage. Under the plan, before the beginning of the calendar year, *E* elects family health coverage for *E*, *F*, and *G*. *E* and *F* divorce during the year and *F* loses eligibility for coverage under *P*'s plan. *G* does not lose eligibility for health coverage under *P*'s plan upon the divorce. *E* now wants to revoke *E*'s election under the cafeteria plan and elect no coverage.

(ii) The divorce is a change in status under paragraph (c)(2)(i). A change in the cafeteria plan election to cancel health coverage for *F* is consistent with that change in status. However, an election change to cancel *E*'s or *G*'s health coverage does not satisfy the consistency rule under paragraph (c)(3)(iii) of this section regarding cancellation of coverage for an employee's other dependents in the event of divorce. Therefore, the cafeteria plan may not permit *E* to elect no coverage. However, an election to change to employee-plus-one-dependent health coverage would correspond with the change in status, and thus the cafeteria plan may permit *E* to elect employee-plus-one-dependent health coverage.

(iii) In addition, under paragraph (f)(4) of this section, if *F* makes an election change to cover *G* under *F*'s employer's plan, then *E* may make a corresponding change to elect employee-only coverage under *P*'s cafeteria plan.

Example 4. (i) Employer *R* maintains a calendar year cafeteria plan under which full-time employees may elect coverage under one of three benefit package options provided under an accident or health plan: an indemnity option or either of two HMO options for employees who work in the respective service areas of the two HMOs. Employee *A*, who works in the service area of HMO #1, elects the HMO #1 option. During the year, *A* is transferred to another work location which is outside the HMO #1 service area and inside the HMO #2 service area.

(ii) The transfer is a change in status under paragraph (c)(2)(iii) of this section (relating to a change in worksite), and, under the consistency rule in paragraph (c)(3) of this section, the cafeteria plan may permit *A* to make an election change to elect the indemnity option or HMO #2 or to cancel accident or health coverage.

(iii) The change in work location has no effect on *A*'s eligibility under *R*'s health FSA, so no change in *A*'s health FSA is authorized under this paragraph (c).

Example 5. (i) Employer *S* maintains a calendar year cafeteria plan that allows employees to elect coverage under an accident or health plan providing indemnity coverage and coverage under a health FSA. Prior to the beginning of the calendar year, Employee *B* elects employee-only indemnity coverage, and elects salary reduction contributions of $600 during the year to fund coverage under the health FSA for up to $600 of reimbursements for the year. Employee *B*'s spouse, *C*, has employee-only coverage under an accident or health plan maintained by *C*'s employer. During the year, *C* terminates employment and loses coverage under that plan. *B* now wants to elect family coverage under *S*'s accident or health plan and increase *B*'s FSA election.

(ii) *C*'s termination of employment is a change in status under paragraph (c)(2)(iii) of this section, and the election change satisfies the consistency rule of paragraph (c)(3) of this section. Therefore, the cafeteria plan may permit *B* to elect family coverage under *S*'s accident or health plan and to increase *B*'s FSA coverage.

Example 6. (i) Employer *T* provides group-term life insurance coverage as described under section 79. Under *T*'s plan, an employee may elect life insurance coverage in an amount up to $50,000. *T* also maintains a calendar year cafeteria plan under which qualified benefits, including the group-term life insurance coverage, are funded through salary reduction. Employee *D* has a spouse and a child. Before the beginning of the year, *D* elects $10,000 of group-term life insurance coverage. During the year, *D* is divorced.

(ii) The divorce is a change in status under paragraph (c)(2)(i) of this section. Under paragraph (c)(3)(iii) of this section, either an increase or a decrease in coverage is consistent with this change in status. Thus, *T*'s cafeteria plan may permit *D* to increase or to decrease *D*'s group-term life insurance coverage.

Example 7. (i) Employee *E* is married to *F* and they have one child, *G*. Employee *E*'s employer, *U*, maintains a cafeteria plan under which employees may elect no coverage, employee-only coverage, or family coverage under a group health plan maintained by *U*, and may make a separate vision coverage election under the plan. Before the beginning of the calendar year, *E* elects family health coverage and no vision coverage under *U*'s cafeteria plan. Employee *F*'s employer, *V*, maintains a cafeteria plan under which employees may elect no coverage, employee-only coverage, or family coverage under a group health plan maintained by *V*, and may make a separate vision coverage election under the plan. Before the beginning of the calendar year, *F* elects no health coverage and employee-only vision coverage under *V*'s plan. During the year, *F* terminates employment with *V* and loses vision coverage under *V*'s plan. Employee *E* now wants to elect family vision coverage under *U*'s group health plan.

(ii) *F*'s termination of employment is a change in status under paragraph (c)(2)(iii) of this section, and the election change satisfies the consistency rule of paragraph (c)(3) of this section. Therefore, *U*'s cafeteria plan may permit *E* to elect family vision coverage (covering *E* and *G* as well as *F*) under *U*'s group health plan.

Example 8. (i) Before the beginning of the year, Employee *H* elects to participate in a cafeteria plan maintained by *H*'s employer, *W*. However, in order to change the election during the year so as to cancel coverage, and by prior understanding with *W*, *H* terminates employment and resumes employment one week later.

(ii) In this *Example 8*, under the facts and circumstances, a principal purpose of the termination of employment was to alter the election, and reinstatement of employment was understood at the time of termination. Accordingly, *H* does not have a change in status under paragraph (c)(2)(iii) of this section.

(iii) However, *H*'s termination of employment would constitute a change in status, permitting a cancellation of coverage during the period of unemployment, if *H*'s original cafeteria plan election for the period of coverage was reinstated upon resumption of employment (for example, if *W*'s cafeteria plan contains a provision requiring an employee who resumes employment within 30 days, without any other intervening event that would permit a change in election, to return to the election in effect prior to termination of employment).

(iv) If, instead, *H* terminates employment and cancels coverage during a period of unemployment, and then returns to work more than 30 days following termination of employment, the cafeteria plan may permit *H* the option of returning to the election in effect prior to termination of employment or making a new election under the plan. Alternatively, the cafeteria plan may prohibit *H* from returning to the plan during that plan year.

Example 9. (i) Employee *A* has one child, *B*. Employee *A*'s employer, *X*, maintains a calendar year cafeteria plan that allows employees to elect coverage under a dependent care FSA. Prior to the beginning of the calendar year, *A* elects salary reduction contributions of $4,000 during the year to fund coverage under the dependent care FSA for up to $4,000 of reimbursements for the year. During the year, *B* reaches the age of 13, and *A* wants to cancel coverage under the dependent care FSA.

(ii) When *B* turns 13, *B* ceases to satisfy the definition of qualifying individual under section 21(b)(1) of the Internal Revenue Code. Accordingly, *B*'s attainment of age 13 is a change in status under paragraph (c)(2)(iv) of this section that affects *A*'s employment-related expenses as defined in section 21(b)(2). Therefore, *A* may make a corresponding change under *X*'s cafeteria plan to cancel coverage under the dependent care FSA.

Example 10. (i) Employer *Y* maintains a calendar year cafeteria plan under which full-time employees may elect coverage under either an indemnity option or an HMO. Employee *C* elects the employee-only indemnity option. During the year, *C* marries *D*. *D* has two children from a previous marriage, and has family group health coverage in a cafeteria plan sponsored by *D*'s employer, *Z*. *C* wishes to change from employee-only indemnity coverage to HMO coverage for the family. *D* wishes to cease coverage in *Z*'s group health plan and certifies to *Z* that *D* will have family coverage under *C*'s plan (and *Z* has no reason to believe the certification is incorrect).

(ii) The marriage is a change in status under paragraph (c)(2)(i) of this section. Under the consistency rule in paragraph (c)(3) of this section, *Y*'s cafeteria plan may permit *C* to change his or her salary reduction contributions to reflect the change from employee-only indemnity to HMO family coverage, and *Z* may permit *D* to revoke coverage under *Z*'s cafeteria plan.

(d) *Judgment, decree, or order*—(1) *Conforming election change.* This paragraph (d) applies to a judgment, decree, or order (order) resulting from a divorce, legal separation, annulment, or change in legal custody (including a qualified medical child support order as defined in section 609 of the Employee Retirement Income Security Act of 1974 (Public Law 93-406 (88 Stat. 829))) that requires accident or health coverage for an employee's child or for a foster child who is a dependent of the employee. A cafeteria plan will not fail to satisfy section 125 if it—

(i) Changes the employee's election to provide coverage for the child if the order requires coverage for the child under the employee's plan; or

(ii) Permits the employee to make an election change to cancel coverage for the child if the order requires the spouse, former spouse, or other individual to provide coverage for the child.

(ii) Permits the employee to make an election change to cancel coverage for the child if:

(A) The order requires the spouse, former spouse, or other individual to provide coverage for the child; and

(B) That coverage is, in fact, provided.

(2) *Example.* The following example illustrates the application of this paragraph (d):

Example. (i) Employer *M* maintains a calendar year cafeteria plan that allows employees to elect no health coverage, employee-only coverage, employee-plus-one-dependent coverage, or family coverage. *M*'s employee, *A*, is married to *B* and they have one child, *C*. Before the beginning of the year, *A* elects employee-only health coverage. Employee *A* divorces *B* during the year and, pursuant to *A*'s divorce agreement with *B*, *M*'s health plan receives a qualified medical child support order (as defined in section 609 of the Employee Retirement Income Security Act of 1974) during the plan year. The order requires *M*'s health plan to cover *C*.

(ii) Under this paragraph (d), *M*'s cafeteria plan may change *A*'s election from employee-only health coverage to employee-plus-one-dependent coverage in order to cover *C*.

(e) *Entitlement to Medicare or Medicaid.* If an employee, spouse, or dependent who is enrolled in an accident or health plan of the employer becomes entitled to coverage (i.e., becomes enrolled) under Part A or Part B of Title XVIII of the Social Security Act (Medicare) (Public Law 89-97 (79 Stat. 291)) or Title XIX of the Social Security Act (Medicaid) (Public Law 89-97 (79 Stat. 343)), other than coverage consisting solely of benefits under section 1928 of the Social Security Act (the program for distribution of pediatric vaccines), a cafeteria plan may permit the employee to make a prospective election change to cancel or reduce coverage of that employee, spouse, or dependent under the accident or health plan. In addition, if an employee, spouse, or dependent who has been entitled to such coverage under Medicare or Medicaid loses eligibility for such coverage, the cafeteria plan may permit the employee to make a prospective election to commence or increase coverage of that employee, spouse, or dependent under the accident or health plan.

(f) *Significant cost or coverage changes*—(1) *In general.* Paragraphs (f)(2) through (5) of this section set forth rules for election changes as a result of changes in cost or coverage. This paragraph (f) does not apply to an election change with respect to a health FSA (or on account of a change in cost or coverage under a health FSA).

(2) *Cost changes*—(i) *Automatic changes.* If the cost of a qualified benefits plan increases (or decreases) during a period of coverage and, under the terms of the plan, employees are required to make a corresponding change in their payments, the cafeteria plan may, on a reasonable and consistent basis, automatically make a prospective increase (or decrease) in affected employees' elective contributions for the plan.

(ii) *Significant cost changes.* If the cost charged to an employee for a benefit package option (as defined in paragraph (i)(2) of this section) significantly increases or significantly decreases during a period of coverage, the cafeteria plan may permit the employee to make a corresponding change in election under the cafeteria plan. Changes that may be made include commencing participation in the cafeteria plan for the option with a decrease in cost, or, in the case of an increase in cost, revoking an election for that coverage and, in lieu thereof, either receiving on a prospective basis coverage under another benefit package option providing similar coverage or dropping coverage if no other benefit package option providing similar coverage is available. For example, if the cost of an indemnity option under an accident or health plan significantly increases during a period of coverage, employees who are covered by the indemnity option may make a corresponding prospective increase in their payments or may instead elect to revoke their election for the indemnity option and, in lieu thereof, elect coverage under another benefit package option including an HMO option (or drop coverage under the accident or health plan if no other benefit package option is offered).

(iii) *Application of cost changes.* For purposes of paragraphs (f)(2)(i) and (ii) of this section, a cost increase or decrease refers to an increase or decrease in the amount of the elective contributions under the cafeteria plan, whether that increase or decrease results from an action taken by the employee (such as switching between full-time and part-time status) or from an action taken by an employer (such as reducing the amount of employer contributions for a class of employees).

(iv) *Application to dependent care.* This paragraph (f)(2) applies in the case of a dependent care assistance plan only if the cost change is imposed by a dependent care provider who is not a relative of the employee. For this purpose, a relative is an individual who is related as described in section 152(a)(1) through (8), incorporating the rules of section 152(b)(1) and (2).

(3) *Coverage changes*—(i) *Significant curtailment without loss of coverage.* If an employee (or an employee's spouse or dependent) has a significant curtailment of coverage under a plan during a period of coverage that is not a loss of coverage as described in paragraph (f)(3)(ii) of this section (for example, there is a significant increase in the deductible, the copay, or the out-of-pocket cost sharing limit under an accident or health plan), the cafeteria plan may permit any employee who had been participating in the plan and receiving that coverage to revoke his or her election for that coverage and, in lieu thereof, to elect to receive on a prospective basis coverage under another benefit package option providing similar coverage. Coverage under a plan is significantly curtailed only if there is an overall reduction in coverage provided under the plan so as to constitute reduced coverage generally. Thus, in most cases, the loss of one particular physician in a network does not constitute a significant curtailment.

(ii) *Significant curtailment with loss of coverage.* If an employee (or the employee's spouse or dependent) has a significant curtailment that is a loss of coverage, the plan may permit that employee to revoke his or her election under the cafeteria plan and, in lieu thereof, to elect either to receive on a prospective basis coverage under another benefit package option providing similar coverage or to drop coverage if no similar benefit package option is available. For purposes of this paragraph (f)(3)(ii), a loss of coverage means a complete loss of coverage under the benefit package option or other coverage option (including the elimination of a benefits package option, an HMO ceasing to be available in the area where the individual resides, or the individual losing all coverage under the option by reason of an overall lifetime or annual limitation). In addition, the cafeteria plan may, in its discretion, treat the following as a loss of coverage—

(A) A substantial decrease in the medical care providers available under the option (such as a major hospital ceasing to be a member of a preferred provider network or a substantial decrease in the physicians participating in a preferred provider network or an HMO);

(B) A reduction in the benefits for a specific type of medical condition or treatment with respect to which the employee or the employee's spouse or dependent is currently in a course of treatment; or

(C) Any other similar fundamental loss of coverage.

(iii) *Addition or improvement of a benefit package option.* If a plan adds a new benefit package option or other coverage option, or if coverage under an existing benefit package option or other coverage option is significantly improved during a period of coverage, the cafeteria plan may permit eligible employees (whether or not they have previously made an election under the cafeteria plan or have previously elected the benefit package option) to revoke their election under the cafeteria plan and, in lieu thereof, to make an election on a prospective basis for coverage under the new or improved benefit package option.

(4) *Change in coverage under another employer plan.* A cafeteria plan may permit an employee to make a prospective election change that is on account of and corresponds with a change made under another employer plan (including a plan of the same employer or of another employer) if—

(i) The other cafeteria plan or qualified benefits plan permits participants to make an election change that would be permitted under paragraphs (b) through (g) of this section (disregarding this paragraph (f)(4)); or

(ii) The cafeteria plan permits participants to make an election for a period of coverage that is different from the period of coverage under the other cafeteria plan or qualified benefits plan.

(5) *Loss of coverage under other group health coverage.* A cafeteria plan may permit an employee to make an election on a prospective basis to add coverage under a cafeteria plan for the employee, spouse, or dependent if the employee, spouse, or dependent loses coverage under any group health coverage sponsored by a governmental or educational institution, including the following—

(i) A State's children's health insurance program (SCHIP) under Title XXI of the Social Security Act;

(ii) A medical care program of an Indian Tribal government (as defined in section 7701(a)(40)), the Indian Health Service, or a tribal organization;

(iii) A State health benefits risk pool; or

(iv) A Foreign government group health plan.

(6) *Examples.* The following examples illustrate the application of this paragraph (f):

Example 1. (i) A calendar year cafeteria plan is maintained pursuant to a collective bargaining agreement for the benefit of Employer *M*'s employees. The cafeteria plan offers various benefits, including indemnity health insurance and a health FSA. As a result of mid-year negotiations, premiums for the indemnity health insurance are reduced in the middle of the year, insurance co-payments for office visits are reduced under the indemnity plan by an amount which constitutes a significant benefit improvement, and an HMO option is added.

(ii) Under these facts, the reduction in health insurance premiums is a reduction in cost. Accordingly, under paragraph (f)(2)(i) of this section, the cafeteria plan may automatically decrease the amount of salary reduction contributions of affected participants by an amount that corresponds to the premium change. However, the plan may not permit employees to change their health FSA elections to reflect the mid-year change in copayments under the indemnity plan.

(iii) Also, the decrease in co-payments is a significant benefit improvement and the addition of the HMO option is an addition of a benefit package option. Accordingly, under paragraph (f)(3)(ii) of this section, the cafeteria plan may permit eligible employees to make an election change to elect the indemnity plan or the new HMO option. However, the plan may not permit employees to change their health FSA elections to reflect differences in co-payments under the HMO option.

Example 2. (i) Employer *N* sponsors an accident or health plan under which employees may elect either employee-only coverage or family health coverage. The 12-month period of coverage under *N*'s cafeteria plan begins January 1, 2001. *N*'s employee, *A*, is married to *B*. Employee *A* elects employee-only coverage under *N*'s plan. *B*'s employer, *O*, offers health coverage to *O*'s employees under its accident or health plan under which employees may elect either employee-only coverage or family coverage. *O*'s plan has a 12-month period of coverage beginning September 1, 2001. *B* maintains individual coverage under *O*'s plan at the time *A* elects coverage under *N*'s plan, and wants to elect no coverage for the plan year beginning on September 1, 2001, which is the next period of coverage under *O*'s accident or health plan. *A* certifies to *N* that *B* will elect no coverage under *O*'s accident or health plan for the plan year beginning on September 1, 2001 and *N* has no reason to believe that *A*'s certification is incorrect.

(ii) Under paragraph (f)(4)(ii) of this section, *N*'s cafeteria plan may permit *A* to change *A*'s election prospectively to family coverage under that plan effective September 1, 2001.

Example 3. (i) Employer *P* sponsors a calendar year cafeteria plan under which employees may elect either employee-only or family health coverage. Before the beginning of the year, *P*'s employee, *C*, elects family coverage under *P*'s cafeteria plan. *C* also elects coverage under the health FSA for up to $200 of reimbursements for the year to be funded by salary reduction contributions of $200 during the year. *C* is married to *D*, who is employed by Employer *Q*. *Q* does not maintain a cafeteria plan, but does maintain an accident or health plan providing its employees with employee-only coverage. During the calendar year, *Q* adds family coverage as an option under its health plan. *D* elects family coverage under *Q*'s plan, and *C* wants to revoke *C*'s election for health coverage and elect no health coverage under *P*'s cafeteria plan for the remainder of the year.

(ii) *Q*'s addition of family coverage as an option under its health plan constitutes a new coverage option described in paragraph (f)(3)(ii) of this section. Accordingly, pursuant to paragraph (f)(4)(i) of this section, *P*'s cafeteria plan may permit *C* to revoke *C*'s health coverage election if *D* actually elects family health coverage under *Q*'s accident or health plan. Employer *P*'s plan may not permit *C* to change *C*'s health FSA election.

Example 4. (i) Employer *R* maintains a cafeteria plan under which employees may elect accident or health coverage under either an indemnity plan or an HMO. Before the beginning of the year, *R*'s employee, *E* elects coverage under the HMO at a premium cost of $100 per month. During the year, *E* decides to switch to the indemnity plan, which charges a premium of $140 per month.

(ii) *E*'s change from the HMO to indemnity plan is not a change in cost or coverage under this paragraph (f), and none of the other election change rules under paragraphs (b) through (e) of this section apply.

(iii) Although *R*'s health plan may permit *E* to make the change from the HMO to the indemnity plan, *R*'s cafeteria plan may not permit *E* to make an election change to reflect the increased premium. Accordingly, if *E* switches from the HMO to the indemnity plan, *E* may pay the $40 per month additional cost on an after-tax basis.

Example 5. (i) Employee *A* is married to Employee *B* and they have one child, *C*. Employee *A*'s employer, *M*, maintains a calendar year cafeteria plan that allows employees to elect coverage under a dependent care FSA. Child *C* attends *X*'s on site child care center at an annual cost of $3,000. Prior to the beginning of the year, *A* elects salary reduction contributions of $3,000 during the year to fund coverage under the dependent care FSA for up to $3,000 of reimbursements for the year. Employee *A* now wants to revoke *A*'s election of coverage under the dependent care FSA, because *A* has found a new child care provider.

(ii) The availability of dependent care services from the new child care provider (whether the new provider is a household employee or family member of *A* or *B* or a person who is independent of *A* and *B*) is a significant change in coverage similar to a benefit package option becoming available. Because the FSA is a dependent care FSA rather than a health FSA, the coverage rules of this section apply and *M*'s cafeteria plan may permit *A* to elect to revoke *A*'s previous election of coverage under the dependent care FSA, and make a corresponding new election to reflect the cost of the new child care provider.

Example 6. (i) Employee *D* is married to Employee *E* and they have one child, *F*. Employee *D*'s employer, *N*, maintains a calendar year cafeteria plan that allows employees to elect coverage under a dependent care FSA. Child *F* is cared for by *Y*, *D*'s household employee, who provides child care services five days a week from 9 a.m. to 6 p.m. at an annual cost in excess of $5,000. Prior to the beginning of the year, *D* elects salary reduction contributions of $5,000 during the year to fund coverage under the dependent care FSA for up to $5,000 of reimbursements for the year. During the year, *F* begins school and, as a result, *Y*'s regular hours of work are changed to five days a week from 3 p.m. to 6 p.m. Employee *D* now wants to revoke *D*'s election under the dependent care FSA, and make a new election under the dependent care FSA to an annual cost of $4,000 to reflect a reduced cost of child care due to *Y*'s reduced hours.

(ii) The change in the number of hours of work performed by *Y* is a change in coverage. Thus, *N*'s cafeteria plan may permit *D* to reduce *D*'s previous election under the dependent care FSA to $4,000.

Example 7. (i) Employee *G* is married to Employee *H* and they have one child, *J*. Employee *G*'s employer, *O*, maintains a calendar year cafeteria plan that allows employees to elect coverage under a dependent care FSA. Child *J* is cared for by *Z*, *G*'s household employee, who is not a relative of *G* and who provides child care services at an annual cost of $4,000. Prior to the beginning of the year, *G* elects salary reduction contributions of $4,000 during the year to fund coverage under the dependent care FSA for up to $4,000 of reimbursements for the year. During the year, *G* raises *Z*'s salary. Employee *G* now wants to revoke *G*'s election under the dependent care FSA, and make a new election under the dependent care FSA to an annual amount of $4,500 to reflect the raise.

(ii) The raise in *Z*'s salary is a significant increase in cost under paragraph (f)(2)(i) of this section, and an increase in election to reflect the raise corresponds with that change in status. Thus, *O*'s cafeteria plan may permit *G* to elect to increase *G*'s election under the dependent care FSA.

Example 8. (i) Employer *P* maintains a calendar year cafeteria plan that allows employees to elect employee-only, employee plus one dependent, or family coverage under an indemnity plan. During the middle of the year, Employer *P* gives its employees the option to select employee-only or family coverage from an HMO plan. *P*'s employee, *J*, who had elected employee-plus-one-dependent coverage under the indemnity plan, decides to switch to family coverage under the HMO plan.

(ii) Employer *P*'s midyear addition of the HMO option is an addition of a benefit package option. Under paragraph (f) of this section, Employee *J* may change his or her salary reduction contributions to reflect the change from indemnity to HMO coverage, and also to reflect the change from employee-plus-one-dependent to family coverage (however, an election of employee-only coverage under the new option would not correspond with the addition of a new option). Employer *P* may not permit *J* to change *J*'s health FSA election.

(g) *Special requirements relating to the Family and Medical Leave Act.* An employee taking leave under the Family and Medical Leave Act (FMLA) (Public Law 103-3 (107 Stat. 6)) may revoke an existing election of accident or health plan coverage and make such other election for the remaining portion of the period of coverage as may be provided for under the FMLA.

(h) *Elective contributions under a qualified cash or deferred arrangement.* The provisions of this section do not apply with respect to elective contributions under a qualified cash or deferred arrangement (within the meaning of section 401(k)) or employee contributions subject to section 401(m). Thus, a cafeteria plan may permit an employee to modify or revoke elections in accordance with section 401(k) and (m) and the regulations thereunder.

(i) *Definitions.* Unless otherwise provided, the definitions in paragraphs (i)(1) though (8) of this section apply for purposes of this section.

(1) *Accident or health coverage.* Accident or health coverage means coverage under an accident or health plan as defined in regulations under section 105.

(2) *Benefit package option.* A benefit package option means a qualified benefit under section 125(f) that is offered under a cafeteria plan, or an option for coverage under an underlying accident or health plan (such as an indemnity option, an HMO option, or a PPO option under an accident or health plan).

(3) *Dependent.* A dependent means a dependent as defined in section 152, except that, for purposes of accident or health coverage, any child to whom section 152(e) applies is treated as a dependent of both parents, and, for purposes of dependent care assistance provided through a cafeteria plan, a dependent means a qualifying individual (as defined in section 21(b)(1)) with respect to the employee.

(4) *Disability coverage.* Disability coverage means coverage under an accident or health plan that provides benefits due to personal injury or sickness, but does not reimburse expenses incurred for medical care (as defined in section 213(d)) of the employee or the employee's spouse and dependents. For purposes of this section, disability coverage includes payments described in section 105(c).

(5) *Family member plan.* A family member plan means a cafeteria plan or qualified benefit plan sponsored by the employer of the employee's spouse or the employee's dependent.

(6) *FSA, health FSA.* An FSA means a qualified benefits plan that is a flexible spending arrangement as defined in section 106(c)(2). A health FSA means a health or accident plan that is an FSA.

(7) *Placement for adoption.* Placement for adoption means placement for adoption as defined in regulations under section 9801.

(8) *Qualified benefits plan.* A qualified benefits plan means an employee benefit plan governing the provision of one or more benefits that are qualified benefits under section 125(f). A plan does not fail to be a qualified benefits plan merely because it includes an FSA, assuming that the FSA meets the requirements of section 125 and the regulations thereunder.

(9) *Similar coverage.* Coverage for the same category of benefits for the same individuals (e.g., family to family or single to single). For example, two plans that provide coverage for major medical are considered to be similar coverage. For purposes of this definition, a health FSA is not similar coverage with respect to an accident or health plan that is not a health FSA. A plan may treat coverage by another employer, such as a spouse's or dependent's employer, as similar coverage.

(j) *Effective date*—(1) *General rule.* Except as provided in paragraph (j)(2) of this section, this section is applicable for cafeteria plan years beginning on or after January 1, 2001.

(2) *Delayed effective date for certain provisions.* The following provisions are applicable for cafeteria plan years beginning on or after January 1, 2002: paragraph (c) of this section to the extent applicable to qualified benefits other than an accident or health plan or a group-term life insurance plan; paragraph (d)(1)(ii)(B) of this section (relating to a spouse, former spouse, or other individual obtaining accident or health coverage for an employee's child in response to a judgment, decree, or order); paragraph (f) of this section (rules for election changes as a result of cost or coverage changes); and paragraph (i)(9) of this section (defining similar coverage).

Appendix N

IRS Notice 2002-45 and Revenue Ruling 2002-41

In June 2002, the IRS simultaneously released Notice 2002-45 and Revenue Ruling 2002-41 describing the correct operation of employer-funded Health Reimbursement Arrangements (HRAs) that include a rollover feature. The text of the press release, the notice, and the revenue ruling, follows.

> Today the Treasury Department and the Internal Revenue Service issued guidance that clarifies the tax treatment of health reimbursement arrangements (HRAs) in which the employee's health benefit arrangement provides for employee-controlled reimbursement of medical costs.
>
> "With this new guidance, we clear the way for employers to adopt health plans with patient-directed features so that employees have more choice and greater control over their health care coverage," stated Treasury Secretary Paul O'Neill.
>
> The guidance, consisting of a notice and a revenue ruling, provides that medical benefits paid by Health Reimbursement Arrangements (HRAs) that meet certain requirements are not taxable. The guidance also clarifies that HRAs generally are not subject to the complex design requirements for health Flexible Spending Arrangements funded through salary reduction under a cafeteria plan.
>
> The primary requirements for an HRA are that (1) the plan must be funded solely by the employer and cannot be funded by salary reduction, and (2) the plan may only provide benefits for substantiated medical expenses. If the plan provides for payments or other benefits irrespective of medical expenses, all amounts paid by the plan become taxable, including prior medical reimbursements.
>
> Under this guidance HRAs can:

- Allow the carryover of unused amounts to later years (i.e., the "use-it-or-lose-it rule" does not apply) and
- Reimburse employees for the purchase of health insurance.

In addition, the guidance provides that:

- HRAs may allow former employees, including retirees, continued access to unused reimbursements;
- HRAs may provide that an FSA funded by salary reduction reimburses expenses before the HRA; and
- HRAs are group health plans subject to the COBRA continuation requirements.

Notice 2002-45

Part III—Administrative, Procedural, and Miscellaneous Health Reimbursement Arrangements

Notice 2002-45

PURPOSE

This notice provides basic information about a type of employer-provided health reimbursement arrangement (HRA) described below. Published elsewhere in this bulletin is a revenue ruling providing guidance involving an HRA.

This notice is divided into eight parts. Part I of the notice describes HRAs and their general tax treatment. Part II of the notice outlines the benefits that may be offered under an HRA. Part III details who may be covered under an HRA. Part IV deals with the interaction between HRAs and cafeteria plans. Part V covers ordering rules for reimbursement from HRAs and § 125 health flexible spending arrangements. Part VI relates to the applicability of § 105(h) non-discrimination rules to HRAs. Part VII explains how to provide COBRA continuation coverage under HRAs. Part VIII addresses certain other matters.

I. Tax Treatment of HRAs Generally

An HRA is an arrangement that: (1) is paid for solely by the employer and not provided pursuant to salary reduction election or otherwise under a § 125 cafeteria plan; (2) reimburses the employee for medical care expenses (as defined by § 213(d) of the Internal Revenue Code) incurred by the employee and the employee's spouse and dependents (as defined in § 152); and (3) provides reimbursements up to a maximum dollar amount for a coverage period and any unused portion of the maximum dollar amount at the end of a coverage period is carried forward to increase the maximum reimbursement amount in subsequent coverage periods. To the extent that an HRA is an employer-provided accident or health plan, coverage and reimbursements of medical care expenses of an employee and the employee's spouse and dependents are generally excludable from the employee's gross income under §§ 106 and 105. Assuming that the maximum amount of reimbursement which is reasonably available to a participant under an HRA is not substantially in excess of the value of coverage under the HRA, an HRA is a flexible spending arrangement (FSA) as defined in § 106(c)(2).

II. Benefits under an HRA

To qualify for the exclusions under §§ 106 and 105, an HRA may only provide benefits that reimburse expenses for medical care as defined in § 213(d). Each medical care expense submitted for reimbursement must be substantiated. An HRA may not reimburse a medical care expense that is attributable to a deduction allowed under § 213 for any prior taxable year. Additionally, an HRA may neither reimburse a medical care expense that is incurred before the date the HRA is in existence nor reimburse a medical care expense that is incurred before the date an employee first becomes enrolled under the HRA. Reimbursements for insurance covering medical care expenses as defined in § 213(d)(1)(D) are allowable reimbursements under an HRA, including amounts paid for premiums for accident or health coverage for current employees, retirees, and COBRA qualified beneficiaries. However, see Part IV for a discussion relating to cases in which an employer provides an HRA in conjunction with another accident or health plan. If an HRA is an FSA, reimbursable medical care expenses may not include expenses for qualified long-term care services as defined in § 7702B(c). See §§ 106(c) and 213(d)(1)(C).

An HRA does not qualify for the exclusion under § 105(b) if any person has the right to receive cash or any other taxable or non-taxable benefit under the arrangement other than the reimbursement of medical care expenses. If any person has such a right under an arrangement currently or for any future year, all distributions to all persons made from the arrangement in the current tax year are included in gross income, even amounts paid to reimburse medical care expenses. For example, if an arrangement pays a death benefit without regard to medical care expenses, no amounts paid under the arrangement to any person are reimbursements for medical care expenses excluded under § 105(b). See § 1.105-2 of the Income Tax Regulations. Arrangements formally outside the HRA that provide for the adjustment of an employee's compensation or an employee's receipt of any other benefit will be considered in determining whether the arrangement is an HRA and whether the benefits are eligible for the exclusions under §§ 106 and 105(b). If, for example, in the year an employee retires, the employee receives a bonus and the amount of the bonus is related to that employee's maximum reimbursement amount remaining in an HRA at the time of retirement, no amounts paid under the arrangement are reimbursements for medical care expenses for purposes of § 105(b). Similarly, if an employer provides severance pay only to employees who have reimbursement amounts remaining in a purported HRA at the time of termination of employment, no amounts paid under the arrangement are reimbursements for medical care expenses for purposes of § 105(b).

III. Coverage under an HRA

Medical care expense reimbursements under an HRA are excludable under § 105(b) to the extent the reimbursements are provided to the following individuals: current and former employees (including retired employees), their spouses and dependents (as defined in § 152 as modified by the last sentence of § 105(b)), and the spouses and dependents of deceased employees. The term "employee" does not include a self-employed individual as defined in § 401(c). See § 105(g).

An HRA may continue to reimburse former employees or retired employees for medical care expenses after termination of employment or retirement (even if the employee does not elect COBRA continuation coverage). For example, an HRA may have a provision that reimburses a former employee for medical care expenses only up to an amount equal to the unused reimbursement amount remaining at retirement or other termination of employment. The plan may also provide that the maximum reimbursement amount available after retirement or other termination of employment is reduced for any administrative costs of continuing such coverage. Additionally, an HRA may or may not provide for an increase in the amount available for reimbursement of medical care expenses after the employee retires or otherwise terminates employment (even if the employee does not elect COBRA continuation coverage).

IV. HRAs and Cafeteria Plans

Employer contributions to an HRA may not be attributable to salary reduction or otherwise provided under a § 125 cafeteria plan. An accident or health plan funded pursuant to salary reduction is not an HRA and is subject to the rules under § 125. However, an HRA is not considered to be paid for pursuant to salary reduction merely because it is provided in conjunction with a cafeteria plan. Additionally, if an employer offers employees a choice between employer-provided non-taxable benefits (e.g., coverage under an HRA and coverage under a health maintenance organization (HMO)), with no cash or other taxable benefits available to employees, the choice is not an election to which § 125 applies.

If an employer provides an HRA only in conjunction with another accident or health plan and that other plan is provided pursuant to a salary reduction election under a cafeteria plan, then all the facts and circumstances are considered in determining whether the salary reduction is attributable to the HRA. Assuming that the terms of the salary reduction election indicate that the salary reduction is used only to pay for the specified accident or health plan offered in conjunction with the HRA and not to pay for the HRA itself, the mere fact that an employee may participate in the HRA only if the employee participates in a specified accident or health plan funded pursuant to a salary reduction election does not necessarily result in the salary reduction being attributed to the HRA. In such situations, if the salary reduction election for a coverage period to fund the specified accident or health plan offered in conjunction with the HRA exceeds the actual cost of the specified accident or health plan coverage for such coverage period, the salary reduction is attributable to the HRA. For purposes of this rule, "salary reduction" includes a choice to forgo receipt of any benefits that would be taxable but for the fact they are offered under a § 125 cafeteria plan.

For any coverage period, for purposes solely of determining whether a salary reduction election exceeds the cost of coverage, the actual cost of the specified accident or health plan coverage for the coverage period may be determined pursuant to the rules for determining the COBRA applicable premium under § 4980B(f)(4). For example, assume that an employer offers an HRA and an employee who participates in the HRA must also participate in the corresponding employee-only or family coverage offered in a high-deductible accident and health plan. If the COBRA applicable premium for the high-deductible accident and health coverage would be $1,800 for the employee-only coverage and $4,500 for family coverage if such coverage were offered separately from the HRA, then the annual maximum allowable salary reduction election in this case is $1,800 for employee-only coverage and $4,500 for family coverage in order for the salary reduction to be treated as not attributable to the HRA.

An arrangement is not treated as an HRA if the arrangement interacts with a cafeteria plan in such a way as to permit employees to use salary reduction indirectly to fund the HRA. Therefore, where an employee who participates in a reimbursement arrangement has a choice among two or more specified accident or health plans to be used in conjunction with the reimbursement arrangement (or a choice among various maximum reimbursement amounts credited for a coverage period) and there is a correlation between the maximum reimbursement amount available under the HRA for the coverage period (disregarding amounts carried forward from previous coverage periods) and the amount of salary reduction election for the specified accident and health plan, then the salary reduction is attributed to the reimbursement arrangement even if the amount of salary reduction election is equal to or less than the actual cost of the other accident or health coverage.

For example, assume an employer offers a reimbursement arrangement plus other specified accident or health plan coverage with the actual cost for family coverage for the specified accident or health plan being $4,500 and the employee having a choice to salary reduce $2,500 or $3,500 to fund this coverage. An employee who elects family coverage and $2,500 salary reduction receives a $1,000 maximum reimbursement amount under the reimbursement arrangement for the coverage period and an employee who elects family coverage and $3,500 salary reduction receives a $2,000 maximum reimbursement amount under the reimbursement arrangement for the coverage period. In this case, although the maximum allowable salary reduction is not exceeded, a portion of the salary reduction is attributed to the reimbursement arrangement because the increase in salary reduction election is related to a larger maximum reimbursement amount in the reimbursement arrangement for the coverage period. This arrangement is not an HRA and is subject to § 125.

Similarly, assume an employer provides a reimbursement arrangement in conjunction with another accident or health plan. Employees participating in the reimbursement arrangement are reimbursed up to $1,000 each year for substantiated § 213(d) medical care expenses and unused amounts remaining at the end of the year are carried forward for reimbursements in later years. The employee-share of the annual premium for the other accident or health plan is $1,500. Employees have a choice either to use amounts in the reimbursement arrangement to pay for the premium for the other accident or health plan or to pay that premium pursuant to a salary reduction election. Under this plan, the reimbursement arrangement does not reimburse any portion of the premium paid by salary reduction. Because an employee may use the reimbursement arrangement to pay a portion of the premium in lieu of electing to salary reduce, the reimbursement arrangement is indirectly funded pursuant to salary reduction. This arrangement does not meet the definition of an HRA because it is funded by salary reduction and it is subject to the rules under § 125.

Further, if the amount credited to a reimbursement arrangement is directly or indirectly based on the amount forfeited under a § 125 FSA, the arrangement will be treated as funded by salary reduction. For purposes of making this determination, facts and circumstances taken into consideration include the manner in which salary reduction is implemented for other accident or health plans offered by the employer.

Because an HRA is paid for solely by the employer and not pursuant to salary reduction, the following restrictions on health FSAs under § 125 are not applicable to HRAs: (1) the prohibition against a benefit that defers compensation by permitting employees to carry over unused elective contributions or plan benefits from one plan year to another plan year; (2) the requirement that the maximum amount of reimbursement must be available at all times during the coverage period; (3) the mandatory twelve-month period of coverage; and (4) except as otherwise provided in this notice, the limitation that medical expenses reimbursed must be incurred during the period of coverage. As a result, the maximum reimbursement amount for a coverage period (not including amounts carried forward from previous coverage periods) need not be available at all times during the coverage period. Also, an HRA may specify a coverage period for a reimbursement amount that is less than a year. Although claims incurred during one coverage period may be reimbursed in a later coverage period, an unreimbursed claim may be reimbursed in a later coverage period only if the individual was covered under the HRA when the claim was incurred. Additionally, the maximum reimbursement amount credited under the HRA in the future (not including amounts carried forward from previous coverage periods) may be increased or decreased. However, see § 1.105-11(c)(3)(ii) regarding operational discrimination in favor of highly compensated individuals (as defined in § 105(h)). Thus, if an increase in maximum reimbursement amounts in an HRA favors one or more highly compensated individuals, the HRA may violate these non-discrimination rules.

V. Ordering Rules for HRAs and § 125 Health FSAs

A medical care expense may not be reimbursed from a § 125 health FSA if the expense has been reimbursed or is reimbursable under any other accident or health plan. If coverage is provided under both an HRA and a § 125 health FSA for the same medical care expenses, amounts available under an HRA must be exhausted before reimbursements may be made from the FSA. However, a § 125 health FSA will not violate this rule if coverage is provided under both an HRA and a § 125 health FSA and the FSA reimburses a medical care expense which is not reimbursable by the HRA. In no case may an employee be reimbursed for the same medical care expense by both an HRA and a § 125 health FSA.

Consistent with these rules, before a § 125 health FSA plan year begins, the plan document for the HRA may specify that coverage under the HRA is available only after expenses exceeding the dollar amount of the § 125 FSA have been paid. For example, if an employer sponsors a § 125 health FSA and an HRA, both of which provide coverage for the same medical care expenses, and the HRA plan document includes a provision that the HRA is not available for reimbursements of medical care expenses that are covered by the § 125 health FSA until after expenses exceeding the dollar amount of the § 125 FSA have been paid, then those medical care expenses may be reimbursed first from the § 125 health FSA and then from the HRA when the amount available under the § 125 FSA is exhausted.

VI. Nondiscrimination Rules Applicable to HRAs

Section 105(h) sets forth nondiscrimination rules for self-insured medical expense reimbursement plans. To the extent an HRA is a self-insured medical expense reimbursement plan, the nondiscrimination rules under § 105(h) apply to the HRA. See § 1.105-11.

VII. COBRA Continuation Coverage

An HRA is a group health plan generally subject to the COBRA continuation coverage requirements. If an individual elects COBRA continuation coverage, an HRA complies with these COBRA requirements by providing for the continuation of the maximum reimbursement amount for an individual at the time of the COBRA qualifying event and by increasing that maximum amount at the same time and by the same increment that it is increased for similarly situated non-COBRA beneficiaries (and by decreasing it for claims reimbursed). Premiums are determined under the existing rules in § 4980B. An HRA complies with the COBRA requirements for calculating the applicable premium under § 4980B if the applicable premium is the same for qualified beneficiaries with different total reimbursement amounts available from the HRA (and otherwise also satisfies the requirements of § 4980B). For example, if the annual additional reimbursement amount credited under an HRA is $1,000 and the maximum reimbursement amount remaining for two similarly situated qualified beneficiaries at the time of their qualifying events is $500 and $5,000, the applicable premium is the same for each individual.

The plan rules of an HRA may provide for continued reimbursements after a COBRA qualifying event regardless of whether a qualified beneficiary elects continuation coverage. For example, an HRA might allow reimbursements up to the unused maximum reimbursement amount following termination of employment. In such a situation, an HRA subject to COBRA must still comply with the COBRA continuation coverage requirements. If a qualified beneficiary elects COBRA continuation coverage in addition to the continued reimbursement amount already available, an HRA complies with the COBRA requirements by increasing the maximum reimbursement amount at the same time and by the same increment that it is increased for similarly situated non-COBRA beneficiaries (and by decreasing it for claims reimbursed).

VIII. Other Matters

Accident or health plans that meet the definition of an HRA are subject to a variety of statutory rules and provisions, many of which are not addressed in this notice. Among the statutory provisions not addressed in this notice are:

- The deduction limitations under §§ 419 and 419A (for employer contributions to welfare benefit funds) and under § 404 (for amounts paid or accrued under plans providing for deferred benefits that are not provided through a welfare benefit fund).
- The application of the nondiscrimination requirements under the Health Insurance Portability and Accountability Act of 1996 (HIPAA), including the extent to which underwritten individual health insurance policies purchased and reimbursed by an HRA are treated as health insurance coverage offered under a group health plan.
- Other requirements under HIPAA, including the requirement that a group health plan provide certificates of creditable coverage.
- The requirements for welfare benefit plans under the Employee Retirement Income Security Act of 1974 (ERISA).

The proposed regulations relating to health FSAs under § 125 state that certain requirements apply whether or not the health FSA is part of a cafeteria plan. Future guidance will modify the proposed regulation under § 125 to clarify that while those rules continue to apply to health FSAs provided pursuant to salary reduction election under a § 125 cafeteria plan, they do not apply to HRAs.

COMMENTS REQUESTED

Comments are requested about the rules set forth in this notice. Send comments to: CC:DOM:CORP:R (Notice 2002-45), Room 5226, Internal Revenue Service, POB 7604, Ben Franklin Station, Washington, DC 20044. Comments may be hand-delivered between the hours of 8 a.m. and 5 p.m. to: CC:DOM:CORT:R (Notice 2002-45), Courier's Desk, Internal Revenue Service, 1111 Constitution Avenue, NW, Washington, D.C. Alternatively, taxpayers may submit comments electronically at:

Notice.Comments@irscounsel.treas.gov (a Service Comments e-mail address).

DRAFTING INFORMATION

The principal author of this notice is Lorianne D. Masano of the Office of Division Counsel/Associate Chief Counsel (Tax Exempt and Government Entities). For further information regarding this notice contact Lorianne D. Masano at (202) 622-6080 (not a toll-free call).

Revenue Ruling 2002-41

Part I

Section 105.—Amounts Received under Accident and Health Plans

(Also: 106—Contributions by employer to accident and health plans, 125—Cafeteria plans)

Rev. Rul. 2002-41

ISSUE

Whether employer-provided coverage and medical care expense reimbursements made under a reimbursement arrangement that allows unused amounts to be carried forward, as described in Situations 1 and 2 below, are excludable from gross income under §§ 106 and 105 of the Internal Revenue Code, respectively.

FACTS

Situation 1: An employer sponsors a major medical plan for all employees that provides coverage under a policy of accident and health insurance for certain medical care expenses described in § 213(d)(1)(A) and (B). The major medical plan has a $2,000 annual deductible for employee-only coverage and a $4,000 annual deductible for family coverage. However, certain preventive care benefits (e.g., annual physicals and well-baby visits) are covered without regard to the plan's deductible. The major medical plan is paid for in part pursuant to salary reduction elections under the employer's cafeteria plan. The election form provides that salary reduction elections are used only to pay for the major medical plan. To participate in the major medical plan, an employee must make a $1,000 annual salary reduction election for employee-only coverage or a $3,500 annual salary reduction election for family coverage.

In addition to the major medical plan, the employer also sponsors a health reimbursement arrangement (HRA) that reimburses the medical care expenses of all participating employees and their spouses and dependents up to an annual maximum reimbursement amount that is fixed on January 1 of each year. The HRA is available only to employees who participate in the major medical plan. The HRA meets the nondiscrimination requirements of § 105(h).

The HRA is paid for by the employer and employees do not make any salary reduction election to pay for the HRA. The HRA operates on a calendar year basis. Employees have no right to receive cash or any benefit other than reimbursement for medical care expenses under the HRA.

The expenses reimbursable under the HRA are any medical care expenses that would be covered by the major medical plan but for the major medical plan's deductible, limitation to expenses that are "usual, customary and reasonable," or any other similar dollar limitation imposed by the major medical plan. Only expenses that are substantiated are reimbursed.

The maximum reimbursement amount for the first year in which an employee participates in the HRA is $1,000 for an employee who has employee-only coverage under the major medical plan and $2,000 for an employee who has family coverage under the major medical plan. Unused reimbursement amounts from one year are carried forward for use in later years. Therefore, in each year after the first year, the maximum reimbursement amount under the HRA equals $1,000 for an employee who has employee-only coverage under the major medical plan and $2,000 for an employee who has family coverage under the major medical plan, increased by the unused amount from the previous year. If an employee retires or otherwise terminates employment, any unused reimbursement amount remaining in the HRA is unavailable thereafter.

Under the terms of the plans, a qualified beneficiary who chooses to elect COBRA continuation coverage may only elect the HRA in conjunction with the major medical plan. However, a qualified beneficiary may choose to elect COBRA continuation coverage for only the major medical plan. The COBRA applicable premium for continuation of the major medical plan is $1,800 for employee-only coverage and $4,500 for family coverage.

Situation 2: The facts are the same as Situation 1, except that any portion of the maximum reimbursement amount under the HRA that is not applied to reimburse medical care expenses before an employee retires or otherwise terminates employment continues to be available after retirement or termination for any medical care expense under § 213(d)(1)(A),(B), and (D) incurred by the former employee or the former employee's spouse and dependents. However, after the employee retires or otherwise terminates employment, the maximum reimbursement amount is not increased unless COBRA continuation coverage is elected.

LAW AND ANALYSIS

Section 61(a)(1) and § 1.61-21(a)(3) of the Income Tax Regulations provide that, except as otherwise provided in subtitle A, gross income includes compensation for services, including fees, commissions, fringe benefits, and similar items.

Section 106 provides that "gross income of an employee does not include employer-provided coverage under an accident or health plan."

Section 1.106-1 provides that the gross income of an employee does not include contributions which the employee's employer makes to an accident or health plan for compensation (through insurance or otherwise) to the employee for personal injuries or sickness incurred by the employee or the employee's spouse or dependents (as defined in § 152).

Section 105(a) provides that, except as otherwise provided in § 105, "amounts received by an employee through accident or health insurance for personal injuries or sickness shall be included in gross income to the extent such amounts (1) are attributable to contributions by the employer which were not includible in the gross income of the employee, or (2) are paid by the employer."

Section 105(e) states that amounts received under an accident or health plan for employees are treated as amounts received through accident or health insurance for purposes of § 105 (and § 104 relating to compensation for injuries and sickness). Section 1.105-5(a) provides that an accident or health plan is an arrangement for the payment of amounts to employees in the event of personal injuries or sickness.

Section 105(b) states that except in the case of amounts attributable to (and not in excess of) deductions allowed under § 213 (relating to medical expenses) for any prior taxable year, gross income does not include amounts referred to in subsection (a) if such amounts are paid, directly or indirectly, to the taxpayer to reimburse the taxpayer for expenses incurred by the taxpayer for the medical care (as defined in § 213(d)) of the taxpayer or the taxpayer's spouse or dependents (as defined in § 152).

Section 1.105-2 provides that only amounts that are paid specifically to reimburse the taxpayer for expenses incurred by the taxpayer for the prescribed medical care are excludable from gross income. Thus, § 105(b) does not apply to amounts that the taxpayer would be entitled to receive irrespective of whether or not the taxpayer incurs expenses for medical care.

Section 105(h)(1) provides that, unless the plan satisfies the nondiscrimination requirements of § 105(h)(2), amounts paid under a self-insured medical expense reimbursement plan to a highly compensated individual will not be excludable from that individual's gross income under § 105(b) to the extent they constitute excess reimbursements.

Coverage provided under an accident and health plan to former employees and their spouses and dependents are excludable from gross income under § 106. See, Rev. Rul. 82-196, 1982-2 C.B. 53; Rev. Rul. 85-121, 1985-2 C.B. 57.

Under the facts described above, the HRA is an employer-provided accident and health plan used exclusively to reimburse expenses incurred for medical care as defined under § 213(d). Under the HRA, no benefits other than reimbursements for medical care expenses are available either in the form of cash or other non-taxable or taxable benefits at any time.

For purposes of determining whether any part of the salary reduction for the major medical plan is attributable to the HRA, under the facts and circumstances, the applicable premium for COBRA continuation coverage may be used as the actual cost of the major medical plan. Under the facts described above, the actual cost of the major medical plan for one year is $1,800 for employee-only coverage and $4,500 for family coverage. The amount of salary reduction election for employee-only coverage ($1,000) is less than $1,800 and the amount of salary reduction election for family coverage ($3,500) is less than $4,500. Also, the cafeteria plan election form states that salary reduction elections are used only to pay for the major medical plan. Under these facts and circumstances, the HRA reimbursement amounts are not attributable to the salary reduction contributions made to pay for the major medical plan.

In Situation 2, the employer provides accident and health coverage under the HRA for former employees. This coverage is provided based on the former employee's prior employment relationship with the employer. The HRA is used to reimburse the former employee only for medical care expenses of the former employee or the former employee's spouse or dependents. Neither the former employee nor the former employee's spouse or dependents receive any other benefits from the HRA at any time.

HOLDING

Employer-provided coverage and medical care expense reimbursements made under the reimbursement arrangement that allows unused amounts to be carried forward, as described in Situations 1 and 2, are excludable from gross income under §§ 106 and 105, respectively.

See Notice 2002-45 published elsewhere in this Internal Revenue Bulletin for further information and guidance concerning HRAs.

DRAFTING INFORMATION

The principal author of this revenue ruling is Lorianne D. Masano of the Office of Division Counsel/Associate Chief Counsel (Tax Exempt and Government Entities). For further information regarding this revenue ruling contact Lorianne D. Masano (202) 622-6080 (not a toll-free call).

Appendix O

Final Treasury Regulations Section 54.4980B-2, Q&A 8—Plans that Must Comply

On January 9, 2001, the IRS finalized regulations implementing COBRA continuation provisions. A portion of the regulations with direct application to Section 125 plans (cafeteria plans) is reproduced here.

§ 54.4980B-2. Plans that must comply

Q 8 How do the COBRA continuation coverage requirements apply to cafeteria plans and other flexible benefit arrangements?

A-8: (a)(1) The provision of health care benefits does not fail to be a group health plan merely because those benefits are offered under a cafeteria plan (as defined in section 125) or under any other arrangement under which an employee is offered a choice between health care benefits and other taxable or nontaxable benefits. However, the COBRA continuation coverage requirements apply only to the type and level of coverage under the cafeteria plan or other flexible benefit arrangement that a qualified beneficiary is actually receiving on the day before the qualifying event. See paragraphs (b) through (e) of this Q & A-8 for rules limiting the obligations of certain health flexible spending arrangements.

(2) The rules of this paragraph (a) are illustrated by the following example:

Example. (i) Under the terms of a cafeteria plan, employees can choose among life insurance coverage, membership in a health maintenance organization (HMO), coverage for medical expenses under an indemnity arrangement, and cash compensation. Of these available choices, the HMO and the indemnity arrangement are the arrangements providing health care. The instruments governing the HMO and indemnity arrangements indicate that they are separate group health plans. These group health plans are subject to

COBRA. The employer does not provide any group health plan outside of the cafeteria plan. *B* and *C* are unmarried employees. *B* has chosen the life insurance coverage, and *C* has chosen the indemnity arrangement.

(ii) *B* does not have to be offered COBRA continuation coverage upon terminating employment, nor is a subsequent open enrollment period for active employees required to be made available to *B*. However, if *C* terminates employment and the termination constitutes a qualifying event, *C* must be offered an opportunity to elect COBRA continuation coverage under the indemnity arrangement. If *C* makes such an election and an open enrollment period for active employees occurs while *C* is still receiving the COBRA continuation coverage, *C* must be offered the opportunity to switch from the indemnity arrangement to the HMO (but not to the life insurance coverage because that does not constitute coverage provided under a group health plan).

(b) If a health flexible spending arrangement (health FSA), within the meaning of section 106(c)(2), satisfies the two conditions in paragraph (c) of this Q & A-8 for a plan year, the obligation of the health FSA to make COBRA continuation coverage available to a qualified beneficiary who experiences a qualifying event in that plan year is limited in accordance with paragraphs (d) and (e) of this Q & A-8, as illustrated by an example in paragraph (f) of this Q & A-8. To the extent that a health FSA is obligated to make COBRA continuation coverage available to a qualified beneficiary, the health FSA must comply with all the applicable rules of §§ 5 4.4980B-1 through 54.4980B-10, including the rules of Q & A-3 in § 54.498OB-5 (relating to limits).

(c) The conditions of this paragraph (c) are satisfied if—

(1) Benefits provided under the health FSA are excepted benefits within the meaning of sections 9831 and 9832; and

(2) The maximum amount that the health FSA can require to be paid for a year of COBRA continuation coverage under Q & A-1 of § 54.4980B-8 equals or exceeds the maximum benefit available under the health FSA for the year.

(d) If the conditions in paragraph (c) of this Q & A-8 are satisfied for a plan year, then the health FSA is not obligated to make COBRA continuation coverage available for any subsequent plan year to any qualified beneficiary who experiences a qualifying event during that plan year.

(e) If the conditions in paragraph (c) of this Q & A-8 are satisfied for a plan year, the health FSA is not obligated to make COBRA continuation coverage available for that plan year to any qualified beneficiary who experiences a qualifying event during that plan year unless, as of the date of the qualifying event, the qualified beneficiary can become entitled to receive during the remainder of the plan year a benefit that exceeds the maximum amount that the health FSA is permitted to require to be paid for COBRA continuation coverage for the remainder of the plan year. In determining the amount of the benefit that a qualified beneficiary can become entitled to receive during the remainder of the plan year, the health FSA may deduct from the maximum benefit available to that qualified beneficiary for the year (based on the election made under the health FSA for that qualified beneficiary before the date of the qualifying event) any reimbursable claims submitted to the health FSA for that plan year before the date of the qualifying event.

(f) The rules of paragraphs (b), (c), (d), and (e) of this Q & A-8 are illustrated by the following example:

> **Example.** (i) An employer maintains a group health plan providing major medical benefits and a group health plan that is a health FSA, and the plan year for each plan is the calendar year. Both the plan providing major medical benefits and the health FSA are subject to COBRA. Under the health FSA, during an open season before the beginning of each calendar year, employees can elect to reduce their compensation during the upcoming year by up to $1200 per year and have that same amount contributed to a health flexible spending account. The employer contributes an additional amount to the account equal to the employee's salary reduction election for the year. Thus, the maximum amount available to an employee under the health FSA for a year is two times the amount of the employee's salary reduction election for the year. This amount may be paid to the employee during the year as reimbursement for health expenses not covered by the employer's major medical plan (such as deductibles, copayments, prescription drugs, or eyeglasses). The employer determined, in accordance with section 4980B(f)(4), that a reasonable estimate of the cost of providing coverage for similarly situated nonCOBRA beneficiaries for 2002 under this health FSA is equal to two times their salary reduction election for 2002 and, thus, that two times the salary reduction election is the applicable premium for 2002.
>
> (ii) Because the employer provides major medical benefits under another group health plan, and because the maximum benefit that any employee can receive under the health FSA is not greater than two times the employee's salary reduction election for the plan year, benefits under this health FSA are excepted benefits within the meaning of sections 9831 and 9832. Thus, the first condition of paragraph (c) of this Q & A-8 is satisfied for the year. The maximum amount that a plan can require to be paid for coverage (outside of coverage required to be made available due to a disability extension) under Q & A-1 of § 54.4980B-8 is 102 percent of the applicable premium. Thus, the maximum amount that the health FSA can require to be paid for coverage for the 2002 plan year is 2.04 times the employee's salary reduction election for the plan year. Because the maximum benefit available under the health FSA is 2.0 times the employee's salary reduction election for the year, the maximum benefit available under the health FSA for the year is less than the maximum amount that the health FSA can require to be paid for coverage for the year. Thus, the second condition in paragraph (c) of this Q & A-8 is also satisfied for the 2002 plan year. Because both conditions in paragraph (c) of this Q & A-8 are satisfied for 2002, with respect to any qualifying event

occurring in 2002, the health FSA is not obligated to make COBRA continuation coverage available for any year after 2002.

(iii) Whether the health FSA is obligated to make COBRA continuation coverage available in 2002 to a qualified beneficiary with respect to a qualifying event that occurs in 2002 depends upon the maximum benefit that would be available to the qualified beneficiary under COBRA continuation coverage for that plan year. *Case 1:* Employee *B* has elected to reduce *B*'s salary by $1200 for 2002. Thus, the maximum benefit that *B* can become entitled to receive under the health FSA during the entire year is $2400. *B* experiences a qualifying event that is the termination of *B*'s employment on May 31, 2002. As of that date, *B* had submitted $300 of reimbursable expenses under the health FSA. Thus, the maximum benefit that *B* could become entitled to receive for the remainder of 2002 is $2100. The maximum amount that the health FSA can require to be paid for COBRA continuation coverage for the remainder of 2002 is 102 percent times 1/12 of the applicable premium for 2002 times the number of months remaining in 2002 after the date of the qualifying event. In *B*'s case, the maximum amount that the health FSA can require to be paid for COBRA continuation coverage for 2002 is 2.04 times $1200, or $2448. One-twelfth of $2448 is $204. Because seven months remain in the plan year, the maximum amount that the health FSA can require to be paid for *B*'s coverage for the remainder of the year is seven times $204, or $1428. Because $1428 is less than the maximum benefit that *B* could become entitled to receive for the remainder of the year ($2100), the health FSA is required to make COBRA continuation coverage available to *B* for the remainder of 2002 (but not for any subsequent year).

(iv) *Case 2:* The facts are the same as in *Case 1* except that *B* had submitted $1000 of reimbursable expenses as of the date of the qualifying event. In that case, the maximum benefit available to *B* for the remainder of the year would be $1400 instead of $2100. Because the maximum amount that the health FSA can require to be paid for *B*'s coverage is $1428, and because the $1400 maximum benefit for the remainder of the year does not exceed $1428, the health FSA is not obligated to make COBRA continuation coverage available to *B* in 2002 (or any later year). (Of course, the administrator of the health FSA is permitted to make COBRA continuation coverage available to every qualified beneficiary in the year that the qualified beneficiary's qualifying event occurs in order to avoid having to determine the maximum benefit available for each qualified beneficiary for the remainder of the plan year.)

Appendix P

Final Treasury Regulations § 1.132-9

On January 10, 2001, final regulations for transportation fringe benefits were released. [TD 8933 (Jan 10, 2001)] These final regulations replace proposed regulations issued in 2000.

§ 1.132-9. Qualified transportation fringes

(a) *Table of contents.* This section contains a list of the questions and answers in §1.132-9.

(1) *General rules.*

Q-1. What is a qualified transportation fringe?

Q-2. What is transportation in a commuter highway vehicle?

Q-3. What are transit passes?

Q-4. What is qualified parking?

Q-5. May qualified transportation fringes be provided to individuals who are not employees?

Q-6. Must a qualified transportation fringe benefit plan be in writing?

(2) *Dollar limitations.*

Q-7. Is there a limit on the value of qualified transportation fringes that may be excluded from an employee's gross income?

Q-8. What amount is includible in an employee's wages for income and employment tax purposes if the value of the qualified transportation fringe exceeds the applicable statutory monthly limit?

Q-9. Are excludable qualified transportation fringes calculated on a monthly basis?

Q-10. May an employee receive qualified transportation fringes from more than one employer?

(3) *Compensation reduction.*

Q-11. May qualified transportation fringes be provided to employees pursuant to a compensation reduction agreement?

Q-12. What is a compensation reduction election for purposes of section 132(f)?

Q-13. Is there a limit to the amount of the compensation reduction?

Q-14. When must the employee have made a compensation reduction election and under what circumstances may the amount be paid in cash to the employee?

Q-15. May an employee whose qualified transportation fringe costs are less than the employee's compensation reduction carry over this excess amount to subsequent periods?

(4) *Expense reimbursements.*

Q-16. How does section 132(f) apply to expense reimbursements?

Q-17. May an employer provide nontaxable cash reimbursement under section 132(f) for periods longer than one month?

Q-18. What are the substantiation requirements if an employer distributes transit passes?

Q-19. May an employer choose to impose substantiation requirements in addition to those described in this regulation?

(5) *Special rules for parking and vanpools.*

Q-20. How is the value of parking determined?

Q-21. How do the qualified transportation fringe rules apply to van pools?

(6) *Reporting and employment taxes.*

Q-22. What are the reporting and employment tax requirements for qualified transportation fringes?

(7) *Interaction with other fringe benefits.*

Q-23. How does section 132(f) interact with other fringe benefit rules?

(8) *Application to individuals who are not employees.*

Q-24. May qualified transportation fringes be provided to individuals who are partners, 2-percent shareholders of S-corporations, or independent contractors?

(9) *Effective date.*

Q-25. What is the effective date of this section?

(b) *Questions and answers.*

Q-1. What is a qualified transportation fringe?

A-1. (a) The following benefits are qualified transportation fringe benefits:

(1) Transportation in a commuter highway vehicle.

(2) Transit passes.

(3) Qualified parking.

(b) An employer may simultaneously provide an employee with any one or more [of] these three benefits.

Q-2. What is transportation in a commuter highway vehicle?

A-2. Transportation in a commuter highway vehicle is transportation provided by an employer to an employee in connection with travel between the employee's residence and place of employment. A commuter highway vehicle is a highway vehicle with a seating capacity of at least 6 adults (excluding the driver) and with respect to which at least 80 percent of the vehicle's mileage for a year is reasonably expected to be—

(a) For transporting employees in connection with travel between their residences and their place of employment; and

(b) On trips during which the number of employees transported for commuting is at least one-half of the adult seating capacity of the vehicle (excluding the driver).

Q-3. What are transit passes?

A-3. A transit pass is any pass, token, farecard, voucher, or similar item (including an item exchangeable for fare media) that entitles a person to transportation—

(a) On mass transit facilities (whether or not publicly owned); or

(b) Provided by any person in the business of transporting persons for compensation or hire in a highway vehicle with a seating capacity of at least 6 adults (excluding the driver).

Q-4. What is qualified parking?

A-4. (a) Qualified parking is parking provided to an employee by an employer—

(1) On or near the employer's business premises; or

(2) At a location from which the employee commutes to work (including commuting by carpool, commuter highway vehicle, mass transit facilities, or transportation provided by any person in the business of transporting persons for compensation or hire).

(b) For purposes of section 132(f), parking on or near the employer's business premises includes parking on or near a work location at which the employee provides services for the employer. However, qualified parking does not include—

(1) The value of parking provided to an employee that is excludable from gross income under section 132(a)(3) (as a working condition fringe), or

(2) Reimbursement paid to an employee for parking costs that is excludable from gross income as an amount treated as paid under an accountable plan. See §1.62-2.

(c) However, parking on or near property used by the employee for residential purposes is not qualified parking.

(d) Parking is provided by an employer if—

(1) The parking is on property that the employer owns or leases;

(2) The employer pays for the parking; or

(3) The employer reimburses the employee for parking ex- penses (see Q/A-16 of this section for rules relating to cash reimbursements).

Q-5. May qualified transportation fringes be provided to individuals who are not employees?

A-5. An employer may provide qualified transportation fringes only to individuals who are currently employees of the employer at the time the qualified transportation fringe is provided. The term employee for purposes of qualified transportation fringes is defined in §1.132-1(b)(2)(i). This term includes only common law employees and other statutory employees, such as officers of corporations. See Q/A-24 of this section for rules regarding partners, 2-percent shareholders, and independent contractors.

Q-6. Must a qualified transportation fringe benefit plan be in writing?

A-6. No. Section 132(f) does not require that a qualified transportation fringe benefit plan be in writing.

Q-7. Is there a limit on the value of qualified transportation fringes that may be excluded from an employee's gross income?

A-7. (a) *Transportation in a commuter highway vehicle and transit passes.* Before January 1, 2002, up to $65 per month is excludable from the gross income of an employee for transportation in a commuter highway vehicle and transit passes provided by an employer. On January 1, 2002, this amount is increased to $100 per month.

(b) *Parking.* Up to $175 per month is excludable from the gross income of an employee for qualified parking.

(c) *Combination.* An employer may provide qualified parking benefits in addition to transportation in a commuter highway vehicle and transit passes.

(d) *Cost-of-living adjustments*. The amounts in paragraphs (a) and (b) of this Q/A-7 are adjusted annually, beginning with 2000, to reflect cost-of-living. The adjusted figures are announced by the Service before the beginning of the year.

Q-8. What amount is includible in an employee's wages for income and employment tax purposes if the value of the qualified transportation fringe exceeds the applicable statutory monthly limit?

A-8. (a) Generally, an employee must include in gross income the amount by which the fair market value of the benefit exceeds the sum of the amount, if any, paid by the employee and any amount excluded from gross income under section 132(a)(5). Thus, assuming no other statutory exclusion applies, if an employer provides an employee with a qualified transportation fringe that exceeds the applicable statutory monthly limit and the employee does not make any payment, the value of the benefits provided in excess of the applicable statutory monthly limit is included in the employee's wages for income and employment tax purposes. See § 1.61-21(b)(1).

(b) The following examples illustrate the principles of this Q/A-8:

Example 1. (i) For each month in a year in which the statutory monthly transit pass limit is $100 (i.e., a year after 2001), Employer *M* provides a transit pass valued at $110 to Employee D, who does not pay any amount to Employer M for the transit pass.

(ii) In this *Example 1,* because the value of the monthly transit pass exceeds the statutory monthly limit by $10, $120 ($110–$100, times 12 months) must be included in D's wages for income and employment tax purposes for the year with respect to the transit passes.

Example 2. (i) For each month in a year in which the statutory monthly qualified parking limit is $175, Employer M provides qualified parking valued at $195 to Employee E, who does not pay any amount to M for the parking.

(ii) In this *Example 2,* because the fair market value of the qualified parking exceeds the statutory monthly limit by $20, $240 ($195–$175, times 12 months) must be included in Employee E's wages for income and employment tax purposes for the year with respect to the qualified parking.

Example 3. (i) For each month in a year in which the statutory monthly qualified parking limit is $175, Employer P provides qualified parking with a fair market value of $220 per month to its employees, but charges each employee $45 per month.

(ii) In this *Example 3,* because the sum of the amount paid by an employee ($45) plus the amount excludable for qualified parking ($175) is not less than the fair market value of the monthly benefit, no amount is includible in the employee's wages for income and employment tax purposes with respect to the qualified parking.

Q-9. Are excludable qualified transportation fringes calculated on a monthly basis?

A-9. (a) *In general.* Yes. The value of transportation in a commuter highway vehicle, transit passes, and qualified parking is calculated on a monthly basis to determine whether the value of the benefit has exceeded the applicable statutory monthly limit on qualified transportation fringes. Except in the case of a transit pass provided to an employee, the applicable statutory monthly limit applies to qualified transportation fringes used by the employee in a month. Monthly exclusion amounts are not combined to provide a qualified transportation fringe for any month exceeding the statutory limit. A month is a calendar month or a substantially equivalent period applied consistently.

(b) *Transit passes.* In the case of transit passes provided to an employee, the applicable statutory monthly limit applies to the transit passes provided by the employer to the employee in a month for that month or for any previous month in the calendar year. In addition, transit passes distributed in advance for more than one month, but not for more than twelve months, are qualified transportation fringes if the requirements in paragraph (c) of this Q/A-9 are met (relating to the income tax and employment tax treatment of advance transit passes). The applicable statutory monthly limit under section 132(f)(2) on the combined amount of transportation in a commuter highway vehicle and transit passes may be calculated by taking into account the monthly limits for all months for which the transit passes are distributed. In the case of a pass that is valid for more than one month, such as an annual pass, the value of the pass may be divided by the number of months for which it is valid for purposes of determining whether the value of the pass exceeds the statutory monthly limit.

(c) *Rule if employee's employment terminates*—(1) *Income tax treatment.* The value of transit passes provided in advance to an employee with respect to a month in which the individual is not an employee is included in the employee's wages for income tax purposes.

(2) *Reporting and employment tax treatment.* Transit passes distributed in advance to an employee are excludable from wages for employment tax purposes under sections 3121, 3306, and 3401 (FICA, FUTA, and income tax withholding) if the employer distributes transit passes to the employee in advance for not more than three months and, at the time the transit passes are distributed, there is not an established date that the employee's employment will terminate (for example, if the employee has given notice of retirement) which will occur before the beginning of the last month of the period for which the transit passes are provided. If the employer distributes transit passes to an employee in advance for not more than three months and at the time the transit passes are distributed there is an established date that the employee's employment will terminate, and the employee's employment does terminate before the beginning of the last month of the period for which the transit passes are provided, the value of transit passes provided for months beginning after the date of termination during which the employee is not employed by the employer

is included in the employee's wages for employment tax purposes. If transit passes are distributed in advance for more than three months, the value of transit passes provided for the months during which the employee is not employed by the employer is includible in the employee's wages for employment tax purposes regardless of whether at the time the transit passes were distributed there was an established date of termination of the employee's employment.

(d) *Examples.* The following examples illustrate the principles of this Q/A-9:

Example 1. (i) Employee E incurs $150 for qualified parking used during the month of June of a year in which the statutory monthly parking limit is $175, for which E is reimbursed $150 by Employer R. Employee E incurs $180 in expenses for qualified parking used during the month of July of that year, for which E is reimbursed $180 by Employer R.

(ii) In this *Example 1,* because monthly exclusion amounts may not be combined to provide a benefit in any month greater than the applicable statutory limit, the amount by which the amount reimbursed for July exceeds the applicable statutory monthly limit ($180 minus $175 equals $5) is includible in Employee E's wages for income and employment tax purposes.

Example 2. (i) Employee F receives transit passes from Employer G with a value of $195 in March of a year (for which the statutory monthly transit pass limit is $65) for January, February, and March of that year. F was hired during January and has not received any transit passes from G.

(ii) In this *Example 2,* the value of the transit passes (three months times $65 equals $195) is excludable from F's wages for income and employment tax purposes.

Example 3. (i) Employer S has a qualified transportation fringe benefit plan under which its employees receive transit passes near the beginning of each calendar quarter for that calendar quarter. All employees of Employer S receive transit passes from Employer S with a value of $195 on March 31 for the second calendar quarter covering the months April, May, and June (of a year in which the statutory monthly transit pass limit is $65).

(ii) In this *Example 3,* because the value of the transit passes may be calculated by taking into account the monthly limits for all months for which the transit passes are distributed, the value of the transit passes (three months times $65 equals $195) is excludable from the employees' wages for income and employment tax purposes.

Example 4. (i) Same facts as in *Example 3,* except that Employee T, an employee of Employer S, terminates employment with S on May 31. There was not an established date of termination for Employee T at the time the transit passes were distributed.

(ii) In this *Example 4,* because at the time the transit passes were distributed there was not an established date of termination for Employee T, the value of the transit passes provided for June ($65) is excludable from T's wages for employment tax purposes. However, the value of the transit passes distributed to Employee T for June ($65) is not excludable from T's wages for income tax purposes.

(iii) If Employee T's May 31 termination date was established at the time the transit passes were provided, the value of the transit passes provided for June ($65) is included in T's wages for both income and employment tax purposes.

Example 5. (i) Employer F has a qualified transportation fringe benefit plan under which its employees receive transit passes semi-annually in advance of the months for which the transit passes are provided. All employees of Employer F, including Employee X, receive transit passes from F with a value of $390 on June 30 for the 6 months of July through December (of a year in which the statutory monthly transit pass limit is $65). Employee X's employment terminates and his last day of work is August 1. Employer F's other employees remain employed throughout the remainder of the year.

(ii) In this *Example 5,* the value of the transit passes provided to Employee X for the months September, October, November, and December ($65 times 4 months equals $260) of the year is included in X's wages for income and employment tax purposes. The value of the transit passes provided to Employer F's other employees is excludable from the employees' wages for income and employment tax purposes.

Example 6. (i) Each month during a year in which the statutory monthly transit pass limit is $65, Employer R distributes transit passes with a face amount of $70 to each of its employees. Transit passes with a face amount of $70 can be purchased from the transit system by any individual for $65.

(ii) In this *Example 6,* because the value of the transit passes distributed by Employer R does not exceed the applicable statutory monthly limit ($65), no portion of the value of the transit passes is included as wages for income and employment tax purposes.

Q-10. May an employee receive qualified transportation fringes from more than one employer?

A-10. (a) *General rule.* Yes. The statutory monthly limits described in Q/A-7 of this section apply to benefits provided by an employer to its employees. For this purpose, all employees treated as employed by a single employer under section 414(b), (c), (m), or (o) are treated as employed by a single employer. See section 414(t) and §1.132-1(c). Thus, qualified transportation fringes paid by entities under common control under section 414(b), (c), (m), or (o) are combined for purposes of applying the applicable statutory monthly limit. In addition, an individual who is treated as a leased employee of the employer under section 414(n) is treated as an employee of that employer for purposes of section 132. See section 414(n)(3)(C).

(b) *Examples.* The following examples illustrate the principles of this Q/A-10:

Example 1. (i) During a year in which the statutory monthly qualified parking limit is $175, Employee E works for Employers M and N, who are unrelated and not treated as a single employer under section 414(b), (c), (m), or (o). Each month, M and N each provide qualified parking benefits to E with a value of $100.

(ii) In this *Example 1,* because M and N are unrelated employers, and the value of the monthly parking benefit provided by each is not more than the applicable statutory monthly limit, the parking benefits provided by each employer are excludable as qualified transportation fringes assuming that the other requirements of this section are satisfied.

Example 2. (i) Same facts as in Example 1, except that Employers M and N are treated as a single employer under section 414(b).

(ii) In this *Example 2,* because M and N are treated as a single employer, the value of the monthly parking benefit provided by M and N must be combined for purposes of determining whether the applicable statutory monthly limit has been exceeded. Thus, the amount by which the value of the parking benefit exceeds the monthly limit ($200 minus the monthly limit amount of $175 equals $25) for each month in the year is includible in E's wages for income and employment tax purposes.

Q-11. May qualified transportation fringes be provided to employees pursuant to a compensation reduction agreement?

A-11. Yes. An employer may offer employees a choice between cash compensation and any qualified transportation fringe. An employee who is offered this choice and who elects qualified transportation fringes is not required to include the cash compensation in income if—

(a) The election is pursuant to an arrangement described in Q/A-12 of this section;

(b) The amount of the reduction in cash compensation does not exceed the limitation in Q/A-13 of this section;

(c) The arrangement satisfies the timing and reimbursement rules in Q/A-14 and 16 of this section; and

(d) The related fringe benefit arrangement otherwise satisfies the requirements set forth elsewhere in this section.

Q-12. What is a compensation reduction election for purposes of section 132(f)?

A-12. (a) *Election requirements generally.* A compensation reduction arrangement is an arrangement under which the employer provides the employee with the right to elect whether the employee will receive either a fixed amount of cash compensation at a specified future date or a fixed amount of qualified transportation fringes to be provided for a specified future period (such as qualified parking to be used during a future calendar month). The employee's election must be in writing or another form, such as electronic, that includes, in a permanent and verifiable form, the information required to be in the election. The election must contain the date of the election, the amount of the compensation to be reduced, and the period for which the benefit will be provided. The election must relate to a fixed dollar amount or fixed percentage of compensation reduction. An election to reduce compensation for a period by a set amount for such period may be automatically renewed for subsequent periods.

(b) *Automatic election permitted.* An employer may provide under its qualified transportation fringe benefit plan that a compensation reduction election will be deemed to have been made if the employee does not elect to receive cash compensation in lieu of the qualified transportation fringe, provided that the employee receives adequate notice that a compensation reduction will be made and is given adequate opportunity to choose to receive the cash compensation instead of the qualified transportation fringe.

Q-13. Is there a limit to the amount of the compensation reduction?

A-13. Yes. Each month, the amount of the compensation reduction may not exceed the combined applicable statutory monthly limits for transportation in a commuter highway vehicle, transit passes, and qualified parking. For example, for a year in which the statutory monthly limit is $65 for transportation in a commuter highway vehicle and transit passes, and $175 for qualified parking, an employee could elect to reduce compensation for any month by no more than $240 ($65 plus $175) with respect to qualified transportation fringes. If an employee were to elect to reduce compensation by $250 for a month, the excess $10 ($250 minus $240) would be includible in the employee's wages for income and employment tax purposes.

Q-14. When must the employee have made a compensation reduction election and under what circumstances may the amount be paid in cash to the employee?

A-14. (a) The compensation reduction election must satisfy the requirements set forth under paragraphs (b), (c), and (d) of this Q/A-14.

(b) *Timing of election.* The compensation reduction election must be made before the employee is able currently to receive the cash or other taxable amount at the employee's discretion. The determination of whether the employee is able currently to receive the cash does not depend on whether it has been constructively received for purposes of section 451. The election must specify that the period (such as a calendar month) for which the qualified transportation fringe will be provided must not begin before the election is made. Thus, a compensation reduction election must relate to qualified transportation fringes to be provided after the election. For this purpose, the date a qualified transportation fringe is provided is—

(1) The date the employee receives a voucher or similar item; or

(2) In any other case, the date the employee uses the qualified transportation fringe.

(c) *Revocability of elections.* The employee may not revoke a compensation reduction election after the employee is able currently to receive the cash or other taxable amount at the employee's discretion. In addition, the election may not be revoked after the beginning of the period for which the qualified transportation fringe will be provided.

(d) *Compensation reduction amounts not refundable.* Unless an election is revoked in a manner consistent with paragraph (c) of this Q/A-14, an employee may not subsequently receive the compensation (in cash or any form other than by payment of a qualified transportation fringe under the employer's plan). Thus, an employer's qualified transportation fringe benefit plan may not provide that an employee who ceases to participate in the employer's qualified transportation fringe benefit plan (such as in the case of termination of employment) is entitled to receive a refund of the amount by which the employee's compensation reductions exceed the actual qualified transportation fringes provided to the employee by the employer.

(e) *Examples.* The following examples illustrate the principles of this Q/A-14:

Example 1. (i) Employer P maintains a qualified transportation fringe benefit arrangement during a year in which the statutory monthly limit is $100 for transportation in a commuter highway vehicle and transit passes (2002 or later) and $180 for qualified parking. Employees of P are paid cash compensation twice per month, with the payroll dates being the first and the fifteenth day of the month. Under P's arrangement, an employee is permitted to elect at any time before the first day of a month to reduce his or her compensation payable during that month in an amount up to the applicable statutory monthly limit ($100 if the employee elects coverage for transportation in a commuter highway vehicle or a mass transit pass, or $180 if the employee chooses qualified parking) in return for the right to receive qualified transportation fringes up to the amount of the election. If such an election is made, P will provide a mass transit pass for that month with a value not exceeding the compensation reduction amount elected by the employee or will reimburse the cost of other qualified transportation fringes used by the employee on or after the first day of that month up to the compensation reduction amount elected by the employee. Any compensation reduction amount elected by the employee for the month that is not used for qualified transportation fringes is not refunded to the employee at any future date.

(ii) In this *Example 1,* the arrangement satisfies the requirements of this Q/A-14 because the election is made before the employee is able currently to receive the cash and the election specifies the future period for which the qualified transportation fringes will be provided. The arrangement would also satisfy the requirements of this Q/A-14 and Q/A-13 of this section if employees are allowed to elect to reduce compensation up to $280 per month ($100 plus $180).

(iii) The arrangement would also satisfy the requirements of this Q/A-14 (and Q/A-13 of this section) if employees are allowed to make an election at any time before the first or the fifteenth day of the month to reduce their compensation payable on that payroll date by an amount not in excess of one-half of the applicable statutory monthly limit (depending on the type of qualified transportation fringe elected by the employee) and P provides a mass transit pass on or after the applicable payroll date for the compensation reduction amount elected by the employee for the payroll date or reimburses the cost of other qualified transportation fringes used by the employee on or after the payroll date up to the compensation reduction amount elected by the employee for that payroll date.

Example 2. (i) Employee Q elects to reduce his compensation payable on March 1 of a year (for which the statutory monthly mass transit limit is $65) by $195 in exchange for a mass transit voucher to be provided in March. The election is made on the preceding February 27. Employee Q was hired in January of the year. On March 10 of the year, the employer of Employee Q delivers to Employee Q a mass transit voucher worth $195 for the months of January, February, and March.

(ii) In this *Example 2,* $65 is included in Employee Q's wages for income and employment tax purposes because the compensation reduction election fails to satisfy the requirement in this Q/A-14 and Q/A-12 of this section that the period for which the qualified transportation fringe will be provided not begin before the election is made to the extent the election relates to $65 worth of transit passes for January of the year. The $65 for February is not taxable because the election was for a future period that includes at least one day in February.

(iii) However, no amount would be included in Employee Q's wages as a result of the election if $195 worth of mass transit passes were instead provided to Q for the months of February, March, and April (because the compensation reduction would relate solely to fringes to be provided for a period not beginning before the date of the election and the amount provided does not exceed the aggregate limit for the period, i.e., the sum of $65 for each of February, March, and April). See Q/A-9 of this section for rules governing transit passes distributed in advance for more than one month.

Example 3. (i) Employee R elects to reduce his compensation payable on March 1 of a year (for which the statutory monthly parking limit is $175) by $185 in exchange for reimbursement by Employer T of parking expenses incurred by Employee R for parking on or near Employer T's business premises during the period beginning after the date of the election through March. The election is made on the preceding February 27. Employee R incurs $10 in parking expenses on February 28 of the year, and $175 in parking expenses during the month of March. On April 5 of the year, Employer T reimburses Employee R $185 for the parking expenses incurred on February 28, and during March, of the year.

(ii) In this *Example 3,* no amount would be includible in Employee R's wages for income and employment tax purposes because the compensation reduction related solely to parking on or near Employer R's business premises used during a period not beginning before the date of the election and the amount reimbursed for parking used in any one month does not exceed the statutory monthly limitation.

Q-15. May an employee whose qualified transportation fringe costs are less than the employee's compensation reduction carry over this excess amount to subsequent periods?

A-15. (a) Yes. An employee may carry over unused compensation reduction amounts to subsequent periods under the plan of the employee's employer.

(b) The following example illustrates the principles of this Q/A-15:

Example. (i) By an election made before November 1 of a year for which the statutory monthly mass transit limit is $65, Employee E elects to reduce compensation in the amount of $65 for the month of November. E incurs $50 in employee-operated commuter highway vehicle expenses during November for which E is reimbursed $50 by Employer R, E's employer. By an election made before December, E elects to reduce compensation by $65 for the month of December. E incurs $65 in employee-operated commuter highway vehicle expenses during December for which E is reimbursed $65 by R. Before the following January, E elects to reduce compensation by $50 for the month of January. E incurs $65 in employee-operated commuter highway vehicle expenses during January for which E is reimbursed $65 by R because R allows E to carry over to the next year the $15 amount by which the compensation reductions for November and December exceeded the employee-operated commuter highway vehicle expenses incurred during those months.

(ii) In this *Example,* because Employee E is reimbursed in an amount not exceeding the applicable statutory monthly limit, and the reimbursement does not exceed the amount of employee-operated commuter highway vehicle expenses incurred during the month of January, the amount reimbursed ($65) is excludable from E's wages for income and employment tax purposes.

Q-16. How does section 132(f) apply to expense reimbursements?

A-16. (a) *In general.* The term qualified transportation fringe includes cash reimbursement by an employer to an employee for expenses incurred or paid by an employee for transportation in a commuter highway vehicle or qualified parking. The term qualified transportation fringe also includes cash reimbursement for transit passes made under a bona fide reimbursement arrangement, but, in accordance with section 132(f)(3), only if permitted under paragraph (b) of this Q/A-16. The reimbursement must be made under a bona fide reimbursement arrangement which meets the rules of paragraph (c) of this Q/A-16. A payment made before the date an expense has been incurred or paid is not a reimbursement. In addition, a bona fide reimbursement arrangement does not include an arrangement that is dependent solely upon an employee certifying in advance that the employee will incur expenses at some future date.

(b) *Special rule for transit passes*—(1) *In general.* The term *qualified transportation fringe* includes cash reimbursement for transit passes made under a bona fide reimbursement arrangement, but, in accordance with section 132(f)(3), only if no voucher or similar item that may be exchanged only for a transit pass is readily available for direct distribution by the employer to employees. If a voucher is readily available, the requirement that a voucher be distributed in-kind by the employer is satisfied if the voucher is distributed by the employer or by another person on behalf of the employer (for example, if a transit operator credits amounts to the employee's fare card as a result of payments made to the operator by the employer).

(2) *Voucher or similar item.* For purposes of the special rule in paragraph (b) of this Q/A-16, a transit system voucher is an instrument that may be purchased by employers from a voucher provider that is accepted by one or more mass transit operators (e.g., train, subway, and bus) in an area as fare media or in exchange for fare media. Thus, for example, a transit pass that may be purchased by employers directly from a voucher provider is a transit system voucher.

(3) *Voucher provider.* The term voucher provider means any person in the trade or business of selling transit system vouchers to employers, or any transit system or transit operator that sells vouchers to employers for the purpose of direct distribution to employees. Thus, a transit operator might or might not be a voucher provider. A voucher provider is not, for example, a third-party employee benefits administrator that administers a transit pass benefit program for an employer using vouchers that the employer could obtain directly.

(4) *Readily available.* For purposes of this paragraph (b), a voucher or similar item is readily available for direct distribution by the employer to employees if and only if an employer can obtain it from a voucher provider that—

(i) does not impose fare media charges that cause vouchers to not be readily available as described in paragraph (b)(5) of this section; and

(ii) does not impose other restrictions that cause vouchers to not be readily available as described in paragraph (b)(6) of this section.

(5) *Fare media charges.* For purposes of paragraph (b)(4) of this section, fare media charges relate only to fees paid by the employer to voucher providers for vouchers. The determination of whether obtaining a voucher would result in fare media charges that cause vouchers to not be readily available as described in this paragraph (b) is made with respect to each transit system voucher. If more than one transit system voucher is available for direct distribution to employees, the employer must consider the fees imposed for the lowest cost monthly voucher for purposes of determining whether the fees imposed by the voucher provider satisfy this paragraph. However, if transit system vouchers for multiple transit systems are required in an area to meet the transit needs of the

individual employees in that area, the employer has the option of averaging the costs applied to each transit system voucher for purposes of determining whether the fare media charges for transit system vouchers satisfy this paragraph. Fare media charges are described in this paragraph (b)(5), and therefore cause vouchers to not be readily available, if and only if the average annual fare media charges that the employer reasonably expects to incur for transit system vouchers purchased from the voucher provider (disregarding reasonable and customary delivery charges imposed by the voucher provider, e.g., not in excess of $15) are more than 1 percent of the average annual value of the vouchers for a transit system.

(6) *Other restrictions.* For purposes of paragraph (b)(4) of this section, restrictions that cause vouchers to not be readily available are restrictions imposed by the voucher provider other than fare media charges that effectively prevent the employer from obtaining vouchers appropriate for distribution to employees. Examples of such restrictions include—

(i) *Advance purchase requirements.* Advance purchase requirements cause vouchers to not be readily available only if the voucher provider does not offer vouchers at regular intervals or fails to provide the voucher within a reasonable period after receiving payment for the voucher. For example, a requirement that vouchers may be purchased only once per year may effectively prevent an employer from obtaining vouchers for distribution to employees. An advance purchase requirement that vouchers be purchased not more frequently than monthly does not effectively prevent the employer from obtaining vouchers for distribution to employees.

(ii) *Purchase quantity requirements.* Purchase quantity requirements cause vouchers to not be readily available if the voucher provider does not offer vouchers in quantities that are reasonably appropriate to the number of the employer's employees who use mass transportation (for example, the voucher provider requires a $1,000 minimum purchase and the employer seeks to purchase only $200 of vouchers).

(iii) *Limitations on denominations of vouchers that are available.* If the voucher provider does not offer vouchers in denominations appropriate for distribution to the employer's employees, vouchers are not readily available. For example, vouchers provided in $5 increments up to the monthly limit are appropriate for distribution to employees, while vouchers available only in a denomination equal to the monthly limit are not appropriate for distribution to employees if the amount of the benefit provided to the employer's employees each month is normally less than the monthly limit.

(7) *Example.* The following example illustrates the principles of this paragraph (b):

Example. (i) Company C in City X sells mass transit vouchers to employers in the metropolitan area of X in various denominations appropriate for distribution to employees. Employers can purchase vouchers monthly in reasonably appropriate quantities. Several different bus, rail, van pool, and ferry operators service X, and a number of the operators accept the vouchers either as fare media or in exchange for fare media. To cover its operating expenses, C imposes on each voucher a 50 cents charge, plus a reasonable and customary $15 charge for delivery of each order of vouchers. Employer M disburses vouchers purchased from C to its employees who use operators that accept the vouchers and M reasonably expects that $55 is the average value of the voucher it will purchase from C for the next calendar year.

(ii) In this *Example,* vouchers for X are readily available for direct distribution by the employer to employees because the expected cost of the vouchers disbursed to M's employees for the next calendar year is not more than 1 percent of the value of the vouchers (50 cents divided by $55 equals 0.91 percent), the delivery charges are disregarded because they are reasonable and customary, and there are no other restrictions that cause the vouchers to not be readily available. Thus, any reimbursement of mass transportation costs in X would not be a qualified transportation fringe.

(c) *Substantiation requirements.* Employers that make cash reimbursements must establish a bona fide reimbursement arrangement to establish that their employees have, in fact, incurred expenses for transportation in a commuter highway vehicle, transit passes, or qualified parking. For purposes of section 132(f), whether cash reimbursements are made under a bona fide reimbursement arrangement may vary depending on the facts and circumstances, including the method or methods of payment utilized within the mass transit system. The employer must implement reasonable procedures to ensure that an amount equal to the reimbursement was incurred for transportation in a commuter highway vehicle, transit passes, or qualified parking. The expense must be substantiated within a reasonable period of time. An expense substantiated to the payor within 180 days after it has been paid will be treated as having been substantiated within a reasonable period of time. An employee certification at the time of reimbursement in either written or electronic form may be a reasonable reimbursement procedure depending on the facts and circumstances. Examples of reasonable reimbursement procedures are set forth in paragraph (d) of this Q/A-16.

(d) *Illustrations of reasonable reimbursement procedures.* The following are examples of reasonable reimbursement procedures for purposes of paragraph (c) of this Q/A-16. In each case, the reimbursement is made at or within a reasonable period after the end of the events described in paragraphs (d)(1) through (d)(3) of this section.

(1) An employee presents to the employer a parking expense receipt for parking on or near the employer's business premises, the employee certifies that the parking was used by the employee, and the employer has no reason to doubt the employee's certification.

(2) An employee either submits a used time-sensitive transit pass (such as a monthly pass) to the employer and certifies that he or she purchased it or

presents an unused or used transit pass to the employer and certifies that he or she purchased it and the employee certifies that he or she has not previously been reimbursed for the transit pass. In both cases, the employer has no reason to doubt the employee's certification.

(3) If a receipt is not provided in the ordinary course of business (e.g., if the employee uses metered parking or if used transit passes cannot be returned to the user), the employee certifies to the employer the type and the amount of expenses incurred, and the employer has no reason to doubt the employee's certification.

Q-17. May an employer provide nontaxable cash reimbursement under section 132(f) for periods longer than one month?

A-17. (a) *General rule.* Yes. Qualified transportation fringes include reimbursement to employees for costs incurred for transportation in more than one month, provided the reimbursement for each month in the period is calculated separately and does not exceed the applicable statutory monthly limit for any month in the period. See Q/A-8 and 9 of this section if the limit for a month is exceeded.

(b) *Example.* The following example illustrates the principles of this Q/A-17:

Example. (i) Employee R pays $100 per month for qualified parking used during the period from April 1 through June 30 of a year in which the statutory monthly qualified parking limit is $175. After receiving adequate substantiation from Employee R, R's employer reimburses R $300 in cash on June 30 of that year.

(ii) In this *Example,* because the value of the reimbursed expenses for each month did not exceed the applicable statutory monthly limit, the $300 reimbursement is excludable from R's wages for income and employment tax purposes as a qualified transportation fringe.

Q-18. What are the substantiation requirements if an employer distributes transit passes?

A-18. There are no substantiation requirements if the employer distributes transit passes. Thus, an employer may distribute a transit pass for each month with a value not more than the statutory monthly limit without requiring any certification from the employee regarding the use of the transit pass.

Q-19. May an employer choose to impose substantiation requirements in addition [to] those described in this regulation?

A-19. Yes.

Q-20. How is the value of parking determined?

A-20. Section 1.61-21(b)(2) applies for purposes of determining the value of parking.

Q-21. How do the qualified transportation fringe rules apply to van pools?

A-21. (a) *Van pools generally.* Employer and employee-operated van pools, as well as private or public transit-operated van pools, may qualify as qualified transportation fringes. The value of van pool benefits which are qualified transportation fringes may be excluded up to the applicable statutory monthly limit for transportation in a commuter highway vehicle and transit passes, less the value of any transit passes provided by the employer for the month.

(b) *Employer-operated van pools.* The value of van pool transportation provided by or for an employer to its employees is excludable as a qualified transportation fringe, provided the van qualifies as a commuter highway vehicle as defined in section 132(f)(5)(B) and Q/A-2 of this section. A van pool is operated by or for the employer if the employer purchases or leases vans to enable employees to commute together or the employer contracts with and pays a third party to provide the vans and some or all of the costs of operating the vans, including maintenance, liability insurance and other operating expenses.

(c) *Employee-operated van pools.* Cash reimbursement by an employer to employees for expenses incurred for transportation in a van pool operated by employees independent of their employer are excludable as qualified transportation fringes, provided that the van qualifies as a commuter highway vehicle as defined in section 132(f)(5)(B) and Q/A-2 of this section. See Q/A-16 of this section for the rules governing cash reimbursements.

(d) *Private or public transit-operated van pool transit passes.* The qualified transportation fringe exclusion for transit passes is available for travel in van pools owned and operated either by public transit authorities or by any person in the business of transporting persons for compensation or hire. In accordance with paragraph (b) of Q/A-3 of this section, the van must seat at least 6 adults (excluding the driver). See Q/A-16(b) and (c) of this section for a special rule for cash reimbursement for transit passes and the substantiation requirements for cash reimbursement.

(e) *Value of van pool transportation benefits.* Section 1.61-21(b)(2) provides that the fair market value of a fringe benefit is based on all the facts and circumstances. Alternatively, transportation in an employer-provided commuter highway vehicle may be valued under the automobile lease valuation rule in §1.61-21(d), the vehicle cents-per-mile rule in §1.61-21(e), or the commuting valuation rule in §11.61-21(f). If one of these special valuation rules is used, the employer must use the same valuation rule to value the use of the commuter highway vehicle by each employee who shares the use. See §1.61-21(c)(2)(i)(B).

(f) *Qualified parking prime member.* If an employee obtains a qualified parking space as a result of membership in a car or van pool, the applicable statutory monthly limit for qualified parking applies to the individual to whom the parking space is assigned. This individual is the prime member. In determining the tax consequences to the prime member, the statutory monthly limit amounts of each car pool member may not be combined. If the employer provides access to the space and the space is not assigned to a particular individual, then the employer must designate one of its employees as the prime member who will bear the tax consequences. The employer may not designate more than one prime member for a car or van pool during a month. The employer of the prime member is responsible for including the value of the qualified parking in excess of the statutory monthly limit in the prime member's wages for income and employment tax purposes.

Q-22. What are the reporting and employment tax requirements for qualified transportation fringes?

A-22. (a) *Employment tax treatment generally.* Qualified transportation fringes not exceeding the applicable statutory monthly limit described in Q/A-7 of this section are not wages for purposes of the Federal Insurance Contributions Act (FICA), the Federal Unemployment Tax Act (FUTA), and federal income tax withholding. Any amount by which an employee elects to reduce compensation as provided in Q/A-11 of this section is not subject to the FICA, the FUTA, and federal income tax withholding. Qualified transportation fringes exceeding the applicable statutory monthly limit described in Q/A-7 of this section are wages for purposes of the FICA, the FUTA, and federal income tax withholding and are reported on the employee's Form W-2, Wage and Tax Statement.

(b) *Employment tax treatment of cash reimbursement exceeding monthly limits.* Cash reimbursement to employees (for example, cash reimbursement for qualified parking) in excess of the applicable statutory monthly limit under section 132(f) is treated as paid for employment tax purposes when actually or constructively paid. See §§31.3121(a)-2(a), 31.3301-4, 31.3402(a)-1(b) of this chapter. Employers must report and deposit the amounts withheld in addition to reporting and depositing other employment taxes. See Q/A-16 of this section for rules governing cash reimbursements.

(c) *Noncash fringe benefits exceeding monthly limits.* If the value of noncash qualified transportation fringes exceeds the applicable statutory monthly limit, the employer may elect, for purposes of the FICA, the FUTA, and federal income tax withholding, to treat the noncash taxable fringe benefits as paid on a pay period, quarterly, semi-annual, annual, or other basis, provided that the benefits are treated as paid no less frequently than annually.

Q-23. How does section 132(f) interact with other fringe benefit rules?

A-23. For purposes of section 132, the terms working condition fringe and de minimis fringe do not include any qualified transportation fringe under section 132(f). If, however, an employer provides local transportation other than transit passes (without any direct or indirect compensation reduction election), the value of the benefit may be excludable, either totally or partially, under fringe benefit rules other than the qualified transportation fringe rules under section 132(f). See §§1.132-6(d)(2)(i) (occasional local transportation fare), 1.132-6(d)(2)(iii) (transportation provided under unusual circumstances), and 1.61-21(k) (valuation of local transportation provided to qualified employees). See also Q/A-4(b) of this section.

Q-24. May qualified transportation fringes be provided to individuals who are partners, 2-percent shareholders of S-corporations, or independent contractors?

A-24. (a) *General rule.* Section 132(f)(5)(E) states that self-employed individuals who are employees within the meaning of section 401(c)(1) are not employees for purposes of section 132(f). Therefore, individuals who are partners, sole proprietors, or other independent contractors are not employees for purposes of section 132(f). In addition, under section 1372(a), 2-percent shareholders of S corporations are treated as partners for fringe benefit purposes. Thus, an individual who is both a 2-percent shareholder of an S corporation and a common law employee of that S corporation is not considered an employee for purposes of section 132(f). However, while section 132(f) does not apply to individuals who are partners, 2-percent shareholders of S corporations, or independent contractors, other exclusions for working condition and de minimis fringes may be available as described in paragraphs (b) and (c) of this Q/A-24. See §§1.132-1(b)(2) and 1.132-1(b)(4).

(b) *Transit passes.* The working condition and de minimis fringe exclusions under section 132(a)(3) and (4) are available for transit passes provided to individuals who are partners, 2-percent shareholders, and independent contractors. For example, tokens or farecards provided by a partnership to an individual who is a partner that enable the partner to commute on a public transit system (not including privately-operated van pools) are excludable from the partner's gross income if the value of the tokens and farecards in any month does not exceed the dollar amount specified in §1.132-6(d)(1). However, if the value of a pass provided in a month exceeds the dollar amount specified in §1.132-6(d)(1), the full value of the benefit provided (not merely the amount in excess of the dollar amount specified in §1.132-6(d)(1)) is includible in gross income.

(c) *Parking.* The working condition fringe rules under section 132(d) do not apply to commuter parking. See §1.132-5(a)(1). However, the de minimis fringe rules under section 132(e) are available for parking provided to individuals who are partners, 2-percent shareholders, or independent contractors that qualifies under the de minimis rules. See §1.132-6(a) and (b).

(d) *Example.* The following example illustrates the principles of this Q/A-24:

Example. (i) Individual G is a partner in partnership P. Individual G commutes to and from G's office every day and parks free of charge in P's lot.

(ii) In this *Example,* the value of the parking is not excluded under section 132(f), but may be excluded under section 132(e) if the parking is a de minimis fringe under §1.132-6.

Q-25. What is the effective date of this section?

A-25. (a) Except as provided in paragraph (b) of this Q/A-25, this section is applicable for taxable years beginning after December 31, 2001.

(b) The last sentence of paragraph (b)(5) of Q/A-16 of this section (relating to whether transit system vouchers for transit passes are readily available) is effective for taxable years beginning after December 31, 2003.

Index

[*References are to question numbers.*]

A

B

C

D

E

F

G

H

I

K

L

M

Q

R

S

W